READINGS IN
THE PHILOSOPHY
OF RELIGION

READINGS IN
THE PHILOSOPHY
OF RELIGION

 AN ANALYTIC APPROACH

Edited by

Baruch A. Brody

Massachusetts Institute of Technology

PRENTICE-HALL, INC., *Englewood Cliffs, New Jersey*

Library of Congress Cataloging in Publication Data

BRODY, BARUCH A   comp.
  Readings in the philosophy of religion.

  Bibliography: p. 664
  1. Religion—Philosophy—Collected works.
I. Title.
BL51.B758   200'.1   73-20485
ISBN 0-13-759340-6

© 1974 by PRENTICE-HALL, INC., *Englewood Cliffs, N.J.*

10 9 8 7 6 5 4 3 2 1

Printed in the United States of America

PRENTICE-HALL INTERNATIONAL, INC., *London*
PRENTICE-HALL OF AUSTRALIA, PTY. LTD., *Sydney*
PRENTICE-HALL OF CANADA, LTD., *Toronto*
PRENTICE-HALL OF INDIA PRIVATE LIMITED, *New Delhi*
PRENTICE-HALL OF JAPAN, INC., *Tokyo*

TO MY IN-LAWS

In Appreciation for the Very Special Gift
They Gave Me Eight Years Ago

PREFACE

Traditionally, the philosophy of religion has been one of the central areas of philosophy. This is not surprising. For throughout history people have turned to the study of philosophy with the hope that it would shed light upon some fundamental problems encountered in connection with their religious beliefs. In the twentieth century, however, philosophy of religion lost its traditional centrality within Anglo-American philosophy.

What brought about this change? I think it can be attributed to several factors: (1) For centuries, a principal issue in traditional religious philosophy had been whether one could prove the truth or falsity of a variety of fundamental doctrines (the existence of God, the immortality of the soul, etc.). During the forties and fifties, the verifiability theory of meaning convinced many philosophers that such religious claims are cognitively meaningless and therefore neither true nor false. There remained, of course, conjectures as to what type of meaning these religious statements do have, but this question did not arouse much interest. And even when the verifiability theory of meaning was abandoned, many continued to neglect the philosophy of religion. (2) Another factor is that very few working philosophers in the analytic school have had a personal religious commitment. Consequently, with the exception of those fervent nonbelievers who were concerned with proselytizing for their cause (the most notable example being Bertrand Russell), the philosophy of religion was neglected because analytical philosophers simply took little interest in religious matters.

All of this has changed in recent years. With the complete rejection of verificationism, the question of the truth and falsity of religious doctrines is now once more recognized as a legitimate question, and there is a growing number of analytical philosophers who have a real personal interest in theological issues and would like to apply to those issues the methods of the analytic school. Consequently, some very fine work in the philosophy of religion has been published in recent years.

As one scans this literature, two things emerge very clearly. The first is that there is a real affinity between recent analytic work and much of the writings of medieval theologians and rationalist and empiricist philosophers of the seventeenth and eighteenth centuries: both groups are keenly concerned with the careful analysis of the meaning and implications of religious doctrines, and with the question of whether or not different doctrines are consistent with each other; both groups are very much involved in the careful elaboration and critical analysis of proofs of the truth and falsity of religious doctrines. The second is that it is impossible to do good work in the philosophy of religion without taking into account the important advances of recent years in metaphysical analysis, in the philosophy of logic, and in philosophical psychology. Issues in the philosophy of religion tend to be intertwined with issues in all of these areas.

There have been several recent attempts to collect the new analytic material in the philosophy of religion, but they all suffer from two main defects that make them unsuitable for classroom use. First, they fail to cover systematically the major issues in the philosophy of religion, but offer merely a series of unrelated, unintegrated articles. Secondly, they fail to include some of the traditional writings that serve as background for the recent analytic discussions. This anthology, by the careful organization of materials and by the juxtaposition of classical and contemporary discussions, tries to show the student the continuity of philosophical thinking that he may fail to perceive in other texts.

CONTENTS

PART FOUR: GOD'S RELATION
TO THE WORLD   429

INTRODUCTION   430

Creation

Miracles

PART FIVE: MAN'S RELATION TO GOD   471

INTRODUCTION   472

Religious Experience

Prayer and Ritual

Morality and Religion

PART SIX: THE END OF THINGS   605

Immortality and Resurrection

PART ONE

THE EXISTENCE
OF GOD

INTRODUCTION

In western religions the most fundamental theological claim is that there is an all-perfect being, God. For that reason, one of the most fundamental questions, if not the most fundamental question, in the philosophy of religion centers around the truth and falsity of that belief. Is there any reason to suppose that God exists, any proof of his existence? Or is there perhaps some reason to suppose that he does not exist, some proof of his nonexistence? And if neither of these proofs exists, what ought a reasonable person to do? Should he have faith in God's existence, is he free to believe what he wants about this issue, or should he simply remain in doubt? Part 1 of this book is devoted to a consideration of these questions.

There are three classical proofs of the existence of God. One of these, the cosmological argument, argues that there must be a God to create the world or nothing would exist in the world. Another, the teleological argument, argues that there must be a God or the world would not be the orderly, harmonious, purposively adaptive place that it is. Both of these arguments are attempts by philosophers to state, in a clear and rigorous fashion, the intuitive arguments that religious believers normally offer for their beliefs. But the ontological argument, the first argument that we will consider carefully, is different in this respect; it bears no relation to the intuitive arguments that ordinary religious believers offer. It is a product purely of philosophical thought.

The classical statement of the ontological argument occurs in the *Proslogium* of St. Anselm of Canterbury (1033–1109). Anselm begins with the very conception of God as all-perfect—as that being than which nothing greater can be conceived—and goes on to argue that God must exist, and that His existence is entailed by His nature. Indeed, says Anselm, the very claim that God does not exist cannot have any more meaning than the equally contradictory claim that fire is water.

Anselm offers several versions of his argument in the first selection in this section. We shall later consider whether or not he really has more than one argument. One thing that should be kept in mind, however, is that in all of his discussion Anselm makes no appeal to any facts about the nature and existence of the world. His proof is a purely a priori proof—a proof based upon pure reason without any appeal to what experience has taught us about the world.

Anselm's argument has been criticized in many different ways. During his own lifetime, a monk named Gaunilon challenged the argument and Anselm responded to his challenge. Two things should be especially noted about this response. The first is Gaunilon's claim that, if Anselm's argument works, it could also be used to prove such absurd conclusions as the existence of an island greater than which none can be conceived. The other is Anselm's reformulation of his argument at the beginning of his reply, for there are many who claim that we get there still another new version of the argument.

It is generally thought that the ontological argument was decisively refuted by Immanuel Kant in his *Critique of Pure Reason*. The basic idea behind Kant's objection seems, moreover, to be pretty clear. Anselm, says Kant, is supposing that existence is a perfection—a property that a perfect being must, by its very nature, have. But existence is not a property at all, and therefore certainly not a perfection. So the ontological argument is mistaken.

Kant's claim obviously involves two parts. The first is the idea that the ontological argument really does suppose that existence is a property, a real predicate. The second is the idea that this presupposition is false. But Kant offers no careful analysis of Anselm's argument so it is difficult to see whether his first claim is true. The recent analytic literature has seen a variety of attempts to carefully formulate the argument; these attempts conclude that Kant was wrong in supposing there to be some objectionable claim about existence being a property that is presupposed by the Anselmian argument.

Alvin Plantinga's article is an attempt to formulate the argument in chapter 2 of the *Proslogium*. Having formulated the argument, Plantinga goes on to consider what might be meant by the claim that existence is not a property. He rejects that claim on certain interpretations of it, and asserts that, on the other interpretations according to which it is true that existence is not a property, the argument that he reconstructs from Anselm does not presuppose that it is a property.

Norman Malcolm takes a different approach. He concedes that Anselm's argument presupposes that existence is a perfection and that Anselm is wrong in thinking that this is so. But, claims Malcolm, Anselm offered a different argument in chapter 3 of the *Proslogium* based upon the idea that necessary existence is a perfection and concluding, therefore, that God must possess necessary existence—that God exists necessarily. And, Malcolm goes on to argue, while existence is not a property and not therefore a perfection, necessary existence is both.

It is interesting to note that Malcolm and Plantinga differ as to whether or not the argument in the second chapter of the *Proslogium* presupposes that existence is a perfection. The reader should certainly review the text of the *Proslogium* at this point to see whether Malcolm's or Plantinga's interpretation of chapter 2 is correct, and whether Malcolm is right in supposing that the argument in chapter 3 is a different argument.

There are two other objections that have been raised against ontological arguments of any form, one due to Kant (that all necessity is only hypothetical necessity) and the other due to Leibniz (that the argument presupposes that the very concept of God is coherent). Malcolm offers his replies to these two objections as well.

In the last few years, attempts have been made to find new fallacies in the ontological argument. One of the most interesting attempts to do so is in the paper of David Lewis. Lewis presents his own formalization of the argument and asks the reader to carry out a similar analysis for other formalizations of the argument. The intuitive idea behind Lewis's objection is the following: A crucial step in the ontological argument is the idea that since we can conceive of God, he, a perfect being, exists in our understanding. Anselm goes on to conclude that God's perfection entails that he exists in reality as well. But what does it mean to say that a perfect being exists in the understanding? It might mean (a) that there is a being in our understanding which is, in some possible world in which it exists, greater than any possible being in any possible world; or (b) that there is a being in our understanding which is, in our actual world, greater than any possible being in any possible world. Lewis shows that if it means (a), the conclusion of the ontological argument does not follow, but if it means (b), there is no reason to suppose that God exists in our understanding just because we can conceive of him. So the ontological argument fails for this new reason.

In the course of his discussion of (b), Lewis has some very important things to say about the nature of actuality and about confusions regarding the nature of actuality that make (b) plausible. While not directly related to the ontological argument, these are important points that should be noted carefully.

We turn then to the cosmological argument. The classical statement of the cosmological argument comes in the first two of St. Thomas Aquinas's five ways. Both of these arguments begin with noticing some fact about the world. In the case of the first way, what is noted is that some change is occurring. In the case of the second way, what is noted is that something exists. Then, some causal principle (either that changes are caused or that the existence of things is caused) is invoked, and we therefore conclude that there is a series of causes and effects that precede the original thing noted. But, says St. Thomas, there cannot be an infinite regression of causes. So there must be a first cause, and that is God.

There is an obvious objection that can be raised at this point. A crucial assumption of the cosmological argument seems to be the claim that there could not have been an infinite causal regression. But what reason is there to believe that this is so? Why couldn't there be one? Samuel Clarke, in his

A Demonstration of the Being and Attributes of God, attempted to reformulate the argument so as to meet this objection. Let us concede, says Clarke, that there is no reason why there could not have been an infinite causal regression. And, to be sure, every member of that infinite series has, as its cause, the previous member of the series. This still leaves unanswered, however, one fundamental question. What is the cause of the existence of the whole series? To answer this question, says Clarke, we must bring in God. To put Clarke's point another way, even if we have, in our infinite sequence, a cause of each particular object and of each particular change, we still have to find a cause for everything taken together, for the whole universe. This cause is God.

The standard objection to Clarke's reformulation of the argument was first raised by David Hume and then elaborated by Paul Edwards. It points out that Clarke's argument presupposes that, having explained every member of the causal sequence, we would still have something else left to explain, viz., the sequence as a whole. But, say Hume and Edwards, that is just a confusion. Once we have explained why each member exists, there is nothing left to explain.

In an extremely important article, William Rowe sets out to defend Clarke's argument against this line of criticism. He begins by clarifying the meaning of the question, "Why does the sequence exist at all?" For Rowe, this question is equivalent to the question, "Why does the sequence have any members at all?" Given this interpretation, argues Rowe, the question as to the cause of the existence of the sequence is perfectly meaningful. Now, says Rowe, imagine an infinite causal sequence, each member of which is caused by an earlier member. Given all of this causal information, we would still not know why the sequence has any members rather than none at all, for all of our causal knowledge would already involve members of the sequence whose existence we are trying to explain. So, contra Russell and Edwards, even if we have an explanation of the existence of each member of the sequence, we still wouldn't know why the sequence as a whole exists, and to answer that question we must appeal to the existence of God.

St. Thomas was, himself, aware of the objection that there might be an infinite causal regress. Thus, in the course of presenting the first two ways, rather than concede that possibility and make a Clarkian move, he argues against that possibility. The argument that he presents is very obscure. To begin with, as Edwards shows, the argument is, on its simplest interpretation, a very bad one. But secondly, and even more importantly, there are well-known texts in which St. Thomas allows not only for the possibility of there being infinite series but even for the possibility of there being certain types of infinite causal regresses.

Patterson Brown's article is concerned with doing two things: (a) explaining the difference between those infinite causal regresses that St. Thomas is prepared to allow as possible and those that he is not; and (b) offering an account of why St. Thomas would object to the second type of infinite causal regress. Brown's crucial idea is that St. Thomas recognized a type of causation in which one did not have the real cause at all until one found the first member of the causal sequence. So, if there were an infinite causal regress, then the event in question would have no real cause (in this special Thomistic sense of cause).

Brown recognizes that this interpretation of St. Thomas leads to an obvious problem: is there any reason to suppose that events do have a cause (in this special Thomistic sense)? If there is not, then the cosmological argument will fail for a new reason, viz., its dependence upon the unsupported claim that every event must have a cause of this special type. Having said that, however, we are immediately reminded that there is still a further general issue about the cosmological argument, one alluded to by Rowe at the beginning of his article. Since every cosmological argument employs some version or another of the principle that every event has a cause, no version of the argument will work unless such a principle can be supported. The reader is referred to the bibliography for reference to further discussions of this vital issue of the status of the causal principle.

We come, finally, to the third famous argument for the existence of God, the teleological argument. Its basic idea is that we must suppose that the universe was created by a wise creator, God, in order to explain the presence in it of order and of purposive adaptiveness—the fact that the parts of natural objects are made and put together in such a way as to enable these objects to perform a variety of tasks. There are many different statements of the argument. We shall study the famous version of it presented by William Paley.

Paley begins by asking us to contrast our reactions when we stumble across a stone and when we stumble across a watch. In the case of the watch, but not of the stone, we would say that it is an artifact—an entity made by some creator and made so as to be able to do certain things. Paley wants to claim that the very reasons that lead us to make such a statement in the case of the watch, the ways in which the parts are designed and put together so as to perform a task, should lead us to make the same statement in the case of the universe as a whole.

Paley goes on to claim that our conclusion would not be weakened in the case of the watch (and should not, therefore, in the case of the universe) just because we had never seen a watch made, or because it didn't always work just right, or because we didn't know the purpose of some parts, etc. But there are other, more serious, objections that might be raised. Is it at all legitimate to suppose that the objects are created for the purposes we ascribe to them or would it be better to say—in the case of the natural objects, as opposed to artifacts like watches—that they are used for these purposes just because they happened to be suitable for them? And couldn't we explain the occurrence of this purposive adaptiveness as the result of chance—as one of many possibilities that came about by accident but which continue, unlike the others that died out, just because they work so well? Paley is aware of these objections and he offers his response to them.

There is still a final question about the argument that Paley considers. Let us grant, for the moment, that the teleological argument succeeds in proving the existence of the creator of the universe. What right has one to suppose that this creator is God, that all-perfect being that is postulated in the Judeo-Christian tradition? Certainly the argument does not prove that. Paley takes a very interesting line in response to this objection. He concedes the point, and suggests that all that the religious person has to suppose about God, such as the immensity of his power and knowledge, is proven by the argument, and that the ideas of infinite power, infinite wisdom, etc., need not be taken literally. The question as to whether these weakened claims are, as Paley suggests, sufficient to capture the conception of God needed for religious persons is something that the reader will have to decide.

Some of the objections that Paley considered are among those raised by David Hume in his classical critique of the teleological argument in his *Dialogues Concerning Natural Religion.* In a large number of ways, Hume was trying to argue that the analogy between artifacts and natural objects that the teleological argument rests upon is not strong enough to support its conclusion. While it has generally been conceded that Hume was right, there has been a recent reevaluation of that claim. R. G. Swinburne's recent article presents an analysis of the logic of analogical arguments and goes on to claim with some force that, in light of this analysis, none of the objections that Hume presents are satisfactory.

There is one further aspect of this issue that is not adequately discussed in the literature presented below, although it is discussed to some degree by each of our authors. Hume raises the possibility of alternative explanations of the order and harmony and purposive adaptiveness in the universe. These alternative explanations involve the idea of the universe existing for a long time, and the realization of many possibilities of which only the orderly and purposively adaptive ones survive. Indeed, as Hume describes it, his conception bears a real resemblance to evolutionary biology and historical cosmology as we know those subjects today. Paley, as we pointed out above, attempts to rule out this alternative, but the arguments that he offers are not satisfactory in light of our contemporary scientific knowledge. In order to meet this objection, Swinburne distinguishes two types of order: regularities of co-presence (the type of purposive adaptiveness that Paley was talking about and for which we can offer scientific explanations), and regularities of succession (the facts about the ways in which objects always behave over a period of time in accordance with scientific laws). Swinburne wants to claim that, while ordinary regularities of succession can be explained in terms of more basic regularities of succession, the fact that objects obey these most basic regularities of succession can be explained only by the supposition that God created them to behave in such a way.

Swinburne's argument raises certain fundamental issues that need further discussion: (a) are there really such things as the basic regularities of succession or is it the case that, for each such regularity, there is an even more basic one in terms of which the former can be explained? and (b) if there are basic regularities of succession, is there any reason to suppose that they can be explained? Before Swinburne's argument can be accepted, these issues would have to be clarified.

We have so far been considering arguments for the existence of God. We turn now to a consideration of the arguments against the existence of God. There is really only one argument that deserves careful consideration, the argument from evil. In a way, this argument is the inverse of the teleological argument. While the teleological argument claims that the nature of the universe indicates that there is a deity, the argument from evil claims that the nature of the universe indicates that there is no deity. In particular, the evil and suffering in the universe indicates that he does not exist.

It is important to understand that the argument from evil is a serious problem just because of the nature of God in the Judeo-Christian tradition. God is all-wise, so he should know how to avoid these evils; he is all-powerful, so he should be able to see that they do not occur; and he is all-good, so he should want to see that they do not occur. Then, if he exists, how is it that they do exist? If, of course, the conception of God were different—if it were supposed that the God that existed did not literally have these properties—then the argument would collapse. And one of the characters, Philo, in a dialogue by Hume in which this problem is raised, suggests that the way out of it is to suppose that God does not have these attributes in the way that people do, and that God's true nature is a mystery.

But many theologians have wanted to avoid these conclusions. If God's nature is such a mystery then what is the content of the belief that God exists? Instead, they have attempted to show that the problem can be avoided in other ways. Many of their attempts are surveyed in the articles by Professors Mackie and McCloskey. Let us look briefly at some of these defenses. But before doing so, it is important to note the important distinction between two types of evils drawn by McCloskey: moral evils (the evil of bad actions and the bad consequences they produce), and physical evils (evils due to other causes).

The following seem to be the major ways that theologians have adopted for avoiding the problem of evil: (a) evil is an illusion; (b) evil is merely the privation of good; (c) evil has to exist as a counterpart of the good; (d) evil is the by-product of the operations of the laws of nature which are intrinsically good; (e) the presence of evil brings out the good in people; (f) evil is a warning to man or is man's punishment for his sin; and (g) evil is due to man's free will. Of all of these, the only one that really has any plausibility is the last. The others are easily shown to be inadequate by Mackie and McCloskey.

What precisely is the free-will solution to the problem of evil? It seems to come to the following: the mere existence of free will, or some of its consequences, are great goods—goods that outweigh any evils that might result from their presence. But the existence of free will entails the possibility of men's doing evil actions. It is the actual performance of these actions that produces the evil that exists in the world.

Mackie and McCloskey raise a variety of objections to this solution. To begin with, it is at best only a solution to the problem of moral evil; it says nothing at all about the problem of physical evil. Secondly, the claim that free will is a great enough good to outweigh the evil it might produce (and even the evil that it *does* produce) is questionable. Thirdly, couldn't God have so ordered things (by making the world less conducive to the practice of evil, by making us a bit more predisposed to do the good thing, etc.) that, although we are free, less evil is actually performed? Fourthly, and perhaps most importantly, given that it is possible that all men freely choose to do the right thing, why didn't God see to it that it was this possibility that was actualized? Then, even though there would be free will (with all its attendant goods) and the possibility of evil, there wouldn't be any actual evil.

Professor Plantinga's article is an important attempt to respond to many of these objections. He begins by considering the crucial fourth objection. His crucial point in response to it is that there are certain logically possible states of affairs that are such that it is logically impossible even for God to bring them about, and that one of these is the state of affairs that all men freely choose to do the right thing. Having done that, he then goes on to demonstrate that the free-will defense must be satisfactory. It cannot be incoherent, as Mackie and McCloskey claim, because it is easy to see that under certain conditions it would be true.

Besides dealing with this crucial fourth objection (and, in a derivative fashion, with the third objection), Plantinga suggests that there is also a way to deal with the first objection. It is, he says, at least logically possible that the physical evil in the world is due to the free actions of the devil or other nonhuman spirits. As Plantinga points out, all that is required to defend the free-will solution is that this be a possibility.

There is another solution to the problem of evil that is often suggested by religious people. It is suggested by certain passages in the book of *Job* and runs roughly as follows: for all we know, it may be the case that the evil in the world is necessary for some greater good, and that is why God created the world as it is. As Professor Pike points out, the existence of evil raises a problem for the belief in the existence of God only if one supposes that there cannot be any morally sufficient reasons for permitting its existence—only if one supposes that its presence cannot be necessary for some greater good that outweighs it. And since the proponent of the argument from evil is in no position to justify these assumptions (the best that he can show is that we do not know of any such reasons), the argument from evil against the existence of God collapses.

Pike's claim has recently been challenged by Professor Penelhum. Penelhum points out that the traditional theist is also committed to a large number of moral and valuational claims that are quite specific about what does and does not constitute an adequate reason for allowing certain evils in the world. Therefore, in a given context, it may be possible to show that none of the limited number of possible morally adequate reasons are actually present and, therefore, that Pike's response will not do in those contexts.

It is interesting to note that Penelhum does not actually carry out, for a given case of evil, the argument that he says can be given. It would be instructive, I suggest, for the reader to try to carry it out and see whether Penelhum's claim is actually true.

In conclusion, then, we have not been able to find any arguments for or against the existence of God that are satisfactory. This leads us, in a way, to the following question. Given that there are no satisfactory proofs on either side, what ought a reasonable person to do? In a way, one has three options: one can believe anyway in the existence of God (meaning that one has a theistic faith); or one can believe in the nonexistence of God (meaning that one has an atheistic faith); or one can hold no beliefs at all on the question (in which case one is an agnostic). Is there some reason for preferring one of these courses of action over the others?

There is a classical argument advanced by Pascal that purports to show that the only reasonable course of action is to hold a theistic faith. Pascal points out that if you do anything else, you run the risk of losing (if you are wrong) eternal life and suffering eternal damnation. But if you have a theistic faith, even if you are wrong, there is little that you will really have lost. In short, belief in God is the only reasonable course of action open.

There are a variety of classical objections to this argument. To begin with, is Pascal right in supposing that the nonbeliever will lose eternal salvation because of his nonbelief? Given that there is no evidence either way, would it be just of God to condemn the nonbeliever for his nonbelief? And if God would not do that, then Pascal's argument collapses. Secondly, of what purpose is this argument? Can a person choose what he is going to believe? And if he cannot, then how will he be led to a religious belief by virtue of Pascal's argument?

Professor Swinburne's article attempts to show that these objections can be met. More generally, and more importantly, Swinburne presents Pascal's argument in the context of the general theory of rational action that had been developed in recent years, and shows that the argument is far more serious than it is normally thought to be. But, he concludes, the argument is not persuasive in the way that Pascal thought it was because (a) Pascal failed to take into account the possibility that one might lose a great deal (perhaps even eternal life) for holding certain theological beliefs, and (b) Pascal assumed that his was the only possible way of evaluating the consequences of the courses of action under consideration. In short, says Professor Swinburne, Pascal's approach is correct, but his conclusion does not necessarily follow.

At the end of his article, Swinburne raises the issue of the morality of holding beliefs without adequate evidence or against the probable evidence. This theme plays a central role in the debate between William Clifford and William James about the morality of religious faith. Clifford argued against having faith and for agnosticism on the basis of a moral claim that it is always wrong to believe anything upon insufficient evidence.

Clifford begins his argument by presenting a case in which a person acts upon a sincerely held belief, but one that he has no real reason to believe is true, and terrible results come about that harm many people. In that case, we clearly condemn the person. He wants to go on to argue that we should make the same judgment even if the belief does not result in any action and even if other people are not harmed. His essential point is that the mere fact that we hold a belief without evidence for it is harmful because it contributes to that great enemy of human progress, credulity.

By way of contrast, William James wants to claim that there are at least some cases in which we may legitimately come to hold a belief even though the evidence on that issue is inconclusive. Such cases involve options which are living (both the belief in question and its denial are ones which you could come to believe), forced (there is really no alternative but coming to believe one or the other), and momentous (the stake is great and one chooses now or not at all). James wants to claim that religious beliefs give rise to such cases, and that it is therefore legitimate to hold such beliefs if we want to, even though the evidence is not present.

The crucial point in his argument is that religious belief poses us a forced choice and that the option of agnosticism is not a third real option between belief and disbelief. His basis for making this claim is that we lose the supposed benefits of religious belief whether we are agnostics or atheists. Whether this claim is true is something that the reader will have to decide for himself.

Throughout all of our discussion of religious faith so far, we have been working with the following model: religious beliefs are true or false, and their truth or falsity is determined by some reality that exists or fails to exist independently of any belief that we have. The question is whether or not we should hold such a belief given the lack of evidence. It is just this whole model and approach that is challenged in the writings of Kierkegaard.

Kierkegaard is concerned instead with what he calls subjective truth. A belief is subjectively true, in his account of the matter, if it is held in the proper way, and the question of the objective truth of the belief (its correspondence to reality) then becomes irrelevant. Kierkegaard even goes so far as to claim that such a subjectively true belief may, from the point of view of normal reasoning processes, be paradoxical, and that should still not bother the believer.

In effect, Kierkegaard has posed a fundamental challenge here. I think that there are few religious people who would not want to agree with his claim that, even if one held the objectively true religious beliefs, if one did not hold them with the proper religious attitudes and commitments there would be something lacking in one's beliefs. But most religious thinkers would also want to say that it is still important that your beliefs be objectively true—that their mere subjective truth (in the Kierkegaardian sense) is not enough. It is, of course, just in this way that they disagree with Kierkegaard, and who is right is something that the reader will have to come to his own conclusions about.

ARGUMENTS FOR HIS EXISTENCE

The Ontological Argument

ST. ANSELM

1.1 *Presentation of the Argument*

> Truly there is a God, although the fool hath said in his heart, There
> is no God.

And so, Lord, do thou, who dost give understanding to faith, give me, so far
as thou knowest it to be profitable, to understand that thou art as we believe;
and that thou art that which we believe. And, indeed, we believe that thou
art a being than which nothing greater can be conceived. Or is there no such
nature, since the fool hath said in his heart, there is no God? (Psalm xiv. 1).
But, at any rate, this very fool, when he hears of this being of which I speak
—a being than which nothing greater can be conceived—understands what he
hears, and what he understands is in his understanding; although he does not
understand it to exist.

For, it is one thing for an object to be in the understanding, and another to
understand that the object exists. When a painter first conceives of what he
will afterwards perform, he has it in his understanding, but he does not yet
understand it to be, because he has not yet performed it. But after he has made
the painting, he both has it in his understanding, and he understands that it
exists, because he has made it.

Hence, even the fool is convinced that something exists in the understanding,
at least, than which nothing greater can be conceived. For, when he hears of
this, he understands it. And whatever is understood, exists in the understanding. And assuredly that, than which nothing greater can be conceived,

---

From Chapters II–IV of St. Anselm's *Proslogium*.

cannot exist in the understanding alone. For, suppose it exists in the understanding alone: then it can be conceived to exist in reality; which is greater.

Therefore, if that, than which nothing greater can be conceived, exists in the understanding alone, the very being, than which nothing greater can be conceived, is one, than which a greater can be conceived. But obviously this is impossible. Hence, there is no doubt that there exists a being, than which nothing greater can be conceived, and it exists both in the understanding and in reality.

> God cannot be conceived not to exist.—God is that, than which nothing greater can be conceived.—That which can be conceived not to exist is not God.

And it assuredly exists so truly, that it cannot be conceived not to exist. For, it is possible to conceive of a being which cannot be conceived not to exist; and this is greater than one which can be conceived not to exist. Hence, if that, than which nothing greater can be conceived, can be conceived not to exist, it is not that, than which nothing greater can be conceived. But this is an irreconcilable contradiction. There is, then, so truly a being than which nothing greater can be conceived to exist, that it cannot even be conceived not to exist; and this being thou art, O Lord, our God.

So truly, therefore, dost thou exist, O Lord, my God, that thou canst not be conceived not to exist; and rightly. For, if a mind could conceive of a being better than thee, the creature would rise above the Creator; and this is most absurd. And, indeed, whatever else there is, except thee alone, can be conceived not to exist. To thee alone, therefore, it belongs to exist more truly than all other beings, and hence in a higher degree than all others. For, whatever else exists does not exist so truly, and hence in a less degree it belongs to it to exist. Why, then, has the fool said in his heart, there is no God (Psalm xiv. 1), since it is so evident, to a rational mind, that thou dost exist in the highest degree of all? Why, except that he is dull and a fool?

> How the fool has said in his heart what cannot be conceived.—A thing may be conceived in two ways: (1) when the word signifying it is conceived; (2) when the thing itself is understood. As far as the word goes, God can be conceived not to exist; in reality he cannot.

But how has the fool said in his heart what he could not conceive; or how is it that he could not conceive what he said in his heart? since it is the same to say in the heart, and to conceive.

But, if really, nay, since really, he both conceived, because he said in his heart; and did not say in his heart, because he could not conceive; there is more than one way in which a thing is said in the heart or conceived. For, in one sense, an object is conceived, when the word signifying it is conceived; and in another, when the very entity, which the object is, is understood.

In the former sense, then, God can be conceived not to exist; but in the latter, not at all. For no one who understands what fire and water are can conceive fire to be water, in accordance with the nature of the facts themselves, although this is possible according to the words. So, then, no one who understands what God is can conceive that God does not exist, although he says these words in his heart, either without any, or with some foreign, signification. For, God is that than which a greater cannot be conceived. And he who thoroughly understands this, assuredly understands that this being so truly exists, that not even in concept can it be non-existent. Therefore, he who understands that God so exists, cannot conceive that he does not exist.

I thank thee, gracious Lord, I thank thee; because what I formerly believed by thy bounty, I now so understand by thine illumination, that if I were unwilling to believe that thou dost exist, I should not be able not to understand this to be true.

GAUNILON AND ST. ANSELM

1.2   *Controversy over the Argument*

GAUNILON:

1. If one doubts or denies the existence of a being of such a nature that nothing greater than it can be conceived, he receives this answer:

The existence of this being is proved, in the first place, by the fact that he himself, in his doubt or denial regarding this being, already has it in his understanding; for in hearing it spoken of he understands what is spoken of. It is proved, therefore, by the fact that what he understands must exist not only in his understanding, but in reality also.

And the proof of this is as follows.—It is a greater thing to exist both in the understanding and in reality than to be in the understanding alone. And if this being is in the understanding alone, whatever has even in the past existed in reality will be greater than this being. And so that which was greater than all beings will be less than some being, and will not be greater than all: which is a manifest contradiction.

And hence, that which is greater than all, already proved to be in the understanding, must exist not only in the understanding, but also in reality: for otherwise it will not be greater than all other beings.

From the appendix to St. Anselm's *Proslogium*.

2. The fool might make this reply:

This being is said to be in my understanding already, only because I understand what is said. Now could it not with equal justice be said that I have in my understanding all manner of unreal objects, having absolutely no existence in themselves, because I understand these things if one speaks of them, whatever they may be?

Unless indeed it is shown that this being is of such a character that it cannot be held in concept like all unreal objects, or objects whose existence is uncertain: and hence I am not able to conceive of it when I hear of it, or to hold it in concept; but I must understand it and have it in my understanding; because, it seems, I cannot conceive of it in any other way than by understanding it, that is, by comprehending in my knowledge its existence in reality.

But if this is the case, in the first place there will be no distinction between what has precedence in time—namely, the having of an object in the understanding—and what is subsequent in time—namely, the understanding that an object exists; as in the example of the picture, which exists first in the mind of the painter, and afterwards in his work.

Moreover, the following assertion can hardly be accepted: that this being, when it is spoken of and heard of, cannot be conceived not to exist in the way in which even God can be conceived not to exist. For if this is impossible, what was the object of this argument against one who doubts or denies the existence of such a being?

Finally, that this being so exists that it cannot be perceived by an understanding convinced of its own indubitable existence, unless this being is afterwards conceived of—this should be proved to me by an indisputable argument, but not by that which you have advanced: namely, that what I understand, when I hear it, already is in my understanding. For thus in my understanding, as I still think, could be all sorts of things whose existence is uncertain, or which do not exist at all, if some one whose words I should understand mentioned them. And so much the more if I should be deceived, as often happens, and believe in them: though I do not yet believe in the being whose existence you would prove.

3. Hence, your example of the painter who already has in his understanding what he is to paint cannot agree with this argument. For the picture, before it is made, is contained in the artificer's art itself; and any such thing, existing in the art of an artificer, is nothing but a part of his understandng itself. A joiner, St. Augustine says, when he is about to make a box in fact, first has it in his art. The box which is made in fact is not life; but the box which exists in his art is life. For the artificer's soul lives, in which all these things are, before they are produced. Why, then, are these things life in the living soul of the artificer, unless because they are nothing else than the knowledge or understanding of the soul itself?

With the exception, however, of those facts which are known to pertain to

the mental nature, whatever, on being heard and thought out by the understanding, is perceived to be real, undoubtedly that real object is one thing, and
the understanding itself, by which the object is grasped, is another. Hence, even
if it were true that there is a being than which a greater is inconceivable: yet
to this being, when heard of and understood, the not yet created picture in
the mind of the painter is not analogous.

4. Let us notice also the point touched on above, with regard to this being
which is greater than all which can be conceived, and which, it is said, can be
none other than God himself. I, so far as actual knowledge of the object,
either from its specific or general character, is concerned, am as little able to
conceive of this being when I hear of it, or to have it in my understanding, as
I am to conceive of or understand God himself: whom, indeed, for this very
reason I can conceive not to exist. For I do not know that reality itself which
God is, nor can I form a conjecture of that reality from some other like reality.
For you yourself assert that that reality is such that there can be nothing else
like it.

For, suppose that I should hear something said of a man absolutely unknown to me, of whose very existence I was unaware. Through that special
or general knowledge by which I know what man is, or what men are, I could
conceive of him also, according to the reality itself, which man is. And yet it
would be possible, if the person who told me of him deceived me, that the man
himself, of whom I conceived, did not exist; since that reality according to
which I conceived of him, though a no less indisputable fact, was not that man,
but any man.

Hence, I am not able, in the way in which I should have this unreal being
in concept or in understanding, to have that being of which you speak in concept or in understanding, when I hear the word *God* or the words, *a being
greater than all other beings.* For I can conceive of the man according to a fact
that is real and familiar to me: but of God, or a being greater than all others,
I could not conceive at all, except merely according to the word. And an object
can hardly or never be conceived according to the word alone.

For when it is so conceived, it is not so much the word itself (which is,
indeed, a real thing—that is, the sound of the letters and syllables) as the
signification of the word, when heard, that is conceived. But it is not conceived
as by one who knows what is generally signified by the word; by whom, that
is, it is conceived according to a reality and in true conception alone. It is conceived as by a man who does not know the object, and conceives of it only
in accordance with the movement of his mind produced by hearing the word,
the mind attempting to image for itself the signification of the word that is
heard. And it would be surprising if in the reality of fact it could ever attain
to this.

Thus, it appears, and in no other way, this being is also in my understanding, when I hear and understand a person who says that there is a being greater than all conceivable beings. So much for the assertion that this supreme nature already is in my understanding.

5. But that this being must exist, not only in the understanding but also in reality, is thus proved to me:

If it did not so exist, whatever exists in reality would be greater than it. And so the being which has been already proved to exist in my understanding, will not be greater than all other beings.

I still answer: if it should be said that a being which cannot be even conceived in terms of any fact, is in the understanding, I do not deny that this being is, accordingly, in my understanding. But since through this fact it can in no wise attain to real existence also, I do not yet concede to it that existence at all, until some certain proof of it shall be given.

For he who says that this being exists, because otherwise the being which is greater than all will not be greater than all, does not attend strictly enough to what he is saying. For I do not yet say, no, I even deny or doubt that this being is greater than any real object. Nor do I concede to it any other existence than this (if it should be called existence) which it has when the mind, according to a word merely heard, tries to form the image of an object absolutely unknown to it.

How, then, is the veritable existence of that being proved to me from the assumption, by hypothesis, that it is greater than all other beings? For I should still deny this, or doubt your demonstration of it, to this extent, that I should not admit that this being is in my understanding and concept even in the way in which many objects whose real existence is uncertain and doubtful, are in my understanding and concept. For it should be proved first that this being itself really exists somewhere; and then, from the fact that it is greater than all, we shall not hesitate to infer that it also subsists in itself.

6. For example: it is said that somewhere in the ocean is an island, which, because of the difficulty, or rather the impossibility, of discovering what does not exist, is called the lost island. And they say that this island has an inestimable wealth of all manner of riches and delicacies in greater abundance than is told of the Islands of the Blest; and that having no owner or inhabitant, it is more excellent than all other countries, which are inhabited by mankind, in the abundance with which it is stored.

Now if some one should tell me that there is such an island, I should easily understand his words, in which there is no difficulty. But suppose that he went on to say, as if by a logical inference: "You can no longer doubt that this island which is more excellent than all lands exists somewhere, since you have no doubt that it is in your understanding. And since it is more excellent not to be in the understanding alone, but to exist both in the understanding and in reality, for this reason it must exist. For if it does not exist, any land which really exists will be more excellent than it; and so the island already under-stood by you to be more excellent will not be more excellent."

If a man should try to prove to me by such reasoning that this island truly exists, and that its existence should no longer be doubted, either I should believe that he was jesting, or I know not which I ought to regard as the greater fool: myself, supposing that I should allow this proof; or him, if he should suppose that he had established with any certainty the existence of this island. For he ought to show first that the hypothetical excellence of this island exists as a real and indubitable fact, and in no wise as any unreal object, or one whose existence is uncertain, in my understanding.

7. This, in the mean time, is the answer the fool could make to the arguments urged against him. When he is assured in the first place that this being is so great that its non-existence is not even conceivable, and that this in turn is proved on no other ground than the fact that otherwise it will not be greater than all things, the fool may make the same answer, and say:

When did I say that any such being exists in reality, that is, a being greater than all others?—that on this ground it should be proved to me that it also exists in reality to such a degree that it cannot even be conceived not to exist? Whereas in the first place it should be in some way proved that a nature which is higher, that is, greater and better, than all other natures, exists; in order that from this we may then be able to prove all attributes which necessarily the being that is greater and better than all possesses.

Moreover, it is said that the non-existence of this being is inconceivable. It might better be said, perhaps, that its non-existence, or the possibility of its non-existence, is unintelligible. For according to the true meaning of the word, unreal objects are unintelligible. Yet their existence is conceivable in the way in which the fool conceived of the non-existence of God. I am most certainly aware of my own existence; but I know, nevertheless, that my non-existence is possible. As to that supreme being, moreover, which God is, I understand without any doubt both his existence, and the impossibility of his non-existence. Whether, however, so long as I am positively aware of my existence, I can conceive of my non-existence, I am not sure. But if I can, why can I not conceive of the non-existence of whatever else I know with the same certainty? If, however, I cannot, God will not be the only being of which it can be said, it is impossible to conceive of his non-existence.

8. The other parts of this book are argued with such truth, such brilliancy, such grandeur; and are so replete with usefulness, so fragrant with a certain perfume of devout and holy feeling, that though there are matters in the beginning which, however rightly sensed, are weakly presented, the rest of the work should not be rejected on this account. The rather ought these earlier matters to be reasoned more cogently, and the whole to be received with great respect and honor.

ST. ANSELM:

A general refutation of Gaunilon's argument. It is shown that a being than which a greater cannot be conceived exists in reality.

You say—whosoever you may be, who say that a fool is capable of making these statements—that a being than which a greater cannot be conceived is not in the understanding in any other sense than that in which a being that is altogether inconceivable in terms of reality, is in the understanding. You say that the inference that this being exists in reality, from the fact that it is in the understanding, is no more just than the inference that a lost island most certainly exists, from the fact that when it is described the hearer does not doubt that it is in his understanding.

But I say: if a being than which a greater is inconceivable is not understood or conceived, and is not in the understanding or in concept, certainly either God is not a being than which a greater is inconceivable, or else he is not understood or conceived, and is not in the understanding or in concept. But I call on your faith and conscience to attest that this is most false. Hence, that than which a greater cannot be conceived is truly understood and conceived, and is in the understanding and in concept. Therefore either the grounds on which you try to controvert me are not true, or else the inference which you think to base logically on those grounds is not justified.

But you hold, moreover, that supposing that a being than which a greater cannot be conceived is understood, it does not follow that this being is in the understanding; nor, if it is in the understanding, does it therefore exist in reality.

In answer to this, I maintain positively: if that being can be even conceived to be, it must exist in reality. For that than which a greater is inconceivable cannot be conceived except as without beginning. But whatever can be conceived to exist, and does not exist, can be conceived to exist through a beginning. Hence what can be conceived to exist, but does not exist, is not the being than which a greater cannot be conceived. Therefore, if such a being can be conceived to exist, necessarily it does exist.

Furthermore: if it can be conceived at all, it must exist. For no one who denies or doubts the existence of a being than which a greater is inconceivable, denies or doubts that if it did exist, its non-existence, either in reality or in the understanding, would be impossible. For otherwise it would not be a being than which a greater cannot be conceived. But as to whatever can be conceived, but does not exist—if there were such a being, its non-existence, either in reality or in the understanding, would be possible. Therefore if a being than which a greater is inconceivable can be even conceived, it cannot be non-existent.

But let us suppose that it does not exist, even if it can be conceived. Whatever can be conceived, but does not exist, if it existed, would not be a being than which a greater is inconceivable. If, then, there were a being a greater than which is inconceivable, it would not be a being than which a greater is inconceivable: which is most absurd. Hence, it is false to deny that a being than which a greater cannot be conceived exists, if it can be even conceived; much the more, therefore, if it can be understood or can be in the understanding.

Moreover, I will venture to make this assertion: without doubt, whatever at any place or at any time does not exist—even if it does exist at some place or at some time—can be conceived to exist nowhere and never, as at some place and at some time it does not exist. For what did not exist yesterday, and exists to-day, as it is understood not to have existed yesterday, so it can be apprehended by the intelligence that it never exists. And what is not here, and is elsewhere, can be conceived to be nowhere, just as it is not here. So with regard to an object of which the individual parts do not exist at the same places or times: all its parts and therefore its very whole can be conceived to exist nowhere or never.

For, although time is said to exist always, and the world everywhere, yet time does not as a whole exist always, nor the world as a whole everywhere. And as individual parts of time do not exist when others exist, so they can be conceived never to exist. And so it can be apprehended by the intelligence that individual parts of the world exist nowhere, as they do not exist where other parts exist. Moreover, what is composed of parts can be dissolved in concept, and be non-existent. Therefore, whatever at any place or at any time does not exist as a whole, even if it is existent, can be conceived not to exist.

But that than which a greater cannot be conceived, if it exists, cannot be conceived not to exist. Otherwise, it is not a being than which a greater cannot be conceived: which is inconsistent. By no means, then, does it at any place or at any time fail to exist as a whole: but it exists as a whole everywhere and always.

Do you believe that this being can in some way be conceived or understood, or that the being with regard to which these things are understood can be in concept or in the understanding? For if it cannot, these things cannot be understood with reference to it. But if you say that it is not understood and that it is not in the understanding, because it is not thoroughly understood; you should say that a man who cannot face the direct rays of the sun does not see the light of day, which is none other than the sunlight. Assuredly a being than which a greater cannot be conceived exists, and is in the understanding, at least to this extent—that these statements regarding it are understood.

> The argument is continued. It is shown that a being than which a greater
> is inconceivable can be conceived, and also, in so far, exists.

I have said, then, in the argument which you dispute, that when the fool hears mentioned a being than which a greater is inconceivable, he understands what he hears. Certainly a man who does not understand when a familiar language is spoken, has no understanding at all, or a very dull one. Moreover, I have said that if this being is understood, it is in the understanding. Is that in no understanding which has been proved necessarily to exist in the reality of fact?

But you will say that although it is in the understanding, it does not follow that it is understood. But observe that the fact of its being understood does necessitate its being in the understanding. For as what is conceived, is conceived by conception, and what is conceived by conception, as it is conceived, so is in conception; so what is understood, is understood by understanding, and what is understood by understanding, as it is understood, so is in the understanding. What can be more clear than this?

After this, I have said that if it is even in the understanding alone, it can be conceived also to exist in reality, which is greater. If, then, it is in the understanding alone, obviously the very being than which a greater cannot be conceived is one than which a greater can be conceived. What is more logical? For if it exists even in the understanding alone, can it not be conceived also to exist in reality? And if it can be so conceived, does not he who conceives of this conceive of a thing greater than that being, if it exists in the understanding alone? What more consistent inference, then, can be made than this: that if a being than which a greater cannot be conceived is in the understanding alone, it is not that than which a greater cannot be conceived?

But, assuredly, in no understanding is a being than which a greater is conceivable a being than which a greater is inconceivable. Does it not follow, then, that if a being than which a greater cannot be conceived is in any understanding, it does not exist in the understanding alone? For if it is in the understanding alone, it is a being than which a greater can be conceived, which is inconsistent with the hypothesis.

> A criticism of Gaunilon's example, in which he tries to show that in this
> way the real existence of a lost island might be inferred from the fact
> of its being conceived.

But, you say, it is as if one should suppose an island in the ocean, which surpasses all lands in its fertility, and which, because of the difficulty, or rather the impossibility, of discovering what does not exist, is called a lost island; and should say that there can be no doubt that this island truly exists in reality, for this reason, that one who hears it described easily understands what he hears.

Now I promise confidently that if any man shall devise anything existing either in reality or in concept alone (except that than which a greater cannot be conceived) to which he can adapt the sequence of my reasoning, I will discover that thing, and will give him his lost island, not to be lost again.

But it now appears that this being than which a greater is inconceivable cannot be conceived not to be, because it exists on so assured a ground of truth; for otherwise it would not exist at all.

Hence, if anyone says that he conceives this being not to exist, I say that at the time when he conceives of this either he conceives of a being than which a greater is inconceivable, or he does not conceive at all. If he does not conceive, he does not conceive of the non-existence of that of which he does not conceive. But if he does conceive, he certainly conceives of a being which cannot be even conceived not to exist. For if it could be conceived not to exist, it could be conceived to have a beginning and an end. But this is impossible.

He, then, who conceives of this being conceives of a being which cannot be even conceived not to exist; but he who conceives of this being does not conceive that it does not exist; else he conceives what is inconceivable. The non-existence, then, of that than which a greater cannot be conceived is inconceivable.

> The difference between the possibility of conceiving of non-existence, and understanding non-existence.

You say, moreover, that whereas I assert that this supreme being cannot be *conceived* not to exist, it might better be said that its non-existence, or even the possibility of its non-existence, cannot be *understood*.

But it was more proper to say, it cannot be conceived. For if I had said that the object itself cannot be understood not to exist, possibly you yourself, who say that in accordance with the true meaning of the term what is unreal cannot be understood, would offer the objection that nothing which is can be understood not to be, for the non-existence of what exists is unreal: hence God would not be the only being of which it could be said, it is impossible to understand its non-existence. For thus one of those beings which most certainly exist can be understood not to exist in the same way in which certain other real objects can be understood not to exist.

But this objection, assuredly, cannot be urged against the term *conception,* if one considers the matter well. For although no objects which exist can be understood not to exist, yet all objects, except that which exists in the highest degree, can be conceived not to exist. For all those objects, and those alone, can be conceived not to exist, which have a beginning or end or composition of parts: also, as I have already said, whatever at any place or at any time does not exist as a whole.

That being alone, on the other hand, cannot be conceived not to exist, in which any conception discovers neither beginning nor end nor composition of parts, and which any conception finds always and everywhere as a whole.

Be assured, then, that you can conceive of your own non-existence, although you are most certain that you exist. I am surprised that you should have admitted that you are ignorant of this. For we conceive of the non-existence of many objects which we know to exist, and of the existence of many which we know not to exist; not by forming the opinion that they so exist, but by imagining that they exist as we conceive of them.

And indeed, we can conceive of the non-existence of an object, although we know it to exist, because at the same time we can conceive of the former and know the latter. And we cannot conceive of the non-existence of an object, so long as we know it to exist, because we cannot conceive at the same time of existence and non-existence.

If, then, one will thus distinguish these two senses of this statement, he will understand that nothing, so long as it is known to exist, can be conceived not to exist; and that whatever exists, except that being than which a greater cannot be conceived, can be conceived not to exist, even when it is known to exist.

So, then, of God alone it can be said that it is impossible to conceive of his non-existence; and yet many objects, so long as they exist, in one sense cannot be conceived not to exist. But in what sense God is to be conceived not to exist, I think has been shown clearly enough in my book.

A particular discussion of certain statements of Gaunilon's. In the first place, he misquoted the argument which he undertook to refute.

The nature of the other objections which you, in behalf of the fool, urge against me it is easy, even for a man of small wisdom, to detect; and I had therefore thought it unnecessary to show this. But since I hear that some readers of these objections think they have some weight against me, I will discuss them briefly.

In the first place, you often repeat that I assert that what is greater than all other beings is in the understanding; and if it is in the understanding, it exists also in reality, for otherwise the being which is greater than all would not be greater than all.

Nowhere in all my writings is such a demonstration found. For the real existence of a being which is said to be *greater than all other beings* cannot be demonstrated in the same way with the real existence of one that is said to be *a being than which a greater cannot be conceived.*

If it should be said that a being than which a greater cannot be conceived has no real existence, or that it is possible that it does not exist, or even that it can be conceived not to exist, such an assertion can be easily refuted. For the non-existence of what does not exist is possible, and that whose non-existence is possible can be conceived not to exist. But whatever can be conceived not to exist, if it exists, is not a being than which a greater cannot be conceived; but if it does not exist, it would not, even if it existed, be a being than which a greater cannot be conceived. But it cannot be said that a being than which a greater is inconceivable, if it exists, is not a being than which a greater is inconceivable; or that if it existed, it would not be a being than which a greater is inconceivable.

It is evident, then, that neither is it non-existent, nor is it possible that it does not exist, nor can it be conceived not to exist. For otherwise, if it exists, it is not that which it is said to be in the hypothesis; and if it existed, it would not be what it is said to be in the hypothesis.

But this, it appears, cannot be so easily proved of a being which is said to be *greater than all other beings.* For it is not so evident that what can be con-

ceived not to exist is not greater than all existing beings, as it is evident that
it is not a being than which a greater cannot be conceived. Nor is it so indubitable that if a being greater than all other beings exists, it is no other than
the being than which a greater cannot be conceived; or that if it were such a
being, some other might not be this being in like manner; as it is certain with
regard to a being which is hypothetically posited as one than which a greater
cannot be conceived.

For consider: if one should say that there is a being greater than all other
beings, and that this being can nevertheless be conceived not to exist; and that
a being greater than this, although it does not exist, can be conceived to exist:
can it be so clearly inferred in this case that this being is therefore not a being
greater than all other existing beings, as it would be most positively affirmed
in the other case, that the being under discussion is not, therefore, a being
than which a greater cannot be conceived?

For the former conclusion requires another premise than the predication,
greater than all other beings. In my argument, on the other hand, there is no
need of any other than this very predication, *a being than which a greater
cannot be conceived.*

If the same proof cannot be applied when the being in question is predicated
to be greater than all others, which can be applied when it is predicated to be
a being than which a greater cannot be conceived, you have unjustly censured
me for saying what I did not say; since such a predication differs so greatly
from that which I actually made. If, on the other hand, the other argument is
valid, you ought not to blame me so for having said what can be proved.

Whether this can be proved, however, he will easily decide who recognises
that this being than which a greater cannot be conceived is demonstrable. For
by no means can this being than which a greater cannot be conceived be
understood as any other than that which alone is greater than all. Hence, just
as that than which a greater cannot be conceived is understood, and is in the
understanding, and for that reason is asserted to exist in the reality of fact:
so what is said to be greater than all other beings is understood and is in the
understanding, and therefore it is necessarily inferred that it exists in reality.

You see, then, with how much justice you have compared me with your
fool, who, on the sole ground that he understands what is described to him,
would affirm that a lost island exists.

> A discussion of Gaunilon's argument in his second chapter: that any
> unreal beings can be understood in the same way, and would, to that
> extent, exist.

Another of your objections is that any unreal beings, or beings whose existence
is uncertain, can be understood and be in the understanding in the same way
with that being which I discussed. I am surprised that you should have conceived this objection, for I was attempting to prove what was still uncertain,
and contented myself at first with showing that this being is understood in

any way, and is in the understanding. It was my intention to consider, on these grounds, whether this being is in the understanding alone, like an unreal object, or whether it also exists in fact, as a real being. For if unreal objects, or objects whose existence is uncertain, in this way are understood and are in the understanding, because, when they are spoken of, the hearer understands what the speaker means, there is no reason why that being of which I spoke should not be understood and be in the understanding.

How, moreover, can these two statements of yours be reconciled: (1) the assertion that if a man should speak of any unreal objects, whatever they might be, you would understand, and (2) the assertion that on hearing of that being which does exist, and not in that way in which even unreal objects are held in concept, you would not say that you conceive of it or have it in concept; since, as you say, you cannot conceive of it in any other way than by understanding it, that is, by comprehending in your knowledge its real existence?

How, I ask, can these two things be reconciled: that unreal objects are understood, and that understanding an object is comprehending in knowledge its real existence? The contradiction does not concern me: do you see to it. But if unreal objects are also in some sort understood, and your definition is applicable, not to every understanding, but to a certain sort of understanding, I ought not to be blamed for saying that a being than which a greater cannot be conceived is understood and is in the understanding, even before I reached the certain conclusion that this being exists in reality.

> In answer to another objection: that the supremely great being may be conceived not to exist, just as by the fool God is conceived not to exist.

Again, you say that it can probably never be believed that this being, when it is spoken of and heard of, cannot be conceived not to exist in the same way in which even God may be conceived not to exist.

Such an objection could be answered by those who have attained but little skill in disputation and argument. For is it compatible with reason for a man to deny the existence of what he understands, because it is said to be that being whose existence he denies because he does not understand it? Or, if at some times its existence is denied, because only to a certain extent is it understood, and that which is not at all understood is the same to him: is not what is still undetermined more easily proved of a being which exists in some understanding than of one which exists is no understanding?

Hence it cannot be credible that any man denies the existence of a being than which a greater cannot be conceived, which, when he hears of it, he understands in a certain degree: it is incredible, I say, that any man denies the existence of this being because he denies the existence of God, the sensory perception of whom he in no wise conceives of.

Or if the existence of another object, because it is not at all understood, is denied, yet is not the existence of what is understood in some degree more easily proved than the existence of an object which is in no wise understood?

Not irrationally, then, has the hypothesis of a being a greater than which cannot be conceived been employed in controverting the fool, for the proof of the existence of God: since in some degree he would understand such a being, but in no wise could he understand God.

> The example of the picture, treated in Gaunilon's third chapter, is examined.—From what source a notion may be formed of the supremely great being, of which Gaunilon inquired in his fourth chapter.

Moreover, your so careful demonstration that the being than which a greater cannot be conceived is not analogous to the not yet executed picture in the understanding of the painter, is quite unnecessary. It was not for this purpose that I suggested the preconceived picture. I had no thought of asserting that the being which I was discussing is of such a nature; but I wished to show that what is not understood to exist can be in the understanding.

Again, you say that when you hear of a being than which a greater is inconceivable, you cannot conceive of it in terms of any real object known to you either specifically or generally, nor have it in your understanding. For, you say, you neither know such a being in itself, nor can you form an idea of it from anything like it.

But obviously this is not true. For everything that is less good, in so far as it is good, is like the greater good. It is therefore evident to any rational mind, that by ascending from the lesser good to the greater, we can form a considerable notion of a being than which a greater is inconceivable.

For instance, who (even if he does not believe that what he conceives of exists in reality) supposing that there is some good which has a beginning and an end, does not conceive that a good is much better, which, if it begins, does not cease to be? And that as the second good is better than the first, so that good which has neither beginning nor end, though it is ever passing from the past through the present to the future, is better than the second? And that far better than this is a being—whether any being of such a nature exists or not—which in no wise requires change or motion, nor is compelled to undergo change or motion?

Is this inconceivable, or is some being greater than this conceivable? Or is not this to form a notion from objects than which a greater is conceivable, of the being than which a greater cannot be conceived? There is, then, a means of forming a notion of a being than which a greater is inconceivable.

So easily, then, can the fool who does not accept sacred authority be refuted, if he denies that a notion may be formed from other objects of a being than which a greater is inconceivable. But if any Catholic would deny this, let him remember that the invisible things of God, from the creation of the world, are clearly seen, being understood by the things that are made, even his eternal power and Godhead. (Romans i. 20.)

The possibility of understanding and conceiving of the supremely great being. The argument advanced against the fool is confirmed.

But even if it were true that a being than which a greater is inconceivable cannot be conceived or understood; yet it would not be untrue that a being than which a greater cannot be conceived is conceivable and intelligible. There is nothing to prevent one's saying *ineffable*, although what is said to be ineffable cannot be spoken of. *Inconceivable* is conceivable, although that to which the word *inconceivable* can be applied is not conceivable. So, when one says, *that than which nothing greater is conceivable*, undoubtedly what is heard is conceivable and intelligible, although that being itself, than which a greater is inconceivable, cannot be conceived or understood.

Or, though there is a man so foolish as to say that there is no being than which a greater is inconceivable, he will not be so shameless as to say that he cannot understand or conceive of what he says. Or, if such a man is found, not only ought his words to be rejected, but he himself should be contemned.

Whoever, then, denies the existence of a being than which a greater cannot be conceived, at least understands and conceives of the denial which he makes. But this denial he cannot understand or conceive of without its component terms; and a term of this statement is *a being than which a greater cannot be conceived*. Whoever, then, makes this denial, understands and conceives of that than which a greater is inconceivable.

Moreover, it is evident that in the same way it is possible to conceive of and understand a being whose non-existence is impossible; but he who conceives of this conceives of a greater being than one whose non-existence is possible. Hence, when a being than which a greater is inconceivable is conceived, if it is a being whose non-existence is possible that is conceived, it is not a being than which a greater cannot be conceived. But an object cannot be at once conceived and not conceived. Hence he who conceives of a being than which a greater is inconceivable, does not conceive of that whose non-existence is possible, but of that whose non-existence is impossible. Therefore, what he conceives of must exist; for anything whose non-existence is possible, is not that of which he conceives.

The certainty of the foregoing argument.—The conclusion of the book.

I believe that I have shown by an argument which is not weak, but sufficiently cogent, that in my former book I proved the real existence of a being than which a greater cannot be conceived; and I believe that this argument cannot be invalidated by the validity of any objection. For so great force does the signification of this reasoning contain in itself, that this being which is the subject of discussion, is of necessity, from the very fact that it is understood or conceived, proved also to exist in reality, and to be whatever we should believe of the divine substance.

For we attribute to the divine substance anything of which it can be conceived that it is better to be than not to be that thing. For example: it is better to be eternal than not eternal; good, than not good; nay, goodness itself, than not goodness itself. But it cannot be that anything of this nature is not a property of the being than which a greater is inconceivable. Hence, the being than which a greater is inconceivable must be whatever should be attributed to the divine essence.

ALVIN PLANTINGA

**1.3   Kant's Objection
to the Ontological Argument**

The Ontological Argument for the existence of God has fascinated and puzzled philosophers ever since it was first formulated by St. Anselm. I suppose most philosophers have been inclined to reject the argument, although it has an illustrious line of defenders extending to the present and presently terminating in Professors Malcolm and Hartshorne. Many philosophers have tried to give *general* refutations of the argument—refutations designed to show that no version of it can possibly succeed—of which the most important is, perhaps, Kant's objection, with its several contemporary variations. I believe that none of these general refutations are successful; in what follows I shall support this belief by critically examining Kant's objection.

Anselm's argument, it seems to me, is best construed as a *reductio ad absurdum*. Let us use the term 'God' as an abbreviation for 'the being than which none greater can be conceived'. The argument then proceeds (in Anselm's own terms as much as possible) as follows:

(1) God exists in the understanding but not in reality.

(assumption for *reductio*)

(2) Existence in reality is greater than existence in the understanding alone.

(premise)

(3) A being having all of God's properties plus existence in reality can be conceived.   (premise)

(4) A being having all of God's properties plus existence in reality is greater than God.   (from 1 and 2)

From *The Journal of Philosophy* 63 (1966): 537–46. Copyright © 1966 by Journal of Philosophy, Inc. Reprinted by permission of the author and the editors.

(5) A being greater than God can be conceived. (3, 4)

(6) It is false that a being greater than God can be conceived.

(by definition of 'God')

(7) Hence, it is false that God exists in the understanding but not in reality.

(1–6 *reductio ad absurdum*)

And so, if God exists in the understanding, he also exists in reality; but clearly enough he does exist in the understanding (as even the fool will testify); accordingly, he exists in reality as well.

A couple of preliminary comments: to say that a state of affairs is conceivable is to say that there is no logical impossibility in the supposition that it obtains. And to say specifically that a being having all of God's properties plus existence in reality is conceivable, is simply to say that it is possible that there is a being having all of God's properties plus existence in reality—i.e., it is possible that God exists. To say that a being greater than God can be conceived, on the other hand, is to say that it is possible that there exist a being greater than the being than which it is not possible that there exist a greater—which certainly seems unlikely. We should note further that premise 2 of the argument is susceptible of several interpretations, each yielding a different version of the argument. For example, it may be taken as 2a:

(2a) If x exists and y does not, then x is greater than y.

It can also be taken as a weaker claim. Suppose we select some properties—call them "*g*-properties"—whose possession makes for greatness. Then we might read 2 as

(2b) If x has every g-property y has, and x exists and y does not, then x is greater than y.[1]

And of course there are many other possible interpretations.

The most famous attack upon the Ontological Argument is contained in a few pages of the *Critique of Pure Reason*—an attack which many think conclusive. The heart of Kant's objection is contained in the following passage:

> "*Being*" is obviously not a real predicate; that is, it is not a concept of something which could be added to the concept of a thing. It is merely the positing of a thing, or of certain determinations, as existing in themselves. Logically, it is merely the copula of a judgment. The proposition "God is omnipotent" contains two concepts, each of which has its object—God and omnipotence. The small word "is" adds no new predicate, but only serves to posit the predicate *in its relation* to the subject. If, now, we take the subject (God) with all its predicates (among which is omnipotence), and say "God is," or "There is a God," we attach no new predicate to the concept of God, but only posit the

---

[1]This version of 2 was suggested to me by Peter De Vos.

subject in itself with all its predicates, and indeed, posit it as an *object* that stands in relation to my *concept*. The content of both must be one and the same; nothing can have been added to the concept, which expresses merely what is possible, by my thinking its object (through the expression "it is") as given absolutely. Otherwise stated, the real contains no more than the merely possible. A hundred real thalers do not contain the least coin more than a hundred possible thalers. For as the latter signify the concept and the former the object and the positing of the concept, should the former contain more than the latter, my concept would not, in that case, express the whole object, and would not therefore be an adequate concept of it. My financial position, however, is affected very differently by a hundred real thalers than it is by the mere concept of them (that is, of their possibility). For the object, as it actually exists, is not analytically contained in my concept, but is added to my concept (which is a determination of my state) synthetically; and yet the conceived hundred thalers are not themselves in the least increased through thus acquiring existence outside my concept.

By whatever and by however many predicates we may think a thing—even if we completely determine it—we do not make the least addition to the thing when we further declare that this thing *is*. Otherwise it would not be exactly the same thing that exists, but something more than we had thought in the concept: and we could not, therefore, say that the exact object of my concept exists. If we think in a thing every feature of reality except one, the missing reality is not added by my saying that this defective thing exists. [2]

How, exactly, is what Kant says here relevant to Anselm's Ontological Argument? And how are we to understand what he says? The point of the passage seems to be that being or existence is not a real predicate; Kant apparently thinks this follows from (or is equivalent to) what he puts variously as "the real *contains* no more than the merely possible," "the *content* of both (i.e., concept and object) must be one and the same," "being is not the concept of something that could be *added to* the concept of a thing," etc. An adequate concept, Kant believes, must contain as much content as the thing of which it is the concept; the content of the concept of a thing remains the same whether the thing exists or not; and the existence of the object of a concept is not part of the content of that concept. But what *is* the content of a concept, or of an object? In what way do objects and concepts have content? Kant gives us very little help, in the passage under consideration, in understanding what it is to *add something* to a concept, what it means to say that a concept *contains* as much as an object, or what it is for a concept and its object both to have *content*—the *same* content.

Perhaps what he means is something like this: the content of a concept is the set of properties a thing must have to fall under or be an instance of that concept. The content of the concept *crevasse*, for example, includes, among others, the properties of *occurring on or in glaciers*, and *being more than one foot deep*. The content of the concept *the tallest man in Boston*, will include, among others, the properties of *being a man, being in Boston*, and *being taller*

---

[2]Kemp Smith translation (London: Macmillan, 1929), pp. 504–5.

than any other man in Boston. The content of an *object*, on the other hand, is the set of properties that object has; and a thing *a has* (at least) *as much content as* or *contains as much as* a thing *b* if every member of *b*'s content is a member of *a*'s content. But here we immediately encounter difficulty. For of course it will not be true that the concept of an object contains as much content as the object itself. Consider, for example, the concept *horse.* Any real horse will have many properties not contained in that concept; any real horse will be either more than 16 hands high or else 16 hands or less. But neither of these properties is in the content of the concept *horse* (although of course the property of being either more than 16 hands high or else 16 hands or less will be). Similarly for the tallest man in Boston: he will have the property of being married or else the property of being unmarried; but neither of these properties is part of the content of the concept *the tallest man in Boston.* This suggestion, therefore, requires amendment.

"By whatever and by however many predicates we may think a thing—even if we completely determine it—we do not make the least addition to the thing when we further declare that this thing *is.*" This sentence provides a clue. We might note that to every object there corresponds its *whole concept:* the concept whose content includes all (and only) the properties the object in question has. And where *C* is the whole concept of some object *O*, suppose we say that *a whole concept of O diminished with respect to P* is any concept whose content is a largest subset of the content of *C* that does not entail[3] *P*— that is, its content is a subset of *C* that does not entail *P*, and is such that the addition of any other member of the content of *C* yields a set that does entail *P*. Very roughly and inaccurately, a whole concept diminished with respect to *P* is what remains of the whole concept when *P* is deleted from its content.

Now suppose we consider a domain *D* of objects some of which really exist and some of which are merely mythological; among its members we may find, e.g., Pegasus, the Taj Mahal, Lyndon Johnson, Santa Claus, Bucephalos, and King Arthur. Suppose also that we define an existential quantifier over this domain as follows: "$(\exists x)x$ is pink" is to be read as "some existing member of *D* is pink." (If we went on to embed this quantifier in an appropriate lower functional calculus, the result would be what has been called "free logic.") Suppose, furthermore, that the Taj Mahal is pink; and let C, C^{-E}, and C^{-P} be, respectively, the whole concept of the Taj Mahal, a whole concept of the Taj Mahal diminished with respect to existence, and a whole concept of the Taj Mahal diminished with respect to pinkness. Finally, let Cx, $C^{-E}x$ and $C^{-P}x$, respectively, ascribe to *x* all the properties in C, C^{-E}, and C^{-P}. Now perhaps Kant means to point out that existence differs from pinkness in the following respect. Evidently there are possible circumstances in which $(\exists x)C^{-P}x$ would be true but $(\exists x)Cx$ false; perhaps these circumstances would obtain if the Taj

---

[3]Where a set *S* of properties entails a property *P* if the proposition that a thing *x* has *P* follows from the proposition that *x* has every property in *S*.

Mahal were green, for example. But the same does not hold for $(\exists x)C^{-E}x$; it cannot be true unless $(\exists x)Cx$ is too. It is possible that a whole concept of the Taj Mahal diminished with respect to pinkness be exemplified by some existing member of D when the whole concept of the Taj Mahal is not. But here existence differs from pinkness; if any whole concept of the Taj Mahal diminished with respect to existence is exemplified, then so is the whole concept. A whole concept diminished with respect to existence, unlike a whole concept diminished with respect to pinkness, is *existentially equivalent* to the corresponding whole concept. And perhaps this fact yields an explanation of the claim that existence is not a real property or predicate; we might say that P is a *real* property or predicate just in case it is false that any whole concept diminished with respect to P is existentially equivalent to the corresponding whole concept ($D1$). It then turns out that existence, unlike pinkness, is not a real property; it "is not a concept of something that could be added to the concept of a thing."

But here we must consider an objection that runs as follows. It is certainly true that, on the proffered definitions, existence is not a real quality. But that this is so is, given these definitions, a mere triviality that in no significant way distinguishes existence from other properties. To see this, let us return to our domain of objects. We defined a quantifier over this domain in such a way that "$(\exists x)Qx$" is to mean that some existent member of the domain has Q. We could also define a "quantifier" $(\exists^r x)$ (the quotation marks may serve to mollify the purist) in such a way that '$(\exists^r x)Qx$' is to mean that some *pink* member of the domain has Q. Then, even if no *existent* member of D were pink, it would still be true that $(\exists^r x)$ ($x =$ Valhalla) since, as is well known, the walls of Valhalla are pink. And now we note that $(\exists^r x)C^{-P}x$ can be true if and only if $(\exists^r x)Cx$ is true; we might say that a whole concept diminished with respect to pinkness is *pinksistentially equivalent* to the corresponding whole concept. Of course the same is not true for a whole concept diminished with respect to existence. There are possible circumstances in which $(\exists^r x)C^{-E}x$ but not $(\exists^r x)Cx$ would hold; these circumstances might have obtained, for example, had the Taj Mahal been the merely mythological dwelling place of some legendary Indian prince. And if we said that P is a real property or predicate just in case it is false that any whole concept diminished with respect to P is pinksistentially equivalent to the corresponding whole concept ($D2$), then existence, but not pinkness, would be a real property or predicate.

We might put the charge of triviality as follows. To say, under ($D1$), that pinkness is a real predicate but existence is not, really comes to saying that the proposition *all existent members of D exist* is necessarily true but *all existent members of D are pink* is not. This is indeed so; but it seems no more illuminating, in the present context, than the parallel remark that, although *all pink members of D are pink* is necessarily true, *all pink members of D exist* is not.

If we accept this objection, then, Kant's claim begins to look like an insignificant triviality with which Anselm scarcely need concern himself. But should we accept it? Kant is not, it seems to me, entirely without a reply; there is a fairly plausible refinement of his claim that may evade the charge of triviality. For consider any merely mythological creature such as Santa Claus, and ask whether he has the property of wearing a size-ten shoe. The legends and stories say nothing at all about the size of Santa's feet. Does Santa wear a size-10 shoe? There seems no reason for supposing that he does, but also no reason for supposing the contrary. There seems, furthermore, to be no way to investigate the question. And perhaps it is plausible to suggest that it's not merely that we don't *know* whether Santa wears a size-ten shoe—there is nothing *to* know here. That Santa wears a size-ten shoe is neither true nor false; he has neither the property of wearing a size-ten shoe nor the complement of that property. And, it might be added, here is the crucial difference between any existent and any nonexistent object. Where O is any existent object and P any property, either O has P or O has the complement $\bar{P}$ of P, (and if O's having P is absurd or necessarily false, as in the case of President Johnson and the property of being a real number, then O has $\bar{P}$). But if O is a merely fictional object such as Pegasus or Santa Claus, then there is at least one property P such that O has neither P nor $\bar{P}$; there is at least one property P such that O *has* P is neither true nor false.

I know of no very strong arguments either for or against this view. But suppose for the moment that it is true. Then a certain difference between existence and pinkness emerges. First of all, the whole concept of an existing object will be *maximal* in the sense that, for any property P, either P or $\bar{P}$ will be a member of it; since this is false for any whole concept of a nonexistent being, a whole concept of an existent is larger than any whole concept of a nonexistent. To put the same point differently, any consistent maximal concept contains existence. This is not true for pinkness, of course; it is not true that any consistent maximal concept contains pinkness.

Furthermore, a whole concept diminished with respect to existence will be smaller than a whole concept diminished with respect to pinkness. For consider any pair of whole concepts diminished with respect to pinkness and existence respectively: suppose we call them C^{-P} and C^{-E}. The result of adding *non-existence* to C^{-E} is a consistent concept, since it is possible that D contain an object that has every property in C^{-E} and lacks existence. But this new concept cannot be maximal; for, if it were, then on the doctrine under consideration it would contain existence; since it also contains nonexistence, the result would be inconsistent. So we cannot construct a maximal concept by adding non-existence to a whole concept diminished with respect to existence. On the other hand, it is possible to show that we *can* construct a maximal concept by adding nonpinkness to some whole concept diminished with respect to pinkness. In this respect, therefore, a whole concept diminished with respect to existence is smaller than one diminished with respect to pinkness.

We could dramatize this difference by redefining 'whole concept diminished with respect to *P*' as "set of properties such that (1) it is a largest subset of *C* that does not entail *P*, and (2) the addition of *P̄* to it yields a maximal concept." Then there would *be* no whole concepts diminished with respect to existence; and then the dictum that existence is not a property could be understood as the claim that what distinguishes existence from a real property such as pinkness is just that there are no whole concepts diminished with respect to existence.

Giving a clear and fairly plausible explanation of the claim that existence is not a real predicate, this interpretation also suggests an interesting respect in which existence may differ from other predicates or properties. Unfortunately, it seems to have no particular bearing on Anselm's argument. For Anselm can certainly agree, so far as his argument is concerned, that existence is not a real predicate in the explained sense. Anselm maintains that the concept *the being than which none greater can be conceived* is necessarily exemplified; that this is so is in no way inconsistent with the suggestion that existence differs in the way just explained from pinkness. Anselm argues that the proposition *God exists* is necessarily true; but neither this claim nor his argument for it entails or presupposes that existence is a predicate in the sense just explained.

Finally I wish to make a desultory gesture (space permits no more) in the direction of another way of understanding Kant's objection. "Being is obviously not a real predicate; that is, it is not a concept of something that could be added to the concept of a thing. It is merely the positing of a thing, or of certain determinations, as existing in themselves." Conceivably Gottlob Frege means to echo this sentiment when he writes that "Affirmation of existence is in fact nothing but a denial of the number nought. Because existence is a property of concepts [and not of objects] the ontological argument for the existence of God breaks down."[4] Now, in saying that existence is not a property of objects, Frege does not mean to say, of course, that propositions of the form *x exists* are all nonsensical or false. He means rather that any proposition of that form is equivalent to one that predicates *being instantiated* or *having some number other than nought* of a concept. And he means to say further that the second way of putting the matter is more revealing or more "basic" than the first. But how does this bear on Anselm's proof? It seems to show only that an equivalent (and perhaps more "basic") form of the argument may be obtained by replacing every phrase of the form '*x* exists', in the argument, by some such phrase as 'the concept of *x* is not instantiated'. Now, if this procedure is to reveal some impropriety in Anselm's argument, then the resulting argument must display some glaring deficiency not apparent in the original. But what sort of deficiency would this be? Possibly Frege thinks that, upon translating the argument in the suggested way, we see the futility of premise 2:

---

[4]*The Foundation of Arithmetic*, tr. J. L. Austin, rev. ed. (London: Blackwell & Mott. 1953; New York: Harper, TB 534, 1962), p. 65.

(2) Existence is greater than nonexistence.

Now to function properly in the argument, 2 must be construed along the following lines:

(2a) For any objects *A* and *B*, if *A* exists and *B* does not, then *A* is greater than *B*.

And, given Frege's claim about existence, 2a must be understood as

(2′) If the concept of *A* is instantiated and the concept of *B* is not, then *A* is greater than *B*.

Now perhaps Frege's query is as follows: If the concept of *B* is not instantiated, with what are we comparing *A*? There seems to be nothing relevant with which to compare it. If the concept of *B* is not instantiated, then it makes no sense, it may be said, to try to compare an object *A* with *B* with respect to greatness or, indeed, any other property.

C. D. Broad concurs in this suggestion:

> (1) No comparison can be made between a non-existent term and anything else except on the hypothesis that it exists and (2) on this hypothesis it is meaningless to compare it with anything in respect of the presence or absence of existence.[5]

But this claim is surely false. One certainly *can* compare, for example, Hamlet with Louis XIV in point of the number of books written about each. And this comparison need not be hypothetical in Broad's sense; when a man says *more books have been written about Hamlet than about Louis XIV*, he certainly need not commit himself to the supposition that if Hamlet had existed more books would have been written about him than about Louis XIV. (If Hamlet really existed, people might find him something of a bore.) And while it is true that Superman is a comic-book figure much stronger than any actual man, it is probably false that if Superman really existed he would be a comic book figure much stronger than any actual man. Finally, one certainly *can* compare an existent and a nonexistent with respect to existence; to do this is only to point out that the one really exists while the other does not. One of the principal differences between Cerberus and Governor Wallace, for example, is that the latter (for better or worse) really exists.

If we return to our domain *D* of objects we may see another way of putting this point. We have defined two quantifiers over *D*: (∃x) and (∃ᵖx). We

---

[5]*Religion, Philosophy and Psychical Research* (New York: Harcourt, Brace, 1953), p. 181.

member of D has Q. And now we may put the present point as follows: Kant, Frege, and Broad (if we have understood them) have confused the first of these quantifiers with the third. It is perhaps excusable to hold that if Louis XIV and Hamlet are to be compared, some appropriate domain must contain them both; (Ex) ($x =$ Hamlet) and (Ex) ($x =$ Louis XIV) must both be true. But this does not entail the false claim that ($\exists x$) ($x =$ Hamlet) must be true if we are to compare Hamlet with some other member of D. Frege too, then, fails to provide a sense of 'is a predicate' such that, in that sense, it is clear both that existence is not a predicate and that Anselm's argument requires it to be one.

What *does* Kant's argument show, then? How could anyone be led to suppose that Kant's claim did dispose of the Ontological Argument? This last question is not altogether easy to answer. What Kant's argument does show, however, is that one cannot "define things into existence"; it shows that one cannot, by adding existence to a concept that has application contingently if at all, get a concept that is necessarily exemplified. For let C be any whole concept and C^{-E} be that whole concept diminished with respect to existence. If the proposition ($\exists x$)$C^{-E}x$ is contingent, so is ($\exists x$)Cx. Kant's argument shows that the proposition *there exists an object to which C applies* is logically equivalent to *there exists an object to which C^{-E} applies*; hence, if either is contingent, so is the other. And this result can be generalized. For *any* concept C, singular or general, if it is a contingent truth that C is exemplified, it is also a contingent truth that the concept derived from C by annexing existence to it is exemplified. From a concept that has application contingently—e.g., *crow* —we can't, by annexing existence to it, get a concept that necessarily applies; for if it is a contingent truth that there exist some crows, it is also a contingent truth that there are existent crows.

But of course Anselm needn't have thought otherwise. Schopenhauser describes the Ontological Argument as follows: "On some occasion or other someone excogitates a conception, composed out of all sorts of predicates, among which, however, he takes care to include the predicate actuality or existence, either openly or wrapped up for decency's sake in some other predicate, such as perfection, immensity, or something of the kind."[6] If this *were* Anselm's procedure—if he started with some concept that has instances contingently if at all and then annexed *existence* to it—then indeed his argument would be subject to Kant's criticism. But he didn't, and it isn't. And Kant's objection shows neither that there are no necessary existential propositions nor that the proposition *God exists* is not necessary—any more than it shows that *there is a prime between 50 and 55* is a contingent proposition.

---

[6]"The Fourfold Root of the Principle of Sufficient Reason," tr. Mme. Carl Hildebrand, reprinted in A. Plantinga, ed., *The Ontological Argument* (New York: Doubleday, 1965), pp. 66–67.

NORMAN MALCOLM

1.4   Anselm's Ontological Arguments

I believe that in Anselm's *Proslogion* and *Responsio editoris* there are two different pieces of reasoning which he did not distinguish from one another, and that a good deal of light may be shed on the philosophical problem of "the ontological argument" if we do distinguish them. In Chapter 2 of the *Proslogion*[1] Anselm says that we believe that God is *something a greater than which cannot be conceived*. (The Latin is *aliquid quo nihil maius cogitari posit.* Anselm sometimes uses the alternate expressions *aliquid quo maius nihil cogitari potest, id quo maius cogitari nequit, aliquid quo maius cogitari non valet.*) Even the fool of the Psalm who says in his heart there is no God, when he hears this very thing that Anselm says, namely, "something a greater than which cannot be conceived," understands what he hears, and what he understands is in his understanding though he does not understand that it exists.

Apparently Anselm regards it as tautological to say that whatever is understood is in the understanding (*quidquid intelligitur in intellectu est*): he uses *intelligitur* and *initellectu est* as interchangeable locutions. The same holds for another formula of his: whatever is thought is in thought (*quidquid cogitatur in cogitatione est*).[2]

Of course many things may exist in the understanding that do not exist in reality; for example, elves. Now, says Anselm, something a greater than which cannot be conceived exists in the understanding. But it cannot exist *only* in the understanding, for to exist in reality is greater. Therefore that thing a greater than which cannot be conceived cannot exist only in the understanding, for then a greater thing could be conceived: namely, one that exists both in the understanding and in reality.[3]

From *The Philosophical Review*, 69 (1960). Reprinted by permission of the author and the editors.

[1]I have consulted the Latin text of the *Proslogion*, of *Gaunilonis Pro Insipiente*, and of the *Responsio editoris*, in S. Anselmi, *Opera Omnia*, edited by F. C. Schmitt (Secovii, 1938), vol. I. With numerous modifications, I have used the English translation by S. N. Deane: *St. Anselm* (La Salle, Illinois, 1948).

[2]See *Proslogion* 1 and *Responsio* 2.

[3]Anselm's actual words are: "Et certe id quo maius cogitari nequit, non potest esse in solo intellectu. Si enim vel in solo intellectu est, potest cogitari esse et in re, quod maius est. Si ergo id quo maius cogitari non potest, est in solo intellectu: id ipsum quo maius cogitari non potest, est quo maius cogitari potest. Sed certe hoc esse non potest." *Proslogion* 2.

Here I have a question. It is not clear to me whether Anselm means that (a) existence in reality by itself is greater than existence in the understanding, or that (b) existence in reality and existence in the understanding together are greater than existence in the understanding alone. Certainly he accepts (b). But he might also accept (a), as Descartes apparently does in *Meditation III* when he suggests that the mode of being by which a thing is "objectively in the understanding" is *imperfect*.[4] Of course Anselm might accept both (a) and (b). He might hold that in general something is greater if it has both of these "modes of existence" than if it has either one alone, but also that existence in reality is a more perfect mode of existence than existence in the understanding.

In any case, Anselm holds that something is greater if it exists both in the understanding and in reality than if it exists merely in the understanding. An equivalent way of putting this interesting proposition, in a more current terminology, is: something is greater if it is both conceived of and exists than if it is merely conceived of. Anselm's reasoning can be expressed as follows: *id quo maius cogitari nequit* cannot be merely conceived of and not exist, for then it would not be *id quo maius cogitari nequit*. The doctrine that something is greater if it exists in addition to being conceived of, than if it is only conceived of, could be called the doctrine that *existence is a perfection*. Descartes maintained, in so many words, that existence is a perfection,[5] and presumably he was holding Anselm's doctrine, although he does not, in *Meditation V* or elsewhere, argue in the way that Anselm does in *Proslogion 2*.

When Anselm says, "And certainly, that than which nothing greater can be conceived cannot exist merely in the understanding. For suppose it exists merely in the understanding, then it can be conceived to exist in reality, which is greater,"[6] he is claiming that if I conceived of a being of great excellence, that being would be *greater* (more excellent, more perfect) if it existed than if it did not exist. His supposition that "it exists merely in the understanding" is the supposition that it is conceived of but does not exist. Anselm repeated this claim in his reply to the criticism of the monk Gaunilo. Speaking of the being a greater than which cannot be conceived, he says:

> I have said that if it exists merely in the understanding it can be conceived to exist in reality, which is greater. Therefore, if it exists merely in the understanding obviously the very being a greater than which cannot be conceived, is one a greater than which can be conceived. What, I ask, can follow better than that? For if it exists merely in the understanding, can it not be conceived to exist in reality? And if it can be so conceived does not he who conceives of this conceive of a thing greater than it, if it does exist merely in the understanding? Can anything follow better than this: that if a being a greater than which cannot be conceived exists merely in the understanding, it is something a greater than which can be conceived? What could be plainer?[7]

---

[4]Haldane and Ross, *The Philosophical Works of Descartes*, 2 vols. (Cambridge, 1931), I, 163.

[5]*Op. cit.*, p. 182.

[6]*Proslogion 2*; Deane, p. 8.

[7]*Responsio 2*; Deane, pp. 157–58.

He is implying, in the first sentence, that if I conceive of something which does not exist then it is possible for it to exist, and *it will be greater if it exists than if it does not exist.*

The doctrine that existence is a perfection is remarkably queer. It makes sense and is true to say that my future house will be a better one if it is insulated than if it is not insulated; but what could it mean to say that it will be a better house if it exists than if it does not? My future child will be a better man if he is honest than if he is not; but who would understand the saying that he will be a better man if he exists than if he does not? Or who understands the saying that if God exists He is more perfect than if He does not exist? One might say, with some intelligibility, that it would be better (for oneself or for mankind) if God exists than if He does not—but that is a different matter.

A king might desire that his next chancellor should have knowledge, wit, and resolution; but it is ludicrous to add that the king's desire is to have a chancellor who exists. Suppose that two royal councilors, A and B, were asked to draw up separately descriptions of the most perfect chancellor they could conceive, and that the descriptions they produced were identical except that A included existence in his list of attributes of a perfect chancellor and B did not. (I do not mean that B put nonexistence in his list.) One and the same person could satisfy both descriptions. More to the point, any person who satisfied A's description would *necessarily* satisfy B's description and *vice versa!* This is to say that A and B did not produce descriptions that differed in any way but rather one and the same description of necessary and desirable qualities in a chancellor. A only made a show of putting down a desirable quality that B had failed to include.

I believe I am merely restating an observation that Kant made in attacking the notion that "existence" or "being" is a "real predicate." He says:

> By whatever and by however many predicates we may think a thing—even if we completely determine it—we do not make the least addition to the thing when we further declare that this thing *is*. Otherwise, it would not be exactly the same thing that exists, but something more than we had thought in the concept; and we could not, therefore, say that the exact object of my concept exists. [8]

Anselm's ontological proof of *Proslogion 2* is fallacious because it rests on the false doctrine that existence is a perfection (and therefore that "existence" is a "real predicate"). It would be desirable to have a rigorous refutation of the doctrine but I have not been able to provide one. I am compelled to leave the matter at the more or less intuitive level of Kant's observation. In any case, I believe that the doctrine does not belong to Anselm's other formulation of the ontological argument. It is worth noting that Gassendi anticipated Kant's criticism when he said, against Descartes:

---

[8] *The Critique of Pure Reason*, tr. by Norman Kemp Smith (London, 1929), p. 505.

> Existence is a perfection neither in God nor in anything else; it is rather that in the absence of which there is no perfection. . . . Hence neither is existence held to exist in a thing in the way that perfections do, nor if the thing lacks existence is it said to be imperfect (or deprived of a perfection), so much as to be nothing.[9]

II

I take up now the consideration of the second ontological proof, which Anselm presents in the very next chapter of the *Proslogion*. (There is no evidence that he thought of himself as offering two different proofs.) Speaking of the being a greater than which cannot be conceived, he says:

> And it so truly exists that it cannot be conceived not to exist. For it is possible to conceive of a being which cannot be conceived not to exist; and this is greater than one which can be conceived not to exist. Hence, if that, than which nothing greater can be conceived, can be conceived not to exist, it is not that than which nothing greater can be conceived. But this is a contradiction. So truly, therefore, is there something than which nothing greater can be conceived, that it cannot even be conceived not to exist.
> And this being thou art, O Lord, our God.[10]

Anselm is saying two things: first, that a being whose nonexistence is logically impossible is "greater" than a being whose nonexistence is logically possible (and therefore that a being a greater than which cannot be conceived must be one whose nonexistence is logically impossible); second, that *God* is a being than which a greater cannot be conceived.

In regard to the second of these assertions, there certainly is *a* use of the word "God," and I think far the more common use, in accordance with which the statements "God is the greatest of all beings," "God is the most perfect being," "God is the supreme being," are *logically* necessary truths, in the same sense that the statement "A square has four sides" is a logically necessary truth. If there is a man named "Jones" who is the tallest man in the world, the statement "Jones is the tallest man in the world" is merely true and is not a logically necessary truth. It is a virtue of Anselm's unusual phrase, "a being a greater than which cannot be conceived,"[11] to make it explicit that the sentence "God is the greatest of all beings" expresses a logically necessary truth and not a mere matter of fact such as the one we imagined about Jones.

With regard to Anselm's first assertion (namely, that a being whose nonexistence is logically impossible is greater than a being whose nonexistence is logically possible) perhaps the most puzzling thing about it is the use of the

---

[9]Haldane and Ross, II, 186.

[10]*Proslogion* 3; Deane, pp. 8–9.

[11]Professor Robert Calhoun has pointed out to me that a similar locution had been used by Augustine. In *De moribus Manichaeorum* (Bk. II, ch. xi, sec. 24), he says that God is a being *quo esse aut cogitari melius nihil possit* (*Patrologiae Patrum Latinorum*, ed. by J. P. Migne, Paris, 1841–1845, vol. 32: *Augustinus*, vol. 1).

word "greater." It appears to mean exactly the same as "superior," "more excellent," "more perfect." This equivalence by itself is of no help to us, however, since the latter expressions would be equally puzzling here. What is required is some explanation of their use.

We do think of *knowledge*, say, as an excellence, a good thing. If A has more knowledge of algebra than B we express this in common language by saying that A has a *better* knowledge of algebra than B, or that A's knowledge of algebra is *superior* to B's, whereas we should not say that B has a better or superior *ignorance* of algebra than A. We do say "greater ignorance," but here the word "greater" is used purely quantitatively.

Previously I rejected *existence* as a perfection. Anselm is maintaining in the remarks last quoted, not that existence is a perfection, but that *the logical impossibility of nonexistence is a perfection*. In other words, *necessary existence* is a perfection. His first ontological proof uses the principle that a thing is greater if it exists than if it does not exist. His second proof employs the different principle that a thing is greater if it necessarily exists than if it does not necessarily exist.

Some remarks about the notion of *dependence* may help to make this latter principle intelligible. Many things depend for their existence on other things and events. My house was built by a carpenter: its coming into existence was dependent on a certain creative activity. Its continued existence is dependent on many things: that a tree does not crush it, that it is not consumed by fire, and so on. If we reflect on the common meaning of the word "God" (no matter how vague and confused this is), we realize that it is incompatible with this meaning that God's existence should *depend* on anything. Whether we believe in Him or not we must admit that the "almighty and everlasting God" (as several ancient prayers begin), the "Maker of heaven and earth, and of all things visible and invisible" (as is said in the Nicene Creed), cannot be thought of as being brought into existence by anything or as depending for His continued existence on anything. To conceive of anything as dependent upon something else for its existence is to conceive of it as a lesser being than God.

If a housewife has a set of extremely fragile dishes, then as dishes they are *inferior* to those of another set like them in all respects except that they are *not* fragile. Those of the first set are *dependent* for their continued existence on gentle handling; those of the second set are not. There is a definite connection in common language between the notions of dependency and inferiority, and independence and superiority. To say that something which was dependent on nothing whatever was superior to ("greater than") anything that was dependent in any way upon anything is quite in keeping with the everyday use of the terms "superior" and "greater." Correlative with the notions of dependence and independence are the notions of *limited* and *unlimited*. An engine requires fuel and this is a limitation. It is the same thing to say that an engine's operation is *dependent* on as that it is *limited* by its fuel supply. An engine that could accomplish the same work in the same time and was in other respects satisfactory, but did not require fuel, would be a *superior* engine.

God is usually conceived of as an *unlimited* being. He is conceived of as a being who *could not* be limited, that is, as an absolutely unlimited being. This is no less than to conceive of Him as *something a greater than which cannot be conceived.* If God is conceived to be an absolutely unlimited being He must be conceived to be unlimited in regard to His existence as well as His operation. In this conception it will not make sense to say that He depends on anything for coming into or continuing in existence. Nor, as Spinoza observed, will it make sense to say that something could *prevent* Him from existing.[12] Lack of moisture can prevent trees from existing in a certain region of the earth. But it would be contrary to the concept of God as an unlimited being to suppose that anything other than God Himself could prevent Him from existing, and it would be self-contradictory to suppose that He Himself could do it.

Some may be inclined to object that although nothing could prevent God's existence, still it might just *happen* that He did not exist. And if He did exist that too would be by chance. I think, however, that from the supposition that it could happen that God did not exist it would follow that, if He existed, He would have mere duration and not eternity. It would make sense to ask, "How long has He existed?," "Will He still exist next week?," "He was in existence yesterday but how about today?," and so on. It seems absurd to make God the subject of such questions. According to our ordinary conception of Him, He is an eternal being. And eternity does not mean endless duration, as Spinoza noted. To ascribe eternity to something is to exclude as senseless all sentences that imply that it has duration. If a thing has duration then it would be merely a *contingent* fact, if it was a fact, that its duration was endless. The moon could have endless duration but not eternity. If something has endless duration it will *make sense* (although it will be false) to say that it will cease to exist, and it will make sense (although it will be false) to say that something will *cause* it to cease to exist. A being with endless duration is not, therefore, an absolutely unlimited being. That God is conceived to be eternal follows from the fact that He is conceived to be an absolutely unlimited being.

I have been trying to expand the argument of *Proslogion* 3. In *Responsio* 1 Anselm adds the following acute point: if you can conceive of a certain thing and this thing does not exist then if it *were* to exist its nonexistence would be *possible.* It follows, I believe, that if the thing were to exist it would depend on other things both for coming into and continuing in existence, and also that it would have duration and not eternity. Therefore it would not be, either in reality or in conception, an unlimited being, *aliquid quo nihil maius cogitari possit.*

Anselm states his argument as follows:

---

[12]*Ethics*, pt. I, prop. 11.

If it [the thing a greater than which cannot be conceived] can be conceived at all it must exist. For no one who denies or doubts the existence of a being a greater than which is inconceivable, denies or doubts that if it did exist its non-existence, either in reality or in the understanding, would be impossible. For otherwise it would not be a being a greater than which cannot be conceived. But as to whatever can be conceived but does not exist: if it were to exist its non-existence either in reality or in the understanding would be possible. Therefore, if a being a greater than which cannot be conceived, can even be conceived, it must exist.[13]

What Anselm has proved is that the notion of contingent existence or of contingent nonexistence cannot have any application to God. His existence must either be logically necessary or logically impossible. The only intelligible way of rejecting Anselm's claim that God's existence is necessary is to maintain that the concept of God, as a being a greater than which cannot be conceived, is self-contradictory or nonsensical.[14] Supposing that this is false, Anselm is right to deduce God's necessary existence from his characterization of Him as a being a greater than which cannot be conceived.

Let me summarize the proof. If God, a being a greater than which cannot be conceived, does not exist then He cannot *come* into existence. For if He did He would either have been *caused* to come into existence or have *happened* to come into existence, and in either case He would be a limited being, which by our conception of Him He is not. Since He cannot come into existence, if He does not exist His existence is impossible. If He does exist He cannot have come into existence (for the reasons given), nor can He cease to exist, for nothing could cause Him to cease to exist nor could it just happen that He ceased to exist. So if God exists His existence is necessary. Thus God's existence is either impossible or necessary. It can be the former only if the concept of such a being is self-contradictory or in some way logically absurd. Assuming that this is not so, it follows that He necessarily exists.

It may be helpful to express ourselves in the following way: to say, not that *omnipotence* is a property of God, but rather that *necessary omnipotence* is; and to say, not that omniscience is a property of God, but rather that *necessary omniscience* is. We have criteria for determining that a man knows this and that and can do this and that, and for determining that one man has greater knowledge and abilities in a certain subject than another. We could think of

---

[13]*Responsio* 1; Deane, pp. 154–55.

[14]Gaunilo attacked Anselm's argument on this very point. He would not concede that a being a greater than which cannot be conceived existed in his understanding (*Gaunilonis Pro Insipiente*, secs. 4 and 5; Deane, pp. 148–50). Anselm's reply is: "I call on your faith and conscience to attest that this is most false" (*Responsio* 1; Deane, p. 154). Gaunilo's faith and conscience will attest that it is false that "God is not a being a greater than which is inconceivable," and false that "He is not understood (*intelligitur*) or conceived (*cogitatur*)" (*ibid.*). Descartes also remarks that one would go to "strange extremes" who denied that we understand the words "*that thing which is the most perfect that we can conceive*; for that is what all men call God" (Haldane and Ross, II, 129).

various tests to give them. But there is nothing we should wish to describe, seriously and literally, as "testing" God's knowledge and powers. That God is omniscient and omnipotent has not been determined by the application of criteria: rather these are requirements of our conception of Him. They are internal properties of the concept, although they are also rightly said to be properties of God. *Necessary existence* is a property of God in the *same sense* that *necessary omnipotence* and *necessary omniscience* are His properties. And we are not to think that "God necessarily exists" means that it follows necessarily from something that God exists *contingently*. The a priori proposition "God necessarily exists" entails the proposition "God exists," if and only if the latter also is understood as an a priori proposition: in which case the two propositions are equivalent. In this sense Anselm's proof is a proof of God's existence.

Descartes was somewhat hazy on the question of whether existence is a property of things that exist, but at the same time he saw clearly enough that *necessary existence* is a property of God. Both points are illustrated in his reply to Gassendi's remark, which I quoted above:

> I do not see to what class of reality you wish to assign existence, nor do I see why it may not be said to be a property as well as omnipotence, taking the word property as equivalent to any attribute or anything which can be predicated of a thing, as in the present case it should be by all means regarded. Nay, necessary existence in the case of God is also a true property in the strictest sense of the word, because it belongs to Him and forms part of His essence alone.[15]

Elsewhere he speaks of "the necessity of existence" as being "that crown of perfections without which we cannot comprehend God."[16] He is emphatic on the point that necessary existence applies solely to "an absolutely perfect Being."[17]

III

I wish to consider now a part of Kant's criticism of the ontological argument which I believe to be wrong. He says:

> If, in an identical proposition, I reject the predicate while retaining the subject, contradiction results; and I therefore say that the former belongs necessarily to the latter. But if we reject subject and predicate alike, there is no contradiction; for nothing is then left that can be contradicted. To post a triangle, and yet to reject its three angles, is self-contradictory; but there is no contradiction in rejecting the triangle together with its three angles. The same holds true of the concept of an absolutely necessary being. If its existence is rejected, we reject the thing itself with all its predicates; and no question of contradiction can

---

[15]Haldane and Ross, II, 228.

[16]*Ibid.*, I, 445.

[17]E.g., *ibid.*, Principle 15, p. 225.

then arise. There is nothing outside it that would then be contradicted, since the necessity of the thing is not supposed to be derived from anything external; nor is there anything internal that would be contradicted, since in rejecting the thing itself we have at the same time rejected all its internal properties. "God is omnipotent" is a necessary judgment. The omnipotence cannot be rejected if we posit a Deity, that is, an infinite being; for the two concepts are identical. But if we say, "There is no God," neither the omnipotence nor any other of its predicates is given; they are one and all rejected together with the subject, and there is therefore not the least contradiction in such a judgment. [18]

To these remarks the reply is that when the concept of God is correctly understood one sees that one cannot "reject the subject." "There is no God" is seen to be a necessarily false statement. Anselm's demonstration proves that the proposition "God exists" has the same a priori footing as the proposition "God is omnipotent."

Many present-day philosophers, in agreement with Kant, declare that existence is not a property and think that this overthrows the ontological argument. Although it is an error to regard existence as a property of things that have contingent existence, it does not follow that it is an error to regard necessary existence as a property of God. A recent writer says, against Anselm, that a proof of God's existence "based on the necessities of thought" is "universally regarded as fallacious: it is not thought possible to build bridges between mere abstractions and concrete existence."[19] But this way of putting the matter obscures the distinction we need to make. Does "concrete existence" mean contingent existence? Then to build bridges between concrete existence and mere abstractions would be like inferring the existence of an island from the concept of a perfect island, which both Anselm and Descartes regarded as absurd. What Anselm did was to give a demonstration that the proposition "God necessarily exists" is entailed by the proposition "God is a being a greater than which cannot be conceived" (which is equivalent to "God is an absolutely unlimited being"). Kant declares that when "I think a being as the supreme reality, without any defect, the question still remains whether it exists or not."[20] But once one has grasped Anselm's proof of the necessary existence of a being a greater than which cannot be conceived, no question remains as to whether it exists or not, just as Euclid's demonstration of the existence of an infinity of prime numbers leaves no question on that issue.

Kant says that "every reasonable person" must admit that "all existential propositions are synthetic."[21] Part of the perplexity one has about the ontological argument is in deciding whether or not the proposition "God necessarily exists" is or is not an "existential proposition." But let us look around.

---

[18] *Op. cit.*, p. 502.

[19] J. N. Findlay, "Can God's Existence Be Disproved?," *New Essays in Philosophical Theology*, ed. by A. N. Flew and A. MacIntyre (London, 1955), p. 47.

[20] *Op. cit.*, pp. 505–6.

[21] *Ibid.*, pp. 504.

Is the Euclidean theorem in number theory, "There exists an infinite number of prime numbers," an "existential proposition"? Do we not want to say that *in some sense* it asserts the existence of something? Cannot we say, with equal justification, that the proposition "God necessarily exists" asserts the existence of something, *in some sense?* What we need to understand, in each case, is the particular sense of the assertion. Neither proposition has the same sort of sense as do the propositions, "A low pressure area exists over the Great Lakes," "There still exists some possibility that he will survive," "The pain continues to exist in his abdomen." One good way of seeing the difference in sense of these various propositions is to see the variously different ways in which they are proved or supported. It is wrong to think that all assertions of existence have the same kind of meaning. There are as many kinds of existential propositions as there are kinds of subjects of discourse.

Closely related to Kant's view that all existential propositions are "synthetic" is the contemporary dogma that all existential propositions are contingent. Professor Gilbert Ryle tells us that "Any assertion of the existence of something, like any assertion of the occurrence of something, can be denied without logical absurdity."[22] "All existential statements are contingent," says Mr. I. M. Crombie.[23] Professor J. J. C. Smart remarks that "Existence is not a property" and then goes on to assert that "There can never be any *logical contradiction* in denying that God exists."[24] He declares that "The concept of a logically necessary being is a self-contradictory concept, like the concept of a round square. . . . No existential proposition can be logically necessary," he maintains, for "the truth of a logically necessary proposition depends only on our symbolism, or to put the same thing in another way, on the relationship of concepts" (p. 38). Professor K. E. M. Baier says, "It is no longer seriously in dispute that the notion of a logically necessary being is self-contradictory. Whatever can be conceived of as existing can equally be conceived of as not existing."[25] This is a repetition of Hume's assertion, "Whatever we conceive as existent, we can also conceive as non-existent. There is no being, therefore, whose non-existence implies a contradiction."[26]

Professor J. N. Findlay ingeniously constructs an ontological *dis*proof of God's existence, based on a "modern view of the nature of "necessity in propositions": the view, namely, that necessity in propositions "merely reflects our use of words, the arbitrary conventions of our language."[27] Findlay undertakes to characterize what he calls "religious attitude," and here there is a striking agreement between his observations and some of the things I have said in expounding Anselm's proof. Religious attitude, he says, presumes *su-*

---

[22] *The Nature of Metaphysics*, ed. by D. F. Pears (New York, 1957), p. 150.
[23] *New Essays in Philosophical Theology*, p. 114.
[24] *Ibid.*, p. 34.
[25] *The Meaning of Life*, Inaugural Lecture, Canberra University College (Canberra, 1957), p. 8.
[26] *Dialogues Concerning Natural Religion*, pt. IX.
[27] Findlay, *op. cit.*, p. 54.

periority in its object and superiority so great that the worshiper is in comparison as nothing. Religious attitude finds it "anomalous to worship anything *limited* in any unthinkable manner. . . . And hence we are led on irresistibly to demand that our religious object should have an *unsurpassable* supremacy along all avenues, that it should tower *infinitely* above all other objects" (p. 51). We cannot help feeling that "the worthy object of our worship can never be a thing that merely *happens* to exist, nor one on which all other objects merely *happen* to depend. The true object of religious reverence must not be one, merely, to which no *actual* independent realities stand opposed: it must be one to which such opposition is totally *inconceivable*. . . . And not only must the existence of *other* things be unthinkable without Him, but His own non-existence must be wholly unthinkable in any circumstances" (p. 52). And now, says Findlay, when we add up these various requirements, what they entail is "not only that there isn't a God, but that the Divine Existence is either senseless or impossible" (p. 54). For on the one hand, "if God is to satisfy religious claims and needs, He must be a being in every way inescapable, One whose existence and whose possession of certain excellences we cannot possibly conceive away." On the other hand, "modern views make it self-evidently absurd (if they don't make it ungrammatical) to speak of such a Being and attribute existence to Him. It was indeed an ill day for Anselm when he hit upon his famous proof. For on that day he not only laid bare something that is of the essence of an adequate religious object, but also something that entails its necessary non-existence" (p. 55).

Now I am inclined to hold the "modern" view that logically necessary truth "merely reflects our use of words" (although I do not believe that the conventions of language are always *arbitrary*). But I confess that I am unable to see how that view is supposed to lead to the conclusion that "the Divine existence is either senseless or impossible." Findlay does not explain how this result comes about. Surely he cannot mean that this view entails that nothing can have necessary properties: for this would imply that mathematics is "senseless or impossible," which no one wants to hold. Trying to fill in the argument that is missing from his article, the most plausible conjecture I can make is the following: Findlay thinks that the view that logical necessity "reflects the use of words" implies, not that nothing has necessary properties, but that *existence* cannot be a necessary property of anything. That is to say, every proposition of the form "*x* exists," including the proposition "God exists," must be *contingent*.[28] At the same time, our concept of God requires that His existence be *necessary*, that is, that "God exists" be a necessary truth. Therefore, the modern view of necessity proves that what the concept of God requires *cannot* be fulfilled. It proves that God *cannot* exist.

---

[28]The other philosophers I have just cited may be led to this opinion by the same thinking. Smart, for example, says that "the truth of a logically necessary proposition depends only on our symbolism, or to put the same thing in another way, on the relationship of concepts" (*supra*). This is very similar to saying that it "reflects our use of words."

The correct reply is that the view that logical necessity merely reflects the use of words cannot possibly have the implication that every existential proposition must be contingent. That view requires us to *look at* the use of words and not manufacture a priori theses about it. In the Ninetieth Psalm it is said: "Before the mountains were brought forth, or ever thou hadst formed the earth and the world, even from everlasting to everlasting, thou art God." Here is expressed the idea of the necessary existence and eternity of God, an idea that is essential to the Jewish and Christian religions. In those complex systems of thought, those "language-games," God has the status of a necessary being. Who can doubt that? Here we must say with Wittgenstein, "This language-game is played!"[29] I believe we may rightly take the existence of those religious systems of thought in which God figures as a necessary being to be a disproof of the dogma, affirmed by Hume and others, that no existential proposition can be necessary.

Another way of criticizing the ontological argument is the following. "Granted that the concept of necessary existence follows from the concept of a being a greater than which cannot be conceived, this amounts to no more than granting the *a priori* truth of the *conditional* proposition, 'If such a being exists then it necessarily exists.' This proposition, however, does not entail the *existence* of *anything*, and one can deny its antecedent without contradiction." Kant, for example, compares the proposition (or "judgment," as he calls it) "A triangle has three angles" with the proposition "God is a necessary being." He allows that the former is "absolutely necessary" and goes on to say:

> The absolute necessity of the judgment is only a conditional necessity of the thing, or of the predicate in the judgment. The above proposition does not declare that three angles are absolutely necessary, but that, under the condition that there is a triangle (that is, that a triangle is given), three angles will necessarily be found in it.[30]

He is saying, quite correctly, that the proposition about triangles is equivalent to the conditional proposition, "If a triangle exists, it has three angles." He then makes the comment that there is no contradiction "in rejecting the triangle together with its three angles." He proceeds to draw the alleged parallel: "The same holds true of the concept of an absolutely necessary being. If its existence is rejected, we reject the thing itself with all its predicates; and no question of contradiction can then arise."[31] The priest, Caterus, made the same objection to Descartes when he said:

> Though it be conceded that an entity of the highest perfection implies its existence by its very name, yet it does not follow that that very existence is anything actual in the real world, but merely that the concept of existence is inseparably united with the concept of highest being. Hence you cannot infer

---

[29]*Philosophical Investigations* (New York, 1953), sec. 654.
[30]*Op. cit.*, pp. 501–2.
[31]*Ibid.*, p. 502.

that the existence of God is anything actual, unless you assume that that highest being actually exists; for then it will actually contain all its perfections, together with this perfection of real existence.[32]

I think that Caterus, Kant, and numerous other philosophers have been mistaken in supposing that the proposition "God is a necessary being" (or "God necessarily exists") is equivalent to the conditional proposition "If God exists then He necessarily exists."[33] For how do they want the antecedent clause, "*If* God exists," to be understood? Clearly they want it to imply that it is *possible* that God does *not* exist.[34] The whole point of Kant's analysis is to try to show that it is possible to "reject the subject." Let us make this implication explicit in the conditional proposition, so that it reads: "If God exists (and it is possible that He does not) then He necessarily exists." But now it is apparent, I think, that these philosophers have arrived at a self-contradictory position. I do not mean that this conditional proposition, taken alone, is self-contradictory. Their position is self-contradictory in the following way. On the one hand, they agree that the proposition "God necessarily exists" is an a priori truth; Kant implies that it is "absolutely necessary," and Caterus says that God's existence is implied by His very name. On the other hand, they think that it is correct to analyze this proposition in such a way that it will entail the proposition "It is possible that God does not exist." But so far from its being the case that the proposition "God necessarily exists" entails the proposition "It is possible that God does not exist," it is rather the case that they are *incompatible* with one another! Can anything be clearer than the conjunction "God necessarily exists but it is possible that He does not exist" is self-con-

---

[32]Haldane and Ross, II, 7.

[33]I have heard it said by more than one person in discussion that Kant's view was that it is really a misuse of language to speak of a "necessary being," on the grounds that necessity is properly predicated only of propositions (judgments) not of *things*. This is not a correct account of Kant. (See his discussion of "The Postulates of Empirical Thought in General," *op. cit.*, pp. 239–56, esp. p. 239 and pp. 247–48.) But if he had held this, as perhaps the above philosophers think he should have then presumably his view would not have been that the pseudo-proposition "God is a necessary being" is equivalent to the conditional "If God exists then He necessarily exists." Rather his view would have been that the genuine proposition " 'God exists' is necessarily true" is equivalent to the conditional "If God exists then He exists" (*not* "If God exists then He *necessarily* exists," which would be an illegitimate formulation, on the view imaginatively attributed to Kant).

"If God exists then He exists" is a foolish tautology which says nothing different from the tautology "If a new earth satellite exists then it exists." If "If God exists then He exists" were a correct analysis of " 'God exists' is necessarily true," then "If a new earth satellite exists then it exists" would be a correct analysis of " 'A new earth satellite exists' is necessarily true." If the *analysans* is necessarily true then the *analysandum* must be necessarily true, provided the analysis is correct. If this proposed Kantian analysis of " 'God exists' is necessarily true" were correct, we should be presented with the consequence that not only is it necessarily true that God exists, but also it is necessarily true that a new earth satellite exists: which is absurd.

[34]When summarizing Anselm's proof (in part II, *supra*) I said: "If God exists He necessarily exists." But there I was merely stating an entailment. "If God exists" did not have the implication that it is possible He does not exist. And of course I was not regarding the conditional as *equivalent* to "God necessarily exists."

tradictory? Is it not just as plainly self-contradictory as the conjunction "A square necessarily has four sides but it is possible for a square not to have four sides"? In short, this familiar criticism of the ontological argument is self-contradictory, because it accepts *both* of two incompatible propositions.[35]

One conclusion we may draw from our examination of this criticism is that (contrary to Kant) there is a lack of symmetry, in an important respect, between the propositions "A triangle has three angles" and "God has necessary existence," although both are a priori. The former can be expressed in the conditional assertion "If a triangle exists (and it is possible that none does) it has three angles." The latter cannot be expressed in the corresponding conditional assertion without contradiction.

IV

I turn to the question of whether the idea of a being a greater than which cannot be conceived is self-contradictory. Here Leibniz made a contribution to the discussion of the ontological argument. He remarked that the argument of Anselm and Descartes

> is not a paralogism, but it is an imperfect demonstration, which assumes something that must still be proved in order to render it mathematically evident; that is, it is tacitly assumed that this idea of the all-great or all-perfect being is possible, and implies no contradiction. And it is already something that by this remark it is proved that, assuming that God is possible, he exists, which is the privilege of divinity alone.[36]

Leibniz undertook to give a proof that God is possible. He defined a *perfection* as a simple, positive quality in the highest degree.[37] He argued that since perfections are *simple* qualities they must be compatible with one another. Therefore the concept of a being possessing all perfections is consistent.

I will not review his argument because I do not find his definition of a perfection intelligible. For one thing, it assumes that certain qualities or attributes are "positive" in their intrinsic nature, and others "negative" or "privative," and I have not been able clearly to understand that. For another thing, it assumes that some qualities are intrinsically simple. I believe that Wittgenstein has shown in the *Investigations* that nothing is *intrinsically* simple, but that whatever has the status of a simple, an indefinable, in one system of concepts, may have the status of a complex thing, a definable thing, in another system of concepts.

---

[35]This fallacious criticism of Anselm is implied in the following remarks by Gilson: "To show that the affirmation of necessary existence is analytically implied in the idea of God, would be . . . to show that God is necessary if He exists, but would not prove that He does exist" (E. Gilson, *The Spirit of Medieval Philosophy*, New York, 1940, p. 62).

[36]*New Essays Concerning the Human Understanding*, Bk. IV, ch. 10; ed. by A. G. Langley (La Salle, Illinois, 1949), p. 504.

[37]See *Ibid.*, Appendix X, p. 714.

I do not know how to demonstrate that the concept of God—that is, of a being a greater than which cannot be conceived—is not self-contradictory. But I do not think that it is legitimate to demand such a demonstration. I also do not know how to demonstrate that either the concept of a material thing or the concept of *seeing* a material thing is not self-contradictory, and philosophers have argued that both of them are. With respect to any particular reasoning that is offered for holding that the concept of seeing a material thing, for example, is self-contradictory, one may try to show the invalidity of the reasoning and thus free the concept from the charge of being self-contradictory *on that ground*. But I do not understand what it would mean to demonstrate *in general*, and not in respect to any particular reasoning, that the concept is not self-contradictory. So it is with the concept of God. I should think there is no more of a presumption that it is self-contradictory than is the concept of seeing a material thing. Both concepts have a place in the thinking and the lives of human beings.

But even if one allows that Anselm's phrase may be free of self-contradiction, one wants to know how it can have any *meaning* for anyone. Why is it that human beings have even *formed* the concept of an infinite being, a being a greater than which cannot be conceived? This is a legitimate and important question. I am sure there cannot be a deep understanding of that concept without an understanding of the phenomena of human life that give rise to it. To give an account of the latter is beyond my ability. I wish, however, to make one suggestion (which should not be understood as autobiographical).

There is the phenomenon of feeling guilt for something that one has done or thought or felt or for a disposition that one has. One wants to be free of this guilt. But sometimes the guilt is felt to be so great that one is sure that nothing one could do oneself, nor any forgiveness by another human being, would remove it. One feels a guilt that is beyond all measure, a guilt "a greater than which cannot be conceived." Paradoxically, it would seem, one nevertheless has an intense desire to have this incomparable guilt removed. One requires a forgiveness that is beyond all measure, a forgiveness "a greater than which cannot be conceived." Out of such a storm in the soul, I am suggesting, there arises the conception of a forgiving mercy that is limitless, beyond all measure. This is one important feature of the Jewish and Christian conception of God.

I wish to relate this thought to a remark made by Kierkegaard, who was speaking about belief in Christianity but whose remark may have a wider application. He says:

> There is only one proof of the truth of Christianity and that, quite rightly, is from the emotions, when the dread of sin and a heavy conscience torture a man into crossing the narrow line between despair bordering upon madness— and Christendom. [38]

---

[38] *The Journals*, tr. by A. Dru (Oxford, 1938), sec. 926.

One may think it absurd for a human being to feel a guilt of such magnitude, and even more absurd that, if he feels it, he should *desire* its removal. I have nothing to say about that. It may also be absurd for people to fall in love, but they do it. I wish only to say that there *is* that human phenomenon of an unbearably heavy conscience and that it is importantly connected with the genesis of the concept of God, that is, with the formation of the "grammar" of the word "God." I am sure that this concept is related to human experience in other ways. If one had the acuteness and depth to perceive these connections one could grasp the *sense* of the concept. When we encounter this concept as a problem in philosophy, we do not consider the human phenomena that lie behind it. It is not surprising that many philosophers believe that the idea of a necessary being is an arbitrary and absurd construction.

What is the relation of Anselm's ontological argument to religious belief? This is a difficult question. I can imagine an atheist going through the argument, becoming convinced of its validity, acutely defending it against objections, yet remaining an atheist. The only effect it could have on the fool of the Psalm would be that he stopped saying in his heart "There is no God," because he would now realize that this is something he cannot meaningfully say or think. It is hardly to be expected that a demonstrative argument should, in addition, produce in him a living faith. Surely there is a level at which one can view the argument as a piece of logic, following the deductive moves but not being touched religiously? I think so. But even at this level the argument may not be without religious value, for it may help to remove some philosophical scruples that stand in the way of faith. At a deeper level, I suspect that the argument can be thoroughly understood only by one who has a view of that human "form of life" that gives rise to the idea of an infinitely great being, who views it from the *inside* not just from the outside and who has, therefore, at least some inclination to *partake* in that religious form of life. This inclination, in Kierkegaard's words, is "from the emotions." This inclination can hardly be an *effect* of Anselm's argument, but is rather presupposed in the fullest understanding of it. It would be unreasonable to require that the recognition of Anselm's demonstration as valid must produce a conversion.

DAVID LEWIS

1.5   *Anselm and Actuality*[1]

1. INTRODUCTION

Philosophy abounds in troublesome modal arguments—endlessly debated, perennially plausible, perennially suspect. The standards of validity for modal reasoning have long been unclear; they become clear only when we provide a semantic analysis of modal logic by reference to possible worlds and to possible things therein.[2] Thus insofar as we understand modal reasoning at all, we understand it as disguised reasoning about possible beings. But if these are intelligible enough to provide modal logic with foundations, they are intelligible enough to be talked about explicitly. Modal reasoning can be replaced by nonmodal, ordinary reasoning about possible things. Given an obscure modal argument, we can translate it into a nonmodal argument—or into several nonmodal arguments, if the given argument was ambiguous. Once we have a nonmodal argument, we have clear standards of validity; and once we have nonmodal translations of the premises, we can understand them well enough to judge whether they are credible. Foremost among our modal headaches is Anselm's ontological argument. How does it fare under the translation treatment I have prescribed? It turns out to have two principal nonmodal translations. One is valid; the other has credible premises; the difference between the two is subtle. No wonder the argument has never been decisively refuted; no wonder it has never convinced the infidel.

2. FORMULATION OF THE ARGUMENT

The ontological argument notoriously comes in countless versions. We shall confine our attention to one of the arguments that can, with some plausibility, be extracted from Chapter II of the *Proslogion*—not the only one, but the one I take to be both simplest and soundest. The reader must judge for himself whether what I say can be adapted to his own favorite ontological argument.

From *Nous* 4 (1970): 175–88. Reprinted by permission of the author, the editor of *Nous*, and the Wayne State University Press.

[1] I am grateful to Alvin Plantinga for his criticisms of an earlier version of this paper.

[2] See, for instance, Saul Kripke, "Semantical Considerations on Modal Logic," *Acta Philosophica Fennica* 16 (1963): 83–94.

The version we shall work on has the merit of bypassing some familiar difficulties that are not at the heart of the matter. It will have no chance to be invalid in some of the ways that ontological arguments have been said to be invalid. The proper name "God" will not appear, so we will not have to worry about the form or content of its definition. In fact, there will be no defining of anything. We will also not have to worry about the logic of definite descriptions. If I say "That which is red is not green" I might just mean "Whatever is red is not green," neither implying nor presupposing that at least or at most one thing is red. Similarly, we can construe Anselm's "that, than which nothing greater can be conceived" not as a definite description but rather as an idiom of universal quantification.

Our argument is as follows:

Premise 1.   Whatever exists in the understanding can be conceived to exist in reality.

Premise 2.   Whatever exists in the understanding would be greater if it existed in reality than if it did not.

Premise 3.   Something exists in the understanding, than which nothing greater can be conceived.

Conclusion.   Something exists in reality, than which nothing greater can be conceived.

3. THE FIRST PREMISE

It is our plan to reason explicitly about possible worlds and possible things therein. These possible beings will be included in our domain of discourse. The idioms of quantification, therefore, will be understood as ranging over all the beings we wish to talk about, whether existent or nonexistent.

In the context at hand, the appropriate sense of possibility is conceivability. Possible worlds are conceivable worlds. If some otherwise possible worlds are inconceivable—say, seventeen-dimensional worlds—we should not count those; whereas if some otherwise impossible worlds are conceivable—say, worlds in which there is a largest prime—we should count those. Given any statement about what may be conceived to be the case, we translate it into a statement about what is the case in some conceivable world.

Thus to say that something can be conceived to exist in reality is to say that in some conceivable world, it does exist. This makes sense only if existence is taken to be a relation between beings and worlds, so that we can say that something exists in one world but not in another.[3]

Premise 1 tells us that whatever exists in the understanding exists in some

---

[3]We will not need to settle the question whether anything—or any nonabstract thing—ever exists in more than one world, or in none, or partly in one and partly in another. For consideration of such questions, see my "Counterpart Theory and Quantified Modal Logic," *Journal of Philosophy* 65 (1968): 113–26.

conceivable world or other. Thus the beings that may be said to exist in the understanding are among the beings we have already admitted into our domain of discourse. It is ill-advised to speak of them as existing in the understanding: they do not bear to the understanding the same relation which something existing in a world bears to that world! Let us simply call them *understandable* beings.

We are ready now to give a nonmodal translation of Premise 1, as follows:

1. $\forall x \, (\, Ux \supset \exists w \, (\, Ww \, \& \, xEw \,) \,)$

(For any understandable being x, there is a world w such that x exists in w.)

Is the premise credible? I have no wish to contest it. Someone might say that a round square is an understandable being that does not exist in any conceivable world; and perhaps there is enough latitude in the notions of understandability and conceivability so that he might be within his rights. But the ontological arguer who construes those notions so that Premise 1 is a necessary truth is also within his rights, and that is what matters. It is not for me, but for the ontological arguer, to explain what existing in the understanding is supposed to be, and what is supposed to be the relation between the existence in one's understanding of a possible being and one's understanding of some or all descriptions that would apply to that being. I am willing to grant that he can give some adequate account.

He might wish to do so in such a way that the understandability of a given possible being is a contingent matter, so that a being might be *understandable in* one world but not in another. I may grant him this; but we shall only be concerned with actual understandability, understandability in the actual world. Hence the predicate "U" need not be relativized to worlds.[4]

4. THE SECOND PREMISE

In some versions of the ontological argument, it seems that a hypothetical nonexistent God is supposed to be excelled in greatness by some *other* conceivable being: one that exists, but otherwise is just like the hypothetical nonexistent God. I am unable to see how this strategy could yield an argument close enough to soundness to be interesting. Moreover, it is not Anselm's strategy; he writes: "For suppose it exists in the understanding alone: then *it* can be conceived to exist in reality; which is greater." What excels a hypothetical nonexistent God is not some other being; it is that same being, conceived as existent.

To capture this idea, beings must have their greatness relative to worlds.

---

[4]Similar remarks apply to "W". The ontological arguer might choose to explain conceivability in such a way that a world sometimes is *conceivable from* one world but not from another. However, we will be concerned only with actual conceivability of worlds; that is, conceivability from the actual world.

Premise 2 says that any understandable being is greater in worlds in which it exists than in worlds in which it does not. We have the following nonmodal translation of Premise 2:

2. $\forall x \, \forall w \, \forall v \, (\, Ux \, \& \, Ww \, \& \, Wv \, \& \, xEw \, \& \, \sim xEv \, \supset \, xwGxv \,)$

(For any understandable being x, and for any worlds w and v, if x exists in w but x does not exist in v, then the greatness of x in w exceeds the greatness of x in v.)

We need not regard the seeming hypostatization of greatnesses as more than a figure of speech, since we can take "the greatness of . . . in . . . exceeds the greatness of . . . in . . ." as an indivisible 4-place predicate.

I have no wish to dispute the second premise. In saying what makes for greatness, the ontological arguer is merely expounding his standards of greatness. Within wide limits, he is entitled to whatever standards of greatness he wants. All we can demand is that he stick to fixed standards throughout his argument, and throughout his subsequent account of the theological significance of the conclusion thereof.

5. THE THIRD PREMISE

The third premise says that there is some understandable being x whose greatness cannot be conceived to be exceeded by the greatness of anything. That is, the greatness of x is not exceeded by the greatness in any conceivable world w of any being y. We have seen that greatnesses, as thought of by the ontological arguer, belong to beings paired with worlds; according to the third premise, no such pair has a greatness exceeding the greatness of a certain understandable being x.

But if greatnesses belong to beings relative to worlds, what are we talking about when we say: the greatness of x? *Which* greatness of x? The greatness of x in which conceivable world? Different answers to the question yield different nonmodal translations of Premise 3.

We might construe Premise 3 as saying that what is unexceeded is the *actual* greatness of x, the greatness of x here in the actual world. If we speak of the greatness of something without mentioning a world, surely we ordinarily mean its greatness in the actual world; for we are ordinarily not talking about any worlds except the actual world. So it is plausible that even when other worlds *are* under discussion, we are speaking about the actual world unless we say otherwise. Thus, introducing a name "@" for the actual world, we obtain this first nonmodal translation of Premise 3:

3A. $\exists x \, (\, Ux \, \& \, \sim \exists w \, \exists y \, (\, Ww \, \& \, ywGx@ \,) \,)$

(There is an understandable being x, such that for no world w and being y does the greatness of y in w exceed the greatness of x in the actual world.)

Alternatively, we might construe Premise 3 as saying something weaker: that what is unexceeded is the *greatest* greatness of x, the greatness of x in any one of the worlds in which x is at its greatest. That is equivalent to saying merely that the greatness of x in some world v is unexceeded; for if the greatness of x in v is unexceeded, v is one of the worlds in which x is at its greatest. Thus we obtain a second nonmodal translation of Premise 3:

3B. ∃x ∃v (Ux & Wv & ~ ∃w ∃y (Ww & ywGxv))

(There are an understandable being x and a world v, such that for no world w and being y does the greatness of y in w exceed the greatness of x in v.)

Or we might construe Premise 3 as saying something stronger: that what is unexceeded is *any* greatness of x, the greatness of x in any world whatever. Thus we obtain a third nonmodal translation of Premise 3:

3C. ∃x (Ux & ~ ∃v ∃w ∃y (Ww & Ww & ywGxv))

(There is an understandable being x such that for no worlds v and w and being y does the greatness of y in w exceed the greatness of x in v.)

Under the auxiliary premise 4, which we shall take for granted henceforth,

4. W @

(The actual world is a world.)

3C implies 3A, but not conversely, and 3A implies 3B, but not conversely.

Perhaps there is one more possibility: For any world w, the greatness in w of x is not exceeded by the greatness in w of anything. Thus we obtain a fourth translation:

3D. ∃x (Ux & ~ ∃w ∃y (Ww & ywGxv))

(There is an understandable being x such that for no world w and being y does the greatness of y in w exceed the greatness of x in w.)

3D is not a plausible translation, since it might be true even if the greatness of anything x in any world w is exceeded by the greatness of something else elsewhere.

Premise 3B, at least, is moderately credible. It says that there is a highest grade of greatness, and that this grade of greatness is occupied, in some world, by an understandable being. If, above some level, we were prepared to discriminate only finitely many grades of greatness (no matter how many), and if we were prepared to admit that any grade of greatness, however high, could be occupied by an understandable being, then we would thereby be committed to accepting 3B. I have no wish to dispute 3B.

We postpone consideration of the credibility of the stronger translations 3A and 3C of Premise 3. We will not need to consider whether 3D is credible.

6. THE CONCLUSION

The conclusion says that there is some being x, existing in the actual world, whose greatness cannot be conceived to be exceeded by the greatness of anything. (We need not add that x is an understandable being, though that would follow if the rest did.) That is, the greatness of x is not exceeded by the greatness in any conceivable world w of any being y.

We ask again: *which* greatness of x? But this time the answer clearly should be: the *actual* greatness of x, the greatness of x here in the actual world. Other versions of the conclusion would either imply this version or be of no theological interest. The fool would not mind being convinced that there is an actual being who might conceivably have been—is, in some conceivable world —of unexcelled greatness. So our nonmodal translation of the conclusion resembles 3A, our first version of Premise 3:

C. $\exists x \, (\, x \, E \, @ \, \& \sim \exists w \, \exists y \, (\, Ww \, \& \, ywGx@ \,) \,)$

(There is a being x existing in the actual world such that for no world w and being y does the greatness of y in w exceed the greatness of x in the actual world.)

7. VALIDITY OF THE ARGUMENT

We now have four precise, nonmodal translations of our original argument, one for each alternative translation of Premise 3. It is a routine matter to determine, by ordinary nonmodal logic, which are valid and which are not. It turns out that the arguments from 3A and 3C

$$\frac{1, \ 2, \ 3A, \ 4}{\therefore \ C} \qquad\qquad \frac{1, \ 2, \ 3C, \ 4}{\therefore \ C}$$

are valid, whereas the arguments from 3B and 3D

$$\frac{1, \ 2, \ 3B, \ 4}{\therefore \ C} \qquad\qquad \frac{1, \ 2, \ 3D, \ 4}{\therefore \ C}$$

are not valid. Hence, we shall not consider the arguments from 3B and 3D further, despite the moderate credibility of 3B. Moreover, since 3C implies 3A and the argument from 3A is already valid, we need not consider the argument from 3C separately. Rather, we shall regard the inference from 3C to 3A as a possible preliminary to the argument from 3A, and ask whether 3C has any credibility to pass on to 3A.

8. CREDIBILITY OF THE THIRD PREMISE

The success of our form of the ontological argument therefore turns out to depend on the credibility of 3A, our first nonmodal translation of the premise that something exists in the understanding, than which nothing greater can be conceived. Why might an ontological arguer accept 3A?

He might infer 3A from 3C, if 3C were credible. Why might he accept 3C?

He might infer 3C from premises he accepts concerning the existence and nature of God. But in that case he could not argue from 3C without circularity.

He might assume that for every description he understands, there is some understandable being answering to that description. But what of such well-understood descriptions as "largest prime" or "round square"? Possibly he can give some account of understandable beings such that one of them answers to any understood description; but if so, we can hardly continue to grant him Premise 1, according to which every understandable being can be conceived to exist. Premise 1 is indispensable to the argument from 3C, since without Premise 1, 3C might be true by virtue of a supremely great understandable being existing in no conceivable world.

He might obtain 3C by using the following *Principle of Saturation:* any sentence saying that there exists an understandable being of so-and-so description is true unless provably false. Such a principle would, of course, permit a much simpler ontological argument than ours: apply it to the description "Divine being existing in every world." But the Principle of Saturation can as easily be used to refute 3C as to defend it. Consider the sentence (*) saying that there is an understandable being which is greater than anything else in some world, but is exceeded in greatness in another world.

(*) $\quad \exists x \, \exists w \, \exists v \, (\, Ux \, \& \, Ww \, \& \, Wv \, \& \, \forall y \, (\, y \neq x \supset xwGyw \,) \, \& \, \exists y \, yvGxv \,)$

If the Principle of Saturation supports 3C,[5] it should equally well support (*); otherwise it makes a discrimination unjustified by any visibly relevant difference between 3C and (*). But (*) is incompatible with 3C. So if the Principle of Saturation supports 3C, then it is a bad principle.

I know of no other way to defend 3C. Therefore let us turn to the question whether 3A, unsupported by 3C, is credible in its own right.

---

[5] I argue conditionally since we cannot say whether the Principle of Saturation supports 3C (and (*)) until we have formulated the Principle more precisely. In particular, we would have to settle whether the provability mentioned in the Principle is to include provability by means of the Principle itself.

The ontological arguer might accept 3A with or without also accepting G, a generalization over all worlds of which 3A is the instance pertaining to the actual world.

G. $\forall v (Wv \supset \exists x (Ux \& \sim \exists w \exists y (Ww \& ywGxv)))$

(For any world v, there is an understandable being x such that for no world w and being y does the greatness of y in w exceed the greatness of x in v.)

Why might he accept G? He might infer it from 3C; but we know of no non-circular reasons for him to believe 3C. Unless inferred from 3C, G does not seem credible. Let v be a bad world—say, one containing nothing but a small chunk of mud—and let w be the most splendid conceivable world. Then according to G there is some understandable being whose greatness in v is unexceeded by the greatness in w of anything—even the greatest of the inhabitants of w. What could this understandable being be? By 1 and 2 (which the ontological arguer accepts) it is something that exists in v. Is it part of the mud? Or is it an abstract entity that exists everywhere? If the latter, then there is no reason for it to be especially great at v, while if it is equally great everywhere then we are back to arguing from 3C. It seems that in order to believe G without inferring it from 3C, the ontological arguer would need to adopt standards of greatness so eccentric as to rob his conclusion of its expected theological import. If some mud in its mud-world is deemed to be as great as the greatest angel in his heavenly world, then it does not matter whether or not something exists in reality than which nothing greater—by *these* standards of greatness—can be conceived.

If the ontological arguer accepts 3A without also accepting G, then he is claiming that the actual world possesses a distinction which at least some other worlds lack: the actual world is one of those worlds at which something achieves a greatness unexceeded by the greatness of anything anywhere. For short: the actual world, unlike some other worlds, is a *place of greatest greatness*. Why is this credible? What is special about the actual world, compared to some others, that should lead us to think it a place of greatest greatness?

It will not do for the ontological arguer to cite various features of the actual world that impress him: its tall mountains, beautiful women, wise philosophers or what not. In the first place, the actual world is greatly excelled in all such respects by other worlds—it is possible for mountains to be taller than they actually are, and so on. In the second place, the ontological arguer is not supposed to be giving us empirical theology; we wish to know whether his premises are at all credible *a priori*.

It remains for the ontological arguer to hold that the actual world is special, and a fitting place of greatest greatness, precisely because it, alone out of the worlds, is actual. This reason seems *prima facie* to have some force: whatever actuality may be, it is something we deem tremendously important, and there *is* only one world that has it. We picture the actual world—indefensibly—as the one solid, vivid, energetic world among innumerable ghostly, faded, wispy, "merely" possible worlds. Therefore it may well seem plausible that the actual world, being special by its unique actuality, might also be special by being a place of greatest greatness. This does not pretend to be a proof of 3A, but we do not demand proof; we wish to know if the ontological arguer has any reason at all to accept 3A, even a reason that does no more than appeal to his sense of fitness.

9. THE NATURE OF ACTUALITY

But this last reason to accept 3A is not only weak; it is mistaken. It is true that our world alone is actual; but that does not make our world special, radically different from all other worlds.

I suggest that "actual" and its cognates should be analyzed as *indexical* terms: terms whose reference varies, depending on relevant features of the context of utterance. The relevant feature of context, for the term "actual", is the world at which a given utterance occurs. According to the indexical analysis I propose, "actual" (in its primary sense) refers at any world w to the world w. "Actual" is analogous to "present", an indexical term whose reference varies depending on a different feature of context: "present" refers at any time t to the time t. "Actual" is analogous also to "here", "I", "you", "this", and "aforementioned"—indexical terms depending for their reference respectively on the place, the speaker, the intended audience, the speaker's acts of pointing, and the aforegoing discourse.[6]

I do not mean to say that "actual" has different meanings in the languages used in different worlds, so that for any world w, "the actual world" is a proper name of w in the native language of w. That is false. (Just as it would be false to say that "today" changes its meaning every midnight.) Rather, the *fixed* meaning we give to "actual" is such that, at any world w, "actual" refers in *our* language to w.

I use "refers" broadly to cover various semantic relations for indexical terms of various grammatical categories. To speak more precisely: at any world w, the name "the actual world" *denotes* or *names* w; the predicate "is actual" *designates* or *is true of* w and whatever exists in w; the operator "actually" *is true of* propositions true at w, and so on for cognate terms of other categories. Similarly, at any time t the name "the present time" denotes t, the predicate "is present" is true of t and whatever exists at t, the operator "presently" is true of propositions true at t, and so on.

A complication: we can distinguish primary and secondary senses of "ac-

---

[6]For a general account of indexicality, see Richard Montague. "Pragmatics," *Contemporary Philosophy*, ed. Raymond Klibansky (Florence: La Nuova Italie Editrice, 1968). A. N. Prior states the indexical analysis of actuality in "Modal Logic and the Logic of Applicability," *Theoria* 34 (1968): 191–92; but, sadly, he goes on to say "this seems a tall story, and . . . I doubt whether anyone seriously believes it."

tual" by asking what world "actual" refers to at a world w in a context in which some other world v is under consideration. In the primary sense, it still refers to w, as in "If Max ate less, he would be thinner than he actually is". In the secondary sense it shifts its reference to the world v under consideration, as in "If Max ate less, he would actually enjoy himself more". A similar distinction occurs among temporal indexicals: the unaccompanied present tense does, and the present tense accompanied by "now" does not, tend to shift its reference from the time of an utterance to another time under consideration.[7] "It will be the case in 2100 A.D. that there are men on Mars," said now, is probably true, whereas "It will be the case in 2100 A.D. that there are now men on Mars," said now, is probably false. The secondary, shifting sense of "actual" is responsible for our translation 3D. If we set out on the route that leads to 3A, we get "There is an understandable being x, such that for no world w and being y does the greatness of y in w exceed the actual greatness of x." Then if we take "actual" in the secondary sense, it shifts from referring to our own world to referring to the world w under consideration, thereby yielding 3D rather than 3A.

The strongest evidence for the indexical analysis of actuality is that it explains why skepticism about our own actuality is absurd. How do we know that we are not the unactualized possible inhabitants of some unactualized possible world? We can give no evidence: whatever feature of our world we may mention, it is shared by other worlds that are not actual. Some unactualized grass is no less green, some unactualized dollars buy no less (unactualized) bread, some unactualized philosophers are no less sure they are actual. Either we know in some utterly mysterious way that we are actual; or we do not know it at all.

But of course we do know it. The indexical analysis of actuality explains how we know it: in the same way I know that I am me, that *this* time is the present, or that I am here. All such sentences as "This is the actual world," "I am actual," "I actually exist," and the like are true on any possible occasion of utterance in any possible world. That is why skepticism about our own actuality is absurd.

"This is the actual world" is true whenever uttered in any possible world. That is not to say, of course, that all worlds are actual. "All worlds are actual" is *false* whenever uttered in any world. Everyone may truly call his own world actual, but no one, wherever located, may truly call all the worlds actual. It is the same with time. Sometimes it seems to the novice that indexical analysts of "present" are pretending that all times alike are present. But no: although "This time is present" is always true, "All times are present" is never true. If we take a timeless point of view and ignore our own location in time, the big difference between the present time and other times vanishes. That is not

---

[7] I owe this distinction to J. A. W. Kamp, "The treatment of 'now' as a 1-place sentential operator" (1967, unpublished). It is discussed also by A. N. Prior in "'Now'," *Nous* 2 (1968): 101–19.

because we regard all times as equally present, but rather because if we ignore our own location in time we cannot use temporally indexical terms like "present" at all. And similarly, I claim, if we take an *a priori* point of view and ignore our own location among the worlds the big difference between the actual world and other worlds should vanish. That is not because we regard all worlds as equally actual[8] but rather because if we ignore our own location among the worlds we cannot use indexical terms like "actual".

If I am right, the ontological arguer who says that his world is special because his world alone is the actual world is as foolish as a man who boasts that he has the special fortune to be alive at a unique moment in history: the present. The actual world is not special in itself, but only in the special relation it bears to the ontological arguer. Other worlds bear the same relation to other ontological arguers. The ontological arguer has no reason to regard his own actual world as special except in its relation to him. Hence he has not even a weak reason to think that his world differs from some other worlds in being a place of greatest greatness—that is, not even a weak reason to accept 3A without also accepting its generalization G. We have already found that he has no reason to accept G without 3C and no good, noncircular reason to accept 3C. We should conclude, therefore, that the argument from 3A is a valid argument from a premise we have no noncircular reason to accept.

10. CONCLUSION

Of the alternative nonmodal translations of our ontological argument, the best are the arguments from 3A and 3B. The premises of the argument from 3B enjoy some credibility, but the argument is invalid. The argument from 3A is valid, but 3A derives its credibility entirely from the illusion that because our world alone is actual, therefore our world is radically different from all other worlds—special in a way that makes it a fitting place of greatest greatness. But once we recognize the indexical nature of actuality, the illusion is broken and the credibility of 3A evaporates. It is true of *any* world, at that world but not elsewhere, that that world alone is actual. The world an ontological arguer calls actual is special only in that the ontological arguer resides there—and it is no great distinction for a world to harbor an ontological arguer. Think of an ontological arguer in some dismally mediocre world—there are such ontological arguers—arguing that his world alone is actual, hence special, hence a fitting place of greatest greatness, hence a world wherein something exists than which no greater can be conceived to exist. He is wrong to argue thus. So are we.

---

[8]Prior slips here in presenting the indexical analysis (as a tall story). He writes, "this word 'actual' must not be taken as signifying that the world in question is any more 'real' than those other worlds. . . ." But "real" (even in scare-quotes) is presumably indexical in the same way as "actual". Hence we can no more say that all worlds are equally real than we can say that all worlds alike are actual.

The Cosmological Argument

ST. THOMAS AQUINAS

1.6 The Five Ways

We proceed thus to the Third Article:—

Objection 1. It seems that God does not exist; because if one of two contraries be infinite, the other would be altogether destroyed. But the name *God* means that He is infinite goodness. If, therefore, God existed, there would be no evil discoverable; but there is evil in the world. Therefore God does not exist.

Obj. 2. Further, it is superfluous to suppose that what can be accounted for by a few principles has been produced by many. But it seems that everything we see in the world can be accounted for by other principles, supposing God did not exist. For all natural things can be reduced to one principle, which is nature; and all voluntary things can be reduced to one principle, which is human reason, or will. Therefore there is no need to suppose God's existence.

On the contrary, It is said in the person of God: *I am Who am* (*Exod.* iii. 14).

I answer that, The existence of God can be proved in five ways.

The first and more manifest way is the argument from motion. It is certain, and evident to our senses, that in the world some things are in motion. Now whatever is moved is moved by another, for nothing can be moved except it is in potentiality to that towards which it is moved; whereas a thing moves inasmuch as it is in act. For motion is nothing else than the reduction of something from potentiality to actuality. But nothing can be reduced from potentiality to actuality, except by something in a state of actuality. Thus that which is actually hot, as fire, makes wood, which is potentially hot, to be actually hot, and thereby moves and changes it. Now it is not possible that the same thing should be at once in actuality and potentiality in the same respect, but only in different respects. For what is actually hot cannot simultaneously be potenially hot; but it is simultaneously potentially cold. It is therefore impossible that in the same respect and in the same way a thing should be both mover and moved, *i.e.*, that it should move itself. Therefore, whatever is moved must be moved by another. If that by which it is moved be itself moved, then this also must needs be moved by another, and that by another again. But

From *Summa Theologica*, Part I, trans. Dominican Fathers of English Province (New York: Benzinger, Inc., 1947). Reprinted by permission of the publisher.

this cannot go on to infinity, because then there would be no first mover, and, consequently, no other mover, seeing that subsequent movers move only inasmuch as they are moved by the first mover; as the staff moves only because it is moved by the hand. Therefore it is necessary to arrive at a first mover, moved by no other; and this everyone understands to be God.

The second way is from the nature of efficient cause. In the world of sensible things we find there is an order of efficient causes. There is no case known (neither is it, indeed, possible) in which a thing is found to be the efficient cause of itself; for so it would be prior to itself, which is impossible. Now in efficient causes it is not possible to go on to infinity, because in all efficient causes following in order, the first is the cause of the intermediate cause, and the intermediate is the cause of the ultimate cause, whether the intermediate cause be several, or one only. Now to take away the cause is to take away the effect. Therefore, if there be no first cause among efficient causes, there will be no ultimate, nor any intermediate, cause. But if in efficient causes it is possible to go on to infinity, there will be no first efficient cause, neither will there be an ultimate effect, nor any intermediate efficient causes; all of which is plainly false. Therefore it is necessary to admit a first efficient cause, to which everyone gives the name of God.

The third way is taken from possibility and necessity, and runs thus. We find in nature things that are possible to be and not to be, since they are found to be generated, and to be corrupted, and consequently, it is possible for them to be and not to be. But it is impossible for these always to exist, for that which can not-be at some time is not. Therefore, if everything can not-be, then at one time there was nothing in existence. Now if this were true, even now there would be nothing in existence, because that which does not exist begins to exist only through something already existing. Therefore, if at one time nothing was in existence, it would have been impossible for anything to have begun to exist; and thus even now nothing would be in existence—which is absurd. Therefore, not all beings are merely possible, but there must exist something the existence of which is necessary. But every necessary thing either has its necessity caused by another, or not. Now it is impossible to go on to infinity in necessary things which have their necessity caused by another, as has been already proved in regard to efficient causes. Therefore we cannot but admit the existence of some being having of itself its own necessity, and not receiving it from another, but rather causing in others their necessity. This all men speak of as God.

The fourth way is taken from the gradation to be found in things. Among beings there are some more and some less good, true, noble, and the like. But *more* and *less* are predicated of different things according as they resemble in their different ways something which is the maximum, as a thing is said to be hotter according as it more nearly resembles that which is hottest; so that there is something which is truest, something best, something noblest, and, consequently, something which is most being, for those things that are greatest in truth are greatest in being, as it is written in *Metaph. ii.* Now the maximum in any genus is the cause of all in that genus, as fire, which is the maximum of heat, is the cause of all hot things, as is said in the same book. Therefore there must also be something which is to all beings the cause of their being, goodness, and every other perfection; and this we call God.

The fifth way is taken from the governance of the world. We see that things which lack knowledge, such as natural bodies, act for an end, and this is evident from their acting always, or nearly always, in the same way, so as to obtain the best result. Hence it is plain that they achieve their end, not fortuitously, but designedly. Now whatever lacks knowledge cannot move towards an end, unless it be directed by some being endowed with knowledge and intelligence; as the arrow is directed by the archer. Therefore some intelligent being exists by whom all natural things are directed to their end; and this being we call God.

Reply Obj. 1. As Augustine says: *Since God is the highest good, He would not allow any evil to exist in His works, unless His omnipotence and goodness were such as to bring good even out of evil.* This is part of the infinite goodness of God, that He should allow evil to exist, and out of it produce good.

Reply Obj. 2. Since nature works for a determinate end under the direction of a higher agent, whatever is done by nature must be traced back to God as to its first cause. So likewise whatever is done voluntarily must be traced back to some higher cause other than human reason and will, since these can change and fail; for all things that are changeable and capable of defect must be traced back to an immovable and self-necessary first principle, as has been shown.

SAMUEL CLARKE

1.7   An Improved Version of the Argument

There has existed from eternity some one unchangeable and independent being. For since something must needs have been from eternity; as hath been already proved, and is granted on all hands: either there has always existed one unchangeable and *independent* Being, from which all other beings that are or ever were in the universe, have received their original; or else there has been an infinite succession of changeable and *dependent* beings, produced one from another in an endless progression, without any original cause at all: which latter supposition is so very absurd, that tho' all atheism must in its account

---

From Samuel Clarke, *A Demonstration of the Being and Attributes of God* (1705), Part II.

of most things (as shall be shown hereafter) terminate in it, yet I think very few atheists ever were so weak as openly and directly to defend it. For it is plainly impossible and contradictory to itself. I shall not argue against it from the supposed impossibility of infinite succession, *barely and absolutely considered in itself*; for a reason which shall be mentioned hereafter: but, if we consider such an infinite progression, as *one* entire endless *series* of *dependent* beings; 'tis plain this whole *series* of beings can have no cause *from without,* of its existence; because in it are supposed to be included *all things* that are or ever were in the universe: and 'tis plain it can have no reason *within itself,* of its existence; because no one being in this infinite succession is supposed to be self-existent or *necessary* (which is the only ground or reason of existence of any thing, that can be imagined *within the thing itself*, as will presently more fully appear), but every one *dependent* on the foregoing: and where *no part* is necessary, 'tis manifest *the whole* cannot be necessary; absolute necessity of existence, not being an outward, relative, and accidental determination; but an inward and essential property of the nature of the thing which so exists. An infinite succession therefore of merely *dependent* beings, without any original independent cause; is a *series* of beings, that has neither necessity nor cause, nor any reason *at all* of its existence, neither *within itself* nor *from without:* that is, 'tis an express contradiction and impossibility; 'tis a supposing *something* to be *caused,* (because it's granted in every one of its stages of succession, not to be necessary and from itself); and yet that in the whole it is caused *absolutely by nothing*: Which every man knows is a contradiction to be done *in time*; and because duration in this case makes no difference, 'tis equally a contradiction to suppose it done from eternity: And consequently there must *on the contrary*, of necessity have existed from eternity, *some one* immutable and *independent* Being: Which, what it is, remains in the next place to be inquired.

DAVID HUME

1.8 Criticism of Clarke's Argument

But if so many difficulties attend the argument *a posteriori*, said Demea, had we not better adhere to that simple and sublime argument *a priori* which, by offering to us infallible demonstration, cuts off at once all doubt and difficulty? By this argument, too, we may prove the *infinity* of the Divine attributes,

From David Hume, *Dialogues Concerning Natural Religion* (1779), Part IX.

which, I am afraid, can never be ascertained with certainty from any other topic. For how can an effect which either is finite or, for aught we know, may be so—how can such an effect, I say, prove an infinite cause? The unity, too, of the Divine Nature it is very difficult, if not absolutely impossible, to deduce merely from contemplating the works of nature; nor will the uniformity alone of the plan, even were it allowed, give us any assurance of that attribute. Whereas the argument *a priori* . . .

You seem to reason, Demea, interposed Cleanthes, as if those advantages and conveniences in the abstract argument were full proofs of its solidity. But it is first proper, in my opinion, to determine what argument of this nature you choose to insist on; and we shall afterwards, from itself, better than from its *useful* consequences, endeavor to determine what value we ought to put upon it.

The argument, replied Demea, which I would insist on is the common one. Whatever exists must have a cause or reason of its existence, it being absolutely impossible for anything to produce itself or be the cause of its own existence. In mounting up, therefore, from effects to causes, we must either go on in tracing an infinite succession, without any ultimate cause at all, or must at last have recourse to some ultimate cause that is *necessarily* existent. Now, that the first supposition is absurd may be thus proved. In the infinite chain or succession of causes and effects, each single effect is determined to exist by the power and efficacy of that cause which immediately preceded; but the whole eternal chain or succession, taken together, is not determined or caused by anything; and yet it is evident that it requires a cause or reason, as much as any particular object which begins to exist in time. The question is still reasonable why this particular succession of causes existed from eternity, and not any other succession or no succession at all. If there be no necessarily existent being, any supposition which can be formed is equally possible; nor is there any more absurdity in nothing's having existed from eternity than there is in that succession of causes which constitutes the universe. What was it, then, which determined something to exist rather than nothing, and bestowed being on a particular possibility, exclusive of the rest? *External causes*, there are supposed to be none. *Chance* is a word without a meaning. Was it *nothing?* But that can never produce anything. We must, therefore, have recourse to a necessarily existent Being who carries the *reason* of his existence in himself; and who cannot be supposed not to exist, without an express contradiction. There is, consequently, such a Being—that is, there is a Deity.

I shall not leave it to Philo, said Cleanthes (though I know that the starting objections is his chief delight), to point out the weakness of this metaphysical reasoning. It seems to me so obviously ill-grounded, and at the same time of so little consequence to the cause of true piety and religion, that I shall myself venture to show the fallacy of it.

I shall begin with observing that there is an evident absurdity in pretending to demonstrate a matter of fact, or to prove it by any arguments *a priori*.

Nothing is demonstrable unless the contrary implies a contradiction. Nothing that is distinctly conceivable implies a contradiction. Whatever we conceive as existent, we can also conceive as non-existent. There is no being, therefore, whose non-existence implies a contradiction. Consequently there is no being whose existence is demonstrable. I propose this argument as entirely decisive, and am willing to rest the whole controversy upon it.

It is pretended that the Deity is a necessarily existent being; and this necessity of his existence is attempted to be explained by asserting that, if we knew his whole essence or nature, we should perceive it to be as impossible for him not to exist, as for twice two not to be four. But it is evident that this can never happen, while our faculties remain the same as at present. It will still be possible for us, at any time, to conceive the non-existence of what we formerly conceived to exist; nor can the mind ever lie under a necessity of supposing any object to remain always in being; in the same manner as we lie under a necessity of always conceiving twice two to be four. The words, therefore, *necessary existence* have no meaning; or, which is the same thing, none that is consistent.

But further, why may not the material universe be the necessarily existent Being, according to this pretended explication of necessity? We dare not affirm that we know all the qualities of matter; and, for aught we can determine, it may contain some qualities which, were they known, would make its non-existence appear as great a contradiction as that twice two is five. I find only one argument employed to prove that the material world is not the necessarily existent Being; and this argument is derived from the contingency both of the matter and the form of the world. "Any particle of matter", it is said, "may be *conceived* to be annihilated, and any form may be *conceived* to be altered. Such an annihilation or alteration, therefore, is not impossible."[1] But it seems a great partiality not to perceive that the same argument extends equally to the Deity, so far as we have any conception of him; and that the mind can at least imagine him to be non-existent, or his attributes to be altered. It must be some unknown, inconceivable qualities which can make his non-existence appear impossible or his attributes unalterable: And no reason can be assigned why these qualities may not belong to matter. As they are altogether unknown and inconceivable, they can never be proved incompatible with it.

Add to this that in tracing an eternal succession of objects it seems absurd to inquire for a general cause or first author. How can anything that exists from eternity have a cause, since that relation implies a priority in time and a beginning of existence?

In such a chain, too, or succession of objects, each part is caused by that which preceded it, and causes that which succeeds it. Where then is the difficulty? But the *whole*, you say, wants a cause. I answer that the uniting of these parts into a whole, like the uniting of several distinct countries into one king-

---

[1]Dr. Clarke.

dom, or several distinct members into one body, is performed merely by an arbitrary act of the mind, and has no influence on the nature of things. Did I show you the particular causes of each individual in a collection of twenty particles of matter, I should think it very unreasonable should you afterwards ask me what was the cause of the whole twenty. This is sufficiently explained in explaining the cause of the parts.

Though the reasonings which you have urged, Cleanthes, may well excuse me, said Philo, from starting any further difficulties; yet I cannot forbear insisting still upon another topic. It is observed by arithmeticians that the products of 9 compose always either 9 or some lesser product of 9 if you add together all the characters of which any of the former products is composed. Thus, of 18, 27, 36, which are products of 9, you make 9 by adding 1 to 8, 2 to 7, 3 to 6. Thus 369 is a product also of 9; and if you add 3, 6, and 9, you make 18, a lesser product of 9.[2] To a superficial observer so wonderful a regularity may be admired as the effect either of chance or design; but a skillful algebraist immediately concludes it to be the work of necessity, and demonstrates that it must forever result from the nature of these numbers. Is it not probable, I ask, that the whole economy of the universe is conducted by a like necessity, though no human algebra can furnish a key which solves the difficulty? And instead of admiring the order of natural beings, may it not happen that, could we penetrate into the intimate nature of bodies, we should clearly see why it was absolutely impossible they could ever admit of any other disposition? So dangerous is it to introduce this idea of necessity into the present question! and so naturally does it afford an inference directly opposite to the religious hypothesis!

But dropping all these abstractions, continued Philo, and confining ourselves to more familiar topics, I shall venture to add an observation that the argument *a priori* has seldom been found very convincing, except to people of a metaphysical head who have accustomed themselves to abstract reasoning, and who, finding from mathematics that the understanding frequently leads to truth through obscurity, and contrary to first appearances, have transferred the same habit of thinking to subjects where it ought not to have place. Other people, even of good sense and the best inclined to religion, feel always some deficiency in such arguments, though they are not perhaps able to explain distinctly where it lies—a certain proof that men ever did and ever will derive their religion from other sources than from this species of reasoning.

---

[2]*République des Lettres*, Aut 1685.

PAUL EDWARDS

1.9 The Cosmological Argument

The so-called "cosmological proof" is one of the oldest and most popular arguments for the existence of God. It was forcibly criticized by Hume,[1] Kant,[2] and Mill,[3] but it would be inaccurate to consider the argument dead or even moribund. Catholic philosophers, with hardly any exception, appear to believe that it is as solid and conclusive as ever. Thus Father F. C. Copleston confidently championed it in his Third Programme debate with Bertrand Russell,[4] and in America, where Catholic writers are more sanguine, we are told by a Jesuit professor of physics that "the existence of an intelligent being as the First Cause of the universe can be established by *rational scientific inference.*"[5]

> I am absolutely convinced [the same writer continues] that any one who would give the same consideration to that proof (the cosmological argument), as outlined for example in William Brosnan's *God and Reason*, as he would give to a line of argumentation found in the *Physical Review* or the *Proceedings of the Royal Society* would be forced to admit that the cogency of this argument for the existence of God far outstrips that which is found in the reasoning which Chadwick uses to prove the existence of the neutron, which today is accepted as certain as any conclusion in the physical sciences.[6]

Mild theists like the late Professor Dawes Hicks[7] and Dr. [A. C.] Ewing,[8] who concede many of Hume's and Kant's criticisms, nevertheless contend that the argument possesses a certain core of truth. In popular discussions it also crops up again and again—for example, when believers address atheists with such questions as "You tell me where the universe came from!" Even philosophers who reject the cosmological proof sometimes embody certain of its confusions in the formulation of their own position. In the light of all this,

---

From *The Rationalist Annual*, 1959 (London: Pemberton Publishing Co. Ltd.). Reprinted by permission of the publisher.

[1]*Dialogues Concerning Natural Religion*, Part IX.
[2]*The Critique of Pure Reason*, Transcendental Dialectic, Book II, Chapter III.
[3]"Theism," *Three Essays on Religion*, Part I.
[4]Reprinted in the British edition of Russell's *Why I Am Not a Christian*.
[5]J. S. O'Connor, "A Scientific Approach to Religion," *The Scientific Monthly* (1940), p. 369; my italics.
[6]*Ibid.*, pp. 369–70.
[7]*The Philosophical Bases of Theism*, Lecture V.
[8]*The Fundamental Questions of Philosophy*, Chapter XI.

it may be worth while to undertake a fresh examination of the argument with special attention to the fallacies that were not emphasized by the older critics.

II

The cosmological proof has taken a number of forms, the most important of which are known as the "causal argument" and "the argument from contingency," respectively. In some writers, in Samuel Clarke for example, they are combined, but it is best to keep them apart as far as possible. The causal argument is the second of the "five ways" of Aquinas and roughly proceeds as follows: we find that the things around us come into being as the result of the activity of other things. These causes are themselves the result of the activity of other things. But such a causal series cannot "go back to infinity." Hence there must be a first member, a member which is not itself caused by any preceding member—an uncaused or "first" cause.

It has frequently been pointed out that even if this argument were sound it would not establish the existence of *God*. It would not show that the first cause is all-powerful or all-good or that it is in any sense personal. Somebody believing in the eternity of atoms, or of matter generally, could quite consistently accept the conclusion. Defenders of the causal argument usually concede this and insist that the argument is not in itself meant to prove the existence of God. Supplementary arguments are required to show that the first cause must have the attributes assigned to the deity. They claim, however, that the argument, if valid, would at least be an important step towards a complete proof of the existence of God.

Does the argument succeed in proving so much as a first cause? This will depend mainly on the soundness of the premise that an infinite series of causes is impossible. Aquinas supports this premise by maintaining that the opposite belief involves a plain absurdity. To suppose that there is an infinite series of causes logically implies that nothing exists now; but we know that plenty of things do exist now; and hence any theory which implies that nothing exists now must be wrong. Let us take some causal series and refer to its members by the letters of the alphabet:

$$A \longrightarrow B \ldots W \longrightarrow X \longrightarrow Y \longrightarrow Z$$

Z stands here for something presently existing, e.g. Margaret Truman. Y represents the cause or part of the cause of Z, say Harry Truman. X designates the cause or part of the cause of Y, say Harry Truman's father, etc. Now, Aquinas reasons, whenever we take away the cause, we also take away the effect: if Harry Truman had never lived, Margaret Truman would never have been born. If Harry Truman's father had never lived, Harry Truman and Margaret Truman would never have been born. If A had never existed, none of the subsequent members of the series would have come into existence. But it is precisely A that the believer in the infinite series is "taking away." For in maintaining that the series is infinite he is denying that it has a first member; he is denying that there is such a thing as a first cause; he is in other words denying the existence of A. Since without A, Z could not have existed, his position implies that Z does not exist now; and that is plainly false.

This argument fails to do justice to the supporter of the infinite series of causes. Aquinas has failed to distinguish between the two statements:

(1) A did not exist, and
(2) A is not uncaused.

To say that the series is infinite implies (2), but it does not imply (1). The following parallel may be helpful here: Suppose Captain Spaulding had said, "I am the greatest explorer who ever lived," and somebody replied, "No, you are not." This answer would be denying that the Captain possessed the exalted attribute he had claimed for himself, but it would not be denying his existence. It would not be "taking him away." Similarly, the believer in the infinite series is not "taking A away." He is taking away the privileged status of A; he is taking away its "first causiness." He does not deny the *existence* of A or of any particular member of the series. He denies that A or anything else *is the first member* of the series. Since he is not taking A away, he is not taking B away, and thus he is also not taking X, Y, or Z away. His view, then, does not commit him to the absurdity that nothing exists now, or more specifically, that Margaret Truman does not exist now. It may be noted in this connection that a believer in the infinite series is not necessarily denying the existence of supernatural beings. He is merely committed to denying that such a being, if it exists, is uncaused. He is committed to holding that whatever other impressive attributes a supernatural being might possess, the attribute of being a first cause is not among them.

The causal argument is open to several other objections. Thus, even if otherwise valid, the argument would not prove a *single* first cause. For there does not seem to be any good ground for supposing that the various causal series in the universe ultimately merge. Hence even if it is granted that no series of causes can be infinite the possibility of a plurality of first members has not been ruled out. Nor does the argument establish the *present* existence of the first cause. It does not prove this, since experience clearly shows that an effect may exist long after its cause has been destroyed.

III

Many defenders of the causal argument would contend that at least some of these criticisms rest on a misunderstanding. They would probably go further and contend that the argument was not quite fairly stated in the first place— or at any rate that if it was fair to some of its adherents it was not fair to others. They would in this connection distinguish between two types of causes —what they call "causes *in fieri*" and what they call "causes *in esse*." A cause *in fieri* is a factor which brought or helped to bring an effect into existence. A cause in *esse* is a factor which "sustains" or helps to sustain the effect "in being." The parents of a human being would be an example of a cause *in fieri*. If somebody puts a book in my hand and I keep holding it up, his putting it there would be the cause *in fieri*, and my holding it would be the cause *in esse* of the book's position. To quote Father [G. H.] Joyce:

> If a smith forges a horse-shoe, he is only a cause *in fieri* of the shape given to the iron. That shape persists after his action has ceased. So, too, a builder is a cause *in fieri* of the house which he builds. In both these cases the substances employed act as causes *in esse* as regards the continued existence of the effect produced. Iron, in virtue of its natural rigidity, retains in being the shape which it has once received; and, similarly, the materials employed in building retain in being the order and arrangement which constitute them into a house.[9]

Using this distinction, a defender of the argument now reasons in the following way. To say that there is an infinite series of causes *in fieri* does not lead to any absurd conclusions. But Aquinas is concerned only with causes *in esse* and an infinite series of *such* causes is impossible. In the words of the contemporary American Thomist, R. P. Phillips:

> Each member of the series of causes possesses being solely by virtue of the actual present operation of a superior cause. . . . Life is dependent, *inter alia,* on a certain atmospheric pressure, this again on the continual operation of physical forces, whose being and operation depends on the position of the earth in the solar system, which itself must endure relatively unchanged, a state of being which can only be continuously produced by a definite—if unknown—constitution of the material universe. This constitution, however, cannot be its own cause. That a thing should cause itself is impossible: for in order that it may cause it is necessary for it to exist, which it cannot do, on the hypothesis, until it has been caused. So it must *be* in order to cause itself. Thus, not being uncaused nor yet its own cause, it must be caused by another, which produces and preserves it. It is plain, then, that as no member of this series possesses being except in virtue of the actual present operation of a superior cause, if there be no first cause actually operating none of the dependent causes could operate either. We are thus irresistibly led to posit a first efficient cause which, while itself uncaused, shall impart causality to a whole series. . . .
>
> The series of causes which we are considering is not one which stretches back into the past; so that we are not demanding a beginning of the world at some definite moment reckoning back from the present, but an actual cause now operating, to account for the present being of things.[10]

Professor Phillips offers the following parallel to bring out his point:

[9]*The Principles of Natural Theology*, p. 58.
[10]*Modern Thomistic Philosophy*, Vol. II, pp. 284–85.

In a goods train each truck is moved and moves by the action of the one immediately in front of it. If then we suppose the train to be infinite, i.e. that there is no end to it, and so no engine which starts the motion, it is plain that no truck will move. To lengthen it out to infinity will not give it what no member of it possesses of itself, viz. the power of drawing the truck behind it. If then we see any truck in motion we know there must be an end to the series of trucks which gives causality to the whole.[11]

Father Joyce introduces an illustration from Aquinas to explain how the present existence of things may be compatible with an infinite series of causes *in fieri* but not with an infinite series of causes *in esse*.

When a carpenter is at work, the series of efficient causes on which his work depends is necessarily limited. The final effect, e.g. the fastening of a nail is caused by a hammer: the hammer is moved by the arm: and the motion of his arm is determined by the motor-impulses communicated from the nerve centres of the brain. Unless the subordinate causes were limited in number, and were connected with a starting-point of motion, the hammer must remain inert; and the nail will never be driven in. If the series be supposed infinite, no work will ever take place. But if there is question of causes on which the work is not essentially dependent, we cannot draw the same conclusion. We may suppose the carpenter to have broken an infinite number of hammers, and as often to have replaced the broken tool by a fresh one. There is nothing in such a supposition which excludes the driving home of the nail.[12]

The supporter of the infinite series of causes, Joyce also remarks, is

... asking us to believe that although each link in a suspended chain is prevented from falling simply because it is attached to the one above it, yet if only the chain be long enough, it will, taken as a whole, need no support, but will hang loose in the air suspended from nothing.[13]

This formulation of the causal argument unquestionably circumvents one of the objections mentioned previously. If Y is the cause *in esse* of an effect, Z, then it must exist as long as Z exists. If the argument were valid in this form it would therefore prove the present and not merely the past existence of a first cause. In this form the argument is, however, less convincing in another respect. To maintain that all "natural" or "phenomenal" objects— things like tables and mountains and human beings—require a cause *in fieri* is not implausible, though even here Mill and others have argued that strictly speaking only *changes* require a causal explanation. It is far from plausible, on the other hand, to claim that all natural objects require a cause *in esse*. It may be granted that the air around us is a cause *in esse* of human life and further that certain gravitational forces are among the causes *in esse* of the air being where it is. But when we come to gravitational forces or, at any rate, to material particles like atoms or electrons it is difficult to see what cause

---

[11]*Op. cit.*, p. 278.
[12]*Op. cit.*, pp. 67–68.
[13]*Op. cit.*, p. 82.

in esse they require. To those not already convinced of the need for a supernatural First Cause some of the remarks by Professor Phillips in this connection appear merely dogmatic and question-begging. Most people would grant
that such particles as atoms did not cause themselves, since, as Professor
Phillips observes, they would in that event have had to exist before they began
existing. It is not at all evident, however, that these particles cannot be uncaused. Professor Phillips and all other supporters of the causal argument immediately proceed to claim that there is something else which needs no cause
in esse. They themselves admit thus, that there is nothing self-evident about the
proposition that everything must have a cause *in esse*. Their entire procedure
here lends substance to Schopenhauer's gibe that supporters of the cosmological argument treat the law of universal causation like "a hired cab which we
dismiss when we have reached our destination."[14]

But waiving this and all similar objections, the restatement of the argument
in terms of causes *in esse* in no way avoids the main difficulty which was
previously mentioned. A believer in the infinite series would insist that his
position was just as much misrepresented now as before. He is no more removing the member of the series which is supposed to be the first cause *in
esse* than he was removing the member which had been declared to be the
first cause *in fieri*. He is again merely denying a privileged status to it. He is
not denying the reality of the cause *in esse* labelled "A." He is not even necessarily denying that it possesses supernatural attributes. He is again merely
taking away its "first causiness."

The advocates of the causal argument in either form seem to confuse an
infinite series with one which is long but finite. If a book, Z, is to remain in
its position, say 100 miles up in the air, there must be another object, say
another book, Y, underneath it to serve as its support. If Y is to remain where
it is, it will need another support, X, beneath it. Suppose that this series of
supports, one below the other, continues for a long time, but eventually, say
after 100,000 members, comes to a first book which is not resting on any
other book or indeed on any other support. In that event the whole collection
would come crashing down. What we seem to need is a first member of the
series, a first support (such as the earth) which does not need another member
as *its* support, which in other words is "self-supporting."

This is evidently the sort of picture that supporters of the First Cause argument have before their minds when they rule out the possibility of an infinite
series. But such a picture is not a fair representation of the theory of the
infinite series. A *finite* series of books would indeed come crashing down, since
the first or lowest member would not have a predecessor on which it could
be supported. If the series, however, were infinite this would not be the case.
In that event every member *would* have a predecessor to support itself on and

---

[14]*The Fourfold Root of the Principle of Sufficient Reason*, pp. 42–43. My attention to
this passage was drawn by Professor C. J. Ducasse. See his excellent discussion of the
arguments for the existence of God in *A Philosophical Scrutiny of Religion*, Chapter 15.

there would be no crash. That is to say: a crash can be avoided either by a finite series with a first self-supporting member or by an infinite series. Similarly, the present existence of motion is equally compatible with the theory of a first unmoved mover and with the theory of an infinite series of moving objects; and the present existence of causal activity is compatible with the theory of a first cause *in esse* as much as with the theory of an infinite series of such causes.

The illustrations given by Joyce and Phillips are hardly to the point. It is true that a carpenter would not, *in a finite time-span*, succeed in driving in a nail if he had to carry out an infinite number of movements. For that matter, he would not accomplish this goal in a finite time if he broke an infinite number of hammers. However, to make the illustrations relevant we must suppose that he has infinite time at his disposal. In that case he would succeed in driving in the nail even if he required an infinite number of movements for this purpose. As for the goods train, it may be granted that the trucks do not move unless the train has an engine. But this illustration is totally irrelevant as it stands. A relevant illustration would be that of engines, each moved by the one in front of it. Such a train would move if it were infinite. For every member of this series there would be one in front capable of drawing it along. The advocate of the infinite series of causes does not, as the original illustration suggests, believe in a series whose members are not really causally connected with one another. In the series he believes in every member is genuinely the cause of the one that follows it.

IV

No staunch defender of the cosmological argument would give up at this stage. Even if there were an infinite series of causes *in fieri* or *in esse*, he would contend, this still would not do away with the need for an ultimate, a first cause. As Father Copleston put it in his debate with Bertrand Russell:

> Every object has a phenomenal cause, if you insist on the infinity of the series. But the series of phenomenal causes is an insufficient explanation of the series. Therefore, the series has not a phenomenal cause, but a transcendent cause. . . . [15]
> An infinite series of contingent beings will be, to my way of thinking, as unable to cause itself as one contingent being. [16]

The demand to find the cause of the series as a whole rests on the erroneous assumption that the series is something over and above the members of which it is composed. It is tempting to suppose this, at least by implication, because the word "series" is a noun like "dog" or "man." Like the expression "this dog" or "this man" the phrase "this series" is easily taken to designate an

---

[15]*Why I Am Not a Christian*, pp. 152–53.
[16]*Ibid.*, p. 151.

individual object. But reflection shows this to be an error. If we have explained the individual members there is nothing additional left to be explained. Supposing I see a group of five Eskimos standing on the corner of Sixth Avenue and 50th Street and I wish to explain why the group came to New York. Investigation reveals the following stories:

> Eskimo No. 1 did not enjoy the extreme cold in the polar region and decided to move to a warmer climate.
> No. 2 is the husband of Eskimo No. 1. He loves her dearly and did not wish to live without her.
> No. 3 is the son of Eskimos 1 and 2. He is too small and too weak to oppose his parents.
> No. 4 saw an advertisement in the *New York Times* for an Eskimo to appear on television.
> No. 5 is a private detective engaged by the Pinkerton Agency to keep an eye on Eskimo No. 4.

Let us assume that we have now explained in the case of each of the five Eskimos why he or she is in New York. Somebody then asks: "All right, but what about the group as a whole; why is *it* in New York?" This would plainly be an absurd question. There is no group over and above the five members, and if we have explained why each of the five members is in New York we have *ipso facto* explained why the group is there. It is just as absurd to ask for the cause of the series as a whole as distinct from asking for the causes of individual members.

V

It is most unlikely that a determined defender of the cosmological line of reasoning would surrender even here. He would probably admit that the series is not a thing over and above its members and that it does not make sense to ask for the cause of the series if the cause of each member has already been found. He would insist, however, that when he asked for the explanation of the entire series, he was not asking for its *cause*. He was really saying that a series, finite or infinite, is not "intelligible" or "explained" if it consists of nothing but "contingent" members. To quote Father Copleston once more:

> What we call the world is intrinsically unintelligible apart from the existence of God. The infinity of the series of events, if such an infinity could be proved, would not be in the slightest degree relevant to the situation. If you add up chocolates, you get chocolates after all, and not a sheep. If you add up chocolates to infinity, you presumably get an infinite number of chocolates. So, if you add up contingent beings to infinity, you still get contingent beings, not a necessary being.[17]

This last quotation is really a summary of the "contingency argument," the other main form of the cosmological proof and the third of the five ways of

---

[17]*Op. cit.*, p. 151.

Aquinas. It may be stated more fully in these words: All around us we perceive contingent beings. This includes all physical objects and also all human minds. In calling them "contingent" we mean that they might not have existed. We mean that the universe can be *conceived* without this or that physical object, without this or that human being, however certain their actual existence may be. These contingent beings we can trace back to other contingent beings— e.g. a human being to his parents. However, since these other beings are also contingent, they do not provide a real or full explanation. The contingent beings we originally wanted explained have not yet become intelligible, since the beings to which they have been traced back are no more necessary than they were. It is just as true of our parents, for example, as it is of ourselves, that they might not have existed. We can then properly explain the contingent beings around us only by tracing them back ultimately to some necessary being, to something which exists necessarily, which has "the reason for its existence within itself." The existence of contingent beings, in other words, implies the existence of a necessary being.

This form of the cosmological argument is even more beset with difficulties than the causal variety. In the first place, there is the objection, stated with great force by Kant, that it really commits the same error as the ontological argument in tacitly regarding existence as an attribute or characteristic. To say that there is a necessary being is to say that it would be a self-contradiction to deny its existence. This would mean that at least one existential statement is a necessary truth; and this in turn presupposes that in at least one case existence is contained in a concept. But only a characteristic can be contained in a concept and it has seemed plain to most philosophers since Kant that existence is not a characteristic, that it can hence never be contained in a concept, and that hence no existential statement can ever be a necessary truth. To talk about anything "existing necessarily" is in their view about as sensible as to talk about round squares, and they have concluded that the contingency-argument is quite absurd.

It would lead too far to discuss here the reasons for denying that existence is a characteristic. I will assume that this difficulty can somehow be surmounted and that the expression "necessary being," as it is intended by the champions of the contingency-argument, might conceivably apply to something. There remain other objections which are of great weight. I shall try to state these by first quoting again from the debate between Bertrand Russell and Father Copleston:

> RUSSELL: . . . It all turns on this question of sufficient reason, and I must say you haven't defined "sufficient reason" in a way that I can understand—what do you mean by sufficient reason? You don't mean cause?
> COPLESTON: Not necessarily. Cause is a kind of sufficient reason. Only contingent being can have a cause. God is his own sufficient reason; and he is not cause of himself. By sufficient reason in the full sense I mean an explanation adequate for the existence of some particular being.

RUSSELL: But when is an explanation adequate? Suppose I am about to make a flame with a match. You may say that the adequate explanation of that is that I rub it on the box.

COPLESTON: Well for practical purposes—but theoretically, that is only a partial explanation. An adequate explanation must ultimately be a total explanation, to which nothing further can be added.

RUSSELL: Then I can only say that you're looking for something which can't be got, and which one ought not to expect to get.

COPLESTON: To say that one has not found it is one thing; to say that one should not look for it seems to me rather dogmatic.

RUSSELL: Well, I don't know. I mean, the explanation of one thing is another thing which makes the other thing dependent on yet another, and you have to grasp this sorry scheme of things entire to do what you want, and that we can't do. [18]

Russell's main point here may be expanded in the following way. The contingency-argument rests on a misconception of what an explanation is and does, and similarly on what it is that makes phenomena "intelligible." Or else it involves an obscure and arbitrary redefinition of "explanation," "intelligible," and related terms. Normally, we are satisfied that we have explained a phenomenon if we have found its cause or if we have exhibited some other uniform or near-uniform connection between it and something else. Confining ourselves to the former case, which is probably the most common, we might say that a phenomenon, Z, has been explained if it has been traced back to a group of factors, a, b, c, d, etc., which are its cause. These factors are the full and real explanation of Z, quite regardless of whether they are pleasing or displeasing, admirable or contemptible, necessary or contingent. The explanation would not be adequate only if the factors listed are not really the cause of Z. If they are the cause of Z, the explanation would be adequate, even though each of the factors is merely a "contingent" being.

Let us suppose that we have been asked to explain why General Eisenhower won the elections of 1952. "He was an extremely popular general," we might answer, "while Stevenson was relatively little known; moreover there was a great deal of resentment over the scandals in the Truman Administration." If somebody complained that this was only a partial explanation we might mention additional antecedents, such as the widespread belief that the Democrats had allowed communist agents to infiltrate the State Department, that Eisenhower was a man with a winning smile, and that unlike Stevenson he had shown the good sense to say one thing on race relations in the North and quite another in the South. Theoretically, we might go further and list the motives of all American voters during the weeks or months preceding the elections. If we could do this we would have explained Eisenhower's victory. We would have made it intelligible. We would "understand" why he won and why Stevenson lost. Perhaps there is a sense in which we might make Eisenhower's victory even more intelligible if we went further back and discussed

---

[18]*Op. cit.*, p. 150.

such matters as the origin of American views on Communism or of racial attitudes in the North and South. However, to explain the outcome of the election in any ordinary sense, loose or strict, it would not be necessary to go back to prehistoric days or to the amœba or to a first cause, if such a first cause exists. Nor would our explanation be considered in any way defective because each of the factors mentioned was a "contingent" and not a necessary being. The only thing that matters is whether the factors were really the cause of Eisenhower's election. If they were, then it has been explained although they are contingent beings. If they were not the cause of Eisenhower's victory, we would have failed to explain it even if each of the factors were a necessary being.

If it is granted that, in order to explain a phenomenon or to make it intelligible, we need not bring in a necessary being, then the contingency-argument breaks down. For a series, as was already pointed out, is not something over and above its members; and every contingent member of it could in that case be explained by reference to other contingent beings. But I should wish to go further than this and it is evident from Russell's remarks that he would do so also. Even if it were granted, both that the phrase "necessary being" is meaningful and that all explanations are defective unless the phenomena to be explained are traced back to a necessary being, the conclusion would still not have been established. The conclusion follows from this premise together with the additional premise that *there are* explanations of phenomena in the special sense just mentioned. It is this further premise which Russell (and many other philosophers) would question. They do not merely question, as Copleston implies, whether human beings can ever obtain explanations in this sense, but whether they *exist*. To assume without further ado that phenomena have explanations or an explanation in this sense is to beg the very point at issue. The use of the same word "explanation" in two crucially different ways lends the additional premise a plausibility it does not really possess. It may indeed be highly plausible to assert that phenomena have explanations, whether we have found them or not, in the ordinary sense in which this usually means that they have causes. It is then tempting to suppose, because of the use of the same word, that they also have explanations in a sense in which this implies dependence on a necessary being. But this is a gross *non sequitur*.

VI

It is necessary to add a few words about the proper way of formulating the position of those who reject the main premise of the cosmological argument, in either of the forms we have considered. It is sometimes maintained in this connection that in order to reach a "self-existing" entity it is not necessary to go beyond the universe: the universe itself (or "Nature") is "self-existing." And this in turn is sometimes expanded into the statement that while all individual things "within" the universe are caused, the universe itself is uncaused. Statements of this kind are found in Büchner, Bradlaugh, Haeckel, and other free-thinkers of the nineteenth and early twentieth century. Sometimes the assertion that the universe is "self-existing" is elaborated to mean that *it* is the "necessary being." Some eighteenth-century unbelievers, apparently accepting the view that there is a necessary being, asked why Nature or the material universe could not fill the bill as well or better than God.

> "Why," asks one of the characters in Hume's *Dialogues,* "may not the material universe be the necessarily existent Being? . . . We dare not affirm that we know all the qualities of matter; and for aught we can determine, it may contain some qualities, which, were they known, would make its non-existence appear as great a contradiction as that twice two is five."[19]

Similar remarks can be found in Holbach and several of the Encyclopedists.

The former of these formulations immediately invites the question why the universe, alone of all "things," is exempted from the universal sway of causation. "The strong point of the cosmological argument," writes Dr. Ewing, "is that after all it does remain incredible that the physical universe should just have happened. . . . It calls out for some further explanation of some kind."[20] The latter formulation is exposed to the criticism that there is nothing any more "necessary" about the existence of the universe or Nature as a whole than about any particular thing within the universe.

I hope some of the earlier discussions in this article have made it clear that in rejecting the cosmological argument one is not committed to either of these propositions. If I reject the view that there is a supernatural first cause, I am not thereby committed to the proposition that there is a *natural* first cause, and even less to the proposition that a mysterious "thing" called "the universe" qualifies for this title. I may hold that there is no "universe" over and above individual things of various sorts; and, accepting the causal principle, I may proceed to assert that all these things are caused by other things, and these other things by yet other things, and so on, *ad infinitum.* In this way no arbitrary exception is made to the principle of causation. Similarly, if I reject the assertion that God is a "necessary being," I am not committed to the view that the universe is such an entity. I may hold that it does not make sense to speak of anything as a "necessary being" and that even if there were such a thing as the universe it could not be properly considered a necessary being.

However, in saying that nothing is uncaused or that there is no necessary being, one is not committed to the view that everything, or for that matter anything, is merely a "brute fact." Dr. Ewing laments that "the usual modern philosophical views opposed to theism do not try to give any rational explanation of the world at all, but just take it as a brute fact not to be explained." They thus fail to "rationalize" the universe. Theism, he concedes, cannot com-

---

[19]*Op. cit.,* Part IX.
[20]*Op. cit.,* p. 225.

pletely rationalize things either since it does not show "how God can be his own cause or how it is that he does not need a cause."[21] Now, if one means by "brute fact" something for which there *exists* no explanation (as distinct from something for which no explanation is in our possession), then the theists have at least one brute fact on their hands, namely God. Those who adopt Büchner's formulation also have one brute fact on their hands, namely "the universe." Only the position I have been supporting dispenses with brute facts altogether. I don't know if this is any special virtue, but the defenders of the cosmological argument seem to think so.

[21]*Op. cit.*, p. 225.

WILLIAM L. ROWE

1.10   Two Criticisms of the Cosmological Argument

In this paper I wish to consider two major criticisms which have been advanced against the Cosmological Argument for the existence of God, criticisms which many philosophers regard as constituting a decisive refutation of that argument. Before stating and examining these objections it will be helpful to have before us a version of the Cosmological Argument. The Cosmological Argument has two distinct parts. The first part is an argument to establish the existence of a necessary being. The second part is an argument to establish that this necessary being is God. The two objections I shall consider are directed against the first part of the Cosmological Argument. Using the expression "dependent being" to mean "a being which has the reason for its existence in the causal efficacy or nature of some other being," and that expression "independent being" to mean "a being which has the reason for its existence within its own nature," we may state the argument for the existence of a necessary being as follows:

1. Every being is either a dependent being or an independent being; therefore,
2. Either there exists an independent being or every being is dependent;
3. It is false that every being is dependent; therefore,
4. There exists an independent being; therefore,
5. There exists a necessary being.

From *The Monist* 54 (1970). Reprinted by permission of the author and The Open Court Publishing Company.

This argument consists of two premises—propositions (1) and (3)—and three inferences. The first inference is from (1) to (2), the second from (2) and (3) to (4), and the third inference is from (4) to (5). Of the premises neither is obviously true, and of the inferences only the first and second are above suspicion. Before discussing the main subject of this paper—the reasoning in support of proposition (3) and the two major objections which have been advanced against that reasoning—I want to say something about the other questionable parts of the argument; namely, proposition (1) and the inference from (4) to (5).

Proposition (1) expresses what we may call the strong form of the Principle of Sufficient Reason. It insists not only that those beings which begin to exist must have a cause or explanation (the weak form of the Principle of Sufficient Reason) but that absolutely every being must have an explanation of its existing rather than not existing—the explanation lying either within the causal efficacy of some other being or within the thing's own nature. In an earlier paper I examined this Principle in some detail.[1] The objections I wish to consider in this paper are, I believe, independent of the Principle of Sufficient Reason. That is, these objections are meant to refute the argument even if the first premise is true. This being so, it will facilitate our examination of these two objections if we take proposition (1) as an unquestioned premise throughout our discussion. Accordingly, in this paper proposition (1) will function as an axiom in our reasoning. This, of course, should not be taken as implying that I think the first premise of the argument is true.

The inference from proposition (4) to proposition (5) is not considered in this paper. Indeed, for purposes of this paper we could have ended the statement of the argument with proposition (4). I have included the inference from (4) to (5) simply because it is an important element in the first part of the Cosmological Argument. Proposition (4) asserts the existence of a being which has the reason or explanation of its existence within its own nature. Proposition (5) asserts the existence of a necessary being. By "a necessary being" is meant a being whose nonexistence is a logical impossibility.[2] Many

---

[1]See "The Cosmological Argument and the Principle of Sufficient Reason," *Man and World*, I, No. 2 (1968).

[2]Not all versions of the Cosmological Argument employ the notion of a logically necessary being. It seems likely, for example, that in Aquinas' Third Way the expression "necessary being" is not used to mean a logically necessary being. (See P. Brown, "St. Thomas' Doctrine of Necessary Being," *Philosophical Review*, 73 [1964], 76–90.) But in the version we are considering, it is clear that by "necessary being" is meant a being whose existence is logically necessary. Thus Samuel Clarke, from whose work our version has been adapted, remarks: ". . . the only true idea of a self-existent or necessarily existing being, is the idea of a being the supposition of whose not-existing is an express contradiction" (Samuel Clarke, *A Demonstration of the Being and Attributes of God*, 4th edition, p. 17). David Hume also understands the notion of a necessary being this way. Thus in his statement of the argument, which he adapted from Clarke, he has Demea conclude, "We must, therefore, have recourse to a necessarily existent being, who carries the reason of his existence in himself, and who cannot be supposed not to exist, without an express contradiction" (*Dialogues Concerning Natural Religion*, Part IX).

philosophers have argued that it is logically impossible for there to be a necessary being in this sense of "necessary being." Hence, even if the two objections I shall examine in this paper can be met, the defender of the Cosmological Argument must still face objections not only to the inference from (4) to (5) but to (5) itself. But again, this is a matter which I shall not pursue in this paper. Unlike proposition (1), however, which I treat as an unquestioned assumption, neither proposition (5) nor the inference from (4) to (5) will be appealed to in this paper. In what follows we may simply ignore that part of the argument. Indeed, our attention will be focused entirely on proposition (3), the reasoning which supports it, and the two major criticisms which have been advanced against that reasoning.

Proposition (3) asserts that it is false that every being is dependent. For what reasons? Well, if every being which exists (or ever existed) is dependent, then the whole of existing things, it would seem, consists of a collection of dependent beings, that is, a collection of beings each member of which exists by reason of the causal efficacy of some other being. This collection would have to contain an infinite number of numbers. For suppose it contained a finite number, let us say three a, b, and c. Now if in Scotus' phrase "a circle of causes is inadmissible" then if c is caused by b and b by a, a would exist without a cause, there being no other member of the collection that could be its cause. But in that case a would not be what by supposition it is, namely a *dependent* being. Hence, if we grant that a circle of causes is inadmissible it is impossible that the whole of existing things should consist of a collection of dependent beings *finite* in number.

Suppose, then, that the dependent beings making up the collection are infinite in number. Why is it impossible that the whole of existing things should consist of such a collection? The proponent of the Cosmological Argument answers as follows.[3] The infinite collection *itself*, he argues, requires an explanation of its existence. For since it is true of each member of the collection that it might not have existed, it is true of the whole infinite collection that it might not have existed. But if the entire infinite collection might not have existed there must be some explanation of why it exists rather than not. The explanation cannot lie in the causal efficacy of some being outside of the collection since by supposition the collection includes every being which is or ever was. Nor can the explanation of why there is an infinite collection be found within the collection itself, for since no member of the collection is independent, has the reason of its existence within itself, the collection as a whole cannot have the reason of its existence within itself. Thus the conception of an infinite collection of dependent beings is the conception of something whose existence has no explanation whatever. But since premise (1) tells us that whatever exists has an explanation for its existence, either within itself

---

[3]See, for example, Samuel Clarke's discussion of Propositions II and III in his *Demonstration*. This discussion is summarized by Hume in Part IX of his *Dialogues*.

or in the causal efficacy of some other being, it cannot be that the whole of existing things consists of an infinite collection of dependent beings.

The reasoning developed here is exhibited as follows:

1. If every being is dependent then the whole of existing things consists of an infinite collection of dependent beings;
2. If the whole of existing things consists of an infinite collection of dependent beings then the infinite collection itself must have an explanation of its existence;
3. If the existence of the infinite collection of dependent beings has an explanation then the explanation must lie either in the causal efficacy of some being outside the collection or it must lie within the infinite collection itself;
4. The explanation of the existence of the infinite collection of dependent beings cannot lie in the causal efficacy of some being outside the collection;
5. The explanation of the existence of the infinite collection of dependent beings cannot lie within the collection itself; therefore,
6. There is no explanation of the infinite collection of dependent beings (from 3, 4, and 5); therefore,
7. It is false that the whole of existing things consists of an infinite collection of dependent beings (from 2 and 6); therefore,
8. It is false that every being is dependent (from 1 and 7).

Perhaps every premise in this argument is open to criticism. I propose here, however, to consider what I regard as the two major criticisms advanced against this reasoning in support of proposition (3) of the main argument. The first of these criticisms may be construed as directed against premise (2) of the above argument. According to this criticism it *makes no sense* to apply the notion of cause or explanation to the totality of things, and the arguments used to show that the whole of existing things must have a cause or explanation are *fallacious*. Thus in his B.B.C. debate with Father Copleston, Bertrand Russell took the view that the concept of cause is inapplicable to the universe conceived of as the total collection of things. When pressed by Copleston as to how he could rule out "the legitimacy of asking the question how the total, or anything at all comes to be there," Russell responded: "I can illustrate what seems to me your fallacy. Every man who exists has a mother, and it seems to me your argument is that therefore the human race must have a mother, but obviously the human race hasn't a mother—that's a different logical sphere."[4]

The second major criticism is directed at premise (5). According to this criticism it is *intelligible* to ask for an explanation of the existence of the infinite collection of dependent beings. But the answer to this question, so the criticism goes, is provided once we learn that each member of the infinite collection has an explanation of its existence. Thus Hume remarks: "Did I show you

---

[4]"The Existence of God, A Debate between Bertrand Russell and Father F. C. Copleston," in John Hick (ed.), *The Existence of God* (New York: Macmillan, 1964), p. 175. The debate was originally broadcast by the British Broadcasting Corporation in 1948. References are to the debate as reprinted in *The Existence of God*.

the particular causes of each individual in a collection of twenty particles of matter, I should think it very unreasonable, should you afterwards ask me, what was the cause of the whole twenty. This is sufficiently explained in explaining the cause of the parts."[5]

These two criticisms express the major reasons philosophers have given for rejecting what undoubtedly is the most important part of the Cosmological Argument—namely, that portion of the argument which seeks to establish that not every being can be a dependent being. In this paper my aim is to defend the Cosmological Argument against both of these criticisms. I shall endeavor to show that each of these criticisms rests on a philosophical mistake.

The first criticism draws attention to what appears to be a fatal flaw in the Cosmological Argument. It seems that the proponent of the argument (*i*) ascribes to the infinite collection itself a property (having a cause or explanation) which is applicable only to the members of that collection, and (*ii*) does so by means of a fallacious inference from a proposition about the members of the collection to a proposition about the collection itself. There are, then, two alleged mistakes committed here. The first error is, perhaps, a category mistake—the ascription to the collection of a property applicable only to the members of the collection. As Russell would say, the collection, in comparison with its members, belongs to a "different logical sphere." The second error is apparently what leads the proponent of the Cosmological Argument to make the first error. He ascribes the property of having an explanation to the infinite collection because he *infers* that the infinite collection must have a cause or explanation from the premise that each of its members has a cause. But to infer this, Russell suggests, is as fallacious as to infer that the human race must have a mother because each member of the human race has a mother.

That the proponent of the Cosmological Argument ascribes the property of having a cause or explanation to the infinite collection of dependent beings is certainly true. That to do so is a category mistake is, I think, questionable. But before pursuing this point I want to deal with the second charge. The main question we must consider in connection with the second charge is whether the Cosmological Argument involves the inference: Every member of the infinite collection has an explanation of its existence; therefore, the infinite collection itself has an explanation of its existence. As we have seen, Russell thinks that Copleston has employed this inference in coming to the conclusion that there must be an explanation for the totality of things, and not simply for each of the things making up that totality.

Perhaps some proponents of the Cosmological Argument have used the argument which Russell regards as fallacious. But not all of them have.[6] Moreover, there is no need to employ such an inference since in its first premise the Cosmological Argument has available a principle from which it follows

---

[5]*Dialogues*, Part IX.

[6]Samuel Clarke did not. Nor do we find Hume appealing to this inference in the course of presenting the Cosmological Argument in Part IX of the *Dialogues*.

that the infinite collection of dependent beings must have an explanation of its existence. Thus one famous exponent of the argument—Samuel Clarke— reasons that the infinite collection of beings must have an explanation of its existence by appealing to the strong form of the Principle of Sufficient Reason. The principle assures us that whatever exists has an explanation of its existence. But if there exists an infinite succession or collection of dependent beings then that collection or succession, Clarke reasons, must have an explanation of its existence. Hence, we can, I think, safely dismiss the charge that the Cosmo- logical Argument involves an erroneous inference from the premise that the members of a collection have a certain property to the conclusion that the col- lection itself must have that property.

We must now deal with the question whether it makes *sense* to ascribe the property of having an explanation or cause to the infinite collection of de- pendent beings. Clearly only if it does make sense is the reasoning in support of proposition (3) of the main argument acceptable. Our question, then, is whether it makes sense to ask for a cause or explanation of the entire universe, conceiving the universe as an infinite collection of dependent beings.

One recent critic of the Cosmological Argument, Ronald Hepburn, has stated our problem as follows:

> When we are seriously speaking of absolutely everything there is, are we speaking of something that requires a cause, in the way that events *in* the universe may require causes? What indeed can be safely said at all about the totality of things? For a great many remarks that one can make with perfect propriety about limited things quite obviously can*not* be made about the cosmos itself. It cannot, for instance, be said meaningfully to be "above" or "below" anything, although things-in-the-universe can be so related to one another. Whatever we might claim to be "*below* the universe" would turn out to be just some more *universe*. We should have been relating part to part, instead of relating the whole to something not-the-universe. The same applies to "outside the universe." We can readily imagine a boundary, a garden wall, shall we say, round something that we want to call the universe. But if we imagine ourselves boring a hole through that wall and pushing a stick out *beyond* it into a nameless zone "outside," we should still not in fact have given meaning to the phrase "outside the universe." For the place into which the stick was intruding would deserve to be called a part of the universe (even if consisting of empty space, no matter) just as much as the area within the walls. We should have demonstrated *not* that the universe has an outside, but that what we took to be the whole universe was not really the whole.
>
> Our problem is this. Supposing we could draw up a list of questions that can be asked about objects in the universe, but cannot be asked about the *whole* universe: would the question, "Has it a cause?" be on that list? One thing is clear. Whether or not this question is on the proscribed list, we are not entitled to argue as the Cosmological Argument does that *because* things in the world have causes, therefore the sum of things must also have *its* cause. No more (as we have just seen) can we argue from the fact that things in the world have tops and bottoms, insides and outsides, and are related to other

things, to the belief that the universe has its top and bottom, inside and outside, and is related to a supra-cosmical something.[7]

In this passage Hepburn (*i*) points out that some properties (e.g., "above,"
"below," etc.) of things in the universe cannot properly be ascribed to the total
universe, (*ii*) raises the question whether "having a cause" is such a property,
and (*iii*) concludes that ". . . we are not entitled to argue as the Cosmological
Argument does that *because* things in the world have causes, therefore, the
sum of things must also have *its* cause." We noted earlier that the Cosmological
Argument (i.e., the version we are examining) does not argue that the sum
of things (the infinite collection of dependent beings) must have a cause *because* each being in the collection has a cause. Thus we may safely ignore
Hepburn's main objection. However, his other two points are well taken.
There certainly are properties which it makes sense to apply to things within
a collection but which it makes no sense to apply to the collection itself. What
assurance do we have that "having a cause" is not such a property?

Suppose we are holding in our hands a collection of ten marbles. Not only
would each marble have a definite weight but the collection itself would have
a weight. Indeed, from the premise that each marble weighs more than one
ounce we could infer validly that the collection itself weighs more than an
ounce. This example shows that it is not always fallacious to infer that a collection has a certain property from the premise that each member of the
collection has that property.[8] But the collection in this example is, we might
say, *concrete* rather than *abstract*. That is, we are here considering the collection as itself a physical entity, an aggregate of marbles. This, of course, is not
a collection in the sense of a class or set of things. Holding several marbles in
my hands I can consider the *set* whose members are those marbles. The set
itself, being an *abstract* entity, rather than a physical heap, has no weight.
Just as the set of human beings has no mother, so the set whose members are
marbles in my hand has no weight. Therefore, in considering whether it makes
sense to speak of the infinite collection of dependent beings as having a cause
or explanation of its existence it is important to decide whether we are speaking of a collection as a *concrete* entity—for example, a physical whole or aggregate—or an *abstract* entity.

Suppose we view the infinite collection of dependent beings as itself a concrete entity. As far as the Cosmological Argument is concerned, one advantage
of so viewing it is that it is understandable why it might have the property of
having a cause or explanation of its existence. For concrete entities—physical
objects, events, physical heaps—can be caused. Thus if the infinite collection

---

[7]Ronald W. Hepburn, *Christianity and Paradox* (London: Watts, 1958), pp. 167–68.

[8]For a consideration of inferences of this sort in connection with the fallacy of composition see my paper "The Fallacy of Composition," *Mind*, 71 (January 1962). For some
needed corrections of my paper see Yehoshua Bar-Hillel, "More on the Fallacy of Composition," *Mind*, 73 (January 1964).

is a concrete entity it may well make sense to ascribe to it the property of having a cause or explanation.

But such a view of the infinite collection is implausible, if not plainly incorrect. Many collections of physical things cannot possibly be themselves concrete entities. Think, for example, of the collection whose members are the largest prehistoric beast, Socrates, and the Empire State Building. By any stretch of the imagination can we view this collection as itself a concrete thing? Clearly we cannot. Such a collection must be construed as an *abstract* entity, a class or set.[9] But if there are many collections of beings which cannot be concrete entities, what grounds have we for thinking that on the supposition that every being that is or ever was is dependent the collection of those beings would itself be a concrete thing such as a physical heap? At any rate our knowledge of the things (both past and present) comprising the universe and their interrelations would have to be much greater than it currently is before we would be entitled to view the *sum* of concrete things, past and present, as itself something *concrete*.

But if the infinite collection of dependent beings is to be understood as an abstract entity, say the set whose members include all the beings that are or ever were, haven't we conceded the point to Russell? A set or class conceived of as an abstract entity has no weight, is not below or above anything, and cannot be thought of as being caused or brought into being. Thus if the infinite collection is a set, an abstract entity, is not Russell right in charging that it makes no more sense to ascribe the property of having a cause or an explanation to the infinite collection than it does to ascribe the property of having a mother to the human race?

Suppose that every being that is or ever was is dependent. Suppose further that the number of such beings is infinite. Let A be the set consisting of these beings. Thus no being exists or ever existed which is not a member of A. Does it make *sense* to ask for an explanation of A's existence? We do, of course, ask questions about sets which are equivalent to questions about their members. For example, "Is set X included in set Y?" is equivalent to the question "Is every member of X a member of Y?" I suggest that the question "Why does A exist?" be taken to mean "Why does A have the members that it does rather than some other members or none at all?" Consider, for example, the set of men. Let M be this set. The question "Why does M exist?" is perhaps odd if we understand it as a request for an explanation of the existence of an abstract entity. But the question "Why does M exist?" may be taken to mean "Why does M have the members it has rather than some other members or none at all?" So understood the form of words "Why does M exist?" does, I think, ask an intelligible question. It is a contingent fact that Hitler existed.

---

[9] Of course, the three members of this collection, unlike the members of the collection of dependent beings, presumably are causally unrelated. But it is equally easy to think of collections which cannot possibly be concrete entities whose members are causally related—e.g., the collection whose members are the ancestors of a given man.

Indeed, it is a contingent fact that any men exist at all. One of Leibniz' logically possible worlds is a world which includes some members of M, for example Socrates and Plato, but not others, say Hitler and Stalin. Another is a world in which the set of men is entirely empty and therefore identical with the null set. Why is it, then, that M exists? That is, why does M have just the members it has rather than some other members or none at all? Not only is this question intelligible but we seem to have some idea of what its answer is. Presumably, the theory of evolution might be a part of the explanation of why M is not equivalent to the null set and why its members have certain properties rather than others.

But if the question "Why does M exist?" makes sense, why should not the question "Why does A exist?" also make sense? A is the set of dependent beings. In asking why A exists we are not asking for an explanation of the existence of an abstract entity; we are asking why A has the members it has rather than some other members or none at all. I submit that this question does make sense. Moreover, I think that it is precisely this question which the proponents of the Cosmological Argument were asking when they asked for an explanation of the existence of the infinite collection or succession of dependent beings.[10] Of course, it is one thing for a question to make sense and another thing for there to be an answer to it.

The interpretation I have given to the question "Why does A exist?" is somewhat complex. For according to this interpretation what is being asked is not simply why does A have members rather than having none, but also why does A have just the members it has rather than having some other members. Although the proponents of the Cosmological Argument do seem to interpret the question in this way, it will facilitate our discussion if we simplify the interpretation somewhat by focusing our attention solely on the question why A has the members it has rather than having none. Hence, for purposes of simplification, in what follows I shall take the question "Why does A exist?" to mean "Why does A have the members it has rather than not having any?"

For any being to be a member of A it is necessary and sufficient that it have the reason of its existence in the causal efficacy of some other being. Imagine the following state of affairs. A has exactly three members: a_1, a_2, and a_3. a_3 exists by reason of the causal efficacy of a_2, and a_2 exists by reason of the causal efficacy of a_1. There exists an *eternal* being b which does not exist by reason of the causal efficacy of any other being. Since b is not a dependent being, b is not a member of A. At a certain time a_1 came into existence by reason of the causal efficacy of b. Clearly the question "Why does A exist?" when taken to mean "Why does A have the members it has rather than none

---

[10]Thus in speaking of the infinite succession, Hume has Demea say: "... and yet it is evident that it requires a cause or reason, as much as any particular object which begins to exist in time. The question is still reasonable, *why this particular succession of causes existed from eternity, and not any other succession, or no succession at all*" (*Dialogues*, Part IX; italics mine).

at all?" makes sense when asked within the context of this imagined state of affairs. Indeed, part of the answer to the question would involve reference to *b* and its causal efficacy in bringing about the existence of one of the members of A, namely a_1.

What this case shows is that the question "Why does A exist?" is not always (i.e., in every context) meaningless. If Russell holds that the question is meaningless in the framework of the Cosmological Argument it must be because of some special assumption about A which forms part of the context of the Cosmological Argument. The assumption in question undoubtedly is that absolutely every being is dependent. On this assumption every being which is or ever was has membership in A and A has an infinite number of members.

Perhaps Russell's view is that within the context of the assumption that *every* being is dependent it makes no sense to ask why A has the members it has rather than none at all. It makes no sense, he might argue, for two reasons. First, on the assumption that every being is dependent there could not be such a thing as the *set* A whose members are all dependent beings. For the set A is, although abstract, presumably a being. But if every being is dependent then A would have to be dependent and therefore a member of itself. But apart from whatever difficulties arise when a set is said to be a member of itself, it would seem to make little sense to think of an abstract entity, such as a set, as being caused, as having the reason of its existence within the causal efficacy of some other being.

Second, Russell might argue that the assumption that every being is dependent and therefore a member of A rules out the possibility of any answer to the question why A has the members it has rather than none at all. For on that assumption our question about A is in effect a question about the totality of things. And, as Russell observes, "I see no reason whatsoever to suppose that the total has any cause whatsoever."[11]

Neither of these reasons suffices to show that our question about A is meaningless. The first reason does, however, point up the necessity of introducing some restriction on the assumption "Every being is dependent" in order that abstract entities like numbers and sets not fall within the scope of the expression "Every being." Such a restriction will obviate the difficulty that A is said to be both a member of itself and dependent. I propose the following rough restriction. In speaking of beings we shall restrict ourselves to beings that *could be caused* to exist by some other being or *could be causes* of the existence of other beings. God (if he exists), a man, the sun, a stone are beings of this sort. Presumably, numbers, sets, and the like are not. The assumption that every being is dependent is to be understood under this restriction. That is, we are here assuming that every being of the sort described by the restriction is *in fact* a being which exists by reason of the causal efficacy of some other being. The second reason given confuses the issue of whether a question makes

---

[11]"Debate," p. 175.

sense, is meaningful, with the issue of whether a question has an answer. Of course, given the assumption that every being is a member of A we cannot expect to find the cause or reason of A's existence in some being which is not a member of A. If the explanation for A's existence cannot be found within A itself then we must conclude that there can be no explanation for the infinite collection of dependent beings. But this is to say only that on our assumption that every being is dependent there is no answer to the question "Why does A exist?" It is one thing for a question not to have an answer and quite another thing for the question to be *meaningless*.

We have been examining the first of the two major criticisms philosophers have directed at the reasoning the Cosmological Argument provides in support of the proposition that not every being is dependent. The heart of this criticism is that it *makes no sense* to ascribe the property of having a cause or explanation to the infinite collection of dependent beings. This criticism, I think, has been shown to be correct in one way, but incorrect in another. If we construe the infinite collection of dependent beings as an abstract entity, a set, it perhaps does not make sense to claim that something caused the existence of this abstract entity. But the question "Why does A exist?" may be interpreted to mean "Why does A have the members it has rather than none at all?" I have argued that taken in this way the question "Why does A exist?" is a *meaningful* question.

According to the Principle of Sufficient Reason there must be an answer to the question "Why does A exist?," an explanation of the existence of the infinite collection of dependent beings. Moreover, the explanation either must lie in the causal efficacy of some being outside of the collection or it must lie within the collection itself. But since by supposition every being is dependent— and therefore in the collection—there is no being outside the collection whose causal efficacy might explain the existence of the collection. Therefore, either the collection has the explanation of its existence within itself or there can be no explanation of its existence. If the first alternative is rejected then, since the Principle of Sufficient Reason requires that everything has an explanation of its existence, we must reject the supposition that every being is dependent. For on that supposition there is no explanation for why there is an infinite collection of dependent beings.

The second major criticism argues that the proponent of the Cosmological Argument is mistaken in thinking that the explanation of the existence of the infinite collection cannot be found within the collection itself. The explanation of the existence of the collection is provided, so the criticism goes, once we learn what the explanation is of each of the members of the collection. As we noted earlier, this criticism was succinctly expressed by Hume in his remark: "Did I show you the particular causes of each individual in a collection of twenty particles of matter, I should think it very unreasonable, should you afterwards ask me, what was the cause of the whole twenty. This is sufficiently explained in explaining the cause of the parts." Applying this objection to the infinite collection of dependent beings, we obtain the result that to explain the existence of the infinite collection, A, amounts to no more than explaining the existence of each of its members. Now, of course, A is unlike Hume's collection of twenty particles in that we cannot give *individual* explanations for each of the members of A. For since A has an infinite number of members we would have to give an infinite number of explanations. But our inability to give a particular explanation for each of the members of A does not imply that there is any member of A for whose existence there is no explanation. Indeed, from the fact that each member of A is dependent (i.e., has the reason of its existence in the causal efficacy of some other being), we know that every member of A has an explanation of its existence; from the assumption that every being is a member of A we know that for each member of A the explanation lies in the causal efficacy of some other member of A. But, so the criticism goes, if every member of A has an explanation of its existence then the existence of A has been sufficiently explained. For to explain why a certain collection of things exists it is sufficient to explain the existence of each of its members. Hence, since we know that the existence of every one of A's members is explained we know that the existence of the collection A is explained.

This forceful criticism, originally advanced by Hume, has gained wide acceptance in contemporary philosophy. Indeed, the only remaining problem seems to be to explain why the proponents of the Cosmological Argument failed to see that to explain the existence of all the members of a collection is to explain the existence of the collection. In restating Hume's criticism, Paul Edwards suggests that perhaps they may have been misled by grammar.

> The demand to find the cause of the series as a whole rests on the erroneous assumption that the series is something over and above the members of which it is composed. It is tempting to suppose this, at least by implication, because the word "series" is a noun like "dog" or "man." Like the expression "this dog" or "this man" the phrase "this series" is easily taken to designate an individual object. But reflection shows this to be an error. If we have explained the individual members there is nothing additional left to be explained. Suppose I see a group of five Eskimos standing on the corner of Sixth Avenue and 50th Street and I wish to explain why the group came to New York. Investigation reveals the following stories:
> Eskimo No. 1 did not enjoy the extreme cold in the polar region and decided to move to a warmer climate.
> No. 2 is the husband of Eskimo No. 1. He loves her dearly and did not wish to live without her.
> No. 3 is the son of Eskimos 1 and 2. He is too small and too weak to oppose his parents.
> No. 4 saw an advertisement in the *New York Times* for an Eskimo to appear on television.
> No. 5 is a private detective engaged by the Pinkerton Agency to keep an eye on Eskimo No. 4.
> Let us assume that we have now explained in the case of each of the five Eskimos why he or she is in New York. Somebody then asks: "All right, but

what about the group as a whole; why is *it* in New York?" This would plainly be an absurd question. There is no group over and above the five members, and if we have explained why each of the five members is in New York we have *ipso facto* explained why the group is there. It is just as absurd to ask for the cause of the series as a whole as distinct from asking for the causes of the individual members.[12]

The principle underlying the Hume-Edwards criticism may be stated as follows: *If the existence of every member of a set is explained the existence of that set is thereby explained.* This principle seems to be a corollary of our interpretation of the question "Why does this set exist?" For on our interpretation, once it is explained why the set has the members it has rather than none at all it is thereby explained why the set exists. And it would seem that if a set A has, say, three members, a_1, a_2 and a_3, then if we explain the existence of a_1, a_2, and a_3 we have explained why A has the members it has rather than none at all. Thus the principle which underlies the second major criticism seems to be implied by our conception of what is involved in explaining the existence of a set.

The principle underlying the Hume-Edwards criticism seems plausible enough when restricted to finite sets, i.e., sets with a finite number of members. But the principle is false, I believe, when extended to infinite sets in which the explanation of each member's existence is found in the causal efficacy of some other member. Consider M, the set of men. Suppose M consists of an infinite number of members, each member owing its existence to some other member which generated it. Suppose further that to explain the existence of a given man it is sufficient to note that he was begotten by some other man. That is, where x and y are men and x begat y we allow that the existence of y is explained by the causal efficacy of x. On these suppositions it is clear that the antecedent of the principle is satisfied with respect to M. For every member of M has an explanation of its existence. But does it follow that the existence of M has an explanation? I think not. We do not have an explanation of the existence of M until we have an explanation of why M has the members it has rather than none at all. But clearly if *all* we know is that there always have been men and that every man's existence is explained by the causal efficacy of some other man, we do not know *why* there always have been men rather than none at all. If I ask why M has the members it has rather than none, it is no answer to say that M always had members. We may, I suppose, answer the question "Why does M have the *currently existing* members it has?" by saying that M always had members and there were men who generated the currently existing men. But in asking why M has the members it has rather than none at all we are not asking why M has the currently existing members it has. To make this clear, we may rephrase our question as follows: "Why is it

---

[12]Paul Edwards, "The Cosmological Argument," in Donald R. Burrill (ed.), *The Cosmological Arguments* (New York: Doubleday, 1967), pp. 113–14. Edwards' paper was originally published in *The Rationalist Annual for the Year 1959.*

that M has now and always had members rather than never having had any members at all?" Surely we have not learned the answer to this question when we have learned that there always have been members of M and that each member's existence is explained by the causal efficacy of some other member.

What we have just seen is that from the fact that the existence of each member of a collection is explained it does not follow that the existence of the collection is thereby explained. It does not follow because when the collection (set) has an infinite number of members, each member's existence having its explanation in the causal efficacy of *some other member*, it is true that the existence of every member has an explanation, and yet it is still an open question whether the existence of the set has an explanation. To explain the existence of a set we must explain why it has the members it has rather than none. But clearly if every member's existence is explained by some other *member*, then although the existence of every member has an explanation it is still unexplained why the set has the members it has, rather than none at all.

Put somewhat differently, we have seen that the fact (assuming for the moment that it is a fact) that there always have been men, each man's existence brought about by some other man, is insufficient to explain *why* it is a fact that there always have been men rather than a fact that there never have been any men. If someone asks us to explain why there always have been men rather than never having been any it would not suffice for us to observe that there always have been men and each man has been brought into existence by some other man.

I have argued that the second major criticism rests on a false principle, namely, that if the existence of every member of a set is explained then the existence of that set is thereby explained. This principle, so far as I can determine, is true when restricted to sets with a *finite* number of members. For example, if a set A has two members, a_1 and a_2, and if we explain a_2 by a_1 and a_1 by some being *b* that caused a_1, then, I think, we have explained the existence of A. In any case we have explained why A has members rather than none at all. Thus I am not claiming that the principle underlying Hume's objection is always false. Indeed, as I have just indicated, it is easy to provide an example of a finite set of which the principle is true. And perhaps it is just this feature of the principle—i.e., its plausibility when applied to finite sets such as Hume's collection of twenty particles and Edwards' five Eskimos —which has led Hume and many philosophers since Hume to reject the Cosmological Argument's thesis that even if every member of the infinite succession of dependent beings has an explanation the infinite succession itself is not thereby explained. If so, then the mistake Hume and his successors have made is to assume that a principle which is true of all finite sets also is true of all infinite sets.

We know, for example, that if we have a set B consisting of five members and a set C consisting of three of the members of B, the members of C cannot be put in one-to-one correspondence with those of B. In reflecting on this fact, we are tempted to conclude that for *any* two sets X and Y, if all the members of X are members of Y but some members of Y are not members of X then the members of X cannot be put in one-to-one correspondence with those of Y. Indeed, so long as X and Y are restricted to *finite* sets the principle just stated is true. But if we let X be the set of *even* natural numbers—2, 4, 6, . . . —and Y be the set of natural numbers—1, 2, 3, . . . —the principle is shown to be false. For although all the members of X are members of Y and some members of Y—the odd integers—are not members of X, it is not true that the members of X cannot be put in one-to-one correspondence with those of Y. What this example illustrates is that a principle which holds of all finite sets may not hold of all infinite sets. The principle underlying the second major criticism is, I have argued, such a principle.

One final point concerning my reply to the second major criticism needs to be made clear. In rejecting the principle on which the criticism rests I have contended that when a set has an *infinite* number of members, every one of which has an explanation of its existence, it *does not follow* that the existence of the set is thereby explained. In saying this I do not mean to imply that in explaining the existence of every member of an infinite set we never thereby explain the existence of the set, only that we *sometimes* do not. Specifically, we do not, I think, when we explain the existence of each member of the set by some other member of *that set*. Recall our example of M, the set of men. If we think of the members of this set as forming a temporal series stretching infinitely back in time, each member's existence explained by the causal efficacy of the preceding member, we have an example, I think, in which an explanation of the existence of each member of M does not constitute an explanation of the existence of M. Let us suppose that each man is produced not by another man but by some superior being, say a god. What we are supposing is that M is described as before except that instead of every member having the explanation of its existence in some preceding member of M the explanation is found in the causal efficacy of some member of the set of gods. From eternity, then, gods have been producing men. There have always been members of M and every member has an explanation of its existence. Here it does seem true to say that in explaining the existence of every member of M we have thereby explained the existence of M. If someone asks why there now are and always have been men rather than never having been any, we can say in response that there always have been men because there always have been gods producing them. This, if true, would explain why M has always had members.

In this paper I have examined two criticisms which have been advanced against that part of the Cosmological Argument which seeks to establish that not every being can be a dependent being. I have argued that each of these criticisms is mistaken and, therefore, fails as a refutation of the Cosmological Argument. If my arguments are correct, it does not follow, of course, that the Cosmological Argument is a good argument for its conclusion. But it does follow that those philosophers who have rejected the argument for either of the two criticisms discussed in this paper need to re-examine the argument and, if they continue to reject it, provide some *good* reasons for doing so.

PATTERSON BROWN

1.11   Infinite Causal Regression

> The whole modern conception of the world is founded on the illusion that the so-called laws of nature are the explanations of natural phenomena. Thus people today stop at the laws of nature, treating them as something inviolable, just as God and Fate were treated in past ages. And in fact both are right and both wrong: though the view of the ancients is clearer in so far as they have a clear and acknowledged terminus, while the modern system tries to make it look as if *everything* were explained.
>   WITTGENSTEIN, *Tractatus*, 6.371–6.372

Arguments concerning the possibility of an infinite regress of causes have always played a crucial role in metaphysics and in natural theology. And of course this issue was once important in the sciences as well, namely in Aristotelianism. Indeed, the most influential reasons which have been adduced by philosophers and theologians against infinite causal regressions—as, for example, St. Thomas' well-known Five Ways—arose directly and explicitly out of Aristotelian scientific considerations; they are meta-physical proofs, that is, proofs which are supposed to follow on theorizations in physical science. The gist of them is that, if there were an infinite regress of causes, then no adequate scientific explanation would be possible, and observed phenomena would thus be unintelligible—which consequence is absurd. In this paper I shall attempt to delineate the medieval elaboration of this argument, as given by such men as Avicenna, Averroes, Maimonides, Aquinas, and Duns Scotus.

I

The *locus classicus* of the scholastic discussion was the following passage from Aristotle's *Metaphysics*, wherein he claims that a so-called ascending series of any of his four types of cause must have a first member:

> One thing [cannot] proceed from another, as from matter, *ad infinitum*, . . . nor can the sources of movement form an endless series. . . . Similarly the final causes cannot go on *ad infinitum*. . . . And the case of the essence [that is, of

From *The Philosophical Review* 75 (1966): 510–25. Reprinted by permission of the editors.

formal causes] is similar. For in the case of intermediates, which have a last
term and a term prior to them, the prior must be the cause of the later terms.
For if we had to say which of the three is the cause, we should say the first;
surely not the last, for the final term is the cause of none; nor even the intermediate, for it is the cause only of one. (It makes no difference whether
there is one intermediate or more, nor whether they are finite or infinite in
number.) But of series which are infinite in this way, . . . all the parts down
to that now present are alike intermediates; so that if there is no first there
is no cause at all. [1]

Early in the eleventh century, Avicenna drew a distinction, as Aristotle had
not, between the causality of a *mover* and that of a *maker*.[2] The latter was
then called an "efficient" or "agent" cause, and Aristotle's same line of reasoning was directed against there being an infinite regress of such causes of being
(see, for example, Aquinas' Second Way). There was, then, one basic argument
which the medieval Aristotelians held to demonstrate that neither efficient,
moving, formal, final, nor material causal series can regress infinitely.

It is perhaps commonplace nowadays to assume that the Aristotelian schoolmen were unconditionally opposed to beginningless series, or at least to beginningless causal series. Thus we find W. I. Matson laconically stating that the
"contention is defensible only if it is logically impossible for a series to have
no first member, . . . such as the series of all negative integers."[3] This criticism
is clearly ineffectual against the Aristotelians, none of whom wished to deny
that some series—for example, mathematical ones—may have no termini.
After all, consider Aristotle's own definition of an infinite quantity: "A quantity
is infinite if it is such that we can always take a part outside what has already
been taken."[4] The application of this to the series of negative integers is self-
evident. As John Hick has realized, however, the claim was in fact limited to
causal series: "Aquinas excludes the possibility of an infinite regress of causes,
and so concludes that there must be a first cause, which we call God."[5] Even
Hick's remark, however, must be considerably qualified if we are to reach any
understanding of the argument, for it was only some among causal series which
were held to require a first member. In the course of proving that the world
might in principle be everlasting, St. Thomas wrote:

In efficient causes it is impossible to proceed to infinity *per se*. Thus, there
cannot be an infinite number of causes that are *per se* required for a certain
effect; for instance, that a stone be moved by a stick, the stick by the hand,

---

[1]994a2–19. All quotations from Aristotle will be from R. McKeon (ed.), *The Basic
Works of Aristotle* (New York, 1941). "Ascent" in a causal series was defined as proceeding from effect to cause, while "descent" meant proceeding from cause to effect.
[2]Cf. E. Gilson, *History of Christian Philosophy in the Middle Ages* (New York, 1955),
pp. 210–12.
[3]*The Existence of God* (Ithaca, N.Y., 1965), p. 59.
[4]*Physics*, 207a8. See also Aquinas, *Summa Theologica*, ed. by A. C. Pegis (New York,
1945), I, Q. 7, Art. 4, Obj. 1 and Reply (hereafter referred to as *ST*).
[5]*Philosophy of Religion* (Englewood Cliffs, N.J., 1963), p. 20.

and so on to infinity. But it is not impossible to proceed to infinity *accidentally* as regards efficient causes. . . . [It is, for example,] accidental to this particular man as generator to be generated by another man; for he generates as a man, and not as the son of another man. For all men generating hold one grade in the order of efficient causes—viz., the grade of a particular generator. Hence it is not impossible for a man to be generated by man to infinity.[6]

The claim is, then, that causal regresses like a's being begotten by b, b's being begotten by c, and so forth, can go on to infinity, whereas causal regresses like z's being moved by y, y's being moved by x, and so forth, cannot. So not only did the Aristotelians admit the possibility of infinite regresses in general (like -1, -2, -3, and so forth, and even—as we shall see—today, yesterday, day before yesterday, and so forth), but they also admitted the possibility of certain infinite *causal* regresses.

It is important to note that it is the composite causal series, and not the individual constituent causes, which Aquinas is contrasting as either *per se* or *per accidens* in the above quotation. Aristotle had of course differentiated between essential and accidental causes, meaning by the latter an accidental attribute of an essential cause,[7] but that is not the distinction to which St. Thomas is here alluding. This is confirmed by Duns Scotus' comment in his presentation of the argument:

> It is one thing to speak of incidental causes (*causae per accidens*) as contrasted with those which are intended by their nature to produce a certain effect (*causae per se*). It is quite another to speak of causes which are ordered to one another essentially or of themselves (*per se*) and those which are ordered only accidentally (*per accidens*).[8]

There is, then, a difference between essential and accidental *causes* on the one hand, and essential and accidental *ordering* of causes on the other. Moreover, it is the latter distinction which is supposed to be germane to the impossibility of certain infinite causal regressions; infinite causal regression *per accidens* is said to be possible, while infinite causal regression *per se* is said to be impossible. Scotus fortunately tells us in some detail what was understood by the crucial contrast:

> *Per se* or essentially ordered causes differ from accidentally ordered causes. . . .
> In essentially ordered causes, the second depends upon the first precisely in its act of causation. In accidentally ordered causes this is not the case, although the second may depend upon the first for its existence, or in some other way.

---

[6]*ST*, I, Q. 46, Art. 2, Reply Obj. 7.

[7]Cf. *Physics*, 195a27 ff., 196b24–29, and 224a21–36, as well as *Metaphysics*, 1013b29. In St. Thomas' words, "If A is the cause of B *per se*, whatever is accidental to A is the accidental cause of B"—*Summa contra Gentiles* (Garden City, N.Y., 1955), III, ch. 14 (hereafter referred to as *SCG*).

[8]*Opus Oxoniense*, I, Dist. II, Q. 1, as found in A. Wolter (ed.), *Duns Scotus: Philosophical Writings* (Edinburgh, 1962), p. 40.

Thus a son depends upon his father for existence but is not dependent upon him in exercising his own causality [that is, in himself begetting a son], since he can act just as well whether his father be living or dead.[9]

I shall now quote what is perhaps the best scholastic statement of the Aristotelian argument against an infinite regress of essentially ordered causes, as found in Aquinas' *Summa contra Gentiles:*

> In an ordered series of movers and things moved (this is a series in which one is moved by another according to an order), it is necessarily the fact that, when the first mover is removed or ceases to move, no other mover will move [another] or be [itself] moved. For the first mover is the cause of motion for all the others. But, if there are movers and things moved following an order to infinity, there will be no first mover, but all would be as intermediate movers. . . . [Now] that which moves [another] as an instrumental cause cannot [so] move unless there be a principal moving cause. But, if we proceed to infinity among movers and things moved, all movers will be as instrumental causes, because they will be moved movers and there will be nothing as a principal mover. Therefore, nothing will be moved [which consequence is patently false.][10]

II

Before going on to consider this argument in any detail, let us first repudiate perhaps the three most common criticisms of it. The first of these[11] takes off from statements like the following, found in St. Thomas' Second Way: "To take away the cause is to take away the effect. Therefore, if there be no first cause among efficient causes, there will be no ultimate, nor any intermediate, cause."[12] This passage may seem to contain an equivocation on "taking away the first cause." It is certainly true that, in any causal sequence, to take away any of the earlier causes—in the sense of removing it from the chain altogether—would break the progression; and this would then preclude any of the subsequent members of the series from coming about at all. But if, with regard to any such catena, we take away any first cause—in the sense of denying that any member is first, that is, uncaused—we do not thereby remove any of the links from the causal chain; the progression is not broken, and so the

---

[9]*Ibid.*, pp. 40–41. From this fundamental criterion Scotus then claims to derive two more: that in essentially ordered causes each step must be to a new order of cause, and that a series of *per se* ordered causes must be instantaneous. See also the selection from Scotus' *Tractatus De Primo Principio*, ch. iii, included in A. Freemantle, *The Age of Belief* (New York, 1955), pp. 189 ff. I gather that this analysis of variously ordered series originated with Avicenna, in Bk. VI of his *Metaphysics*, but no copy of that important work has been available to me.

[10]I, ch. xiii; cf. *ST*, I, Q. 2, Art. 3, First Way. See also Averroes' version in his *Tahafut Al-Tahafut* (London, 1954), I, the Fourth Discussion.

[11]It may be found, e.g., in Paul Edwards' introduction to the section entitled "The Existence of God," in P. Edwards & A. Pap (eds.), *A Modern Introduction to Philosophy* (Glencoe, Ill., 1957), pp. 450–51.

[12]*ST*, I, Q. 2, Art. 3, Second Way.

later members are not precluded. In the hand-stick-stone case, for example, we must differentiate between taking away the stick, and denying that the stick is an uncaused cause of the stone's motion. We might thus think that the Aristotelian rejection of an infinite regress of causes rests on an equivocation between "taking away any first cause" (that is, denying that any cause is first) and "taking away one of the causes" (that is, removing one of the members from the causal series).

Even if we could believe that this glaring fallacy could have gone undetected for two millennia, however, it will hardly do as an objection to the argument. For the above-mentioned polemic cannot account for the distinction between essentially and accidentally ordered causal regresses. If Jacob or Isaac or Abraham *vel cetera* had not copulated, this would in fact have precluded Joseph's existence—just as taking away the motion of the stick or the hand would in fact have resulted in the stone's not moving. In both cases a statement of the effect materially implies a statement of all the string of causes (although in neither instance is there a strict implication; the stone could equally well be caused to move by a hand or a foot, just as Joseph could equally well be descended from Adam or a baboon). It seems highly unlikely that Aristotle and the others would have equivocated in contending that there must be a first mover, and yet have avoided exactly the same type of fallacy in admitting that there need not be a first ancestor.

The second standard criticism of the argument is voiced, for example, by Hick, in his retort that time may never have begun. "The weakness of the argument as Aquinas states it," he writes, "lies in the difficulty (which he himself elsewhere acknowledges) of excluding as impossible an endless regress of events requiring no beginning."[13] A similar point is made by W. T. Blackstone, who objects that "it is perfectly conceivable that time has no beginning, and that every event was preceded by an earlier event."[14] Such comments simply cannot be reconciled with the texts. For of course the Aristotelians notoriously held that causal efficacy must be instantaneous rather than chronological. Aristotle says that "the motion of the moved and the motion of the movent must proceed simultaneously (for the movent is causing motion and the moved is being moved simultaneously)."[15] St. Thomas concurs: "It is clear that when a thing moves because it is moved, the mover and the mobile object are moved simultaneously. For example, if the hand by its own motion moves a staff, the hand and the staff are moved simultaneously."[16] After all, it was only on these grounds that Aristotle could argue

---

[13]*Op. cit.*, p. 21; the clause in parentheses is footnoted by Hick: *ST*, I, Q. 46, Art. 2, and *SCG*, II, ch. xxxviii.

[14]*The Problem of Religious Knowledge* (Englewood Cliffs, N.J., 1963), p. 164.

[15]*Physics*, 242a23–26.

[16]*Commentary on Aristotle's "Physics"* (New Haven, 1963), Bk. VIII, lec. 2, #892 (hereafter referred to as *On Physics*). Cf. n. 9, *supra*, for Scotus' parallel claim.

both for a First Cause and for the perpetuity of the world.[17] This also explains why Aquinas held it to be of no theological concern that we cannot demonstrate whether or not the world had a beginning in time (leaving it a matter to be settled by revelation alone).[18] The requirement for a Prime Cause is, he thought, the same in either case, since causal chains are necessarily confined to one instant. This same doctrine was later defended by Descartes when he wrote that "all the moments of [the world's] duration are [causally] independent the one from the other";[19] for, he held, "any motion involves a kind of circulation of matter all moving simultaneously."[20]

The third commonplace objection is found, for example, in the following remark by C. J. F. Williams:

> The flaw in this argument is its use of the term *moventia secunda* in an attempt to prove the impossibility of an infinite series of causes. For not until we know that such a series is impossible can we know that all movers are properly described as either "a first mover" or as "second movers." This however, is precisely what the argument assumes.[21]

The gravamen of this criticism is, I gather, that to designate anything as a second (intermediate, instrumental, dependent) mover must involve a *petitio principii*, since "second mover" just means "mover dependent for its efficacy on an unmoved mover." This, however, is simply not what the Aristotelians understood by "second mover"; this phrase meant merely "mover dependent for its efficacy on another," with no question-begging stipulation that this other be itself unmoved. In Aquinas' words, "everything which both moves [another] and is moved [by yet another] has the nature of an instrument."[22] Thus, if the hand pushes a stick, the stick in turn pushes a stone, and the stone in turn pushes a clod, then the stone is called an "intermediate" mover just because it depends on the stick for its efficacy; what makes the stick move, and *a fortiori* whether there is an infinite regress of movers, is entirely irrelevant to the classification of the stone as a second mover. There is therefore no begging of the issue in the very introduction of the phrase "second mover."

---

[17]Cf. *Physics*, 250b11 ff. and 256a4 ff. Some critics have gone so far as explicitly to claim that Aristotle contradicted himself here; see, e.g., S. van Den Bergh's introduction to Averroes, *op. cit.*, I, xvi.

[18]*ST*, I, Q. 46, *passim*.

[19]Letter to Chanut, quoted by F. Copleston, *History of Philosophy* (London, 1960), IV, 134.

[20]*Principles of Philosophy*, Pt. T. II, xxxix, as found in G. E. M. Anscombe and P. T. Geach (eds.), *Descartes: Philosophical Writings* (Edinburgh, 1954), p. 217; cf. all of pp. 213–19. For a similar doctrine, cp. Aristotle, *Physics*, 214a25–32, 217a10–19, 242a23, and 267a21–b9.

[21]"*Hic autem* . . . (St. Thomas Aquinas)," *Mind*, LXIX (1960), 403.

[22]*On Physics*, Bk. VIII, lec. 9, #1044.

III

It is evident that we cannot hope to understand the argument against infinite causal regresses without first getting straight on the supposedly critical contrast between causal series ordered *per se* and those ordered *per accidens*. So let us examine the previously quoted explanation by Scotus that "in essentially ordered series the second [that is, the posterior] depends upon the first [the prior] precisely in its act of causation." I assume that the entire argument would be laid bare if we fully understood this criterion and its application to the two paradigm cases, propulsion and genealogy.

The criterion delineated by Scotus seems straightforward enough; it is simply that each member of an essential series (except of course the first and last *if* there be such) is causally dependent upon its predecessor for its own causal efficacy regarding its successor. The members are each intermediate (secondary, instrumental, dependent) in the sense discussed above. In an accidental series, however, each member is not dependent upon its predecessor for its own causal efficacy—though it may be dependent in some other regard. Thus a causal series is *per se* ordered if and only if it is throughout of the form: w's being F causes x to be G, x's being G causes y to be H, y's being H causes z to be I, . . . (here $F\hat{x}$, $G\hat{x}$, $H\hat{x}$, and $I\hat{x}$ may be identical or differing functions). A causal series is ordered *per accidens*, however, if and only if it is throughout of the form: w's being F causes x to be G, x's being H causes y to be I, y's being J causes z to be K, . . . (here $G\hat{x} \neq H\hat{x}$ and $I\hat{x} \neq J\hat{x}$, but otherwise $F\hat{x}$, $G\hat{x}$, $H\hat{x}$, $I\hat{x}$, $J\hat{x}$, and $K\hat{x}$ may be identical or differing functions). In other words, the two functions of each individual variable must be identical in the essential case, but must differ in the accidental case.

Consider the paradigm case where one's hand pushes a stick which in turn pushes a stone. This causal series is *per se* because it is the same function of the stick (namely, its locomotion) which both is caused by the movement of the hand and causes the movement of the stone. Again, a series where the fire heats the pot and the pot in turn heats the stew, causing it to boil, is also essentially ordered; for the warmth of the pot is both caused by the warmth of the fire and cause of the warmth of the stew, while the warmth of the stew is both caused by the warmth of the pot and cause of the stew's boiling.

On the other hand, consider the paradigm case of Abraham's begetting Isaac, who in turn begets Jacob. Here the series is accidentally ordered because that function of Isaac (namely, his copulating) which causes Jacob's birth is not caused by Abraham's copulation; the latter results in Isaac's *birth*, whereas it is Isaac's *copulation* which causes Jacob to be born. Genealogical series like the following are thus *per accidens*: Abraham's copulation causes Isaac's birth, Isaac's copulation causes Jacob's birth, Jacob's copulation causes Joseph's birth. Each member has one attribute qua effect (being born) and quite another attribute qua cause (copulating).

Now Aristotle and his followers held as a critically important thesis that the constituent relations in an essentially ordered series are *transitive*. This is, I suggest, the point of Aristotle's statement that "everything that is moved is moved by the movent that is further back in the series as well as by that which immediately moves it."[23] If, to use the standard example, the hand propels the stick and the stick in turn propels the stone, then the hand propels the stone by means of the stick. Again, if the fire heats the pot, which heats the stew, which causes the stew to boil, then the fire causes the stew to boil. St. Thomas makes this point in the following passage:

> If that which was given as moved locally is moved by the nearest mover which is increased, and that again is moved by something which is altered, and that again is moved by something which is moved in place, then that which is moved with respect to place will be moved more by the first thing which is moved with respect to place than by the second thing which is altered or by the third thing which is increased.[24]

Here we have an undisguised claim that "*x* moves *y*" is a transitive causal relation.

The Aristotelians claimed such transitivity not only for "*x* moves *y*" (moving causation), but also for "*x* creates *y*" (Avicennian efficient causation), "*y* is made out of *x*" (material causation), "*x* is the form of *y*" (formal causation), and "*x* is the goal of *y*" (final causation). Maimonides writes:

> A cause must . . . be sought for each of the four divisions of causes. When we have found for any existing thing those four causes which are in immediate connexion with it, we find for these again causes, and for these again other causes, and so on until we arrive at the first causes. E.g., a certain production has its *agens*, this *agens* has again its *agens*, and so on and on until at last we arrive at a first *agens*, which is the true *agens* throughout all the intervening links. If the letter *aleph* be moved by *bet, bet* by *gimel, gimel* by *dalet*, and *dalet* by *hé*—and as the series does not extend to infinity, let us stop at *hé*— there is no doubt that the *hé* moves [each of] the letters *aleph, bet, gimel*, and *dalet*, and we say correctly that the *aleph* is moved by *hé*. In that sense everything occurring in the universe, although indirectly produced by certain nearer causes, is ascribed to the Creator. . . . [By parity of reasoning] we arrive at length at that form which is necessary for the existence of all intermediate forms, which are the causes of the present [that is, last] form. That form to which the forms of all existing things are traced is God. . . . The same argument holds good in reference to all final causes.[25]

So, in an essentially ordered series of any type of cause, each member is supposed to be the cause of all those which follow on it, owing to the transitivity of the relations involved. And then, of course, if there is or must be a

---

[23]*Physics*, 257a10–12.
[24]*On Physics*, Bk. VIII, lec. 9, #1047.
[25]*The Guide for the Perplexed* (New York, 1956), I, ch. lxix.

first member of such series, the transitivity would make it natural to say that the first member was the ultimate cause of every one of the others.

It might be questioned whether these various causal relations are really always transitive. We may suspect that a careful examination of the ordinary uses of, for example, "*x* moves *y*" would show it sometimes to be used transitively and sometimes not. But such a discovery would, I think, be irrelevant to the argument, because Aristotle and the others are employing these causal relation statements in refined ways. It can simply be stipulated that "*x* moves *y*" and the others be invariably transitive within the Aristotelian scientific model. Nor would this be to use those expressions in ways greatly different from their employment in ordinary language, for they are commonly—even if perhaps not universally—used transitively.

As a counterpart of the foregoing, the Aristotelians held that the constituent relations in an accidentally ordered causal series are *intransitive*. Thus, regarding the paradigm case of "*x* begets *y*," if Abraham begets Isaac, who in turn begets Jacob, then Abraham clearly does not beget Jacob.

IV

Why was an infinite regress thought to be impossible in essentially ordered series, but not in accidentally ordered ones? It has been widely believed that it was the purported simultaneity in the former case which was held to be decisive.[26] Some of Aquinas' statements in particular might seem to support this interpretation; at one place, for instance, he says:

> It is impossible to proceed to infinity in the order of efficient causes which act together at the same time, because in that case the effect would have to depend on an infinite number of actions simultaneously existing. And such cases are essentially infinite, because their infinity is required for the effect caused by them. On the other hand, in the sphere of non-simultaneously acting causes, it is not . . . impossible to proceed to infinity. And the infinity here is accidental to the causes; thus it is accidental to Socrates' father that he is another man's son or not. But it is not accidental to the stick, in moving the stone, that it be moved by the hand; for the stick moves [the stone] just so far as it is moved [by the hand].[27]

The gist of this argument would seem to be that an instantaneous causal series would have to be essentially ordered, and furthermore that all *per se* ordered series must have a first member. But this is not at all to claim that essentially ordered series must have a beginning just because they are instantaneous; on the contrary, the contention is that instantaneous series must have a beginning just because they are always *per se* ordered. Whatever it is, therefore, that requires essentially ordered causal series to have a first term, we know that it is not their (purported) simultaneity. For example, the argument was not that

[26]E.g., by Ockham; see his *Quaestiones in lib. I Physicorum*, Qs. 132–36, included in P. Boehner (ed.), *Ockham: Philosophical Writings* (Edinburgh, 1957), pp. 115–25.
[27]*SCG*, II, ch. xxxviii; see *ST*, I, Q. 7, Arts. 3 & 4.

an infinite series of essentially ordered causes, being instantaneous, would involve an impossible concurrent infinity, whereas an infinite series of accidentally ordered causes, being chronological, would not involve this absurd consequence. For Aristotle and his disciples explicitly state that the argument for a first cause has nothing to do with whether an infinite number of concurrent intermediate causes is possible. Aristotle writes that "it makes no difference whether there is one intermediate or more, nor whether they are infinite or finite in number."[28] St. Thomas concurs, asserting that it does not "make any difference whether there are a finite or an infinite number of intermediates, because so long as they have the nature of intermediate they cannot be the first cause of motion."[29] Finally, we may record Scotus' claim that, "even if the group of beings caused were infinite, they would still depend on something outside the group."[30] I therefore conclude that the argument does not rest on the supposed simultaneity of causal series ordered *per se*. Hence it cannot be simply an application of the well-known Aristotelian doctrine that an actualized infinity is impossible.[31]

An interesting recent proposal by G. E. M. Anscombe and P. T. Geach is that the argument involves a composition or grouping together of the members of the causal chain. Anscombe and Geach suggest the following as a paraphrase of the reasoning involved:

> If B is the cause of a process going on in A, or of A's coming to be, then it may be that this happens because of a process in B that is caused by a further thing C; and C in turn may act because of a process in C caused by D; and so on. But now let us lump together the chain of things B, C, D, . . . , and call it X. We may predicate of each one of the causes B, C, D, . . . , *and also* of X as a whole, that it causes a process in A (or the coming-to-be of A) in virtue of being *itself* in process of change. But what is it that maintains this process of change in X? Something that cannot itself be in process of change: for if it were, it would just be one of the things in process of change that causes the process in A (or the coming-to-be of A).[32]

Our first reaction to this presentation of the proof might be to object that it commits the fallacy of composition, in that an inference is made from a common property of the parts B, C, D, . . . to X's having that same attribute. It was this maneuver which Hume had in mind when he wrote: "But the whole [chain of causes and effects], you say, wants a cause. I answer that the uniting of these parts into a whole . . . is performed merely by an arbitrary act of the mind, and has no influence on the nature of things."[33] Ockham had raised a similar objection: "I reply that the whole multitude of both essentially and accidentally ordered causes is caused, but not by some one thing which is

---

[28]See n. 1, *supra*.
[29]*Commentary on the Metaphysics of Aristotle* (Chicago, 1961), Bk. II, lec. 3, #303.
[30]Wolter, *op. cit.*, p. 42.
[31]See *Physics*, Bk. III, chs. iv–viii.
[32]*Three Philosophers* (Oxford, 1961), pp. 113–14.
[33]*Dialogues Concerning Natural Religion* (New York, 1948), Pt. IX.

part of this multitude, or which is outside this multitude, but one part is caused by one thing which is part of this multitude, and another by another thing, and so on *ad infinitum.*"[34]

It is not at all certain, however, that the Ockhamist-Humean criticism is effective. For although inferences of the form "All the parts of X have the property P, so therefore X has the property P" are not formally valid, yet many are valid in virtue of the meanings of the arguments substituted for "X" and "P."[35] This is the case with, for example, "All the bricks in that wall are red, and so the wall itself is red," and similarly with "Every part of the United States is in the Northern Hemisphere, so therefore the whole U.S. is in the Northern Hemisphere." On the other hand, many such inferences are quite invalid—as, for example, "Every brick in that wall weighs one pound, and so the entire wall weighs one pound," and "Every part of the U.S. is either east or west of the Mississippi, so therefore the whole U.S. is either east or west of the Mississippi." Thus if the Aristotelian argument really is based on an inference of composition, it cannot be rejected out of hand; each such proof must be considered on its own merits.

It seems to me, however, that Anscombe and Geach have introduced a superfluous issue in making the argument appear to rest primarily on an inference of composition. The *working* parts of their version of the proof are merely the following: the whole world, or at least some substantial part of it, X, is "itself in process of change. But what is it that maintains this process of change in X? Something that cannot itself be in process of change." The grouping together of $B, C, D, \ldots$ to form X is in fact a cog having no important connection with the clockworks; it is merely used to prove the truism that the whole X is undergoing change. Now a mainspring composition argument would be: each part $B, C, D, \ldots$ of X is moved by another, so therefore X itself is moved by another. But neither Aristotle nor his medieval disciples nor Anscombe and Geach even suggest such an inference. The only grouping together employed by the latter pair is the trivial: $B, C, D, \ldots$ are each changing, and so X is changing. This is a sound composition inference, but hardly succeeds in demonstrating the existence of an unchanging cause of X's changing.

V

I want now to suggest a reading of the argument against infinite causal regresses on the basis of our earlier understanding of the contrast between *per se* and *per accidens* ordering of causal series. I think that the substance of the proof was as follows, again using moving causation as our paradigmatic

---

[34]Boehner, *op. cit.*, p. 124.

[35]I am indebted to Geach for bringing this point to my attention. For recent discussion, see W. L. Rowe, "The Fallacy of Composition," *Mind*, LXXI (1962), 87; Y. Bar-Hillel, "More on the Fallacy of Composition," *Mind*, LXXIII (1964), 125; and R. Cole, "A Note on Informal Fallacies," *Mind*, LXXIV (1965), 432.

example. Parallel arguments could obviously be constructed regarding Aristotle's other types of cause, and also regarding Avicennian efficient causes.

The Aristotelian scientific model stipulates that all motions are to be given causal explanations, and that such explanations are to be of the form "*x* moves *y*." (Compare the analogous Newtonian stipulation that all accelerations are to be explained in terms of equations of the form "$F = ma$.") Suppose then that we observe something, *a*, to be moving, and we wish to explain this phenomenon by means of the Aristotelian physics. The explanation must be of the form "*x* moves *a*." Suppose further that *a* is moved by *b, b* is in turn moved by *c, c* in turn by *d*, and so on indefinitely. The issue is whether this series can continue *ad infinitum*. We now ask, what moves *a*? Well, it has already been stated that *b* moves *a*; so it may be suggested that "*b* moves *a*" is the desired explanation of *a*'s motion, the desired value of "*x* moves *a*." But this would be an inadequate account of the matter. For *b* is itself being moved by *c*, which—owing to the transitivity of "*x* moves *y*"—thus yields the implication that *a* is moved by *c*, with *b* serving merely as an instrument or intermediate. But in turn *d* moves *c*; and so *d* moves *a*. But *e* moves *d;* therefore *e* moves *a*. And so on indefinitely. Now, so long as this series continues, we have not found the real mover of *a*; that is to say, we have not found the *explaining* value of the function "*x* moves *a*." The regress is thus a vicious one, in that the required explanation of *a*'s motion is deferred so long as the series continues. With regard to any *x* which moves *a*, if there is a *y* such that *y* moves *x*, then we must infer that *y* moves *a*. And if for any *x* such that *x* moves *a* there were a *y* such that *y* moved *x* (and therefore moved *a* as well), then no explanation of *a*'s motion would be possible with the Aristotelian model. There would of course be any number of *true* statements of the form "*x* moves *a*"—namely, "*b* moves *a*," "*c* moves *a*," "*d* moves *a*," and so forth. But none of these is to count as the Aristotelian *explanation* of *a*'s motion. Nor, it must be noted, is any such explanation given merely by asserting that there is an infinite regress of movers of *a*. "An infinite regress of movers move *a*" is not a possible value of the function "*x* moves *a*," for the variable in the latter ranges over individuals, not classes (and *a fortiori* not over series, finite or infinite). An uncaused motion, however, is no motion at all; in other words, an inexplicable motion would be an unintelligible motion. There must be, therefore, an unmoved mover of *a*.

The foregoing case is to be contrasted with giving an explanation of, for example, Jacob's birth. Such an account is to be of the form "*x* begat Jacob." The complete and unique explanation of that form is that Isaac begat Jacob. We do not get a new value for the function on the grounds that Abraham in turn begat Isaac, since this does not imply that Abraham begat Jacob; on the contrary, it implies that he did not do so. So a full explanation of Jacob's birth can be given regardless of whether his family tree extends back to infinity. An explanation of Isaac's copulation is still required, of course; but that will center on his actions with Rebecca, rather than on his having been sired by Abraham. (The Aristotelians would contend that Isaac's copulation, being a locomotion, must be the termination of an essentially ordered *moving* series. This means that there indeed is a *per se* series which terminates in Jacob's birth, but it does not ascend through Isaac, Abraham, Terah, and so on; rather, it goes back through Isaac's copulation and thence instantaneously back through a series of contiguous movers reaching up to the celestial spheres. Aquinas writes that "whatever generates here below, moves to the production of the species as the instrument of a heavenly body. Thus the Philosopher says that 'man and the sun generate man.' "[36] God is then in turn causally responsible for the locomotion of the heavenly spheres—though not of course by himself changing.[37] In this way each man is supposed to be efficiently caused by God via an essentially ordered series of movers, regardless of whether he has an infinite regress of ancestors in an accidentally ordered genealogy series.)

VI

What are we to say of the foregoing argument, once so widely accepted? I want to suggest that its salient feature (aside of course, from the transitivity of the relevant causal relations) is the quasi-*legalistic* connotation of "cause" which is employed. It is precisely the sense of a cause as *responsible* for its effect—as against its being merely a concomitant of its effect—which entails that *b*'s being moved by *c* renders the *true* statement "*b* moves *a*" unacceptable as the Aristotelian explanation of *a*'s motion. As it were, the *responsibility* for *a*'s motion is passed on back to *c*, and then on back to *d*, and so on back through the transitive series. Hence Aristotle's assertion: "It is clear that everything that is moved is moved by the movent that is further back in the series as well as by that which immediately moves it; in fact *the earlier movent is that which more strictly moves it*."[38] This seems to be a way of saying that an unmoved mover has some sort of causal *responsibility* in a way that a moved mover has not.

Consider the following case. Mr. Alpha is in his automobile, stopped at an intersection. Immediately behind him sits Mr. Beta in his own car. Behind Mr. Beta is Mr. Gamma, behind whom is Mr. Delta, and so on indefinitely. Suddenly Alpha's car is rammed from the rear, damaging his bumper. So Alpha, desiring to recover the expense of repairing his automobile, accuses Beta of having caused the accident, and brings suit against him. Beta, how-

---

[36]*ST*, I, Q. 115, Art. 3, Reply Obj. 2; the quotation from Aristotle is from *Physics*, 194b13. See also *ST*, I, Q. 118, Art. 1, Reply Obj. 3, where Aquinas asserts that the act of begetting is "concurrent with the power of a heavenly body."

[37]Aristotle held that God is merely the final cause of the celestial rotations; cf. *Metaphysics*, 1072a19 ff. The medievals tended to abuse Avicenna's distinction (n. 2, *supra*) by saying that God is somehow the efficient cause of that locomotion, though perhaps with the intelligences (angels) as intermediates; see E. Gilson, *The Elements of Christian Philosophy* (New York, 1963), pp. 71–74.

[38]*Physics*, 257a10–13; my italics. See also n. 24, *supra*. The etymology of "αἰτί-α" supports my thesis, I think.

ever, successfully defends himself in court on the grounds that he had himself been rammed into Alpha by Gamma. So Alpha now sues Gamma. But the latter, it turns out, had in turn been rammed by Delta. So Alpha takes legal action against Delta. And so on indefinitely. Now, if this series of rammings extended *ad infinitum*, there would be no one whom Alpha could successfully sue as having caused the dent in his bumper; there would, in short, have been *no* cause for the accident at all. But if there were no cause, no mover, then there would be no effect, no moved, either—which is patently false, since Alpha's bumper *is* dented and his car *was* moved. Therefore there cannot be a regress to infinity of ramming automobiles, but rather someone was the first cause of the whole series of accidents; someone can properly be said to have moved Beta into Alpha, Gamma into Beta, Delta into Gamma, and so on. Therefore there is someone from whom Mr. Alpha can collect his expenses.

In this rather queer argument the legalistic sense of "cause" is manifest; the cause of the damage to Alpha's car will lie wherever legal responsibility lies, in this sense of "cause." It seems to me to be an allied (though not identical) notion of causation which is being employed in the Aristotelian argument against infinite regresses in all *per se* ordered causal series.

If my interpretation of the argument is correct, there arise two questions regarding its soundness: (1) whether it is *proper* in scientific explanation to employ a sense of "cause" as being responsible for its effect, or whether only concomitances may be mentioned; and even if the former be proper, (2) whether there could be any *a priori* guarantee that there will always be a *successful* employment of that sense of causation regarding observed phenomena. But answering these questions would obviously require giving a full analysis of the notions of causation and of explanation in natural science—a task far beyond the scope of this paper. I close the present discussion with the following remarks made in another context by J. L. Austin:

> My general opinion about this doctrine is that it is a typically *scholastic* view, attributable, first, to an obsession with a few particular words, the uses of which are over-simplified, not really understood or carefully studied or correctly described; and second, to an obsession with a few (and nearly always the same) half-studied "facts." (I say "scholastic," but I might just as well have said "philosophical"; over-simplification, schematization, and constant obsessive repetition of the same small range of jejune "examples" are . . . far too common to be dismissed as an occasional weakness of philosophers.)[39]

---

[39]*Sense and Sensibilia* (Oxford, 1962), p. 3. See also the comment in Wittgenstein's *Philosophical Investigations* (Oxford, 1963), #593: "A main cause of philosophical disease —a one-sided diet: one nourishes one's thinking with only one kind of example." One wonders whether the lines of attack mentioned in my last paragraph could be forestalled by elaborating on the next-to-last paragraph of section III above—that is, by means of recently familiar talk about stipulations, conventions, theoretical entities, and the like. So, e.g.: is the Aristotelian God perhaps a theoretical entity in a way not unlike a Newtonian force? Cf. the succinct discussion of "The Nature of Scientific Theory, Illustrated by the Case of Mechanics" in M. Black, *A Companion to Wittgenstein's Tractatus* (Ithaca, 1964), ch. lxxxi.

The Teleological Argument

WILLIAM PALEY

1.12   *The Analogy of the Watch*

CHAPTER ONE

In crossing a heath, suppose I pitched my foot against a *stone* and were asked how the stone came to be there, I might possibly answer that for anything I knew to the contrary it had lain there forever; nor would it, perhaps, be very easy to show the absurdity of this answer. But suppose I had found a *watch* upon the ground, and it should be inquired how the watch happened to be in that place, I should hardly think of the answer which I had before given, that for anything I knew the watch might have always been there. Yet why should not this answer serve for the watch as well as for the stone; why is it not as admissible in the second case as in the first? For this reason, and for no other, namely, that when we come to inspect the watch, we perceive— what we could not discover in the stone—that its several parts are framed and put together for a purpose, e.g., that they are so formed and adjusted as to produce motion, and that motion so regulated as to point out the hour of the day; that if the different parts had been differently shaped from what they are, or placed after any other manner or in any other order than that in which they are placed, either no motion at all would have been carried on in the machine, or none which would have answered the use that is now served by it. To reckon up a few of the plainest of these parts and of their offices, all tending to one result: we see a cylindrical box containing a coiled elastic spring, which, by its endeavor to relax itself, turns round the box. We next observe a flexible chain—artificially wrought for the sake of flexure—com- municating the action of the spring from the box to the fusee. We then find a series of wheels, the teeth of which catch in and apply to each other, con- ducting the motion from the fusee to the balance and from the balance to the pointer, and at the same time, by the size and shape of those wheels, so regulating that motion as to terminate in causing an index, by an equable and measured progression, to pass over a given space in a given time. We take notice that the wheels are made of brass, in order to keep them from rust;

From William Paley, *Natural Theology* (1802).

the springs of steel, no other metal being so elastic; that over the face of the watch there is placed a glass, a material employed in no other part of the work, but in the room of which, if there had been any other than a transparent substance, the hour could not be seen without opening the case. This mechanism being observed—it requires indeed an examination of the instrument, and perhaps some previous knowledge of the subject, to perceive and understand it; but being once, as we have said, observed and understood—the inference we think is inevitable, that the watch must have had a maker—that there must have existed, at some time and at some place or other, an artificer or artificers who formed it for the purpose which we find it actually to answer, who completely comprehended its construction and designed its use.

I. Nor would it, I apprehend, weaken the conclusion, that we had never seen a watch made—that we had never known an artist capable of making one—that we were altogether incapable of executing such a piece of workmanship ourselves, or of understanding in what manner it was performed; all this being no more than what is true of some exquisite remains of ancient art, of some lost arts, and, to the generality of mankind, of the more curious productions of modern manufacture. Does one man in a million know how oval frames are turned? Ignorance of this kind exalts our opinion of the unseen and unknown artist's skill, if he be unseen and unknown, but raises no doubt in our minds of the existence and agency of such an artist, at some former time and in some place or other. Nor can I perceive that it varies at all the inference, whether the question arise concerning a human agent or concerning an agent of a different species, or an agent possessing in some respects a different nature.

II. Neither, secondly, would it invalidate our conclusion, that the watch sometimes went wrong or that it seldom went exactly right. The purpose of the machinery, the design, and the designer might be evident, and in the case supposed, would be evident, in whatever way we accounted for the irregularity of the movement, or whether we could account for it or not. It is not necessary that a machine be perfect in order to show with what design it was made: still less necessary, where the only question is whether it were made with any design at all.

III. Nor, thirdly, would it bring any uncertainty into the argument, if there were a few parts of the watch, concerning which we could not discover or had not yet discovered in what manner they conduced to the general effect; or even some parts, concerning which we could not ascertain whether they conduced to that effect in any manner whatever. For, as to the first branch of the case, if by the loss, or disorder, or decay of the parts in question, the movement of the watch were found in fact to be stopped, or disturbed, or retarded, no doubt would remain in our minds as to the utility or intention of these parts, although we should be unable to investigate the manner according to which, or the connection by which, the ultimate effect depended upon their action or assistance; and the more complex the machine, the more likely is this obscurity to arise. Then, as to the second thing supposed, namely, that there were parts which might be spared without prejudice to the movement of the watch, and that we had proved this by experiment, these superfluous parts, even if we were completely assured that they were such, would not vacate the reasoning which we had instituted concerning other parts. The indication of contrivance remained, with respect to them, nearly as it was before.

IV. Nor, fourthly, would any man in his senses think the existence of the watch with its various machinery accounted for, by being told that it was one out of possible combinations of material forms; that whatever he had found in the place where he found the watch, must have contained some internal configuration or other; and that this configuration might be the structure now exhibited, namely, of the works of a watch, as well as a different structure.

V. Nor, fifthly, would it yield his inquiry more satisfaction, to be answered that there existed in things a principle of order, which had disposed the parts of the watch into their present form and situation. He never knew a watch made by the principle of order; nor can he even form to himself an idea of what is meant by a principle of order distinct from the intelligence of the watchmaker.

VI. Sixthly, he would be surprised to hear that the mechanism of the watch was no proof of contrivance, only a motive to induce the mind to think so:

VII. And not less surprised to be informed that the watch in his hand was nothing more than the result of the laws of *metallic* nature. It is a perversion of language to assign any law as the efficient, operative cause of any thing. A law presupposes an agent, for it is only the mode according to which an agent proceeds: it implies a power, for it is the order according to which that power acts. Without this agent, without this power, which are both distinct from itself, the *law* does nothing, is nothing. The expression, "the law of metallic nature," may sound strange and harsh to a philosophic ear; but it seems quite as justifiable as some others which are more familiar to him, such as "the law of vegetable nature," "the law of animal nature," or, indeed, as "the law of nature" in general, when assigned as the cause of phenomena, in exclusion of agency and power, or when it is substituted into the place of these.

VIII. Neither, lastly, would our observer be driven out of his conclusion or from his confidence in its truth by being told that he knew nothing at all about the matter. He knows enough for his argument; he knows the utility of the end; he knows the subserviency and adaptation of the means to the end. These points being known, his ignorance of other points, his doubts concerning other points affect not the certainty of his reasoning. The consciousness of knowing little need not beget a distrust of that which he does know.

CHAPTER TWO

Suppose, in the next place, that the person who found the watch should after some time discover that, in addition to all the properties which he had hitherto observed in it, it possessed the unexpected property of producing in the course of its movement another watch like itself—the thing is conceivable; that it contained within it a mechanism, a system of parts—a mold, for instance, or a complex adjustment of lathes, files, and other tools—evidently and separately calculated for this purpose; let us inquire what effect ought such a discovery to have upon his former conclusion.

I. The first effect would be to increase his admiration of the contrivance, and his conviction of the consummate skill of the contriver. Whether he regarded the object of the contrivance, the distinct apparatus, the intrticate, yet in many parts intelligible mechanism by which it was carried on, he would perceive in this new observation nothing but an additional reason for doing what he had already done—for referring the construction of the watch to design and to supreme art. If that construction *without* this property, or, which is the same thing, before this property had been noticed, proved intention and art to have been employed about it, still more strong would the proof appear when he came to the knowledge of this further property, the crown and perfection of all the rest.

II. He would reflect that, though the watch before him were *in some sense* the maker of the watch which was fabricated in the course of its movements, yet it was in a very different sense from that in which a carpenter, for instance, is the maker of a chair—the author of its contrivance, the cause of the relation of its parts to their use. With respect to these, the first watch was no cause at all to the second; in no such sense as this was it the author of the constitution and order, either of the parts which the new watch contained, or of the parts by the aid and instrumentality of which it was produced. We might possibly say, but with great latitude of expression, that a stream of water ground corn; but no latitude of expression would allow us to say, no stretch of conjecture could lead us to think that the stream of water built the mill, though it were too ancient for us to know who the builder was. What the stream of water does in the affair is neither more nor less than this: by the application of an unintelligent impulse to a mechanism previously arranged, arranged independently of it and arranged by intelligence, an effect is produced, namely, the corn is ground. But the effect results from the arrangement. The force of the stream cannot be said to be the cause or the author of the effect, still less of the arrangement. Understanding and plan in the formation of the mill were not the less necessary for any share which the water has in grinding the corn; yet is this share the same as that which the watch would have contributed to the production of the new watch, upon the supposition assumed in the last section. Therefore,

III. Though it be now no longer probable that the individual watch which our observer had found was made immediately by the hand of an artificer, yet this alteration does not in anywise affect the inference that an artificer had been originally employed and concerned in the production. The argument from design remains as it was. Marks of design and contrivance are no more accounted for now than they were before. In the same thing, we may ask for the cause of different properties. We may ask for the cause of the color of a body, of its hardness, of its heat; and these causes may be all different. We are now asking for the cause of that subserviency to a use, that relation to an end, which we have remarked in the watch before us. No answer is given to this question by telling us that a preceding watch produced it. There cannot be design without a designer; contrivance without a contriver; order without choice; arrangement without anything capable of arranging; subserviency and relation to a purpose without that which could intend a purpose; means suitable to an end, and executing their office in accomplishing that end, without the end ever having been contemplated or the means accommodated to it. Arrangement, disposition of parts, subserviency of means to an end, relation of instruments to a use imply the presence of intelligence and mind. No one, therefore, can rationally believe that the insensible, inanimate watch, from which the watch before us issued, was the proper cause of the mechanism we so much admire in it—could be truly said to have constructed the instrument, disposed its parts, assigned their office, determined their order, action, and mutual dependency, combined their several motions into one result, and that also a result connected with the utilities of other beings. All these properties, therefore, are as much unaccounted for as they were before.

IV. Nor is anything gained by running the difficulty farther back, that is, by supposing the watch before us to have been produced from another watch, that from a former, and so on indefinitely. Our going back ever so far brings us no nearer to the least degree of satisfaction upon the subject. Contrivance is still unaccounted for. We still want a contriver. A designing mind is neither supplied by this supposition nor dispensed with. If the difficulty were diminished the farther we went back, by going back indefinitely we might exhaust it. And this is the only case to which this sort of reasoning applies. Where there is a tendency, or, as we increase the number of terms, a continual approach toward a limit, *there*, by supposing the number of terms to be what is called infinite, we may conceive the limit to be attained; but where there is no such tendency or approach, nothing is effected by lengthening the series. There is no difference as to the point in question, whatever there may be as to many points, between one series and another—between a series which is finite and a series which is infinite. A chain composed of an infinite number of links can no more support itself than a chain composed of a finite number of links. And of this we are assured, though we never *can* have tried the experiment; because, by increasing the number of links, from ten, for instance, to a hundred, from a hundred to a thousand, etc., we make not the smallest approach, we observe not the smallest tendency toward self-support. There is no difference in this respect—yet there may be a great difference in several respects—between a chain of a greater or less length, between one chain and another, between one that is finite and one that is infinite. This very much resembles the case before us. The machine which we are inspecting demonstrates, by its construction, contrivance and design. Contrivance must have had a contriver, design a designer, whether the machine immediately proceeded from another machine or not. That circumstance alters not the case. That other machine may, in like manner, have proceeded from a former machine: nor does that alter the case; the contrivance must have had a contriver. That former one from one preceding it: no alteration still; a contriver is still necessary. No tendency is perceived, no approach toward a diminution of this necessity. It is the same with any and every succession of these machines—a succession of ten, of a hundred, of a thousand; with one series, as with another—a series which is finite, as with a series which is infinite. In whatever other respects they may differ, in this they do not. In all equally, contrivance and design are unaccounted for.

The question is not simply, how came the first watch into existence?— which question, it may be pretended, is done away by supposing the series of watches thus produced from one another to have been infinite, and consequently to have had no such *first* for which it was necessary to provide a cause. This, perhaps, would have been nearly the state of the question, if nothing had been before us but an unorganized, unmechanized substance, without mark or indication of contrivance. It might be difficult to show that such substance could not have existed from eternity, either in succession— if it were possible, which I think it is not, for unorganized bodies to spring from one another—or by individual perpetuity. But that is not the question now. To suppose it to be so is to suppose that it made no difference whether he had found a watch or a stone. As it is, the metaphysics of that question have no place; for, in the watch which we are examining are seen contrivance, design, an end, a purpose, means for the end, adaptation to the purpose. And the question which irresistibly presses upon our thoughts is, whence this contrivance and design? The thing required is the intending mind, the adapted hand, the intelligence by which that hand was directed. This question, this demand is not shaken off by increasing a number or succession of substances destitute of these properties; nor the more, by increasing that number to infinity. If it be said that, upon the supposition of one watch being produced from another in the course of that other's movements and by means of the mechanism within it, we have a cause for the watch in my hand, namely, the watch from which it proceeded; I deny that for the design, the contrivance, the suitableness of means to an end, the adaptation of instruments to a use, all of which we discover in the watch, we have any cause whatever. It is in vain, therefore, to assign a series of such causes or to allege that a series may be carried back to infinity; for I do not admit that we have yet any cause at all for the phenomena, still less any series of causes either finite or infinite. Here is contrivance but no contriver; proofs of design, but no designer.

V. Our observer would further also reflect that the maker of the watch before him was in truth and reality the maker of every watch produced from it: there being no difference, except that the latter manifests a more exquisite skill, between the making of another watch with his own hands, by the mediation of files, lathes, chisels, etc., and the disposing, fixing, and inserting of these instruments, or of others equivalent to them, in the body of the watch already made, in such a manner as to form a new watch in the course of the movements which he had given to the old one. It is only working by one set of tools instead of another.

The conclusion which the *first* examination of the watch, of its works, construction, and movement, suggested, was that it must have had, for cause and author of that construction, an artificer who understood its mechanism and designed its use. This conclusion is invincible. A *second* examination presents us with a new discovery. The watch is found, in the course of its movement, to produce another watch similar to itself; and not only so, but we perceive in it a system or organization separately calculated for that purpose. What effect would this discovery have or ought it to have upon our former inference? What, as has already been said, but to increase beyond measure our admiration of the skill which had been employed in the formation of such a machine? Or shall it, instead of this, all at once turn us round to an opposite conclusion, namely, that no art or skill whatever has been concerned in the business, although all other evidences of art and skill remain as they were, and this last and supreme piece of art be now added to the rest? Can this be maintained without absurdity? Yet this is atheism.

CHAPTER FIVE

Every observation which was made in our first chapter concerning the watch may be repeated with strict propriety concerning the eye, concerning animals, concerning plants, concerning, indeed, all the organized parts of the works of nature. As,

I. When we are inquiring simply after the *existence* of an intelligent Creator, imperfection, inaccuracy, liability to disorder, occasional irregularities may subsist in a considerable degree without inducing any doubt into the question; just as a watch may frequently go wrong, seldom perhaps exactly right, may be faulty in some parts, defective in some, without the smallest ground of suspicion from thence arising that it was not a watch, or not made for the purpose ascribed to it. When faults are pointed out, and when a question is started concerning the skill of the artist or the dexterity with which the work is executed, then, indeed, in order to defend these qualities from accusation, we must be able either to expose some intractableness and imperfection in the materials or point out some invincible difficulty in the execution, into which imperfection and difficulty the matter of complaint may be resolved; or, if we cannot do this, we must adduce such specimens of consummate art and contrivance proceeding from the same hand as may convince the inquirer of the existence, in the case before him, of impediments like those which we have mentioned, although, what from the nature of the case is very likely to happen, they be unknown and unperceived by him. This we must do in order to vindicate the artist's skill, or at least the perfection of it; as we must also judge of his intention and of the provisions employed in fulfilling that intention, not from an instance in which they fail but from the great plurality of instances in which they succeed. But, after all, these are different questions from the question of the artist's existence; or, which is the same, whether the thing before us be a work of art or not; and the questions ought always to be kept separate in the mind. So likewise it is in the works of nature. Irregularities and imperfections are of little or no weight in the consideration when that consideration relates simply to the existence of a Creator. When the argument respects his attributes, they are of weight; but are then to be taken in conjunction—the attention is not to rest upon them, but they are to be taken in conjunction with the unexceptional evidences which we possess of skill, power, and benevolence displayed in other instances; which evidences may, in strength, number, and variety, be such and may so overpower apparent blemishes as to induce us, upon the most reasonable ground, to believe that these last ought to be referred to some cause, though we be ignorant of it, other than defect of knowledge or of benevolence in the author.

II. There may be also parts of plants and animals, as there were supposed to be of the watch, of which in some instances the operation, in others the use, is unknown. These form different cases; for the operation may be unknown, yet the use be certain. Thus it is with the lungs of animals. It does not, I think, appear that we are acquainted with the action of the air upon the blood, or in what manner that action is communicated by the lungs; yet we find that a very short suspension of their office destroys the life of the animal. In this case, therefore, we may be said to know the use, nay, we experience the necessity of the organ though we be ignorant of its operation. Nearly the same thing may be observed of what is called the lymphatic system. We suffer grievous inconveniences from its disorder, without being informed of the office which it sustains in the economy of our bodies. There may possibly also be some few examples of the second class in which not only the operation is unknown, but in which experiments may seem to prove that the part is not necessary; or may leave a doubt how far it is even useful to the plant or animal in which it is found. This is said to be the case with the spleen, which has been extracted from dogs without any sensible injury to their vital functions. Instances of the former kind, namely, in which we cannot explain the operation, may be numerous; for they will be so in proportion to our ignorance. They will be more or fewer to different persons, and in different stages of science. Every improvement of knowledge diminishes their number. There is hardly, perhaps, a year passes that does not in the works of nature bring some operation or some mode of operation to light, which was before undiscovered—probably unsuspected. Instances of the second kind, namely, where the part appears to be totally useless, I believe to be extremely rare; compared with the number of those of which the use is evident, they are beneath any assignable proportion and perhaps have been never submitted to trial and examination sufficiently accurate, long enough continued, or often enough repeated. No accounts which I have seen are satisfactory. The mutilated animal may live and grow fat—as was the case of the dog deprived of its spleen—yet may be defective in some other of its functions, which, whether they can all, or in what degree of vigor and perfection, be performed, or how long preserved without the extirpated organ, does not seem to be ascertained by experiment. But to this case, even were it fully made out, may be applied the consideration which we suggested concerning the watch, namely, that these superfluous parts do not negative the reasoning which we instituted concerning those parts which are useful, and of which we know the use; the indication of contrivance with respect to them remains as it was before.

III. One atheistic way of replying to our observations upon the works of nature, and to the proofs of a Deity which we think that we perceive in them, is to tell us that all which we see must necessarily have had some form, and that it might as well be its present form as any other. Let us now apply this answer to the eye, as we did before to the watch. Something or other must have occupied that place in the animal's head, must have filled up, as we say, the socket; we will say also, that it must have been of that sort of substance which we call animal substance, as flesh, bone, membrane, or cartilage, etc. But that it should have been an *eye*, knowing as we do what an eye comprehends, namely, that it should have consisted, first, of a series of transparent lenses—very different, by the by, even in their substance, from the opaque materials of which the rest of the body is, in general at least, composed, and with which the whole of its surface, this single portion of it excepted, is covered; secondly, of a black cloth or canvas—the only membrane in the body which is black—spread out behind these lenses, so as to receive the image formed by pencils of light transmitted through them, and at which alone a distinct image could be formed, namely, at the concourse of the refracted rays; thirdly, of a large nerve communicating between this membrane and the brain, without which the action of light upon the membrane, however modified by the organ, would be lost to the purposes of sensation; that this fortunate conformation of parts should have been the lot not of one individual out of many thousand individuals, like the great prize in a lottery or like some singularity in nature, but the happy chance of a whole species; nor of one species out of many thousand species with which we are acquainted, but of by far the greatest number of all that exist, and that under varieties not causal or capricious, but bearing marks of being suited to their respective exigencies; that all this should have taken place merely because something must have occupied these points on every animal's forehead, or that all this should be thought to be accounted for by the short answer that "whatever was there must have had some form or other" is too absurd to be made more so by any argumentation. We are not contented with this answer; we find no satisfaction in it, by way of accounting for appearances of organization far short of those of the eye, such as we observe in fossil shells, petrified bones, or other substances which bear the vestiges of animal or vegetable recrements, but which, either in respect to utility or of the situation in which they are discovered, may seem accidental enough. It is no way of accounting even for these things, to say that the stone, for instance, which is shown to us—supposing the question to be concerning a petrifaction—must have contained some internal conformation or other. Nor does it mend the answer to add, with respect to the singularity of the conformation, that after the event it is no longer to be computed what the chances were against it. This is always to be computed when the question is whether a useful or imitative conformation be the product of chance or not: I desire no greater certainty in reasoning than that by which chance is excluded from the present disposition of the natural world. Universal experience is against it. What does chance ever do for us? In the human body, for instance, chance, that is, the operation of causes without design, may produce a wen, a wart, a mole, a pimple, but never an eye. Among inanimate substances, a clod, a pebble, a liquid drop might be; but never was a watch, a telescope, an organized body of any kind, answering a valuable purpose by a complicated mechanism, the effect of chance. In no assignable instance has such a thing existed without intention somewhere.

IV. There is another answer which has the same effect as the resolving of things into chance, which answer would persuade us to believe that the eye, the animal to which it belongs, every other animal, every plant, indeed every organized body which we see are only so many out of the possible varieties and combinations of being which the lapse of infinite ages has brought into existence; that the present world is the relic of that variety; millions of other bodily forms and other species having perished, being, by the defect of their constitution, incapable of preservation, or of continuance by generation. Now there is no foundation whatever for this conjecture in any thing which we observe in the works of nature; no such experiments are going on at present —no such energy operates as that which is here supposed, and which should be constantly pushing into existence new varieties of beings. Nor are there any appearances to support an opinion that every possible combination of vegetable or animal structure has formerly been tried. Multitudes of conformation, both of vegetables and animals, may be conceived capable of existence and succession, which yet do not exist. Perhaps almost as many forms of plants might have been found in the fields as figures of plants can be delineated upon paper. A countless variety of animals might have existed which do not exist. Upon the supposition here stated, we should see unicorns and mermaids, sylphs and centaurs, the fancies of painters and the fables of poets, realized by examples. Or, if it be alleged that these may transgress the bounds of possible life and propagation, we might at least have nations of human beings without nails upon their fingers, with more or fewer fingers and toes than ten, some with one eye, others with one ear, with one nostril, or without the sense of smelling at all. All these and a thousand other imaginable varieties might live and propagate. We may modify any one species many different ways, all consistent with life, and with the actions necessary to preservation, although affording different degrees of conveniency and enjoyment to the animal. And if we carry these modifications through the different species which are known to subsist, their number would be incalculable. No reason can be given why, if these deperdits ever existed, they have now disappeared. Yet, if all possible existences have been tried, they must have formed part of the catalogue.

But, moreover, the division of organized substances into animals and vegetables, and the distribution and subdistribution of each into genera and species, which distribution is not an arbitrary act of the mind, but founded in the order which prevails in external nature, appear to me to contradict the supposition of the present world being the remains of an indefinite variety of existences—of a variety which rejects all plan. The hypothesis teaches that every possible variety of being has at one time or other found its way into existence—by what cause or in what manner is not said—and that those which were badly formed perished; but how or why those which survived should be cast, as we see that plants and animals are cast, into regular classes, the hypothesis does not explain; or rather the hypothesis is inconsistent with this phenomenon.

The hypothesis, indeed, is hardly deserving of the consideration which we have given it. What should we think of a man who, because we had never ourselves seen watches, telescopes, stocking mills, steam engines, etc., made, knew not how they were made, nor could prove by testimony when they were made, or by whom, would have us believe that these machines, instead of deriving their curious structures from the thought and design of their inventors and contrivers, in truth derive them from no other origin than this: namely, that a mass of metals and other materials having run, when melted, into all possible figures, and combined themselves in all possible forms and shapes and proportions, these things which we see are what were left from the incident, as best worth preserving, and as such are become the remaining stock of a magazine which at one time or other, has by this means contained every mechanism, useful and useless, convenient and inconvenient, into which such like materials could be thrown? I cannot distinguish the hypothesis, as applied to the works of nature, from this solution, which no one would accept as applied to a collection of machines.

V. To the marks of contrivance discoverable in animal bodies, and to the argument deduced from them in proof of design and of a designing Creator, this turn is sometimes attempted to be given, namely, that the parts were not intended for the use, but that the use arose out of the parts. This distinction is intelligible. A cabinetmaker rubs his mahogany with fish skin; yet it would be too much to assert that the skin of the dogfish was made rough and granulated on purpose for the polishing of wood, and the use of cabinet-makers. Therefore the distinction is intelligible. But I think that there is very little place for it in the works of nature. When roundly and generally affirmed of them, as it has sometimes been, it amounts to such another stretch of assertion as it would be to say that all the implements of the cabinetmaker's workshop, as well as his fish skin, were substances accidentally configurated, which he had picked up and converted to his use; that his adzes, saws, planes, and gimlets were not made, as we suppose, to hew, cut, smooth, shape out, or bore wood with, but that, these things being made, no matter with what design, or whether with any, the cabinetmaker perceived that they were applicable to his purpose and turned them to account.

But, again, so far as this solution is attempted to be applied to those parts of animals the action of which does not depend upon the will of the animal, it is fraught with still more evident absurdity. Is it possible to believe that the eye was formed without any regard to vision; that it was the animal itself which found out that, though formed with no such intention, it would serve to see with; and that the use of the eye as an organ of sight resulted from this discovery, and the animal's application of it? The same question may be asked of the ear; the same of all the senses. None of the senses fundamentally depend upon the election of the animal; consequently neither upon his sagacity nor his experience. It is the impression which objects make upon them that constitutes their use. Under that impression he is passive. He may bring objects to the sense, or within its reach; he may select these objects; but over the impression itself he has no power, or very little; and that properly is the sense.

Secondly, there are many parts of animal bodies which seem to depend upon the will of the animal in a greater degree than the senses do, and yet with respect to which this solution is equally unsatisfactory. If we apply the solution to the human body, for instance, it forms itself into questions upon which no reasonable mind can doubt: such as, whether the teeth were made expressly for the mastication of food, the feet for walking, the hands for holding; or whether, these things as they are being in fact in the animal's possession, his own ingenuity taught him that they were convertible to these purposes, though no such purposes were contemplated in their formation.

All that there is of the appearance of reason in this way of considering the subject is that, in some cases, the organization seems to determine the habits of the animal and its choice to a particular mode of life which in a certain sense may be called "the use arising out of the part." Now, to all the instances in which there is any place for this suggestion, it may be replied that the organization determines the animal to habits beneficial and salutary to itself, and that this effect would not be seen so regularly to follow, if the several organizations did not bear a concerted and contrived relation to the substance by which the animal was surrounded. They would, otherwise, be capacities without objects—powers without employment. The webfoot determines, you say, the duck to swim; but what would that avail if there were no water to swim in? The strong hooked bill and sharp talons of one species of bird determine it to prey upon animals; the soft straight bill and weak claws of another species determine it to pick up seeds; but neither determination could take effect in providing for the sustenance of the birds, if animal bodies and vegetable seeds did not lie within their reach. The peculiar conformation of the bill and tongue and claws of the woodpecker determines that bird to search for his food among the insects lodged behind the bark or in the wood of decayed trees; but what would this profit him if there were no trees, no decayed trees, no insects lodged under their bark or in their trunk? The proboscis with which the bee is furnished determines him to seek for honey; but what would that signify if flowers supplied none? Faculties thrown down upon animals at random, and without reference to the objects amidst which they are placed, would not produce to them the services and benefits which we see; and if there be that reference, then there is intention.

Lastly, the solution fails entirely when applied to plants. The parts of plants answer their uses without any concurrence from the will or choice of the plant.

VI. Others have chosen to refer every thing to a *principle of order* in nature. A principle of order is the word; but what is meant by a principle of order as different from an intelligent Creator has not been explained either by definition or example; and without such explanation it should seem to be a mere substitution of words for reasons, names for causes. Order itself is only the adaptation of means to an end: a principle of order, therefore, can only signify the mind and intention which so adapts them. Or, were it capable of being explained in any other sense, is there any experience, any analogy, to sustain it? Was a watch ever produced by a principle of order; and why might not a watch be so produced as well as an eye?

Furthermore, a principle of order, acting blindly and without choice, is negatived by the observation that order is not universal, which it would be if it issued from a constant and necessary principle, nor indiscriminate, which it would be if it issued from an unintelligent principle. Where order is wanted, there we find it; where order is not wanted, that is, where if it prevailed, it would be useless, there we do not find it. In the structure of the eye—for we adhere to our example—in the figure and position of its several parts, the most exact order is maintained. In the forms of rocks and mountains, in the lines which bound the coasts of continents and islands, in the shape of bays and promontories, no order whatever is perceived, because it would have been superfluous. No useful purpose would have arisen from molding rocks and mountains into regular solids, bounding the channel of the ocean by geometrical curves, or from the map of the world resembling a table of diagrams in Euclid's *Elements* or Simpson's "Conic Sections."

VII. Lastly, the confidence which we place in our observations upon the works of nature, in the marks which we discover of contrivance, choice, and design, and in our reasoning upon the proofs afforded us, ought not to be shaken, as it is sometimes attempted to be done, by bringing forward to our view our own ignorance, or rather the general imperfection of our knowledge of nature. Nor, in many cases, ought this consideration to affect us even when it respects some parts of the subject immediately under our notice. True fortitude of understanding consists in not suffering what we know, to be disturbed by what we do not know. If we perceive a useful end, and means adapted to that end, we perceive enough for our conclusion. If these things be clear, no matter what is obscure. The argument is finished. For instance, if the utility of vision to the animal which enjoys it, and the adaptation of the *eye* to this office, be evident and certain—and I can mention nothing which is more so—ought it to prejudice the inference which we draw from these premises, that we cannot explain the use of the spleen? Nay, more, if there be parts of the eye, namely, the cornea, the crystalline, the retina, in their substance, figure and position, manifestly suited to the formation of an image by the refraction of rays of light, at least as manifestly as the glasses and tubes of a dioptric telescope are suited to that purpose, it concerns not the proof which these afford of design, and of a designer, that there may perhaps be other parts, certain muscles, for instance, or nerves in the same eye, of the agency or effect of which we can give no account, any more than we should be inclined to doubt, or ought to doubt, about the construction of a telescope, namely, for what purpose it was constructed, or whether it was constructed at all, because there belonged to it certain screws and pins, the use or action of which we did not comprehend. I take it to be a general way of infusing doubts and scruples into the mind, to recur to its own ignorance, its own imbecility—to tell us that upon these subjects we know little; that little imperfectly; or rather, that we know nothing properly about the matter. These suggestions so fall in with our consciousness as sometimes to produce a general distrust of our faculties and our conclusions. But this is an unfounded jealousy. The uncertainty of one thing does not necessarily affect the certainty of another thing. Our ignorance of many points need not suspend our assurance of a few. Before we yield, in any particular instance, to the skepticism which this sort of insinuation would induce, we ought accurately to ascertain whether our ignorance or doubt concern those precise points upon which our conclusion rests. Other points are nothing. Our ignorance of other points may be of no consequence to these, though they be points, in various respects, of great importance. A just reasoner removes from his consideration not only what he knows, but what he does not know, touching matters not strictly connected with his argument, that is, not forming the very steps of his deduction: beyond these, his knowledge and his ignorance are alike relative.

DAVID HUME

1.13   Criticisms of the Analogy

Not to lose any time in circumlocutions, said Cleanthes, addressing himself to Demea, much less in replying to the pious declamations of Philo, I shall briefly explain how I conceive this matter. Look round the world: Contemplate the whole and every part of it: You will find it to be nothing but one great machine, subdivided into an infinite number of lesser machines, which again admit of subdivisions to a degree beyond what human senses and faculties can trace and explain. All these various machines, and even their most minute parts, are adjusted to each other with an accuracy which ravishes into admiration all men who have ever contemplated them. The curious adapting of means to ends, throughout all nature, resembles exactly, though it much exceeds, the productions of human contrivance—of human design, thought, wisdom, and intelligence. Since therefore the effects resemble each other, we are led to infer, by all the rules of analogy, that the causes also resemble, and that the Author of Nature is somewhat similar to the mind of man, though possessed of much larger faculties, proportioned to the grandeur of the work which he has executed. By this argument a posteriori, and by this argument alone, do we prove at once the existence of a Deity and his similarity to human mind and intelligence.

I shall be so free, Cleanthes, said Demea, as to tell you that from the beginning I could not approve of your conclusion concerning the similarity of the Deity to men, still less can I approve of the mediums by which you endeavor to establish it. What! No demonstration of the Being of God! No abstract arguments! No proofs a priori! Are these which have hitherto been so much insisted on by philosophers all fallacy, all sophism? Can we reach no farther in this subject than experience and probability? I will say not that this is betraying the cause of a Deity; but surely, by this affected candor, you

From David Hume, *Dialogues Concerning Natural Religion* (1779), Parts II, V, and VIII.

give advantages to atheists which they never could obtain by the mere dint of argument and reasoning.

What I chiefly scruple in this subject, said Philo, is not so much that all religious arguments are by Cleanthes reduced to experience, as that they appear not to be even the most certain and irrefragable of that inferior kind. That a stone will fall, that fire will burn, that the earth has solidity, we have observed a thousand and a thousand times; and when any new instance of this nature is presented, we draw without hesitation the accustomed inference. The exact similarity of the cases gives us a perfect assurance of a similar event, and a stronger evidence is never desired nor sought after. But wherever you depart, in the least, from the similarity of the cases, you diminish proportionably the evidence; and may at last bring it to a very weak *analogy,* which is confessedly liable to error and uncertainty. After having experienced the circulation of the blood in human creatures, we make no doubt that it takes place in Titius and Maevius; but from its circulation in frogs and fishes it is only a presumption, though a strong one, from analogy that it takes place in men and other animals. The analogical reasoning is much weaker when we infer the circulation of the sap in vegetables from our experience that the blood circulates in animals; and those who hastily followed that imperfect analogy are found, by more accurate experiments, to have been mistaken.

If we see a house, Cleanthes, we conclude, with the greatest certainty, that it had an architect or builder because this is precisely that species of effect which we have experienced to proceed from that species of cause. But surely you will not affirm that the universe bears such a resemblance to a house that we can with the same certainty infer a similar cause, or that the analogy is here entire and perfect. The dissimilitude is so striking that the utmost you can here pretend to is a guess, a conjecture, a presumption concerning a similar cause; and how that pretension will be received in the world, I leave you to consider.

It would surely be very ill received, replied Cleanthes; and I should be deservedly blamed and detested did I allow that the proofs of a Deity amounted to no more than a guess or conjecture. But is the whole adjustment of means to ends in a house and in the universe so slight a resemblance? the economy of final causes? the order, proportion, and arrangement of every part? Steps of a stair are plainly contrived that human legs may use them in mounting; and this inference is certain and infallible. Human legs are also contrived for walking and mounting; and this inference, I allow, is not altogether so certain because of the dissimilarity which you remark; but does it, therefore, deserve the name only of presumption or conjecture?

Good God! cried Demea, interrupting him, where are we? Zealous defenders of religion allow that the proofs of a Deity fall short of perfect evidence! And you, Philo, on whose assistance I depended in proving the adorable mysteriousness of the Divine Nature, do you assent to all these extravagant opinions of Cleanthes? For what other name can I give them?

or, why spare my censure when such principles are advanced, supported by such an authority, before so young a man as Pamphilus?

You seem not to apprehend, replied Philo, that I argue with Cleanthes in his own way, and, by showing him the dangerous consequences of his tenets, hope at last to reduce him to our opinion. But what sticks most with you, I observe, is the representation which Cleanthes has made of the argument *a posteriori*; and, finding that the argument is likely to escape your hold and vanish into air, you think it so disguised that you can scarcely believe it to be set in its true light. Now, however much I may dissent, in other respects, from the dangerous principle of Cleanthes, I must allow that he has fairly represented that argument, and I shall endeavor so to state the matter to you that you will entertain no further scruples with regard to it.

Were a man to abstract from everything which he knows or has seen, he would be altogether incapable, merely from his own ideas, to determine what kind of scene the universe must be, or to give the preference to one state or situation of things above another. For as nothing which he clearly conceives could be esteemed impossible or implying a contradiction, every chimera of his fancy would be upon an equal footing; nor could he assign any just reason why he adheres to one idea or system, and rejects the others which are equally possible.

Again, after he opens his eyes and contemplates the world as it really is, it would be impossible for him at first to assign the cause of any one event, much less of the whole of things, or of the universe. He might set his fancy a rambling, and she might bring him in an infinite variety of reports and representations. These would all be possible; but, being all equally possible, he would never of himself give a satisfactory account for his preferring one of them to the rest. Experience alone can point out to him the true cause of any phenomenon.

Now, according to this method of reasoning, Demea, it follows (and is, indeed, tacitly allowed by Cleanthes himself) that order, arrangement, or the adjustment of final causes, is not of itself any proof of design, but only so far as it has been experienced to proceed from that principle. For aught we can know *a priori*, matter may contain the source or spring of order originally within itself, as well as mind does; and there is no more difficulty in conceiving that the several elements, from an internal unknown cause, may fall into the most exquisite arrangement, than to conceive that their ideas, in the great universal mind, from a like internal unknown cause, fall into that arrangement. The equal possibility of both these suppositions is allowed. But, by experience, we find (according to Cleanthes) that there is a difference between them. Throw several pieces of steel together, without shape or form, they will never arrange themselves so as to compose a watch. Stone and mortar and wood, without an architect, never erect a house. But the ideas in a human mind, we see, by an unknown, inexplicable economy, arrange themselves so as to form the plan of a watch or house. Experience, therefore, proves that there is an original principle of order in mind, not in matter.

From similar effects we infer similar causes. The adjustment of means to ends is alike in the universe, as in a machine of human contrivance. The causes, therefore, must be resembling.

I was from the beginning scandalized, I must own, with this resemblance which is asserted between the Deity and human creatures, and must conceive it to imply such a degradation of the Supreme Being as no sound theist could endure. With your assistance, therefore, Demea, I shall endeavor to defend what you justly call the adorable mysteriousness of the Divine Nature, and shall refute this reasoning of Cleanthes, provided he allows that I have made a fair representation of it.

When Cleanthes had assented, Philo, after a short pause, proceeded in the following manner.

That all inferences, Cleanthes, concerning fact are founded on experience, and that all experimental reasonings are founded on the supposition that similar causes prove similar effects, and similar effects similar causes, I shall not at present much dispute with you. But observe, I entreat you, with what extreme caution all just reasoners proceed in the transferring of experiments to similar cases. Unless the cases be exactly similar, they repose no perfect confidence in applying their past observation to any particular phenomenon. Every alteration of circumstances occasions a doubt concerning the event; and it requires new experiments to prove certainly that the new circumstances are of no moment or importance. A change in bulk, situation, arrangement, age, disposition of the air, or surrounding bodies—any of these particulars may be attended with the most unexpected consequences. And unless the objects be quite familiar to us, it is the highest temerity to expect with assurance, after any of these changes, an event similar to that which before fell under our observation. The slow and deliberate steps of philosophers here, if anywhere, are distinguished from the precipitate march of the vulgar, who, hurried on by the smallest similitude, are incapable of all discernment or consideration.

But can you think, Cleanthes, that your usual phlegm and philosophy have been preserved in so wide a step as you have taken when you compared to the universe houses, ships, furniture, machines; and, from their similarity in some circumstances, inferred a similarity in their causes? Thought, design, intelligence, such as we discover in men and other animals, is no more than one of the springs and principles of the universe, as well as heat or cold, attraction or repulsion, and is a hundred others which fall under daily observation. It is an active cause by which some particular parts of nature, we find, produce alterations on other parts. But can a conclusion, with any propriety, be transferred from parts to the whole? Does not the great disproportion bar all comparison and inference? From observing the growth of a hair, can we learn anything concerning the generation of a man? Would the manner of a leaf's blowing, even though perfectly known, afford us any instruction concerning the vegetation of a tree? But allowing that we were to take the *operations* of one part of nature upon another for the foundation of our judgment concerning the *origin* of the whole (which never can be admitted), yet why select so minute, so weak, so bounded a principle as the reason and design of animals is found to be upon this planet? What peculiar privilege has this little agitation of the brain which we call *thought*, that we must thus make it the model of the whole universe? Our partiality in our own favor does indeed present it on all occasions, but sound philosophy ought carefully to guard against so natural an illusion.

So far from admitting, continued Philo, that the operations of a part can afford us any just conclusion concerning the origin of the whole, I will not allow any one part to form a rule for another part if the latter be very remote from the former. Is there any reasonable ground to conclude that the inhabitants of other planets possess thought, intelligence, reason, or anything similar to these faculties in men? When nature has so extremely diversified her manner of operation in this small globe, can we imagine that she incessantly copies herself throughout so immense a universe? And if thought, as we may well suppose, be confined merely to this narrow corner and has even there so limited a sphere of action, with what propriety can we assign it for the original cause of all things? The narrow views of a peasant who makes his domestic economy the rule for the government of kingdoms is in comparison a pardonable sophism.

But were we ever so much assured that a thought and reason resembling the human were to be found throughout the whole universe, and were its activity elsewhere vastly greater and more commanding than it appears in this globe; yet I cannot see why the operations of a world constituted, arranged, adjusted, can with any propriety be extended to a world which is in its embryo-state, and is advancing towards that constitution and arrangement. By observation we know somewhat of the economy, action, and nourishment of a finished animal; but we must transfer with great caution that observation to the growth of a foetus in the womb, and still more to the formation of an animalcule in the loins of its male parent. Nature, we find, even from our limited experience, possesses an infinite number of springs and principles which incessantly discover themselves on every change of her position and situation. And what new and unknown principles would actuate her in so new and unknown a situation as that of the formation of a universe, we cannot, without the utmost temerity, pretend to determine.

A very small part of this great system, during a very short time, is very imperfectly discovered to us; and do we thence pronounce decisively concerning the origin of the whole?

Admirable conclusion! Stone, wood, brick, iron, brass, have not, at this time, in this minute globe of earth, an order or arrangement without human art and contrivance; therefore, the universe could not originally attain its order and arrangement without something similar to human art. But is a part of nature a rule for another part very wide of the former? Is it a rule for the whole? Is a very small part a rule for the universe? Is nature in one situation a certain rule for nature in another situation vastly different from the former?

And can you blame me, Cleanthes, if I here imitate the prudent reserve of Simonides, who, according to the noted story, being asked by Hiero, *What God was?* desired a day to think of it, and then two days more; and after that manner continually prolonged the term, without ever bringing in his definition or description? Could you even blame me if I had answered, at first, *that I did not know*, and was sensible that this subject lay vastly beyond the reach of my faculties? You might cry out sceptic and railer, as much as you pleased; but, having found in so many other subjects much more familiar the imperfections and even contradictions of human reason, I never should expect any success from its feeble conjectures in a subject so sublime and so remote from the sphere of our observation. When two *species* of objects have always been observed to be conjoined together, I can *infer*, by custom, the existence of one wherever I *see* the existence of the other; and this I call an argument from experience. But how this argument can have place where the objects, as in the present case, are single, individual, without parallel or specific resemblance, may be difficult to explain. And will any man tell me with a serious countenance that an orderly universe must arise from some thought and art like the human because we have experience of it? To ascertain this reasoning it were requisite that we had experience of the origin of worlds; and it is not sufficient, surely, that we have seen ships and cities arise from human art and contrivance. . . .

Now, Cleanthes, said Philo, with an air of alacrity and triumph, mark the consequences. *First*, by this method of reasoning you renounce all claim to infinity in any of the attributes of the Deity. For, as the cause ought only to be proportioned to the effect, and the effect, so far as it falls under our cognizance, is not infinite, what pretensions have we, upon your suppositions, to ascribe that attribute to the divine Being? You will still insist that, by removing him so much from all similarity to human creatures, we give in to the most arbitrary hypothesis, and at the same time weaken all proofs of his existence.

Secondly, you have no reason, on your theory, for ascribing perfection to the Deity, even in his finite capacity; or for supposing him free from every error, mistake, or incoherence, in his undertakings. There are many inexplicable difficulties in the works of nature which, if we allow a perfect author to be proved *a priori*, are easily solved, and become only seeming difficulties from the narrow capacity of man, who cannot trace infinite relations. But according to your method of reasoning, these difficulties become all real; and, perhaps, will be insisted on as new instances of likeness to human art and contrivance. At least, you must acknowledge that it is impossible for us to tell, from our limited views, whether this system contains any great faults or deserves any considerable praise if compared to other possible and even real systems. Could a peasant, if the *Aeneid* were read to him, pronounce that poem to be absolutely faultless, or even assign to it its proper rank among the productions of human wit, he who had never seen any other production? But were this world ever so perfect a production, it must still remain uncertain whether all the excellences of the work can justly be ascribed to the workman. If we survey a ship, what an exalted idea must we form of the ingenuity of the carpenter who framed so complicated, useful, and beautiful a machine? And what surprise must we feel when we find him a stupid mechanic who imitated others, and copied an art which, through a long succession of ages, after multiplied trials, mistakes, corrections, deliberations, and controversies, had been gradually improving? Many worlds might have been botched and bungled, throughout an eternity, ere this system was struck out; much labor lost; many fruitless trials made; and a slow but continued improvement carried on during infinite ages in the art of world-making. In such subjects, who can determine where the truth, nay, who can conjecture where the probability lies, amidst a great number of hypotheses which may be proposed, and a still greater which may be imagined?

And what shadow of an argument, continued Philo, can you produce from your hypothesis to prove the unity of the Deity? A great number of men join in building a house or ship, in rearing a city, in framing a commonwealth; why may not several deities combine in contriving and framing a world? This is only so much greater similarity to human affairs. By sharing the work among several, we may so much further limit the attributes of each, and get rid of that extensive power and knowledge which must be supposed in one deity, and which, according to you, can only serve to weaken the proof of his existence. And if such foolish, such vicious creatures as man can yet often unite in framing and executing one plan, how much more those deities or demons, whom we may suppose several degrees more perfect?

To multiply causes without necessity is indeed contrary to true philosophy, but this principle applies not to the present case. Were one deity antecedently proved by your theory who were possessed of every attribute requisite to the production of the universe, it would be needless, I own (though not absurd), to suppose any other deity existent. But while it is still a question whether all these attributes are united in one subject or dispersed among several independent beings; by what phenomena in nature can we pretend to decide the controversy? Where we see a body raised in a scale, we are sure that there is in the opposite scale, however concealed from sight, some counterposing weight equal to it; but it is still allowed to doubt whether that weight be an aggregate of several distinct bodies or one uniform united mass. And if the weight requisite very much exceeds anything which we have ever seen conjoined in any single body, the former supposition becomes still more probable and natural. An intelligent being of such vast power and capacity as is necessary to produce the universe—or, to speak in the language of ancient philosophy, so prodigious an animal—exceeds all analogy and even comprehension.

But further, Cleanthes, men are mortal, and renew their species by generation; and this is common to all living creatures. The two great sexes of male and female, says Milton, animate the world. Why must this circumstance, so universal, so essential, be executed from those numerous and limited deities? Behold, then, the theogeny of ancient times brought back upon us.

And why not become a perfect anthropomorphite? Why not assert the deity or deities to be corporeal, and to have eyes, a nose, mouth, ears, etc.? Epicurus maintained that no man had ever seen reason but in a human figure; therefore, the gods must have a human figure. And this argument, which is deservedly so much ridiculed by Cicero, becomes, according to you, solid and philosophical.

In a word, Cleanthes, a man who follows your hypothesis is able, perhaps, to assert or conjecture that the universe sometime arose from something like design; but beyond that position he cannot ascertain one single circumstance, and is left afterwards to fix every point of his theology by the utmost license of fancy and hypothesis. This world, for aught he knows, is very faulty and imperfect, compared to a superior standard; and was only the first rude essay of some infant deity who afterwards abandoned it, ashamed of his lame performance; it is the work only of some dependent, inferior deity, and is the object of derision to his superiors; it is the production of old age and dotage in some superannuated deity; and ever since his death has run on at adventures, from the first impulse and active force which it received from him. You justly give signs of horror, Demea, at these strange suppositions; but these, and a thousand more of the same kind, are Cleanthes' suppositions, not mine. From the moment the attributes of the Deity are supposed finite, all these have place. And I cannot, for my part, think that so wild and unsettled a system of theology is, in any respect, preferable to none at all. . . .

What you ascribe to the fertility of my invention, replied Philo, is entirely owing to the nature of the subject. In subjects adapted to the narrow compass of human reason there is commonly but one determination which carries probability or conviction with it; and to a man of sound judgment all other suppositions but that one appear entirely absurd and chimerical. But in such questions as the present, a hundred contradictory views may preserve a kind of imperfect analogy, and invention has here full scope to exert itself. Without any great effort of thought, I believe that I could, in an instant, propose other systems of cosmogony which would have some faint appearance of truth; though it is a thousand, a million to one if either yours or any one of mine be the true system.

For instance, what if I should revive the old Epicurean hypothesis? This is commonly, and I believe justly, esteemed the most absurd system that has yet been proposed; yet I know not whether, with a few alterations, it might not be brought to bear a faint appearance of probability. Instead of supposing matter infinite, as Epicurus did, let us suppose it finite. A finite number of particles is only susceptible of finite transpositions; and it must happen, in an eternal duration, that every possible order or position must be tried an infinite number of times. This world, therefore, with all its events, even the

most minute, has before been produced and destroyed, and will again be produced and destroyed, without any bounds and limitations. No one who has
a conception of the powers of infinite, in comparison of finite, will ever
scruple this determination.

But this supposes, said Demea, that matter can acquire motion without
any voluntary agent or first mover.

And where is the difficulty, replied Philo, of that supposition? Every event,
before experience, is equally difficult and incomprehensible; and every event,
after experience, is equally easy and intelligible. Motion, in many instances,
from gravity, from elasticity, from electricity, begins in matter, without any
known voluntary agent; and to suppose always, in these cases, an unknown
voluntary agent is mere hypothesis—and hypothesis attended with no advantages. The beginning of motion in matter itself is as conceivable *a priori*
as its communication from mind and intelligence.

Besides, why may not motion have been propagated by impulse through
all eternity, and the same stock of it, or nearly the same, be still upheld in the
universe? As much as is lost by the composition of motion, as much is gained
by its resolution. And whatever the causes are, the fact is certain that matter
is and always has been in continual agitation, as far as human experience or
tradition reaches. There is not probably, at present, in the whole universe,
one particle of matter at absolute rest.

And this very consideration, too, continued Philo, which we have stumbled
on in the course of the argument suggests a new hypothesis of cosmogony
that is not absolutely absurd and improbable. Is there a system, an order, an
economy of things, by which matter can preserve that perpetual agitation
which seems essential to it, and yet maintain a constancy in the forms which
it produces? There certainly is such an economy, for this is actually the case
with the present world. The continual motion of matter, therefore, in less
than infinite transpositions, must produce this economy or order; and, by its
very nature, that order, when once established, supports itself for many ages
if not to eternity. But wherever matter is so poised, arranged, and adjusted, as
to continue in perpetual motion, and yet preserve a constancy in the forms,
its situation must, of necessity, have all the same appearance of art and contrivance which we observe at present. All the parts of each form must have a
relation to each other and to the whole; and the whole itself must have a relation to the other parts of the universe, to the element in which the form subsists, to the materials with which it repairs its waste and decay, and to every
other form which is hostile or friendly. A defect in any of these particulars
destroys the form; and the matter of which it is composed is again set loose,
and is thrown into irregular motions and fermentations till it unite itself to
some other regular form. If no such form be prepared to receive it, and if
there be a great quantity of this corrupted matter in the universe, the universe
itself is entirely disordered, whether it be the feeble embryo of a world in its
first beginnings that is thus destroyed or the rotten carcass of one languishing

in old age and infirmity. In either case, a chaos ensues till infinite though innumerable revolutions produce, at last, some forms whose parts and organs are so adjusted as to support the forms amidst a continued succession of matter.

Suppose (for we shall endeavor to vary the expression) that matter were thrown into any position by a blind, unguided force; it is evident that this first position must, in all probability, be the most confused and most disorderly imaginable, without any resemblance to those works of human contrivance which, along with a symmetry of parts, discover an adjustment of means to ends and a tendency to self-preservation. If the actuating force cease after this operation, matter must remain forever in disorder, and continue an immense chaos, without any proportion or activity. But suppose that the actuating force, whatever it be, still continues in matter, this first position will immediately give place to a second which will likewise, in all probability, be as disorderly as the first, and so on through many successions of changes and revolutions. No particular order or position ever continues a moment unaltered. The original force, still remaining in activity, gives a perpetual restlessness to matter. Every possible situation is produced, and instantly destroyed. If a glimpse or dawn of order appears for a moment, it is instantly hurried away and confounded by that never-ceasing force which actuates every part of matter.

Thus the universe goes on for many ages in a continued succession of chaos and disorder. But is it not possible that it may settle at last, so as not to lose its motion and active force (for that we have supposed inherent in it), yet so as to preserve a uniformity of appearance, amidst the continual motion and fluctuation of its parts? This we find to be the case with the universe at present. Every individual is perpetually changing, and every part of every individual; and yet the whole remains, in appearance, the same. May we not hope for such a position or rather be assured of it from the eternal revolutions of unguided matter; and may not this account for all the appearing wisdom and contrivance which is in the universe? Let us contemplate the subject a little, and we shall find that this adjustment if attained by matter of a seeming stability in the forms, with a real and perpetual revolution or motion of parts, affords a plausible, if not a true, solution of the difficulty.

It is in vain, therefore, to insist upon the uses of the parts in animals or vegetables, and their curious adjustment to each other. I would fain know how an animal could subsist unless its parts were so adjusted? Do we not find that it immediately perishes whenever this adjustment ceases, and that its matter, corrupting, tries some new form? It happens indeed that the parts of the world are so well adjusted that some regular form immediately lays claim to this corrupted matter; and if it were not so, could the world subsist? Must it not dissolve, as well as the animal, and pass through new positions and situations till in great but finite succession it fall, at last, into the present or some such order?

It is well, replied Cleanthes, you told us that this hypothesis was suggested on a sudden, in the course of the argument. Had you had leisure to examine it, you would soon have perceived the insuperable objections to which it is exposed. No form, you say, can subsist unless it possess those powers and organs requisite for its subsistence; some new order or economy must be tried, and so on, without intermission, till at last some order which can support and maintain itself is fallen upon. But according to this hypothesis, whence arise the many conveniences and advantages which men and all animals possess? Two eyes, two ears are not absolutely necessary for the subsistence of the species. Human race might have been propagated and preserved without horses, dogs, cows, sheep, and those innumerable fruits and products which serve to our satisfaction and enjoyment. If no camels had been created for the use of man in the sandy deserts of Africa and Arabia, would the world have been dissolved? If no loadstone had been framed to give that wonderful and useful direction to the needle, would human society and the human kind have been immediately extinguished? Though the maxims of nature be in general very frugal, yet instances of this kind are far from being rare; and any one of them is a sufficient proof of design—and of a benevolent design—which gave rise to the order and arrangement of the universe.

At least, you may safely infer, said Philo, that the foregoing hypothesis is so far incomplete and imperfect, which I shall not scruple to allow. But can we ever reasonably expect greater success in any attempts of this nature? Or can we ever hope to erect a system of cosmogony that will be liable to no exceptions, and will contain no circumstance repugnant to our limited and imperfect experience of the analogy of nature? Your theory itself cannot surely pretend to any such advantage; even though you have run into *anthropomorphism*, the better to preserve a conformity to common experience. Let us once more put it to trial. In all instances which we have ever seen, ideas are copied from real objects, and are ectypal, not archetypal, to express myself in learned terms. You reverse this order and give thought the precedence. In all instances which we have ever seen, thought has no influence upon matter except where that matter is so conjoined with it as to have an equal reciprocal influence upon it. No animal can move immediately anything but the members of its own body; and, indeed, the equality of action and reaction seems to be an universal law of nature; but your theory implies a contradiction to this experience. These instances, with many more which it were easy to collect (particularly the supposition of a mind or system of thought that is eternal or, in other words, an animal ingenerable and immortal)—these instances, I say, may teach all of us sobriety in condemning each other, and let us see that as no system of this kind ought ever to be received from a slight analogy, so neither ought any to be rejected on account of a small incongruity. For that is an inconvenience from which we can justly pronounce no one to be exempted.

All religious systems, it is confessed, are subject to great and insuperable difficulties. Each disputant triumphs in his turn, while he carries on an offensive war, and exposes the absurdities, barbarities, and pernicious tenets of his antagonist. But all of them, on the whole, prepare a complete triumph for the *sceptic*, who tells them that no system ought ever to be embraced with regard to such subjects; for this plain reason, that no absurdity ought ever to be assented to with regard to any subject. A total suspense of judgment is here our only reasonable resource. And if every attack, as is commonly observed, and no defence among theologians is successful, how complete must be *his* victory who remains always, with all mankind, on the offensive, and has himself no fixed station or abiding city which he is ever, on any occasion, obliged to defend?

R. G. SWINBURNE

1.14   *The Argument from Design*

The object of this paper[1] is to show that there are no valid formal objections to the argument from design, so long as the argument is articulated with sufficient care. In particular I wish to analyse Hume's attack on the argument in *Dialogues Concerning Natural Religion* and to show that none of the formal objections made therein by Philo have any validity against a carefully articulated version of the argument.

The argument from design is an argument from the order or regularity of things in the world to a god or, more precisely, a very powerful free non-embodied rational agent, who is responsible for that order. By a body I understand a part of the material universe subject, at any rate partially, to an agent's direct control, to be contrasted with other parts not thus subject. An agent's body marks the limits to what he can directly control; he can only control other parts of the universe by moving his body. An agent who could directly control any part of the universe would not be embodied. Thus ghosts, if they existed, would be non-embodied agents, because there are no particular pieces of matter subject to their direct control, but any piece of matter may be so subject. I use the word "design" in such a way that it is not analytic that if anything evinces design, an agent designed it, and so it becomes a synthetic question whether the design of the world shows the activity of a designer.

The argument, taken by itself, as was admitted in the *Dialogues* by

From *Philosophy* 43 (1968). Reprinted by permission of the author and the editors.
[1]I am most grateful to Christopher Williams and to colleagues at Hull for their helpful criticisms of an earlier version of this paper.

Cleanthes the proponent of the argument, does not show that the designer of the world is omnipotent, omniscient, totally good, etc. Nor does it show that he is the God of Abraham, Isaac, and Jacob. To make these points, further arguments would be needed. The isolation of the argument from design from the web of Christian apologetic is perhaps a somewhat unnatural step, but necessary in order to analyse its structure. My claim is that the argument does not commit any formal fallacy, and by this I mean that it keeps to the canons of argument about matters of fact and does not violate any of them. It is, however, an argument by analogy. It argues from an analogy between the order of the world and the products of human art to a god responsible for the former, in some ways similar to man who is responsible for the latter. And even if there are no formal fallacies in the argument, one unwilling to admit the conclusion might still claim that the analogy was too weak and remote for him to have to admit it, that the argument gave only negligible support to the conclusion which remained improbable. In defending the argument I will leave to the objector this way of escape from its conclusion.

I will begin by setting forward the argument from design in a more careful and precise way than Cleanthes did.

There are in the world two kinds of regularity or order, and all empirical instances of order are such because they evince one or other or both kinds of order. These are the regularities of co-presence or spatial order, and regularities of succession, or temporal order. Regularities of co-presence are patterns of spatial order at some one instant of time. An example of a regularity of co-presence would be a town with all its roads at right angles to each other, or a section of books in a library arranged in alphabetical order of authors. Regularities of succession are simple patterns of behaviour of objects, such as their behaviour in accordance with the laws of nature—for example, Newton's law of gravitation, which holds universally to a very high degree of approximation, that all bodies attract each other with forces proportional to the product of their masses and inversely proportional to the square of their distance apart.

Many of the striking examples of order in the world evince an order which is the result both of a regularity of co-presence and of a regularity of succession. A working car consists of many parts so adjusted to each other that it follows the instructions of the driver delivered by his pulling and pushing a few levers and buttons and turning a wheel to take passengers whither he wishes. Its order arises because its parts are so arranged at some instant (regularity of co-presence) that, the laws of nature being as they are (regularity of succession), it brings about the result neatly and efficiently. The order of living animals and plants likewise results from regularities of both types.

Men who marvel at the order of the world may marvel at either or both of the regularities of co-presence and of succession. The men of the eighteenth century, that great century of "reasonable religion," were struck almost exclusively by the regularities of co-presence. They marvelled at the design and orderly operations of animals and plants; but since they largely took for granted the regularities of succession, what struck them about the animals and plants, as to a lesser extent about machines made by men, was the subtle and coherent arrangement of their millions of parts. Paley's *Natural Theology* dwells mainly on details of comparative anatomy, on eyes and ears and muscles and bones arranged with minute precision so as to operate with high efficiency, and Hume's Cleanthes produces the same kind of examples: "Consider, anatomise the eye, survey its structure and contrivance, and tell me from your own feeling, if the idea of a contriver does not immediately flow in upon you with a force like that of sensation."[2]

Those who argue from the existence of regularities of copresence other than those produced by men to the existence of a god who produced them are, however, in many respects on slippery ground when compared with those who rely for their premises on regularities of succession. We shall see several of these weaknesses later in considering Hume's objections to the argument, but it is worth while noting two of them at the outset. First, although the world contains many striking regularities of co-presence (some few of which are caused by human agency), it also contains many examples of spatial disorder. The uniform distribution of the galactic clusters is a marvellous example of spatial order, but the arrangement of trees in an African jungle is a marvellous example of spatial disorder. Although the proponent of the argument may then proceed to argue that in an important sense or from some point of view (e.g., utility to man) the order vastly exceeds the disorder, he has to argue for this in-no-way-obvious proposition.

Secondly the proponent of the argument runs the risk that the regularities of co-presence may be explained in terms of something else by a normal scientific explanation[3] in a way that the regularities of succession could not possibly be. A scientist could show that a regularity of co-presence R arose from an apparently disordered state D by means of the normal operation of the laws of nature. This would not entirely "explain away" the regularity of co-presence, because the proponent of this argument from design might then argue that the apparently disordered state D really had a latent order, being the kind of state which, when the laws of nature operate, turns into a manifestly ordered one. As long as only few of the physically possible states of apparent disorder were states of latent order, the existence of many states of latent order would be an important contingent fact which could form a premiss for an argument from design. But there is always the risk that sci-

---

[2]David Hume, *Dialogues Concerning Natural Religion*, ed. H. D. Aiken (New York, 1948), p. 28.

[3]I understand by a "normal scientific explanation" one conforming to the pattern of deductive or statistical explanation utilised in paradigm empirical sciences such as physics and chemistry, elucidated in recent years by Hempel, Braithwaite, Popper, and others. Although there are many uncertain points about scientific explanation, those to which I appeal in the text are accepted by all philosophers of science.

entists might show that most states of apparent disorder were states of latent order, that is, that if the world lasted long enough considerable order must emerge from whichever of many initial states it began. If a scientist showed that, he would have explained by normal scientific explanation the existence of regularities of co-presence in terms of something completely different. The eighteenth-century proponents of the argument from design did not suspect this danger, and hence the devastating effect of Darwin's Theory of Evolution by Natural Selection on those who accepted their argument. For Darwin showed that the regularities of co-presence of the animal and plant kingdoms had evolved by natural processes from an apparently disordered state and would have evolved equally from many other apparently disordered states. Whether all regularities of co-presence can be fully explained in this kind of way no one yet knows, but the danger remains for the proponent of an argument from design of this kind that they can be.

However, those who argue from the operation of regularities of succession other than those produced by men to the existence of a god who produces them do not run into either of these difficulties. Regularities of succession (other than those produced by men), unlike regularities of co-presence, are all-pervasive. Simple natural laws rule almost all successions of events. Nor can regularities of succession be given a normal scientific explanation in terms of something else. For the normal scientific explanation of the operation of a regularity of succession is in terms of the operation of a yet more general regularity of succession. Note too that a normal scientific explanation of the existence of regularities of co-presence in terms of something different, if it can be provided, is explanation in terms of regularities of succession.

For these reasons the proponent of the argument from design does much better to rely for his premiss more on regularities of succession. St. Thomas Aquinas, wiser than the men of the eighteenth century, did just this. He puts forward an argument from design as his fifth and last way to prove the existence of God, and gives his premiss as follows:

"The fifth way is based on the guidedness of nature. An orderedness of actions to an end is observed in all bodies obeying natural laws, even when they lack awareness. For their behaviour hardly ever varies, and will practically always turn out well; which shows that they truly tend to a goal, and do not merely hit it by accident."[4] If we ignore any value judgment in "practically always turn out well," St. Thomas' argument is an argument from regularities of succession.

The most satisfactory premiss for the argument from design is then the operation of regularities of succession other than those produced by men, that is, the operation of natural laws. Almost all things almost always obey simple natural laws and so behave in a strikingly regular way. Given the

---

[4]St. Thomas Aquinas, *Summa Theologiae*, Ia.2.3. Trans. Timothy McDermott, o.p. (London, 1964).

premiss, what is our justification for proceeding to the conclusion that a very powerful free non-embodied rational agent is responsible for their behaving in that way? The justification which Aquinas gives is that "Nothing . . . that lacks awareness tends to a goal, except under the direction of someone with awareness and with understanding; the arrow, for example, requires an archer. Everything in nature, therefore, is directed to its goal by someone with understanding, and this we call 'God'."[5] A similar argument has been given by many religious apologists since Aquinas, but clearly as it stands it is guilty of the grossest *petitio principii*. Certainly *some* things which tend to a goal, tend to a goal because of a direction imposed upon them by someone "with awareness and with understanding." Did not the archer place the arrow and pull the string in a certain way the arrow would not tend to its goal. But whether *all* things which tend to a goal tend to a goal for this reason is the very question at issue, and that they do cannot be used as a premiss to prove the conclusion. We must therefore reconstruct the argument in a more satisfactory way.

The structure of any plausible argument from design can only be that the existence of a god responsible for the order in the world is a hypothesis well-confirmed on the basis of the evidence—viz., that contained in the premiss which we have now stated, and better confirmed than any other hypothesis. I shall begin by showing that there can be no other possible explanation for the operation of natural laws than the activity of a god, and then see to what extent the hypothesis is well confirmed on the basis of the evidence.

Almost all phenomena can, as we have seen, be explained by a normal scientific explanation in terms of the operation of natural laws on preceding states. There is, however, one other way of explaining natural phenomena, and that is explaining in terms of the rational choice of a free agent. When a man marries Jane rather than Anne, becomes a solicitor rather than a barrister, kills rather than shows mercy after considering arguments in favour of each course, he brings about a state of the world by his free and rational choice. To all appearances this is an entirely different way whereby states of the world may come about than through the operation of laws of nature on preceding states. Someone may object that it is necessary that physiological or other scientific laws operate in order for the agent to bring about effects. My answer is that certainly it is necessary that such laws operate in order for effects brought about directly by the agent to have ulterior consequences. But unless there are some effects which the agent brings about directly without the operation of scientific laws' acting on preceding physical states bringing them about, then these laws and states could fully explain the effects and there would be no need to refer in explaining them to the rational choice of an agent. True, the apparent freedom and rationality of the human will *may* prove an illusion. Man may have no more option what to do than a machine

---

[5]*Ibid.*

and be guided by an argument no more than is a piece of iron. But this has never yet been shown, and, in the absence of good philosophical and scientific argument to show it, I assume, what is apparent, that when a man acts by free and rational choice, his agency is the operation of a different kind of causality from that of scientific laws. The free choice of a rational agent is the only way of accounting for natural phenomena other than the way of normal scientific explanation, which is recognised as such by all men and has not been reduced to normal scientific explanation.

Almost all regularities of succession are the result of the normal operation of scientific laws. But to say this is simply to say that these regularities are instances of more general regularities. The operation of the most fundamental regularities clearly cannot be given a normal scientific explanation. If their operation is to receive an explanation and not merely to be left as a brute fact, that explanation must therefore be in terms of the rational choice of a free agent. What, then, are grounds for adopting this hypothesis, given that it is the only possible one?

The grounds are that we can explain some few regularities of succession as produced by rational agents and that the other regularities cannot be explained except in this way. Among the typical products of a rational agent acting freely are regularities both of co-presence and of succession. The alphabetical order of books on a library shelf is the result of the activity of the librarian who chose to arrange them thus. The order of the cards of a pack by suits and seniority in each suit is the result of the activity of the card-player who arranged them thus. Among examples of regularities of succession produced by men are the notes of a song sung by a singer or the movements of a dancer's body when he performs a dance in time with the accompanying instrument. Hence, knowing that some regularities of succession have such a cause, we postulate that they all have. An agent produces the celestial harmony like a man who sings a song. But at this point an obvious difficulty arises. The regularities of succession, such as songs which are produced by men, are produced by agents of comparatively small power, whose bodies we can locate. If an agent is responsible for the operation of the laws of nature, he must act directly on the whole universe, as we act directly on our bodies. Also he must be of immense power and intelligence compared with men. Hence he can only be somewhat similar to men, having, like them, intelligence and freedom of choice, yet unlike them in the degree of these and in not possessing a body. For a body, as I have distinguished it earlier, is a part of the universe subject to an agent's direct control, to be contrasted with other parts not thus subject. The fact that we are obliged to postulate on the basis of differences in the effects, differences in the causes, men and the god, weakens the argument. How much it weakens it depends on how great these differences are.

Our argument thus proves to be an argument by analogy and to exemplify a pattern common in scientific inference. As are caused by Bs. A*s are similar to As. Therefore—given that there is no more satisfactory explanation of the existence of A*s—they are produced by B*s similar to Bs. B*s are postulated to be similar in all respects to Bs except in so far as shown otherwise, viz., except in so far as the dissimilarities between As and A*s force us to postulate a difference. A well-known scientific example of this type of inference is as follows. Certain pressures (As) on the walls of containers are produced by billiard balls (Bs) with certain motions. Similar pressures (A*s) are produced on the walls of containers which contain not billiard balls but gases. Therefore, since we have no better explanation of the existence of the pressures, gases consist of particles (B*s) similar to billiard balls except in certain respects—e.g., size. By similar arguments, scientists have argued for the existence of many unobservables. Such an argument becomes weaker in so far as the properties which we are forced to attribute to the B*s because of the differences between the As and the A*s become different from those of the Bs. Nineteenth-century physicists postulated the existence of an elastic solid, the aether, to account for the propagation of light. But the way in which light was propagated turned out to have such differences (despite the similarities) from the way in which waves in solids are normally propagated that the physicists had to say that if there was an aether it had very many peculiar properties not possessed by normal liquids or solids. Hence they concluded that the argument for its existence was very weak. The proponent of the argument from design stresses the similarities between the regularities of succession produced by man and those which are laws of nature and so between men and the agent which he postulates as responsible for the laws of nature. The opponent of the argument stresses the dissimilarities. The degree of support which the conclusion obtains from the evidence depends on how great the similarities are.

The degree of support for the conclusion of an argument from analogy does not, however, depend merely on the similarities between the types of evidence but on the degree to which the resulting theory makes explanation of empirical matters more simple and coherent. In the case of the argument from design, the conclusion has an enormous simplifying effect on explanations of empirical matters. For if the conclusion is true, if a very powerful non-embodied rational agent is responsible for the operation of the laws of nature, then normal scientific explanation would prove to be personal explanation. That is, explanation of some phenomenon in terms of the operation of a natural law would ultimately be an explanation in terms of the operation of an agent. Hence (given an initial arrangement of matter) the principles of explanation of phenomena would have been reduced from two to one. It is a basic principle of explanation that we should postulate as few as possible kinds of explanation. To take a more mundane example—if we have as possible alternatives to explain physical phenomena by the operation of two kinds of force, the electromagnetic and the gravitational, and to explain physical phenomena in terms of the operation of only one kind of force, the gravitational, we ought always—*ceteris paribus*—to prefer the latter alternative. Since, as we have seen, we are obliged, at any rate at present, to use explanation in terms of the free choice of a rational agent in explaining many empirical phenomena, then if the amount of similarity between the order in the universe not produced by human agents and that produced by human agents makes it at all plausible to do so, we ought to postulate that an agent is responsible for the former as well as for the latter. So then in so far as regularities of succession produced by the operation of natural laws are similar to those produced by human agents, to postulate that a rational agent is responsible for them would indeed provide a simple unifying and coherent explanation of natural phenomena. What is there against taking this step? Simply that celebrated principle of explanation—*entia non sunt multiplicanda praeter necessitatem*—do not add a god to your ontology unless you have to. The issue turns on whether the evidence constitutes enough of a *necessitas* to compel us to multiply entities. Whether it does depends on how strong the analogy is between the regularities of succession produced by human agents and those produced by the operation of natural laws. I do not propose to assess the strength of the analogy but only to claim that everything turns on it. I claim that the inference from natural laws to a god responsible for them is of a perfectly proper type for inference about matters of fact, and that the only issue is whether the evidence is strong enough to allow us to affirm that it is probable that the conclusion is true.

Now that I have reconstructed the argument from design in what is, I hope, a logically impeccable form, I turn to consider Hume's criticisms of it, and I shall argue that all his criticisms alleging formal fallacies in the argument do not apply to it in the form in which I have stated it. This, we shall see, is largely because the criticisms are bad criticisms of the argument in any form but also in small part because Hume directed his fire against that form of the argument which used as its premiss the existence of regularities of co-presence other than those produced by men, and did not appeal to the operation of regularities of succession. I shall begin by considering one general point which he makes only in the *Enquiry* and then consider in turn all the objections which appear on the pages of the *Dialogues*.

1. The point which appears at the beginning of Hume's discussion of the argument in section XI of the *Enquiry* is a point which reveals the fundamental weakness of Hume's sceptical position. In discussing the argument, Hume puts forward as a general principle that "when we infer any particular cause from an effect, we must proportion the one to the other, and can never be allowed to ascribe to the cause any qualities but what are exactly sufficient to produce the effect."[6] Now, it is true that Hume uses this principle mainly to show that we are not justified in inferring that the god responsible for the

---

[6]David Hume, *An Enquiry Concerning Human Understanding*, ed. L. A. Selby-Bigge (2nd ed., 1902), p. 136.

design of the universe is totally good, omnipotent, and omniscient. I accept, as Cleanthes did, that the argument does not by itself lead to that conclusion. But Hume's use of the principle tends to cast doubt on the validity of the argument in the weaker form in which I am discussing it, for it seems to suggest that although we may conclude that whatever produced the regularity of the world was a regularity-producing object, we cannot go further and conclude that it is an agent who acts by choice, etc., for this would be to suppose more than we need in order to account for the effect. It is, therefore, important to realise that the principle is clearly false on our normal understanding of what are the criteria of inference about empirical matters. For the universal adoption of this celebrated principle would lead to the abandonment of science. Any scientist who told us only that the cause of E and E-producing characteristics would not add an iota to our knowledge. Explanation of matters of fact consists in postulating on reasonable grounds that the cause of an effect has certain characteristics other than those sufficient to produce the effect.

2. Two objections seem to be telescoped in the following passage of the *Dialogues*. "When two *species* of objects have always been observed to be conjoined together, I can *infer* by custom the existence of one wherever I *see* the existence of the other; and this I call an argument from experience. But how this argument can have place where the objects, as in the present case, are single, individual, without parallel or specific resemblance, may be difficult to explain."[7] One argument here seems to be that we can only infer from an observed A to an unobserved B when we have frequently observed As and Bs together, and that we cannot infer to a B unless we have actually observed other Bs. Hence we cannot infer from regularities of succession to an unobserved god on the analogy of the connection between observed regularities and human agents, unless we have observed at other times other gods. This argument, like the first, reveals Hume's inadequate appreciation of scientific method. As we saw in the scientific examples which I cited, a more developed science than Hume knew has taught us that when observed As have a relation R to observed Bs, it is often perfectly reasonable to postulate that observed A*s, similar to As, have the same relation to unobserved and unobservable B*s similar to Bs.

3. The other objection which seems to be involved in the above passage is that we cannot reach conclusions about an object which is the only one of its kind, and, as the universe is such an object, we cannot reach conclusions about the regularities characteristic of it as a whole.[8] But cosmologists are reaching very well-tested scientific conclusions about the universe as a whole, as are physical anthropologists about the origins of our human race, even

---

[7] *Dialogues*, p. 23.
[8] For this argument see also *Enquiry*, pp. 147f.

though it is the only human race of which we have knowledge and perhaps the only human race there is. The principle quoted in the objections is obviously wrong. There is no space here to analyze its errors in detail, but suffice it to point out that it becomes hopelessly confused by ignoring the fact that uniqueness is relative to description. Nothing describable is unique under all descriptions (the universe is, like the solar system, a number of material bodies distributed in empty space), and everything describable is unique under some description.

4. The next argument which we meet in the *Dialogues* is that the postulated existence of a rational agent who produces the order of the world would itself need explaining. Picturing such an agent as a mind, and a mind as an arrangement of ideas, Hume phrases the objection as follows: "a mental world or Universe of ideas requires a cause as much as does a material world or Universe of objects."[9] Hume himself provides the obvious answer to this— that it is no objection to explaining X by Y that we cannot explain Y. But then he suggests that the Y in this case, the mind, is just as mysterious as the ordered universe. Men never "thought it satisfactory to explain a particular effect by a particular cause which was no more to be accounted for than the effect itself."[10] On the contrary, scientists have always thought it reasonable to postulate entities merely to explain effects, so long as the postulated entities accounted simply and coherently for the characteristics of the effects. The existence of molecules with their characteristic behaviour was "no more to be accounted for" than observable phenomena, but the postulation of their existence gave a neat and simple explanation of a whole host of chemical and physical phenomena, and that was the justification for postulating their existence.

5. Next, Hume argues that if we are going to use the analogy of a human agent we ought to go the whole way and postulate that the god who gives order to the universe is like men in many other respects. "Why not become a perfect anthropomorphite? Why not assert the deity or deities to be corporeal, and to have eyes, a nose, mouths, ears, etc."[11] The argument from design is, as we have seen, an argument by analogy. All analogies break down somewhere; otherwise they would not be analogies. In saying that the relation of A to B is analogous to a relation of A* to a postulated B*, we do not claim that B* is in all respects like B, but only in such respects as to account for the existence of the relation and also in other respects except in so far as we have contrary evidence. For the activity of a god to account for the regularities, he must be free, rational, and very powerful. But it is not necessary that he, like men, should only be able to act on a limited part of the universe,

---

[9]*Dialogues*, p. 33.
[10]*Ibid.*, p. 36.
[11]*Ibid.*, p. 40.

a body, and by acting on that control the rest of the universe. And there is good reason to suppose that the god does not operate in this way. For, if his direct control was confined to a part of the universe, scientific laws outside his control must operate to ensure that his actions have effects in the rest of the universe. Hence the postulation of the existence of the god would not explain the operations of those laws: yet to explain the operation of all scientific laws was the point of postulating the existence of the god. The hypothesis that the god is not embodied thus explains more and explains more coherently than the hypothesis that he is embodied. Hume's objection would, however, have weight against an argument from regularities of co-presence which did not appeal to the operation of regularities of succession. For one could suppose an embodied god just as well as a disembodied god to have made the animal kingdom and then left it alone, as a man makes a machine, or, like a landscape gardener, to have laid out the galactic cluster.s The explanatory force of such an hypothesis is as great as that of the hypothesis that a disembodied god did these things, and argument from analogy would suggest the hypothesis of an embodied god to be more probable. Incidentally, a god whose prior existence was shown by the existence of regularities of co-presence might now be dead, but a god whose existence was shown by the present operation of regularities of succession could not be, since the existence of an agent is contemporaneous with the temporal regularities which he produces.

6. Hume urges: why should we not postulate many gods to give order to the universe, not merely one? "A great number of men join in building a house or a ship, in rearing a city, in framing a commonwealth, why may not several deities combine in framing a world?"[12] Hume again is aware of the obvious counter-objection to his suggestion—"To multiply causes without necessity is . . . contrary to true philosophy."[13] He claims, however, that the counter-objection does not apply here, because it is an open question whether there is a god with sufficient power to put the whole universe in order. The principle, however, still applies whether or not we have prior information that a being of sufficient power exists. When postulating entities, postulate as few as possible. Always suppose only one murderer, unless the evidence forces you to suppose a second. If there were more than one deity responsible for the order of the universe, we should expect to see characteristic marks of the handiwork of different deities in different parts of the universe, just as we see different kinds of workmanship in the different houses of a city. We should expect to find an inverse square law of gravitation obeyed in one part of the universe, and in another part a law which was just short of being an inverse square law—without the difference's being explicable in terms of a

---

[12] *Ibid.*, p. 39.
[13] *Ibid.*, p. 40.

more general law. But it is enough to draw this absurd conclusion to see how ridiculous the Humean objection is.

7. Hume argues that there are in the universe other things than rational agents which bestow order. "A tree bestows order and organisation on that tree which springs from it, without knowing the order; an animal in the same manner on its offspring."[14] It would, therefore, Hume argues, be equally reasonable if we are arguing from analogy, to suppose the cause of the regularities in the world "to be something similar or analogous to generation or vegetation."[15] This suggestion makes perfectly good sense if it is the regularities of co-presence which we are attempting to explain. But as analogous processes to explain regularities of succession, generation or vegetation will not do, because they only produce regularities of co-presence—and those through the operation of regularities of succession outside their control. The seed only produces the plant because of the continued operation of the laws of biochemistry.

8. The last distinct objection which I can discover in the *Dialogues* is the following. Why should we not suppose, Hume urges, that this ordered universe is a mere accident among the chance arrangements of eternal matter? In the course of eternity, matter arranges itself in all kinds of ways. We just happen to live in a period when it is characterised by order, and mistakenly conclude that matter is always ordered. Now, as Hume phrases this objection, it is directed against an argument from design which uses as its premiss the existence of the regularities of co-presence. "The continual motion of matter . . . in less than infinite transpositions must produce this economy or order, and by its very nature, that order, when once established supports itself for many ages if not to eternity."[16] Hume thus relies here partly on chance and partly on the operation of regularities of succession (the preservation of order) to account for the existence of regularities of co-presence. In so far as it relies on regularities of succession to explain regularities of co-presence, such an argument has, as we saw earlier, some plausibility. But in so far as it relies on chance, it does not—if the amount of order to be accounted for is very striking. An attempt to attribute the operation of regularities of succession to chance would not thus be very plausible. The claim would be that there are no laws of nature which always apply to matter; matter evinces in the course of eternity all kinds of patterns of behaviour; it is just chance that at the moment the states of the universe are succeeding each other in a regular way. But if we say that it is chance that in 1960 matter is behaving in a regular way, our claim becomes less and less plausible as we find that in 1961 and 1962 and so on it continues to behave in a regular way. An appeal

---

[14]*Ibid.*, p. 50.
[15]*Ibid.*, p. 47.
[16]*Ibid.*, p. 53.

to chance to account for order becomes less and less plausible, the greater the order. We would be justified in attributing a typewritten version of collected works of Shakespeare to the activity of monkeys typing eternally on eternal typewriters if we had some evidence of the existence of an infinite quantity of paper randomly covered with type, as well as the collected works. In the absence of any evidence that matter behaved irregularly at other temporal periods, we are not justified in attributing its present regular behaviour to chance.

In addition to the objections which I have stated, the *Dialogues* contain a lengthy presentation of the argument that the existence of evil in the world shows that the god who made it and gave it order is not both totally good and omnipotent. But this does not affect the argument from design which, as Cleanthes admits, does not purport to show that the designer of the universe does have these characteristics. The eight objections which I have stated are all the distinct objections to the argument from design which I can find in the *Enquiry* and in the *Dialogues*, which claim that in some formal respect the argument does not work. As well as claiming that the argument from design is deficient in some formal respect, Hume makes the point that the analogy of the order produced by men to the other order of the universe is too remote for us to postulate similar causes.[17] I have argued earlier that if there is a weakness in the argument it is here that it is to be found. The only way to deal with this point would be to start drawing the parallels or stressing the dissimilarities, and these are perhaps tasks more appropriate for the preacher and the poet than for the philosopher. The philosopher will be content to have shown that though perhaps weak, the argument has some force. How much force depends on the strength of the analogy.

---

[17]See, for example, *Dialogues*, pp. 18 and 37.

DAVID HUME

1.15   The Argument from Evil

It is my opinion, I own, replied Demea, that each man feels, in a manner, the truth of religion within his own breast; and, from a consciousness of his imbecility and misery rather than from any reasoning, is led to seek protection from that Being on whom he and all nature are dependent. So anxious or so

---

From David Hume, *Dialogues Concerning Natural Religion* (1779), Part X.

tedious are even the best scenes of life that futurity is still the object of all
our hopes and fears. We incessantly look forward and endeavor, by prayers,
adoration, and sacrifice, to appease those unknown powers whom we find, by
experience, so able to afflict and oppress us. Wretched creatures that we are!
What resource for us amidst the innumerable ills of life did not religion suggest some methods of atonement, and appease those terrors with which we are
incessantly agitated and tormented?

I am indeed persuaded, said Philo, that the best and indeed the only method
of bringing everyone to a due sense of religion is by just representations of
the misery and wickedness of men. And for that purpose a talent of eloquence
and strong imagery is more requisite than that of reasoning and argument.
For is it necessary to prove what everyone feels within himself? It is only
necessary to make us feel it, if possible, more intimately and sensibly.

The people, indeed, replied Demea, are sufficiently convinced of this great
and melancholy truth. The miseries of life, the unhappiness of man, the general corruptions of our nature, the unsatisfactory enjoyment of pleasures,
riches, honors—these phrases have become almost proverbial in all languages.
And who can doubt of what all men declare from their own immediate feeling
and experience?

In this point, said Philo, the learned are perfectly agreed with the vulgar;
and in all letters, *sacred* and *profane*, the topic of human misery has been
insisted on with the most pathetic eloquence that sorrow and melancholy
could inspire. The poets, who speak from sentiment, without a system, and
whose testimony has therefore the more authority, abound in images of this
nature. From Homer down to Dr. Young, the whole inspired tribe have ever
been sensible that no other representation of things would suit the feeling
and observation of each individual.

As to authorities, replied Demea, you need not seek them. Look round
this library of Cleanthes. I shall venture to affirm that, except authors of
particular sciences, such as chemistry or botany, who have no occasion to
treat of human life, there is scarce one of those innumerable writers from
whom the sense of human misery has not, in some passage or other, extorted
a complaint and confession of it. At least, the chance is entirely on that side;
and no one author has ever, so far as I can recollect, been so extravagant as
to deny it.

There you must excuse me, said Philo: Leibniz has denied it, and is perhaps
the first[1] who ventured upon so bold and paradoxical an opinion; at least,
the first who made it essential to his philosophical system.

And by being the first, replied Demea, might he not have been sensible of
his error? For is this a subject in which philosophers can propose to make
discoveries especially in so late an age? And can any man hope by a simple

---

[1]That sentiment had been maintained by Dr. King and some few others before Leibniz,
though by none of so great fame as that German philosopher.

denial (for the subject scarcely admits of reasoning) to bear down the united testimony of mankind, founded on sense and consciousness?

And why should man, added he, pretend to an exemption from the lot of all other animals? The whole earth, believe me, Philo, is cursed and polluted. A perpetual war is kindled amongst all living creatures. Necessity, hunger, want stimulate the strong and courageous; fear, anxiety, terror agitate the weak and infirm. The first entrance into life gives anguish to the new-born infant and to its wretched parent; weakness, impotence, distress attend each stage of that life, and it is, at last, finished in agony and horror.

Observe, too, says Philo, the curious artifices of nature in order to embitter the life of every living being. The stronger prey upon the weaker and keep them in perpetual terror and anxiety. The weaker, too, in their turn, often prey upon the stronger, and vex and molest them without relaxation. Consider that innumerable race of insects, which either are bred on the body of each animal or, flying about, infix their stings in him. These insects have others still less than themselves which torment them. And thus on each hand, before and behind, above and below, every animal is surrounded with enemies which incessantly seek his misery and destruction.

Man alone, said Demea, seems to be, in part, an exception to this rule. For by combination in society he can easily master lions, tigers, and bears, whose greater strength and agility naturally enable them to prey upon him.

On the contrary, it is here chiefly, cried Philo, that the uniform and equal maxims of nature are most apparent. Man, it is true, can, by combination, surmount all his *real* enemies and become master of the whole animal creation; but does he not immediately raise up to himself *imaginary* enemies, the demons of his fancy, who haunt him with superstitious terrors and blast every enjoyment of lfe? His pleasure, as he imagines, becomes in their eyes a crime; his food and repose give them umbrage and offence; his very sleep and dreams furnish new materials to anxious fear; and even death, his refuge from every other ill, presents only the dread of endless and innumerable woes. Nor does the wolf molest more the timid flock than superstition does the anxious beast of wretched mortals.

Besides, consider, Demea: This very society by which we surmount those wild beasts, our natural enemies, what new enemies does it not raise to us? What woe and misery does it not occasion? Man is the greatest enemy of man. Oppression, injustice, contempt, contumely, violence, sedition, war, calumny, treachery, fraud—by these they mutually torment each other, and they would soon dissolve that society which they had formed were it not for the dread of still greater ills which must attend their separation.

But though these external insults, said Demea, from animals, from men, from all the elements, which assault us form a frightful catalogue of woes, they are nothing in comparison of those which arise within ourselves, from the distempered condition of our mind and body. How many lie under the lingering torment of disease? Hear the pathetic enumeration of the great poet.

Intestine stone and ulcer, colic-pangs,
Demoniac frenzy, moping melancholy,
And moon-struck madness, pining atrophy,
Marasmus, and wide-wasting pestilence.
Dire was the tossing, deep the groans: *Despair*
Tended the sick, busiest from couch to couch.
And over them triumphant *Death* his dart
Shook: but delay'd to strike, though oft invok'd
With vows, as their chief good and final hope.

The disorders of the mind, continued Demea, though more secret, are not perhaps less dismal and vexatious. Remorse, shame, anguish, rage, disappointment, anxiety, fear, dejection, despair—who has ever passed through life without cruel inroads from these tormentors? How many have scarcely ever felt any better sensations? Labor and poverty, so abhorred by everyone, are the certain lot of the far greater number; and those few privileged persons who enjoy ease and opulence never reach contentment or true felicity. All the goods of life united would not make a very happy man, but all the ills united would make a wretch indeed; and any one of them almost (and who can be free from every one), nay, often the absence of one good (and who can possess all) is sufficient to render life ineligible.

Were a stranger to drop on a sudden into this world, I would show him, as a specimen of its ills, a hospital full of diseases, a prison crowded with malefactors and debtors, a field of battle strewed with carcases, a fleet foundering in the ocean, a nation languishing under tyranny, famine, or pestilence. To turn the gay side of life to him and give him a notion of its pleasures—whither should I conduct him? To a ball, to an opera, to court? He might justly think that I was only showing him a diversity of distress and sorrow.

There is no evading such striking instances, said Philo, but by apologies which still further aggravate the charge. Why have all men, I ask, in all ages, complained incessantly of the miseries of life? . . . They have no just reason, says one: These complaints proceed only from their discontented, repining, anxious disposition. . . . And can there possibly, I reply, be a more certain foundation of misery than such a wretched temper?

But if they were really as unhappy as they pretend, says my antagonist, why do they remain in life? . . .

Not satisfied with life, afraid of death.

This is the secret chain, say I, that holds us. We are terrified, not bribed to the continuance of our existence.

It is only a false delicacy, he may insist, which a few refined spirits indulge, and which has spread these complaints among the whole race of mankind. . . . And what is this delicacy, I ask, which you blame? Is it anything but a greater sensibility to all the pleasures and pains of life? And if the man of a delicate, refined temper, by being so much more alive than the rest of the world, is only so much more unhappy, what judgment must we form in general of human life?

Let men remain at rest, says our adversary, and they will be easy. They are willing artificers of their own misery. . . . No! reply I: An anxious languor follows their repose; disappointment, vexation, trouble, their activity and ambition.

I can observe something like what you mention in some others, replied Cleanthes; but I confess I feel little or nothing of it in myself, and hope that it is not so common as you represent it.

If you feel not human misery yourself, cried Demea, I congratulate you on so happy a singularity. Others, seemingly the most prosperous, have not been ashamed to vent their complaints in the most melancholy strains. Let us attend to the great, the fortunate emperor, Charles V, when, tired with human grandeur, he resigned all his extensive dominions into the hands of his son. In the last harangue which he made on that memorable occasion, he publicly avowed *that the greatest prosperities which he had ever enjoyed had been mixed with so many adversities that he might truly say he had never enjoyed any satisfaction or contentment.* But did the retired life in which he sought for shelter afford him any greater happiness? If we may credit his son's account, his repentance commenced the very day of his resignation.

Cicero's fortune, from small beginnings, rose to the greatest luster and renown; yet what pathetic complaints of the ills of life do his familiar letters, as well as philosophical discourses, contain? And suitably to his own experience, he introduces Cato, the great, the fortunate Cato protesting in his old age that had he a new life in his offer he would reject the present.

Ask yourself, ask any of your acquaintance, whether they would live over again the last ten or twenty years of their life. No! but the next twenty, they say, will be better:

> And from the dregs of life, hope to receive
> What the first sprightly running could not give.

Thus, at last, they find (such is the greatness of human misery, it reconciles even contradictions) that they complain at once of the shortness of life and of its vanity and sorrow.

And is it possible, Cleanthes, said Philo, that after all these reflections, and infinitely more which might be suggested, you can still persevere in your anthropomorphism, and assert the moral attributes of the Deity, his justice, benevolence, mercy, and rectitude, to be of the same nature with these virtues in human creatures? His power, we allow, is infinite; whatever he wills is executed; but neither man nor any other animal is happy; therefore, he does not will their happiness. His wisdom is infinite; he is never mistaken in choosing the means to any end; but the course of nature tends not to human or animal felicity; therefore, it is not established for that purpose. Through the whole compass of human knowledge there are no inferences more certain and infallible than these. In what respect, then, do his benevolence and mercy resemble the benevolence and mercy of men?

Epicurus' old questions are yet unanswered.

Is he willing to prevent evil, but not able? then is he impotent. Is he able, but not willing? then is he malevolent. Is he both able and willing? whence then is evil?

You ascribe, Cleanthes (and I believe justly), a purpose and intention to nature. But what, I beseech you, is the object of that curious artifice and machinery which she has displayed in all animals—the preservation alone of individuals, and propagation of the species? It seems enough for her purpose, if such a rank be barely upheld in the universe, without any care or concern for the happiness of the members that compose it. No resource for this purpose: no machinery in order merely to give pleasure or ease: no fund of pure joy and contentment: no indulgence without some want or necessity accompanying it. At least, the few phenomena of this nature are overbalanced by opposite phenomena of still greater importance.

Our sense of music, harmony, and indeed beauty of all kinds, gives satisfaction, without being absolutely necessary to the preservation and propagation of the species. But what racking pains, on the other hand, arise from gouts, gravels, megrims, toothaches, rheumatisms, where the injury to the animal machinery is either small or incurable? Mirth, laughter, play, frolic seem gratuitous satisfactions which have no further tendency; spleen, melancholy, discontent, superstition are pains of the same nature. How then does the divine benevolence display itself, in the sense of you anthropomorphites? None but we mystics, as you were pleased to call us, can account for this strange mixture of phenomena, by deriving it from attributes infinitely perfect but incomprehensible.

And have you, at last, said Cleanthes smiling, betrayed your intentions, Philo? Your long agreement with Demea did indeed a little surprise me, but I find you were all the while erecting a concealed battery against me. And I must confess that you have now fallen upon a subject worthy of your noble spirit of opposition and controversy. If you can make out the present point, and prove mankind to be unhappy or corrupted, there is an end at once of all religion. For to what purpose establish the natural attributes of the Deity, while the moral are still doubtful and uncertain?

You take umbrage very easily, replied Demea, at opinions the most innocent and the most generally received, even amongst the religious and devout themselves; and nothing can be more surprising than to find a topic like this— concerning the wickedness and misery of man—charged with no less than atheism and profaneness. Have not all pious divines and preachers who have indulged their rhetoric on so fertile a subject; have they not easily, I say, given a solution of any difficulties which may attend it? This world is but a point in comparison of the universe; this life but a moment in comparison of eternity. The present evil phenomena, therefore, are rectified in other regions, and in some future period of existence. And the eyes of men, being then opened to larger views of things, see the whole connection of general laws, and trace, with adoration, the benevolence and rectitude of the Deity through all the mazes and intricacies of his providence.

No! replied Cleanthes, no! These arbitrary suppositions can never be admitted, contrary to matter of fact, visible and uncontroverted. Whence can any cause be known but from its known effects? Whence can any hypothesis be proved but from the apparent phenomena? To establish one hypothesis upon another is building entirely in the air; and the utmost we ever attain by these conjectures and fictions is to ascertain the bare possibility of our opinion, but never can we, upon such terms, establish its reality.

The only method of supporting divine benevolence—and it is what I willingly embrace—is to deny absolutely the misery and wickedness of man. Your representations are exaggerated; your melancholy views mostly fictitious; your inferences contrary to fact and experience. Health is more common than sickness; pleasure than pain; happiness than misery. And for one vexation which we meet with, we attain, upon computation, a hundred enjoyments.

Admitting your position, replied Philo, which yet is extremely doubtful, you must at the same time allow that, if pain be less frequent than pleasure, it is infinitely more violent and durable. One hour of it is often able to outweigh a day, a week, a month of our common insipid enjoyments; and how many days, weeks, and months are passed by several in the most acute torments? Pleasure, scarcely in one instance, is ever able to reach ecstasy and rapture; and in no one instance can it continue for any time at its highest pitch and altitude. The spirits evaporate, the nerves relax, the fabric is disordered, and the enjoyment quickly degenerates into fatigue and uneasiness. But pain often, good God, how often! rises to torture and agony; and the longer it continues, it becomes still more genuine agony and torture. Patience is exhausted, courage languishes, melancholy seizes us, and nothing terminates our misery but the removal of its cause or another event which is the sole cure of all evil, but which, from our natural folly, we regard with still greater horror and consternation.

But not to insist upon these topics, continued Philo, though most obvious, certain, and important, I must use the freedom to admonish you, Cleanthes, that you have put the controversy upon a most dangerous issue, and are unawares introducing a total scepticism into the most essential articles of natural and revealed theology. What! no method of fixing a just foundation for religion unless we allow the happiness of human life, and maintain a continued existence even in this world, with all our present pains, infirmities, vexations, and follies, to be eligible and desirable! But this is contrary to everyone's feeling and experience; it is contrary to an authority so established as nothing can subvert. No decisive proofs can ever be produced against this authority;

nor is it possible for you to compute, estimate, and compare all the pains and all the pleasures in the lives of all men and of all animals; and thus, by your resting the whole system of religion on a point which, from its very nature, must forever be uncertain, you tacitly confess that that system is equally uncertain.

But allowing you what never will be believed, at least, what you never possibly can prove, that animal or, at least, human happiness in this life exceeds its misery, you have yet done nothing; for this is not, by any means, what we expect from infinite power, infinite wisdom, and infinite goodness. Why is there any misery at all in the world? Not by chance, surely. From some cause then. Is it from the intention of the Deity? But he is perfectly benevolent. Is it contrary to his intention? But he is almighty. Nothing can shake the solidity of this reasoning, so short, so clear, so decisive, except we assert that these subjects exceed all human capacity, and that our common measures of truth and falsehood are not applicable to them—a topic which I have all along insisted on, but which you have, from the beginning, rejected with scorn and indignation.

But I will be contented to retire still from this intrenchment, for I deny that you can ever force me in it. I will allow that pain or misery in man is *compatible* with infinite power and goodness in the Deity, even in your sense of these attributes: what are you advanced by all these concessions? A mere possible compatibility is not sufficient. You must *prove* these pure, unmixed and uncontrollable attributes from the present mixed and confused phenomena, and from these alone. A hopeful undertaking! Were the phenomena ever so pure and unmixed, yet, being finite, they would be insufficient for that purpose. How much more, where they are also so jarring and discordant!

Here, Cleanthes, I find myself at ease in my argument. Here I triumph. Formerly, when we argued concerning the natural attributes of intelligence and design, I needed all my sceptical and metaphysical subtilty to elude your grasp. In many views of the universe and of its parts, particularly the latter, the beauty and fitness of final causes strike us with such irresistible force that all objections appear (what I believe they really are) mere cavils and sophisms; nor can we then imagine how it was ever possible for us to repose any weight on them. But there is no view of human life or of the condition of mankind from which, without the greatest violence, we can infer the moral attributes or learn that infinite benevolence, conjoined with infinite power and infinite wisdom, which we must discover by the eyes of faith alone. It is your turn now to tug the laboring oar, and to support your philosophical subtilties against the dictates of plain reason and experience.

J. L. MACKIE

1.16   *Evil and Omnipotence*

The traditional arguments for the existence of God have been fairly thoroughly criticised by philosophers. But the theologian can, if he wishes, accept this criticism. He can admit that no rational proof of God's existence is possible. And he can still retain all that is essential to his position, by holding that God's existence is known in some other, non-rational way. I think, however, that a more telling criticism can be made by way of traditional problem of evil. Here it can be shown, not that religious beliefs lack rational support, but that they are positively irrational, that the several parts of the essential theological doctrine are inconsistent with one another, so that the theologian can maintain his position as a whole only by a much more extreme rejection of reason than in the former case. He must now be prepared to believe, not merely what cannot be proved, but what can be *disproved* from other beliefs that he also holds.

The problem of evil, in the sense in which I shall be using the phrase, is a problem only for someone who believes that there is a God who is both omnipotent and wholly good. And it is a logical problem, the problem of clarifying and reconciling a number of beliefs: it is not a scientific problem that might be solved by further observations, or a practical problem that might be solved by a decision or an action. These points are obvious; I mention them only because they are sometimes ignored by theologians, who sometimes parry a statement of the problem with such remarks as "Well, can you solve the problem yourself?" or "This is a mystery which may be revealed to us later" or "Evil is something to be faced and overcome, not to be merely discussed."

In its simplest form the problem is this: God is omnipotent; God is wholly good; and yet evil exists. There seems to be some contradiction between these three propositions, so that if any two of them were true the third would be false. But at the same time all three are essential parts of most theological positions: the theologian, it seems, at once *must* adhere and *cannot consistently* adhere to all three. (The problem does not arise only for theists, but I shall discuss it in the form in which it presents itself for ordinary theism.)

However, the contradiction does not arise immediately; to show it we need

From *Mind* 64 (1955). Reprinted by permission of Basil Blackwell (London), publisher.

some additional premises, or perhaps some quasi-logical rules connecting the terms 'good', 'evil', and 'omnipotent'. These additional principles are that good is opposed to evil, in such a way that a good thing always eliminates evil as far as it can, and that there are no limits to what an omnipotent thing can do. From these it follows that a good omnipotent thing eliminates evil completely, and then the propositions that a good omnipotent thing exists, and the evil exists, are incompatible.

A. ADEQUATE SOLUTIONS

Now once the problem is fully stated it is clear that it can be solved, in the sense that the problem will not arise if one gives up at least one of the propositions that constitute it. If you are prepared to say that God is not wholly good, or not quite omnipotent, or that evil does not exist, or that good is not opposed to the kind of evil that exists, or that there are limits to what an omnipotent thing can do, then the problem of evil will not arise for you.

There are, then, quite a number of adequate solutions of the problem of evil, and some of these have been adopted, or almost adopted, by various thinkers. For example, a few have been prepared to deny God's omnipotence, and rather more have been prepared to keep the term 'omnipotence' but severely to restrict its meaning, recording quite a number of things that an omnipotent being cannot do. Some have said that evil is an illusion, perhaps because they held that the whole world of temporal, changing things is an illusion, and that what we call evil belongs only to this world, or perhaps because they held that although temporal things *are* much as we see them, those that we call evil are not really evil. Some have said that what we call evil is merely the privation of good, that evil in a positive sense, evil that would really be opposed to good, does not exist. Many have agreed with Pope that disorder is harmony not understood, and that partial evil is universal good. Whether any of these views is *true* is, of course, another question. But each of them gives an adequate solution of the problem of evil in the sense that if you accept it this problem does not arise for you, though you may, of course, have *other* problems to face.

But often enough these adequate solutions are only *almost* adopted. The thinkers who restrict God's power, but keep the term 'omnipotence', may reasonably be suspected of thinking, in other contexts, that his power is really unlimited. Those who say that evil is an illusion may also be thinking, inconsistently, that this illusion is itself an evil. Those who say that "evil" is merely privation of good may also be thinking, inconsistently, that privation of good is an evil. (The fallacy here is akin to some forms of the "naturalistic fallacy" in ethics, where some think, for example, that "good" is just what contributes to evolutionary progress, and that evolutionary progress is itself good.) If Pope meant what he said in the first line of his couplet, that "disorder" is only harmony not understood, the "partial evil" of the second line must, for consistency, mean "that which, taken in isolation, falsely appears to be evil," but it would more naturally mean "that which, in isolation, really is evil." The second line, in fact, hesitates between two views, that "partial evil" isn't really evil, since only the universal quality is real, and that "partial evil" is really an evil, but only a little one.

In addition, therefore, to adequate solutions, we must recognise unsatis- factory inconsistent solutions, in which there is only a half-hearted or temporary rejection of one of the propositions which together constitute the problem. In these, one of the constituent propositions is explicitly rejected, but it is covertly re-asserted or assumed elsewhere in the system.

B. FALLACIOUS SOLUTIONS

Besides these half-hearted solutions, which explicitly reject but implicitly assert one of the constituent propositions, there are definitely fallacious solutions which explicitly maintain all the constituent propositions, but implicitly reject at least one of them in the course of the argument that explains away the problem of evil.

There are, in fact, many so-called solutions which purport to remove the contradiction without abandoning any of its constituent propositions. These must be fallacious, as we can see from the very statement of the problem, but it is not so easy to see in each case precisely where the fallacy lies. I suggest that in all cases the fallacy has the general form suggested above: in order to solve the problem one (or perhaps more) of its constituent propositions is given up, but in such a way that it appears to have been retained, and can therefore be asserted without qualification in other contexts. Sometimes there is a further complication: the supposed solution moves to and fro between, say, two of the constituent propositions, at one point asserting the first of these but covertly abandoning the second, at another point asserting the second but covertly abandoning the first. These fallacious solutions often turn upon some equivocation with the words "good" and "evil," or upon some vagueness about the way in which good and evil are opposed to one another, or about how much is meant by "omnipotence." I propose to examine some of these so-called solutions, and to exhibit their fallacies in detail. Incidentally, I shall also be considering whether an adequate solution could be reached by a minor modification of one or more of the constituent propositions, which would, however, still satisfy all the essential requirements of ordinary theism.

1. "Good cannot exist without evil" or "Evil is necessary as a counterpart to good."

It is sometimes suggested that evil is necessary as a counterpart to good, that if there were no evil there could be no good either, and that this solves the problem of evil. It is true that it points to an answer to the question "Why should there be evil?" But it does so only by qualifying some of the propositions that constitute the problem.

First, it sets a limit to what God can do, saying that God *cannot* create good without simultaneously creating evil, and this means either that God is not omnipotent or that there are *some* limits to what an omnipotent thing can do. It may be replied that these limits are always presupposed, that omnipotence has never meant the power to do what is logically impossible, and on the present view the existence of good without evil would be a logical impossibility. This interpretation of omnipotence may, indeed, be accepted as a modification of our original account which does not reject anything that is essential to theism, and I shall in general assume it in the subsequent discussion. It is, perhaps, the most common theistic view, but I think that some theists at least have maintained that God can do what is logically impossible. Many theists, at any rate, have held that logic itself is created or laid down by God, that logic is the way in which God arbitrarily chooses to think. (This is, of course, parallel to the ethical view that morally right actions are those which God arbitrarily chooses to command, and the two views encounter similar difficulties). And *this* account of logic is clearly inconsistent with the view that God is bound by logical necessities—unless it is possible for an omnipotent being to bind himself, an issue which we shall consider later, when we come to the Paradox of Omnipotence. This solution of the problem of evil cannot, therefore, be consistently adopted along with the view that logic is itself created by God.

But, secondly, this solution denies that evil is opposed to good in our original sense. If good and evil are counterparts, a good thing will not "eliminate evil as far as it can." Indeed, this view suggests that good and evil are not strictly qualities of things at all. Perhaps the suggestion is that good and evil are related in much the same way as great and small. Certainly, when the term "great" is used relatively as a condensation of "greater than so-and-so," and "small" is used correspondingly, greatness and smallness are counterparts and cannot exist without each other. But in this sense greatness is not a quality, not an intrinsic feature of anything; and it would be absurd to think of a movement in favour of greatness and against smallness in this sense. Such a movement would be self-defeating, since relative greatness can be promoted only by a simultaneous promotion of relative smallness. I feel sure that no theists would be content to regard God's goodness as analogous to this—as if what he supports were not the *good* but the *better*, and as if he had the paradoxical aim that all things should be better than other things.

This point is obscured by the fact that "great" and "small" seem to have an absolute as well as a relative sense. I cannot discuss here whether there is absolute magnitude or not, but if there is, there could be an absolute sense for "great," it could mean of at least a certain size, and it would make sense to speak of all things getting bigger, of a universe that was expanding all over, and therefore it would make sense to speak of promoting greatness. But in *this* sense great and small are not logically necessary counterparts: either quality could exist without the other. There would be no logical impossibility in everything's being small or in everything's being great.

Neither in the absolute nor in the relative sense, then, of "great" and "small" do these terms provide an analogy of the sort that would be needed to support this solution of the problem of evil. In neither case are greatness and smallness *both* necessary counterparts *and* mutually opposed forces or possible objects for support and attack.

It may be replied that good and evil are necessary counterparts in the same way as any quality and its logical opposite: redness can occur, it is suggested, only if non-redness also occurs. But unless evil is merely the privation of good, they are not logical opposites, and some further argument would be needed to show that they are counterparts in the same way as genuine logical opposites. Let us assume that this could be given. There is still doubt of the correctness of the metaphysical principle that a quality must have a real opposite: I suggest that it is not really impossible that everything should be, say, red, that the truth is merely that if everything were red we should not notice redness, and so we should have no word "red"; we observe and give names to qualities only if they have real opposites. If so, the principle that a term must have an opposite would belong only to our language or to our thought, and would not be an ontological principle, and, correspondingly, the rule that good cannot exist without evil would not state a logical necessity of a sort that God would just have to put up with. God might have made everything good, though *we* should not have noticed it if he had.

But, finally, even if we concede that this *is* an ontological principle, it will provide a solution for the problem of evil only if one is prepared to say, "Evil exists, but only just enough evil to serve as the counterpart of good." I doubt whether any theist will accept this. After all, the *ontological* requirement that non-redness should occur would be satisfied even if all the universe, except for a minute speck, were red, and, if there were a corresponding requirement for evil as a counterpart to good, a minute dose of evil would presumably do. But theists are not usually willing to say, in all contexts, that all the evil that occurs is a minute and necessary dose.

2. "Evil is necessary as a means to good."

It is sometimes suggested that evil is necessary for good not as a counterpart but as a means. In its simple form this has little plausibility as a solution of the problem of evil, since it obviously implies a severe restriction of God's power. It would be a *causal* law that you cannot have a certain end without a certain means, so that if God has to introduce evil as a means to good, he must be subject to at least some causal laws. This certainly conflicts with what a theist normally means by omnipotence. This view of God as limited by causal laws also conflicts with the view that causal laws are themselves made by God, which is more widely held than the corresponding view about the laws of logic. This conflict, would, indeed, be resolved if it were possible for an omnipotent being to bind himself, and this possiblity has still to be considered. Unless a favourable answer can be given to this question, the suggestion that evil is necessary as a means to good solves the problem of evil only by denying one of its constituent propositions, either that God is omnipotent or that "omnipotent" means what it says.

> 3. "The universe is better with some evil in it than it could be if there were no evil."

Much more important is a solution which at first seems to be a mere variant of the previous one, that evil may contribute to the goodness of a whole in which it is found, so that the universe as a whole is better as it is, with some evil in it, than it would be if there were no evil. This solution may be developed in either of two ways. It may be supported by an aesthetic analogy, by the fact that contrasts heighten beauty, that in a musical work, for example, there may occur discords which somehow add to the beauty of the work as a whole. Alternatively, it may be worked out in connexion with the notion of progress, that the best possible organisation of the universe will not be static, but progressive, that the gradual overcoming of evil by good is really a finer thing than would be the eternal unchallenged supremacy of good.

In either case, this solution usually starts from the assumption that the evil whose existence gives rise to the problem of evil is primarily what is called physical evil, that is to say, pain. In Hume's rather half-hearted presentation of the problem of evil, the evils that he stresses are pain and disease, and those who reply to him argue that the existence of pain and disease makes possible the existence of sympathy, benevolence, heroism, and the gradually successful struggle of doctors and reformers to overcome these evils. In fact, theists often seize the opportunity to accuse those who stress the problem of evil of taking a low, materialistic view of good and evil, equating these with pleasure and pain, and of ignoring the more spiritual goods which can arise in the struggle against evils.

But let us see exactly what is being done here. Let us call pain and misery 'first order evil' or 'evil (1).' What contrasts with this, namely, pleasure and happiness, will be called 'first order good' or 'good (1).' Distinct from this is 'second order good' or 'good (2)' which somehow emerges in a complex situation in which evil (1) is a necessary component—logically, not merely causally, necessary. (Exactly *how* it emerges does not matter: in the crudest version of this solution good (2) is simply the heightening of happiness by the contrast with misery, in other versions it includes sympathy with suffering, heroism in facing danger, and the gradual decrease of first order evil and increase of first order good.) It is also being assumed that second order good is more important than first order good or evil, in particular that it more than outweighs the first order evil it involves.

Now this is a particularly subtle attempt to solve the problem of evil. It defends God's goodness and omnipotence on the ground that (on a sufficiently long view) this is the best of all logically possible worlds, because it includes the important second order goods, and yet it admits that real evils, namely first order evils, exist. But does it still hold that good and evil are opposed? Not, clearly, in the sense that we set out originally: good does not tend to eliminate evil in general. Instead, we have a modified, a more complex pattern. First order good (*e.g.* happiness) *contrasts with* first order evil *(e.g.* misery): these two are opposed in a fairly mechanical way; some second order goods (*e.g.* benevolence) try to maximize first order good and minimize first order evil; but God's goodness is not this, it is rather the will to maximize *second* order good. We might, therefore, call God's goodness an example of a third order goodness, or good (3). While this account is different from our original one, it might well be held to be an improvement on it, to give a more accurate description of the way in which good is opposed to evil, and to be consistent with the essential theist position.

There might, however, be several objections to this solution.

First, some might argue that such qualities as benevolence—and a *fortiori* the third order goodness which promotes benevolence—have a merely derivative value, that they are not higher sorts of good, but merely means to good (1), that is, to happiness, so that it would be absurd for God to keep misery in existence in order to make possible the virtues of benevolence, heroism, etc. The theist who adopts the present solution must, of course, deny this, but he can do so with some plausibility, so I should not press this objection.

Secondly, it follows from this solution that God is not in our sense benevolent or sympathetic: he is not concerned to minimise evil (1), but only to promote good (2); and this might be a disturbing conclusion for some theists.

But, thirdly, the fatal objection is this. Our analysis shows clearly the possibility of the existence of a *second* order evil, an evil (2) contrasting with good (2) as evil (1) contrasts with good (1). This would include malevolence, cruelty, callousness, cowardice, and states in which good (1) is decreasing an evil (1) increasing. And just as good (2) is held to be the important kind of good, the kind that God is concerned to promote, so evil (2) will, by analogy, be the important kind of evil, the kind which God, if he were wholly good and omnipotent, would eliminate. And yet evil (2) plainly exists, and indeed most theists (in other contexts) stress its existence more than that of evil (1). We should, therefore, state the problem of evil in terms of second order evil, and against this form of the problem the present solution is useless.

An attempt might be made to use this solution again, at a higher level, to explain the occurrence of evil (2): indeed the next main solution that we shall examine does just this, with the help of some new notions. Without any fresh notions, such a solution would have little plausibility: for example, we could hardly say that the really important good was a good (3), such as the increase of benevolence in proportion to cruelty, which logically required for its occurrence the occurrence of some second order evil. But even if evil (2) could be explained in this way, it is fairly clear that there would be third order evils contrasting with this third order good: and we should be well on the way to an infinite regress, where the solution of a problem of evil, stated in terms of evil (n), indicated the existence of an evil ($n + 1$), and a further problem to be solved.

4. "Evil is due to human freewill."

Perhaps the most important proposed solution of the problem of evil is that evil is not to be ascribed to God at all, but to the independent actions of human beings, supposed to have been endowed by God with freedom of the will. This solution may be combined with the preceding one: first order evil (e.g. pain) may be justified as a logically necessary component in second order good (e.g. sympathy) while second order evil (e.g. cruelty) is not justified, but is so ascribed to human beings that God cannot be held responsible for it. This combination evades my third criticism of the preceding solution.

The freewill solution also involves the preceding solution at a higher level. To explain why a wholly good God gave men freewill although it would lead to some important evils, it must be argued that it is better on the whole that men should act freely, and sometimes err, than that they should be innocent automata, acting rightly in a wholly determined way. Freedom, that is to say, is now treated as a third order good, and as being more valuable than second order goods (such as sympathy and heroism) would be if they were deterministically produced, and it is being assumed that second order evils, such as cruelty, are logically necessary accompaniments of freedom, just as pain is a logically necessary pre-condition of sympathy.

I think that this solution is unsatisfactory primarily because of the incoherence of the notion of freedom of the will: but I cannot discuss this topic adequately here, although some of my criticisms will touch upon it.

First I should query the assumption that second order evils are logically necessary accompaniments of freedom. I should ask this: if God has made men such that in their free choices they sometimes prefer what is good and sometimes what is evil, why could he not have made men such that they always freely choose the good? If there is no logical impossibility in a man's freely choosing the good on one, or on several, occasions, there cannot be a logical impossibility in his freely choosing the good on every occasion. God was not, then, faced with a choice between making innocent automata and makng beings who, in acting freely, would sometimes go wrong: there was open to him the obviously better possibility of making beings who would act freely but always go right. Clearly, his failure to avail himself of this possibility is inconsistent with his being both omnipotent and wholly good.

If it is replied that this objection is absurd, that the making of some wrong choices is logically necessary for freedom, it would seem that 'freedom' must here mean complete randomness or indeterminacy, including randomness with regard to the alternatives good and evil, in other words that men's choices and consequent actions can be "free" only if they are not determined by their characters. Only on this assumption can God escape the responsibility for men's actions; for if he made them as they are, but did not determine their wrong choices, this can only be because the wrong choices are not determined by men as they are. But then if freedom is randomness, how can it be a characteristic of *will?* And, still more, how can it be the most important good? What value or merit would there be in free choices if these were random actions which were not determined by the nature of the agent?

I conclude that to make this solution plausible two different senses of 'freedom' must be confused, one sense which will justify the view that freedom is a third order good, more valuable than other goods would be without it, and another sense, sheer randomness, to prevent us from ascribing to God a decision to make men such that they sometimes go wrong when he might have made them such that they would always freely go right.

This criticism is sufficient to dispose of this solution. But besides this there is a fundamental difficulty in the notion of an omnipotent God creating men with free will, for if men's wills are really free this must mean that even God cannot control them, that is, that God is no longer omnipotent. It may be objected that God's gift of freedom to men does not mean that he *cannot* control their wills, but that he always *refrains* from controlling their wills. But why, we may ask, should God refrain from controlling evil wills? Why should he not leave men free to will rightly, but intervene when he sees them beginning to will wrongly? If God could do this, but does not, and if he is wholly good, the only explanation could be that even a wrong free act of will is not really evil, that its freedom is a value which outweighs its wrongness, so that there would be a loss of value if God took away the wrongness and the freedom together. But this is utterly opposed to what theists say about sin in other contexts. The present solution of the problem of evil, then, can be maintained only in the form that God has made men so free that he *cannot* control their wills.

This leads us to what I call the Paradox of Omnipotence: can an omnipotent being make things which he cannot subsequently control? Or, what is practically equivalent to this, can an omnipotent being make rules which then bind himself? (These are practically equivalent because any such rules could be regarded as setting certain things beyond his control, and *vice versa*.) The second of these formulations is relevant to the suggestions that we have already met, that an omnipotent God creates the rules of logic or causal laws, and is then bound by them.

It is clear that this is a paradox: the questions cannot be answered satisfactorily either in the affirmative or in the negative. If we answer "Yes", it follows that if God actually makes things which he cannot control, or makes rules which bind himself, he is not omnipotent once he has made them: there are *then* things which he cannot do. But if we answer "No", we are immediately asserting that there are things which he cannot do, that is to say that he is already not omnipotent.

It cannot be replied that the question which sets this paradox is not a proper question. It would make perfectly good sense to say that a human mechanic has made a machine which he cannot control: if there is any difficulty about the question it lies in the notion of omnipotence itself.

This, incidentally, shows that although we have approached this paradox from the free will theory, it is equally a problem for a theological determinist. No one thinks that machines have free will, yet they may well be beyond the control of their makers. The determinist might reply that anyone who makes anything determines its ways of acting, and so determines its subsequent behaviour: even the human mechanic does this by his *choice* of materials and structure for his machine, though he does not know all about either of these: the mechanic thus determines, though he may not foresee, his machine's actions. And since God is omniscient, and since his creation of things is total, he both determines and foresees the ways in which his creatures will act. We may grant this, but it is beside the point. The question is not whether God *originally* determined the future actions of his creatures, but whether he can *subsequently* control their actions, or whether he was able in his original creation to put things beyond his subsequent control. Even on determinist principles the answers "Yes" and "No" are equally irreconcilable with God's omnipotence.

Before suggesting a solution of this paradox, I would point out that there is a parallel Paradox of Sovereignty. Can a legal sovereign make a law restricting its own future legislative power? For example, could the British parliament make a law forbidding any future parliament to socialise banking, and also forbidding the future repeal of this law itself? Or could the British parliament, which was legally sovereign in Australia in, say, 1899, pass a valid law, or series of laws, which made it no longer sovereign in 1933? Again, neither the affirmative nor the negative answer is really satisfactory. If we were to answer "Yes", we should be admitting the validity of a law which, if it were actually made, would mean that parliament was no longer sovereign. If we were to answer "No", we should be admitting that there is a law, not logically absurd, which parliament cannot validly make, that is, that parliament is not now a legal sovereign. This paradox can be solved in the following way. We should distinguish between first order laws, that is laws governing the actions of individuals and bodies other than the legislature, and second order laws, that is laws about laws, laws governing the actions of the legislature itself. Correspondingly, we should distinguish two orders of sovereignty, first order sovereignty (sovereignty (1)) which is unlimited authority to make first order laws, and second order sovereignty (sovereignty (2)) which is unlimited authority to make second order laws. If we say that parliament is sovereign we might mean that any parliament at any time has sovereignty (1), or we might mean that parliament has both sovereignty (1) and sovereignty (2) at present, but we cannot without contradiction mean both that the present parliament has sovereignty (2) and that every parliament at every time has sovereignty (1), for if the present parliament has sovereignty (2) it may use it to take away the sovereignty (1) of later parliaments. What the paradox shows is that we cannot ascribe to any continuing institution legal sovereignty in an inclusive sense.

The analogy between omnipotence and sovereignty shows that the paradox of omnipotence can be solved in a similar way. We must distinguish between first order omnipotence (omnipotence (1)), that is unlimited power to act, and second order omnipotence (omnipotence (2)), that is unlimited power to determine what powers to act things shall have. Then we could consistently say that God all the time has omnipotence (1), but if so no beings at any time have powers to act independently of God. Or we could say that God at one time had omnipotence (2), and used it to assign independent powers to act to certain things, so that God thereafter did not have omnipotence (1). But what the paradox shows is that we cannot consistently ascribe to any continuing being omnipotence is an inclusive sense.

An alternative solution of this paradox would be simply to deny that God is a continuing being, that any times can be assigned to his actions at all. But on this assumption (which also has difficulties of its own) no meaning can be given to the assertion that God made men with wills so free that he could not control them. The paradox of omnipotence can be avoided by putting God outside time, but the freewill solution of the problem of evil cannot be saved in this way, and equally it remains impossible to hold that an omnipotent God *binds himself* by causal or logical laws.

CONCLUSION

Of the proposed solutions of the problem of evil which we have examined, none has stood up to criticism. There may be other solutions which require examination, but this study strongly suggests that there is no valid solution of the problem which does not modify at least one of the constituent propositions in a way which would seriously affect the essential core of the theistic position.

Quite apart from the problem of evil, the paradox of omnipotence has shown that God's omnipotence must in any case be restricted in one way or another, that unqualified omnipotence cannot be ascribed to any being that continues through time. And if God and his actions are not in time, can omnipotence, or power of any sort, be meaningfuly ascribed to him?

H. J. MCCLOSKEY

1.17   God and Evil

A. THE PROBLEM STATED

Evil is a problem for the theist in that a contradiction is involved in the fact of evil on the one hand, and the belief in the omnipotence and perfection of God on the other. God cannot be both all-powerful and perfectly good if evil is real. This contradiction is well set out in its detail by Mackie in his discussion of the problem.[1] In his discussion Mackie seeks to show that this contradiction cannot be resolved in terms of man's free will. In arguing in this way Mackie neglects a large number of important points, and concedes far too much to the theist. He implicitly allows that whilst physical evil creates a problem, this problem is reducible to the problem of moral evil and that therefore the satisfactoriness of solutions of the problem of evil turns on the compatibility of free will and absolute goodness. In fact physical evils create a number of distinct problems which are not reducible to the problem of moral evil. Further, the proposed solution of the problem of moral evil in terms of free will renders the attempt to account for physical evil in terms of moral good, and the attempt thereby to reduce the problem of evil to the problem of moral evil, completely untenable. Moreover, the account of moral evil in terms of free will breaks down on more obvious and less disputable grounds than those indicated by Mackie. Moral evil can be shown to remain a problem whether or not free will is compatible with absolute goodness. I therefore propose in this paper to reopen the discussion of "the problem of evil," by approaching it from a more general standpoint, examining a wider variety of solutions than those considered by Mackie and his critics.

The fact of evil creates a problem for the theist; but there are a number of

From *The Philosophical Quarterly* 10 (1960). Reprinted by permission of the author and the editor.
[1]Evil and Omnipotence," *Mind*, 1955.

simple solutions available to a theist who is content seriously to modify his theism. He can either admit a limit to God's power, or he can deny God's moral perfection. He can assert either (1) that God is not powerful enough to make a world that does not contain evil, or (2) that God created only the good in the universe and that some other power created the evil, or (3) that God is all-powerful but morally imperfect, and chose to create an imperfect universe. Few Christians accept these solutions, and this is no doubt partly because such "solutions" ignore the real inspiration of religious beliefs, and partly because they introduce embarrassing complications for the theist in his attempts to deal with other serious problems. However, if any one of these "solutions" is accepted, then the problem of evil is avoided, and a weakened version of theism is made secure from attacks based upon the fact of the occurrence of evil.

For more orthodox theism, according to which God is both omnipotent and perfectly good, evil creates a real problem; and this problem is well-stated by the Jesuit, Father G. H. Joyce. Joyce writes:

> The existence of evil in the world must at all times be the greatest of all problems which the mind encounters when it reflects on God and His relation to the world. If He is, indeed, all-good and all-powerful, how has evil any place in the world which He has made? Whence came it? Why is it here? If He is all-good why did He allow it to arise? If all-powerful why does He not deliver us from the burden? Alike in the physical and moral order creation seems so grievously marred that we find it hard to understand how it can derive in its entirety from God. [2]

The facts which give rise to the problem are of two general kinds, and give rise to two distinct types of problem. These two general kinds of evil are usually referred to as "physical" and as "moral" evil. These terms are by no means apt—suffering for instance is not strictly physical evil—and they conceal significant differences. However, this terminology is too widely accepted, and too convenient to be dispensed with here, the more especially as the various kinds of evil, whilst important as distinct kinds, need not for our purposes be designated by separate names.

Physical evil and moral evil then are the two general forms of evil which independently and jointly constitute conclusive grounds for denying the existence of God in the sense defined, namely as an all-powerful, perfect Being. The acuteness of these two general problems is evident when we consider the nature and extent of the evils of which account must be given. To take physical evils, looking first at the less important of these.

(a) *Physical evils*. Physical evils are involved in the very constitution of the earth and animal kingdom. There are deserts and icebound areas; there are dangerous animals of prey, as well as creatures such as scorpions and snakes.

---

[2]Joyce: *Principles of Natural Theology*, ch. XVII. All subsequent quotations from Joyce in this paper are from this chapter of this work.

physical—scientific explanation
moral

There are also pests such as flies and fleas and the hosts of other insect pests, as well as the multitude of lower parasites such as tapeworms, hookworms and the like. Secondly, there are the various natural calamities and the immense human suffering that follows in their wake—fires, floods, tempests, tidal-waves, volcanoes, earthquakes, droughts and famines. Thirdly, there are the vast numbers of diseases that torment and ravage man. Diseases such as leprosy, cancer, poliomyelitis, appear *prima facie* not to be creations which are to be expected of a benevolent Creator. Fourthly, there are the evils with which so many are born—the various physical deformities and defects such as misshapen limbs, blindness, deafness, dumbness, mental deficiency and insanity. Most of these evils contribute towards increasing human pain and suffering: but not all physical evils are reducible simply to pain. Many of these evils are evils whether or not they result in pain. This is important, for it means that, unless there is one solution to such diverse evils, it is both inaccurate and positively misleading to speak of *the* problem of physical evil. Shortly I shall be arguing that no one "solution" covers all these evils, so we shall have to conclude that physical evils create not one problem but a number of distinct problems for the theist.

The nature of the various difficulties referred to by the theist as the problem of physical evil is indicated by Joyce in a way not untypical among the more honest, philosophical theists, as follows:

> The actual amount of suffering which the human race endures is immense. Disease has store and to spare of torments for the body: and disease and death are the lot to which we must all look forward. At all times, too, great numbers of the race are pinched by want. Nor is the world ever free for very long from the terrible sufferings which follow in the track of war. If we concentrate our attention on human woes, to the exclusion of the joys of life, we gain an appalling picture of the ills to which the flesh is heir. So too if we fasten our attention on the sterner side of nature, on the pains which men endure from natural forces—on the storms which wreck their ships, the cold which freezes them to death, the fire which consumes them—if we contemplate this aspect of nature alone we may be led to wonder how God came to deal so harshly with His Creatures as to provide them with such a home.

Many such statements of the problem proceed by suggesting, if not by stating, that the problem arises at least in part by concentrating one's attention too exclusively on one aspect of the world. This is quite contrary to the facts. The problem is not one that results from looking at only one aspect of the universe. It may be the case that over-all pleasure predominates over pain, and that physical goods in general predominate over physical evils, but the opposite may equally well be the case. It is both practically impossible and logically impossible for this question to be resolved. However, it is not an unreasonable presumption, with the large bulk of mankind inadequately fed and housed and without adequate medical and health services, to suppose that physical evils at present predominate over physical goods. In the light of the facts at our disposal, this would seem to be a much more reasonable conclusion than the conclusion hinted at by Joyce and openly advanced by less cautious theists, namely, that physical goods in fact outweigh physical evils in the world.

However, the question is not, Which predominates, physical good or physical evil? The problem of physical evil remains a problem whether the balance in the universe is on the side of physical good or not, because the problem is that of accounting for the fact that physical evil occurs at all.

(*b*) *Moral evil.* Physical evils create one of the groups of problems referred to by the theist as "the problem of evil." Moral evil creates quite a distinct problem. Moral evil is simply immorality—evils such as selfishness, envy, greed, deceit, cruelty, callousness, cowardice and the larger scale evils such as wars and the atrocities they involve.

Moral evil is commonly regarded as constituting an even more serious problem than physical evil. Joyce so regards it, observing:

> The man who sins thereby offends God. . . . We are called on to explain how God came to create an order of things in which rebellion and even final rejection have such a place. Since a choice from among an infinite number of possible worlds lay open to God, how came He to choose one in which these occur? Is not such a choice in flagrant opposition to the Divine Goodness?

Some theists seek a solution by denying the reality of evil or by describing it as a "privation" or absence of good. They hope thereby to explain it away as not needing a solution. This, in the case of most of the evils which require explanation, seems to amount to little more than an attempt to sidestep the problem simply by changing the name of that which has to be explained. It can be exposed for what it is simply by describing some of the evils which have to be explained. That is why a survey of the data to be accounted for is a most important part of the discussion of the problem of evil.

In *The Brothers Karamazov*, Dostoievsky introduces a discussion of the problem of evil by reference to some then recently committed atrocities. Ivan states the problem:

> "By the way, a Bulgarian I met lately in Moscow," Ivan went on . . . "told me about the crimes committed by Turks in all parts of Bulgaria through fear of a general rising of the Slavs. They burn villages, murder, outrage women and children, and nail their prisoners by the ears to the fences, leave them till morning, and in the morning hang them—all sorts of things you can't imagine. People talk sometimes of bestial cruelty, but that's a great injustice and insult to the beasts; a beast can never be so cruel as a man, so artistically cruel. The tiger only tears and gnaws and that's all he can do. He would never think of nailing people by the ears, even if he were able to do it. These Turks took a pleasure in torturing children too; cutting the unborn child from the mother's womb, and tossing babies up in the air and catching them on the points of their

bayonets before their mothers' eyes. Doing it before the mother's eyes was what gave zest to the amusement. Here is another scene that I thought very interesting. Imagine a trembling mother with her baby in her arms, a circle of invading Turks around her. They've planned a diversion: they pet the baby to make it laugh. They succeed; the baby laughs. At that moment, a Turk points a pistol four inches from the baby's face. The baby laughs with glee, holds out its little hands to the pistol, and he pulls the trigger in the baby's face and blows out its brains. Artistic, wasn't it?"[3]

Ivan's statement of the problem was based on historical events. Such happenings did not cease in the nineteenth century. *The Scourge of the Swastika* by Lord Russell of Liverpool contains little else than descriptions of such atrocities; and it is simply one of a host of writings giving documented lists of instances of evils, both physical and moral.

Thus the problem of evil is both real and acute. There is a clear *prima facie* case that evil and God are incompatible—both cannot exist. Most theists admit this, and that the onus is on them to show that the conflict is not fatal to theism; but a consequence is that a host of proposed solutions are advanced.

The mere fact of such a multiplicity of proposed solutions, and the widespread repudiation of each other's solutions by theists, in itself suggests that the fact of evil is an insuperable obstacle to theism as defined here. It also makes it impossible to treat of all proposed solutions, and all that can be attempted here is an examination of those proposed solutions which are most commonly invoked and most generally thought to be important by theists.

Some theists admit the reality of the problem of evil, and then seek to sidestep it, declaring it to be a great mystery which we poor humans cannot hope to comprehend. Other theists adopt a rational approach and advance rational arguments to show that evil, properly understood, is compatible with, and even a consequence of God's goodness. The arguments to be advanced in this paper are directed against the arguments of the latter theists; but in so far as these arguments are successful against the rational theists, to that extent they are also effective in showing that the non-rational approach in terms of great mysteries is positively irrational.

B. PROPOSED SOLUTIONS TO THE PROBLEM OF PHYSICAL EVIL

Of the large variety of arguments advanced by theists as solutions to the problem of physical evil, five popularly used and philosophically significant solution will be examined. They are, in brief: (i) Physical good (pleasure) requires physical evil (pain) to exist at all; (ii) Physical evil is God's punishment of sinners; (iii) Physical evil is God's warning and reminder to man; (iv) Physical evil is the result of the natural laws, the operations of which are on the whole good; (v) Physical evil increases the total good.

(i) *Physical Good is Impossible without Physical Evil*. Pleasure is possible

---

[3]P. 244, Garnett translation, Heinemann.

only by way of contrast with pain. Here the analogy of colour is used. If everything were blue we should, it is argued, understand neither what colour is nor what blue is. So with pleasure and pain.

The most obvious defect of such an argument is that it does not cover all physical goods and evils. It is an argument commonly invoked by those who think of physical evil as creating only one problem, namely the problem of human pain. However, the problems of physical evils are not reducible to the one problem, the problem of pain; hence the argument is simply irrelevant to much physical evil. Disease and insanity are evils, but health and sanity are possible in the total absence of disease and insanity. Further, if the argument were in any way valid even in respect of pain, it would imply the existence of only a speck of pain, and not the immense amount of pain in the universe. A speck of yellow is all that is needed for an appreciation of blueness and of colour generally. The argument is therefore seen to be seriously defective on two counts even if its underlying principle is left unquestioned. If its underlying principle is questioned, the argument is seen to be essentially invalid. Can it seriously be maintained that if an individual were born crippled and deformed and never in his life experienced pleasure, that he could not experience pain, not even if he were severely injured? It is clear that pain is possible in the absence of pleasure. It is true that it might not be distinguished by a special name and called "pain," but the state we now describe as a painful state would nonetheless be possible in the total absence of pleasure. So too the converse would seem to apply. Plato brings this out very clearly in Book 9 of the *Republic* in respect of the pleasures of taste and smell. These pleasures seem not to depend for their existence on any prior experience of pain. Thus the argument is unsound in respect of its main contention; and in being unsound in this respect, it is at the same time ascribing a serious limitation to God's power. It maintains that God cannot create pleasure without creating pain, although as we have seen, pleasure and pain are not correlatives.

(ii) *Physical Evil is God's Punishment for Sin.* This kind of explanation was advanced to explain the terrible Lisbon earthquake in the 18th century, in which 40,000 people were killed. There are many replies to this argument, for instance Voltaire's. Voltaire asked: "Did God in this earthquake select the 40,000 least virtuous of the Portuguese citizens?" The distribution of disease and pain is in no obvious way related to the virtue of the persons afflicted, and popular saying has it that the distribution is slanted in the opposite direction. The only way of meeting the fact that evils are not distributed proportunately to the evil of the sufferer is by suggesting that all human beings, including children, are such miserable sinners, that our offenses are of such enormity, that God would be justified in punishing all of us as severely as it is possible for humans to be punished; but even then, God's apparent caprice in the selection of His victims requires explanation. In any case it is by no means clear that young children who very often suffer severely are guilty of sin of such an enormity as would be necessary to justify their sufferings as punishment.

Further, many physical evils are simultaneous with birth—insanity, mental defectiveness, blindness, deformities, as well as much disease. No crime or sin of *the child* can explain and justify these physical evils as punishment; and, for a parent's sin to be punished in the child is injustice or evil of another kind.

Similarly, the sufferings of animals cannot be accounted for as punishment. For these various reasons, therefore, this argument must be rejected. In fact it has dropped out of favour in philosophical and theological circles, but it continues to be invoked at the popular level.

(iii) *Physical Evil is God's Warning to Men.* It is argued, for instance of physical calamities, that "they serve a moral end which compensates the physical evil which they cause. The awful nature of these phenomena, the overwhelming power of the forces at work, and man's utter helplessness before them, rouse him from the religious indifference to which he is so prone. They inspire a reverential awe of the Creator who made them, and controls them, and a salutary fear of violating the laws which He has imposed" (Joyce). This is where immortality is often alluded to as justifying evil.

This argument proceeds from a proposition that is plainly false; and that the proposition from which it proceeds is false is conceded implicitly by most theologians. Natural calamities do not necessarily turn people to God, but rather present the problem of evil in an acute form; and the problem of evil is said to account for more defections from religion than any other cause. Thus if God's object in bringing about natural calamities is to inspire reverence and awe, He is a bungler. There are many more reliable methods of achieving this end. Equally important, the use of physical evil to achieve this object is hardly the course one would expect a benevolent God to adopt when other, more effective, less evil methods are available to Him, for example, miracles, special revelation, etc.

(iv) *Evils are the Results of the Operation of Laws of Nature.* This fourth argument relates to most physical evil, but it is more usually used to account for animal suffering and physical calamities. These evils are said to result from the operation of the natural laws which govern these objects, the relevant natural laws being the various causal laws, the law of pleasure-pain as a law governing sentient beings, etc. The theist argues that the non-occurrence of these evils would involve either the constant intervention by God in a miraculous way, and contrary to his own natural laws, or else the construction of a universe with different components subject to different laws of nature; for God, in creating a certain kind of being, must create it subject to its appropriate laws; He cannot create it and subject it to any law of His own choosing. Hence He creates a world which has components and laws good in their total effect, although calamitous in some particular effects.

Against this argument three objections are to be urged. First, it does not cover all physical evil. Clearly not all disease can be accounted for along these lines. Secondly, it is not to give a reason against God's miraculous intervention simply to assert that it would be unreasonable for Him constantly to intervene in the operation of His own laws. Yet this is the only reason that theists seem to offer here. If, by intervening in respect to the operation of His laws, God could thereby eliminate an evil, it would seem to be unreasonable and evil of Him not to do so. Some theists seek a way out of this difficulty by denying that God has the power miraculously to intervene; but this is to ascribe a severe limitation to His power. It amounts to asserting that when His Creation has been effected, God can do nothing else except contemplate it. The third objection is related to this, and is to the effect that it is already to ascribe a serious limitation to God's omnipotence to suggest that He could not make sentient beings which did not experience pain, nor sentient beings without deformities and deficiencies, nor natural phenomena with different laws of nature governing them. There is no reason why better laws of nature governing the existing objects are not possible on the divine hypothesis. Surely, if God is all-powerful, He could have made a better universe in the first place, or one with better laws of nature governing it, so that the operation of its laws did not produce calamities and pain. To maintain this is not to suggest that an omnipotent God should be capable of achieving what is logically impossible. All that has been indicated here is logically possible, and therefore not beyond the powers of a being Who is really omnipotent.

This fourth argument seeks to exonerate God by explaining that He created a universe sound on the whole, but such that He had no direct control over the laws governing His creations, and had control only in His selection of His creations. The previous two arguments attribute the detailed results of the operations of these laws directly to God's will. Theists commonly use all three arguments. It is not without significance that they betray such uncertainty as to whether God is to be *commended* or *exonerated*.

(v) *The Universe is Better with Evil in it*. This is the important argument. One version of it runs:

> Just as the human artist has in view the beauty of his composition as a whole, not making it his aim to give to each several part the highest degree of brilliancy, but that measure of adornment which most contributes to the combined effect, so it is with God. [Joyce]

Another version of this general type of argument explains evil not so much as *a component* of a good whole, seen out of its context as a mere component, but rather as *a means* to a greater good. Different as these versions are, they may be treated here as one general type of argument, for the same criticisms are fatal to both versions.

This kind of argument if valid simply shows that some evil may enrich the Universe; it tells us nothing about *how much evil* will enrich this particular

universe, and how much will be too much. So, even if valid in principle—
and shortly I shall argue that it is not valid—such an argument does not in
itself provide a justification for the evil in the universe. It shows simply that
the evil which occurs might have a justification. In view of the immense
amount of evil the probabilities are against it.

This is the main point made by Wisdom in his discussion of this argument.
Wisdom sums up his criticism as follows:

> It remains to add that, unless there are independent arguments in favour
> of this world's being the best logically possible world, it is probable that some
> of the evils in it are not logically necessary to a compensating good; it is
> probable because there are so many evils. [4]

Wisdom's reply brings out that the person who relies upon this argument
as a conclusive and complete argument is seriously mistaken. The argument,
if valid, justifies only some evil. A belief that it justifies all the evil that occurs
in the world is mistaken, for a second argument, by way of a supplement to it,
is needed. This supplementary argument would take the form of a proof that
all the evil that occurs is *in fact* valuable and necessary as a means to greater
good. Such a supplementary proof is in principle impossible; so, at best, this
fifth argument can be taken to show only that some evil *may be* necessary
for the production of good, and that the evil in the world may perhaps have
a justification on this account. This is not to justify a physical evil, but simply
to suggest that physical evil might nonetheless have a justification, although
we may never come to know this justification.

Thus the argument even if it is valid as a general form of reasoning is unsatisfactory because inconclusive. It is, however, also unsatisfactory in that it
follows on the principle of the argument that, just as it is possible that evil
in the total context contributes to increasing the total ultimate good, so
equally, it will hold that good in the total context may increase the ultimate
evil. Thus if the principle of the argument were sound, we could never know
whether evil is really evil, or good really good. (Aesthetic analogies may be
used to illustrate this point.) By implication it follows that it would be dangerous to eliminate evil because we may thereby introduce a discordant element into the divine symphony of the universe; and, conversely, it may be
wrong to condemn the elimination of what is good, because the latter may
result in the production of more, higher goods.

So it follows that, even if the general principle of the argument is not questioned, it is still seen to be a defective argument. On the one hand, it proves
too little—it justifies only some evil and not necessarily all the evil in the
universe; on the other hand it proves too much because it creates doubts
about the goodness of apparent goods. These criticisms in themselves are
fatal to the argument as a solution to the problem of physical evil. However,
because this is one of the most popular and plausible accounts of physical evil,

---

[4] *Mind*, 1931.

it is worthwhile considering whether it can properly be claimed to establish even the very weak conclusion indicated above.

Why, and in what way, is it supposed that physical evils such as pain and misery, disease and deformity, will heighten the total effect and add to the value of the moral? The answer given is that physical evil enriches the whole by giving rise to moral goodness. Disease, insanity, physical suffering and the like are said to bring into being the noble moral virtues—courage, endurance, benevolence, sympathy and the like. This is what the talk about the enriched whole comes to. W. D. Niven makes this explicit in his version of the argument:

> Physical evil has been the goad which has impelled men to most of those achievements which made the history of man so wonderful. Hardship is a stern but fecund parent of invention. Where life is easy because physical ills are at a minimum we find man degenerating in body, mind, and character.

And Niven concludes by asking:

> Which is preferable—a grim fight with the possibility of splendid triumph; or no battle at all?[5]

Joyce's corresponding argument runs:

> Pain is the great stimulant to action. Man no less than animals is impelled to work by the sense of hunger. Experience shows that, were it not for this motive the majority of men would be content to live in indolent ease. Man must earn his bread.
> One reason plainly why God permits suffering is that man may rise to a height of heroism which would otherwise have been beyond his scope. Nor are these the only benefits which it confers. That sympathy for others which is one of the most precious parts of our experience, and one of the most fruitful sources of well-doing, has its origin in the fellow-feeling engendered by endurance of similar trials. Furthermore, were it not for these trials, man would think little enough of a future existence, and of the need of striving after his last end. He would be perfectly content with his existence, and would reck little of any higher good. These considerations here briefly advanced suffice at least to show how important is the office filled by pain in human life, and with what little reason it is asserted that the existence of so much suffering is irreconcilable with the wisdom of the Creator.

And:

> It may be asked whether the Creator could not have brought man to perfection without the use of suffering. Most certainly He could have conferred upon him a similar degree of virtue without requiring any effort on his part. Yet it is easy to see that there is a special value attaching to a conquest of difficulties such as man's actual demands, and that in God's eyes this may well be an adequate reason for assigning this life to us in preference to another.... Pain has value in respect to the next life, but also in respect to this. The advance of scientific discovery, the gradual improvement of the organization of the community, the growth of material civilization are due in no small degree to the stimulus afforded by pain.

The argument is: Physical evil brings moral good into being, and in fact is an essential precondition for the existence of some moral goods. Further, it is

---

[5]W. D. Niven, *Encyclopedia of Religion and Ethics.*

sometimes argued in this context that those moral goods which are possible in the total absence of physical evils are more valuable in themselves if they are achieved as a result of a struggle. Hence physical evil is said to be justified on the grounds that moral good plus physical evil is better than the absence of physical evil.

A common reply, and an obvious one, is that urged by Mackie.[6] Mackie argues that whilst it is true that moral good plus physical evil together are better than physical good alone, the issue is not as simple as that, for physical evil also gives rise to and makes possible many moral evils that would not or could not occur in the absence of physical evil. It is then urged that it is not clear that physical evils (for example, disease and pain) plus some moral goods (for example courage) plus some moral evil (for example, brutality) are better than physical good and those moral goods which are possible and which would occur in the absence of physical evil.

This sort of reply, however, is not completely satisfactory. The objection it raises is a sound one, but it proceeds by conceding too much to the theist, and by overlooking two more basic defects of the argument. It allows implicitly that the problem of physical evil may be reduced to the problem of moral evil; and it neglects the two objections which show that the problem of physical evil cannot be so reduced.

The theist therefore happily accepts this kind of reply, and argues that, if he can give a satisfactory account of moral evil he will then have accounted for both physical and moral evil. He then goes on to account for moral evil in terms of the value of free will and/or its goods. This general argument is deceptively plausible. It breaks down for the two reasons indicated here, but it breaks down at another point as well. If free will alone is used to justify moral evil, then even if no moral good occurred, moral evil would still be said to be justified; but physical evil would have no justification. Physical evil is not essential to free will; it is only justified if moral good actually occurs, and if the moral good which results from physical evils outweighs the moral evils. This means that the argument from free will cannot alone justify physical evil along these lines; and it means that the argument from free will and its goods does not justify physical evil, because such an argument is incomplete, and necessarily incomplete. It needs to be supplemented by factual evidence that it is logically and practically impossible to obtain.

The correct reply, therefore, is first that the argument is irrelevant to many instances of physical evil, and secondly that it is not true that physical evil plus the moral good it produces is better than physical good and its moral goods. Much pain and suffering, in fact much physical evil generally, for example in children who die in infancy, animals and the insane passes unnoticed; it therefore has no morally uplifting effects upon others, and cannot by virtue of the examples chosen have such effects on the sufferers. Further,

---

[6]Mackie, "Evil and Omnipotence," *Mind*, 1955.

there are physical evils such as insanity and much disease to which the argument is inapplicable. So there is a large group of significant cases not covered by the argument. And where the argument is relevant, its premiss is plainly false. It can be shown to be false by exposing its implications in the following way.

We either have obligations to lessen physical evil or we have not. If we have obligations to lessen physical evil then we are thereby reducing the total good in the universe. If, on the other hand, our obligation is to increase the total good in the universe it is our duty to prevent the reduction of physical evil and possibly even to increase the total amount of physical evil. Theists usually hold that we are obliged to reduce the physical evil in the universe; but in maintaining this, the theist is, in terms of this account of physical evil, maintaining that it is his duty to reduce the total amount of real good in the universe, and thereby to make the universe worse. Conversely, if by eliminating the physical evil he is not making the universe worse, then that amount of evil which he eliminates was unnecessary and in need of justification. It is relevant to notice here that evil is not always eliminated for morally praiseworthy reasons. Some discoveries have been due to positively unworthy motives, and many other discoveries which have resulted in a lessening of the sufferings of mankind have been due to no higher a motive than a scientist's desire to earn a reasonable living wage.

This reply to the theist's argument brings out its untenability. The theist's argument is seen to imply that war plus courage plus the many other moral virtues war brings into play are better than peace and its virtues; that famine and its moral virtues are better than plenty; that disease and its moral virtues are better than health. Some Christians in the past, in consistency with this mode of reasoning, opposed the use of anaesthetics to leave scope for the virtues of endurance and courage, and they opposed state aid to the sick and needy to leave scope for the virtues of charity and sympathy. Some have even contended that war is a good in disguise, again in consistency with this argument. Similarly the theist should, in terms of this fifth argument, in his heart if not aloud regret the discovery of the Salk polio vaccine because Dr. Salk has in one blow destroyed infinite possibilities of moral good.

There are three important points that need to be made concerning this kind of account of physical evil. (a) We are told, as by Niven, Joyce and others, that pain is a goad to action and that part of its justification lies in this fact. This claim is empirically false as a generalization about all people and all pain. Much pain frustrates action and wrecks people and personalities. On the other hand many men work and work well without being goaded by pain or discomfort. Further, to assert that men need goading is to ascribe another evil to God, for it is to claim that God made men naturally lazy. There is no reason why God should not have made men naturally industrious; the one is no more incompatible with free will than the other. Thus the argument from physical evil being a goad to man breaks down on three distinct counts. Pain often frustrates human endeavour, pain is not essential as a goad with many men, and where pain is a goad to higher endeavours, it is clear that less evil means to this same end are available to an omnipotent God. (*b*) The real fallacy in the argument is in the assumption that all or the highest moral excellence results from physical evil. As we have already seen, this assumption is completely false. Neither all moral goodness nor the highest moral goodness is triumph in the face of adversity or benevolence towards others in suffering. Christ Himself stressed this when He observed that the two great commandments were commandments to love. Love does not depend for its possibility on the existence and conquest of evil. (*c*) The "negative" moral virtues which are brought into play by the various evils—courage, endurance, charity, sympathy and the like—besides not representing the highest forms of moral virtue, are in fact commonly supposed by the theist and atheist alike not to have the value this fifth argument ascribes to them. We—theists and atheists alike—reveal our comparative valuations of these virtues and of physical evil when we insist on state aid for the needy; when we strive for peace, for plenty, and for harmony within the state.

In brief, the good man, the morally admirable man, is he who loves what is good knowing that it is good and preferring it because it is good. He does not need to be torn by suffering or by the spectacle of another's sufferings to be morally admirable. Fortitude in his own sufferings, and sympathetic kindness in others' may reveal to us his goodness; but his goodness is not necessarily increased by such things.

Five arguments concerning physical evil have now been examined. We have seen that the problem of physical evil is a problem in its own right, and one that cannot be reduced to the problem of moral evil; and further, we have seen that physical evil creates not one but a number of problems to which no one nor any combination of the arguments examined offers a solution.

C. PROPOSED SOLUTIONS TO THE PROBLEM OF MORAL EVIL

The problem of moral evil is commonly regarded as being the greater of the problems concerning evil. As we shall see, it does create what appears to be insuperable difficulties for the theist; but so too, apparently, do physical evils.

For the theist moral evil must be interpreted as a breach of God's law and as a rejection of God himself. It may involve the eternal damnation of the sinner, and in many of its forms it involves the infliction of suffering on other persons. Thus it aggravates the problem of physical evil, but its own peculiar character consists in the fact of sin. How could a morally perfect, all-powerful God create a universe in which occur such moral evils as cruelty, cowardice and hatred, the more especially as these evils constitute a rejection of God Himself by His creations, and as such involve them in eternal damnation? The two main solutions advanced relate to free will and to the fact that moral evil is a consequence of free will. There is a third kind of solution more often invoked implicitly than as an explicit and serious argument, which need not be examined here as its weaknesses are plainly evident. This third solution is to the effect that moral evils and even the most brutal atrocities have their justification in the moral goodness they make possible or bring into being.

(i) *Free will alone provides a justification for moral evil.* This is perhaps the more popular of the serious attempts to explain moral evil. The argument in brief runs: men have free will; moral evil is a consequence of free will; a universe in which men exercise free will even with lapses into moral evil is better than a universe in which men become *automata* doing good aways because predestined to do so. Thus on this argument it is the mere fact of the supreme value of free will itself that is taken to provide a justification for its corollary moral evil.

(ii) *The goods made possible by free will provide a basis for accounting for moral evil.* According to this second argument, it is not the mere fact of free will that is claimed to be of such value as to provide a justification of moral evil, but the fact that free will makes certain goods possible. Some indicate the various moral virtues as the goods that free will makes possible, whilst others point to beatitude, and others again to beatitude achieved by man's own efforts or the virtues achieved as a result of one's own efforts. What all these have in common is the claim that the good consequences of free will provide a justification of the bad consequences of free will, namely moral evil.

Each of these two proposed solutions encounters two specific criticisms, which are fatal to their claims to be real solutions.

(i) To consider first the difficulties to which the former proposed solution is exposed. (*a*) A difficulty for the first argument—that it is free will alone that provides a justification for moral evil—lies in the fact that the theist who argues in this way has to allow that it is logically possible on the free will hypothesis that all men should always will what is evil, and that even so, a universe of completely evil men possessing free will is better than one in which men are predestined to virtuous living. It has to be contended that the value of free will itself is so immense that it more than outweights the total moral evil, the eternal punishment of the wicked, and the sufferings inflicted on others by the sinners in their evilness. It is this paradox that leads to the formulation of the second argument; and it is to be noted that the explanation of moral evil switches to the second argument or to a combination of the first and second argument, immediately the theist refuses to face the logical possibility of complete wickedness, and insists instead that in fact men do not always choose what is evil.

(*b*) The second difficulty encountered by the first argument relates to the possibility that free will is compatible with less evil, and even with no evil, that is, with absolute goodness. If it could be shown that free will is compatible with absolute goodness, or even with less moral evil than actually occurs, then all or at least some evil will be left unexplained by free will alone.

Mackie, in his recent paper, and Joyce, in his discussion of this argument, both contend that free will is compatible with absolute goodness. Mackie argues that if it is not possible for God to confer free-will on men and at the same time ensure that no moral evil is committed, He cannot really be omnipotent. Joyce directs his argument rather to fellow-theists, and it is more of an *ad hominem* argument addressed to them. He writes:

> Free will need not (as is often assumed) involve the power to choose wrong. Our ability to misuse the gift is due to the conditions under which it is exercised here. In our present state we are able to reject what is truly good, and exercise our power of preference in favour of some baser attraction. Yet it is not necessary that it should be so. And all who accept Christian revelation admit that those who attain their final beatitude exercise freedom of will, and yet cannot choose aught but what is truly good. They possess the knowledge of Essential Goodness; and to it, not simply to good in general, they refer every choice. Moreover, even in our present condition it is open to omnipotence so to order our circumstances and to confer on the will such instinctive impulses that we should in every election adopt the right course and not the wrong one.

To this objection, that free will is compatible with absolute goodness and that therefore a benevolent, omnipotent God would have given man free will and ensured his absolute virtue, it is replied that God is being required to perform what is logically impossible. It is logically impossible, so it is argued, for free will and absolute goodness to be combined, and hence, if God lacks omnipotence only in this respect. He cannot be claimed to lack omnipotence in any sense in which serious theists have ascribed it to Him.

Quite clearly, if free will and absolute goodness are logically incompatible, then God, in not being able to confer both on man does not lack omnipotence in any important sense of the term. However, it is not clear that free will and absolute goodness are logically opposed; and Joyce does point to considerations which suggest that they are not logical incompatibles. For my own part I am uncertain on this point; but my uncertainty is not a factual one but one concerning a point of usage. It is clear that an omnipotent God could create rational agents predestined always to make virtuous "decisions"; what is not clear is whether we should describe such agents as having free will. The considerations to which Joyce points have something of the status of test cases, and they would suggest that we should describe such agents as having free will. However, no matter how we resolve the linguistic point, the question remains—Which is more desirable, free will and moral evil and the physical evil to which free will gives rise, or this special free will or pseudo-free will which goes with absolute goodness? I suggest that the latter is clearly preferable. Later I shall endeavour to defend this conclusion; for the moment I am content to indicate the nature of the value judgement on which the question turns at this point.

The second objection to the proposed solution of the problem of moral evil in terms of free will alone, related to the contention that free will is compatible with less moral evil than occurs, and possibly with no moral evil. We have seen what is involved in the latter contention. We may now consider what is involved in the former. It may be argued that free will is compatible with less moral evil than in fact occurs on various grounds. (1) God, if He were all-powerful, could miraculously intervene to prevent some or perhaps all moral evil; and He is said to do so on occasion in answer to prayers, (for example, to prevent wars) or of His own initiative (for instance, by producing calamities which serve as warnings, or by working miracles, etc.). (2) God has made man with a certain nature. This nature is often interpreted by theologians as having a bias to evil. Clearly God could have created man with a strong bias to good, whilst still leaving scope for a decision to act evilly. Such a bias to good would be compatible with freedom of the will. (3) An omnipotent God could so have ordered the world that it was less conducive to the practice of evil.

These are all considerations advanced by Joyce, and separately and jointly, they establish that God could have conferred free will upon us, and at least very considerably *reduced* the amount of moral evil that would have resulted from the exercise of free will. This is sufficient to show that *not all* the moral evil that exists can be justified by reference to free will alone. This conclusion is fatal to the account of moral evil in terms of free will alone. The more extreme conclusion that Mackie seeks to establish—that absolute goodness is compatible with free will—is not essential as a basis for refuting the free will argument. The difficulty is as fatal to the claims of theism whether all moral evil or only some moral evil is unaccountable. However, whether Mackie's contentions are sound is still a matter of logical interest, although not of any real moment in the context of the case against theism, once the fact that less moral evil is compatible with free will has been established.

(ii) The second free will argument arises out of an attempt to circumvent these objections. It is not free will, but the value of the goods achieved through free will that is said to be so great as to provide a justification for moral evil.

(*a*) This second argument meets a difficulty in that it is now necessary for it to be supplemented by a proof that the number of people who practice moral virtue or who attain beatitude and/or virtue after a struggle is sufficient to outweigh the evilness of moral evil, the evilness of their eternal damnation and the physical evil they cause to others. This is a serious defect in the argument, because it means that the argument can at best show that moral evil *may have* a justification, and not that it has a justification. It is both logically and practically impossible to supplement and complete the argument. It is necessarily incomplete and inconclusive even if its general principle is sound.

(*b*) This second argument is designed also to avoid the other difficulty of the first argument—that free will may be compatible with no evil and certainly with less evil. It is argued that even if free will is compatible with absolute goodness it is still better that virtue and beatitude be attained after a genuine personal struggle; and this, it is said, would not occur if God is conferring free will nonetheless prevented moral evil or reduced the risk of it. Joyce argues in this way:

> To receive our final beatitude as the fruit of our labours, and as the recompense of a hard-won victory, is an incomparably higher destiny than to receive it without any effort on our part. And since God in His wisdom has seen fit to give us such a lot as this, it was inevitable that man should have the power to choose wrong. We could not be called to merit the reward due to victory without being exposed to the possibility of defeat.

There are various objections which may be urged here. First, this argument implies that the more intense the struggle, the greater is the triumph and resultant good, and the better the world; hence we should apparently, on this argument, court temptation and moral struggles to attain greater virtue and to be more worthy of our reward. Secondly, it may be urged that God is being said to be demanding too high a price for the goods produced. He is omniscient. He knows that many will sin and not attain the goods or the Good free will is said to make possible. He creates men with free will, with the natures men have, in the world as it is constituted, knowing that in His doing so He is committing many to moral evil and eternal damnation. He could avoid all this evil by creating men with rational wills predestined to virtue, or He could eliminate much of it by making men's natures and the conditions in the world more conducive to the practice of virtue. He is said not to choose to do this. Instead, at the cost of the sacrifice of the many, He is said to have ordered things so as to allow fewer men to attain this higher virtue and higher beatitude that result from the more intense struggle.

In attributing such behaviour to God, and in attempting to account for moral evil along these lines, theist are, I suggest, attributing to God immoral behaviour of a serious kind—of a kind we should all unhesitatingly condemn in a fellow human being.

We do not commend people for putting temptation in the way of others. On the contrary, anyone who today advocated, or even allowed where he could prevent it, the occurrence of evil and the sacrifice of the many—even as a result of their own freely chosen actions—for the sake of the higher virtue of the few, would be condemned as an immoralist. To put severe temptation in the way of the many, knowing that many and perhaps even most will succumb to the temptation, for the sake of the higher virtue of the few, would be blatant immorality; and it would be immoral whether or not those who yielded to the temptation possessed free will. This point can be brought out by considering how a conscientious moral agent would answer the question: Which should I choose for other people, a world in which there are intense moral struggles and the possibility of magnificent triumphs and the certainty of many defeats, or a world in which there are less intense struggles, less magnificent triumphs and fewer defeats, or a world in which there are no struggles, no triumphs and no defeats? We are constantly answering less easy questions than this in a way that conflicts with the theist's contentions. If by modifying our own behaviour we can save someone else from an intense moral struggle and almost certain moral evil for example if by refraining from gambling or excessive drinking ourselves we can help a weaker person not to become a confirmed gambler or an alcoholic, or if by locking our car and not leaving it unlocked and with the key in it we can prevent people yielding to the temptation to become car thieves, we feel obliged to act accordingly, even though the persons concerned would freely choose the evil course of conduct. How much clearer is the decision with which God is said to be faced—the choice between the higher virtue of some and the evil of others, or the higher but less high virtue of many more, and the evil of many fewer. Neither alternative denies free will to men.

These various difficulties dispose of each of the main arguments relating to moral evil. There are in addition to these difficulties two other objections that might be urged.

If it could be shown that man has not free will both arguments collapse; and even if it could be shown that God's omniscience is incompatible with free will they would still break down. The issues raised here are too great to be pursued in this paper; and they can simply be noted as possible additional grounds for which criticisms of the main proposed solutions of the problem of moral evil may be advanced.

The other general objection is by way of a follow-up to points made in objections (b) to both arguments (i) and (ii). It concerns the relative value of free will and its goods and evils and the value of the best of the alternatives to free will and its goods. Are free will and its goods so much more valuable than the next best alternatives that their superior value can really justify the immense amount of evil that is introduced into the world by free will?

Theologians who discuss this issue ask, Which is better—men with free will striving to work out their own destinies, or automata-machine-like creatures, who never make mistakes because they never make decisions? When put in this form we naturally doubt whether free will plus moral evil plus the possibility of the eternal damnation of the many and the physical evil of untold billions are quite so unjustified after all; but the fact of the matter is that the question has not been fairly put. The real alternative is, on the one hand, rational agents with free wills making many bad and some good decisions on rational and non-rational grounds, and "rational" agents predestined always "to choose" the right things for the right reasons—that is, if the language of automata must be used, rational automata. Predestination does not imply the absence of rationality in all senses of that term. God, were He omnipotent, could preordain the decisions and the reasons upon which they were based; and such a mode of existence would seem to be in itself a worthy mode of existence, and one preferable to an existence with free will, ir-rationality and evil.

D. CONCLUSION

In this paper it has been maintained that God, were He all-powerful and perfectly good, would have created a world in which there was no unnecessary evil. It has not been argued that God ought to have created a perfect world, nor that He should have made one that is in any way logically impossible. It has simply been argued that a benevolent God could, and would, have created a world devoid of superfluous evil. It has been contended that there is evil in this world—unnecessary evil—and that the more popular and philosophically more significant of the many attempts to explain this evil are completely unsatisfactory. Hence we must conclude from the existence of evil that there cannot be an omnipotent, benevolent God.

ALVIN PLANTINGA

1.18   The Free Will Defence

Since the days of Epicurus many philosophers have suggested that the existence of evil constitutes a problem for those who accept theistic belief.[1] Those contemporaries who follow Epicurus here claim, for the most part, to detect logical inconsistency in such belief. So McCloskey:

> Evil is a problem for the theist in that a *contradiction* is involved in the fact of evil, on the one hand, and the belief in the omnipotence and perfection of God on the other.[2]

and Mackie:

> I think, however, that a more telling criticism can be made by way of the traditional problem of evil. Here it can be shown, not that religious beliefs lack rational support, but that they are positively irrational, that the several parts of the essential theological doctrine are *inconsistent* with one another. . . .[3]

From *Philosophy in America*, edited by Max Black. Copyright under the Berne Convention by George Allen & Unwin Ltd. Reprinted by permission of Cornell University Press and George Allen & Unwin Ltd.

[1]David Hume and some of the French encyclopedists, for example, as well as F. H. Bradley, J. McTaggart, and J. S. Mill.

[2]H. J. McCloskey, "God and Evil." *The Philosophical Quarterly*, Vol. 10 (April 1960), p. 97.

[3]"Evil and Omnipotence." J. L. Mackie, *Mind*, Vol. 64, No. 254 (April 1955), p. 200.

and essentially the same charge is made by Professor Aiken in an article entitled "God and Evil."[4]

These philosophers, then, and many others besides, hold that traditional theistic belief is self-contradictory and that the problem of evil, for the theist, is that of deciding which of the relevant propositions he is to abandon. But just which propositions are involved? What is the set of theistic beliefs whose conjunction yields a contradiction? The authors referred to above take the following five propositions to be essential to traditional theism: (*a*) that God exists, (*b*) that God is omnipotent, (*c*) that God is omniscient, (*d*) that God is wholly good, and (*e*) that evil exists. Here they are certainly right: each of these propositions is indeed an essential feature of orthodox theism. And it is just these five propositions whose conjunction is said, by our atheologians,[5] to be self-contradictory.

Apologists for theism, of course, have been quick to repel the charge. A line of resistance they have often employed is called *The Free Will Defence;* in this paper I shall discuss and develop that idea.

First of all, a distinction must be made between *moral evil* and *physical evil*. The former, roughly, is the evil which results from human choice or volition; the latter is that which does not. Suffering due to an earthquake, for example, would be a case of physical evil; suffering resulting from human cruelty would be a case of moral evil. This distinction, of course, is not very clear and many questions could be raised about it; but perhaps it is not necessary to deal with these questions here. Given this distinction, the Free Will Defence is usually stated in something like the following way. A world containing creatures who freely perform both good and evil actions—and do more good than evil—is more valuable than a world containing quasi-automata who always do what is right because they are unable to do otherwise. Now God can create free creatures, but He cannot causally or otherwise determine them to do only what is right; for if he does so then they do not do what is right *freely*. To create creatures capable of moral good, therefore, he must create creatures capable of moral evil; but he cannot create the possibility of moral evil and at the same time prohibit its actuality. And as it turned out, some of the free creatures God created exercised their freedom to do what is wrong: hence moral evil. The fact that free creatures sometimes err, however, in no way tells against God's omnipotence or against his goodness; for he could forestall the occurrence of moral evil only by removing the possibility of moral good.

In this way some traditional theists have tried to explain or justify part of the evil that occurs by ascribing it to the will of man rather than to the will

---

[4]*Ethics*, Vol. 48 (1957–58), p. 79.

[5]*Natural* theology is the attempt to infer central religious beliefs from premises that are either obvious to common sense (e.g., *that some things are in motion*) or logically necessary. *Natural atheology* is the attempt to infer the falsity of such religious beliefs from premises of the same sort.

of God. At least three kinds of objections to this idea are to be found both in the tradition and in the current literature. I shall try to develop and clarify the Free Will Defence by restating it in the face of these objections.

I

The first objection challenges the assumption, implicit in the above statement of the Free Will Defence, that free will and causal determinism are logically incompatible. So Flew:

> ... to say that a person could have helped doing something is not to say that what he did was in principle unpredictable nor that there were no causes anywhere which determined that he would as a matter of fact act in this way. It is to say that if he had chosen to do otherwise he would have been able to do so; that there were alternatives, within the capacities of one of his physical strength, of his I.Q., of his knowledge, open to a person in his situation.
>
> ... There is no contradiction involved in saying that a particular action or choice was: *both* free, and could have been helped, and so on; *and* predictable, or even foreknown, and explicable in terms of caused causes.
>
> ... if it is really logically possible for an action to be both freely chosen and yet fully determined by caused causes, then the keystone argument of the Free Will Defense, that there is contradiction in speaking of God so arranging the laws of nature that all men always as a matter of fact freely choose to do the right, cannot hold. [6]

Flew's objection, I think, can be dealt with in a fairly summary fashion. He does not, in the paper in question, explain what he means by 'causal determination' (and of course in that paper this omission is quite proper and justifiable). But presumably he means to use the locution in question in such a way that to say of Jones' action *A* that it is *causally determined* is to say that the action in question has causes and that given these causes, Jones could not have refrained from doing *A*. That is to say, Flew's use of 'causally determined', presumably, is such that one or both of the following sentences, or some sentences very much like them, express necessarily true propositions:

(*a*) If Jones' action *A* is causally determined, then a set *S* of events has occurred prior to Jones' doing *A* such that, given *S*, it is causally impossible for Jones to refrain from doing *A*.

(*b*) If Jones' action *A* is causally determined, then there is a set *S* of propositions describing events occurring before *A* and a set *L* of propositions expressing natural laws such that

---

[6]"Divine Omnipotence and Human Freedom," in *New Essays in Philosophical Theology,* ed. A. Flew and A. MacIntyre, London 1955, pp. 150, 151, 153.

(1) the conjunction of S's members does not entail that Jones does A, and
(2) the conjunction of the members of S with the members of L does entail that Jones does A.

And Flew's thesis, then, is that there is no contradiction in saying of a man, both that all of his actions are causally determined (in the sense just explained) and that some of them are free.

Now it seems to me altogether paradoxical to say of anyone all of whose actions are causally determined, that on some occasions he acts freely. When we say that Jones acts freely on a given occasion, what we say entails, I should think, that either his action on that occasion is not causally determined, or else he has previously performed an undetermined action which is a causal ancestor of the one in question. But this is a difficult and debatable issue; fortunately we need not settle it in order to assess the force of Flew's objection to the Free Will Defence. The Free Will Defender claims that the sentence 'Not all free actions are causally determined' expresses a necessary truth; Flew denies this claim. This strongly suggests that Flew and the Free Will Defender are not using the words 'free' and 'freedom' in the same way. The Free Will Defender, apparently, uses the words in question in such a way that sentences 'Some of Jones' actions are free' and 'Jones did action A freely' express propositions which are inconsistent with the proposition that all of Jones' actions are causally determined. Flew, on the other hand, claims that with respect to the ordinary use of these words, there is no such inconsistency. It is my opinion that Flew is mistaken here; I think it is he who is using these words in a non-standard, unordinary way. But we need not try to resolve that issue; for the Free Will Defender can simply make Flew a present of the word 'freedom' and state his case using other locutions. He might now hold, for example, not that God made men free and that a world in which men freely do both good and evil is more valuable than a world in which they unfreely do only what is good; but rather that God made men such that some of their actions are *unfettered* (both free in Flew's sense and also causally undetermined) and that a world in which men perform both good and evil unfettered actions is superior to one in which they perform only good, but fettered, actions. By substituting 'unfettered' for 'free' throughout this account, the Free Will Defender can elude Flew's objection altogether.[7] So whether Flew is right or wrong about the ordinary sense of 'freedom' is of no consequence; his objection is in an important sense merely verbal and thus altogether fails to damage the Free Will Defence.

II

Flew's objection, in essence, is the claim that an omnipotent being could have created men in such a way that although free they would be *causally*

---

[7]And since this is so in what follows I shall continue to use the words "free" and "freedom" in the way the Free Will Defender uses them.

determined to perform only right actions. According to a closely allied objection, an omnipotent being could have made men in such a way that although free, and free from any such causal determination, they would nonetheless *freely refrain* from performing any evil actions. Here the contemporary spokesman is Mackie:

> . . . if God has made men such that in their free choices they sometimes prefer what is good and sometimes what is evil, why could he not have made men such that they always freely choose the good? If there is no logical impossibility in a man's freely choosing the good on one, or on several occasions, there cannot be a logical impossibility in his freely choosing the good on every occasion. God was not, then, faced with a choice between making innocent automata and making beings who, in acting freely, would sometimes go wrong; there was open to him the obviously better possibility of making beings who would act freely but always go right. Clearly, his failure to avail himself of this possibility is inconsistent with his being both omnipotent and wholly good. [8]

The objection is more serious than Flew's and must be dealt with more fully. Now the Free Will Defence is an argument for the conclusion that (*a*) is not contradictory or necessarily false. [9]

(*a*) God is omnipotent, omniscient, and all-good and God creates free men who sometimes perform morally evil actions.

What Mackie says, I think, may best be construed as an argument for the conclusion that (*a*) *is* necessarily false; in other words, that *God is omnipotent, omniscient and all good* entails *no free men He creates ever perform morally evil actions*. Mackie's argument seems to have the following structure:

(1) God is omnipotent and omniscient and all-good.
(2) If God is omnipotent, He can create any logically possible state of affairs.
∴.(3) God can create any logically possible state of affairs.   (1, 2)
(4) That all free men do what is right on every occasion is a logically possible state of affairs.
∴.(5) God can create free men such that they always do what is right.   (4, 3)
(6) If God can create free men such that they always do what is right and God is all-good, then any free men created by God always do what is right.
∴.(7) Any free men created by God always do what is right.   (1, 5, 6)
∴.(8) No free men created by God ever perform morally evil actions.   (7)

---

[8]*Op. cit.*, p. 17.
[9]And of course if (*a*) is consistent, so is the set (*a*)–(*e*) mentioned on page 187, for (*a*) entails each member of that set.

Doubtless the Free Will Defender will concede the truth of (4); there is a difficulty with (2), however; for

(*a*) That there are men who are not created by God is a logically possible state of affairs

is clearly true. But (2) and (*a*) entail

(*b*) If God is omnipotent, God can create men who are not created by God.

And (*b*), of course, is false; (2) must be revised. The obvious way to repair it seems to be something like the following:

(2′) If God is omnipotent, then God can create any state of affairs *S* such that *God creates S* is consistent.

Similarly, (3) must be revised:

(3′) God can create any state of affairs *S* such that *God creates S* is consistent.

(1′) and (3′) do not seem to suffer from the faults besetting (1) and (3); but now it is not at all evident that (3′) and (4) entail

(5) God can create free men such that they always do what is right

as the original argument claims. To see this, we must note that (5) is true only if

(5*a*) God creates free men such that they always do what is right

is consistent. But (5*a*), one might think, is equivalent to:

(5*b*) God creates free men and brings it about that they always freely do what is right.

And (5*b*), of course, is *not* consistent; for if God *brings it about* that the men He creates always do what is right, then they do not do what is right *freely*. So if (5*a*) is taken to express (5*b*), then (5) is clearly false and clearly not entailed by (3′) and (4).

On the other hand, (5*a*) could conceivably be used to express:

(5*c*) God creates free men and these free men always do what is right.

(5*c*) is surely consistent; it is indeed logically possible that God creates free men and that the free men created by Him always do what is right. And conceivably the objector is using (5) to express this possibility—i.e., it may be that (5) is meant to express:

(5*d*) the proposition *God creates free men and the free men created by God always do what is right* is consistent.

If (5) is equivalent to (5*d*), then (5) is true—in fact necessarily true (and hence trivially entailed by (3') and (4)). But now the difficulty crops up with respect to (6) which, given the equivalence of (5) and (5*d*) is equivalent to

(6') If God is all-good and the proposition *God creates free men and the free men He creates always do what is right* is consistent, then any free men created by God always do what is right.

Now Mackie's aim is to show that the proposition *God is omnipotent, omniscient and all-good* entails the proposition *no free men created by God ever perform morally evil actions.* His attempt, as I outlined it, is to show this by constructing a valid argument whose premise is the former and whose conclusion is the latter. But then any additional premise appealed to in the deduction must be necessarily true if Mackie's argument is to succeed. (6') is one such additional premise; but there seems to be no reason for supposing that (6') is true at all, let alone necessarily true. Whether the free men created by God would always do what is right would presumably be up to them; for all we know they might sometimes exercise their freedom to do what is wrong. Put in a nutshell the difficulty with the argument is the following. (5*a*) (God creates free men such that they always do what is right) is susceptible of two interpretations ((5*b* and (5*c*)). Under one of these interpretations (5) turns out to be false and the argument therefore fails. Under the other interpretation (6) turns out to be utterly groundless and question begging, and again the argument fails.

So far, then, the Free Will Defence has emerged unscathed from Mackie's objection. One has the feeling, however, that more can be said here; that there is something to Mackie's argument. What more? Well, perhaps something along the following lines. It is agreed that it is logically possible that all men always do only what is right. Now God is said to be omniscient and hence knows, with respect to any person he proposes to create, whether that person would or would not commit morally evil acts. For every person *P* who in fact performs morally evil actions, there is, evidently, a possible person *P'* who is exactly like *P* in every respect except that *P'* never performs any evil actions. If God is omnipotent, He could have created these possible persons instead of the persons He in fact did create. And if He is also all-good, He *would*, presumably, have created them, since they differ from the persons He did create only in being morally better than they are.

Can we make coherent sense out of this revised version of Mackie's objection? What, in particular, could the objector mean by 'possible person'? and what are we to make of the suggestion that God could have created possible persons? I think these questions can be answered. Let us consider first the set of all those properties it is logically possible for human beings to have. Examples of properties *not* in this set are the properties of *being over a mile long; being a hippopotamus; being a prime number; being divisible by four;* and the like. Included in the set are such properties as *having red hair; being present at the Battle of Waterloo; being the President of the United States; being born in 1889*; and *being a pipe-smoker*. Also included are such moral properties as *being kind to one's maiden aunt, being a scoundrel, performing at least one morally wrong action*, and so on. Let us call the properties in this set *H* properties. The complement *P̄* of an *H* property *P* is the property a thing has just in case it does not have *P*. And a *consistent set of H* properties is a set of *H* properties such that it is logically possible that there be a human being having every property in the set. Now we can define "possible person" in the following way:

x is a possible person = *x* is a consistent set of *H* properties such that for every *H* property *P*, either *P* or *P̄* is a member of *x*.

To *instantiate* a possible person *P* is to create a human being having every property in *P*. And a set *S* of possible persons is a *co-possible set of possible persons* just in case it is logically possible that every member of *S* is instantiated.[10]

Given this technical terminology, Mackie's objection can be summarily restated. It is granted by everyone that there is no absurdity in the claim that some man who is free to do what is wrong never, in fact, performs any wrong action. It follows that there are many possible persons containing the property *is free to do wrong but always does right*. And since it is logically possible that all men always freely do what is right, there are presumably several co-possible sets of possible persons such that each member of each set contains the property in question. Now God, if he is omnipotent, can instantiate any possible person and any co-possible set of possible persons he chooses. Hence, if He were all-good, He would have instantiated one of the sets of co-possible persons all of whose members freely do only what is right.

In spite of its imposing paraphernalia the argument, thus restated, suffers from substantially the same defect that afflicts Mackie's original version. There are *some* possible persons God obviously cannot instantiate—those, for example, containing the property *is not created by God*. Accordingly it is *false* that God can instantiate just any possible person, He chooses. But of course the interesting question is whether

---

[10]The definiens must not be confused with: For every member *M* of *S*, it is logically possible that *M* is instantiated.

(1) God can instantiate possible persons containing the property of always freely doing what is right

is true; for perhaps Mackie could substitute (1) for the premise just shown to be false.

Is (1) true? Perhaps we can approach this question in the following way. Let P be any possible person containing the property *always freely does what is right*. Then there must be some action A such that P contains the property of being free with respect to A (i.e., the property of being free to perform A and free to refrain from performing A). The *instantiation* of a possible person, S, I shall say, is a person having every property in S; and let us suppose that if P were instantiated, its instantiation would be doing something morally wrong in performing A. And finally, let us suppose that God wishes to instantiate P. Now P contains many properties in addition to the ones already mentioned. Among them, for example, we might find the following: *is born in 1910, has red hair, is born in Stuttgart, has feeble-minded ancestors, is six feet tall at the age of fourteen,* and the like. And there is no difficulty in God's creating a person with these properties. Further, there is no difficulty in God's bringing it about that this person (let's call him Smith) is free with respect to A. But if God *also* brings it about that Smith refrains from performing A (as he must to be the instantiation of P) then Smith is no longer free with respect to A and is hence not the instantiation of P after all. God cannot cause Smith to refrain from performing A, while allowing him to be free with respect to A; and therefore whether or not Smith does A will be entirely up to Smith; it will be a matter of free choice for him. Accordingly, whether God can instantiate P depends upon what Smith would freely decide to do.

This point may be put more accurately as follows: First, we shall say that an H property Q is *indeterminate* if *God creates a person and causes him to have Q* is necessarily false; an H property is *determinate* if it is not indeterminate. Of the properties we ascribed to P, all are determinate except *freely refrains from doing A* and *always freely does what is right*. Now consider P_1 the subset of P containing just the determinate members of P. In order to instantiate P God must instantiate P_1. It is evident that there is at most one instantiation of P_1, for among the members of P_1 will be some such individuating properties as for example, *is the third son of Richard and Lena Dykstra. P_1* also contains the property of being free with respect to A; and if P_1 is instantiated, its instantiation will either perform A or refrain from performing A. It is, of course, possible that P_1 is such that if it is instantiated its instantiation I will perform A. If so, then if God allows I to remain free with respect to A, I will do A; and if God prevents I from doing A, then I is not free with respect to A and hence not the instantiation of P after all. Hence in neither case does God succeed in instantiating P. And accordingly God can instantiate P only if P_1 is *not* such that if it is instantiated, its instantiation will perform A. Hence it is possible that God cannot instantiate P. And evidently it is also possible, further, that *every* possible person containing the property *always freely does what is right* is such that neither God nor anyone else can instantiate it.

Now we merely supposed that P_1 is such that if it is instantiated, its instantiation will perform A. And this supposition, if true at all, is merely contingently true. It might be suggested, therefore, that God could instantiate P by instantiating P_1 and bringing it about that P_1 is *not* such that if it is instantiated, its instantiation will perform A. But to do this God must instantiate P_1 and bring it about that P_1 is such that if it is instantiated, its instantiation I will *refrain* from performing A. And if God does this then God brings it about that I will not perform A. But then I is not free to perform A and hence once more is not the instantiation of P.

It is possible, then, that God cannot instantiate any possible person containing the property *always freely does what is right*. It is also possible, of course, that He *can* instantiate some such possible persons. But *that* He can, if indeed He can, is a contingent truth. And since Mackie's project is to prove an entailment, he cannot employ any contingent propositions as added premises. Hence the reconstructed argument fails.

Now the difficulty with the reconstructed argument is the fact that God cannot instantiate just any possible person he chooses, and the possibility that God cannot instantiate any possible persons containing the property of always freely doing what is right. But perhaps the objector can circumvent this difficulty.

The H properties that make trouble for the objector are the indeterminate properties—those which God cannot cause anyone to have. It is because possible persons contain indeterminate properties that God cannot instantiate just any possible person He wishes. And so perhaps the objector can reformulate his definition of 'possible person' in such a way that a possible person is a consistent set S of *determinate* properties such that for any determinate H property P or $\bar{P}$ is a member of S. Unfortunately the following difficulty arises. Where I is any indeterminate H property and D a determinate H property, D or I (the property a person has if he has either D or I) is determinate. And so, of course, is D. The same difficulty, accordingly, arises all over again—there will be some possible persons God can't instantiate (those containing the properties *is not created by God or has red hair* and *does not have red hair*, for example). We must add, therefore, that no possible person *entails* an indeterminate property.[11]

Even so our difficulties are not at an end. For the definition as so stated entails that there are no *possible free persons*, i.e., possible persons containing the property *on some occasions free to do what is right and free to do what*

---

[11]Where a set S of properties entails a property P if and only it is necessarily true that anything having every property in S also has P.

is wrong.[12] We may see this as follows: Let P be any possible free person. P then contains the property of being free with respect to some action A. Furthermore, P would contain either the property of performing A (since that is a determinate property) or the property of refraining from performing A. But if P contains the property of performing A and the property of being free with respect to A, then P entails the property of freely performing A—which is an indeterminate property. And the same holds in case P contains the property of refraining from performing A. Hence in either case P entails an indeterminate property and accordingly is not a possible person.

Clearly the objector must revise the definition of 'possible person' in such a way that for any action with respect to which a given possible person P is free, P contains neither the property of performing that action nor the property of refraining from performing it. This may be accomplished in the following way. Let us say that a person S is *free with respect to a property P* just in case there is some action A with respect to which S is free and which is such that S has P if and only if he performs A. So, for example, if a person is free to leave town and free to stay, then he is free with respect to the property *leaves town*. And let us say that a set of properties is free with respect to a given property P just in case it contains the property is *free with respect to P*. Now we can restate the definition of 'possible person' as follows:

x is a possible person $= x$ is a consistent set of determinate H properties such that (1) for every determinate H property P with respect to which x is not free, either P or $\bar{P}$ is a member of x, and (2) x does not entail any indeterminate property.

Now let us add the following new definition:

Possibly person P has indeterminate property $I =$ if P were instantiated, P's instantiation would have I.

Under the revised definition of 'possible person' it seems apparent that God, if he is omnipotent, can instantiate any possible person, and any co-possible set of possible persons, he chooses. But, the objector continues, if God is also all-good, He will, presumably, instantiate only those possible persons who have some such indeterminate H property as that of *always freely doing what is right*. And here the Free Will Defender can no longer make the objection which held against the previous versions of Mackie's argument. For if God can instantiate any possible person he chooses, he can instantiate any possible free person he chooses.

The Free Will Defender can, however raise what is essentially the same

---

difficulty in a new guise: what reason is there for supposing that there are *any* possible persons, in the present sense of 'possible person', having the indeterminate property in question? For it is clear that, given any indeterminate *H* property *I*, the proposition *no possible person has I* is a contingent proposition. Further, the proposition *every possible free person freely performs at least one morally wrong action* is possibly true. But if every *possible* free person performs at least one wrong action, then every *actual* free person also freely performs at least one wrong action; hence if every possible free person performs at least one wrong action, God could create a universe without moral evil only by refusing to create any free persons at all. And, the Free Will Defender adds, a world containing free persons and moral evil (provided that it contained more moral good than moral evil) would be superior to one lacking both free persons and moral good and evil. Once again, then, the objection seems to fail.

The definitions offered during the discussion of Mackie's objection afford the opportunity of stating the Free Will Defence more formally. I said above that the Free Will Defence is in essence an argument for the conclusion that (*a*) is consistent:

(*a*) God is omnipotent, omniscient, and all-good and God creates persons who sometimes perform morally evil actions.

One way of showing (*a*) to be consistent is to show that its first conjunct does not entail the negation of its second conjunct, i.e., that

(*b*) God is omnipotent, omniscient and all-good

does not entail

(*c*) God does not create persons who perform morally evil actions.

Now one can show that a given proposition *p* does not entail another proposition *q* by producing a third proposition *r* which is such that (1) the conjunction of *p* and *r* is consistent and (2) the conjunction of *p* and *r* entails the negation of *q*. What we need here, then, is a proposition whose conjunction with (*b*) is both logically consistent and a logically sufficient condition of the denial of (*c*).

Consider the following argument:

(*b*)   God is omnipotent, omniscient and all-good.
(*r*1)   God creates some free persons.
(*r*2)   Every possible free person performs at least one wrong action.
∴ (*d*)   Every actual free person performs at least one wrong action. (*r*2)
∴ (*e*)   God creates persons who perform morally evil actions. ((*r*1), (*d*))

This argument is valid (and can easily be expanded so that it is *formally* valid). Furthermore, the conjunction of (*b*), (*r*1) and (*r*2) is evidently consistent. And as the argument shows, (*b*), (*r*1) and (*r*2) *jointly entail* (*e*). But (*e*) is the denial of (*c*); hence (*b*) and (*r*) jointly entail the denial of (*c*). Accordingly (*b*) does not entail (*c*), and (*a*) (God is omnipotent, omniscient and all-good and God creates persons who perform morally evil acts) is shown to be consistent. So stated, therefore, the Free Will Defence appears to be successful.

At this juncture it might be objected that even if the Free Will Defence, as explained above, shows that there is no contradiction in the supposition that God, who is all-good, omnipotent and omniscient, creates persons who engage in moral evil, it does nothing to show that an all-good, omnipotent and omniscient Being could create a universe containing as *much* moral evil as this one seems to contain. The objection has a point, although the fact that there seems to be no way of measuring or specifying amounts of moral evil makes it exceedingly hard to state the objection in any way which does not leave it vague and merely suggestive. But let us suppose, for purposes of argument, that there is a way of measuring moral evil (and moral good) and that the moral evil present in the universe amounts to ∅. The problem then is to show that

(*b*) God is omnipresent, omniscient and all-good
is consistent with

(*f*) God creates a set of free persons who produce ∅ moral evil. Here the Free Will Defender can produce an argument to show that (*b*) is consistent with (*f*) which exactly parallels the argument for the consistency of (*b*) with (*c*):

(*b*) God is omnipotent, omniscient and all-good.

(*r*3) God creates a set *S* of free persons such that there is a balance of moral good over moral evil with respect to the members of *S*.

(*r*4) There is exactly one co-possible set *S'* of free possible persons such that there is a balance of moral good over moral evil with respect to its members; and the members of *S'* produce ∅ *moral evil.*

Set *S* is evidently the instantiation of *S'* (i.e. every member of *S* is an instantiation of some members of *S'* and every member of *S'* is instantiated by some member of *S*); hence the members of *S* produce ∅ moral evil. Accordingly, (*b*), (*r*3) and (*r*4) jointly entail (*f*); but the conjunction of (*b*), (*r*3) and (*r*4) is consistent; hence (*b*) is consistent with (*f*).

III

The preceding discussion enables us to conclude, I believe, that the Free Will Defence succeeds in showing that there is no inconsistency in the assertion that God creates a universe containing as much moral evil as the universe in fact contains. There remains but one objection to be considered. Mc-Closkey, Flew and others charge that the Free Will Defence, even if it is successful, accounts for only *part* of the evil we find; it accounts only for moral evil, leaving physical evil as intractable as before. The atheologian can therefore restate his position, maintaining that the existence of *physical evil*, which cannot be ascribed to the free actions of human beings, is inconsistent with the existence of an omniscient, omnipotent and all-good Deity.

To make this claim, however, is to overlook an important part of traditional theistic belief; it is part of much traditional belief to attribute a good deal of the evil we find to Satan, or to Satan and his cohorts. Satan, so the traditional doctrine goes, is a mighty non-human spirit, who, along with many other angels, was created long before God created men. Unlike most of his colleagues, Satan rebelled against God and has since been creating whatever havoc he could; the result, of course, is physical evil. But now we see that the moves available to the Free Will Defender in the case of moral evil are equally available to him in the case of physical evil. First he provides definitions of "possible non-human spirit," "free non-human spirit," etc., which exactly parallel their counterparts where it was moral evil that was at stake. Then he points out that it is logically possible that

(*r5*) God creates a set S of free non-human spirits such that the members of S do more good than evil,
and
(*r6*) there is exactly one co-possible set S' of possible free non-human spirits such that the members of S' do more good than evil and
(*r7*) all of the physical evil in the world is due to the actions of the members of S.

He points out further that (*r5*), (*r6*), and (*r7*) are jointly consistent and that their conjunction is consistent with the proposition that God is omnipotent, omniscient and all-good. But (*r5*) through (*r7*) jointly entail that God creates a universe containing as much physical evil as the universe in fact contains; it follows then, that the existence of physical evil is not inconsistent with the existence of an omniscient, omnipotent, all-good Deity.

Now it must be conceded that views involving devils and other non-human spirits do not at present enjoy either the extensive popularity or the high esteem of (say) the Theory of Relativity. Flew, for example, has this to say about the view in question:

> To make this more than just another desperate *ad hoc* expedient of apologetic it is necessary to produce independent evidence for launching such an hypothesis (if "hypothesis" is not too flattering a term for it).[13]

---

[13]*Op. cit.*, p. 17.

But in the present context this claim is surely incorrect; to rebut the charge of contradiction the theist need not hold that the hypothesis in question is probable or even true. He need hold only that it is not inconsistent with the proposition that God exists. Flew suspects that "hypothesis" may be too flattering a term for the sort of view in question. Perhaps this suspicion reflects his doubts as to the meaningfulness of the proposed view. But it is hard to see how one could plausibly argue that the views in question are nonsensical (in the requisite sense) without invoking some version of the Verifiability Criterion, a doctrine whose harrowing vicissitudes are well known. Furthermore, it is likely that any premises worth considering which yield the conclusion that hypotheses about devils are nonsensical will yield the same conclusion about the hypothesis that God exists. And if *God exists* is nonsensical, then presumably theism is not self-contradictory after all.

We may therefore conclude that the Free Will Defence successfully rebuts the charge of contradiction brought against the theist. The Problem of Evil (if indeed evil constitutes a problem for the theist) does not lie in any inconsistency in the belief that God, who is omniscient, omnipotent and all-good, has created a world containing moral and physical evil.

NELSON PIKE

1.19   Hume on Evil

In Parts X and XI of the *Dialogues Concerning Natural Religion*, Hume sets forth his views on the traditional theological problem of evil. Hume's remarks on this topic seem to me to contain a rich mixture of insight and oversight. It will be my purpose in this paper to disentangle these contrasting elements of his discussion.[1]

PHILO'S FIRST POSITION

A. God, according to the traditional Christian view put forward by Cleanthes in the *Dialogues,* is all-powerful, all-knowing, and perfectly good. And it is clear that for Cleanthes, the terms "powerful," "knowing," and "good" apply to God in exactly the same sense in which these terms apply to men. Philo

From *The Philosophical Review* 72 (1963): 180–97. Reprinted by permission of the author and the editor.

[1]All references to Hume's *Dialogues Concerning Natural Religion* will be to the Hafner Library of Classics edition, ed. H. D. Aiken (New York, 1955).

argues as follows (pp. 61–69): if God is to be all-powerful, all-knowing, and perfectly good (using all key terms in their ordinary sense), then to claim that God exists is to preclude the possibility of admitting that there occur instances of evil; that is, to preclude the possibility of admitting that there occur instances of suffering, pain, superstition, wickedness, and so forth.[2] The statements "God exists" and "There occur instances of suffering" are logically incompatible. Of course, no one could deny that there occur instances of suffering. Such a denial would plainly conflict with common experience.[3] Thus it follows from obvious fact that God (having the attributes assigned to him by Cleanthes) does not exist.

This argument against the existence of God has enjoyed considerable popularity since Hume wrote the *Dialogues*. Concerning the traditional theological problem of evil, F. H. Bradley comments as follows:

> The trouble has come from the idea that the Absolute is a moral person. If you start from that basis, then the relation of evil to the Absolute presents at once an irreducible dilemma. The problem then becomes insoluble, but not because it is obscure or in any way mysterious. To any one who has the sense and courage to see things as they are, and is resolved not to mystify others or himself, *there is really no question to discuss. The dilemma is plainly insoluble because it is based on a clear self-contradition.*[4]

John Stuart Mill,[5] J. E. McTaggart,[6] Antony Flew,[7] H. D. Aiken,[8] J. L. Mackie,[9] C. J. Ducasse,[10] and H. J. McCloskey[11] are but a very few of the many others who have echoed Philo's finalistic dismissal of traditional theism after making reference to the logical incompatibility of "God exists" and "There occur instances of suffering." W. T. Stace refers to Hume's discussion of the matter as follows:

> [Assuming that "good" and "powerful" are used in theology as they are used in ordinary discourse], we have to say that Hume was right. The charge has

---

[2]It is clear that, for Philo, the term "evil" is used simply as a tag for the class containing all instances of suffering, pain, and so on. Philo offers no analysis of "evil" nor does his challenge to Cleanthes rest in the least on the particularities of the logic of his term. On p. 69, e.g., Philo formulates his challenge to Cleanthes without using "evil." Here he speaks only of *misery*. In what is to follow, I shall (following Hume) make little use of "evil." Also, I shall use "suffering" as short for "suffering, pain, superstition, wickedness, and so on."

[3]Had Philo been dealing with "evil" (defined in some special way) instead of "suffering," this move in the argument might not have been open to him.

[4]*Appearance and Reality* (Oxford, 1930), p. 174. Italics mine.

[5]*Theism* (New York, 1957), p. 40. See also *The Utility of Religion* (New York, 1957), pp. 73ff.

[6]*Some Dogmas of Religion* (London, 1906), pp. 212–13.

[7]"Theology and Falsification," in Flew and MacIntyre (eds.), *New Essays in Philosophical Theology* (New York, 1955), p. 108.

[8]"God and Evil: Some Relations between Faith and Morals," *Ethics*, 68 (1958), 77–97.

[9]"Evil and Omnipotence," *Mind*, 64 (1955), 201.

[10]*A Philosophical Scrutiny of Religion* (New York, 1953), ch. 16.

[11]"God and Evil," *Philosophical Quarterly*, 10 (1960), 97–114.

never been answered and never will be. The simultaneous attribution of all-power and all-goodness to the Creator of the whole world is logically incompatible with the existence of evil and pain in the world, for which reason the conception of a finite God, who is not all-powerful . . . has become popular in some quarters.[12]

In the first and second sections of this paper, I shall argue that the argument against the existence of God presented in Part X of the *Dialogues* is quite unconvincing. It is not at all clear that "God exists" and "There occur instances of suffering" are logically incompatible statements.

B. Moving now to the details of the matter, we may, I think, formulate Philo's first challenge to Cleanthes as follows:

(1) The world contains instances of suffering.
(2) God exists—and is omnipotent and omniscient.
(3) God exists—and is perfectly good.

According to the view advanced by Philo, these three statements constitute an "inconsistent triad" (p. 66). Any two of them might be held together. But if any two of them are endorsed, the third must be denied. Philo argues that to say of God that he is omnipotent and omniscient is to say that he *could* prevent suffering if he wanted to. Unless God could prevent suffering, he would not qualify as both omnipotent and omniscient. But, Philo continues, to say of God that he is perfectly good is to say that God *would* prevent suffering if he could. A being who would not prevent suffering when it was within his power to do so would not qualify as perfectly good. Thus, to affirm propositions (2) and (3) is to affirm the existence of a being who both could prevent suffering if he wanted to and would prevent suffering if he could. This, of course, is to deny the truth of proposition (1). By similar reasoning, Philo would insist, to affirm (1) and (2) is to deny the truth of (3). And to affirm (1) and (3) is to deny the truth of (2). But, as conceived by Cleanthes, God is both omnipotent-omniscient and perfectly good. Thus, as understood by Cleanthes, "God exists" and "There occur instances of suffering" are logically incompatible statements. Since the latter of these statements is obviously true, the former must be false. Philo reflects: "Nothing can shake the solidarity of this reasoning, so short, so clear, [and] so decisive" (p. 69).

It seems to me that this argument is deficient. I do not think it follows from the claim that a being is perfectly good that he would prevent suffering if he could.

Consider this case. A parent forces a child to take a spoonful of bitter medicine. The parent thus brings about an instance of discomfort—suffering.

---

[12]*Time and Eternity* (Princeton, 1951), p. 56.

The parent could have refrained from administering the medicine; and he knew that the child would suffer discomfort if he did administer it. Yet, when we are assured that the parent acted in the interest of the child's health and happiness, the fact that he knowingly caused discomfort is not sufficient to remove the parent from the class of perfectly good beings. If the parent fails to fit into this class, it is not because he caused *this* instance of suffering.

Given only that the parent knowingly caused an instance of discomfort, we are tempted to *blame* him for his action—that is, to exclude him from the class of perfectly good beings. But when the full circumstances are known, blame becomes inappropriate. In this case, there is what I shall call a "morally sufficient reason" for the parent's action. To say that there is a morally sufficient reason for his action is simply to say that there is a circumstance or condition which, when known, renders *blame* (though, of course, not *responsibility*) for the action inappropriate. As a general statement, a being who permits (or brings about) an instance of suffering might be perfectly good providing only that there is a morally sufficient reason for his action. Thus, it does not follow from the claim that God is perfectly good that he would prevent suffering if he could. God might fail to prevent suffering, or himself bring about suffering, while remaining perfectly good. It is required only that there be a morally sufficient reason for his action.

C. In the light of these reflections, let us now attempt to put Philo's challenge to Cleanthes in sharper form.

(4) The world contains instances of suffering.
(5) God exists—and is omnipotent, omniscient, and perfectly good.
(6) An omnipotent and omniscient being would have no morally sufficient reason for allowing instances of suffering.

Unlike the first, this sequence is logically tight. Suppose (6) and (4) true. If an omnipotent and omniscient being would have no morally sufficient reason for allowing instances of suffering, then, in a world containing such instances, either there would be no omnipotent and omniscient being or that being would be blameworthy. On either of these last alternatives, proposition (5) would be false. Thus, if (6) and (4) are true, (5) must be false. In similar fashion, suppose (6) and (5) true. If an omnipotent and omniscient being would have no morally sufficient reason for allowing suffering, then, if there existed an omnipotent and omniscient being who was also perfectly good, there would occur no suffering. Thus, if (6) and (5) are true, (4) must be false. Lastly, suppose (5) and (4) true. If there existed an omnipotent and omniscient being who was also perfectly good, then if there occurred suffering, the omnipotent and omniscient being (being also perfectly good) would have to have a morally sufficient reason for permitting it. Thus, if (5) and (4) are true, (6) must be false.

Now, according to Philo (and all others concerned), proposition (4) is surely true. And proposition (6)—well, what about proposition (6)? At this point, two observations are needed.

First, it would not serve Philo's purpose were he to argue the truth of proposition (6) by enumerating a number of reasons for permitting suffering (which might be assigned to an omnipotent and omniscient being) and then by showing that in each case the reason offered is not a morally sufficient reason (when assigned to an omnipotent and omniscient being). Philo could never claim to have examined all the possibilities. And at any given point in the argument, Cleanthes could always claim that God's reason for permitting suffering is one which Philo has not yet considered. A retreat to unexamined reasons would remain open to Cleanthes regardless of how complete the list of examined reasons seemed to be.

Second, the position held by Philo in Part X of the *Dialogues* demands that he affirm proposition (6) as a *necessary truth*. If this is not already clear, consider the following inconsistent triad.

> (7) All swans are white.
> (8) Some swans are not large.
> (9) All white things are large.

Suppose (9) true, but not necessarily true. Either (7) or (8) must be false. But the conjunction of (7) and (8) is not contradictory. If the conjunction of (7) and (8) were contradictory, then (9) would be a necessary truth. Thus, unless (9) is a necessary truth, the conjunction of (7) and (8) is not contradictory. Note what happens to this antilogism when "colored" is substituted for "large." Now (9) becomes a necessary truth and, correspondingly, (7) and (8) become logically incompatible. The same holds for the inconsistent triad we are now considering. As already discovered, Philo holds that "There are instances of suffering" (proposition 4) and "God exists" (proposition 5) are logically incompatible. But (4) and (5) will be logically incompatible only if (6) is a necessary truth. Thus, if Philo is to argue that (4) and (5) are logically incompatible, he must be prepared to affirm (6) as a necessary truth.

We may now reconstitute Philo's challenge to the position held by Cleanthes. Proposition (4) is obviously true. No one could deny that there occur instances of suffering. But proposition (6) is a necessary truth. An omnipotent and omniscient being would have no morally sufficient reason for allowing instances of suffering—just as a bachelor would have no wife. Thus, there exists no being who is, at once, omnipotent, omniscient, and perfectly good. Proposition (5) must be false.

D. This is a formidable challenge to Cleanthes' position. Its strength can best be exposed by reflecting on some of the circumstances or conditions which, in ordinary life, and with respect to ordinary agents, are usually counted as morally sufficient reasons for failing to prevent (or relieve) some given instance of suffering. Let me list five such reasons.

First, consider an agent who lacked physical ability to prevent some instance of suffering. Such an agent could claim to have had a morally sufficient reason for not preventing the instance in question.

Second, consider an agent who lacked knowledge of (or the means of knowing about) a given instance of suffering. Such an agent could claim to have had a morally sufficient reason for not preventing the suffering, even if (on all other counts) he had the ability to prevent it.

Third, consider an agent who knew of an instance of suffering and had the physical ability to prevent it, but did not *realize* that he had this ability. Such an agent could usually claim to have had a morally sufficient reason for not preventing the suffering. Example: if I push the button on the wall, the torment of the man in the next room will cease. I have the physical ability to push the button. I know that the man in the next room is in pain. But I do not know that pushing the button will relieve the torment. I do not push the button and thus do not relieve the suffering.

Fourth, consider an agent who had the ability to prevent an instance of suffering, knew of the suffering, knew that he had the ability to prevent it, but did not prevent it because he believed (rightly or wrongly) that to do so would be to fail to effect some future good which would outweigh the negative value of the suffering. Such an agent might well claim to have had a morally sufficient reason for not preventing the suffering. Example: go back to the case of the parent causing discomfort by administering bitter medicine to the child.

Fifth, consider an agent who had the ability to prevent an instance of suffering, knew of the suffering, knew that he had the ability to prevent it, but failed to prevent it because to do so would have involved his preventing a prior good which outweighed the negative value of the suffering. Such an agent might claim to have had a morally sufficient reason for not preventing the suffering. Example: a parent permits a child to eat some birthday cake knowing that his eating the cake will result in the child's feeling slightly ill later in the day. The parent estimates that the child's pleasure of the moment outweighs the discomfort which will result.

Up to this point, Philo would insist, we have not hit on a circumstance or condition which could be used by Cleanthes when constructing a "theodicy," that is, when attempting to identify the morally sufficient reason God has for permitting instances of suffering.

The first three entries on the list are obviously not available. Each makes explicit mention of some lack of knowledge or power on the part of the agent. Nothing more need be said about them.

A theologian might, however, be tempted to use a reason for the fourth type when constructing a theodicy. He might propose that suffering *results in goods* which outweigh the negative value of the suffering. Famine (hunger) leads man to industry and progress. Disease (pain) leads man to knowledge and understanding. Philo suggests that no theodicy of this kind can be successful (pp. 73–74 and 76). An omnipotent and omniscient being could find other means of bringing about the same results. The mere fact that evils give rise to goods cannot serve as a morally sufficient reason for an omnipotent and omniscient being to permit suffering.

A theologian might also be tempted to use reasons of the fifth type when constructing a theodicy. He might propose that instances of suffering *result from goods* which outweigh the negative value of the suffering. That the world is run in accordance with natural law is good. But any such regular operation will result in suffering. That men have the ability to make free choices is good. But free choice will sometimes result in wrong choice and suffering. Philo argues that it is not at all clear that a world run in accordance with natural law is better than one not so regulated (p. 74). And one might issue a similar challenge with respect to free will. But a more general argument has been offered in the contemporary literature on evil which is exactly analogous to the one suggested by Philo above. According to H. J. McCloskey, an omnipotent and omniscient being could devise a law-governed world which would not include suffering.[13] And according to J. L. Mackie, an omnipotent and omniscient being could create a world containing free agents which would include no suffering or wrong-doing.[14] The import of both these suggestions is that an omnipotent and omniscient being could create a world containing whatever is good (regularity, free will, and so on) without allowing the suffering which (only factually) results from these goods. The mere fact that suffering results from good cannot serve as a morally sufficient reason for an omnipotent and omniscient being to allow suffering.

Though the above reflections may be far from conclusive, let us grant that, of the morally sufficient reasons so far considered, none could be assigned to an omnipotent and omniscient being. This, of course, is not to say that proposition (6) is true—let alone necessarily true. As mentioned earlier, proposition (6) will not be shown true by an enumerative procedure of the above kind. But consider the matter less rigorously. If none of the reasons so far considered could be assigned to an omnipotent and omniscient being, ought this not to raise a suspicion? Might there not be a principle operating in each of these reasons which guarantees that *no* morally sufficient reason for permitting suffering *could* be assigned to an omnipotent and omniscient being? Such a principle immediately suggests itself. Men are sometimes excused for allowing suffering. But in these cases, men are excused only because they lack the knowledge or power to prevent suffering, or because they lack the knowledge or power to bring about goods (which are causally related to suffering) without also bringing about suffering. In other words, men are excusable only

---

[13]"God and Evil," pp. 103–4.
[14]"Evil and Omnipotence," pp. 208–10.

because they are limited. Having a morally sufficient reason for permitting suffering *entails* having some lack of knowledge or power. If this principle is sound (and, indeed, it is initially plausible), then proposition (6) must surely be listed as a necessary truth.

DEMEA'S THEODICY

But the issue is not yet decided. Demea has offered a theodicy which does not fit any of the forms outlined above. And Philo must be willing to consider all proposals if he is to claim "decisiveness" for his argument against Cleanthes. Demea reasons as follows:

> This world is but a point in comparison of the universe; this life but a moment in comparison of eternity. The present evil phenomena, therefore, are rectified in other regions, and in some future period of existence. And the eyes of men, being then opened to larger views of things, see the whole connection of general laws, and trace, with adoration, the benevolence and rectitude of the Deity through all mazes and intricacies of his providence [p. 67].

It might be useful if we had a second statement of this theodicy, one taken from a traditional theological source. In Chapter LXXI of the *Summa contra Gentiles*, St. Thomas argues as follows:

> The good of the whole is of more account than the good of the part. Therefore, it belongs to a prudent governor to overlook a lack of goodness in a part, that there may be an increase of goodness in the whole. Thus, the builder hides the foundation of a house underground, that the whole house may stand firm. Now, if evil were taken away from certain parts of the universe, the perfection of the universe would be much diminished, since its beauty results from the ordered unity of good and evil things, seeing that evil arises from the failure of good, and yet certain goods are occasioned from those very evils through the providence of the governor, even as the silent pause gives sweetness to the chant. Therefore, evil should not be excluded from things by the divine providence.

Neither of these statements seems entirely satisfactory. Demea might be suggesting that the world is good on the whole—that the suffering we discover in our world is, as it were, made up for in other regions of creation. God here appears as the husband who beats his wife on occasion but makes up for it with favors at other times. In St. Thomas' statement, there are unmistakable hints of causal reasoning. Certain goods are "occasioned" by evils, as the foundation of the house permits the house to stand firm. But in both of these statements another theme occurs. Let me state it in my own way without pretense of historical accuracy.

I have a set of ten wooden blocks. There is a T-shaped block, an L-shaped block, an F-shaped block, and so on. No two blocks have the same shape. Let us assign each block a value—say, an aesthetic value—making the T-shaped block most valuable and the L-shaped block least valuable. Now the blocks may be fitted together into formation. And let us suppose that the blocks are so shaped that there is one and only one subset of the blocks which will fit together into a square. The L-shaped block is a member of that subset. Further, let us stipulate that any formation of blocks (consisting of two or more blocks fitted together) will have more aesthetic value than any of the blocks taken individually or any subset of the blocks taken as a mere collection. And, as a last assumption, let us say that the square formation has greater aesthetic value than any other logically possible block formation. The L-shaped block is a necessary component of the square formation; that is, the L-shaped block is logically indispensable to the square formation. Thus the L-shaped block is a necessary component of the best of all possible block formations. Hence, the block with the least aesthetic value is logically indispensable to the best of all possible block formations. Without this very block, it would be logically impossible to create the best of all possible block formations.

Working from this model, let us understand Demea's theodicy as follows. Put aside the claim that instances of suffering are *de facto* causes or consequences of greater goods. God, being a perfectly good, omniscient, and omnipotent being, would create the best of all possible worlds. But the best of all possible worlds must contain instances of suffering: they are logically indispensable components. This is why there are instances of suffering in the world which God created.

What shall we say about this theodicy? Philo expresses no opinion on the subject.

Consider this reply to Demea's reasonings. A world containing instances of suffering as necessary components might be the best of all possible worlds. And if a world containing instances of suffering as necessary components were the best of all possible worlds, an omnipotent and omniscient being would have a morally sufficient reason for permitting instances of suffering. But how are we to know that, in fact, instances of suffering are logically indispensable components of the best of all possible worlds? There would appear to be no way of establishing this claim short of assuming that God does in fact exist, and then concluding (as did Leibniz) that the world (containing suffering) which he did in fact create is the best of all possible worlds. But, this procedure assumes that God exists. And this latter is precisely the question now at issue.

It seems to me that this reply to Demea's theodicy has considerable merit. First, my hypothetical objector is probably right in suggesting that the only way one could show that the best of all possible worlds must contain instances of suffering would be via the above argument in which the existence of God is assumed. Second, I think that my objector is right in allowing that, if instances of suffering were logically indispensable components of the best of all possible worlds, this would provide a morally sufficient reason for an omnipotent and omniscient being to permit instances of suffering. And, third,

I think that my objector exhibits considerable discretion in not challenging the claim that the best of all possible worlds *might* contain instances of suffering as necessary components. I know of no argument which will show this claim to be true. But on the other hand, I know of no argument which will show this claim to be false. (I shall elaborate this last point directly.)

Thus, as I have said, the above evaluation of the theodicy advanced by Demea seems to have considerable merit. But this evaluation, *if correct,* seems to be sufficient to refute Philo's claim that "God exists" and "There occur instances of suffering" are logically incompatible statements. If instances of suffering were necessary components of the best of all possible worlds, then an omnipotent and omniscient being would have a morally sufficient reason for permitting instances of suffering. Thus, if it is *possible* that instances of suffering are necessary components of the best of all possible worlds, then there *might be* a morally sufficient reason for an omnipotent and omniscient being to permit instances of suffering. Thus if the statement "Instances of suffering are necessary components of the best of all possible worlds" is not contradictory, then proposition (6) is not a necessary truth. And, as we have seen, if proposition (6) is not a necessary truth, then "God exists" and "There occur instances of suffering" are not logically incompatible statements.

What shall we say? Is the statement "Instances of suffering are logically indispensable components of the best of all possible worlds" contradictory? That it is, is simply assumed in Philo's first position. But, surely, this is not a trivial assumption. If it is correct, it must be shown to be so; it is not *obviously* correct. And how shall we argue that it is correct? Shall we, for example, assume that any case of suffering contained in any complex of events detracts from the value of the complex? If this principle were analytic, then a world containing an instance of suffering could not be the best of all possible worlds. But G. E. Moore has taught us to be suspicious of any such principle.[15] And John Wisdom has provided a series of counterexamples which tend to show that this very principle is, in fact, not analytic. Example: I believe (rightly or wrongly) that you are in pain, and become unhappy as a result of that belief. The resulting complex would appear to be better by virtue of my unhappiness (suffering) than it would have been had I believed you to be in pain but had not become unhappy (or had become happy) as a result.[16] Philo's argument against the existence of God is not finished. And it is not at all obvious that it is *capable* of effective completion. It is, I submit, far from clear that God and evil could not exist together in the same universe.

PHILO'S SECOND POSITION

At the end of Part X, Philo agrees to "retire" from his first position. He now concedes that "God exists" and "There occur instances of suffering" are not

---

[15]I refer here to Moore's discussion of "organic unities" in *Principia Ethica* (Cambridge, 1903), pp. 28ff.

[16]"God and Evil," *Mind*, 44 (1935), 13–14. I have modified Wisdom's example slightly.

logically incompatible statements (p. 69). (It is clear from the context that this adjustment in Philo's thinking is made only for purposes of argument and not because Hume senses any inadequacy in Philo's first position.) Most contemporary philosophers think that Hume's major contribution to the literature on evil was made in Part X of the *Dialogues*. But it seems to me that what is of really lasting value in Hume's reflections on this subject is to be found, not in Part X, but in the discusison in Part XI which follows Philo's "retirement" from his first position.

A. Consider, first of all, a theology in which the existence of God is accepted on the basis of what is taken to be a conclusive (*a priori*) demonstration. (A theology in which the existence of God is taken as an item of faith can be considered here as well.) On this view, that God exists is a settled matter, not subject to review or challenge. It is, as it were, axiomatic to further theological debate. According to Philo, evil in the world presents no special problem for a theology of this sort:

> Let us allow that, if the goodness of the Deity (I mean a goodness like the human) could be established on any tolerable reasons *a priori*, these (evil) phenomena, however untoward, would not be sufficient to subvert that principle, but might easily, in some unknown manner, be reconcilable to it [p. 78].

This point, I think, is essentially correct, but it must be put more firmly.

Recalling the remarks advanced when discussing the inconsistent nature of propositions (4) through (6) above, a theologian who accepts the existence of God (either as an item of faith or on the basis of an *a priori* argument) must conclude either that there is some morally sufficient reason for God's allowing suffering in the world, or that there are no instances of suffering in the world. He will, of course, choose the first alternative. Thus, in a theology of the sort now under consideration, the theologian begins by affirming the existence of God and by acknowledging the occurrence of suffering. It follows *logically* that God has some morally sufficient reason for allowing instances of suffering. The conclusion is not, as Philo suggests, that there *might be* a morally sufficient reason for evil. The conclusion is, rather, that there *must be* such a reason. It *could* not be otherwise.

What, then, of the traditional theological problem of evil? Within a theology of the above type, the problem of evil can only be the problem of discovering a *specific* theodicy which is adequate—that is, of discovering which, if any, of the specific proposals which might be advanced really describes God's morally sufficient reason for allowing instances of suffering. This problem, of course, is not a major one for the theologian. If the problem of evil is simply the problem of uncovering the specific reason for evil—given assurance that there is (and must be) some such reason—it can hardly be counted as a critical problem. Once it is granted that there is some specific reason for evil, there is a sense in which it is no longer vital to find it. A theologian of the type we are now considering might never arrive at a satisfactory theodicy. (Philo's "unknown" reason might remain forever unknown.) He might condemn as erroneous all existing theodicies and might despair of ever discovering the morally sufficient reason in question. A charge of incompleteness would be the worst that could be leveled at his world view.

B. Cleanthes is not, of course, a theologian of the sort just described. He does not accept the existence of God as an item of faith, nor on the basis of an *a priori* argument. In the *Dialogues*, Cleanthes supports his theological position with an *a posteriori* argument from design. He argues that "order" in the universe provides sufficient evidence that the world was created by an omnipotent, omniscient, and perfectly good being.[17] He proposes the existence of God as a quasi-scientific explanatory hypothesis, arguing its truth via the claim that it provides an adequate explanation for observed facts.

Philo has two comments to make regarding the relevance of suffering in the world for a theology of this kind.

The first is a comment with which Philo is obviously well pleased. It is offered at the end of Part X and is repeated no fewer than three times in Part XI. It is this: even if the existence of God and the occurrence of suffering in the world are logically compatible, one cannot argue from a world containing suffering to the existence of an omnipotent, omniscient, and perfectly good creator. This observation, I think all would agree, is correct. Given only a painting containing vast areas of green, one could not effectively argue that its creator disliked using green. There would be no *logical* conflict in holding that a painter who disliked using green painted a picture containing vast areas of green. But given *only* the picture (and no further information), the hypothesis that its creator disliked using green would be poorly supported indeed.

It is clear that in this first comment Philo has offered a criticism of Cleanthes' *argument* for the existence of God. He explicitly says that this complaint is against Cleanthes' *inference* from a world containing instances of suffering to the existence of an omnipotent, omniscient, and perfectly good creator (p. 73). Philo's second comment, however, is more forceful than this. It is a challenge of the *truth* of Cleanthes' *hypothesis*.

Philo argues as follows:

---

[17]It is interesting to notice that, in many cases, theologians who have used an argument from design have not attempted to argue that "order" in the world proves the existence of a perfectly moral being. For example, in St. Thomas' "fifth way" and in William Paley's *Natural Theology*, "order" is used to show only that the creator of the world was *intelligent*. There are, however, historical instances of the argument from design's being used to prove the goodness as well as the intelligence of a creator. For example, Bishop Berkeley argues this way in the second of the *Dialogues Between Hylas and Philonous*.

Look round this universe. What an immense profusion of beings, animated and organized, sensible and active! You admire this prodigious variety and fecundity. But inspect a little more narrowly these living existences, the only beings worth regarding. How hostile and destructive to each other! How insufficient all of them for their own happiness! . . . There is indeed an opposition of pains and pleasures in the feelings of sensible creatures; but are not all the operations of nature carried on by an opposition of principles, of hot and cold, moist and dry, light and heavy! The true conclusion is that the original Source of all things is entirely indifferent to all these principles, and has no more regard to good above ill than to heat above cold, or to drought above moisture, or to light above heavy [p. 79].

Philo claims that *there is* an "original Source of all things" and that this source is indifferent with respect to matters of good and evil. He pretends to be inferring this conclusion from observed data. This represents a departure from Philo's much professed skepticism in the *Dialogues*. And, no doubt, many of the criticisms of Cleanthes' position which Philo advanced earlier in the *Dialogues* would apply with equal force to the inference Philo has just offered. But I shall not dwell on this last point. I think that the center of Philo's remarks in this passage must be located in their skeptical rather than their metaphysical import. Philo has proposed a hypothesis which is counter to the one offered by Cleanthes. And he claims that his hypothesis is the "true conclusion" to be drawn from the observed data. But the point is not, I think, that Philo's new hypothesis is true, or even probable. The conclusion is, rather, that the hypothesis advanced by Cleanthes is false, or very improbable. When claiming that evil in the world *supports* a hypothesis which is counter to the one offered by Cleanthes, I think Philo simply means to be calling attention to the fact that evil in the world provides *evidence against* Cleanthes' theological position.

Consider the following analogy which, I think, will help expose this point. I am given certain astronomical data. In order to explain the data, I introduce the hypothesis that there exists a planet which has not yet been observed but which will be observable at such and such a place in the sky at such and such a time. No other hypothesis seems as good. The anticipated hour arrives and the telescopes are trained on the designated area. No planet appears. Now, either one of two conclusions may be drawn. First, I might conclude that there is no planet there to be seen. This requires either that I reject the original astronomical data or that I admit that what seemed the best explanation of the data is not, in fact, the true explanation. Second, I might conclude that there is a planet there to be seen, but that something in the observational set-up went amiss. Perhaps the equipment was faulty, perhaps there were clouds, and so on. Which conclusion is correct? The answer is not straightforward. I must check both possibilities.

Suppose I find nothing in the observational set-up which is in the least out of order. My equipment is in good working condition, I find no clouds, and so on. To decide to retain the planet hypothesis in the face of the recalcitrant datum (my failure to observe the planet) is, in part, to decide that there is some circumstance (as yet unknown) which explains the datum *other* than the nonexistence of the planet in question. But a decision to retain the planet hypothesis (in the face of my failure to observe the planet and in the absence of an explicit explanation which "squares" this failure with the planet hypothesis) is made correctly *only* when the *evidence for* the planet hypothesis is such as to render its negation less plausible than would be the assumption of a (as yet unknown) circumstance which explains the observation failure. This, I think, is part of the very notion of dealing reasonably with an explanatory hypothesis.

Now Cleanthes has introduced the claim that there exists an omnipotent, omniscient, and perfectly good being as a way of explaining "order" in the world. And Philo, throughout the *Dialogues* (up to and including most of Part XI), has been concerned to show that this procedure provides very little (if any) solid evidence for the existence of God. The inference from the data to the hypothesis is extremely tenuous. Philo is now set for his final thrust at Cleanthes' position. Granting that God and evil are not logically incompatible, the existence of human suffering in the world must still be taken as a recalcitrant datum with respect to Cleanthes' hypothesis. Suffering, as Philo says, is not what we should antecedently expect in a world created by an omnipotent, omniscient, and perfectly good being (pp. 71–72). Since Cleanthes has offered nothing in the way of an explicit theodicy (that is, an explanation of the recalcitrant datum which would "square" it with his hypothesis) and since the *evidence for* his hypothesis is extremely weak and generally ineffective, there is pretty good reason for thinking that Cleanthes' hypothesis is false.

This, I think, is the skeptical import of Philo's closing remarks in Part XI. On this reading, nothing is said about an "original Source of all things" which is indifferent with respect to matters of good and evil. Philo is simply making clear the negative force of the fact of evil in the world for a hypothesis such as the one offered by Cleanthes.

It ought not to go unnoticed that Philo's closing attack on Cleanthes' position has extremely limited application. Evil in the world has central negative importance for theology only when theology is approached as a quasi-scientific subject, as by Cleanthes. That it is seldom approached in this way will be evident to anyone who has studied the history of theology. Within most theological positions, the existence of God is taken as an item of faith or embraced on the basis of an *a priori* argument. Under these circumstances, where there is nothing to qualify as a "hypothesis" capable of having either negative or positive "evidence," the fact of evil in the world presents no special problem for theology. As Philo himself has suggested, when the existence of God is accepted prior to any rational consideration of the status of evil in the world, the traditional problem of evil reduces to a noncrucial perplexity of relatively minor importance.

TERENCE PENELHUM

1.20 Divine Goodness and the Problem of Evil

The purpose of this paper is not to offer any solution to the problem of evil, or to declare it insoluble. It is rather the more modest one of deciding on its nature. Many writers assume that the problem of evil is one that poses a logical challenge to the theist, rather than a challenge of a moral or scientific sort. If this assumption is correct, and the challenge cannot be met, Christian theism can be shown to be untenable on grounds of inconsistency. This in turn means that it is refutable by philosophers, even if their task is interpreted in the most narrowly analytical fashion. It has recently been argued that the challenge of the problem of evil can be met on logical grounds, and that if the existence of evil is damaging to theism it is not because the recognition of its existence is inconsistent with some essential part of it. I take two examples of this position. The first is in the paper "Hume on Evil" by Nelson Pike;[1] the second I owe to Professor R. M. Chisholm.[2]

Let us first present the problem of evil in its traditional, logical guise. The argument is that it is inconsistent for anyone to believe both of the following two propositions:

I. The world is the creation of a God who is omnipotent, omniscient, and wholly good.
II. The world contains evil.

Both, especially the first, are highly complex propositions, and it is natural that the problem is often put as one of the apparent inconsistency of holding

From *Religious Studies* 2 (1967): 95–107. Reprinted by permission of Cambridge University Press.
[1]Nelson Pike, "Hume on Evil," *Philosophical Review*, vol. LXXII, (no. 2, 1963), pp. 180–97. The argument is also presented in his volume *God and Evil* (Prentice-Hall, Inc., 1964), pp. 85–102.
[2]I learned of this argument through seminar discussion, and Professor Chisholm is not responsible for any inaccuracies in my account of it or any infelicities in my examples.

three or four or more propositions at once. Although the complexity of I is vital, the problem can be stated well enough in this deceptively simple form. Let us begin by recognising two things about the problem as presented. (*a*) Apart from some eminent and disingenuous theologians, proposition II is not itself a challenge to theism. It is a part of it. The existence of evil is not something the facts of life force the theist to admit, in the way in which the facts of the fossil evidence forced some nineteenth century theists to admit the antiquity of the world. The existence of evil is something the theist emphasises. Theists do not see fewer evils in the world than atheists; they see more. It is a necessary truth that they see more. For example, to the theist adultery is not only an offence against another person or persons, but also an offence against a sacrament, and therefore against God; it is therefore a worse offence, because it is a compound of several offences. Atheists can never be against sin, for to atheists there can be no sins, "sin" being a theological concept that only has application if God exists. Only if this is accepted can the problem of evil be represented as a logical problem. For a charge of inconsistency can only be levelled against the theist if he holds both of the allegedly inconsistent propositions *as part of his belief*. The nineteenth century theist who finally accepted the antiquity of the world could not have been accused of logical inconsistency unless a belief like that of the world's beginning in 4004 B.C. were entailed by his form of theism. (*b*) Given this, it is easy to see why the logical challenge the problem of evil presents is so serious. For the theist, in believing in God, believes *both* that God created the world *and* that much that is in the world is deeply deficient in the light of the very standards God himself embodies. The inconsistency seems to result from two distinguishable functions which the idea of God has. It is an ultimate source of explanations of why things are as they are; it is also the embodiment of the very standards by which many of them are found to be wanting.

II

Let us now turn to Pike's argument. Briefly paraphrased, it runs as follows. Propositions I and II are not of themselves incompatible. To get a logically inconsistent set of beliefs we have to add:

III. A being who is omnipotent and omniscient would have no morally sufficient reason for allowing instances of evil.

I, II, and III are, taken together, logically inconsistent, since any two together entail the falsity of the third. For the inconsistency of theism to be demonstrated, Pike argues, III has to be a necessary truth. Unless it is shown to be a necessary truth it is always open to a theist to say that there is some morally sufficient reason why God allows evil, even though he may have no

idea what this reason actually is. He can say that he knows I and II are true
(e.g. I by revelation and II by observation); so III is false: even though God
is omnipotent and omniscient, there is some (mysterious) morally sufficient
reason for the evils which he allows. There just *must* be. This is, Pike argues,
a perfectly adequate retort to the charge of inconsistency unless proposition
III can be *demonstrated*: i.e. unless there is a demonstration that there
cannot be any available morally sufficient reason for an omnipotent and
omniscient being to allow evils.

But how would one set about demonstrating the truth of III? It cannot be
deduced from I or II separately, and in any case to try to do this would be
to beg the question. It obviously cannot be deduced from the conjunction
of I and II, because it is incompatible with this conjunction. The only apparent way of establishing the truth of III is to show in one case after another
that a suggested reason for God's permitting evil is not morally sufficient.
But this is not conclusive, since the theist can always deny that the list of
suggested reasons is complete. This denial can be based on a simple deduction
from I and II taken together, and is compatible with complete agnosticism as
to what God's morally sufficient reason or reasons might be. A theist is not,
in other words, committed to any particular theodicy. The onus is therefore
on the sceptic to show that III is a necessary truth. The theist does not have
to make it seem *plausible* that there is a morally sufficient reason for evil in
order to evade the inconsistency charge. Rather the sceptic has to make the
inconsistency charge take hold by proving that there *cannot* be one.

I think this argument is serious. I shall now summarise Chisholm's argument. The goodness or badness of a state of affairs is, says Chisholm,
defeasible, if it can (logically) be overridden. This can happen when the
state of affairs is combined with another and the resultant complex is of a
value which is either neutral or opposite to that of the first state of affairs,
and is not reduced by the fact that the first state of affairs is a part of it. It
might be held, for example, that the evil of my suffering pain is defeated
by my acquisition of fortitude in the face of it; or that the evil of my suffering
mental distress is defeated by the fact that my distress is due to contrition
for my former sins. Since there is no more good, and perhaps even less good,
in my acquiring fortitude in ways other than that of living through occasions
that require its exercise, then the pain plus the fortitude is better than either
without the other; and since contrition is only possible if some sins have been
committed, the contrite sinner may be a better phenomenon, or no worse
a phenomenon, than the unhumbled innocent.

The theist can argue in the face of the problem of evil in the following
way. Every evil in the world, he can say, is or will be defeated. For every
evil there is a state of affairs which, when combined with it, results in a
conjoint state of affairs which is *either*

(i) not bad and better than either without the other,
or (ii) good and better than either without the other,
or (iii) good and better than any alternative state of affairs.

God can allow evil situations if their defeat is assured in one of these ways; in fact, his goodness would require him to do so.

Chisholm concludes that the problem of evil as a logical challenge is soluble. The moral problem of evil, as he calls it, is harder. This is the problem of suggesting in given cases what states of affairs actually defeat the evils we find in the world; the problem in other words, of finding a specific theodicy. On this he recommends the agnosticism which Pike implicitly recommends. Pike recommends this by classifying the problem thus understood as a "non-crucial perplexity of relatively minor importance."[3]

I would like to suggest that this defence of theism is not successful, since it is not open to the theist to eschew theodicy in the way Pike and Chisholm recommend.

III

Consider the following discussion. To counter the argument that diseases are an indication that the world is not the creation of a wholly good and powerful deity, a believer uses the following obviously bad arguments.

(i) Diseases are a way of reducing populations and preventing undue pressure on world food supplies.

(ii) Some diseases have aesthetically pleasing side-effects: tuberculosis sufferers often acquire a charming pink flush and according to Puccini can often sing better than healthy people.

Both these arguments fail, but for different reasons. The first one fails because it implies what is clearly false, that God could not manage to avoid over-population and food shortage by any means other than allowing epidemics. The second fails because it suggests that aesthetically pleasing side-effects are a morally sufficient reason for allowing the suffering attendant upon diseases. Sceptics often score points against believers by showing that more sophisticated defences end up on examination by committing the same errors. It is very important to stress that the basic challenge that these arguments, and others like them, fail to meet is a logical one rather than a moral or scientific one. This is especially hard to bear in mind in the second sort of case, because people who object to defences of this sort have to appeal to moral considerations in presenting their case. Nevertheless it is the con-

---

[3]Pike, *op. cit.* p. 197.

sistency of theism that is at issue. In the first case the defence fails because it would only work if God were not omnipotent or were not omniscient; and these attributes are built into the *concept* of God. By saying the world is created by God the believer is ruling out this line of defence from the beginning. In the second case we reject the defence because it could only succeed if we were prepared to agree that minor aesthetic advantages could outweigh major moral and physical disadvantages in the assessment of evils like disease. We reject this evaluation, and in doing so we commit ourselves to saying that any being who placed such aesthetic considerations higher on the scale of choices than the physical ones would not be morally good. And moral goodness is also built into the concept of God. It is therefore inconsistent to present a defence of theism which attributes to God this particular preference.

These cases show, therefore, that for all the moral heat the problem of evil gives rise to it is correct to regard it as a logical issue, even though logical issues frequently do not give rise to heatedness. They also show, if they are as typical in form as I think they are, that the concept of God rules out a very large number of theistic defences, because they entail attributing to God limitations or preferences that are incompatible with his stated attributes. So although it may seem plausible for a theist to say, with Pike and Chisholm, that he does not need to commit himself to any particular theodicy, his very theism commits him at the very least to saying that a large number of possible theodicies are false, viz. all those that commit these errors. This entails the view that whatever reason God may have for allowing evils, it is a reason which is compatible with his omnipotence, omniscience, and his moral goodness. The situation regarding the omnipotence and the omniscience are fairly clear, though they generate interesting perplexities. I would like to concentrate here on the more complex attribute of moral goodness.

It is impossible to emphasize too much how deeply our thinking about religious matters has been affected by the absorption of the ideas of moral goodness and omnipotence into the concept of God. From time to time thinkers suggest that there is a God who is all-good but not all-powerful, or who is all-powerful but not all-good. Such suggestions clearly avoid the problem of evil; but we are merely bored by them. The alternatives are always tacitly restricted to two: either there is a God who is all-powerful and all-good, or there is no God at all. Christianity may not have convinced everybody, but it has certainly made us all very finicky. For (as Findlay has so forcibly reminded us[4]) the only God in whose existence we can evince interest is one whom it would be proper to worship. And worship in the Western world does not now mean the appeasing of an angry god or the encouragement of a weak one. It necessarily includes submission and moral reverence.

This important feature of the logic of theism goes so deep that it can be

---

[4] J. N. Findlay, "Can God's Existence be Disproved?" in Flew and MacIntyre, *New Essays in Philosophical Theology* (S. C. M., London, 1955), pp. 47–56.

overlooked or misunderstood. In particular, since the very complexity of the demands made on the concept of deity by most people issues in a tacit rejection of many possible hypotheses intermediate between theism and atheism, there is a tendency for us to overlook the fact that there are a variety of reasons why the concept of God may be thought to have no application. An unbeliever may decide that no being is omnipotent, or that no being is omniscient, or that no being is all-good. Or he may decide that even if there exists a being who is all these things in the eyes of the believers he knows, the policies attributed to him are not such as to merit moral reverence. If he decides this he decides that the object of his friends' worship is not God; God does not exist. This is a *moral* rejection of theism. He may, yet again, reject theism on the ground that no being who was all-powerful, omniscient and all-good *by his friends' standards* would allow the evils that he and his friends both see to exist. *This* would be a logical reason for rejecting theism, even though it would lean, at critical points, on the attribution to God of moral goodness. Let us now explore this attribution with more care.

IV

There is something very odd about suggesting that although someone is morally good I have no idea what he would do in a wide range of situations; though it is quite possible for me to say that I do not know how he would handle some particularly knotty problem. The reason the second is possible is that familiar situations, where the good man's actions are predictable, do not supply precedents that yield ready answers to the knotty problems. In such cases the good man will likely serve as the source of such guidance, his suitability for this role deriving from his rectitude in more readily assessable situations. If this is correct it shows that evaluating someone as morally good may entail a readiness to agree to the wisdom of his decision on a difficult case just because it is he who is making the decision; but it also shows that this cannot cover *all* cases. His very authority derives from our having certified him as good, and this derives from his decisions in straightforward instances. These I acknowledge as good on the basis of *my own* moral standards. If I see that someone else, however consistent or deliberative, acts in straightforward cases in ways that manifest standards different from my own, I will not accept his decisions as a guide, and not evaluate his decisions as morally good. (If I call such a person good I shall refer to his motives not his particular choices, and, what is important here, I shall not regard the reasons he offers for his decisions as morally sound or sufficient, even though I shall not blame him for adhering to them.) The case of God may be different; but I shall put this possibility on one side for the present. What I wish to emphasise at this stage is that the concept of moral goodness, however blessedly general it may look, nevertheless requires, when actually applied to a particular person and his actions *by* some particular person (in other words, when actually used rather than mentioned) the attribution to the person it is applied to of a fairly specific set of choice-patterns. More than this, these choice-patterns are (and this is a necessary truth, and a familiar one) the choice-patterns *of the speaker.* In calling someone morally good, a speaker must have in mind some set of moral standards which the man he calls good follows in his conduct. In Hare's terms, he must have criteria of goodness which the man he calls good satisfies.[5] And these must be criteria he subscribes to himself (though he need not, of course, act on them—he can show he subscribes to them by felling guilty at *not* acting on them). For it is inconsistent to say that someone else's decisions are made in accordance with correct moral standards but that one does not subscribe to these standards oneself. It is true that people's criteria of goodness differ. But in calling someone good I have to use *some* set of criteria. And these have banally, to be my own.

Extrapolating to the divine case is hazardous. But I will nevertheless hazard the following. In calling God good one is not merely applying to him some general epithet of commendation, with no ancillary commitment on what he might be expected to do. Although one cannot require God to do anything, in calling him good one is necessarily expressing the conviction that his behaviour will satisfy a certain set of moral standards; and in this case as in others, it is vacuous to apply the concept of goodness without a fairly detailed idea of what these standards are. These standards are standards which the speaker must regard as applying to himself. If God's actions are approved because it is God who does them, this is the result of his manifesting, in general, the standards to which believers subscribe themselves. I wish to conclude from this set of theses that in calling God good a theist is committed to saying that God's reasons for permitting evils must be reasons that are acceptable according to the believer's own set of moral standards. I wish to argue that in some important cases these are sufficiently restrictive to delineate a definite theodicy, even if it is not worked out in practice.

It is true that people's moral standards differ. But if they do, their concepts of God differ also; and, notoriously, one's concept of the will of God will be affected by one's independent moral judgments and the changes in them. Let us imagine two examples. A doctor, who believes in God, may find it hard to decide whether euthanasia is ever morally permissible. If he decides it never is, he will no doubt say euthanasia is contrary to the will of God. Let us now suppose that after some harrowing experiences he comes to believe that euthanasia is in some cases morally right. How will he describe his state of mind? I think it is clear he will not say, "I used to agree with God that euthanasia is always wrong; but now I see he is mistaken." He will say, if he retains his belief, that he has reversed his view of what God's will is. If he has changed his mind about euthanasia but not about the divine will

---

[5] See *The Language of Morals*, chapter 6 (Oxford, Clarendon Press, 1952).

he must abandon his theism. Secondly, let us imagine a consistent disciple of Oscar Wilde, who believes that aesthetic values can properly take precedence over ethical ones. We can expect such a person, if he believes in God, to ascribe such standards to him, and not, therefore, to repudiate the aesthetic defence of theism that I outlined earlier. 'Good', we are often reminded, is an evaluative term, and evaluations vary; but the concept of the being who gets the highest possible value-rating will vary with the scale of values of those who award the marks.

It should be emphasized that the word 'evil' is also an evaluative term. It is frequently said that observation will establish that the world contains evil. This is no doubt true, but the judgment that certain observed facts in the world are *to be classed as evils* is an evaluative judgment, however much the presence of those facts is established by observation. The theist can only be accused of inconsistency if the scale of values *he* uses commits him to saying that the facts *he* calls evil are allowed by God without reasons that *his* scale of values allows *him* to call morally sufficient; if the states of affairs *he* calls evil ones are undefeated on *his* scale of values by other facts conjoined with them. And of course the theist commits no logical mistake if he rejects the sceptic's value-scale, and insists that certain apparent evils are not evils at all, and certain apparent goods not goods at all. We must avoid posing the problem as one where the theist is attacked for accepting the existence of certain facts which only the critic regards as evil and ascribing to God reasons which only the critic would refuse to accept as morally good. This is a moral disagreement, not a logical one. We must also avoid the suggestion that the recognition of the evil facts is straightforwardly empirical, and their justification something more besides. If the facts are to pose a problem at all, they have to be accepted by the believer as potential counter-examples; and moral agreement here is too readily assumed. This is one of the many places where Christianity is paying a high price for its social success.

It might be agreed thus far that in ascribing the creation of the world to a being he classifies as all-good, the theist is ascribing to God a scale of values akin to his own, and that this circumscribes the range of possible reasons for allowing evil that he can consistently ascribe to God. But this may seem a long way from admitting that the theist is committed in most or any cases to the choice of one or two such reasons, or from admitting that he cannot in the tough cases resort to agnosticism on the grounds that God knows best and we do not understand.

Let us look at the second first. Certainly it seems reasonable in the case of any person endowed with high moral standing and authority to say that he should be the source of advice, and even to go so far as to say that *his* deciding one way rather than the other may serve, now and again, as a criterion of the correctness of the decision. If this can go for wise men, why not for the deity? Certainly there is a strong theological tradition which argues, against Plato, that some things are right because God does them rather than that God does them because they are right. I think the retort to this for our present purpose is not to contest this possibility, but to allow it and contest its relevance. Certainly I might say that I have accepted the Pope's moral authority and must therefore accept what he says on birth control, even though it runs counter to my own intuitions in these matters. This is allowable, but does have one consequence. Having decided that the authority's decision has to stand, I am not at liberty to leave my principles unaffected. If the Pope's stand on birth control is agreed to, so be it; but then I must sacrifice any principles I previously held with which this value-decision is inconsistent. Or I must show that there are no real inconsistencies, only apparent ones. Then of course those who object to the papal pronouncements have a straightforwardly moral disagreement with me—and it follows at once that their concept of God cannot be mine, or (what comes to the same here) that they think the Pope is not the infallible mouthpiece of the Holy Ghost. We do not need to insist that God's moral authority depends on his decisions' coinciding with our moral intuitions; but we do need to insist that if we accept a purported moral decision as coming from God, our moral intuitions have to be put aside as misleading if they do not coincide with that decision. What is necessary is that the moral principles the theist holds to and the ones he ascribes to God are the same. Here again we have to allow for the fact that an omnipotent and omniscient being will not be in situations that compare precisely with any in which we find ourselves (God, in fact, is never "in" situations at all); but the principles he follows must be the same. A rich man with no family and a poor man with a large one will no doubt respond differently to the same request for money; yet their moral principles can be identical.

The problem of internal consistency would arise if some moral decision were ascribed to God which was inconsistent with moral principles the theist could not adjust or abandon, because they were previously held by him to have divine sanction. And it would arise also if the only logically possible reasons for the existence of a given evil were inconsistent with such principles. This would show, if it happened, that there are no morally sufficient reasons possible for the evil in question (that it is indefeasible), and that agnosticism regarding the reasons God actually might have does not provide an escape-route for the theist.

How would we know when such a case was before us? The answer, I think, is "when the system of values adhered to by the believer, and ascribed to God, is one which contains specific guidance on what goods do and do not defeat certain evils, or upon what is and is not a morally sufficient reason for certain evils; when a given evil is agreed to exist, and the goods which might defeat it do not." If this general answer is agreed to, it will readily be seen that some forms of theism would indeed permit a wide range of instances where a prudent agnosticism on matters of theodicy might be possible, and others would not permit any range at all. One could only argue from this point on with particular theists with particular scales of value. Catholics would have much less room for manoeuvre than Unitarians. I propose to discuss the case of a moderately sophisticated biblical Protestant.

V

It would be absurd to attempt a detailed characterisation of Christian ethics here. But two features of it are particularly striking and important. The first is the fact that Christian principles are in many cases rules for assigning priorities in choice, and serve as guides to relatively complex moral situations, not as mere classifications of certain states of affairs as good or bad. To illustrate, let us consider the contrast between Christian ethics and hedonistic ethics. The latter are based upon the fundamentally simple assertions that pleasure is the main or only good and pain the main or only evil. The fundamental principles of Christian ethics, such as the Ten Commandments, deal directly with complex moral situations such as stealing, murder, or adultery, rather than with their ingredients. Notoriously they do not even say unambiguously whether pleasure and pain are good or bad; they direct attention at once onto occasions where we are called upon, as moral agents, to assign a precedence among various possibilities. However good pleasure may be, or however bad frustration may be, if the potential partner in the enterprise is another man's wife, the pleasure is forbidden. The goodness of the pleasure, if any, is defeated by the badness of the violation of the marriage-bond; and the badness, if any, of the frustration, is defeated by the goodness of the observance of it. However good, if at all, the acquisition of property is, the badness of depriving someone to whom it already belongs defeats it. The ethic makes fundamental use of notions such as temptation and resistance, which themselves suggest this sort of complexity of choice. The second feature requiring emphasis here is the fact that as it finds expression in the New Testament, the Christian ethic places uniquely high value on certain personal qualities and relationships, founded upon love. The value assigned to pleasure or pain would seem to depend upon their relationship to these qualities (or to their opposites) in complex situations. Clearly in the Christian tradition pleasure in the infliction of suffering makes the infliction worse, not better; although the same conclusion can be arrived at in a hedonistic ethic, a good deal of casuistic footwork needs to be done to reach it. Christianity obviously rejects the thesis that pleasure is the only good, and does not clearly embrace even the modest thesis that it is good *per se*, i.e. in the absence of bad accompaniments. It even more obviously rejects the principle that pain is the only, or even the greatest, evil, though in enjoining its diminution it would seem to embrace the thesis that it is *per se* bad, i.e. bad when not a means to that which is prized, such as steadfastness, forgiveness or humility.

If these brief characterisations of the ethics associated with one familiar form of theism are correct, it follows, I would suggest, that its adherents are committed to the principles of a familiar form of theodicy, and embroiled thereby in its problems. For they are committed to a moral scheme which requires them to judge the value of certain states of affairs in the light of that of others. This, in turn, will determine their judgments on what are, and (equally importantly) what are not, morally sufficient reasons for certain kinds of action or inaction. As theists they are committed to ascribing this very scheme of moral priorities to God, to ascribing to him, in other words, a set of policies which have to determine what evils have to be allowed by him in his creation. More accurately, they are committed to ascribing to him the particular sorts of reasons which *their* ethic would permit them to regard as sufficient for the evils which his creation can independently be seen to contain. They have to say, in other words, that the universe is run on Christian principles, and when they encounter a state of affairs which, by those principles, is evil, they must in consistency hold that it is permitted by God for reasons which are applications of those principles. This follows from calling God good and this state of affairs evil. More specifically, if certain forms of spiritual life and relationship have the highest place in the application of Christian principles, God too must value them highly, and evils he permits must only *appear* to contravene the ascription of these values to him; when rightly understood they have to be thought of as furthering them. We seem to be involved, therefore, in the traditional theological exercise of regarding all evils as justified, if God exists, by the possibility of some spiritual benefit of which they are the necessary condition.

This is not to say that a commitment to a general theodicy of this sort is tantamount to agreement to any particular theologian's justification of a particular historical evil, like the Lisbon earthquake. It is, however, tantamount to the acceptance of a limited *range* of possible explanations (those that entail ascribing to God a choice good by Christian standards) and the rejection of others. The problem becomes the acute difficulty of internal consistency it is traditionally alleged to be when the permissible range provides no reason that will fit some state of affairs that is admittedly an evil one. (A theodicy emphasising spiritual benefits can perhaps offer reason for human suffering, but seems unable to deal with animal pain, for example. Such an evil may not be in practice the worst, but it may be in theology the most intractable.)

Even this limitation allows a wide range of theological interpretation. Two areas of potential variation should be mentioned. There is, first of all, some ambiguity in the ascription to God of the value-scale of a believer. Our moral principles tell us what to do in certain sets of circumstances. God is not limited by circumstances, but creates them. Some principles tell us what to do in bad circumstances, e.g. the rule that we should forgive injuries. In ascribing such a standard to God we do of course imply that he forgives those who commit offences against him. But do we also imply that he so prizes forgiveness in us that his goodness requires him to provide (or allow) the unpleasant occasions that call for its exercise? Granted that when Smith injures Jones, Jones ought to forgive Smith; is the evil of Smith's injury to Jones justified by the fact that only it, or something like it, could afford Jones an opportunity to show forgiveness? It is at least plausible to argue that a theodicy that would justify the evil by reference to its potential for training men in the right spiritual responses would require us to ascribe to God this very strong sort of adherence to the value of forgiveness; but it is not obviously necessary to do so. Furthermore, the spiritual states most highly prized in the Christian tradition are only possible for free agents; hence the great emphasis on man's freedom of choice in all the major theodicies. This emphasis enables apologists to distinguish between natural evils like pain (evils which can elicit good states of mind but which are not caused by bad states of mind) and moral evils like vengefulness which *are* bad states of mind. The latter can all be blamed on the misuse of human free choice, which is a logically necessary condition of good states of mind like love and forgiveness, or fortitude, which can turn natural evils into ingredients of good situations. From this in turn it follows that the badness of many actual bad states of mind can be regarded as justified by the fact that their very possibility is a necessary condition of the free choice which is logically required for the chance of the good states of mind which have not, on these occasions, materialised. This generates the problem of whether free choice is itself a good which God fosters. It is not obvious what the apologist should say to this. All he *has* to say is that the highest goods in the Christian tradition are states of mind and relationships which cannot exist without free choice; so that the presence of some evils which free choice can lead to (such as revenge instead of forgiveness) is due to the wrong exercise of a faculty which one has to have to achieve the preferred states of mind. This would seem to leave open, and perhaps to render unimportant, the issue of the intrinsic value of free choice itself.

These two areas of potential controversy are enough to show that there is much freedom of theological, manoeuvre even within the fairly specific value scheme of Christian theism. It is nevertheless true, however, that Christian theism, by calling God omnipotent and omniscient *and* wholly good, requires its adherents to hold that he permits such evils as there are for Christian reasons; and that these involve his being said to allow them in the interests of certain spiritual states in his creatures, who have, to participate in these states, to be capable of free choice. A Christian theist, therefore, is committed to some form or other of the traditional 'free-will defence'.

VI

To sum up: I have argued that any theist, in calling his God good, ascribes to him his own moral principles, and implies that the world is created and governed in a way which ideally represents their exercise. Any evils he admits to being in the world must, he must say, be allowed by God because their presence is at least compatible with the furtherance of those ends regarded on the very scale which classes the evils *as* evils, as being supremely good. The existence of any admitted evil not so compatible would refute the believer's theism; for to admit its existence would be to introduce an element of inconsistency into the theist's position. When this is recognised it becomes clear that a theist is committed to a scheme of theodicy in two ways at least. He cannot remain confidently agnostic about the range of purposes for which God would allow evils. And the more specific his moral code is on moral priorities, the more precise he has to be in suggesting possible divine reasons for particular evils. I have suggested that *Christian* theism is quite specific on moral priorities, and that it lays fundamental stress on certain relationships and states of mind. A Christian theist, faced with what he admits to be an evil, has therefore to hold that God allows it because the existence or possibility of it, or of something equally bad, is a necessary condition of some such relationship or state of mind. To admit the existence of an evil which demonstrably cannot have this function would be to admit a proposition inconsistent with Christian theism. For such an evil would be *pointless*. It is logically inconsistent for a theist to admit the existence of a pointless evil.

Pike argued that for the problem of evil to present a logical challenge to the theist, it must be possible to show that his proposition III:

> A being who is omnipotent and omniscient would have no morally suffi-
> cient reason for allowing instances of evil

is a necessary truth; and that it is not possible to show it to be one. In all its high generality it is not. I have tried to show, however, that in a given form of theism the concept of a morally sufficient reason may be sufficiently restricted to render it impossible for an omnipotent and omniscient being to have morally sufficient reasons for some evils. If such evils seem to exist in fact, then the problem of evil presents itself to the theist as the logical difficulty it has traditionally been thought to be.

Similarly, Chisholm's suggestion that a theist can hold that every evil is defeated without claiming to know by what, must contend with the fact that in a given form of theism the range of possible defeating factors may be specifically understood and incorporated in its moral requirements. If it should seem that a particular evil is not so defeasible its existence poses a logical difficulty to the theist as it has traditionally been thought to do.

FAITH

BLAISE PASCAL

1.21 The Wager

Let us speak now according to the light of nature.

If there is a God he is infinitely incomprehensible, since, having neither parts nor limits, he has no proportion to us: we are then, incapable of knowing either what he is, or whether he is. This being true, who will dare to undertake to resolve this question? It is not we, who have no proportion to him.

Who, then, shall blame, as not being able to give a reason for their belief, those Christians, men who profess a religion for which they can give no reason? They declare, in exposing it to the world, that it is a folly, *stultitiam;* and then you complain that they do not prove it! If they proved it, they would not keep their word: it is in lacking proofs, that they do not lack sense. Yes; but though this may excuse those who offer it such, and take away the blame for producing it without reason, this does not excuse those who receive it. Let us examine this point then, and say: God is, or he is not. But to which side shall we incline? Reason cannot decide it at all. There is an infinite chaos that separates us. A game is being played, at the extremity of this infinite distance, in which heads or tails must come up. Which will you take? By reason you can wager on neither; by reason you can hinder neither from winning.

Do not, then, charge with falsehood those who have made a choice; for you know nothing about it.—No: but I blame them for having made, not this choice, but a choice; for, although he who takes heads, and the other, are in the same fault, they are both in fault: the proper way is not to wager.

From Blaise Pascal, *Pensées.*

Yes, but you must wager: this is not voluntary, you are embarked. Which will you take then? Let us see. Since a choice must be made, let us see which interests you the least. You have two things to lose, the true and the good; and two things to stake, your reason and your will, your knowledge and your beatitude; and your nature has two things to shun, error and misery. Your reason is not more wounded, since a choice must necessarily be made, in choosing one rather than the other. Here is a point eliminated; but your beatitude? Let us weigh the gain and the loss, in taking heads that God exists. Let us weigh these two cases: if you gain, you gain all; if you lose, you lose nothing. Wager then that he is, without hesitation.—This is admirable: yes, it is necessary to wager; but perhaps I wager too much.—Let us see. Since there is equal hazard of gaining or losing, if you had to gain but two lives for one, still you might wager. But if there were three to gain, it would be requisite to play (since you are under the necessity of playing), and you would be imprudent, when you are forced to play, not to hazard your life in order to gain three in a play where there is equal hazard of loss and gain. But there is an eternity of life and happiness. And this being true, even were there an infinity of chances, only one of which might be for you, you would still be right in wagering one in order to have two, and you would act foolishly, being obliged to play, to refuse to play one life against three in a game where among an infinity of chances there is one for you, if there was an infinity of life infinitely happy to gain. But there is here an infinity of life infinitely happy to gain, a chance of gain against a finite number of chances of loss, and what you play is finite. This is quite settled: wherever the infinite is, and where there is not an infinity of chances of loss against the chance of gain, there is nothing to balance, we must give all. And thus, when we are forced to play, we must renounce reason in order to keep life rather than to hazard it for the infinite gain, as ready to come as the loss of nothingness.

For there is no use in saying that it is uncertain whether we shall gain, and that it is certain that we hazard; and that the infinite distance between the certainty of what we risk, and the uncertainty of what we shall gain, raises the finite good which we risk with certainty, to an equality with the infinite which is uncertain. It is not so: every player hazards with certainty to gain with uncertainty, and nevertheless he hazards certainly the finite to gain uncertainly the finite, without sinning against reason. The distance is not infinite between this certainty of what we risk and the uncertainty of gain; this is false. There is, in truth, an infinity between the certainty of gaining and the certainty of losing. But the uncertainty of gaining is proportioned to the certainty of what we hazard, according to the proportion of the chances of gain and loss; whence it comes that, if there are as many chances on one side as there are on the other, the game is playing even; and then the certainty of what we hazard is equal to the uncertainty of the gain: so far is it from being infinitely distant. And thus our proposition is of infinite force, when there is the finite to hazard in a play where the chances of gain and loss are equal, and the infinite to gain. This is demonstrative; and if men are capable of any truths, this is one of them.

I confess it, I admit it. But, still, are there no means of seeing the trick of the game?—Yes, the Scripture, and the rest, etc.

Yes; but my hands are tied and my mouth is dumb: I am forced to wager, and I am not at liberty: I am not unfettered and so constituted that I cannot believe. What will you have me do then?

It is true. But learn, at least, your inability to believe, since reason brings you to it, and yet you cannot believe; try then to convince yourself, not by the augmentation of proofs of the existence of God, but by the diminution of your own passions. You would have recourse to faith, but you know not the way: you wish to be cured of infidelity, and you ask for the remedy: learn it from those who have been bound like yourself, and who would wager now all their goods; these know the road that you wish to follow, and are cured of a disease that you wish to be cured of. Follow their course, then, from its beginning; it consisted in doing all things as if they believed in them, in using holy water, in having masses said, etc. Naturally this will make you believe and stupefy you at the same time.—But this is what I fear.—And why? what have you to lose?

But to show you that this leads to it, this will diminish the passions, which are your great obstacles, etc.

Now, what harm will come to you in taking this course? You would be faithful, virtuous, humble, grateful, beneficent, a sincere friend, truthful. Truly, you would not be given up to infectious pleasures, to false glory, or false joys; but would you not have other pleasures?

I say to you that you will gain by it in this life; and that at each step you take in this direction, you will see so much of the certainty of gain, and so much of the nothingness of what you hazard, that you will acknowledge in the end that you have wagered for something certain, infinite, for which you have given nothing.

Oh! this discourse transports me, delights me, etc.

If this discourse pleases you and appears to you strong, know that it is made by a man who has put himself on his knees, before and after, to pray that Being, who is infinite and without parts, and to whom he entirely submits himself, that he would also subject you to himself for your good and his glory; and that thus power accords with this weakness.

R. G. SWINBURNE[1]

1.22   The Christian Wager

On what grounds will the rational man become a Christian? It is often assumed by many, especially non-Christians, that he will become a Christian
if and only if he judges that the evidence available to him shows that it is
more likely than not that the Christian theological system is true, that, in
mathematical terms, on the evidence available to him, the probability of its
truth is greater than half. It is the purpose of this paper to investigate whether
or not this is a necessary and sufficient condition for the rational man to
adopt Christianity.

The Christian is a man who believes a series of propositions (accepts the
Christian theological system as basically correct) and tries to act in a certain
way (sets himself to live the Christian life). Several recent theologians have
claimed that the Christian is a man who enters into a personal relationship
with Christ, not a man who accepts a series of propositions. Now indeed
there is more to faith than mere belief-that ("Thou believest that God is one;
Thou doest well: The devils also believe and shudder." James 2.19). But, as
Professor Price painstakingly pointed out[2]—belief "in" always presupposes
belief "that." Belief in God presupposes the belief that He exists. A man
who believes in the God of the Christians must—of logical necessity—believe
that a being with the defining properties of the God of the Christians exists.
A man who claims to believe in God may indeed mean much more by his
claim than that he believes that God exists; he will often mean that he puts
his confidence in God to help in life's difficulties. But to put one's confidence
in a person is something one does. Putting one's confidence in God is among
the many actions to which the Christian is committed. The man who makes no
effort to do any of these actions, to lead the Christian life, cannot be described
as a Christian, whatever his beliefs. So the Christian is a man who believes a
series of propositions and tries to act in a certain way.

The rational man is the man who pursues a policy if and only if he judges

From *Religious Studies* 4 (1969): 217–28. Reprinted by permission of Cambridge University Press.
[1]I am most grateful to G. Wallace and C. J. F. Williams for their helpful criticisms of
an earlier version of this paper.
[2]H. H. Price, "Belief 'In' and Belief 'That'." *Religious Studies*, 1965, Vol. I, pp. 5–27.

that the expected gain or mathematical expectation from it exceeds the expected gain (positive or negative) from not pursuing the policy. (If the expected gains from pursuing or not pursuing the policy are equal, the rational man may do either.) The expected gain from a policy is the sum of the values of each possible outcome of the policy, each multiplied by the probability of that outcome. The probability of some outcome O of a policy is the probability of the existence of that state of affairs under which O will be the outcome of the policy. The rational man will thus evaluate the probabilities of the existence of the different states and the value of each outcome, calculate the expected gain from pursuing or not pursuing a policy and act accordingly. Now let us suppose to start with, to simplify the picture, that the only considerations relevant are prudential ones. In that case the rational man is the prudent man, the man who pursues his long-term self-interest. Then the value of an outcome of a policy will be the amount of happiness which it brings to the agent. The rational man will seek to pursue those policies which will maximize his happiness.

Let me give a trivial example to illustrate the above points for those unfamiliar with the terms. A man is deciding between two policies—to bet £1 that Eclipse will win the Derby, or not to bet. There are two possible states of affairs—Eclipse will win, Eclipse will not win. After careful study of the form book, the man estimates the probability that Eclipse will win as 0.2 and so the probability that he will not win as 0.8. The odds offered by bookies are 6–1. Hence if the man bets there are two distinct outcomes—if Eclipse wins, he gains £6; if Eclipse loses, he loses £1. If the man does not bet, the two outcomes are identical—he neither gains nor loses. Now if the value of the outcome for him is measured by their monetary value, then the expected gain of betting is £6 × 0.2 − £1 × 0.8 = £0.4, and the expected gain of not betting is £0 × 0.2 − £0 × 0.8 = £0. Hence the man ought to bet. Of course the value of the outcomes may not be measured by their monetary value—the loss of the £1 may be as undesirable a loss as the win of £6 is a desirable gain. In that case we can represent the gain and loss both by one unit of value. In that case the expected gain of betting will be 1 × 0.2 − 1 × 0.8 = − 0.6, and the expected gain of not betting, as before, 0. Hence in that case the rational man will not bet.

Now it is well known that Pascal's claim that the rational man will become a Christian represented the rational man as choosing between the policies of becoming or not becoming a Christian in this kind of way.

> Let us then examine the point and say "God is," or "He is not." But to which side shall we incline? Reason can decide nothing here. . . . A game is being played . . . heads or tails will turn up. What will you wager?[3]

---

[3] B. Pascal, *Pensées*. No. 233.

If you bet on God and win, you win "an infinity of infinitely happy life";[4] whereas if you bet on God and lose, you lose a mere finite amount. If you bet on no God, or, which amounts to the same thing, refuse to bet openly, then, if you win, you gain a mere finite amount, mere temporary happiness, whereas if you lose, you obtain "an eternity of miseries."[5] Hence you ought to bet on God.

> Our proposition is of infinite force: when there is the finite to stake in a game where there are equal risks of gain and loss, and the infinite to gain. This is demonstrable; and if men are capable of any truths this is one.[6]

There is a lot wrong with Pascal's argument, and it is instructive to consider exactly what. I shall ignore, to begin with, the obvious theological objection that God does not consign to eternal Hell those who die non-Christians for no fault of their own. It will later appear that any mistake in describing the fate of non-Christians if the Christian theological system is true, does not necessarily upset the argument.

First, Pascal has stated the alternative states misleadingly. If the alternatives are meant to be "there is a Christian God" and "there is no after-life," then Pascal has ignored other possible states of affairs—e.g. "There is a god who consigns Christians to eternal Hell and non-Christians to eternal Heaven."[7] Alternatively, Pascal may have intended his alternative states to be simply "There is a Christian God" and "There is not a Christian God." But in that case it is unclear what are the outcomes and so the gains and losses on the second alternative of the two policies—Heaven remains a possible outcome for Christian or non-Christian even on this alternative.

Now clearly we can represent the alternative states as two or many or infinite. Yet perhaps the most useful way to represent them is threefold:

(A)   The God of the Christian exists.
(B)   There is no after-life.
(C)   There is an after-life but no Christian God.

The outcomes of the two alternative policies, becoming or not becoming Christian, are then as Pascal stated them for alternatives A and B; but there are a variety of possible outcomes under the third alternative, and we cannot say much definite about them. The outcomes under the alternative policies, however we evaluate them numerically, will be as follows:

---

[4]*Ibid., loc. cit.*
[5]*Ibid.,* No. 195.
[6]B. Pascal, *Pensées,* No. 233.
[7]This point has been well made by (e.g.) Antony Flew. See his *God and Philosophy* (London, 1966), 9.9 *et seq.*

	A	B	C
(1) Becoming Christian	Christian life of worship and service followed by eternal Heaven	Christian life of worship and service	Christian life of worship and service followed by?
(2) Not becoming Christian	Worldly life followed by eternal Hell	Worldly life	Worldly life followed by?

We will indicate by A_1 the value (positive or negative) of the outcome of policy (1) under state of affairs A, and so on.

A second fault in Pascal's argument is this. Pascal assumed that all men would evaluate in the same way as he the various outcomes. But in fact, rightly or wrongly men will put very different values from each other on the different outcomes. Life in the Christian Heaven appeals to some more than others, and the life of worldly bliss enjoyed by the non-believer also appeals to some more than others. Further of course some men (e.g. the rich) have more opportunity than others to profit from the license of unbelief and so will have a gayer time in consequence. Likewise the Christian religion may demand more sacrifices of some (e.g. the rich) than of others. The different courses of action bring different gains to the twentieth-century business man and the negro in the Ghetto.

Thirdly Pascal supposes (by his remarks "There are equal risks of gain and loss" and "Reason can decide nothing here") that the probabilities of his two alternative states are equal. This claim is, to say the least, arguable. Most of natural theology is devoted to arguing about it. But his argument does not depend on this claim. All we need is some estimate of the probability of alternative states to get the argument off the ground, and, as will be seen, we can reach Pascal's conclusion without having his estimate of probabilities.

Now the rational action for a man will be determined by his estimates of the respective probabilities of the three alternative states and his evaluation of the outcomes under them. The difficulty is that we do not know what our fate will be, after death, if the alternative C be true. Nevertheless men may ascribe probabilities to the other alternative states and evaluate the possible outcomes in such a way that they can judge that one policy would be the best, even if they cannot estimate by how much the best. Thus they may ascribe a probability of zero to alternative C—in which case evaluation of gains and losses under it makes no difference to the calculation. Or, more likely, their scale of values may be such that they can say this much about the gains and losses under alternative C—that C_1 cannot exceed A_1 since Heaven is for them the highest possible bliss, that C_2 can only exceed A_1

by an infinitesimal amount since the maximum gain from life after death, if policy (2) be followed in state of affairs C, can at best only equal that obtained if policy (1) be followed in state of affairs A, and that the very slight difference in happiness on Earth can make very very little difference to the eternal balance sheet.

Once we have in this way assessed the probabilities of alternative states and the values of possible outcomes, we can work out expected gain under the two policies. The expected gain under policy (1)—becoming Christian will be

$$P(A) A_1 + P(B) B_1 + P(C) C_1$$

where $P(A)$ is the probability that A is true, etc. If this exceeds the expected gain under policy (2)

$$P(A) A_2 + P(B) B_2 + P(C) C_2$$

we ought to become Christian; otherwise not. Our estimates will depend on how desirable we consider the different outcomes. If we have Pascal's standards, our evaluation can be represented as follows:

$$A_1 = 1 \qquad\qquad B_1 = 0 \qquad\qquad 1 \leq C_1 \leq -1$$
$$A_2 = -1 \qquad\qquad B_2 = 0 \qquad\qquad 1 \leq C_2 \leq -1$$

These standards are Pascal's, since for him the ratio of worldly gains and losses to gains in the life to come, if there is one, is of finite to infinite. It is more convenient for the purposes of my calculation to measure Pascal's comparative evaluations on a scale on which $A_1 = 1$, $B_1 = 0$, etc., rather than one on which $A_1 = \infty$, $B_1 =$ some finite number. However, Pascal's standards are not everyone's, and someone else might evaluate the alternatives as follows:

$$A_1 = 1 \qquad\qquad B_1 = -0.0005 \qquad\qquad 1 \leq C_1 \leq -1$$
$$A_2 = -1 \qquad\qquad B_2 = +0.0005 \qquad\qquad 1 \leq C_2 \leq -1$$

Then on this estimate of probabilities

$$P(A) = 0.1; P(B) = 0.85; P(C) = 0.05,$$

policy (1) ought to be followed. Yet on this estimate $P(A) = 0.0001$, $P(B) = 0.99985$, $P(C) = 0.00005$, policy (2) ought to be followed. On some estimates of probability, it will be unclear which is the rational policy because of the uncertainty of gains and losses, if C be true. In such circumstances, we ought to divide alternative C up into different possible states—e.g. Ca

(After-life rewards distributed according to Hindu scheme), *Cb* (Christians go to Hell, non-Christians cease to exist), etc.—in such a way that we can ascribe values and probabilities, so as to get a clear indication of the best policy. I conclude that Pascal's system of evaluating whether the man concerned with his long-term interests ought to become a Christian is perfectly workable, but it does not necessarily yield Pascal's results.

Two points must now be made to tidy up the argument so far. First, Pascal's supposition that every man who dies a non-Christian goes, if the Christian God exists, to eternal Hell, would be denied by most Christians. Many Christians would say that only the culpable non-Christian goes to eternal Hell for his beliefs, whereas the man who was a non-Christian because the Christian alternative was never presented to him or because he mistakenly judged it irrational to become Christian would not go to Hell for his beliefs. However, if this is the fate of the non-Christian under alternative (*A*), calculations of the best policy based on this supposition will be the same as those based on the original supposition. For the investigator is a man to whom the Christian alternative has been presented and who must assume that he has not made a mistake in his calculations—hence it is irrelevant what happens to the man to whom the Christian alternative has not been presented or to the man who unintentionally miscalculates. But not all Christians believe that anyone will go to Hell. Some Christians would say that the culpable non-Christian merely ceases to exist—this supposition means that $A_2 = B_2$. This supposition may make a different policy the best one— on some estimates of value and probability. Some few Christians would maintain the rather unbiblical view that all men go to Heaven eventually—the man who follows policy (1) simply goes there sooner. On most estimates of probability and evaluations of outcomes on this supposition policy (2) would seem to come out the best. Further of course most Christians today think of Hell, not as the mediaeval place of literal fiery torment, but merely as a state of separation from God. In so far as different suppositions about the fate of the non-Christian on alternative (*A*) make a difference to what is the best policy, the alternative must be subdivided and probabilities and values ascribed to *Aa* (Christians go to eternal Heaven; non-Christians to eternal Hell), *Ab* (Christians go to eternal Heaven; non-Christians cease to exist) etc.

The second relevant point is this. A man who decides to become a Christian does not merely decide to act in a certain way but decides to hold certain beliefs. The convert may not have held, when wondering whether or not to become a Christian, that the Christian theological system was probably true, but in becoming a Christian he must now adopt this view. Is it logically possible for him to do so? Can a man adopt a belief? Certain philosophers from Hume[8] onwards have held that our beliefs are not subject to our control. If

---

[8] David Hume, *A Treatise of Human Nature*, Appendix, p. 624 in the edition edited by L. A. Selby-Bigge (Oxford, 1888).

they are right, it cannot be rational for us to decide to become Christians, unless we are already convinced of the truth of the Christian theological system, for it cannot be rational for us to do what is not logically possible. Now there *may* be something odd about the suggestion that a man could decide to believe something. But there seems nothing odd about the suggestion that a man could decide to take certain action which had the known effect of inducing some belief.[9] A man might, for instance adopt Pascal's own programme—take holy water, have masses said, etc.[10] Or he might say prayers; or he might just think hard about certain kinds of evidence for his proposition. Having considered the difficulty, I shall nevertheless in future, to avoid the cumbersome phrase, often speak of choosing or deciding to believe, rather than of choosing or deciding to take steps with the known effect of inducing a belief. The former expressions are now meant to be mere definitional substitutes for the latter.

So then if the rational man is the prudent man, whether or not he becomes a Christian depends on how he estimates the happiness provided by the different outcomes and how he assigns probabilities to the different alternative states. Now although we shall shortly have to think of the rational man as a less selfish person, the account so far does elucidate two features of Christian apologetic which have been ignored by most philosophers of religion.

The first is that the Christian preacher to the unconverted is often concerned not with proving the Christian religion to be true, but with expounding what it teaches and the new relationship to God and his fellows which the Christian believes that he and only he will enjoy now and hereafter. An extreme form of this kind of preaching, more fashionable in the past than now, was the sermon which contrasted the joys of Heaven with the pains of Hell, and exhorted men to pursue the good life lest they find themselves in Hell forever after death. Another form of such preaching is the sermon which tells of the joy of Christians on Earth and contrasts it with the dreariness of the non-Christian life on Earth. Many sophisticated philosophers of religion would pour scorn on preaching of this kind. What matters, they would urge, is not what the Christian system offers or threatens, but whether or not it is true, and if the preacher is not prepared to produce evidence to show this, his talk is mere rhetoric. If my argument is correct, such philosophers would not be sophisticated enough. What the preacher has been trying to do is to persuade men of the desirability of what the Christian religion offers here and hereafter, and thereby to show it to be rational for men to gamble all to gain it. In so far as the preacher makes men give a higher value to A_1 and a lower value to A_2, then for fixed $P(A)$, he makes it more rational for men to become Christian. The more desirable is Heaven and the less

---

[9]See H. H. Price, "Belief and Will," *Proceedings of the Aristotelian Society Supplementary Volume*, 1954, 28, pp. 1–26, who develops this point at length.
[10]*Ibid.*, No. 233.

desirable is Hell the more sensible it is to risk much to get to Heaven and avoid Hell, for any given probability that the Christian system is true. Further, in telling of the joy of the Christian life and the dreariness of the non-Christian life on Earth the preacher is presenting an immensely powerful argument for becoming Christian. For he is claiming not merely that A_1 vastly exceeds A_2, but that B_1 somewhat exceeds B_2. If he accepts that argument then (if we ignore for a moment the alternative (C), however low he estimates $P(A)$ and however high he estimates $P(B)$,) the rational man will become Christian. The improbability of the truth of the Christian theological system would be quite irrelevant, for the rewards of being Christian exceed the rewards of not being Christian whether or not the Christian theological system is true. This result could be upset by taking alternative C into account, only if—given an after-life but no Christian God—the evidence was that the Christian was less likely to have a happy after-life than was the non-Christian. But, if we ignore this possibility, then, if the preacher can convince men that B_1 exceeds B_2, probabilities are irrelevant and the rational man will straightway become Christian. The humanist is of course perfectly entitled to counter these arguments by pointing out how even Heaven might pall (viz, that A_1 is not very large after all) and by describing the pleasure of his own worldly society.

The second feature of Christian apologetic on which our account sheds light is this. In so far as Christians have attempted to show the truth of their system, they have often been very much concerned to show how much more likely it is to be true than any other religious system, but not so concerned to show that it is more likely to be true than any non-religious system. My analysis brings out why this is so. Non-religious systems limit the duration of human life to life in this world, and hence the gains and losses of following any religious or non-religious policy are, if a non-religious system be true, very small compared with the gains and losses if the Christian system be true. Hence a non-religious system would have to be very much more probable than the Christian system for it to be rational to adopt it. Whereas rival religious systems offer their own eternal rewards and penalties and so, if their probability is anywhere near that of the Christian system, it will be in no way clear which it is rational to adopt. Hence it is important to the Christian preacher to show that their probability is not in that region. If $P(C)$ exceeds $P(A)$ and C_2 considerably exceeds C_1, then the policy of becoming a Christian may be the irrational policy—even if the joys of Christian life in the present exceed the joys of non-Christian life. For $P(A) = 0.05$, $P(B) = 0.85$, $P(C) = 0.1$, $A_1 = +1$, $A_2 = -1$, $B_1 = B_2$, $C_1 = -0.6$, $C_2 = +0.6$, the non-Christian policy will be the rational one. Now, true, in fact $P(C)$ covers many alternatives, on only some of which will the Christian be less well rewarded than the non-Christian, but these alternatives together must be shown to have a low probability, since the rewards and punishments will have a high positive or negative value in the regions respectively of A_1 and A_2. For this reason the Christian must show that Muhammad is no true prophet, and the Book of Mormon no true gospel. From earliest times Christians have been very much concerned to substantiate this kind of claim.

Yet, of course, there is more to religion than prudence. Moral considerations enter into our picture in two crucial ways. First the goals which we ought to seek are not merely those which we judge to be to our long-term advantage, not what we want, but what we ought to want for ourselves as well as for others. The preacher preaching the relative merits of the different systems tells men not merely that they will enjoy, say, Heaven but that life there will alone have meaning and purpose and that it is man's duty to seek such an existence for himself. But introducing morality into the ends does not disturb our calculus. We can use the same calculus to calculate the morally good as to calculate the long-term advantage. Yet although introducing morality into the ends may not upset the form of the calculus, it may make quite a difference to its matter. If we are concerned only with selfish advantage, there may well be some gain in living the non-Christian life. But the preacher may be able to persuade us that there is no moral good in it, and that the only life worth living is the life of Christian service here and hereafter. In that case we would hold that, however small the probability that the Christian theological system is true, we ought to become Christian. On the other hand the humanist preacher may be able to convince us that the Christian ideal of preserving oneself for a life hereafter, albeit a life of service, is not a worthy one. In that case we would hold that, whatever the possible selfish gain from doing so, we ought not to become Christian. Yet, if on the contrary, the evidence shows that the Christian system is probably true, then it shows that all deductive consequences of that system are probably true. One of these is that it is the duty of men to become Christian. However, considerations so far adduced suggest that it could be our duty to become Christian, even when the evidence suggests that the Christian theological system is probably false.

The other moral consideration which enters into our picture is perhaps the most crucial. It is this. We have seen that the Christian is one who believes certain propositions and lives out a certain kind of life. To decide to become a Christian involves—if we do not already believe them—deciding to take steps which would result in believing certain propositions. But even if a man can choose to believe, ought he to do so? Many would consider that it is highly immoral to choose to believe propositions (viz. to regard the evidence as supporting those propositions) when the evidence is now known not to support them. It would seem like lying to oneself. Others may be concerned with the fact that unless one is prepared to sacrifice one's beliefs in the service of the good, one is only half-committed to its pursuit. I do not wish to consider this moral issue in detail, but only to point out the consequences of different views about it. If a man claimed that there was nothing immoral in inducing in oneself any beliefs at all, not supported by present evidence,[11] then the position is as I have so far outlined it in this paper. The joys of Heaven (or the moral desirability of attempting to obtain them) and the horrors of Hell (or the moral wickedness of allowing oneself to risk obtaining them) provide reasons for inducing oneself to believe what seems on the evidence improbable. Many however would consider it morally wrong to induce oneself to believe what seems improbable. Yet these might hold a weaker position, that there is nothing immoral in choosing to believe one of two exhaustive alternatives between which we cannot decide by rational assessment of the evidence. By this I do not mean choosing to believe something with—by agreed standards of estimating probability—a probability of half; but choosing to believe something with—by one method of estimating probability—a probability of more than half, and—by another method of estimating—a probability of less than half, when it seems equally legitimate to use either method of estimating probability.

There are certain paradigm cases of events having on certain evidence certain numerical probabilities, and of events and theories being on certain evidence more probable than other events and theories. It is clear what is the probability relative to certain evidence of throwing two heads in a row or three sixes with three dice. But it is not always clear how we are to extrapolate standards of estimating probability from such simple cases to more complicated ones and on one way, one method of estimating probability, some theory T may have a probability of more than half, and on another way less than half. Yet both methods may appear equally natural ways of extrapolating from the paradigm cases. What ought one to do here? On one view one ought to average out the results given by the different methods. But there may be many methods, and the average result for the probability of theories and events from all methods may be all too often near to a half. To average the results yielded by all possible methods might seem no less arbitrary than to decide to adopt one method of estimating probability, and thereby reach definite conclusions on matters previously unsettled. Such a decision would not be a decision to go against the evidence, but, at most, a decision to go beyond it. Yet such a decision would lead one to adopt beliefs previously not held. A man who felt it immoral to induce in himself beliefs not warranted by the evidence might well not feel it immoral to adopt one method of estimating probability rather than another, and this on grounds of which beliefs it would lead him to adopt.

Now the position in metaphysics may well be that there are various methods of estimating the probability of metaphysical theories and they are equally natural extrapolations from paradigm cases of ascribing probability to events

---

[11]Price adopts this view in the paper referred to in note 9.

and simpler theories. On one natural way of extrapolating from paradigm cases the evidence may indicate that the Christian theological system is probably true and on another way the evidence may indicate that the system is probably false; yet there be no rational grounds for choosing between the ways of assessing probability obtained by extrapolation from paradigm cases. In such circumstances a man might hold that it was not immoral to choose a method of estimating probability. Hence, he would hold, it would not be immoral to choose a method which led to certain assessments of probability rather than others.

Let us see in detail how, given that a man is allowed to choose between two different methods of estimating probability α and β, but not to choose to believe anything shown by both methods to have a probability of less than a half, he will work out the rational religious policy. Let us denote by P_α (A) the probability that state of affairs A holds on the method α of estimating half, he will work out the rational religious policy. Let us denote by $P_\alpha(A)$ probability, and so on. Let $P_\alpha(A) = 0.55, P_\alpha(B) = 0.35, P_\alpha(C) = 0.1, P_\beta(A) = 0.45, P_\beta(B) = 0.45, P_\beta(C) = 0.1$. Let the man's estimates of the values of the outcomes be as follows:

$$A_1 = 1 \qquad B_1 = -0.05 \qquad +1 \leq C_1 \leq -1$$
$$A_2 = -1 \qquad B_2 = +0.05 \qquad +1 \leq C_2 \leq -1$$

Then on method α the expressed gain of policy (1) will lie between 0.6325 and 0.4325 and of policy (2) between -0.4325 and -0.6325. On method β the expected gain of policy (1) will lie between 0.5275 and 0.3275, and of policy (2) between -0.3275 and -0.5275. Thus, whichever method of estimating probability be used, the expected gain of policy (1) will far outweigh the expected gain of policy (2). Hence if it is not immoral on other grounds to adopt it policy 1 ought to be adopted on these grounds. It will be immoral on other grounds only if thereby we decide to believe something shown to have a probability of less than a half by all legitimate methods of estimating probability. We do not do so in this case. We are deciding to believe something which, if we adopt a certain legitimate method of estimating probability, will have a probability of more than a half. It will therefore be rational to adopt that method of estimating probability. The numerical example which I chose is in one respect a simple one since the expected gain of one policy is greater than that of the other on both methods of estimating probability. It would be easy enough to devise an example in which the most rational policy will vary with the method of estimating probability which we adopt for calculating expected gain. In that case the pursuit of either policy would seem equally rational.

A man might however consider that the results of different methods of estimating probability ought always to be averaged arithmetically, in which case there will effectively be one resultant method of estimating probability; and that it is only legitimate to believe some system to be true if on that method the evidence now shows it to be probably true. In this case the rational man will become a Christian only if he judges that the evidence indicates that the Christian religion is probably true. He will not however necessarily become Christian even in that case, if we understand by the rational man the prudent man, for he may value so lowly the lives promised by the Christian theological system that the expected gain of becoming a Christian is outweighed by the gain of not becoming a Christian. Even if he judges that $P(A) > \frac{1}{2}$, B_2 may have such a high value in a man's estimation, that policy (2) is for him the most rational policy—so long as by "rational" policy is meant prudential policy. Yet if a man held that $P(A) > \frac{1}{2}$, he would hold that the consequences of the Christian system were probably true and these include the consequence that all men ought to become Christians. In that case if the rational man is the man who pursues the morally right policy, he would become a Christian.

My problem was whether it was a necessary and sufficient condition for the rational man becoming a Christian that he judges that the evidence available to him shows that the probability that the Christian theological system is true is greater than a half. My conclusion is that it depends on how one interprets "rational" and what are one's views about the morality of believing what is probably false. I have illustrated in detail how these considerations affect the issue, and how on some views on the moral issue the cited condition is not a necessary condition, and how on a non-moral understanding of "rational" it is not a sufficient condition, for the rational man to become a Christian.

W. K. CLIFFORD

1.23   *The Ethics of Belief*

A shipowner was about to send to sea an emigrant-ship. He knew that she was old, and not over-well built at the first; that she had seen many seas and climes, and often had needed repairs. Doubts had been suggested to him that possibly she was not seaworthy. These doubts preyed upon his mind, and made him unhappy; he thought that perhaps he ought to have her thor-

From W. K. Clifford, *Lectures and Essays* (1879).

oughly overhauled and refitted, even though this should put him to great expense. Before the ship sailed, however, he succeeded in overcoming these melancholy reflections. He said to himself that she had gone safely through so many voyages and weathered so many storms that it was idle to suppose she would not come safely home from this trip also. He would put his trust in Providence, which could hardly fail to protect all these unhappy families that were leaving their fatherland to seek for better times elsewhere. He would dismiss from his mind all ungenerous suspicions about the honesty of builders and contractors. In such ways he acquired a sincere and comfortable conviction that his vessel was thoroughly safe and seaworthy; he watched her departure with a light heart, and benevolent wishes for the success of the exiles in their strange new home that was to be; and he got his insurance-money when she went down in mid-ocean and told no tales.

What shall we say of him? Surely this, that he was verily guilty of the death of those men. It is admitted that he did sincerely believe in the soundness of his ship; but the sincerity of his conviction can in no wise help him, because *he had no right to believe on such evidence as was before him.* He had acquired his belief not by honestly earning it in patient investigation, but by stifling his doubts. And although in the end he may have felt so sure about it that he could not think otherwise, yet inasmuch as he had knowingly and willingly worked himself into that frame of mind, he must be held responsible for it.

Let us alter the case a little, and suppose that the ship was not unsound after all; that she made her voyage safely, and many others after it. Will that diminish the guilt of her owner? Not one jot. When an action is once done, it is right or wrong for ever; no accidental failure of its good or evil fruits can possibly alter that. The man would not have been innocent, he would only have been not found out. The question of right or wrong has to do with the origin of his belief, not the matter of it; not what it was, but how he got it; not whether it turned out to be true or false, but whether he had a right to believe on such evidence as was before him.

There was once an island in which some of the inhabitants professed a religion teaching neither the doctrine of original sin nor that of eternal punishment. A suspicion got abroad that the professors of this religion had made use of unfair means to get their doctrines taught to children. They were accused of wresting the laws of their country in such a way as to remove children from the care of their natural and legal guardians; and even of stealing them away and keeping them concealed from their friends and relations. A certain number of men formed themselves into a society for the purpose of agitating the public about this matter. They published grave accusations against individual citizens of the highest position and character, and did all in their power to injure these citizens in the exercise of their professions. So great was the noise they made, that a Commission was appointed to investigate the facts; but after the Commission had carefully inquired into all the evidence that could be got, it appeared that the accused were innocent. Not only had they been accused on insufficient evidence, but the evidence of their innocence was such as the agitators might easily have obtained, if they had attempted a fair inquiry. After these disclosures the inhabitants of that country looked upon the members of the agitating society, not only as persons whose judgment was to be distrusted, but also as no longer to be counted honourable men. For although they had sincerely and conscientiously believed in the charges they had made, yet *they had no right to believe on such evidence as was before them.* Their sincere convictions, instead of being honestly earned by patient inquiring, were stolen by listening to the voice of prejudice and passion.

Let us vary this case also, and suppose, other things remaining as before, that a still more accurate investigation proved the accused to have been really guilty. Would this make any difference in the guilt of the accusers? Clearly not; the question is not whether their belief was true or false, but whether they entertained it on wrong grounds. They would no doubt say, "Now you see that we were right after all; next time perhaps you will believe us." And they might be believed, but they would not thereby become honourable men. They would not be innocent, they would only be not found out. Every one of them, if he chose to examine himself *in foro conscientiae,* would know that he had acquired and nourished a belief, when he had no right to believe on such evidence as was before him; and therein he would know that he had done a wrong thing.

It may be said, however, that in both of these supposed cases it is not the belief which is judged to be wrong, but the action following upon it. The shipowner might say, "I am perfectly certain that my ship is sound, but still I feel it my duty to have her examined, before trusting the lives of so many people to her." And it might be said to the agitator, "However convinced you were of the justice of your cause and the truth of your convictions, you ought not to have made a public attack upon any man's character until you had examined the evidence on both sides with the utmost patience and care."

In the first place, let us admit that, so far as it goes, this view of the case is right and necessary; right, because even when a man's belief is so fixed that he cannot think otherwise, he still has a choice in regard to the action suggested by it, and so cannot escape the duty of investigating on the ground of the strength of his convictions; and necessary, because those who are not yet capable of controlling their feelings and thoughts must have a plain rule dealing with overt acts.

But this being premised as necessary, it becomes clear that it is not sufficient, and that our previous judgment is required to supplement it. For it is not possible so to sever the belief from the action it suggests as to condemn the one without condemning the other. No man holding a strong belief on one side of a question, or even wishing to hold a belief on one side, can investigate it with such fairness and completeness as if he were really in doubt and unbiased; so that the existence of a belief not founded on fair inquiry unfits a man for the performance of this necessary duty.

Nor is that truly a belief at all which has not some influence upon the actions of him who holds it. He who truly believes that which prompts him to an action has looked upon the action to lust after it, he has committed it already in his heart. If a belief is not realized immediately in open deeds, it is stored up for the guidance of the future. It goes to make a part of that aggregate of beliefs which is the link between sensation and action at every moment of all our lives, and which is so organized and compacted together that no part of it can be isolated from the rest, but every new addition modifies the structure of the whole. No real belief, however trifling and fragmentary it may seem, is ever truly insignificant; it prepares us to receive more of its like, confirms those which resembled it before, and weakens others; and so gradually it lays a stealthy train in our inmost thoughts, which may some day explode into overt action, and leave its stamp upon our character for ever.

And no one man's belief is in any case a private matter which concerns himself alone. Our lives are guided by that general conception of the course of things which has been created by society for social purposes. Our words, our phrases, our forms and processes and modes of thought, are common property, fashioned and perfected from age to age; an heirloom which every succeeding generation inherits as a precious deposit and a sacred trust to be handed on to the next one, not unchanged but enlarged and purified, with some clear marks of its proper handiwork. Into this, for good or ill, is woven every belief of every man who has speech of his fellows. An awful privilege, and an awful responsibility, that we should help to create the world in which posterity will live.

In the two supposed cases which have been considered, it has been judged wrong to believe on insufficient evidence, or to nourish belief by suppressing doubts and avoiding investigation. The reason of this judgment is not far to seek: it is that in both these cases the belief held by one man was of great importance to other men. But forasmuch as no belief held by one man, however seemingly trivial the belief, and however obscure the believer, is ever actually insignificant or without its effect on the fate of mankind, we have no choice but to extend our judgment to all cases of belief whatever. Belief, that sacred faculty which prompts the decisions of our will, and knits into harmonious working all the compacted energies of our being, is ours not for ourselves, but for humanity. It is rightly used on truths which have been established by long experience and waiting toil, and which have stood in the fierce light of free and fearless questioning. Then it helps to bind men together, and to strengthen and direct their common action. It is desecrated when given to unproved and unquestioned statements, for the solace and private pleasure of the believer; to add a tinsel splendour to the plain straight road of our life and display a bright mirage beyond it; or even to drown the common sorrows of our kind by a self-deception which allows them not only to cast down, but also to degrade us. Whoso would deserve well of his fellows in this matter will guard the purity of his belief with a very fanaticism of jealous care, lest at any time it should rest on an unworthy object, and catch a stain which can never be wiped away.

It is not only the leader of men, statesman, philosopher, or poet, that owes this bounden duty to mankind. Every rustic who delivers in the village alehouse his slow, infrequent sentences, may help to kill or keep alive the fatal superstitions which clog his race. Every hard-worked wife of an artisan may transmit to her children beliefs which shall knit society together, or rend it in pieces. No simplicity of mind, no obscurity of station, can escape the universal duty of questioning all that we believe.

It is true that this duty is a hard one, and the doubt which comes out of it is often a very bitter thing. It leaves us bare and powerless where we thought that we were safe and strong. To know all about anything is to know how to deal with it under all circumstances. We feel much happier and more secure when we think we know precisely what to do, no matter what happens, than when we have lost our way and do not know where to turn. And if we have supposed ourselves to know all about anything, and to be capable of doing what is fit in regard to it, we naturally do not like to find that we are really ignorant and powerless, that we have to begin again at the beginning, and try to learn what the thing is and how it is to be dealt with—if indeed anything can be learnt about it. It is the sense of power attached to a sense of knowledge that makes men desirous of believing, and afraid of doubting.

This sense of power is the highest and best of pleasures when the belief on which it is founded is a true belief, and has been fairly earned by investigation. For then we may justly feel that it is common property, and hold good for others as well as for ourselves. Then we may be glad, not that *I* have learned secrets by which I am safer and stronger, but that *we men* have got mastery over more of the world; and we shall be strong, not for ourselves, but in the name of Man and in his strength. But if the belief has been accepted on insufficient evidence, the pleasure is a stolen one. Not only does it deceive ourselves by giving us a sense of power which we do not really possess, but it is sinful, because it is stolen in defiance of our duty to mankind. That duty is to guard ourselves from such beliefs as from a pestilence, which may shortly master our own body and then spread to the rest of the town. What would be thought of one who, for the sake of a sweet fruit, should deliberately run the risk of bringing a plague upon his family and his neighbours?

And, as in other such cases, it is not the risk only which has to be considered; for a bad action is always bad at the time when it is done, no matter what happens afterwards. Every time we let ourselves believe for unworthy reasons, we weaken our powers of self-control, of doubting, of judicially and fairly weighing evidence. We all suffer severely enough from the maintenance and support of false beliefs and the fatally wrong actions which they lead to, and the evil born when one such belief is entertained is great and wide. But a greater and wider evil arises when the credulous character is maintained and supported, when a habit of believing for unworthy reasons is fostered and made permanent. If I steal money from any person, there may be no harm done by the mere transfer of possession; he may not feel the loss, or it may prevent him from using the money badly. But I cannot help doing this great wrong towards Man, that I make myself dishonest. What hurts society is not that it should lose its property, but that it should become a den of thieves; for then it must cease to be society. This is why we ought not to do evil that good may come; for at any rate this great evil has come, that we have done evil and are made wicked thereby. In like manner, if I let myself believe anything on insufficient evidence, there may be no great harm done by the mere belief; it may be true after all, or I may never have occasion to exhibit it in outward acts. But I cannot help doing this great wrong towards Man, that I make myself credulous. The danger to society is not merely that it should believe wrong things, though that is great enough; but that it should become credulous, and lose the habit of testing things and inquiring into them; for then it must sink back into savagery.

The harm which is done by credulity in a man is not confined to the fostering of a credulous character in others, and consequent support of false beliefs. Habitual want of care about what I believe leads to habitual want of care in others about the truth of what is told to me. Men speak the truth to one another when each reveres the truth in his own mind and in the other's mind; but how shall my friend revere the truth in my mind when I myself am careless about it, when I believe things because I want to believe them, and because they are comforting and pleasant? Will he not learn to cry, "Peace," to me, when there is no peace? By such a course I shall surround myself with a thick atmosphere of falsehood and fraud, and in that I must live. It may matter little to me, in my cloud-castle of sweet illusions and darling lies; but it matters much to Man that I have made my neighbours ready to deceive. The credulous man is father to the liar and the cheat; he lives in the bosom of this his family, and it is no marvel if he should become even as they are. So closely are our duties knit together, that whoso shall keep the whole law, and yet offend in one point, he is guilty of all.

To sum up: it is wrong always, everywhere, and for anyone, to believe anything upon insufficient evidence.

If a man, holding a belief which he was taught in childhood or persuaded of afterwards, keeps down and pushes away any doubts which arise about it in his mind, purposely avoids the reading of books and the company of men that call in question or discuss it, and regards as impious those questions which cannot easily be asked without disturbing it—the life of that man is one long sin against mankind.

If this judgment seems harsh when applied to those simple souls who have never known better, who have been brought up from the cradle with a horror of doubt, and taught that their eternal welfare depends on *what* they believe, then it leads to the very serious question, *Who hath made Israel to sin?*

It may be permitted me to fortify this judgment with the sentence of Milton—

> A man may be a heretic in the truth; and if he believe things only because his pastor says so, or the assembly so determine, without knowing other reason, though his belief be true, yet the very truth he holds becomes his heresy.

And with this famous aphorism of Coleridge—

> He who begins by loving Christianity better than Truth, will proceed by loving his own sect or Church better than Christianity, and end in loving himself better than all.

Inquiry into the evidence of a doctrine is not to be made once for all, and then taken as finally settled. It is never lawful to stifle a doubt; for either it can be honestly answered by means of the inquiry already made, or else it proves that the inquiry was not complete.

"But," says one, "I am a busy man; I have no time for the long course of study which would be necessary to make me in any degree a competent judge of certain questions, or even able to understand the nature of the arguments." Then he should have no time to believe.

WILLIAM JAMES

1.24 *The Will to Believe*

In the recently published Life by Leslie Stephen of his brother, Fitz-James, there is an account of a school to which the latter went when he was a boy. The teacher, a certain Mr. Guest, used to converse with his pupils in this wise: "Gurney, what is the difference between justification and sanctification?

This essay was originally an address delivered before the Philosophical Clubs of Yale and Brown Universities. It was first published in 1896.

—Stephen, prove the omnipotence of God!" etc. In the midst of our Harvard freethinking and indifference we are prone to imagine that here at your good old orthodox College conversation continues to be somewhat upon this order; and to show you that we at Harvard have not lost all interest in these vital subjects, I have brought with me to-night something like a sermon on justification by faith to read to you,—I mean an essay in justification *of* faith, a defence of our right to adopt a believing attitude in religious matters, in spite of the fact that our merely logical intellect may not have been coerced. "The Will to Believe," accordingly, is the title of my paper.

I have long defended to my own students the lawfulness of voluntarily adopted faith; but as soon as they have got well imbued with the logical spirit, they have as a rule refused to admit my contention to be lawful philosophically, even though in point of fact they were personally all the time chock-full of some faith or other themselves. I am all the while, however, so profoundly convinced that my own position is correct, that your invitation has seemed to me a good occasion to make my statements more clear. Perhaps your minds will be more open than those with which I have hitherto had to deal. I will be as little technical as I can, though I must begin by setting up some technical distinctions that will help us in the end.

I

Let us give the name of *hypothesis* to anything that may be proposed to our belief; and just as the electricians speak of live and dead wires, let us speak of any hypothesis as either *live* or *dead*. A live hypothesis is one which appeals as a real possibility to him to whom it is proposed. If I ask you to believe in the Mahdi, the notion makes no electric connection with your nature,—it refuses to scintillate with any credibility at all. As an hypothesis it is completely dead. To an Arab, however (even if he be not one of the Mahdi's followers), the hypothesis is among the mind's possibilities: it is alive. This shows that deadness and liveness in an hypothesis are not intrinsic properties, but relations to the individual thinker. They are measured by his willingness to act. The maximum of liveness in an hypothesis means willingness to act irrevocably. Practically, that means belief; but there is some believing tendency wherever there is willingness to act at all.

Next, let us call the decision between two hypotheses an *option*. Options may be of several kinds. They may be—1, *living* or *dead*; 2, *forced* or *avoidable*; 3, *momentous* or *trivial*; and for our purposes we may call an option a *genuine* option when it is of the forced, living, and momentous kind.

1. A living option is one in which both hypotheses are live ones. If I say to you: "Be a theosophist or be a Mohammedan," it is probably a dead option, because for you neither hypothesis is likely to be alive. But if I say: "Be an agnostic or be a Christian," it is otherwise: trained as you are, each hypothesis makes some appeal, however small, to your belief.

2. Next, if I say to you: "Choose between going out with your umbrella or without it," I do not offer you a genuine option, for it is not forced. You can easily avoid it by not going out at all. Similarly, if I say, "Either love me or hate me," "Either call my theory true or call it false," your option is avoidable. You may remain indifferent to me, neither loving nor hating, and you may decline to offer any judgment as to my theory. But if I say, "Either accept this truth or go without it," I put on you a forced option, for there is no standing place outside of the alternative. Every dilemma based on a complete logical disjunction, with no possibility of not choosing, is an option of this forced kind.

3. Finally, if I were Dr. Nansen and proposed to you to join my North Pole expedition, your option would be momentous; for this would probably be your only similar opportunity, and your choice now would either exclude you from the North Pole sort of immortality altogether or put at least the chance of it into your hands. He who refuses to embrace a unique opportunity loses the prize as surely as if he tried and failed. *Per contra*, the option is trivial when the opportunity is not unique, when the stake is insignificant, or when the decision is reversible if it later prove unwise. Such trivial options abound in the scientific life. A chemist finds an hypothesis live enough to spend a year in its verification: he believes in it to that extent. But if his experiments prove inconclusive either way, he is quit for his loss of time, no vital harm being done.

It will facilitate our discussion if we keep all these distinctions well in mind.

II

The next matter to consider is the actual psychology of human opinion. When we look at certain facts, it seems as if our passional and volitional nature lay at the root of all our convictions. When we look at others, it seems as if they could do nothing when the intellect had once said its say. Let us take the latter facts up first.

Does it not seem preposterous on the very face of it to talk of our opinions being modifiable at will? Can our will either help or hinder our intellect in its perceptions of truth? Can we, by just willing it, believe that Abraham Lincoln's existence is a myth, and that the portraits of him in McClure's Magazine are all of some one else? Can we, by any effort of our will, or by any strength of wish that it were true, believe ourselves well and about when we are roaring with rheumatism in bed, or feel certain that the sum of the two one-dollar bills in our pocket must be a hundred dollars? We can *say* any of these things, but we are absolutely impotent to believe them; and of just such things is the whole fabric of the truths that we do believe in made up,—matters of fact, immediate or remote, as Hume said, and relations between ideas, which are either there or not there for us if we see them so, and which if not there cannot be put there by any action of our own.

In Pascal's *Thoughts* there is a celebrated passage known in literature as Pascal's wager. In it he tries to force us into Christianity by reasoning as if our concern with truth resembled our concern with the stakes in a game of chance. Translated freely his words are these: You must either believe or not believe that God is—which will you do? Your human reason cannot say. A game is going on between you and the nature of things which at the day of judgment will bring out either heads or tails. Weigh what your gains and your losses would be if you should stake all you have on heads, or God's existence: if you win in such case, you gain eternal beatitude; if you lose, you lose nothing at all. If there were an infinity of chances, and only one for God in this wager, still you ought to stake your all on God; for though you surely risk a finite loss by this procedure, any finite loss is reasonable, even a certain one is reasonable, if there is but the possibility of infinite gain. Go, then, and take holy water, and have masses said; belief will come and stupefy your scruples, —*Cela vous fera croire et vous abêtira.* Why should you not? At bottom, what have you to lose?

You probably feel that when religious faith expresses itself thus, in the language of the gaming-table, it is put to its last trumps. Surely Pascal's own personal belief in masses and holy water had far other springs; and this celebrated page of his is but an argument for others, a last desperate snatch at a weapon against the hardness of the unbelieving heart. We feel that a faith in masses and holy water adopted wilfully after such a mechanical calculation would lack the inner soul of faith's reality; and if we were ourselves in the place of the Deity, we should probably take particular pleasure in cutting off believers of this pattern from their infinite reward. It is evident that unless there be some pre-existing tendency to believe in masses and holy water, the option offered to the will by Pascal is not a living option. Certainly no Turk ever took to masses and holy water on its account; and even to us Protestants these means of salvation seem such foregone impossibilities that Pascal's logic, invoked for them specifically, leaves us unmoved. As well might the Mahdi write to us, saying, "I am the Expected One whom God has created in his effulgence. You shall be infinitely happy if you confess me; otherwise you shall be cut off from the light of the sun. Weigh, then, your infinite gain if I am genuine against your finite sacrifice if I am not!" His logic would be that of Pascal; but he would vainly use it on us, for the hypothesis he offers us is dead. No tendency to act on it exists in us to any degree.

The talk of believing by our volition seems, then, from one point of view, simply silly. From another point of view it is worse than silly, it is vile. When one turns to the magnificent edifice of the physical sciences, and sees how it was reared; what thousands of disinterested moral lives of men lie buried in its mere foundations; what patience and postponement, what choking down of preference, what submission to the icy laws of outer fact are wrought into

its very stones and mortar; how absolutely impersonal it stands in its vast
augustness,—then how besotted and contemptible seems every little senti-
mentalist who comes blowing his voluntary smoke-wreaths, and pretending to
decide things from out of his private dream! Can we wonder if those bred in
the rugged and manly school of science should feel like spewing such sub-
jectivism out of their mouths? The whole system of loyalties which grow up
in the schools of science go dead against its toleration; so that it is only
natural that those who have caught the scientific fever should pass over to
the opposite extreme, and write sometimes as if the incorruptibly truthful
intellect ought positively to prefer bitterness and unacceptableness to the
heart in its cup.

> It fortifies my soul to know
> That, though I perish, Truth is so—

sings Clough, while Huxley exclaims: "My only consolation lies in the reflection that, however bad our posterity may become, so far as they hold by the
plain rule of not pretending to believe what they have no reason to believe,
because it may be to their advantage so to pretend [the word 'pretend' is
surely here redundant], they will not have reached the lowest depth of immortality." And that delicious *enfant terrible* Clifford writes: "Belief is
desecrated when given to unproved and unquestioned statements for the solace
and private pleasure of the believer. . . . Whoso would deserve well of his
fellows in this matter will guard the purity of his belief with a very fanaticism
of jealous care, lest at any time it should rest on an unworthy object, and
catch a stain which can never be wiped away. . . . If [a] belief has been
accepted on insufficient evidence [even though the belief be true, as Clifford
on the same page explains] the pleasure is a stolen one. . . . It is sinful because it is stolen in defiance of our duty to mankind. That duty is to guard
ourselves from such beliefs as from a pestilence which may shortly master
our own body and then spread to the rest of the town. . . . It is wrong always,
everywhere, and for every one, to believe anything upon insufficient evidence."

III

All this strikes one as healthy, even when expressed, as by Clifford, with
somewhat too much of robustious pathos in the voice. Free-will and simple
wishing do seem, in the matter of our credences, to be only fifth wheels to
the coach. Yet if any one should thereupon assume that intellectual insight
is what remains after wish and will and sentimental preference have taken
wing, or that pure reason is what then settles our opinions, he would fly
quite as directly in the teeth of the facts.

It is only our already dead hypotheses that our willing nature is unable
to bring to life again. But what has made them dead for us is for the most

part a previous action of our willing nature of an antagonistic kind. When I say "willing nature," I do not mean only such deliberate volitions as may have set up habits of belief that we cannot now escape from,—I mean all such factors of belief as fear and hope, prejudice and passion, imitation and partisanship, the circumpressure of our caste and set. As a matter of fact we find ourselves believing, we hardly know how or why. Mr. Balfour gives the name of "authority" to all those influences, born of the intellectual climate, that make hypotheses possible or impossible for us, alive or dead. Here in this room, we all of us believe in molecules and the conservation of energy, in democracy and necessary progress, in Protestant Christianity and the duty of fighting for "the doctrine of the immortal Monroe," all for no reasons worthy of the name. We see into these matters with no more inner clearness, and probably with much less, than any disbeliever in them might possess. His unconventionality would probably have some grounds to show for its conclusions; but for us, not insight, but the *prestige* of the opinions, is what makes the spark shoot from them and light up our sleeping magazines of faith. Our reason is quite satisfied, in nine hundred and ninety-nine cases out of every thousand of us, if it can find a few arguments that will do to recite in case our credulity is criticised by some one else. Our faith is faith in some one else's faith, and in the greatest matters this is most the case. Our belief in truth itself, for instance, that there is a truth, and that our minds and it are made for each other,—what is it but a passionate affirmation of desire, in which our social system backs us up? We want to have a truth; we want to believe that our experiments and studies and discussions must put us in a continually better and better position towards it; and on this line we agree to fight out our thinking lives. But if a pyrrhonistic sceptic asks us *how we know* all this, can our logic find a reply? No! certainly it cannot. It is just one volition against another,—we willing to go in for life upon a trust or assumption which he, for his part, does not care to make.[1]

As a rule we disbelieve all facts and theories for which we have no use. Clifford's cosmic emotions find no use for Christian feelings. Huxley belabors the bishops because there is no use for sacerdotalism in his scheme of life. Newman, on the contrary, goes over to Romanism, and finds all sorts of reasons good for staying there, because a priestly system is for him an organic need and delight. Why do so few "scientists" even look at the evidence for telepathy, so called? Because they think, as a leading biologist, now dead, once said to me, that even if such a thing were true, scientists ought to band together to keep it suppressed and concealed. It would undo the uniformity of Nature and all sorts of other things without which scientists cannot carry on their pursuits. But if this very man had been shown something which as a scientist he might *do* with telepathy, he might not only have examined the

---

[1]Compare the admirable p. 310 in S. H. Hodgson's *Time and Space*, London, 1865.

evidence, but even have found it good enough. This very law which the logicians would impose upon us—if I may give the name of logicians to those who would rule out our willing nature here—is based on nothing but their own natural wish to exclude all elements for which they, in their professional quality of logicians, can find no use.

Evidently, then, our non-intellectual nature does influence our convictions. There are passional tendencies and volitions which run before and others which come after belief, and it is only the latter that are too late for the fair, and they are not too late when the previous passional work has been already in their own direction. Pascal's argument, instead of being powerless, then seems a regular clincher, and is the last stroke needed to make our faith in masses and holy water complete. The state of things is evidently far from simple; and pure insight and logic, whatever they might do ideally, are not the only things that really do produce our creeds.

IV

Our next duty, having recognized this mixed-up state of affairs, is to ask whether it be simply reprehensible and pathological, or whether, on the contrary, we must treat it as a normal element in making up our minds. The thesis I defend is, briefly stated, this: *Our passional nature not only lawfully may, but must, decide an option between propositions, whenever it is a genuine option that cannot by its nature be decided on intellectual grounds; for to say, under such circumstances, "Do not decide, but leave the question open," is itself a passional decision,—just like deciding yes or no,—and is attended with the same risk of losing the truth.* The thesis thus abstractly expressed will, I trust, soon become quite clear. But I must first indulge in a bit more of preliminary work.

V

It will be observed that for the purposes of this discussion we are on "dogmatic" ground,—ground, I mean, which leaves systematic philosophical scepticism altogether out of account. The postulate that there is truth, and that it is the destiny of our minds to attain it, we are deliberately resolving to make, though the sceptic will not make it. We part company with him, therefore, absolutely, at this point. But the faith that truth exists, and that our minds can find it, may be held in two ways. We may talk of the *empiricist* way and of the *absolutist* way of believing in truth. The absolutists in this matter say that we not only can attain to knowing truth, but we can *know when* we have attained to knowing it; while the empiricists think that although we may attain it, we cannot infallibly know when. To *know* is one thing, and to know for certain *that* we know is another. One may hold to the first being possible without the second; hence the empiricists and the absolutists, although neither of them is a sceptic in the usual philosophic sense of the term, show very different degrees of dogmatism in their lives.

If we look at the history of opinions, we see that the empiricist tendency has largely prevailed in science, while in philosophy the absolute tendency has had everything in its own way. The characteristic sort of happiness, indeed, which philosophies yield has mainly consisted in the conviction felt by each successive school or system that by it bottom-certitude had been attained. "Other philosophies are collections of opinions, mostly false; *my* philosophy gives standing-ground forever,"—who does not recognize in this the key-note of every system worthy of the name? A system, to be a system at all, must come as a *closed* system, reversible in this or that detail, perchance, but in its essential features never!

Scholastic orthodoxy, to which one must always go when one wishes to find perfectly clear statement, has beautifully elaborated this absolutist conviction in a doctrine which it calls that of "objective evidence." If, for example, I am unable to doubt that I now exist before you, that two is less than three, or that if all men are mortal then I am mortal too, it is because these things illumine my intellect irresistibly. The final ground of this objective evidence possessed by certain propositions is the *adaequatio intellectûs nostri cum rê.* The certitude it brings involves an *aptitudinem ad extorquendum certum assensum* on the part of the truth envisaged, and on the side of the subject a *quietem in cognitione,* when once the object is mentally received, that leaves no possibility of doubt behind; and in the whole transaction nothing operates but the *entitas ipsa* of the object and the *entitas ipsa* of the mind. We slouchy modern thinkers dislike to talk in Latin,—indeed, we dislike to talk in set terms at all; but at bottom our own state of mind is very much like this whenever we uncritically abandon ourselves: You believe in objective evidence, and I do. Of some things we feel that we are certain: we know, and we know that we do know. There is something that gives a click inside of us, a bell that strikes twelve, when the hands of our mental clock have swept the dial and meet over the meridian hour. The greatest empiricists among us are only empiricists on reflection: when left to their instincts, they dogmatize like infallible popes. When the Cliffords tell us how sinful it is to be Christians on such "insufficient evidence," insufficiency is really the last thing they have in mind. For them the evidence is absolutely sufficient, only it makes the other way. They believe so completely in an anti-Christian order of the universe that there is no living option: Christianity is a dead hypothesis from the start.

VI

But now, since we are all such absolutists by instinct, what in our quality of students of philosophy ought we to do about the fact? Shall we espouse and indorse it? Or shall we treat it as a weakness of our nature from which we must free ourselves, if we can?

I sincerely believe that the latter course is the only one we can follow as reflective men. Objective evidence and certitude are doubtless very fine ideals to play with, but where on this moonlit and dream-visited planet are they found? I am, therefore, myself a complete empiricist so far as my theory of human knowledge goes. I live, to be sure, by the practical faith that we must go on experiencing and thinking over our experience, for only thus can our opinions grow more true, but to hold any one of them—I absolutely do not care which—as if it never could be reinterpretable or corrigible, I believe to be a tremendously mistaken attitude, and I think that the whole history of philosophy will bear me out. There is but one indefectibly certain truth, and that is the truth that pyrrhonistic scepticism itself leaves standing,—the truth that the present phenomenon of consciousness exists. That, however, is the bare starting-point of knowledge, the mere admission of a stuff to be philosophized about. The various philosophies are but so many attempts at expressing what this stuff really is. And if we repair to our libraries what disagreement do we discover! Where is a certainly true answer found? Apart from abstract propositions of comparison (such as two and two are the same as four), propositions which tell us nothing by themselves about concrete reality, we find no proposition ever regarded by any one as evidently certain that has not either been called a falsehood, or at least had its truth sincerely questioned by some one else. The transcending of the axioms of geometry, not in play but in earnest, by certain of our contemporaries (as Zöllner and Charles H. Hinton), and the rejection of the whole Aristotelian logic by the Hegelians, are striking instances in point.

No concrete test of what is really true has ever been agreed upon. Some make the criterion external to the moment of perception, putting it either in revelation, the *consensus gentium*, the instincts of the heart, or the systematized experience of the race. Others make the perceptive moment its own test,—Descartes, for instance, with his clear and distinct ideas guaranteed by the veracity of God; Reid with his "common-sense"; and Kant with his forms of synthetic judgment *a priori*. The inconceivability of the opposite; the capacity to be verified by sense; the possession of complete organic unity or self-relation, realized when a thing is its own other,—are standards which, in turn, have been used. The much lauded objective evidence is never triumphantly there; it is a mere aspiration or *Grenzbegriff*, marking the infinitely remote ideal of our thinking life. To claim that certain truths now possess it, is simply to say that when you think them true and they *are* true, then their evidence is objective, otherwise it is not. But practically one's conviction that the evidence one goes by is of the real objective brand, is only one more subjective opinion added to the lot. For what a contradictory array of opinions have objective evidence and absolute certitude been claimed! The world is rational through and through,—its existence is an ultimate brute fact; there is a personal God,—a personal God is inconceivable; there is an extra-mental physical world immediately known,—the mind can only know its own ideas; a moral imperative exists,—obligation is only the resultant of desires; a permanent spiritual principle is in every one,—there are only shifting states of mind; there is an endless chain of causes,—there is an absolute first cause; an eternal necessity,—a freedom; a purpose,—no purpose; a primal One,—a primal Many; a universal continuity,—an essential discontinuity in things; an infinity,—no infinity. There is this,—there is that; there is indeed nothing which some one has not thought absolutely true, while his neighbor deemed it absolutely false; and not an absolutist among them seems ever to have considered that the trouble may all the time be essential, and that the intellect, even with truth directly in its grasp, may have no infallible signal for knowing whether it be truth or no. When, indeed, one remembers that the most striking practical application to life of the doctrine of objective certitude has been the conscientious labors of the Holy Office of the Inquisition, one feels less tempted than ever to lend the doctrine a respectful ear.

But please observe, now, that when as empiricists we give up the doctrine of objective certitude, we do not thereby give up the quest or hope of truth itself. We still pin our faith on its existence, and still believe that we gain an ever better position towards it by systematically continuing to roll up experiences and think. Our great difference from the scholastic lies in the way we face. The strength of his system lies in the principle, the origin, the *terminus a quo* of his thought; for us the strength is in the outcome, the upshot, the *terminus ad quem*. Not where it comes from but what it leads to is to decide. It matters not to an empiricist from what quarter an hypothesis may come to him: he may have acquired it by fair means or by foul; passion may have whispered or accident suggested it; but if the total drift of thinking continues to confirm it, that is what he means by its being true.

VII

One more point, small but important, and our preliminaries are done. There are two ways of looking at our duty in the matter of opinion,—ways entirely different, and yet ways about whose difference the theory of knowledge seems hitherto to have shown very little concern. *We must know the truth*; and *we must avoid error*,—these are our first and great commandments as would-be knowers; but they are not two ways of stating an identical commandment, they are two separable laws. Although it may indeed happen that when we believe the truth *A*, we escape as an incidental consequence from believing the falsehood *B*, it hardly ever happens that by merely disbelieving *B* we necessarily believe *A*. We may in escaping *B* fall into believing other falsehoods, *C* or *D*, just as bad as *B*; or we may escape *B* by not believing anything at all, not even *A*.

Believe truth! Shun error!—these, we see, are two materially different laws; and by choosing between them we may end by coloring differently our whole intellectual life. We may regard the chase for truth as paramount, and the avoidance of error as secondary; or we may, on the other hand, treat the avoidance of error as more imperative, and let truth take its chance. Clifford, in the instructive passage which I have quoted, exhorts us to the latter course. Believe nothing, he tells us, keep your mind in suspense forever, rather than by closing it on insufficient evidence incur the awful risk of believing lies. You, on the other hand, may think that the risk of being in error is a very small matter when compared with the blessings of real knowledge, and be ready to be duped many times in your investigation rather than postpone indefinitely the chance of guessing true. I myself find it impossible to go with Clifford. We must remember that these feelings of our duty about either truth or error are in any case only expressions of our passional life. Biologically considered, our minds are as ready to grind out falsehood as veracity, and he who says, "Better go without belief forever than believe a lie!" merely shows his own preponderant private horror of becoming a dupe. He may be critical of many of his desires and fears, but this fear he slavishly obeys. He cannot imagine any one questioning its binding force. For my own part, I have also a horror of being duped; but I can believe that worse things than being duped may happen to a man in this world: so Clifford's exhortation has to my ears a thoroughly fantastic sound. It is like a general informing his soldiers that it is better to keep out of battle forever than to risk a single wound. Not so are victories either over enemies or over nature gained. Our errors are surely not such awfully solemn things. In a world where we are so certain to incur them in spite of all our caution, a certain lightness of heart seems healthier than this excessive nervousness on their behalf. At any rate, it seems the fittest thing for the empiricist philosopher.

VIII

And now, after all this introduction, let us go straight at our question. I have said, and now repeat it, that not only as a matter of fact do we find our passional nature influencing us in our opinions, but that there are some options between opinions in which this influence must be regarded both as an inevitable and as a lawful determinant of our choice.

I fear here that some of you my hearers will begin to scent danger, and lend an inhospitable ear. Two first steps of passion you have indeed had to admit as necessary,—we must think so as to avoid dupery, and we must think so as to gain truth; but the surest path to those ideal consummations, you will probably consider, is from now onwards to take no further passional step.

Well, of course, I agree as far as the facts will allow. Wherever the option between losing truth and gaining it is not momentous, we can throw the chance of *gaining truth* away, and at any rate save ourselves from any chance of *believing falsehood*, by not making up our minds at all till objective evidence has come. In scientific questions, this is almost always the case; and even in human affairs in general, the need of acting is seldom so urgent that a false belief to act on is better than no belief at all. Law courts, indeed, have to decide on the best evidence attainable for the moment, because a judge's duty is to make law as well as to ascertain it, and (as a learned judge once said to me) few cases are worth spending much time over: the great thing is to have them decided on *any* acceptable principle, and got out of the way. But in our dealings with objective nature we obviously are recorders, not makers, of the truth; and decisions for the mere sake of deciding promptly and getting on to the next business would be wholly out of place. Throughout the breadth of physical nature facts are what they are quite independently of us, and seldom is there any such hurry about them that the risks of being duped by believing a premature theory need be faced. The questions here are always trivial options, the hypotheses are hardly living (at any rate not living for us spectators), the choice between believing truth or falsehood is seldom forced. The attitude of sceptical balance is therefore the absolutely wise one if we would escape mistakes. What difference, indeed, does it make to most of us whether we have or have not a theory of the Röntgen rays, whether we believe or not in mind-stuff, or have a conviction about the causality of conscious states? It makes no difference. Such options are not forced on us. On every account it is better not to make them, but still keep weighing reasons *pro et contra* with an indifferent hand.

I speak, of course, here of the purely judging mind. For purposes of discovery such indifference is to be less highly recommended, and science would be far less advanced than she is if the passionate desires of individuals to get their own faiths confirmed had been kept out of the game. See for example the sagacity which Spencer and Weismann now display. On the other hand, if you want an absolute duffer in an investigation, you must, after all, take the man who has no interest whatever in its results: he is the warranted incapable, the positive fool. The most useful investigator, because the most sensitive observer, is always he whose eager interest in one side of the question is balanced by an equally keen nervousness lest he become deceived.[2] Science has organized this nervousness into a regular *technique*, her so-called method of verification; and she has fallen so deeply in love with the method that one may even say she has ceased to care for truth by itself at all. It is only truth as technically verified that interests her. The truth of truths might come in merely affirmative form, and she would decline to touch it. Such truth as that, she might repeat with Clifford, would be stolen in defiance of her duty to mankind. Human passions, however, are stronger than technical rules. "Le coeur

---

[2] Compare Wilfrid Ward's Essay, "The Wish to Believe," in his *Witnesses to the Unseen*, Macmillan & Co., 1893.

a ses raisons," as Pascal says, "que la raison ne connaît pas"; and however indifferent to all but the bare rules of the game the umpire, the abstract intellect, may be, the concrete players who furnish him the materials to judge of are usually each one of them, in love with some pet "live hypothesis" of his own. Let us agree, however, that wherever there is no forced option, the dispassionately judicial intellect with no pet hypothesis, saving us, as it does, from dupery at any rate, ought to be our ideal.

The question next arises: Are there not somewhere forced options in our speculative questions, and can we (as men who may be interested at least as much in positively gaining truth as in merely escaping dupery) always wait with impunity till the coercive evidence shall have arrived? It seems *a priori* improbable that the truth should be so nicely adjusted to our needs and powers as that. In the great boarding-house of nature, the cakes and the butter and the syrup seldom come out so even and leave the plates so clean. Indeed, we should view them with scientific suspicion if they did.

IX

Moral questions immediately present themselves as questions whose solution cannot wait for sensible proof. A moral question is a question not of what sensibly exists, but of what is good, or would be good if it did exist. Science can tell us what exists; but to compare the *worths*, both of what exists and of what does not exist, we must consult not science, but what Pascal calls our heart. Science herself consults her heart when she lays it down that the infinite ascertainment of fact and correction of false belief are the supreme goods for man. Challenge the statement, and science can only repeat it oracularly, or else prove it by showing that such ascertainment and correction bring man all sorts of other goods which man's heart in turn declares. The question of having moral beliefs at all or not having them is decided by our will. Are our moral preferences true or false, or are they only odd biological phenomena, making things good or bad for *us*, but in themselves indifferent? How can your pure intellect decide? If your heart does not *want* a world of moral reality, your head will assuredly never make you believe in one. Mephistophelian scepticism, indeed, will satisfy the head's play-instincts much better than any rigorous idealism can. Some men (even at the student age) are so naturally cool-hearted that the moralistic hypothesis never has for them any pungent life, and in their supercilious presence the hot young moralist always feels strangely ill at ease. The appearance of knowingness is on their side, of *naïveté* and gullibility on his. Yet, in the inarticulate heart of him, he clings to it that he is not a dupe, and that there is a realm in which (as Emerson says) all their wit and intellectual superiority is no better than the cunning of a fox. Moral scepticism can no more be refuted or proved by logic than intellectual scepticism can. When we stick to it that there *is* truth (be it of either kind), we do so with our whole nature, and resolve to stand or fall by the results. The sceptic with his whole nature adopts the doubting attitude; but which of us is the wiser, Omniscience only knows.

Turn now from these wide questions of good to a certain class of questions of fact, questions concerning personal relations, states of mind between one man and another. *Do you like me or not?*—for example. Whether you do or not depends, in countless instances, on whether I meet you half-way, am willing to assume that you must like me, and show you trust and expectation. The previous faith on my part in your liking's existence is in such cases what makes your liking come. But if I stand aloof, and refuse to budge an inch until I have objective evidence, until you shall have done something apt, as the absolutists say, *ad extorquendum assensum meum*, ten to one your liking never comes. How many women's hearts are vanquished by the mere sanguine insistence of some man that they *must* love him! he will not consent to the hypothesis that they cannot. The desire for a certain kind of truth here brings about that special truth's existence; and so it is in innumerable cases of other sorts. Who gains promotions, boons, appointments, but the man in whose life they are seen to play the part of live hypotheses, who discounts them, sacrifices other things for their sake before they have come, and takes risks for them in advance? His faith acts on the powers above him as a claim, and creates its own verification.

A social organism of any sort whatever, large or small, is what it is because each member proceeds to his own duty with a trust that the other members will simultaneously do theirs. Wherever a desired result is achieved by the co-operation of many independent persons, its existence as a fact is a pure consequence of the precursive faith in one another of those immediately concerned. A government, an army, a commercial system, a ship, a college, an athletic team, all exist on this condition, without which not only is nothing achieved, but nothing is even attempted. A whole train of passengers (individually brave enough) will be looted by a few highwaymen, simply because the latter can count on one another, while each passenger fears that if he makes a movement of resistance, he will be shot before any one else backs him up. If we believed that the whole car-full would rise at once with us, we should each severally rise, and train-robbing would never even be attempted. There are, then, cases where a fact cannot come at all unless a preliminary faith exists in its coming. *And where faith in a fact can help create the fact,* that would be an insane logic which should say that faith running ahead of scientific evidence is the "lowest kind of immorality" into which a thinking being can fall. Yet such is the logic by which our scientific absolutists pretend to regulate our lives!

X

In truths dependent on our personal action, then, faith based on desire is certainly a lawful and possibly an indispensable thing.

But now, it will be said, these are all childish human cases, and have nothing to do with great cosmical matters, like the question of religious faith. Let us then pass on to that. Religions differ so much in their accidents that in discussing the religious question we must make it very generic and broad. What then do we now mean by the religious hypothesis? Science says things are; morality says some things are better than other things; and religion says essentially two things.

First, she says that the best things are the more eternal things, the overlapping things, the things in the universe that throw the last stone, so to speak, and say the final word. "Perfection is eternal,"—this phrase of Charles Secrétan seems a good way of putting this first affirmation of religion, an affirmation which obviously cannot yet be verified scientifically at all.

The second affirmation of religion is that we are better off even now if we believe her first affirmation to be true.

Now, let us consider what the logical elements of this situation are *in case the religious hypothesis in both its branches be really true.* (Of course, we must admit that possibility at the outset. If we are to discuss the question at all, it must involve a living option. If for any of you religion be a hypothesis that cannot, by any living possibility be true, then you need go no farther. I speak to the "saving remnant" alone.) So proceeding, we see, first, that religion offers itself as a *momentous* option. We are supposed to gain, even now, by our belief, and to lose by our non-belief, a certain vital good. Secondly, religion is a *forced* option, so far as that good goes. We cannot escape the issue by remaining sceptical and waiting for more light, because, although we do avoid error in that way *if religion be untrue,* we lose the good, *if it be true,* just as certainly as if we positively chose to disbelieve. It is as if a man should hesitate indefinitely to ask a certain woman to marry him because he was not perfectly sure that she would prove an angel after he brought her home. Would he not cut himself off from that particular angel-possibility as decisively as if he went and married some one else? Scepticism, then, is not avoidance of option; it is option of a certain particular kind of risk. *Better risk loss of truth than chance of error,*—that is your faith-vetoer's exact position. He is actively playing his stake as much as the believer is; he is backing the field against the religious hypothesis, just as the believer is backing the religious hypothesis against the field. To preach scepticism to us as a duty until "sufficient evidence" for religion be found, is tantamount therefore to telling us, when in presence of the religious hypothesis, that to yield to our fear of its being error is wiser and better than to yield to our hope that it may be true. It is not intellect against all passions, then; it is only intellect with one passion laying down its law. And by what, forsooth, is the supreme wisdom of this passion warranted? Dupery for dupery, what proof is there that dupery through hope is so much worse than dupery through fear? I, for one, can see no proof; and I simply refuse obedience to the scientist's command to imitate his kind of option, in a case where my own stake is important enough to give me the right to choose my own form of risk. If religion be true and the evidence for it be still insufficient, I do not wish, by putting your extinguisher upon my nature (which feels to me as if it had after all some business in this matter), to forfeit my sole chance in life of getting upon the winning side,— that chance depending, of course, on my willingness to run the risk of acting as if my passional need of taking the world religiously might be prophetic and right.

All this is on the supposition that it really may be prophetic and right, and that, even to us who are discussing the matter, religion is a live hypothesis which may be true. Now, to most of us religion comes in a still further way that makes a veto on our active faith even more illogical. The more perfect and more eternal aspect of the universe is represented in our religions as having personal form. The universe is no longer a mere *It* to us, but a *Thou,* if we are religious; and any relation that may be possible from person to person might be possible here. For instance, although in one sense we are passive portions of the universe, in another we show a curious autonomy, as if we were small active centres on our own account. We feel, too, as if the appeal of religion to us were made to our own active goodwill, as if evidence might be forever withheld from us unless we met the hypothesis half-way. To take a trivial illustration: just as a man who in a company of gentlemen made no advances, asked a warrant for every concession, and believed no one's word without proof, would cut himself off by such churlishness from all the social rewards that a more trusting spirit would earn,—so here, one who should shut himself up in snarling logicality and try to make the gods extort his recognition willy-nilly, or not get it at all, might cut himself off forever from his only opportunity of making the gods' acquaintance. This feeling, forced on us we know not whence, that by obstinately believing that there are gods (although not to do so would be so easy both for our logic and our life) we are doing the universe the deepest service we can, seems parts of the living essence of the religious hypothesis. If the hypothesis *were* true in all its parts, including this one, then pure intellectualism, with its veto on our making willing advances, would be an absurdity; and some participation of our sympathetic nature would be logically required. I, therefore, for one, cannot see my way to accepting the agnostic rules for truth-seeking, or wilfully agree to keep my willing nature out of the game. I cannot do so for this plain reason, that *a rule of thinking which would absolutely prevent me from acknowledging certain kinds of truth if those kinds of truth were really there, would be an irrational rule.* That for me is the long and short of the formal logic of the situation, no matter what the kinds of truth might materially be.

I confess I do not see how this logic can be escaped. But sad experience makes me fear that some of you may still shrink from radically saying with me, *in abstracto*, that we have the right to believe at our own risk any hypothesis that is live enough to tempt our will. I suspect, however, that if this is so, it is because you have got away from the abstract logical point of view altogether, and are thinking (perhaps without realizing it) of some particular religious hypothesis which for you is dead. The freedom to "believe what we will" you apply to the case of some patent superstition; and the faith you think of is the faith defined by the schoolboy when he said, "Faith is when you believe something that you know ain't true." I can only repeat that this is misapprehension. *In concreto*, the freedom to believe can only cover living options which the intellect of the individual cannot by itself resolve; and living options never seem absurdities to him who has them to consider. When I look at the religious question as it really puts itself to concrete men, and when I think of all the possibilities which both practically and theoretically it involves, then this command that we shall put a stopper on our heart, instincts, and courage, and *wait*—acting of course meanwhile more or less as if religion were *not* true[3]—till doomsday, or till such time as our intellect and senses working together may have raked in evidence enough,—this command, I say, seems to me the queerest idol ever manufactured in the philosophic cave. Were we scholastic absolutists, there might be more excuse. If we had an infallible intellect with its objective certitudes, we might feel ourselves disloyal to such a perfect organ of knowledge in not trusting to it exclusively, in not waiting for its releasing word. But if we are empiricists, if we believe that no bell in us tolls to let us know for certain when truth is in our grasp, then it seems a piece of idle fantasticality to preach so solemnly our duty of waiting for the bell. Indeed we *may* wait if we will,—I hope you do not think that I am denying that,—but if we do so, we do so at our peril as much as if we believed. In either case we *act*, taking our life in our hands. No one of us ought to issue vetoes to the other, nor should we bandy words of abuse. We ought, on the contrary, delicately and profoundly to respect one another's mental freedom: then only shall we bring about the intellectual republic; then only shall we have that spirit of inner tolerance without which all our outer tolerance is soulless, and which is empiricism's glory; then only shall we live and let live, in speculative as well as in practical things.

I began by a reference to Fitz-James Stephen; let me end by a quotation from him. "What do you think of yourself? What do you think of the world? . . . These are questions with which all must deal as it seems good to them.

---

[3]Since belief is measured by action, he who forbids us to believe religion to be true, necessarily also forbids us to act as we should if we did believe it to be true. The whole defence of religious faith hinges upon action. If the action required or inspired by the religious hypothesis is in no way different from that dictated by the naturalistic hypothesis, then religious faith is a pure superfluity, better pruned away, and controversy about its legitimacy is a piece of idle trifling, unworthy of serious minds. I myself believe, of course, that the religious hypothesis gives to the world an expression which specifically determines our reactions, and makes them in a large part unlike what they might be on a purely naturalistic scheme of belief.

They are riddles of the Sphinx, and in some way or other we must deal with them. . . . In all important transactions of life we have to take a leap in the dark. . . . If we decide to leave the riddles unanswered, that is a choice; if we waver in our answer, that, too, is a choice: but whatever choice we make, we make it at our peril. If a man chooses to turn his back altogether on God and the future, no one can prevent him; no one can show beyond reasonable doubt that he is mistaken. If a man thinks otherwise and acts as he thinks, I do not see that any one can prove that *he* is mistaken. Each must act as he thinks best; and if he is wrong, so much the worse for him. We stand on a mountain pass in the midst of whirling snow and blinding mist, through which we get glimpses now and then of paths which may be deceptive. If we stand still we shall be frozen to death. If we take the wrong road we shall be dashed to pieces. We do not certainly know whether there is any right one. What must we do? 'Be strong and of good courage.' Act for the best, hope for the best and take what comes. . . . If death ends all, we cannot meet death better."[4]

---

[4]*Liberty, Equality, Fraternity*, p. 353, 2d ed., London, 1874.

SØREN KIERKEGAARD

1.25   Truth is Subjectivity

The way of objective reflection makes the subject accidental, and thereby transforms existence into something indifferent, something vanishing. Away from the subject the objective way of reflection leads to the objective truth, and while the subject and his subjectivity become indifferent, the truth also becomes indifferent, and this indifference is precisely its objective validity; for all interest, like all decisiveness, is rooted in subjectivity. The way of objective reflection leads to abstract thought, to mathematics, to historical knowledge of different kinds; and always it leads away from the subject, whose existence or non-existence, and from the objective point of view quite rightly, becomes infinitely indifferent. Quite rightly, since as Hamlet says, existence and non-existence have only subjective significance. At its maximum this way will arrive at a contradiction, and in so far as the subject does not become wholly

---

From Søren Kierkegaard, *Concluding Unscientific Postcript*, trans. by David F. Swenson and Walter Lowrie (copyright 1941 © 1969 by Princeton University Press; Princeton Paperback, 1968) pp. 173–82. Reprinted by permission of Princeton University Press and the American Scandinavian Foundation.

indifferent to himself, this merely constitutes a sign that his objective striving is not objective enough. At its maximum this way will lead to the contradiction that only the objective has come into being, while the subjective has gone out; that is to say, the existing subjectivity has vanished, in that it has made an attempt to become what in the abstract sense is called subjectivity, the mere abstract form of an abstract objectivity. And yet, the objectivity which has thus come into being is, from the subjective point of view at the most, either an hypothesis or an approximation, because all eternal decisiveness is rooted in subjectivity.

However, the objective way deems itself to have a security which the subjective way does not have (and, of course, existence and existing cannot be thought in combination with objective security); it thinks to escape a danger which threatens the subjective way, and this danger is at its maximum: madness. In a merely subjective determination of the truth, madness and truth become in the last analysis indistinguishable, since they may both have inwardness.[1] Nevertheless, perhaps I may here venture to offer a little remark, one which would seem to be not wholly superfluous in an objective age. The absence of inwardness is also madness. The objective truth as such, is by no means adequate to determine that whoever utters it is sane; on the contrary, it may even betray the fact that he is mad, although what he says may be entirely true, and especially objectively true. I shall here permit myself to tell a story, which without any sort of adaptation on my part comes direct from an asylum. A patient in such an institution seeks to escape, and actually succeeds in effecting his purpose by leaping out of a window, and prepares to start on the road to freedom, when the thought strikes him (shall I say sanely enough or madly enough?): "When you come to town you will be recognized, and you will at once be brought back here again; hence you need to prepare yourself fully to convince everyone by the objective truth of what you say, that all is in order as far as your sanity is concerned." As he walks along and thinks about this, he sees a ball lying on the ground, picks it up, and puts it into the tail pocket of his coat. Every step he takes the ball strikes him, politely speaking, on his hinder parts, and every time it thus strikes him he says: "Bang, the earth is round." He comes to the city, and at once calls on one of his friends; he wants to convince him that he is not crazy, and therefore walks back and forth, saying continually: "Bang, the earth is round!" But is not the earth round? Does the asylum still crave yet another sacrifice for this opinion, as in the time when all men believed it to be flat as a pancake? Or is a man who hopes to prove that he is sane, by uttering a generally

---

[1] Even this is not really true, however, for madness never has the specific inwardness of the infinite. Its fixed idea is precisely some sort of objectivity, and the contradiction of madness consists in embracing this with passion. The critical point in such madness is thus again not the subjective, but the little finitude which has become a fixed idea, which is something that can never happen to the infinite.

accepted and generally respected objective truth, insane? And yet it was clear to the physician that the patient was not yet cured; though it is not to be thought that the cure would consist in getting him to accept the opinion that the earth is flat. But all men are not physicians, and what the age demands seems to have a considerable influence upon the question of what madness is. Aye, one could almost be tempted sometimes to believe that the modern age, which has modernized Christianity, has also modernized the question of Pontius Pilate, and that its urge to find something in which it can rest proclaims itself in the question: What is madness? When a *Privatdocent*, every time his scholastic gown reminds him that he ought to say something, says *de omnibus dubitandum est*, and at the same time writes away at a system which offers abundant internal evidence in every other sentence that the man has never doubted anything at all: he is not regarded as mad.

Don Quixote is the prototype for a subjective madness, in which the passion of inwardness embraces a particular finite fixed idea. But the absence of inwardness gives us on the other hand the prating madness, which is quite as comical; and it might be a very desirable thing if an experimental psychologist would delineate it by taking a handful of such philosophers and bringing them together. In the type of madness which manifests itself as an aberrant inwardness, the tragic and the comic is that the something which is of such infinite concern to the unfortunate individual is a particular fixation which does not really concern anybody. In the type of madness which consists in the absence of inwardness, the comic is that though the something which the happy individual knows really is the truth, the truth which concerns all men, it does not in the slightest degree concern the much respected prater. This type of madness is more inhuman than the other. One shrinks from looking into the eyes of a madman of the former type lest one be compelled to plumb there the depths of his delirium; but one dares not look at a madman of the latter type at all, from fear of discovering that he has eyes of glass and hair made from carpet-rags; that he is, in short, an artificial product. If you meet someone who suffers from such a derangement of feeling, the derangement consisting in his not having any, you listen to what he says in a cold and awful dread, scarcely knowing whether it is a human being who speaks, or a cunningly contrived walking stick in which a talking machine has been concealed. It is always unpleasant for a proud man to find himself unwittingly drinking a toast of brotherhood with the public hangman; but to find oneself engaged in rational and philosophical conversation with a walking stick is almost enough to make a man lose his mind.

The subjective reflection turns its attention inwardly to the subject, and desires in this intensification of inwardness to realize the truth. And it proceeds in such fashion that, just as in the preceding objective reflection, when the objectivity had come into being, the subjectivity had vanished, so here the subjectivity of the subject becomes the final stage, and objectivity a vanishing factor. Not for a single moment is it forgotten that the subject is an existing individual, and that existence is a process of becoming, and that therefore the notion of the truth as identity of thought and being is a chimera of abstraction, in its truth only an expectation of the creature; not because the truth is not such an identity, but because the knower is an existing individual for whom the truth cannot be such an identity as long as he lives in time. Unless we hold fast to this, speculative philosophy will immediately transport us into the fantastic realism of the I-am-I, which modern speculative thought has not hesitated to use without explaining how a particular individual is related to it; and God knows, no human being is more than such a particular individual.

If an existing individual were really able to transcend himself, the truth would be for him something final and complete; but where is the point at which he is outside himself? The I-am-I is a mathematical point which does not exist, and in so far there is nothing to prevent everyone from occupying this standpoint; the one will not be in the way of the other. It is only momentarily that the particular individual is able to realize existentially a unity of the infinite and the finite which transcends existence. This unity is realized in the moment of passion. Modern philosophy has tried anything and everything in the effort to help the individual to transcend himself objectively, which is a wholly impossible feat; existence exercises its restraining influence, and if philosophers nowadays had not become mere scribblers in the service of a fantastic thinking and its preoccupation, they would long ago have perceived that suicide was the only tolerable practical interpretation of its striving. But the scribbling modern philosophy holds passion in contempt; and yet passion is the culmination of existence for an existing individual—and we are all of us existing individuals. In passion the existing subject is rendered infinite in the eternity of the imaginative representation, and yet he is at the same time most definitely himself. The fantastic I-am-I is not an identity of the infinite and the finite, since neither the one nor the other is real; it is a fantastic rendezvous in the clouds, an unfruitful embrace, and the relationship of the individual self to this mirage is never indicated.

All essential knowledge relates to existence, or only such knowledge as has an essential relationship to existence is essential knowledge. All knowledge which does not inwardly relate itself to existence, in the reflection of inwardness, is, essentially viewed, accidental knowledge; its degree and scope is essentially indifferent. That essential knowledge is essentially related to existence does not mean the above-mentioned identity which abstract thought postulates between thought and being; nor does it signify, objectively, that knowledge corresponds to something existent as its object. But it means that knowledge has a relationship to the knower, who is essentially an existing individual, and that for this reason all essential knowledge is essentially related to existence. Only ethical and ethico-religious knowledge has an essential relationship to the existence of the knower.

Mediation is a mirage, like the I-am-I. From the abstract point of view everything is and nothing comes into being. Mediation can therefore have no place in abstract thought because it presupposes *movement*. Objective knowledge may indeed have the existent for its object; but since the knowing subject is an existing individual, and through the fact of his existence in process of becoming, philosophy must first explain how a particular existing subject is related to a knowledge of mediation. It must explain what he is in such a moment, if not pretty nearly *distrait*; where he is, if not in the moon? There is constant talk of mediation and mediation; is mediation then a man, as Peter Deacon believes that *Imprimatur* is a man? How does a human being manage to become something of this kind? Is this dignity, this great *philosophicum*, the fruit of study, or does the magistrate give it away, like the office of deacon or grave-digger? Try merely to enter into these and other such plain questions of a plain man, who would gladly become mediation if it could be done in some lawful and honest manner, and not either by saying *ein zwei drei kokolorum*, or by forgetting that he is himself an existing human being, for whom existence is therefore something essential, and an ethico-religious existence a suitable *quantum satis*. A speculative philosopher may perhaps find it in bad taste to ask such questions. But it is important not to direct the polemic to the wrong point, and hence not to begin in a fantastic objective manner to discuss *pro* and *contra* whether there is a mediation or not, but to hold fast what it means to be a human being.

In an attempt to make clear the difference of way that exists between an objective and a subjective reflection, I shall now proceed to show how a subjective reflection makes its way inwardly in inwardness. Inwardness in an existing subject culminates in passion; corresponding to passion in the subject the truth becomes a paradox; and the fact that the truth becomes a paradox is rooted precisely in its having a relationship to an existing subject. Thus the one corresponds to the other. By forgetting that one is an existing subject, passion goes by the board and the truth is no longer a paradox; the knowing subject becomes a fantastic entity rather than a human being, and the truth becomes a fantastic object for the knowledge of this fantastic entity.

When the question of truth is raised in an objective manner, reflection is directed objectively to the truth, as an object to which the knower is related. Reflection is not focussed upon the relationship, however, but upon the question of whether it is the truth to which the knower is related. If only the object to which he is related is the truth, the subject is accounted to be in the truth. When the question of the truth is raised subjectively, reflection is directed subjectively to the nature of the individual's relationship; if only the mode of this relationship is in the truth, the individual is in the truth even if he should happen to be thus related to what is not true.[2] Let us take as an example the

---

[2]The reader will observe that the question here is about essential truth, or about the truth which is essentially related to existence, and that it is precisely for the sake of clarifying it as inwardness or as subjectivity that this contrast is drawn.

knowledge of God. Objectively, reflection is directed to the problem of whether this object is the true God; subjectively, reflection is directed to the question whether the individual is related to a something *in such a manner* that his relationship is in truth a God-relationship. On which side is the truth now to be found? Ah, may we not here resort to a mediation, and say: It is on neither side, but in the mediation of both? Excellently well said, provided we might have it explained how an existing individual manages to be in a state of mediation. For to be in a state of mediation is to be finished, while to exist is to become. Nor can an existing individual be in two places at the same time—he cannot be an identity of subject and object. When he is nearest to being in two places at the same time he is in passion; but passion is momentary, and passion is also the highest expression of subjectivity.

The existing individual who chooses to pursue the objective way enters upon the entire approximation-process by which it is proposed to bring God to light objectively. But this is in all eternity impossible, because God is a subject, and therefore exists only for subjectivity in inwardness. The existing individual who chooses the subjective way apprehends instantly the entire dialectical difficulty involved in having to use some time, perhaps a long time, in finding God objectively; and he feels this dialectical difficulty in all its painfulness, because every moment is wasted in which he does not have God.[3] That very instant he has God, not by virtue of any objective deliberation, but by virtue of the infinite passion of inwardness. The objective inquirer, on the other hand, is not embarrassed by such dialectical difficulties as are involved in devoting an entire period of investigation to finding God—since it is possible that the inquirer may die tomorrow; and if he lives he can scarcely regard God as something to be taken along if convenient, since God is precisely that which one takes *à tout prix*, which in the understanding of passion constitutes the true inward relationship to God.

It is at this point, so difficult dialectically, that the way swings off for everyone who knows what it means to think, and to think existentially; which is something very different from sitting at a desk and writing about what one has never done, something very different from writing *de omnibus dubitandum* and at the same time being as credulous existentially as the most sensuous of men. Here is where the way swings off, and the change is marked by the fact that while objective knowledge rambles comfortably on by way of the long road of approximation without being impelled by the urge of passion, subjective knowledge counts every delay a deadly peril, and the decision so

---

[3]In this manner God certainly becomes a postulate, but not in the otiose manner in which this word is commonly understood. It becomes clear rather that the only way in which an existing individual comes into relation with God, is when the dialectical contradiction brings his passion to the point of despair, and helps him to embrace God with the "category of despair" (faith). Then the postulate is so far from being arbitrary that it is precisely a life-necessity. It is then not so much that God is a postulate, as that the existing individual's postulation of God is a necessity.

infinitely important and so instantly pressing that it is as if the opportunity had already passed.

Now when the problem is to reckon up on which side there is most truth, whether on the side of one who seeks the true God objectively, and pursues the approximate truth of the God-idea; or on the side of one who, driven by the infinite passion of his need of God, feels an infinite concern for his own relationship to God in truth (and to be at one and the same time on both sides equally, is as we have noted not possible for an existing individual, but is merely the happy delusion of an imaginary I-am-I): the answer cannot be in doubt for anyone who has not been demoralized with the aid of science. If one who lives in the midst of Christendom goes up to the house of God, the house of the true God, with the true conception of God in his knowledge, and prays, but prays in a false spirit; and one who lives in an idolatrous community prays with the entire passion of the infinite, although his eyes rest upon the image of an idol: where is there most truth? The one prays in truth to God though he worships an idol; the other prays falsely to the true God, and hence worships in fact an idol.

When one man investigates objectively the problem of immortality, and another embraces an uncertainty with the passion of the infinite: where is there most truth, and who has the greater certainty? The one has entered upon a never-ending approximation, for the certainty of immortality lies precisely in the subjectivity of the individual; the other is immortal, and fights for his immortality by struggling with the uncertainty. Let us consider Socrates. Nowadays everyone dabbles in a few proofs; some have several such proofs, others fewer. But Socrates! He puts the question objectively in a problematic manner: *if* there is an immortality. He must therefore be accounted a doubter in comparison with one of our modern thinkers with the three proofs? By no means. On this "if" he risks his entire life, he has the courage to meet death, and he has with the passion of the infinite so determined the pattern of his life that it must be found acceptable—*if* there is an immortality. Is any better proof capable of being given for the immortality of the soul? But those who have the three proofs do not at all determine their lives in conformity therewith; if there is an immortality it must feel disgust over their manner of life: can any better refutation be given of the three proofs? The bit of uncertainty that Socrates had, helped him because he himself contributed the passion of the infinite; the three proofs that the others have do not profit them at all, because they are dead to spirit and enthusiasm, and their three proofs, in lieu of proving anything else, prove just this. A young girl may enjoy all the sweetness of love on the basis of what is merely a weak hope that she is beloved, because she rests everything on this weak hope; but many a wedded matron more than once subjected to the strongest expressions of love, has in so far indeed had proofs, but strangely enough has not enjoyed *quod erat demonstrandum*. The Socratic ignorance, which Socrates held fast with the entire passion of his inwardness, was thus an expression for the principle that the eternal truth is related to an existing individual, and that this truth must therefore be a paradox for him as long as he exists; and yet it is possible that there was more truth in the Socratic ignorance as it was in him, than in the entire objective truth of the System, which flirts with what the times demand and accommodates itself to *Privatdocents*.

The objective accent falls on WHAT is said, the subjective accent on HOW it is said. This distinction holds even in the aesthetic realm, and receives definite expression in the principle that what is in itself true may in the mouth of such and such a person become untrue. In these times this distinction is particularly worthy of notice, for if we wish to express in a single sentence the difference between ancient times and our own, we should doubtless have to say: "In ancient times only an individual here and there knew the truth; now all know it, except that the inwardness of its appropriation stands in an inverse relationship to the extent of its dissemination.[4] Aesthetically the contradiction that truth becomes untruth in this or that person's mouth, is best construed comically: In the ethico-religious sphere, accent is again on the "how." But this is not to be understood as referring to demeanor, expression, or the like; rather it refers to the relationship sustained by the existing individual, in his own existence, to the content of his utterance. Objectively the interest is focused merely on the thought-content, subjectively on the inwardness. At its maximum this inward "how" is the passion of the infinite, and the passion of the infinite is the truth. But the passion of the infinite is precisely subjectivity, and thus subjectivity becomes the truth. Objectively there is no infinite decisiveness, and hence it is objectively in order to annul the difference between good and evil, together with the principle of contradiction, and therewith also the infinite difference between the true and the false. Only in subjectivity is there decisiveness, to seek objectivity is to be in error. It is the passion of the infinite that is the decisive factor and not its content, for its content is precisely itself. In this manner subjectivity and the subjective "how" constitute the truth.

---

[4]*Stages on Life's Way*, Note on p. 426. Though ordinarily not wishing an expression of opinion on the part of reviewers, I might at this point almost desire it, provided such opinions, so far from flattering me, amounted to an assertion of the daring truth that what I say is something that everybody knows, even every child, and that the cultured know infinitely much better. If it only stands fast that everyone knows it, my standpoint is in order, and I shall doubtless make shift to manage with the unity of the comic and the tragic. If there were anyone who did not know it I might perhaps be in danger of being dislodged from my position of equilibrium by the thought that I might be in a position to communicate to someone the needful preliminary knowledge. It is just this which engages my interest so much, this that the cultured are accustomed to say: that everyone knows what the highest is. This was not the case in paganism, nor in Judaism, nor in the seventeen centuries of Christianity. Hail to the nineteenth century! Everyone knows it. What progress has been made since the time when only a few knew it. To make up for this, perhaps, we must assume that no one nowadays does it.

But the "how" which is thus subjectively accentuated precisely because the subject is an existing individual, is also subject to a dialectic with respect to time. In the passionate moment of decision, where the road swings away from objective knowledge, it seems as if the infinite decision were thereby realized. But in the same moment the existing individual finds himself in the temporal order, and the subjective "how" is transformed into a striving, a striving which receives indeed its impulse and a repeated renewal from the decisive passion of the infinite, but is nevertheless a striving.

When subjectivity is the truth, the conceptual determination of the truth must include an expression for the antithesis to objectivity, a memento of the fork in the road where the way swings off; this expression will at the same time serve as an indication of the tension of the subjective inwardness. Here is such a definition of truth: *An objective uncertainty held fast in an appropriation-process of the most passionate inwardness is the truth*, the highest truth attainable for an *existing* individual. At the point where the way swings off (and where this is cannot be specified objectively, since it is a matter of subjectivity), there objective knowledge is placed in abeyance. Thus the subject merely has, objectively, the uncertainty; but it is this which precisely increases the tension of that infinite passion which constitutes his inwardness. The truth is precisely the venture which chooses an objective uncertainty with the passion of the infinite. I contemplate the order of nature in the hope of finding God, and I see omnipotence and wisdom; but I also see much else that disturbs my mind and excites anxiety. The sum of all this is an objective uncertainty. But it is for this very reason that the inwardness becomes as intense as it is, for it embraces this objective uncertainty with the entire passion of the infinite. In the case of a mathematical proposition the objectivity is given, but for this reason the truth of such a proposition is also an indifferent truth.

But the above definition of truth is an equivalent expression for faith. Without risk there is no faith. Faith is precisely the contradiction between the infinite passion of the individual's inwardness and the objective uncertainty. If I am capable of grasping God objectively, I do not believe, but precisely because I cannot do this I must believe. If I wish to preserve myself in faith I must constantly be intent upon holding fast the objective uncertainty, so as to remain out upon the deep, over seventy thousand fathoms of water, still preserving my faith.

PART TWO

TALKING
ABOUT GOD

INTRODUCTION

In Part 1 we talked quite freely of God's existing or nonexisting, and in future sections we shall talk quite freely about God's power, his wisdom, his benevolence, etc. The emphasis in all of these sections is upon the truth and falsity of such claims, their consistency with other religious claims, and the evidence for and against them. But many philosophers of religion feel that another serious issue must be raised in connection with all of these beliefs, viz., the question of their meaningfulness. It is this question that we will consider in Part 2.

There have been two stages in the discussion of this issue. The first took place in the medieval period and was concerned with problems that would arise if one were to attribute any properties to God. It therefore centered about the meaningfulness of attributing properties to God. The second stage arose in this century and was concerned with the fact that religious claims do not seem to lend themselves to any empirical verification or falsification. It therefore centered around the question of how this fact affected the meaningfulness of religious claims.

Let us look at these issues separately. Why did the medievals suppose that problems would arise if we attributed properties to God? There seem to have been several different problems that they envisaged. Maimonides felt the crucial problem was that attributing properties to God would in some way involve God's being a composite being, and the giving up of the idea that God is an absolute unity. St. Thomas envisaged several other problems: (a) all predicates are such that their being predicated of an object presupposes that the object in question has some of the conditions of corporeality (like temporality, composition, etc.)—but since God is incorporeal, he has none of these conditions and the predicates cannot be truly attributed to him; and (b) there is an important sense in which it is true that God is incomprehensible—but if we could attribute properties to him, he would not be incomprehensible, so a problem arises.

There are several classical positions that the medievals adopted on this issue. The first is the view that all attributions of properties to God must really be understood as denying other positive attributions. Thus, to say that God is alive is really to say only that his being is not like the being of dead bodies. This view is expressed by Maimonides in the selection reprinted here. St. Thomas, however, rejects that view for several reasons. To begin with, one could equally well say, on the Maimonidean account, that God is dead since his being is not like the being of living things (people, plants, etc.). Obviously—and this leads us to St. Thomas's second point—we want to say that God is more unlike dead things than living things, i.e., that God is more like a live thing than a dead thing. But then we really are, in some way, saying something positive about what God is like, and Maimonides's theory collapses.

St. Thomas also rejects two other views that had been adopted by other medieval philosophers. The first is that the predicates we positively attribute to God mean the same thing when attributed to him as when attributed to ordinary creatures. This view he rejects, partially because it involves no solution to the problems mentioned above and partially because such a view obscures the way in which God has these properties perfectly and other creatures do not. The second is that the predicates we positively attribute to God mean something entirely different in such attributions from what they mean when they are attributed to other creatures. St. Thomas rejects this view, as well, on the strange grounds (really not argued for) that it would rule out the possibility that we could come to know something about the nature of God from an examination of ordinary creatures.

Aquinas's own solution to this problem is to claim that the predicates, when applied to God, have a meaning analogous to the meaning that they have when applied to ordinary things. Many have felt that this account cannot be accepted as a viable alternative. Professor James Ross has argued, however, that it can. Ross claims that this type of intermediary between univocity and equivocity is a widespread phenomena in language, occurring in certain definite patterns throughout all of language, and that an understanding of these patterns helps us to account for the ways in which the meaning of the predicates as applied to God differ from the meaning of these predicates as applied to other things.

The contemporary discussion about the meaning of religious claims takes its point of departure from a different set of considerations. Professor Flew states the problem succinctly. When one asserts that something is the case, one is also asserting that certain other things are not the case. But it is not clear that this holds for religious claims. When the religious person says that there is a God who loves us as a father loves a child but then says that this doesn't rule out the presence in our world of all types of suffering, etc., one begins to feel that nothing is asserted by his claim because there is nothing whose existence is ruled out by it. His claim becomes like the claim that there exists an invisible, intangible, eternally elusive gardener. And one is inclined to say that neither claim really asserts anything.

Professor Mitchell feels that Flew has missed the point of the religious person's view that the existence of all types of sufferings in the world does not rule out the existence of a loving God. The religious person recognizes that these sufferings count against the claim that there is a God who loves us as a father loves his child. But his faith is that this evidence against that claim is not conclusive. The fact that he concedes that the suffering is evidence against his claim is sufficient to insure that he actually is asserting something when he makes his claim.

One can see the dispute between Flew and Mitchell as follows: Flew insists that, for a claim to be asserting anything, it must rule out certain states of affairs and they must be such that the observation of their occurrence disproves the claim. Mitchell wants to insist that it is sufficient that the observation of the occurrence of these states of affairs challenges the claim, even if it is conceded that it does not disprove it.

A very different approach to Flew's challenge is presented by Professor Hare. Hare wants to claim that there is a special type of statement, a *blik,* which does not really assert anything, but which is nevertheless meaningful; indeed, it is extremely important that we have the right ones. Unfortunately, Hare does not give a precise account of what these statements do. All that he gives us is a variety of analogies. The reader will have to try to work out for himself what, if anything, these analogies point out about the meaning of religious claims.

Professor John Hick, finally, sees Flew's challenge as failing to take into account the full scope of religious belief. Part of the content of classical religious belief is the idea that man will survive his death and will encounter God. This is a type of experience whose occurrence is ruled out by the denial of the religious claim and is asserted by the religious claim, and both the claim and its denial are therefore meaningful and do express assertions. To be sure, they are not assertions that make any difference in this life, but that does not make them any less assertions.

There is one point that should be noticed about this entire discussion. All of the authors, to a greater or lesser degree, use interchangeably the two ideas that statements, if they are to assert anything, must (a) rule out certain states of affairs, and (b) rule out our having certain experiences (in this life or in some other). But if they only required (a), the problem that they are so concerned about would not arise. After all, one could then say that the statement that there is a God who loves us as a father loves a child does rule out certain states of affairs (e.g., meaningless acts of suffering) although it does not rule out our having any particular experiences, since any given act of suffering that we experience may, as we saw in Part 1, have some meaning that we do not know about.

THE MEANING OF PREDICATES
ATTRIBUTED TO GOD

MAIMONIDES

2.1 Negative Predication

More obscure than what preceded. Know that the description of God, may He be cherished and exalted, by means of negations is the correct description —a description that is not affected by an indulgence in facile language and does not imply any deficiency with respect to God in general or in any particular mode. On the other hand, if one describes Him by means of affirmations, one implies, as we have made clear, that He is associated with that which is not He and implies a deficiency in Him. I must make it clear to you in the first place how negations are in a certain respect attributes and how they differ from the affirmative attributes. After that I shall make it clear to you that we have no way of describing Him unless it be through negations and not otherwise.

I shall say accordingly that an attribute does not particularize any object of which it is predicated in such a way that it is not associated by virtue of that particular attribute with other things. On the contrary, the attribute is sometimes attributed to the object of which it is predicated in spite of the fact that the latter has it in common with other things and is not particularized through it. For instance, if you would see a man at some distance and if you would ask: What is this thing that is seen? and were told: This is a living being—this affirmation would indubitably be an attribute predicated of the thing seen though it does not particularize the latter, distinguishing it from everything else. However, a certain particularization is

---

From Maimonides, *Guide of the Perplexed*, Chap. 58, trans. S. Pines (Chicago: University of Chicago Press, 1963). Reprinted by permission of the publisher.

achieved through it; namely, it may be learnt from it that the thing seen is not a body belonging to the species of plants or to that of the minerals. Similarly if there were a man in this house and you knew that some body is in it without knowing what it is and would ask, saying: What is in this house? and the one who answered you would say: There is no mineral in it and no body of a plant—a certain particularization would be achieved and you would know that a living being is in the house though you would not know which animal. Thus the attributes of negation have in this respect something in common with the attributes of affirmation, for the former undoubtedly bring about some particularization even if the particularization due to them only exists in the exclusion of what has been negated from the sum total of things that we had thought of as not being negated. Now as to the respect in which the attributes of negation differ from the attributes of affirmation: The attributes of affirmation, even if they do not particularize, indicate a part of the thing the knowledge of which is sought, that part being either a part of its substance or one of its accidents; whereas the attributes of negation do not give us knowledge in any respect whatever of the essence the knowledge of which is sought, unless this happens by accident as in the example we have given.

After this preface, I shall say that it has already been demonstrated that God, may He be honored and magnified, is existent of necessity and that there is no composition in Him, as we shall demonstrate, and that we are only able to apprehend the fact that He is and cannot apprehend His quiddity. It is consequently impossible that He should have affirmative attributes. For he has no "That" outside of His "What," and hence an attribute cannot be indicative of one of the two; all the more His "What" is not compound so that an attribute cannot be indicative of its two parts; and all the more, He cannot have accidents so that an attribute cannot be indicative of them. Accordingly He cannot have an affirmative attribute in any respect.

As for the negative attributes, they are those that must be used in order to conduct the mind toward that which must be believed with regard to Him, may He be exalted, for no notion of multiplicity can attach to Him in any respect on account of them; and, moreover, they conduct the mind toward the utmost reach that man may attain in the apprehension of Him, may He be exalted. For instance, it has been demonstrated to us that it is necessary that something exists other than those essences apprehended by means of the senses and whose knowledge is encompassed by means of the intellect. Of this thing we say that it exists, the meaning being that its nonexistence is impossible. We apprehend further that this being is not like the being of the elements, for example, which are dead bodies. We say accordingly that this being is living, the meaning being that He, may He be exalted, is not dead. We apprehend further that this being is not like the being of the heaven, which is a living body. We say accordingly that He is not a body. We apprehend further that this being is not like the being of the intellect, which is neither a body nor dead, but is caused. We say accordingly that He, may He be exalted, is eternal, the meaning being that He has no cause that has brought Him into existence. We apprehend further that the existence of this being, which is its essence, suffices not only for His being existent, but also for many other existents flowing from it, and that this overflow—unlike that of heat from fire and unlike the proceeding of light from the sun—is an overflow that, as we shall make clear, constantly procures for those existents duration and order by means of wisely contrived governance. Accordingly we say of Him, because of these notions, that He is powerful and knowing and willing. The intention in ascribing these attributes to Him is to signify that He is neither powerless nor ignorant nor inattentive nor negligent. Now the meaning of our saying that He is not powerless is to signify that His existence suffices for the bringing into existence of things other than He. The meaning of our saying that He is not ignorant is to signify that He apprehends —that is, is living, for every apprehending thing is living. And the meaning of our saying that He is not inattentive or negligent is to signify that all the existent things in question proceed from their cause according to a certain order and governance—not in a neglected way so as to be generated as chance would have it, but rather as all the things are generated that a willing being governs by means of purpose and will. We apprehend further that no other thing is like that being. Accordingly our saying that He is one signifies the denial of multiplicity.

ST. THOMAS AQUINAS

2.2   *Analogical Predication*

After the consideration of those things which belong to the divine knowledge, we now proceed to the consideration of the divine names. For everything is named by us according to our knowledge of it.

Under this head, there are twelve points for inquiry.[1] (1) Whether God can be named by us? (2) Whether any names applied to God are predicated of Him substantially? (3) Whether any names applied to God are said of Him properly, or are all to be taken metaphorically? (4) Whether any names

---

From *Summa Theologica*, Part I, trans. Dominican Fathers of English Province (New York: Benziger, Inc., 1947). Reprinted by permission of the publisher.
[1]Only the first five are included below — ED.

applied to God are synonymous? (5) Whether some names are applied to
God and to creatures univocally or equivocally? (6) Whether, supposing they
are applied analogically, they are applied first to God or to creatures?
(7) Whether any names are applicable to God from time? (8) Whether this
name *God* is a name of nature, or of operation? (9) Whether this name *God*
is a communicable name? (10) Whether it is taken univocally or equivocally
as signifying God, by nature, by participation, and by opinion? (11) Whether
this name, *Who is*, is the supremely appropriate name of God? (12) Whether
affirmative propositions can be formed about God?

1. WHETHER A NAME CAN BE GIVEN TO GOD

We proceed thus to the First Article:—

Objection 1. It seems that no name can be given to God. For Dionysius
says that, *Of Him there is neither name, nor can one be found of Him*; and
it is written: *What is His name, and what is the name of His Son, if thou
knowest?* (*Prov.* xxx. 4).

Obj. 2. Further, every name is either abstract or concrete. But concrete
names do not belong to God, since He is simple, nor do abstract names
belong to Him, since they do not signify any perfect subsisting thing. Therefore no name can be said of God.

Obj. 3. Further, nouns signify substance with quality; verbs and participles
signify substance with time; pronouns the same with demonstration or relation. But none of these can be applied to God, for He has no quality, or
accident, or time; moreover, He cannot be felt, so as to be pointed out; nor
can He be described by relation, inasmuch as relations serve to recall a thing
mentioned before by nouns, participles, or demonstrative pronouns. Therefore God cannot in any way be named by us.

On the contrary, It is written (*Exod.* xv. 3): *The Lord is a man of war,
Almighty is His name.*

I *answer that*, Since, according to the Philosopher, words are signs of ideas,
and ideas the similitudes of things, it is evident that words function in the
signification of things through the conception of the intellect. It follows therefore that we can give a name to anything in so far as we can understand it.
Now it was shown above that in this life we cannot see the essence of God;
but we know God from creatures as their cause, and also by way of excellence and remotion. In this way therefore He can be named by us from
creatures, yet not so that the name which signifies Him expresses the divine
essence in itself in the way that the name *man* expresses the essence of man
in himself, since it signifies the definition which manifests his essence. For
the idea expressed by the name is the definition.

Reply Obj. 1. The reason why God has no name, or is said to be above
being named, is because His essence is above all that we understand about God
and signify in words.

Reply Obj. 2. Because we come to know and name God from creatures, the names we attribute to God signify what belongs to material creatures, of which the knowledge is natural to us, as was shown above. And because in creatures of this kind what is perfect and subsistent is composite, whereas their form is not a complete subsisting thing, but rather is that whereby a thing is, hence it follows that all names used by us to signify a complete subsisting thing must have a concrete meaning, as befits composite things. On the other hand, names given to signify simple forms signify a thing not as subsisting, but as that whereby a thing is; as, for instance, whiteness signifies that whereby a thing is white. And since God is simple and subsisting, we attribute to Him simple and abstract names to signify His simplicity, and concrete names to signify His subsistence and perfection; although both these kinds of names fail to express His mode of being, because our intellect does not know Him in this life as He is.

Reply Obj. 3. To signify substance with quality is to signify the *suppositum* with a nature or determined form in which it subsists. Hence, as some things are said of God in a concrete sense, to signify His subsistence and perfection, so likewise nouns are applied to God signifying substance with quality. Further, verbs and participles, which signify time, are applied to Him because His eternity includes all time. For as we can apprehend and signify simple subsistents only by way of composite things, so we can understand and express simple eternity only by way of temporal things, because our intellect has a natural proportion to composite and temporal things. But demonstrative pronouns are applied to God as pointing to what is understood, not to what is sensed. For we can point to Him only as far as we understand Him. Thus, according as nouns, participles and demonstrative pronouns are applicable to God, so far can He be signified by relative pronouns.

2. WHETHER ANY NAME CAN BE APPLIED TO GOD SUBSTANTIALLY

We proceed thus to the Second Article:—

Objection 1. It seems that no name can be applied to God substantially. For Damascene says: *Everything said of God must not signify His substance, but rather show forth what He is not; or express some relation, or something following from His nature or operation.*

Obj. 2. Further, Dionysius says: *You will find a chorus of holy doctors addressed to the end of distinguishing clearly and praiseworthy the divine processions in the denominations of God.* This means that the names applied by the holy doctors in praising God are distinguished according to the divine processions themselves. But what expresses the procession of anything does not signify anything pertaining to its essence. Therefore the names said of God are not said of Him substantially.

Obj. 3. Further, a thing is named by us according as we understand it. But in this life God is not understood by us in His substance. Therefore neither is any name we can use applied substantially to God.

On the contrary, Augustine says: *For God to be is to be strong or wise, or whatever else we may say of that simplicity whereby His substance is signified.* Therefore all names of this kind signify the divine substance.

I answer that, Names which are said of God negatively or which signify His relation to creatures manifestly do not at all signify His substance, but rather express the distance of the creature from Him, or His relation to something else, or rather, the relation of creatures to Himself.

But as regards names of God said absolutely and affirmatively, as *good, wise,* and the like, various and many opinions have been held. For some have said that all such names, although they are applied to God affirmatively, nevertheless have been brought into use more to remove something from God than to posit something in Him. Hence they assert that when we say that God lives, we mean that God is not like an inanimate thing; and the same in like manner applies to other names. This was taught by Rabbi Moses. Others say that these names applied to God signify His relationship towards creatures: thus in the words, *God is good,* we mean God is the cause of goodness in things; and the same interpretation applies to other names.

Both of these opinions, however, seem to be untrue for three reasons. First, because in neither of them could a reason be assigned why some names more than others should be applied to God. For He is assuredly the cause of bodies in the same way as He is the cause of good things; therefore if the words *God is good* signified no more than, *God is the cause of good things,* it might in like manner be said that God is a body, inasmuch as He is the cause of bodies. So also to say that He is a body implies that He is not a mere potentiality, as is primary matter. Secondly, because it would follow that all names applied to God would be said of Him by way of being taken in a secondary sense, as healthy is secondarily said of medicine, because it signifies only the cause of health in the animal which primarily is called healthy. Thirdly, because this is against the intention of those who speak of God. For in saying that God lives, they assuredly mean more than to say that He is the cause of our life, or that He differs from inanimate bodies.

Therefore we must hold a different doctrine—viz., that these names signify the divine substance, and are predicated substantially of God, although they fall short of representing Him. Which is proved thus. For these names express God, so far as our intellects know Him. Now since our intellect knows God from creatures, it knows Him as far as creatures represent Him. But it was shown above that God prepossesses in Himself all the perfections of creatures, being Himself absolutely and universally perfect. Hence every creature represents Him, and is like Him, so far as it possesses some perfection: yet not so far as to represent Him as something of the same species or genus, but as the excelling source of whose form the effects fall short, although they derive some kind of likeness thereto, even as the forms of inferior bodies represent the power of the sun. This was explained above in treating of the divine perfection. Therefore, the aforesaid names signify the divine substance, but in an imperfect manner, even as creatures represent it imperfectly. So when we say, *God is good*, the meaning is not, *God is the cause of goodness*, or, *God is not evil*; but the meaning is, *Whatever good we attribute to creatures pre-exists in God*, and in a higher way. Hence it does not follow that God is good because He causes goodness; but rather, on the contrary, He causes goodness in things because He is good. As Augustine says, *Because He is good, we are*.

Reply Obj. 1. Damascene says that these names do not signify what God is because by none of these names is what He is perfectly expressed; but each one signifies Him in an imperfect manner, even as creatures represent Him imperfectly.

Reply Obj. 2. In the signification of names, that from which the name is derived is different sometimes from what it is intended to signify, as for instance this name *stone* [*lapis*] is imposed from the fact that it hurts the *foot* [*lædit pedem*]; yet it is not imposed to signify that which hurts the foot, but rather to signify a certain kind of body; otherwise everything that hurts the foot would be a stone. So we must say that such divine names are imposed from the divine processions; for as according to the diverse processions of their perfections, creatures are the representations of God, although in an imperfect manner, so likewise our intellect knows and names God according to each kind of procession. But nevertheless these names are not imposed to signify the processions themselves, as if when we say *God lives*, the sense were, *life proceeds from Him*, but to signify the principle itself of things, in so far as life pre-exists in Him, although it pre-exists in Him a more eminent way than is understood or signified.

Reply Obj. 3. In this life, we cannot know the essence of God as it is in itself, but we know it according as it is represented in the perfections of creatures; and it is thus that the names imposed by us signify it.

3. WHETHER ANY NAME CAN BE APPLIED TO GOD PROPERLY

We proceed thus to the Third Article:—

Objection 1. It seems that no name is applied properly to God. For all names which we apply to God are taken from creatures, as was explained above. But the names of creatures are applied to God metaphorically, as when we say, God is a stone, or a lion, or the like. Therefore names are applied to God in a metaphorical sense.

Obj. 2. Further, no name can be applied properly to anything if it should be more truly denied of it than given to it. But all such names as *good, wise,* and the like, are more truly denied of God than given to Him; as appears from what Dionysius says. Therefore none of these names is said of God properly.

Obj. 3. Further, corporeal names are applied to God in a metaphorical sense only, since He is incorporeal. But all such names imply some kind of corporeal condition; for their meaning is bound up with time and composition and like corporeal conditions. Therefore all these names are applied to God in a metaphorical sense.

On the contrary, Ambrose says, *Some names there are which express evidently the property of the divinity, and some which express the clear truth of the divine majesty; but others there are which are said of God metaphorically by way of similitude.* Therefore not all names are applied to God in a metaphorical sense, but there are some which are said of Him properly.

I answer that, According to the preceding article, our knowledge of God is derived from the perfections which flow from Him to creatures; which perfections are in God in a more eminent way than in creatures. Now our intellect apprehends them as they are in creatures, and as it apprehends them thus does it signify them by names. Therefore, as to the names applied to God, there are two things to be considered–viz., the perfections themselves which they signify, such as goodness, life, and the like, and their mode of signification. As regards what is signified by these names, they belong properly to God, and more properly than they belong to creatures, and are applied primarily to Him. But as regards their mode of signification, they do not properly and strictly apply to God; for their mode of signification befits creatures.

Reply Obj. 1. There are some names which signify these perfections flowing from God to creatures in such a way that the imperfect way in which creatures receive the divine perfection is part of the very signification of the name itself, as stone signifies a material being; and names of this kind can be applied to God only in a metaphorical sense. Other names, however, express the perfections themselves absolutely, without any such mode of participation being part of their signification, as the words *being, good, living,* and the like; and such names can be applied to God properly.

Reply Obj. 2. Such names as these, as Dionysius shows, are denied of God for the reason that what the name signifies does not belong to Him in the ordinary sense of its signification, but in a more eminent way. Hence Dionysius says also that God is above all substance and all life.

Reply Obj. 3. These names which are applied to God properly imply corporeal conditions, not in the thing signified, but as regards their mode of signification; whereas those which are applied to God metaphorically imply and mean a corporeal condition in the thing signified.

4. WHETHER NAMES APPLIED TO GOD ARE SYNONYMOUS

We proceed thus to the Fourth Article:—

Objection 1. It seems that these names applied to God are synonymous names. For synonymous names are those which mean exactly the same. But these names applied to God mean entirely the same thing in God; for the goodness of God is His essence, and likewise it is His wisdom. Therefore these names are entirely synonymous.

Obj. 2. Further, if it be said that these names signify one and the same thing in reality, but differ in idea, it can be objected that an idea to which no reality corresponds is an empty notion. Therefore if these ideas are many, and the thing is one, it seems also that all these ideas are empty notions.

Obj. 3. Further, a thing which is one in reality and in idea is more one than what is one in reality and many in idea. But God is supremely one. Therefore it seems that He is not one in reality and many in idea; and thus the names applied to God do not have different meanings. Hence they are synonymous.

On the contrary, All synonyms united with each other are redundant, as when we say, *vesture clothing.* Therefore if all names applied to God are synonymous, we cannot properly say *good God,* or the like; and yet it is written, *O most mighty, great and powerful, the Lord of hosts is Thy name* (*Jer.* XXXII. 18).

I answer that, These names spoken of God are not synonymous. This would be easy to understand, if we said that these names are used to remove or to express the relation of cause to creatures; for thus it would follow that there are different ideas as regards the diverse things denied of God, or as regards diverse effects connoted. But according to what was said above, namely, that these names signify the divine substance, although in an imperfect manner, it is also clear from what has been said that they have diverse meanings. For the idea signified by the name is the conception in the intellect of the thing signified by the name. But since our intellect knows God from creatures, in order to understand God it forms conceptions proportioned to the perfections flowing from God to creatures. These perfections pre-exist in God unitedly and simply, whereas in creatures they are received divided and multiplied. Just as, therefore, to the diverse perfections of creatures there corresponds one simple principle represented by the diverse perfections of creatures in a various and manifold manner, so also to the various and multiplied conceptions of our intellect there corresponds one altogether simple principle, imperfectly understood through these conceptions. Therefore, although the names applied to God signify one reality, still, because they signify that reality under many and diverse aspects, they are not synonymous.

Thus appears the solution of the First Objection, since synonymous names signify one thing under one aspect; for names which signify different aspects of one thing do not signify primarily and absolutely one thing, because a name signifies a thing only through the medium of the intellectual conception, as was said above.

Reply Obj. 2. The many aspects of these names are not useless and empty, for there corresponds to all of them one simple reality represented by them in a manifold and imperfect manner.

Reply Obj. 3. The perfect unity of God requires that what are manifold and divided in others should exist in Him simply and unitedly. Thus it comes about that He is one in reality, and yet multiple in idea, because our intellect apprehends Him in a manifold manner, as things represent Him.

5. WHETHER WHAT IS SAID OF GOD AND OF CREATURES IS UNIVOCALLY PREDICATED OF THEM

We proceed thus to the Fifth Article:—

Objection 1. It seems that the things attributed to God and creatures are univocal. For every equivocal term is reduced to the univocal, as many are reduced to one: for if the name *dog* be said equivocally of the barking dog and of the dogfish, it must be said of some univocally—viz., of all barking dogs; otherwise we proceed to infinitude. Now there are some univocal agents which agree with their effects in name and definition, as man generates man; and there are some agents which are equivocal, as the sun which causes heat, although the sun is hot only in an equivocal sense. Therefore it seems that the first agent, to which all other agents are reduced, is a univocal agent: and thus what is said of God and creatures is predicated univocally.

Obj. 2. Further, no likeness is understood through equivocal names. There-fore, as creatures have a certain likeness to God, according to the text of *Genesis* (i. 26), *Let us make man to our image and likeness*, it seems that something can be said of God and creatures univocally.

Obj. 3. Further, measure is homogeneous with the thing measured, as is said in *Metaph.* x. But God is the first measure of all beings. Therefore God is homogeneous with creatures; and thus a name may be applied univocally to God and to creatures.

On the contrary, Whatever is predicated of various things under the same name but not in the same sense is predicated equivocally. But no name be-longs to God in the same sense that it belongs to creatures; for instance, wis-dom in creatures is a quality, but not in God. Now a change in genus changes an essence, since the genus is part of the definition; and the same applies to other things. Therefore whatever is said of God and of creatures is predicated equivocally.

Further, God is more distant from creatures than any creatures are from each other. But the distance of some creatures makes any univocal predica-tion of them impossible, as in the case of those things which are not in the same genus. Therefore much less can anything be predicated univocally of God and creatures; and so only equivocal predication can be applied to them.

I answer that, Univocal predication is impossible between God and crea-tures. The reason of this is that every effect which is not a proportioned result of the power of the efficient cause receives the similitude of the agent not in its full degree, but in a measure that falls short; so that what is divided and multiplied in the effects resides in the agent simply, and in an unvaried man-ner. For example, the sun by the exercise of its one power produces manifold and various forms in these sublunary things. In the same way, as was said above, all perfections existing in creatures divided and multiplied pre-exist in God unitedly. Hence, when any name expressing perfection is applied to a creature, it signifies that perfection as distinct from the others according to the nature of its definition; as, for instance, by this term *wise* applied to a man, we signify some perfection distinct from a man's essence, and distinct from his power and his being, and from all similar things. But when we apply *wise* to God, we do not mean to signify anything distinct from His essence or power or being. And thus when this term *wise* is applied to man, in some degree it circumscribes and comprehends the thing signified; whereas this is not the case when it is applied to God, but it leaves the thing signified as uncomprehended and as exceeding the signification of the name. Hence it is evident that this term *wise* is not applied in the same way to God and to man. The same applies to other terms. Hence, no name is predicated univocally of God and of creatures.

Neither, on the other hand, are names applied to God and creatures in a purely equivocal sense, as some have said. Because if that were so, it follows that from creatures nothing at all could be known or demonstrated about God; for the reasoning would always be exposed to the fallacy of equivocation. Such a view is against the Philosopher, who proves many things about God, and also against what the Apostle says: *The invisible things of God are clearly seen being understood by the things that are made (Rom.* i. 20). Therefore it must be said that these names are said of God and creatures in an *analogous* sense, that is, according to proportion.

This can happen in two ways: either according as many things are proportioned to one (thus, for example *healthy* is predicated of medicine and urine in relation and in proportion to health of body, of which the latter is the sign and the former the cause), or according as one thing is proportioned to another (thus, *healthy* is said of medicine and an animal, since medicine is the cause of health in the animal body). And in this way some things are said of God and creatures analogically, and not in a purely equivocal nor in a purely univocal sense. For we can name God only from creatures. Hence, whatever is said of God and creatures is said according as there is some relation of the creature to God as to its principle and cause, wherein all the perfections of things pre-exist excellently. Now this mode of community is a mean between pure equivocation and simple univocation. For in analogies the idea is not, as it is in univocals, one and the same; yet it is not totally diverse as in equivocals; but the name which is thus used in a multiple sense signifies various proportions to some one thing: *e.g., healthy*, applied to urine, signifies the sign of animal health; but applied to medicine, it signifies the cause of the same health.

Reply Obj. 1. Although in predications all equivocals must be reduced to univocals, still in actions the non-univocal agent must precede the univocal agent. For the non-univocal agent is the universal cause of the whole species, as the sun is the cause of the generation of all men. But the univocal agent is not the universal efficient cause of the whole species (otherwise it would be the cause of itself, since it is contained in the species), but is a particular cause of this individual which it places under the species by way of participation. Therefore the universal cause of the whole species is not a univocal agent: and the universal cause comes before the particular cause. But this universal agent, while not univocal, nevertheless is not altogether equivocal (otherwise it could not produce its own likeness); but it can be called an analogical agent, just as in predications all univocal names are reduced to one first non-univocal analogical name which is *being*.

Reply Obj. 2. The likeness of the creature to God is imperfect, for it does not represent the same thing even generically.

Reply Obj. 3. God is not a measure proportioned to the things measured; hence it is not necessary that God and creatures should be in the same genus.

The arguments adduced in the contrary sense prove indeed that these names are not predicated univocally of God and creatures; yet they do not prove that they are predicated equivocally.

JAMES F. ROSS

2.3 *Analogy and the Resolution of Some Cognitivity Problems*

After describing a form in which difficulties with the cognitive significance of religious discourse have been presented recently, I shall sketch a general "analogy of meaning" hypothesis for natural language and indicate how that hypothesis may lead to the resolution of such cognitivity difficulties while avoiding both noncognitivist and nonliteralist interpretations of religious discourse.

I. A RECENT FORM OF THE DIFFICULTY OVER THE COGNITIVE SIGNIFICANCE OF RELIGIOUS DISCOURSE

1. *A Change in Form.* Discussion of the cognitive (as distinct from emotive, evocative, or expressive) meaningfulness of discourse about God and about

From *The Journal of Philosophy* 67 (1970): 725–46. Reprinted by permission of the author and the editors.

the relationships of man and God has advanced with the recognition that the philosophical difficulties are not really centered upon the verifiability, falsifiability, confirmability, or empirical testability of religious statements, but rather upon their continuity of meaning (or lack of it) with discourse environments whose cognitive significance is not sensibly to be questioned. W. P. Alston, for instance, indicating that in religious discourse terms like 'wise', 'good', and 'person', are applicable to God only if certain sorts of action terms, like 'does', 'makes', 'creates', 'knows', 'forgives', and so forth, are also applicable, argues that in religious discourse the latter are used in ways that differ significantly from the ways in which those terms are used in empirically more accessible contexts:[1]

> ... the objective reference of God-sentences is borrowed from the prior application of their predictive terms to human beings (431).
> ... Thus we get, and must get the terms we apply to God from our talk about men ... in talk about God these terms no longer have their primary or literal meaning; their sense as well as their application has shifted (432).
> ... Any theological use of a word is derivative from a non-theological use of *some* word; derivative just in the sense that the former cannot be taught without employing the latter (435).
> ... The basic trouble is that in removing overt behavior from forgiving, commanding, etc. (and even more if we remove temporal sequence too) we have taken these terms out of the language game in which they primarily function without replacing it with another. In etherealizing these action concepts we snip off the rules which normally govern their use (440).

In consequence of transporting terms from epistemically prior environments to religious-discourse environments where the meanings are altered, we are left unclear as to just what conditions of application hold for these terms, and, supposedly, if we want to elucidate their senses, we shall have to perform a more careful analysis of the ways such terms are used in particular cases of religious discourse. (This is Alston's conclusion, 442–43; he does not draw noncognitivist consequences from the difficulty he has described.)

A challenge to the cognitive significance of religious discourse can be based on such premises, however.[2] It would suggest that, when you transport

---

[1]W. P. Alston, "The Elucidation of Religious Statements," in William L. Reese and Eugene Freeman, eds., *The Hartshorne Festschrift: Process and Divinity* (LaSalle, Ill.: Open Court, 1964), pp. 429–43.

[2]By 'cognitively significant' here, I mean that an expression is cognitively significant or cognitively meaningful if it would be appropriate for the speaker or hearer to adopt a positive epistemic attitude toward it, to believe it, doubt it, disbelieve it, know it to be true, and so forth.
John Smith in "The Present Status of Natural Theology," *Journal of Philosophy* LV (1958): 925–36, describes a "discontinuity thesis" favored by the Barthians and by many Protestant theologians: that there is no epistemic pathway from the world we know to the knowledge of God; the linguistic-discontinuity hypothesis described here is simply a generalization of that idea to a semantic counterpart. I do not think that Hare, Smart, McPherson, Braithwaite, Hepburn, and MacIntyre would abandon their noncognitivist inter-

a term from a context where its conditions of applicability are well understood, its implications are definite, etc., and relocate it in an environment where those conditions are certainly changed but are not well understood, you have or may have evacuated the cognitive significance of the term and may have transferred that effect deleteriously to the whole expression in which the term occurs. Religious discourse is a characteristically alien environment for terms with empirical signification.

2. *Similarity to the Medieval Dispute.* Alston's description of the difficulty brings the discussion full circle to a state remarkably similar to the thirteenth-century beginnings of the cognitivity dispute, when it was proposed that the terms applied to God are all equivocal with respect to their creature-applications.[3] Both the medieval equivocation hypothesis and Alston's description of the problem may be regarded as complementary particularized statements of a general *linguistic* discontinuity hypothesis concerning religious discourse: that religious discourse is of suspect cognitive significance because

---

pretations of religious discourse if they found that our understanding of verifiability, falsifiability, or confirmation had so weakened as to allow religious discourse to pass such tests; their conviction *against* the cognitivity of religious discourse is probably stronger than their conviction *for* the cognitivity criteria they have employed; they could then be expected to broaden their challenge by adopting some form of the discontinuity challenge.

Kai Nielsen still insists that an empirical-confirmability test must be faced and will be failed by God-statements, cf. "On Believing that God Exists," *Southern Journal of Philosophy*, v, 3 (Fall 1967): 167–72. Yet the article Nielsen discusses, Norman Malcolm's "Is It a Religious Belief that 'God Exists'?" in John Hick, ed., *Faith and the Philosophers* (New York: St. Martin's, 1964), pp. 103–10, already has moved from exclusive concentration upon empirical confirmation to considering that religious concepts "have a grip on the world" in ways to which "questions of confirmation and disconfirmation" are not relevant (Nielsen, p. 171). Even Nielsen seems prepared to adopt a discontinuity hypothesis, while maintaining that "claims must be open to some possible confirmation or disconfirmation" [p. 203 of "Wittgensteinian Fideism," *Philosophy*, XLII, 161 (July 1967)]; for he quotes, apparently with approval, G. E. Hughes' description of his and Martin's position as follows: "On my approach and on Martin's approach the fact that the pattern of usage of a term such as 'God' does not accord with that of other nontheological terms with which it is taken to be analogous, is made a basis for the charge that the use of the term is logically incoherent." [Nielsen's quotation from p. 215 of Hughes' "Martin's Religious Belief," *Australasian Journal of Philosophy*, LX, 2 (August 1962) on p. 195 of "Wittgensteinian Fideism," *loc. cit.*]. And in "The Intelligibility of God-Talk," *Religious Studies*, VI (March 1970): 1–21, Nielsen says: "The skeptic draws attention to the fact that such discourse utilizes terms like 'persons' and 'acts' which are common to more mundane contexts, but that in the religious contexts they function in a different way and that their very use in such religious contexts is thoroughly perplexing to believer and unbeliever alike . . . Thus in a very natural way—independently of some disputable philosophical criterion of meaning—questions concerning their intelligibility naturally arise" (p. 20).

[3]For instance, St. Thomas argues against that view in a number of places. In chapter 33 of *Contra Gentiles* he offers five reasons against the equivocation view; the fifth most clearly indicates his recognition of the noncognitivist consequences of the equivocation thesis: that "there is no reason to predicate terms of something unless we increase understanding thereby; if the terms were used equivocally of God, there would be no way to show that God is a being, is good, or anything else." Also in *Summa Theologica*, Ia,q.13,a.5 corpus he says: Nothing is predicated of God "purely equivocally as some say. Because, on that view, nothing could be known of God from creatures nor demonstrated; but the fallacy of equivocation would always block the way." He takes the same position in Ia,q.13,a.10; q.13,a.5,ad 1 and I *Sentences*, d,35,q.1.a.4, corpus.

there is a discontinuity between the meanings of its characteristic terms and the meanings those terms have in other discourse environments, some of which are, for most people, epistemically prior.

The discontinuity is illustrated nowadays by contrasting the indefiniteness and even contrariety of the conditions of observation, evidence, behavioral expression, term applicability, implication, and of paraphrase which accompany expressions in religious discourse, with the definiteness of certain epistemically prior nonreligious discourse environments where the same terms occur. In the thirteenth century the discontinuity was illustrated by a contrast of the metaphysical categories and modes of being of God and creatures, leading to the conclusion that a semantic chasm, equivocation, separated talk about God from talk about other things.

Just as the medievals considered the hypothesis that equivocation may be the result of the displacement of terms from an experiential to a transcendental context, so some philosophers today consider that language "goes on a holiday" or breaks loose from the restraints of meaning-conferring language games when terms are similarly displaced. And just as in the thirteenth century an analogy theory was introduced to provide a *via media* between the anthropomorphic doctrine of "univocation" and the agnostic (noncognitivist or nonliteral) doctrine of "equivocation" concerning the divine predicates,[4] so now an analogy doctrine may be used to refute the linguistic-discontinuity hypothesis by helping us to show that religious discourse has no infirmity peculiar to it, that its semantic structure is fully incorporated within the general semantic regularity of natural language.[5]

3. *Some Qualifications about the Statement of the Difficulty.* Alston is right[6] that we do and must "get the terms we apply to God from our talk about men." (432). But I think we should take "primary" meaning to be person-relative and not delude ourselves into thinking that there can be only one primary meaning a term has for a given person. *A* primary meaning of *t* for *S* is any meaning *t* has for *S* that is not learned by *S* through *t*'s already having some other meaning for *S*. Thus a term may have several primary meanings for *S*. That accords well with the simple equivocation of such terms as 'fast' in 'fast car', 'fast day', 'bound fast', 'fast color', and 'fast girl'. And there is a difference between *primacy* of meaning for *S* and *priority* of

---

[4]In the thirteenth century it was the transcendence of God which supported the argument that terms like 'wise', 'knows', 'loves', 'acts', 'does', 'causes', and even 'exists' must be used equivocally when applied to God (as compared with other "experiential" human employments). Aquinas took that argument seriously because he held that our only access to the "sense" (as distinct from "formal," linguistic) meanings of expressions in language is through experience, and, if the terms do not have their meaning originating in experience and continuous with it, then religious expressions would be quite literally unintelligible.

[5]From its medieval beginnings the analogy theory about religious discourse was developed as an alternative to a noncognitivist account. Although the noncognitivist view was not widely held, it may have had some supporters, for Aquinas denies that the terms are used "purely equivocally, *as some say*" (Ia,q.13,a.5, italics mine).

[6]Aquinas argued similarly: Ia,q.13,a.1,ad.

meaning for S with respect to some other meaning t has for S. For one meaning t has for S is *prior* to some other meaning t has for S if the latter is or was learned by S through S's knowledge of the former. Although no meaning of t that is secondary for S may also be a primary meaning of t for S, some meaning of t for S may be primary without being a prior meaning of t for S or being the *only* primary or prior meaning of t for S.[7]

There is no reason to assume that, for terms that have many meanings for most persons competent in the language, there is any one meaning that is primary for all persons or any one meaning that is, for all persons, prior to all other senses the term has for each person. With these qualifications we can agree with Alston that "In talk about God these terms no longer have their primary . . . meaning."[8] But that is simply a general truth and not, as he seems to think, a matter of principle. For it is not impossible that someone should have the divine-predicate sense of 'wise' as a primary sense for him; rather, given our form of life, it is conditionally impossible that *everyone* should have the divine-predicate senses of such terms as primary. And if S's talk about God makes interpersonal sense (and not accidentally) and yet the divine-predicate senses of some of his terms are their primary senses for him, it must be that S belongs to a discoursing community with other persons for whom these terms do not have primary sense, as described above, in talk about God.

Not to disengage the primary senses and literal uses of terms is a mistake. A nonliteral or metaphorical *use* of a term is not, except by stipulation, the same thing as a nonliteral or metaphorical *sense* of a term. I can understand the latter idea only as a comparative, metalinguistic predicate[9] or as a very loose equivalent of 'nonliteral or metaphorical *use*'. It is frequently and mistakenly assumed that metaphorical uses of terms involve changes in the senses of the terms; just the opposite seems to be true. As long as the sense of the term 'lion' remains the same as in (a) 'Leo is a lion in the circus that played here last year', the *use* of 'lion' in (b) 'General MacArthur was a lion' may be metaphorical with respect to its use in (a); but once the sense of 'lion' in (b) is shifted so that its categories are aligned with those of the subject,

---

[7]While I will not develop the point here because it involves diachronic considerations, a different meaning of t for S can be learned by S *from* some prior meaning t has for S only through some process of derivation; I suggest that those processes are regular and that they are the counterparts of the synchronic regularities to be discussed in this paper.

[8]The "omission dots" indicate that I have left "or literal" out of the quotation for reasons to be made clear below.

[9]I have in mind here that, even if the sense of 'lion' were adjusted to the categories or its subject and occurred literally in (b), below in the text, one might still want to say that the meaning of this occurrence of the term as compared with its use in (a) is "metaphorical." Thus we would be indicating that a new sense of the term had arisen, over time, through the metaphorical use of the term in its earlier meaning. See R. A. Hall, Jr., *Introductory Linguistics* (Philadelphia: Chilton Company, 1964), ch. 59, "Changes in Meaning" especially p. 350/I.

'General MacArthur', the use of 'lion', which would formerly have been metaphorical, becomes literal and becomes equivocal with its use in (a).[10] Not only is it incorrect to identify the primary sense and literal meaning in such a way that no derivative meaning will accompany a literal use; it would be even further wrong to suggest that, because both the sense and the application of a pair of same-term occurrences differ, it cannot happen that both members of the pair should be used literally. That would ignore both simple equivocation and meaning derivation, which are to be found in virtually every extended discourse. Thus although we take Alston's description of the difficulty about religious discourse to be astute and suggestive, we have to amend his assumptions about primacy and reject the apparent equivalence of "derived" and "nonliteral" uses of same-terms.

II. WHAT IS THE ANALOGY HYPOTHESIS?

It is a general hypothesis about meaning derivation in natural languages. But we shall consider only the analogy hypothesis for English. The hypothesis will apply to "religious discourse" because it applies to every discourse environment for which natural language is used, including "physical discourse," "gambling discourse," "architectural discourse," and so forth.[11]

The analogy hypothesis is as follows: (1) The sets of same-term occurrences to be found within the available corpus of utterances and inscriptions in English almost universally exhibit internal multiplicity of meanings. (2) That multiplicity of meaning is not a manifestation of simple equivocation in most cases (equivocation by chance, *a casu*), but manifests meaning derivation that results from *meaning-differentiation-in-use* (meaning differentiation, not by a speaker's design, deliberation or intent, but by semantic contagion). (3) The meaning-differentiation-in-use that can be observed within sets of same-term occurrences, exhibits certain regularities which are to be found in a significant sample of sets of same-term occurrences. (4) These regularities of meaning differentiation are *synchronic* regularities (as distinct from the *diachronic* regularities which are exhibited in the evolution of language and

---

[10]Thus for *t* in (b) to be used metaphorically with respect to *t* in (a) it is necessary (but not sufficient) that *t* in (b) be univocal with *t* in (a) and that the conditions of applicability for *t* in (a) *not* all be satisfied for *t* in (b), though for the statement (b) to be true (as a metaphorical claim) *some* of the conditions of applicability of *t* in (a) must be satisfied in (b). Thus, taken literally, a metaphorical expression must be false, and yet it still has truth conditions that govern the metaphorical expression qua a truth expressed metaphorically.

[11]Nothing more is signified by expressions of the form '*F* discourse' than that the modifier '*F*' is to be regarded as a rough and conventional indication of the likely subject-matter, or concerns or occasion for the discourse; thus the same exchanges may simultaneously belong to several "discourse environments," and, depending upon how elaborately one wants to classify discourse environments, there is no restriction upon the number of discourse environments to which a given expression may belong.

which in some cases have corresponding synchronic regularities).[12] (5) When the regularities exhibited by the meaning-differentiation-in-use within sets of same-term occurrences are expressed in law-like or rule-like generalizations, having "initial conditions" and "derivation conditions" to be satisfied by a pair of same-term occurrences, we call the resulting rules *analogy rules* and say that meaning-differentiation-in-use for sets of same-term occurrences in English, considered synchronically, occurs on the whole in accordance with analogy rules.[13] (6) A same-term occurrence t_2 in a discourse context (2) that is meaning-derived with respect to an analogy rule for E from a same-term occurrence t_1 that occurs in a discourse context (1) that is cognitively significant, is also cognitively significant. (Meaning derivation by analogy is cognitivity-preserving.)

Some further explanation of the analogy hypothesis may help.

a. *Identifying same-term occurrences.* It can be determined through distributional analysis by empirical linguists whether elements of two utterances or inscriptions found in a speech or writing sample that is part of the available corpus, are tokens of the same term.[14] No assumption has to be made as to whether the tokens have the same or different meanings. Thus the set of same-term occurrences of 'knows' within the corpus of available discourse in English will consist of all and only the inscription and utterance tokens of that (phonemic-orthographic) term type. I pass over questions concerned with misspelling, shorthand, mispronunciation, accent, dialect, speech defect, mistyping, etc. because these can be moderately well settled by distributional analysis.

b. *Discourse context.* We are considering only term occurrences within discourse contexts. A discourse context for a term is any complete sentential

---

[12]De Saussure first called attention to the difference between these two sorts of regularities and to the fact that in the synchronic regularities we find our best clues to the structure of a language. Cf. John Lyons, *Introduction to Theoretical Linguistics* (New York: Cambridge, 1969), pp. 45–50. It is because linguists have been so successful in the study of structure upon de Saussure's premise that I concentrate upon synchronic regularities in the investigation of meaning derivation. To the doubt that meaning derivation can be analyzed this way because it is essentially a process, I reply that the conjugation of verbs, the alignment of the person and number of verbs and pronoun subjects also occur as processes in the use of the language, but, like meaning derivation, form patterns and regularities to be found within the available corpus.

[13]In case one is led to expect too much, let me warn that I have not been able to put all the regularities I have observed, especially those concerned with semantic contagion, into this form as yet, or to display very many such regularities. The investigation is too near its beginnings to have yielded many specifics; but the ideas of "initial" and "derivation" conditions are broad enough to provide ample latitude for the formulation of the regularities.

[14]Cf. Zellig S. Harris, *Structural Linguistics* (Chicago: University Press, 1961) (originally titled *Methods in Structural Linguistics*), p. 361. Also, see Lyons, *op. cit.*, ch. v. In accord with the current linguistic interest in morphemes as the smallest free variants which are meaningful and which are the units of grammatical analysis, let 'term' be the same as 'morpheme' rather than 'word', which is too vague.

expression in speech or writing in which the term is used (as contrasted with "mentioned") and which is part of the available corpus of English.

c. *Available corpus.* The notion of the *available* corpus is important for this hypothesis. In constructing a dictionary, it is often useful for the compilers to use the corpus of a written language regardless of its distribution over time. But the kind of corpus relevant here is the kind a compiler would use to construct a dictionary of *contemporary* usage. It must, like the former, consist of verifiable quotations, but since we have to allow that there are relevant uses of terms which do not occur within the written corpus, we broaden the notion of "available corpus" to include recorded speech of all sorts, provided it represents contemporary speech: thus, radio tapes, video tapes with sound tracks, movies, newscasts, court transcriptions and recordings, phonograph records, etc., are all included within the corpus. Thus we are not concerned with what someone might say or would say, but directly with what someone has said or does say. At the same time we cannot, in a philosophical inquiry, document every usage of a term with a reference to its actual occurrence within the available corpus; rather, the corpus is the empirical field of test; our usual examples are acceptable provided there is such an occurrence of the terms within the corpus of English; otherwise the examples are unjustified and misleading. Needless to say, the examples in papers such as this cannot be taken as extensions of the corpus of contemporary English; otherwise they will become self-confirming.

d. *Multiplicity of meanings.* When I talk of the multiplicity of meanings within sets of same-term occurrences, I have in mind such things as these:

(a) In the analysis of the amount of damage caused when the train hit the automobile, *the physical force was calculated* according to three different formulas.

(b) In the weeks of the revolution preceding Castro's taking power, *the physical force was calculated* to throw the economy and the bureaucracy into confusion.

(c) After considering the facts carefully, the district attorney decided that *the physical force was calculated*, and proceeded to charge the suspect with aggravated assault with intent to kill.

Whether or not we happen to have three distinct dictionary entries for the three senses of 'physical force' or of 'was calculated', a person who understands the contexts of discourse has no difficulty whatever grasping the differential meanings of these same-term occurrences.

So too with 'has' in: (a) 'John has a comb with him'. (b) 'John has a home of his own'. (c) 'John has a wife already'. (d) 'John has a cold'.

Here is a third example of meaning-differentiation-in-use:

(a) Whatever a man knows, he does not know everything.

(b) Smith is one of those who always knows he is right and seldom is.
(c) The Internal Revenue Service knows that 10 per cent of the taxpayers falsify their income.
(d) No, I do not know Smith, though I am acquainted with him.
(e) (Someone else speaking) Why, yes, I *do* know him, you pointed him out to me yesterday, but I haven't met him yet.

e. *Two senses of 'meaning-differentiation-in-use'.* In one sense, when we speak of meaning-differentiation-in-use, we mean only that, if we inspect in context a fairly wide sample of same-term occurrences, we shall see that, compared with one another, they differ in meaning, not entirely but in ways that represent the differences in their contexts; although they are equivocal with respect to one another, they are not helter-skelter equivocal but equivocal by adaptation. That kind of meaning differentiation is illustrated by the three examples above and can be manufactured without presently discernible limit for almost any of the common terms of English. But when we have before us a large sampling of different meanings for sets of same-term occurrences, it is reasonable to ask whether there are formulable *regularities* within such sets of occurrences. Is meaning differentiation without organizing principles, or does it occur in some regular way? For instance, can the difference in semantical categories for 'physical force' in various contexts be shown to be represented in changes in attached predicates like 'was calculated'? Or, perhaps, in differences in the lists of predicates that would be appropriate in the contexts?

In the second sense of 'meaning-differentiation-in-use', when we say that terms are meaning-differentiated-in-use, we mean that there is *regularity-conforming* meaning differentiation (or analogy of meaning) among the same-term occurrences. To establish that there is meaning-differentiation-in-use (in this sense), we must establish that there are semantical regularities to which meaning-differentiated (sense 1) sets of same-term occurrences conform.

f. *Meaning derivation.* Let it be understood that when I speak of meaning derivation, there is no assumption whatever that, from a speaker's or hearer's point of view, the "derived" sense is consciously or even actually dependent upon some, for him, prior sense. The notion is to be explained entirely in terms of the relationships the same-term occurrences have with respect to certain semantic regularities. Similarly, any true statement can be said to be derived from some other true statement with respect to the rules of logic, since there will always be a true statement which, manipulated according to the rules, will yield the true statements as a conclusion, regardless of whether anyone ever derives that conclusion from that premise or not. Derivation is simply the relationship of the secondary to the primary with respect to some set of ordering principles. One of a pair of equivocal same-term occurrences is derived in meaning from the other with respect to an analogy rule *R* if and only if the one same-term occurrence satisfies the initial conditions of R and the other satisfies its derivation conditions.[15]

g. *Contrast with simple equivocation.* Meaning-derivative pairs of same-term occurrences are to be contrasted with simply equivocal pairs. For instance, 'plow' in 'New England farmers begin to plow in late April' and in 'The Quarterback will begin to plow through the line while the halfbacks feint an end run' is not simply equivocal, since the pair of same-term occurrences is related by semantical regularities, whereas 'piped' in 'The developers piped the sewerage into the stream' and in 'The coxswain piped the captain aboard' is simply equivocal. There is no general semantic regularity with respect to which the one may be considered derived in meaning from the other. The following three identificatory criteria for cases of analogous meaning derivation are illustrative.[16]

h. *Derivation Criteria.* (1) *Generability.* t_1 is derived from t_2 with respect to R if t_1 is generable from t_2 with respect to R. t_1 is generable from t_2 with respect to R if a native speaker of E, who understands the use of t_1 in its context and who understands R (either explicitly or through experience manifested in the correct use of the language) can by following R generate a discourse context (3) in which t_3 occurs univocally with t_2 (and R is an analogy rule extrapolated from synchronic regularities obtaining among same-term-occurrences in use).

(2) *Context Transformability.* t_1 is meaning-derived from t_2 if a person competent in the language who understands the context for t_2 and the relevant regularity can by altering the sentential expression and context of t_1 produce a context containing a same-term-occurrence t_3 that is univocal with t_2.

(3) *Contracted Semantical Contrast.* t_1 can be said to be meaning-derived from t_2 if there is in the context (1) some semantical unit ϕ such that there is a counterpart unit ψ in (2) which is in semantical categorical contrast with ϕ, and t_1 may be considered to have its meaning as an *alteration* of the meaning

---

[15]Here I simply by-pass questions about the various kinds of direct and indirect analogy ordering among sets of same-term occurrences as a whole (such as, 'expected' in 'I expected a guest', 'I expected rain', 'I expected a raise', 'I expected politeness') and related technical matters which are treated inchoately in "A New Theory of Analogy: I" forthcoming in the *Proceedings of the American Catholic Philosophical Association,* 1970, to be reprinted in *Logical Analysis and Contemporary Theism,* edited by John Donnelly.

There are a number of basic questions concerning the analogy hypothesis which are still to be answered. For instance, why may not the initial and derivation conditions be reversed? What determines which are the initial and which the derivation conditions? What distinguishes the semantic regularities that are relevant to the analogy relationships from those which are not? That is why it seems better to talk about an analogy-of-meaning hypothesis rather than a theory at this point, or perhaps even an analogy conjecture or proposal.

[16]Presumably, these are only first approximations of identificatory criteria which would have the requisite generality. They do seem to pick out derived uses in relation to the few analogy rules presently formulated.

of t_2 (only so far as) to bring its semantical categories into accord with ψ
Thus, in the frame 'He caught the ———', the pair of sentences 'He caught$_1$
the cold' and 'He caught$_2$ the thief' have the same term as verb, but the
meanings of the verbs are different. The one is said to be meaning-derived
from the other because the one may be regarded as an alteration of the meaning of the other to accord with the categorically contrasting direct objects.

The kind of meaning derivation that corresponds to this third criterion is
different from some of the sorts of meaning derivation picked out by the first
two criteria. Examples of the regularities contemplated for (1) and (2) are:
"a third-person singular, present-tense, active verb, used to attribute an action
to an agent is also used to attribute an ability, a disposition, or a proclivity
or ability, disposition, proclivity, etc." "An adjective used to indicate an
apparent modification of some thing or state of affairs is also used to indicate
the *actual* modification of such a thing or state of affairs." "An adjective used
to describe the state of some object is used to describe the cause, effect,
symptom, signs, etc., of the object—with morphemic adjustments in some
cases." The quality and property senses of 'red' is an example. So, too 'evil
deed', 'evil man', and so forth. But while in '— flies' we may have one case
where we attribute a present ability to something, ('the SST flies'), and in
another, a habit or disposition or proclivity, changes in the subjects to create
categorial contrasts bring about a different kind of contrast in the senses of
'flies': 'The plane flies too low over the city'; 'The pilot flies too low over
the city'. Here, although both are "dispositional" or "habitual" uses, the *contrast* in the two occurrences of 'flies' is a contracted contrast based upon the
contrast of semantic categories for the subjects. The sentence frame [NP
'flies', Adv.P.] is neutral to the sentence frame [NP 'determines the positions
of the controls'.] neither entailing it nor excluding it. Hence the differential
sense of 'flies' is determined by contagion of the semantical categories of the
subject term, so that 'The pilot determines the positions of the controls' may
be entailed by the second but not by the first expression.

Semantic contagion seems to be of two main kinds: (a) contrast in meaning
contracted from the contrasts in discourse environment, and (b) contrasts in
meaning contracted from semantic units which are elements in the sentential
expressions. *From the discourse environment:* 'It's a steal'. In an environment of baseball discourse, an umpire may settle a dispute over whether a
player's move was legal or not (whether he moved before the completed
pitch) with a decision in those words. Something quite different is meant when
an automobile salesman describes his offer in such terms. The same is true
of the expression 'That's my view' uttered in reply to certain questions about
whether one believes something, and uttered upon first showing a visitor the
vista outside one's home. *From elements within sentential expressions:* This
sort of contracted semantic contrast is based upon the fact that in pairs of
expressions with a common term, there may be other terms in categorial con-

trast whose contrast is contracted by the pair of same-term occurrences. There are a number of ways this happens; for instance:

i. From contrasting subjects to contrast of predicates, 'Holding': 'John is holding the post out of plumb'; 'The crooked sill is holding the post out of plumb'; 'The Comptroller is holding the checks until Monday'; 'The accident is holding the traffic to ten miles an hour'. (The latter two cases involve more than one contrast of the types being enumerated here). Another example: 'His studies were in Arabic' and 'His letters were in Arabic'. Or: 'The foremen worked all day'; 'The truck worked all day'; 'The pump worked all day' (strained).

ii. From contrasting predicates to a contrast of subjects: 'The Church cannot hold that many people'; 'The Church cannot permit doctrinal chaos'. 'My corn is just above ground' (plants); 'My corn is ready to eat' (ears).

iii. From modifiers to subjects or predicates: 'He stared vacantly'; 'He stared angrily' (contrast induced in predicates by modifier-contrast). 'The Arabic language is difficult for the English'; 'The spoken language is deteriorating' (contrast of meaning induced in 'language' by contrasting modifiers 'Arabic' and 'vocal').

iv. From contrasting objects to a contrast of predicates: 'We told him to cancel the appointment'; 'We told him to cancel the check'. 'He negotiated the bonds'; 'He negotiated the curve'. 'He circled the place to sign'; 'He circled the place to land'.

In general, there seem to be two different kinds of meaning-derivation situations, not entirely unlike the two kinds Aquinas had in mind when he distinguished analogy of proportion from analogy of proportionality: (1) differences in mode of ascription; and (2) contracted categorical differences. Thus the ability, disposition, proclivity, cause, sign, expression of, and symptom of, uses of same terms seem to belong to the former kind. So do ascriptions involving the use of the same term from different points of view: 'He did it, unhappily', and 'He did it unhappily'. Similarly, the use of an expression like 'The place to land' to stand for some place and also to stand for some conventional sign of the place (e.g., a mark on a map) belongs to the first sort, meaning differentiation by contrasting *modes of ascription*. And that does seem to be quite different from derived differences in semantical categories for same-term occurrences. For instance, in the frame '*S* read the entire report' substitute 'The announcer', 'The Committee', 'The proofreader', 'The teacher', 'The second-grader', 'The information-storage device'; and in each case we get a contracted difference in the sense of the predicate. There is no set of "truth conditions" for the frame completed with a subject variable that can be satisfied by all substitutions of subjects for the variable.

One of the defects of traditional philosophy of language, apart from quixotic theories of reference, has been the artificial division of expressions into two basic and supposedly independent units of meaning which in combination determine the sentential meaning; namely, subject and predicate. They are not independent in meaning. In 'His . . . was unsound', substitute 'ship' and then 'reasoning', 'foundation', 'melon'; the senses of 'was unsound' differ accordingly, and yet, as the medievals noticed, they are not unrelated. It was this which the "similarity of relations" hypothesis was introduced to explain. I think, eventually, by regarding analogy of meaning as a semantical phenomenon to be explained without recourse to theories about things, we can provide a better account of semantic contagion.

The same effect is observed with contrasting category-determining modifiers for two occurrences of a category-indeterminate term: 'His hand writing was unintelligible'; 'his published writing was unintelligible'. When we consider that we have no difficulty manufacturing endless cases where same predicates are adjusted in meaning to categorically contrasted subjects, we are made to wonder why so much astonishment has been caused by the contrasts between 'God is wise' and 'Socrates is wise'. Given the evident contrast of semantical categories between the two subjects 'Socrates' and 'God', nothing should be more likely.

In our natural language different completions of the sentence frame '. . . knows what I am going to do now' result in different conditions of applicability depending upon categorial contrasts in the subjects: 'My wife', 'My dog', 'My department', 'My bank'. It would certainly not be easy to state precisely the differences in conditions of applicability, the differences in entailments, in appropriate behavioral manifestations, attitudinal commitments (or any of those things Alston used to make his contrast between the determinateness of some employments of terms and the indeterminateness of the religious-discourse employments of those terms).

III. WHAT IS THE RELATIONSHIP OF THE ANALOGY HYPOTHESIS TO THE DISCUSSION OF THE COGNITIVE MEANINGFULNESS OF RELIGIOUS DISCOURSE?

1. The meanings of terms in religious discourse are to a large extent derived. There does not seem to be serious disagreement over that view, adopted by Alston and common to most persons who have discussed the matter.[17] At least minimally, it is believed that one learns how to use such predicates in religious discourse only after having learned some other kind of use for those predicates. And though I have indicated that there might be some exceptions to that generalization, they are parasitic exceptions.

2. The analogy hypothesis is that meaning differentiation for same terms follows semantic regularities and that such derivation is cognitivity-preserving.

---

[17]In fact, I do not know of any philosopher who has denied that the terms in religious discourse are either univocal with or derived from uses of those same terms in nonreligious contexts or who has denied that psychologically and epistemologically, nonreligious uses of the basic terms precede religious uses for most persons.

Here the analogy hypothesis gains its purchase upon the discussion of religious discourse. First, it calls attention to the fact that meaning derivation for same terms is very common indeed, both within and across discourse environments. Secondly, it indicates that meaning derivation is analyzable through certain regularities among sets of same-term occurrences. Thirdly, it calls attention to the fact that changes in both the sense and the application of a term need not result either in a pair (or more) of occurrences that are simply equivocal, or in a pair at least one of which is used nonliterally. (Thus it cuts the ground from under the usual arguments that religious language is essentially nonliteral.) Fourthly, it helps us to notice that there is nothing about the meaning extension of terms in religious discourse that does not have exact and regularity-conforming parallels in kinds of discourse whose meaningfulness is beyond sensible dispute.

In particular, it helps us to notice that when same-term occurrences occur as predicates with categorially distinct subjects, the senses of the predicate-term occurrences are appropriately modified; it is no anomaly, then, that the predicates applied to creatures contract categorial contracts when applied to God.

The analogy hypothesis also causes us to notice that the same transitive predicate term, concatenated with categorially contrasting direct objects, undergoes a contracted adjustment of sense: 'John caught . . .', 'the ball', 'the cold', 'the idea', 'the implication', 'the fear'. So too, in the expression frame, '*S* made *x*', 'made' undergoes one sort of adjustment in relation to categorially contrasted *objects* and another in relation to categorially contrasted *subjects;* both kinds of contagion may obtain simultaneously. '*S* made a chair', *S* made a million dollars', '*S* made the world', '*S* made a mistake', '*S* made a decision'. Now try 'Socrates', 'The University', and 'God' in each frame; sometimes the result is absurd, sometimes obviously false, and sometimes appropriate and carrying a modification of the sense of 'made'. The categorial contrast of the subjects is exhibited by the pattern of contrast in absurdity, falsity, and appropriateness of the results of the substitution.

What Aquinas talked of as adjustment of the *modus significandi* of predicates to the *modus essendi* of their subjects is here clearly seen to have a counterpart among the general features of discourse. It should, therefore, occasion no wonder, but rather a little confidence, that this feature of natural discourse is preserved within religious discourse. Needless to say, it would be just as difficult to provide a precise specification of the conditions of applicability, sentential entailment, paraphrase, evidence, and so forth, for some of the expressions offered as examples above, as it would be to do so for the key expressions of religious discourse.[18]

---

[18]The reason the dispute about the cognitive meaningfulness of religious discourse has not been resolved satisfactorily is that the more general problem of providing an account

Craft-bound discourse. One can convince oneself that unspecifiability of truth conditions, indefiniteness of what is implied, fuzziness in evidential conditions, and vagueness of associated attitudinal commitments is neither peculiar to religious discourse nor associated with deficiencies in cognitive content, by considering the conversation of persons skilled in some art or craft, for instance, type designing, cloth dyeing, weaving, farming, or cello playing. For example, two musicians may be quite able to describe some sound sequence as having one element that is "flat," when the deviation is not apparent to the untutored observer and the conditions they have in mind for so specifying some sound are unstated. Moreover, the musicians, even with the help of a philosopher, will be completely unable to tell you what the precise criteria are for the truth of a statement of that sort, especially when "being flat" is related to the *direction* (up or down-scale) in which the cellist is playing.[19] The same holds for the way farmers use such words as 'mature', 'green', 'texture', 'ripe', and so forth. Access to the descriptive content of such expressions is pretty much limited to initiates in the way of life, the community of experience, in which the utterances have their home. Such craft-bound discourse, like all natural discourse, reflects the forms of human living, has its own specificity and nuances of descriptive (and evaluative) meaning, and, like every other discourse environment that is pretheoretical and whose expressions are used for things considered important, deeply felt, and actually experienced in the life of a *community*, exhibits no linguistic discontinuity with the rest of natural discourse when examined in terms of the semantical regularity of the language. Religious discourse among believing Christians certainly satisfies these conditions. We can conclude from that, that the

---

of meaning-differentiation-in-use has not been resolved in the philosophy of language.

Why should statements in religious discourse have to conform to a standard of cognitive meaningfulness that is not met by the simplest and most common sorts of utterances of ordinary discourse? 'John married Mary because he loved her'. What are the implications, conditions of application, and so forth of 'loved' or of 'because' in that expression? Alston said: "We know perfectly well how to handle furniture sentences in the contexts in which they are commonly used. It is only their 'analysis' in some abstract philosophical sense that is puzzling. But sentences about God are likely to seem strange even in their native habitat. In the course of using them in religion we are apt to become baffled over what implications they have, what they exclude or do not exclude, and how they are appropriately supported or attacked" (*op. cit.* 430). The contrast, despite its similarity to the passage from Nielsen at the end of note 2, above, is exaggerated; we should have the same difficulties about "craft-bound" talk if we were not insiders to the craft; and religious persons in the *practice* of (as distinct from the reflection upon) religion are not often baffled at all. The reflective puzzlement with religious utterances is paralleled in what happens when we reflect upon statements about "the economic system," "the work of art," "the civil society," "the urban environment," "reading disabilities," "the future of graduate education." That is, when we try to provide theoretical analyses, we may become confused in just the way Alston describes; but that can happen in any area of discourse, as the difficulties in the linguistic analysis of ethics, aesthetics, social philosophy, and the philosophy of science make evident.

[19]I am not here prejudging the outcome of a philosophical analysis, but rather indicating that 'is off pitch' has different conditions in different contexts and may be no less difficult to analyze than 'God made the heavens and the earth'.

philosopher who wants to discount the cognitive content of religious discourse because of the fact that he cannot easily discover its conditions of application, truth, evidence, attitudinal commitments, or criteria for paraphrase, must either pretend to be able to do a great deal more, analytically, with the sorts of common discourse I have illustrated with examples or have failed to notice that an easy yield to the analytic embrace is not to be found very often in human discourse.

3. But still it may be argued that, even on the assumption that the analogy hypothesis is correct and that the meaning derivation of religious discourse conforms to general semantic regularities of natural language, the predicates in God-statements will all be categorially contrasted with every other occurrence of those predicates in nonreligious environments; that should certainly establish that religious discourse is in one way discontinuous with discourse of other sorts. But the assumptions of that argument need correction. Not all the predicates in God-statements are equivocal with respect to all their nonreligious uses. 'God is not a body' employs 'body' univocally with its use in 'Socrates has a body', for it is just what Socrates has that God is to be denied. Generally, *negative* assertions about God contain predicates that are used univocally with certain nonreligious occurrences, though this is not universally true, as for instance, when someone says "God is not all-powerful" or "God is not the creator of the world." The claim that the predicates of God-statements are equivocal with all their nonreligious occurrences holds true for all those simple affirmative categorial propositions about God which would be considered correct by orthodox Christians. But equivocation of same-predicates in simple, affirmative, categorial statements results for *any* pair of subjects that are categorially in contrast; so the wrong conclusion has been drawn from that observation about religious discourse. The predicate 'is not finished yet' is vastly different if the category of its subject is a thing, 'the table' or 'the automobile', as distinct from an event, 'the play', the examination'.

It is overemphasized that there is only one member of the God-category; there is only one member of the universe-category too, and the same sort of predicate adjustment is found in expressions with 'the universe' as subject. In general, categorially distinct subjects, in so far as they can have same-term predicates, have predicates that are analogous with one another. In fact the semantic difference between predicates in G-statements and the occurrence of those same predicates in any other sort of statement is a simple consequence of the general semantic regularity that pairs of same-term occurrences as predicates in affirmative sentential expressions containing categorially distinct subjects, contract contrasts of meaning (and therefore, contrasts in conditions of applicability, truth conditions for the whole expression, entailment, paraphrase, etc.) which correspond to the semantical categorial differences in the subjects. We encounter exactly the same phenomenon when we examine the use of certain terms, e.g., 'larger', for numbers in contrast to the use of the same terms for physical objects. The same holds for all the categorial contrasts of subjects, predicates, objects, and some modifiers.[20]

4. But what of the sixth element of the analogy hypothesis: that analogy of meaning is cognitivity-preserving? The expanded claim is that, if a given term occurrence is cognitively significant in a cognitively significant sentential context, then a same-term occurrence that is meaning-derived from the first (with respect to an analogy rule) will itself be cognitively significant. That does not mean that the whole expression in which the term occurs will be cognitively significant, but only that the term does not lose any of its significance by being meaning-adjusted in some regular way, with respect to another occurrence of the same term. Rather, if the meaning adjustment is regular, then, unless cognitive *evacuation* occurs in some regular way, the term will have cognitive significance. And we should be able to determine what, if any, regularities hold for cognitive evacuation.

There is no difficulty about preservation of significance in the "shift-in-mode-of-attribution" kinds of analogy. For if a shift in mode of attribution occurs in accord with a general regularity, nothing *could* have happened that would evacuate cognitive significance. (False and absurd expressions are cognitively significant.)

But the matter is not so clear in the case of semantic contagion, because not every subject of some predicate P (or object O) *can* be adjusted to every categorially contrasting predicate P' (or object O'). Consider: (a) 'John eats wheaties', (b) 'John eats quadratic equations', (c) 'Saturday followed Friday', (d) 'Saturday followed Mary'. Possibly, we could regard (b) as a categorial adjustment of 'eats' to the contrasting object; yet it seems more likely that, in an appropriate context for the expression, we have in (b) a figure of speech. But in (d) there cannot be a categorial adjustment of 'followed' to the object and simultaneously a categorial adjustment to the subject, since the contrast, categorially, of subject and object would demand contradictory adjustments of the predicate. (The ways in which something can "follow" Mary are just the ways in which Saturday cannot "follow" anything except a day; the same is true of 'come after'.) This provides one rock-bottom criterion for whether an expression is nonliteral as a whole. It also tells us that, if there is no con-

---

[20]It is to be regretted that at this stage I can offer no analysis of "categorial contrast" which will not be circular because it employs talk about contrasts of appropriate subjects, predicates, objects, modifiers, etc. This problem will have to be attacked separately. For the time being, let us provisionally adopt the Fodor-Katz notion of "semantic markers" which would occur in an ideal dictionary. Two subjects, predicates, etc., will be in semantic contrast to the degree that their semantic markers differ. I realize that this resolves practically nothing, but at least it indicates that semantic category is not the same thing as the list of predicates, modifiers, and so on, which are appropriate, but logically precedes it. And that is indicated by the fact that when categorially contrasting subjects have the same predicate ('The man worried his wife', 'The dog worried the rope'), we have to *understand* the categorial difference of subjects (and objects) *before* we can say whether the predicates are univocal or not.

flict in the sorts of categorial adjustments that must occur simultaneously, a literal use of the term is possible in that context and the term will not be robbed of its cognitive significance simply by its categorial adjustment.

IV. CONCLUSION

A. *The State of Evidence for the Analogy Hypothesis.* For parts of the analogy hypothesis the evidence available is conclusive; for instance, that multiplicity of meaning is common for sets of same-term occurrences; that the multiple meanings are not the result of simple equivocation, but in some way represent meaning adjustment to the semantical context and, sometimes, to the discourse environment; that the meaning adjustments exhibit some regularity and that the regularities are synchronic.[21] But few of the regularities one would expect have been formulated as yet, probably because there has been no concerted investigation of the matter by philosophers and linguists.

I have not independently argued as to why we should call these regularities, when formulated, "analogy rules," though the similarity of the material to what Aquinas called "analogy of meaning" is probably enough to justify the name, as does the ancient dispute between analogists and anomalists in the study of language in general.[22]

That meaning-differentiation-in-use occurs, on the whole, in English in accord with analogy regularities is nowhere nearly established yet, though I think consideration of the enormous class of meaning derivations available to each of us who is aware of how we use the language should made this an extremely likely conjecture.[23] That the use of a term in a context where

---

[21] I have not in this paper tried to explain how analogous derivation of meaning occurs dynamically or over time (diachronically) but have treated the corpus as *static*, as synchronic, in order to point out that derivation of meaning is ubiquitous, rule-conforming, the same in religious discourse as in other sorts of discourse, associated with no limitation of cognitive significance and a matter of the greatest importance to the philosophy of language.

[22] As Lyons, *op. cit.* p. 6–8, points out, from earliest times there was a dispute between anomalists and analogists over the pervasiveness (and the normative force) of regularity of structure in natural languages, particularly grammatical and morphological regularity. "It was a dispute as to what constitutes 'regularity' in language." On page 31 Lyons remarks: "it came to be realized that 'analogy' was a major factor in the development of languages at all periods and could not be attributed merely to periods of decline and corruption." So too, I want to extend the analogist's claims to the area of semantics and to claim that meaning derivation for same-terms both diachronically and synchronically is regularity conforming. This is the initial reason for calling a theory of meaning derivation an "analogy" theory; other reasons will be encountered in the study of reasoning by analogy and the sorts of comparisons that are commonly called analogies. Moreover, as R. A. Hall, Jr. remarks, "The process by which semantic shifts take place is basically one of analogical extension or contraction of the practical situations in which a form is used" (p. 348, *op. cit.*).

[23] I am presently attempting to gather a large enough sample of such derivation regularities to complete the argument that meaning derivation does occur in accord with certain regularities. The first stone has hardly been turned in the understanding of analogy; the analogy hypothesis has predictive and heuristic value for the discussion of theoretical

the term is related by some analogy rule to a context that is cognitively significant, is also cognitively significant, needs considerably more scrutiny than it has so far received; though it is already clear that it is not *conformity* to the derivation regularities that evacuates significance, but something quite different.

B. *The Analogy Refutation of the Discontinuity Hypothesis.* The main points in the analogy resolution of the dislocation challenge to the cognitive meaningfulness of religious discourse are (1) that there is a demonstrable continuity, conforming to general semantical regularities for English, between the way terms function in religious discourse and the ways the same terms function in other kinds of discourse; (2) that derived meaning for same terms is the rule rather than the exception in natural language; (3) that the kinds of derivation that relate religious discourse to nonreligious discourse, particularly the adjustment of subject and predicate meanings to the contrasting categories of their complements, are found practically everywhere in extended discourse; (4) that those meaning derivations cannot represent linguistic discontinuity any more than a series of physical events known to occur according to the same general principles which govern nature as a whole can be said to be discontinuous physically with the rest of nature; and (5) that if there is some defect in religious discourse because of the categorial adjustment of the meanings of its predicates, then this defect will pervade human discourse in general, and particularly the discourse of the empirical scientist.

Our showing that there is a semantic continuity between expressions in religious discourse and other sorts of discourse does not entail that one can gain adequate *access* to the cognitive content of assertions within religious discourse by some sort of extrapolation from other sorts of discourse; the same experiential base is required as would be required for us to grasp the sense of discourse about the tuning of instruments, proper intonation on the cello, the criticism of the state of crops, the perception of ducks on the horizon, the conditions of ice in Alaska, etc. We manifest our grasp of the significance of what is stated, not in some formal analysis, but in our ability to support, reject, criticize, question, object to, rephrase, translate, paraphrase, alter, amend, correct, and so forth, such utterances in ways that are intelligible within the discoursing community. An analysis is tested by its coherence with those manifestations.

The discontinuity hypothesis is based upon a mistake about what is involved in one's knowing the meaning of what is said; it is also based upon a mistaken contrast between the utterances of religious discourse and those of human discourse in general.

---

vs. observational terms, the explanation of the notions of models and metaphors, the accounting for reasoning by analogy and the justification of the cognitivity of religious, ethical, metaphysical and aesthetic discourse. Practically none of these matters has been approached in a suitably empirical, linguistically informed, and philosophically inventive way.

Inspection of the analogy structure of English discloses no semantical discontinuity to be characteristic of religious discourse, and reveals that the semantic structure of religious discourse is so much like that of other sorts of discourse that doubts about the cognitive significance of religious discourse can be sustained only at the expense of extending them to most other sorts of discourse, a tactic which would weaken the attack by the degree to which it would have to include what is considered unchallengeable.

THE PROBLEM OF VERIFICATION

FLEW, HARE, AND MITCHELL

2.4   The University Discussion

ANTONY FLEW:

Let us begin with a parable. It is a parable developed from a tale told by John Wisdom in his haunting and revelatory article "Gods."[1] Once upon a time two explorers came upon a clearing in the jungle. In the clearing were growing many flowers and many weeds. One explorer says, "Some gardener must tend this plot." The other disagrees, "There is no gardener." So they pitch their tents and set a watch. No gardener is ever seen. "But perhaps he is an invisible gardener." So they set up a barbed-wire fence. They electrify it. They patrol with bloodhounds. (For they remember how H. G. Wells's *The Invisible Man* could be both smelt and touched though he could not be seen.) But no shrieks ever suggest that some intruder has received a shock. No movements of the wire ever betray an invisible climber. The bloodhounds never give cry. Yet still the Believer is not convinced. "But there is a gardener, invisible, intangible, insensible to electric shocks, a gardener who has no scent and makes no sound, a gardener who comes secretly to look after the garden which he loves." At last the Sceptic despairs, "But what remains of your original assertion? Just how does what you call an invisible, intangible, eternally elusive gardener differ from an imaginary gardener or even from no gardener at all?"

This essay entitled, "Theology and Falsification" is from *New Essays in Philosophical Theology*, ed. Antony Flew and Alasdair MacIntyre (London: SCM Press Ltd 1955), pp. 96–105. Reprinted by permission of the publisher.
    [1]*P.A.S.* 1944–45, reprinted as Ch. X of *Logic and Language*, Vol. I (Blackwell, 1951), and in his *Philosophy and Psychoanalysis* (Blackwell, 1953).

In this parable we can see how what starts as an assertion, that something exists or that there is some analogy between certain complexes of phenomena, may be reduced step by step to an altogether different status, to an expression perhaps of a "picture preference."[2] The Sceptic says there is no gardener. The Believer says there is a gardener (but invisible, etc.). One man talks about sexual behaviour. Another man prefers to talk of Aphrodite (but knows that there is not really a superhuman person additional to, and somehow responsible for, all sexual phenomena).[3] The process of qualification may be checked at any point before the original assertion is completely withdrawn and something of that first assertion will remain (Tautology). Mr. Wells's invisible man could not, admittedly, be seen, but in all other respects he was a man like the rest of us. But though the process of qualification may be, and of course usually is, checked in time, it is not always judiciously so halted. Someone may dissipate his assertion completely without noticing that he has done so. A fine brash hypothesis may thus be killed by inches, the death of a thousand qualifications.

And in this, it seems to me, lies the peculiar danger, the endemic evil, of theological utterance. Take such utterances as "God has a plan," "God created the world," "God loves us as a father loves his children." They look at first sight very much like assertions, vast cosmological assertions. Of course, this is no sure sign that they either are, or are intended to be, assertions. But let us confine ourselves to the cases where those who utter such sentences intend them to express assertion. (Merely remarking parenthetically that those who intend or interpret such utterances as crypto-commands, expressions of wishes, disguised ejaculations, concealed ethics, or as anything else but assertions, are unlikely to succeed in making them either properly orthodox or practically effective).

Now to assert that such and such is the case is necessarily equivalent to denying that such and such is not the case.[4] Suppose then that we are in doubt as to what someone who gives vent to an utterance is asserting, or suppose that, more radically, we are sceptical as to whether he is really asserting anything at all, one way of trying to understand (or perhaps it will be to expose) his utterance is to attempt to find what he would regard as counting against, or as being incompatible with, its truth. For if the utterance is indeed an assertion, it will necessarily be equivalent to a denial of the

---

[2] Cf. J. Wisdom, "Other Minds," *Mind*, 1940; reprinted in his *Other Minds* (Blackwell, 1952).
[3] Cf. Lucretius, *De Rerum Natura*, II, 655–60,
 Hic siquis mare Neptunum Cereremque vocare
 Constituet fruges et Bacchi nomine abuti
 Mavolat quam laticis proprium proferre vocamen
 Concedamus ut hic terrarum dictitet orbem
 Esse deum matrem dum vera re tamen ipse
 Religione animum turpi contingere parcat.
[4] For those who prefer symbolism: $p \equiv\, \sim \sim p$.

negation of that assertion. And anything which would count against the assertion, or which would induce the speaker to withdraw it and to admit that it had been mistaken, must be part of (or the whole of) the meaning of the negation of that assertion. And to know the meaning of the negation of an assertion, is as near as makes no matter, to know the meaning of that assertion.[5] And if there is nothing which a putative assertion denies then there is nothing which it asserts either; and so it is not really an assertion. When the Sceptic in the parable asked the Believer, "Just how does what you call an invisible, intangible, eternally elusive gardener differ from an imaginary gardener or even from no gardener at all?" he was suggesting that the Believer's earlier statement had been so eroded by qualification that it was no longer an assertion at all.

Now it often seems to people who are not religious as if there was no conceivable event or series of events the occurrence of which would be admitted by sophisticated religious people to be a sufficient reason for conceding "There wasn't a God after all" or "God does not really love us then." Someone tells us that God loves us as a father loves his children. We are reassured. But then we see a child dying of inoperable cancer of the throat. His earthly father is driven frantic in his efforts to help, but his Heavenly Father reveals no obvious sign of concern. Some qualification is made—God's love is "not a merely human love" or it is "an inscrutable love," perhaps—and we realize that such sufferings are quite compatible with the truth of the assertion that "God loves us as a father (but, of course, . . .)." We are reassured again. But then perhaps we ask: what is his assurance of God's (appropriately qualified) love worth, what is this apparent guarantee really a guarantee against? Just what would have to happen not merely (morally and wrongly) to tempt but also (logically and rightly) to entitle us to say "God does not love us" or even "God does not exist"? I therefore put to the succeeding symposiasts the simple central questions, "What would have to occur or to have occurred to constitute for you a disproof of the love of, or of the existence of, God?"

R. M. HARE:

I wish to make it clear that I shall not try to defend Christianity in particular, but religion in general—not because I do not believe in Christianity, but because you cannot understand what Christianity is, until you have understood what religion is.

I must begin by confessing that, on the ground marked out by Flew, he seems to me to be completely victorious. I therefore shift my ground by relating another parable. A certain lunatic is convinced that all dons want to murder him. His friends introduce him to all the mildest and most respectable dons that they can find, and after each of them has retired, they say, "You

---

[5]For by simply negating $\sim p$ we get $p : \sim \sim \equiv p$.

see, he doesn't really want to murder you; he spoke to you in a most cordial manner; surely you are convinced now?" But the lunatic replies "Yes but that was only his diabolical cunning; he's really plotting against me the whole time, like the rest of them; I know it I tell you." However, many kindly dons are produced, the reaction is still the same.

Now we say that such a person is deluded. But what is he deluded about? About the truth or falsity of an assertion? Let us apply Flew's test to him. There is no behaviour of dons that can be enacted which he will accept as counting against his theory; and therefore his theory, on this test, asserts nothing. But it does not follow that there is no difference between what he thinks about dons and what most of us think about them—otherwise we should not call him a lunatic and ourselves sane, and dons would have no reason to feel uneasy about his presence in Oxford.

Let us call that in which we differ from this lunatic, our respective *bliks*. He has an insane *blik* about dons; we have a sane one. It is important to realize that we have a sane one, not no *blik* at all; for there must be two sides to any argument—if he has a wrong *blik*, then those who are right about dons must have a right one. Flew has shown that a *blik* does not consist in an assertion or system of them; but nevertheless it is very important to have the right *blik*.

Let us try to imagine what it would be like to have different *bliks* about other things than dons. When I am driving my car, it sometimes occurs to me to wonder whether my movements of the steering-wheel will always continue to be followed by corresponding alterations in the direction of the car. I have never had a steering failure, though I have had skids, which must be similar. Moreover, I know enough about how the steering of my car is made, to know the sort of thing that would have to go wrong for the steering to fail—steel joints would have to part, or steel rods break, or something—but how do I know that this won't happen? The truth is, I don't know; I just have a *blik* about steel and its properties, so that normally I trust the steering of my car; but I find it not at all difficult to imagine what it would be like to lose this *blik* and acquire the opposite one. People would say I was silly about steel; but there would be no mistaking the reality of the difference between our respective *bliks*—for example, I should never go in a motor-car. Yet I should hesitate to say that the difference between us was the difference between contradictory assertions. No amount of safe arrivals or bench-tests will remove my *blik* and restore the normal one; for my *blik* is compatible with any finite number of such tests.

It was Hume who taught us that our whole commerce with the world depends upon our *blik* about the world; and that differences between *bliks* about the world cannot be settled by observation of what happens in the world. That was why, having performed the interesting experiment of doubting the ordinary man's *blik* about the world, and showing that no proof could be given to make us adopt one *blik* rather than another, he turned to backgammon to take his mind off the problem. It seems, indeed, to be impossible even to formulate as an assertion the normal *blik* about the world which makes me put my confidence in the future reliability of steel joints, in the continued ability of the road to support my car, and not gape beneath it revealing nothing below; in the general non-homicidal tendencies of dons; in my own continued well-being (in some sense of that word that I may not now fully understand) if I continue to do what is right according to my lights; in the general likelihood of people like Hitler coming to a bad end. But perhaps a formulation less inadequate than most is to be found in the Psalms: "The earth is weak and all the inhabiters thereof: I bear up the pillars of it."

The mistake of the position which Flew selects for attack is to regard this kind of talk as some sort of *explanation*, as scientists are accustomed to use the word. As such, it would obviously be ludicrous. We no longer believe in God as an Atlas—*nous n'avons pas besoin de cette hypothèse*. But it is nevertheless true to say that, as Hume saw, without a *blik* there can be no explanation; for it is by our *bliks* that we decide what is and what is not an explanation. Suppose we believed that everything that happened, happened by pure chance. This would not of course be an assertion; for it is compatible with anything happening or not happening, and so, incidentally, is its contradictory. But if we had this belief, we should not be able to explain or predict or plan anything. Thus, although we should not be *asserting* anything different from those of a more normal belief, there would be a great difference between us; and this is the sort of difference that there is between those who really believe in God and those who really disbelieve in him.

The word "really" is important, and may excite suspicion. I put it in, because when people have had a good Christian upbringing, as have most of those who now profess not to believe in any sort of religion, it is very hard to discover what they really believe. The reason why they find it so easy to think that they are not religious, is that they have never got into the frame of mind of one who suffers from the doubts to which religion is the answer. Not for them the terrors of the primitive jungle. Having abandoned some of the more picturesque fringes of religion, they think that they have abandoned the whole thing—whereas in fact they still have got, and could not live without, a religion of a comfortably substantial, albeit highly sophisticated, kind, which differs from that of many "religious people" in little more than this, that "religious people" like to sing Psalms about theirs—a very natural and proper thing to do. But nevertheless there may be a big difference lying behind—the difference between two people who, though side by side, are walking in different directions. I do not know in what direction Flew is walking; perhaps he does not know either. But we have had some examples recently of various ways in which one can walk away from Christianity, and there are any number of possibilities. After all, man has not changed biologicaly since primitive times; it is his religion that has changed, and it can easily change again. And if you do not think that such changes make a difference, get acquainted with some Sikhs and some Mussulmans of the same Punjabi stock; you will find them quite different sorts of people.

There is an important difference between Flew's parable and my own which we have not yet noticed. The explorers do not *mind* about their garden; they discuss it with interest, but not with concern. But my lunatic, poor fellow, minds about dons; and I mind about the steering of my car; it often has people in it that I care for. It is because I mind very much about what goes on in the garden in which I find myself, that I am unable to share the explorers' detachment.

BASIL MITCHELL:

Flew's article is searching and perceptive, but there is, I think something odd about his conduct of the theologian's case. The theologian surely would not deny that the fact of pain counts against the assertion that God loves men. This very incompatibility generates the most intractable of theological problems—the problem of evil. So the theologian *does* recognize the fact of pain as counting against Christian doctrine. But it is true that he will not allow it —or anything—to count decisively against it; for he is committed by his faith to trust in God. His attitude is not that of the detached observer, but of the believer.

Perhaps this can be brought out by yet another parable. In time of war in an occupied country, a member of the resistance meets one night a stranger who deeply impresses him. They spend that night together in conversation. The Stranger tells the partisan that he himself is on the side of the resistance —indeed that he is in command of it, and urges the partisan to have faith in him no matter what happens. The partisan is utterly convinced at that meeting of the Stranger's sincerity and constancy and undertakes to trust him.

They never meet in conditions of intimacy again. But sometimes the Stranger is seen helping members of the resistance, and the partisan is grateful and says to his friends, "He is on our side."

Sometimes he is seen in the uniform of the police handing over patriots to the occupying power. On these occasions his friends murmur against him: but the partisan still says, "He is on our side." He still believes that, in spite of appearances, the Stranger did not deceive him. Sometimes he asks the Stranger for help and receives it. He is then thankful. Sometimes he asks and does not receive it. Then he says, "The Stranger knows best." Sometimes his friends, in exasperation, say "Well, what *would* he have to do for you to admit that you were wrong and that he is not on our side?" But the partisan refuses to answer. He will not consent to put the Stranger to the test. And sometimes his friends complain, "Well, if *that's* what you mean by his being on our side, the sooner he goes over to the other side the better."

The partisan of the parable does not allow anything to count decisively against the proposition "The Stranger is on our side." This is because he has committed himself to trust the Stranger. But he of course recognizes that the Stranger's ambiguous behaviour *does* count against what he believes about him. It is precisely this situation which constitutes the trial of his faith.

When the partisan asks for help and doesn't get it, what can he do? He can (*a*) conclude that the stranger is not on our side; or (*b*) maintain that he is on our side, but that he has reasons for withholding help.

The first he will refuse to do. How long can he uphold the second position without its becoming just silly?

I don't think one can say in advance. It will depend on the nature of the impression created by the Stranger in the first place. It will depend, too, on the manner in which he takes the Stranger's behaviour. If he blandly dismisses it as of no consequence, as having no bearing upon his belief, it will be assumed that he is thoughtless or insane. And it quite obviously won't do for him to say easily, "Oh, when used of the Stranger the phrase 'is on our side' *means* ambiguous behaviour of this sort." In that case he would be like the religious man who says blandly of a terrible disaster "It is God's will." No, he will only be regarded as sane and reasonable in his belief, if he experiences in himself the full force of the conflict.

It is here that my parable differs from Hare's. The partisan admits that many things may and do count against his belief: whereas Hare's lunatic who has a *blik* about dons doesn't admit that anything counts against his *blik*. Nothing *can* count against *bliks*. Also the partisan has a reason for having in the first instance committed himself, viz. the character of the Stranger; whereas the lunatic has no reason for his *blik* about dons—because, of course, you can't have reasons for *bliks*.

This means that I agree with Flew that theological utterances must be assertions. The partisan is making an assertion when he says, "The Stranger is on our side."

Do I want to say that the partisan's belief about the Stranger is, in any sense, an explanation? I think I do. It explains and makes sense of the Stranger's behaviour: it helps to explain also the resistance movement in the context of which he appears. In each case it differs from the interpretation which the others put upon the same facts.

"God loves men" resembles "the Stranger is on our side" (and many other significant statements, e.g. historical ones) in not being conclusively falsifiable. They can both be treated in at least three different ways: (1) As provisional hypotheses to be discarded if experience tells against them; (2) As significant articles of faith; (3) As vacuous formulae (expressing, perhaps, a desire for reassurance) to which experience makes no difference and which make no difference to life.

The Christian, once he has committed himself, is precluded by his faith from taking up the first attitude: "Thou shalt not tempt the Lord thy God." He is in constant danger, as Flew has observed, of slipping into the third. But he need not; and, if he does, it is a failure in faith as well as in logic.

JOHN HICK

2.5 Theology and Verification

To ask "Is the existence of God verifiable?" is to pose a question which is too imprecise to be capable of being answered.[1] There are many different concepts of God, and it may be that statements employing some of them are open to verification or falsification while statements employing others of them are not. Again, the notion of verifying is itself by no means perfectly clear and fixed; and it may be that on some views of the nature of verification the existence of God is verifiable, whereas on other views it is not.

Instead of seeking to compile a list of the various different concepts of God and the various possible senses of "verify," I wish to argue with regard to one particular concept of deity, namely the Christian concept, that divine existence is in principle verifiable; and as the first stage of this argument I must indicate what I mean by "verifiable."

I

The central core of the concept of verification, I suggest, is the removal of ignorance or uncertainty concerning the truth of some proposition. That p is verified (whether p embodies a theory, hypothesis, prediction, or straightforward assertion) means that something happens which makes it clear that p is true. A question is settled so that there is no longer room for rational doubt concerning it. The way in which grounds for rational doubt are ex-

---

From *Theology Today* 17 (1960). Reprinted by permission of the author and the editor.
[1] In this paper I assume that an indicative sentence expresses a factual assertion if and only if the state in which the universe would be if the putative assertion could correctly be said to be true differs in some experienceable way from the state in which the universe would be if the putative assertion could correctly be said to be false, all aspects of the universe other than that referred to in the putative assertion being the same in either case. This criterion acknowledges the important core of truth in the logical positivist verification principle. "Experienceable" in the above formulation means, in the case of alleged subjective or private facts (*e.g.*, pains, dreams, after-images, etc.), "experienceable by the subject in question" and, in the case of alleged objective or public facts, "capable in principle of being experienced by anyone." My contention is going to be that "God exists" asserts a matter of objective fact.

cluded varies, of course, with the subject matter. But the general feature common to all cases of verification is the ascertaining of truth by the removal of grounds for rational doubt. Where such grounds are removed, we rightly speak of verification having taken place.

To characterize verification in this way is to raise the question whether the notion of verification is purely logical or is both logical and psychological. Is the statement that p is verified simply the statement that a certain state of affairs exists (or has existed), or is it the statement also that someone is aware that this state of affairs exists (or has existed) and notes that its existence establishes the truth of p? A geologist predicts that the earth's surface will be covered with ice in 15 million years time. Suppose that in 15 million years time the earth's surface *is* covered with ice, but that in the meantime the human race has perished, so that no one is left to observe the event or to draw any conclusion concerning the accuracy of the geologist's prediction. Do we now wish to say that his prediction has been verified, or shall we deny that it has been verified, on the ground that there is no one left to do the verifying?

The range of "verify" and its cognates is sufficiently wide to permit us to speak in either way. But the only sort of verification of theological propositions which is likely to interest us is one in which human beings participate. We may therefore, for our present purpose, treat verification as a logico-psychological rather than as a purely logical concept. I suggest, then, that "verify" be construed as a verb which has its primary uses in the active voice: I verify, you verify, we verify, they verify, or have verified. The impersonal passive, it is verified, now becomes logically secondary. To say that p has been verified is to say that (at least) someone has verified it, often with the implication that his or their report to this effect is generally accepted. But it is impossible, on this usage, for p to have been verified without someone having verified it. "Verification" is thus primarily the name for an event which takes place in human consciousness.[2] It refers to an experience, the experience of ascertaining that a given proposition or set of propositions is true. To this extent verification is a psychological notion. But of course it is also a logical notion. For needless to say, not *any* experience is rightly called an experience of verifying p. Both logical and psychological conditions must be fulfilled in order for verification to have taken place. In this respect, "verify" is like "know." Knowing is an experience which someone has or undergoes, or perhaps a dispositional state in which someone is, and it cannot take place without someone having or undergoing it or being in it; but not

---

[2]This suggestion is closely related to Carnap's insistence that, in contrast to "true," "confirmed" is time-dependent. To say that a statement is confirmed, or verified, is to say that it has been confirmed at a particular time—and, I would add, by a particular person. See Rudolf Carnap, "Truth and Confirmation," Feigl and Sellars, *Readings in Philosophical Analysis*, 1949, pp. 119 f.

by any means every experience which people have, or every dispositional state in which they are, is rightly called knowing.

With regard to this logico-psychological concept of verification, such questions as the following arise. When A, but nobody else, has ascertained that p is true, can p be said to have been verified; or is it required that others also have undergone the same ascertainment? How public, in other words, must verification be? Is it necessary that p could in principle be verified by anyone, without restriction, even though perhaps only A has in fact verified it? If so, what is meant here by "in principle"; does it signify, for example, that p must be verifiable by anyone who performs a certain operation; and does it imply that to do this is within everyone's power?

These questions cannot, I believe, be given any general answer applicable to all instances of the exclusion of rational doubt. The answers must be derived in each case from an investigation of the particular subject matter. It will be the object of subsequent sections of this article to undertake such an investigation concerning the Christian concept of God.

Verification is often construed as the verification of a prediction. However, verification, as the exclusion of grounds for rational doubt, does not necessarily consist in the proving correct of a prediction; a verifying experience does not always need to have been predicted in order to have the effect of excluding rational doubt. But when we are interested in the verifiability of propositions as the criterion for their having factual meaning, the notion of prediction becomes central. If a proposition contains or entails predictions which can be verified or falsified, its character as an assertion (though not of course its character as a true assertion) is thereby guaranteed.

Such predictions may be and often are conditional. For example, statements about the features of the dark side of the moon are rendered meaningful by the conditional predictions which they entail to the effect that if an observer comes to be in such a position in space, he will make such-and-such observations. It would in fact be more accurate to say that the prediction is always conditional, but that sometimes the conditions are so obvious and so likely to be fulfilled in any case that they require no special mention, while sometimes they require for their fulfillment some unusual expedition or operation. A prediction, for example, that the sun will rise within twenty-four hours is intended unconditionally, at least as concerns conditions to be fulfilled by the observer; he is not required by the terms of the prediction to perform any special operation. Even in this case, however, there is an implied negative condition that he shall not put himself in a situation (such as immuring himself in the depths of a coal mine) from which a sunrise would not be perceptible. Other predictions, however, are explicitly conditional. In these cases it is true for any particular individual that in order to verify the statement in question he must go through some specified course of action. The prediction is to the effect that if you conduct such an experiment you will obtain such a result; for example, if you go into the next room you will have such-and-such visual experiences, and if you then touch the table which you see you will have such-and-such tactual experiences, and so on. The content of the "if" clause is of course always determined by the particular subject matter. The logic of "table" determines what you must do to verify statements about tables; the logic of "molecule" determines what you must do to verify statements about molecules; and the logic of "God" determines what you must do to verify statements about God.

In those cases in which the individual who is to verify a proposition must himself first perform some operation, it clearly cannot follow from the circumstances that the proposition is true that everybody has in fact verified it, or that everybody will at some future time verify it. For whether or not any particular person performs the requisite operation is a contingent matter.

II

What is the relation between verification and falsification? We are all familiar today with the phrase, "theology and falsification." A. G. N. Flew and others,[3] taking their cue from John Wisdom,[4] have raised instead of the question, "What possible experiences would verify 'God exists'?" the matching question, "What possible experiences would falsify 'God exists'? What conceivable state of affairs would be incompatible with the existence of God?" In posing the question in this way it was apparently assumed that verification and falsification are symmetrically related, and that the latter is apt to be the more accessible of the two.

In the most common cases, certainly, verification and falsification are symmetrically related. The logically simplest case of verification is provided by the crucial instance. Here it is integral to a given hypothesis that if, in specified circumstances, A occurs, the hypothesis is thereby shown to be true, whereas if B occurs the hypothesis is thereby shown to be false. Verification and falsification are also symmetrically related in the testing of such a proposition as "There is a table in the next room." The verifying experiences in this case are experiences of seeing and touching, predictions of which are entailed by the proposition in question, under the proviso that one goes into the next room; and the absence of such experiences in those circumstances serves to falsify the proposition.

But it would be rash to assume, on this basis, that verification and falsification must always be related in this symmetrical fashion. They do not necessarily stand to one another as do the two sides of a coin, so that once the

---

[3]Antony Flew, editor, *New Essays in Philosophical Theology*, 1955, Chapter VI.

[4]"Gods," *Proceedings of the Aristotelian Society*, 1944–45. Reprinted in *Logic and Language*, Antony Flew, editor, First Series, 1951, and in John Wisdom, *Philosophy and Psycho-Analysis*, 1953.

coin is spun it must fall on one side or the other. There are cases in which verification and falsification each correspond to a side on a different coin, so that one can fail to verify without this failure constituting falsification.

Consider, for example, the proposition that "there are three successive sevens in the decimal determination of π." So far as the value of π has been worked out, it does not contain a series of three sevens, but it will always be true that such a series may occur at a point not yet reached in anyone's calculations. Accordingly, the proposition may one day be verified, if it is true, but can never be falsified, if it is false.

The hypothesis of continued conscious existence after bodily death provides an instance of a different kind of such asymmetry, and one which has a direct bearing upon the theistic problem. This hypothesis has built into it a prediction that one will after the date of one's bodily death have conscious experiences, including the experience of remembering that death. This is a prediction which will be verified in one's own experience if it is true, but which cannot be falsified if it is false. That is to say, it can be false, but *that* it is false can never be a fact which anyone has experientially verified. But this circumstance does not undermine the meaningfulness of the hypothesis, since it is also such that if it be true, it will be known to be true.

It is important to remember that we do not speak of verifying logically necessary truths, but only propositions concerning matters of fact. Accordingly verification is not to be identified with the concept of logical certification or proof. The exclusion of rational doubt concerning some matter of fact is not equivalent to the exclusion of the logical possibility of error or illusion. For truths concerning fact are not logically necessary. Their contrary is never self-contradictory. But at the same time the bare logical possibility of error does not constitute ground for rational doubt as to the veracity of our experience. If it did, no empirical proposition could ever be verified, and indeed the notion of empirical verification would be without use and therefore without sense. What we rightly seek, when we desire the verification of a factual proposition, is not a demonstration of the logical impossibility of the proposition being false (for this would be a self-contradictory demand), but such weight of evidence as suffices, in the type of case in question, to exclude rational doubt.

III

These features of the concept of verification—that verification consists in the exclusion of grounds for rational doubt concerning the truth of some proposition; that this means its exclusion from particular minds; that the nature of the experience which serves to exclude grounds for rational doubt depends upon the particular subject matter; that verification is often related to predictions and that such predictions are often conditional; that verification and falsification may be asymmetrically related; and finally, that the verification of a factual proposition is not equivalent to logical certification—are all relevant to the verification of the central religious claim, "God exists." I wish now to apply these discriminations to the notion of eschatological verification, which has been briefly employed by Ian Crombie in his contribution to *New Essays in Philosophical Theology*,[5] and by myself in *Faith and Knowledge*.[6] This suggestion has on each occasion been greeted with disapproval by both philosophers and theologians. I am, however, still of the opinion that the notion of eschatological verification is sound; and further, that no viable alternative to it has been offered to establish the factual character of theism.

The strength of the notion of eschatological verification is that it is not an *ad hoc* invention but is based upon an actually operative religious concept of God. In the language of Christian faith, the word "God" stands at the center of a system of terms, such as Spirit, grace, Logos, incarnation, Kingdom of God, and many more; and the distinctly Christian conception of God can only be fully grasped in its connection with these related terms.[7] It belongs to a complex of notions which together constitute a picture of the universe in which we live, of man's place therein, of a comprehensive divine purpose interacting with human purposes, and of the general nature of the eventual fulfillment of that divine purpose. This Christian picture of the universe, entertaining as it does certain distinctive expectations concerning the future, is a very different picture from any that can be accepted by one who does not believe that the God of the New Testament exists. Further, these differences are such as to show themselves in human experience. The possibility of experiential confirmation is thus built into the Christian concept of God; and the notion of eschatological verification seeks to relate this fact to the logical problem of meaning.

Let me first give a general indication of this suggestion, by repeating a parable which I have related elsewhere,[8] and then try to make it more precise and eligible for discussion. Here, first, is the parable.

Two men are travelling together along a road. One of them believes that it leads to a Celestial City, the other that it leads nowhere; but since this is the only road there is, both must travel it. Neither has been this way before, and therefore neither is able to say what they will find around each next corner. During their journey they meet both with moments of refreshments and delight, and with moments of hardship and danger. All the time one of them thinks of his journey as a pilgrimage to the Celestial City and interprets the pleasant parts as encouragements and the obstacles as trials of his purpose

---

[5]*Op. cit.*, p. 126.

[6]Cornell University Press, 1957, pp. 150–62.

[7]Its clear recognition of this fact, with regard not only to Christianity but to any religion, is one of the valuable features of Ninian Smart's *Reasons and Faiths* (1958). He remarks, for example, that "the claim that God exists can only be understood by reference to many, if not all, other propositions in the doctrinal scheme from which it is extrapolated" (p. 12).

[8]*Faith and Knowledge*, pp. 150 f.

and lessons in endurance, prepared by the king of that city and designed to make of him a worthy citizen of the place when at last he arrives there. The other, however, believes none of this and sees their journey as an unavoidable and aimless ramble. Since he has no choice in the matter, he enjoys the good and endures the bad. But for him there is no Celestial City to be reached, no all-encompassing purpose ordaining their journey; only the road itself and the luck of the road in good weather and in bad.

During the course of the journey the issue between them is not an experimental one. They do not entertain different expectations about the coming details of the road, but only about its ultimate destination. And yet when they do turn the last corner it will be apparent that one of them has been right all the time and the other wrong. Thus although the issue between them has not been experimental, it has nevertheless from the start been a real issue. They have not merely felt differently about the road; for one was feeling appropriately and the other inappropriately in relation to the actual state of affairs. Their opposed interpretations of the road constituted genuinely rival assertions, though assertions whose assertion-status has the peculiar characteristic of being guaranteed retrospectively by a future crux.

This parable has of course (like all parables) strict limitations. It is designed to make only one point: that Christian doctrine postulates an ultimate unambiguous state of existence *in patria* as well as our present ambiguous existence *in via*. There is a state of having arrived as well as a state of journeying, an eternal heavenly life as well as an earthly pilgrimage. The alleged future experience of this state cannot, of course, be appealed to as evidence for theism as a present interpretation of our experience; but it does suffice to render the choice between theism and atheism a real and not a merely empty or verbal choice. And although this does not affect the logic of the situation, it should be added that the alternative interpretations are more than theoretical, for they render different practical plans and policies appropriate now.

The universe as envisaged by the theist, then, differs as a totality from the universe as envisaged by the atheist. This difference does not, however, from our present standpoint within the universe, involve a difference in the objective content of each or even any of its passing moments. The theist and the atheist do not (or need not) expect different events to occur in the successive details of the temporal process. They do not (or need not) entertain divergent expectations of the course of history viewed from within. But the theist does and the atheist does not expect that when history is completed it will be seen to have led to a particular end-state and to have fulfilled a specific purpose, namely that of creating "children of God."

IV

The idea of an eschatological verification of theism can make sense, however, only if the logically prior idea of continued personal existence after death is intelligible. A desultory debate on this topic has been going on for several years in some of the philosophical periodicals. C. I. Lewis has contended that the hypothesis of immortality "is an hypothesis about our own future experience. And our understanding of what would verify it has no lack of clarity."[9] And Morris Schlick agreed, adding, "We must conclude that immortality, in the sense defined [i.e. 'survival after death,' rather than 'never-ending life'], should not be regarded as a 'metaphysical problem' but as an empirical hypothesis, because it possesses logical verifiability. It could be verified by following the prescription: 'Wait until you die!' "[10] However, others have challenged this conclusion, either on the ground that the phrase "surviving death" is self-contradictory in ordinary language or, more substantially, on the ground that the traditional distinction between soul and body cannot be sustained.[11] I should like to address myself to this latter view. The only self of which we know, it is said, is the empirical self, the walking, talking, acting, sleeping individual who lives, it may be, for some sixty to eighty years and then dies. Mental events and mental characteristics are analyzed into the modes of behavior and behavioral disposition of this empirical self. The human being is described as an organism capable of acting in the "high-level" ways which we characterize as intelligent, thoughtful, humorous, calculating, and the like. The concept of mind or soul is thus not the concept of a "ghost in the machine" (to use Gilbert Ryle's loaded phrase[12]), but of the more flexible and sophisticated ways in which human beings behave and have it in them to behave. On this view there is no room for the notion of soul in distinction from body and if there is no soul in distinction from body, there can be no question of the soul surviving the death of the body. Against this philosophical background the specifically Christian (and also Jewish) belief in the resurrection of the flesh, or body, in contrast to the Hellenic notion of the survival of a disembodied soul, might be expected to have attracted more attention than it has. For it is consonant with the conception of man as an indissoluble psychophysical unity, and yet it also offers the possibility of an empirical meaning for the idea of "life after death."

Paul is the chief Biblical expositor of the idea of the resurrection of the body.[13] His view, as I understand it, is this. When someone has died he is, apart from any special divine action, extinct. A human being is by nature mortal and subject to annihilation by death. But in fact God, by an act of

---

[9]"Experience and Meaning," *Philosophical Review*, 1934, reprinted in Feigl and Sellars, *Readings in Philosophical Analysis*, 1949, p. 142.

[10]"Meaning and Verification," *Philosophical Review*, 1936, reprinted in Feigl and Sellars, *op. cit.*, p. 160.

[11]E.g. Antony Flew, "Death," *New Essays in Philosophical Theology*; "Can a Man Witness his own Funeral?" *Hibbert Journal*, 1956.

[12]*The Concept of Mind*, 1949, which contains an important exposition of the interpretation of "mental" qualities as characteristics of behavior.

[13]I Cor. 15.

sovereign power, either sometimes or always resurrects or (better) reconstitutes or recreates him—not, however, as the identical physical organism that he was before death, but as a *soma pneumatikon*, ("spiritual body") embodying the dispositional characteristics and memory traces of the deceased physical organism, and inhabiting an environment with which the *soma pneumatikon* is continuous as the *ante-mortem* body was continuous with our present world. In discussing this notion we may well abandon the word "spiritual," as lacking today any precise established usage, and speak of "resurrection bodies" and of "the resurrection world." The principal questions to be asked concern the relation between the physical world and the resurrection world, and the criteria of personal identity which are operating when it is alleged that a certain inhabitant of the resurrection world is the same person as an individual who once inhabited this world. The first of these questions turns out on investigation to be the more difficult of the two, and I shall take the easier one first.

Let me sketch a very odd possibility (concerning which, however, I wish to emphasize not so much its oddness as its possibility!), and then see how far it can be stretched in the direction of the notion of the resurrection body. In the process of stretching it will become even more odd than it was before; but my aim will be to show that, however odd, it remains within the bounds of the logically possible. This progression will be presented in three pictures, arranged in a self-explanatory order.

First picture: Suppose that at some learned gathering in this country one of the company were suddenly and inexplicably to disappear, and that at the same moment an exact replica of him were suddenly and inexplicably to appear at some comparable meeting in Australia. The person who appears in Australia is exactly similar, as to both bodily and mental characteristics, with the person who disappears in America. There is continuity of memory, complete similarity of bodily features, including even fingerprints, hair and eye coloration and stomach contents, and also of beliefs, habits, and mental propensities. In fact there is everything that would lead us to identify the one who appeared with the one who disappeared, except continuity of occupancy of space. We may suppose, for example, that a deputation of the colleagues of the man who disappeared fly to Australia to interview the replica of him which is reported there, and find that he is in all respects but one exactly as though he had travelled from say, Princeton to Melbourne, by conventional means. The only difference is that he describes how, as he was sitting listening to Dr. Z reading a paper, on blinking his eyes he suddenly found himself sitting in a different room listening to a different paper by an Australian scholar. He asks his colleagues how the meeting had gone after he ceased to be there, and what they had made of his disappearance, and so on. He clearly thinks of himself as the one who was present with them at their meeting in the United States. I suggest that faced with all these circumstances his colleagues would soon, if not immediately, find themselves thinking of him and treating him as the individual who had so inexplicably disappeared from their midst. We should be extending our normal use of "same person" in a way which the postulated facts would both demand and justify if we said that the one who appears in Australia is the same person as the one who disappears in America. The factors inclining us to identify them would far outweigh the factors disinclining us to do this. We should have no reasonable alternative but to extend our usage of "the same person" to cover the strange new case.

Second picture: Now let us suppose that the event in America is not a sudden and inexplicable disappearance, and indeed not a disappearance at all, but a sudden death. Only, at the moment when the individual dies, a replica of him as he was at the moment before his death, complete with memory up to that instant, appears in Australia. Even with the corpse on our hands, it would still, I suggest, be an extension of "same person" required and warranted by the postulated facts, to say that the same person who died has been miraculously recreated in Australia. The case would be considerably odder than in the previous picture, because of the existence of the corpse in America contemporaneously with the existence of the living person in Australia. But I submit that, although the oddness of this circumstance may be stated as strongly as you please, and can indeed hardly be overstated, yet it does not exceed the bounds of the logically possible. Once again we must imagine some of the deceased's colleagues going to Australia to interview the person who has suddenly appeared there. He would perfectly remember them and their meeting, be interested in what had happened, and be as amazed and dumbfounded about it as anyone else; and he would perhaps be worried about the possible legal complications if he should return to America to claim his property; and so on. Once again, I believe, they would soon find themselves thinking of him and treating him as the same person as the dead Princetonian. Once again the factors inclining us to say that the one who died and the one who appeared are the same person would outweigh the factors inclining us to say that they are different people. Once again we should have to extend our usage of "the same person" to cover this new case.

Third picture: My third supposal is that the replica, complete with memory, etc. appears, not in Australia, but as a resurrection replica in a different world altogether, a resurrection world inhabited by resurrected persons. This world occupies its own space, distinct from the space with which we are now familiar. That is to say, an object in the resurrection world is not situated at any distance or in any direction from an object in our present world, although each object in either world is spatially related to each other object in the same world.

Mr. X, then, dies. A Mr. X replica, complete with the set of memory traces which Mr. X had at the last moment before his death, comes into existence. It is composed of other material than physical matter, and is located in a resurrection world which does not stand in any spatial relationship with the physical world. Let us leave out of consideration St. Paul's hint that the resurrection body may be as unlike the physical body as is a full grain of wheat from the wheat seed, and consider the simpler picture in which the resurrection body has the same shape as the physical body.[14]

In these circumstances, how does Mr. X know that he has been resurrected or recreated? He remembers dying; or rather he remembers being on what he took to be his death-bed, and becoming progressively weaker until, presumably, he lost consciousness. But how does he know that (to put it Irishly) his "dying" proved fatal; and that he did not, after losing consciousness, begin to recover strength, and has now simply waked up?

The picture is readily enough elaborated to answer this question. Mr. X meets and recognizes a number of relatives and friends and historical personages whom he knows to have died; and from the fact of their presence, and also from their testimony that he has only just now appeared in their world, he is convinced that he has died. Evidences of this kind could mount up to the point at which they are quite as strong as the evidence which, in pictures one and two, convince the individual in question that he has been miraculously translated to Australia. Resurrected persons would be individually no more in doubt about their own identity than we are now, and would be able to identify one another in the same kinds of ways, and with a like degree of assurance, as we do now.

If it be granted that resurrected persons might be able to arrive at a rationally founded conviction that their existence is *post-mortem*, how could they know that the world in which they find themselves is in a different space from that in which their physical bodies were? How could such a one know that he is not in a like situation with the person in picture number two, who dies in America and appears as a full-blooded replica in Australia, leaving his corpse in the U. S. A.—except that now the replica is situated, not in Australia, but on a planet of some other star?

It is of course conceivable that the space of the resurrection world should have properties which are manifestly incompatible with its being a region of physical space. But on the other hand, it is not of the essence of the notion of a resurrection world that its space should have properties different from those of physical space. And supposing it not to have different properties, it is not evident that a resurrected individual could learn from any direct observations that he was not on a planet of some sun which is at so great a distance from our own sun that the stellar scenery visible from it is quite unlike that which we can now see. The grounds that a resurrected person would have for believing that he is in a different space from physical space (supposing there to be no discernible difference in spatial properties) would be the same as the grounds that any of us may have now for believing this concerning resurrected individuals. These grounds are indirect and consist in

---

[14]As would seem to be assumed, for example, by Irenaeus (*Adversus Haereses*, Bk. II, Ch. 34, Sec. 1).

all those considerations (*e.g.*, Luke 16: 26) which lead most of those who consider the question to reject as absurd the possibility of, for example, radio communication or rocket travel between earth and heaven.

V

In the present context my only concern is to claim that this doctrine of the divine creation of bodies, composed of a material other than that of physical matter, which bodies are endowed with sufficient correspondence of characteristics with our present bodies, and sufficient continuity of memory with our present consciousness, for us to speak of the same person being raised up again to life in a new environment, is not self-contradictory. If, then, it cannot be ruled out *ab initio* as meaningless, we may go on to consider whether and how it is related to the possible verification of Christian theism.

So far I have argued that a survival prediction such as is contained in the *corpus* of Christian belief is in principle subject to future verification. But this does not take the argument by any means as far as it must go if it is to succeed. For survival, simply as such, would not serve to verify theism. It would not necessarily be a state of affairs which is manifestly incompatible with the non-existence of God. It might be taken just as a surprising natural fact. The atheist, in his resurrection body, and able to remember his life on earth, might say that the universe has turned out to be more complex, and perhaps more to be approved of, than he had realized. But the mere fact of survival, with a new body in a new environment, would not demonstrate to him that there is a God. It is fully compatible with the notion of survival that the life to come be, so far as the theistic problem is concerned, essentially a continuation of the present life, and religiously no less ambiguous. And in this event, survival after bodily death would not in the least constitute a final verification of theistic faith.

I shall not spend time in trying to draw a picture of a resurrection existence which would merely prolong the religious ambiguity of our present life. The important question, for our purpose, is not whether one can conceive of after-life experiences which would *not* verify theism (and in point of fact one can fairly easily conceive them), but whether one can conceive of after-life experiences which *would* serve to verify theism.

I think that we can. In trying to do so I shall not appeal to the traditional doctrine, which figures especially in Catholic and mystical theology, of the Beatific Vision of God. The difficulty presented by this doctrine is not so much that of deciding whether there are grounds for believing it, as of deciding what it means. I shall not, however, elaborate this difficulty, but pass directly to the investigation of a different and, as it seems to me, more intelligible possibility. This is the possibility not of a direct vision of God, whatever that might mean, but of a *situation* which points unambiguously to the existence of a loving God. This would be a situation which, so far as its religious significance is concerned, contrasts in a certain important respect with our present situation. Our present situation is one which in some ways seems to confirm and in other ways to contradict the truth of theism. Some events around us suggest the presence of an unseen benevolent intelligence and others suggest that no such intelligence is at work. Our situation is religiously ambiguous. But in order for us to be aware of this fact we must already have some idea, however vague, of what it would be for our situation to be not ambiguous, but on the contrary wholly evidential of God. I therefore want to try to make clearer this presupposed concept of a religiously unambiguous situation.

There are, I suggest, two possible developments of our experience such that, if they occurred in conjunction with one another (whether in this life or in another life to come), they would assure us beyond rational doubt of the reality of God, as conceived in the Christian faith. These are, *first*, an experience of the fulfillment of God's purpose for ourselves, as this has been disclosed in the Christian revelation; in conjunction, *second*, with an experience of communion with God as he has revealed himself in the person of Christ.

The divine purpose for human life, as this is depicted in the New Testament documents, is the bringing of the human person, in society with his fellows, to enjoy a certain valuable quality of personal life, the content of which is given in the character of Christ—which quality of life (*i.e.* life in relationship with God, described in the Fourth Gospel as eternal life) is said to be the proper destiny of human nature and the source of man's final self-fulfillment and happiness. The verification situation with regard to such a fulfillment is asymmetrical. On the one hand, so long as the divine purpose remains unfulfilled, we cannot know that it never will be fulfilled in the future; hence no final falsification is possible of the claim that this fulfillment will occur—unless, of course, the prediction contains a specific time clause which, in Christian teaching, it does not. But on the other hand, if and when the divine purpose *is* fulfilled in our own experience, we must be able to recognize and rejoice in that fulfillment. For the fulfillment would not be for us the promised fulfillment without our own conscious participation in it.

It is important to note that one can say this much without being cognizant in advance of the concrete form which such fulfillment will take. The before-and-after situation is analogous to that of a small child looking forward to adult life and then, having grown to adulthood, looking back upon childhood. The child possesses and can use correctly in various contexts the concept of "being grown-up," although he does not know, concretely, what it is like to be grown-up. But when he reaches adulthood he is nevertheless able to know that he has reached it; he is able to recognize the experience of living a grown-up life even though he did not know in advance just what to expect.

For his understanding of adult maturity grows as he himself matures. Something similar may be supposed to happen in the case of the fulfillment of the divine purpose for human life. That fulfillment may be as far removed from our present condition as is mature adulthood from the mind of a little child; nevertheless, we possess already a comparatively vague notion of this final fulfillment, and as we move towards it our concept will itself become more adequate; and if and when we finally reach that fulfillment, the problem of recognizing it will have disappeared in the process.

The other feature that must, I suggest, be present in a state of affairs that would verify theism, is that the fulfillment of God's purpose be apprehended *as* the fulfillment of God's purpose and not simply as a natural state of affairs. To this end it must be accompanied by an experience of communion with God as he has made himself known to men in Christ.

The specifically Christian clause, "as he has made himself known to men in Christ," is essential, for it provides a solution to the problem of recognition in the awareness of God. Several writers have pointed out the logical difficulty involved in any claim to have encountered God.[15] How could one know that it was *God* whom one had encountered? God is described in Christian theology in terms of various absolute qualities, such as omnipotence, omnipresence, perfect goodness, infinite love, etc., which cannot as such be observed by us, as can their finite analogues, limited power, local presence, finite goodness, and human love. One can recognize that a being whom one "encounters" has a given finite degree of power, but how does one recognize that he has *un*limited power? How does one observe that an encountered being is *omni*present? How does one perceive that his goodness and love, which one can perhaps see to exceed any human goodness and love, are actually infinite? Such qualities cannot be given in human experience. One might claim, then, to have encountered a Being whom one presumes, or trusts, or hopes to be God; but one cannot claim to have encountered a Being whom one recognized to be the infinite, almighty, eternal Creator.

This difficulty is met in Christianity by the doctrine of the Incarnation—although this was not among the considerations which led to the formulation of that doctrine. The idea of incarnation provides answers to the two related questions: "How do we know that God has certain absolute qualities which, by their very nature, transcend human experience?" and "How can there be an eschatological verification of theism which is based upon a recognition of the presence of God in his Kingdom?"

In Christianity God is known as "the God and Father of our Lord Jesus Christ."[16] God is the Being about whom Jesus taught; the Being in relation to whom Jesus lived, and into a relationship with whom he brought his disciples; the Being whose *agape* toward men was seen on earth in the life of

---

[15]For example, H. W. Hepburn, *Christianity and Paradox*, 1958, pp. 56 f.
[16]II Cor. 11:31.

Jesus. In short, God is the transcendent Creator who has revealed himself in Christ. Now Jesus' teaching about the Father is part of that self-disclosure, and it is from this teaching (together with that of the prophets who preceded him) that the Christian knowledge of God's transcendent being is derived. Only God himself knows his own infinite nature; and our human belief about that nature is based upon his self-revelation to men in Christ. As Karl Barth expresses it, "Jesus Christ is the knowability of God."[17] Our beliefs about God's infinite being are not capable of observational verification, being beyond the scope of human experience, but they are susceptible of indirect verification by the removal of rational doubt concerning the authority of Christ. An experience of the reign of the Son in the Kingdom of the Father would confirm that authority, and therewith, indirectly, the validity of Jesus' teaching concerning the character of God in his infinite transcendent nature.

The further question as to how an eschatological experience of the Kingdom of God could be known to be such has already been answered by implication. It is God's union with man in Christ that makes possible man's recognition of the fulfillment of God's purpose for man as being indeed the fulfillment of *God's* purpose for him. The presence of Christ in his Kingdom marks this as being beyond doubt the Kingdom of the God and Father of the Lord Jesus Christ.

It is true that even the experience of the realization of the promised Kingdom of God, with Christ reigning as Lord of the New Aeon, would not constitute a logical certification of his claims nor, accordingly, of the reality of God. But this will not seem remarkable to any philosopher in the empiricist tradition, who knows that it is only a confusion to demand that a factual proposition be an analytic truth. A set of expectations based upon faith in the historic Jesus as the incarnation of God, and in his teaching as being divinely authoritative, could be so fully confirmed in *post-mortem* experience as to leave no grounds for rational doubt as to the validity of that faith.

VI

There remains of course the problem (which falls to the New Testament scholar rather than to the philosopher) whether Christian tradition, and in particular the New Testament, provides a sufficiently authentic "picture" of the mind and character of Christ to make such recognition possible. I cannot here attempt to enter into the vast field of Biblical criticism, and shall confine myself to the logical point, which only emphasizes the importance of the historical question, that a verification of theism made possible by the Incarnation is dependent upon the Christian's having a genuine contact with the person of Christ, even though this is mediated through the life and tradition of the Church.

---

[17]*Church Dogmatics*, Vol. II, Pt. I, p. 150.

One further point remains to be considered. When we ask the question, "*To whom* is theism verified?" one is initially inclined to assume that the answer must be, "To everyone." We are inclined to assume that, as in my parable of the journey, the believer must be confirmed in his belief, and the unbeliever converted from his unbelief. But this assumption is neither demanded by the nature of verification nor by any means unequivocably supported by our Christian sources.

We have already noted that a verifiable prediction may be conditional. "There is a table in the next room" entails conditional predictions of the form: if someone goes into the next room he will see, etc. But no one is compelled to go into the next room. Now it may be that the predictions concerning human experience which are entailed by the proposition that God exists are conditional predictions and that no one is compelled to fulfill those conditions. Indeed we stress in much of our theology that the manner of the divine self-disclosure to men is such that our human status as free and responsible beings is respected, and an awareness of God never is forced upon us. It may then be a condition of *post-mortem* verification that we be already in some degree conscious of God by an uncompelled response to his modes of revelation in this world. It may be that such a voluntary consciousness of God is an essential element in the fulfillment of the divine purpose for human nature, so that the verification of theism which consists in an experience of the final fulfillment of that purpose can only be experienced by those who have already entered upon an awareness of God by the religious mode of apperception which we call faith.

If this be so, it has the consequence that only the theistic believer can find the vindication of his belief. This circumstance would not of course set any restriction upon who can become a believer, but it would involve that while theistic faith can be verified—found by one who holds it to be beyond rational doubt—yet it cannot be proved to the nonbeliever. Such an asymmetry would connect with that strain of New Testament teaching which speaks of a division of mankind even in the world to come.

Having noted this possibility I will only express my personal opinion that the logic of the New Testament as a whole, though admittedly not always its explicit content, leads to a belief in ultimate universal salvation. However, my concern here is not to seek to establish the religious facts, but rather to establish that there are such things as religious facts, and in particular that the existence or non-existence of the God of the New Testament is a matter of fact, and claims as such eventual experiential verification.

PART THREE

THE DIVINE
ATTRIBUTES

INTRODUCTION

However we understand the nature of the predicates attributed to God, religious people have certainly wanted to attribute to God certain fundamental characteristics. Which ones? Essentially, the ones that seem to be implicit in the idea that God is an all-perfect being, a being than which there can be no greater. These characteristics include omnipotence (the power or ability to do anything) and omniscience (the knowledge of everything). There are, however, a variety of problems that arise in connection with each of these characterizations, and we shall be examining these problems in this section.

Let us begin with the problems that arise in connection with the claim that God is omnipotent. One way to understand these problems is to look at certain paradoxes that the idea of omnipotence gives rise to. One is the paradox of the stone—can God create a stone so heavy that he cannot lift it? If he can, then he is not omnipotent (since there is something—lift that stone —that he cannot do); and if he cannot, then he is also not omnipotent (since there is something—create that stone—that he cannot do). In either case, God cannot be omnipotent. The second is the paradox of God's sinning— can God sin? If he can, then he is not all-perfect. If he cannot, then he is still not all-perfect because he cannot do something (sin) and is not therefore omnipotent.

It is obvious that both of these paradoxes raise, each in their own way, the same issue. Do we want to say that God can do anything? And if we do, won't this idea get us into trouble? On the other hand, if we want in some way to limit God's power (so as to avoid these paradoxes), what is left of the idea that God is all-perfect and therefore omnipotent?

St. Thomas Aquinas, like many other theologians, adopted the idea that God can do anything that is logically possible, but that he cannot do anything that is not logically possible. St. Thomas felt that this was really no limitation on God's power, since the logically impossible is not some task that God cannot perform. In light of this Thomistic principle, Professor Mavrodes argues that the paradox of the stone can be resolved, since even if God cannot create a stone so heavy that he cannot lift it, that is no challenge to his omnipotence, since creating a stone so heavy that God cannot lift it is a logically impossible task. Similarly, others (but, interestingly enough, not St. Thomas—his solution will be discussed below) have used this Thomistic thought to deal with the paradox of God's sinning. God, they say, cannot sin, but that is no challenge to his omnipotence, since God's committing a sin is not a logically possible task.

Not all philosophers have, however, been satisfied with this approach. To begin with, as Professor Frankfurt points out, there are many theologians who are unhappy with the idea that God cannot do logically impossible tasks, that he is in this way bound by the laws of logic. Intuitively speaking, their motivation is the following: just as God is not bound in his actions by the laws of nature, since it is only by his will that ordinary objects act in accordance with these laws, so God is not bound by the laws of logic, since it is only by his will that the world is in accordance with these laws. Descartes, for example, held this view. Now it is obvious that this dispute between Aquinas and Descartes hinges upon some fundamental issues having to do with the nature of the laws of logic, so it would seem desirable to see if the paradoxes could be avoided without having to resolve those very difficult issues. Secondly, as Professor Savage points out, there are ways of formulating the argument in the paradox that don't involve any reference to God's not being able to lift the stone, so it is not clear that the Thomistic solution would really work.

Professor Frankfurt's own solution is rather straightforward. Suppose, he says, that God can do the impossible, so he can create the stone so heavy he can't lift it. There would still be no limitation upon his power, for if he can do the impossible, then he can also lift the stone he can't lift. In short, suggests Professor Frankfurt, if we do want to stick with the idea of God being able to do anything at all, we need not be troubled by the paradox of the stone.

A very different approach is adopted by Professor Savage. He agrees with the original Thomistic analysis that God cannot create a stone so heavy that he cannot lift it but claims that this is no limitation upon God's power. But, for Professor Savage, the reasons why this is no limitation are very different. He feels that to say that God cannot create such a stone is just equivalent to saying that God can lift any stone that he creates, and why is this a limitation upon God's power?

In short, then, depending upon your analysis of omnipotence, there are a variety of ways in which one can deal with this paradox. Like all good philosophical paradoxes, however, it is of importance because it has forced us to clarify our concepts—in this case, the concept of omnipotence. The same is true of the paradox of God's sinning. It, too, can be dealt with, but in different ways, which we will now examine.

St. Thomas himself offers several solutions, only one of which is relevant to us. While agreeing that it is impossible for God to sin, St. Thomas feels that it is at least true that he could sin if he wanted to, and that is all that is required to preserve God's omnipotence. Professor Pike claims that St. Thomas's solution is impossible. If, indeed, it is neither possible that God wants to sin nor (and this is more important) that he can sin, then, argues Pike, it could not even be true that he can sin if he wants to. So the problem of reconciling God's omnipotence with his being morally all-perfect remains.

Pike's own solution is that all that is required by God's omnipotence is that he have the ability, the capacity, to commit a sin, and that God can have this even if it is logically impossible that he actually sins. That logical impossibility requires only that it be logically impossible that he ever actually exercize his capacity to sin—and that might be the case (say, because of his nature) even though he has the capacity.

We have so far been concerned with problems that arise in connection with God's omnipotence. There are, however, equally puzzling problems that arise in connection with his omniscience, and we turn now to a consideration of them. One is a problem first raised by St. Thomas but reemphasized by Professor Kretzmann in his article. Religious people have wanted to say that God's perfection implies that he is not only omniscient but also changeless, immutable. But, argues Kretzmann and others, how can he know everything about a changing world? How could he, for example, know what time it is now? More generally, if the world is changing then what one knows, if one knows everything that is going on in the world, seems also to have to be changing. But then, how can God be immutable?

One important issue that has to be raised in connection with this problem is whether or not the religious person is really committed to the view that God cannot change even in this respect. After all, would such a change imply an imperfection in God, either before or after the change? Kretzmann recognizes this possible way out, and merely alludes to, but does not really develop, the idea that the religious person has other reasons for ruling out even this type of change in God.

St. Thomas's own solution is that God knows everything that takes place, but that he knows it in a way different from our knowing. In particular, his knowledge of it does not involve those temporal elements that would lead to a change in God. It would seem that, in these admittedly obscure remarks, St. Thomas is coming very close to Kretzmann's objection C, and if so, his argument seems open to all of the objections Kretzmann raises, in particular, that this account really means that there are severe limitations on what God actually knows.

In a very important article, Professor Castañeda argues that the whole problem is really a pseudo-problem, one raised by Kretzmann's not noticing how "now" and other words like it function in certain types of discourse. Once one gets clear about the logic of these quasi-indicators, argues Castañeda, one can formulate an account of what it is that God knows that truly preserves his omniscience while not making him subject to change. The reader is referred to Castañeda's article for the details of this point.

There is another problem about omniscience that has to be considered at greater length. Religious people often want to claim (although this is not part of their theological beliefs about God) that man is, at least in some cases, free to do what he wants to do. But how can he be free if God knows what he is going to do?

In order to better assess this argument, it is necessary for us to formulate it more exactly. There is one version of it, found in St. Augustine, that is clearly fallacious. It runs as follows:

(1) God has foreknowledge of all future events;
(2) Therefore, if a man is going to do A, then God knows that he will do A;
(3) Whatever God knows must happen;
(4) Hence, if a man is going to do A, then he must necessarily do A;
(5) But then he did not freely do A;
(6) Therefore, he had no free will concerning his doing A.

Since this argument applies equally to each action, it follows from it that a man never has any free will.

Augustine, as Rowe points out, attempted to solve this problem by claiming that, although the man must necessarily do A, it does not follow that he did not freely do A; i.e., (5) does not follow from (4). Rowe attempts to challenge this solution, and substitutes for it another one—one that is also advocated by St. Thomas and Leibniz. It runs as follows: (3) is ambiguous. It may mean simply that for all p, it is necessarily the case that if God knows that p will occur, then p will occur. If this is what it means, then (3) is clearly true but (4) does not follow from (2) and (3). Or it may mean that for all p, if God knows that p will occur, then p occurs necessarily. If that is what it means, however, there seems to be no reason to accept (3).

This solution does not, however, entirely settle the problem, because there is another version of the argument that is not open to this objection. St. Thomas considers this version as well, and it is also forcibly presented in the writings of Jonathan Edwards. It runs as follows:

(a) Everything that has occured is now necessary;
(b) Suppose that a man does A at some future time;
(c) Then God already has known that he will do A;
(d) So it is necessary that God has known that he will do A;
(e) It is necessary that if God has known that he will do A, then he will do A;
(f) Therefore, it is necessary that he will do A;

(g) But then he did not do *A* freely and he had no free will concerning his doing *A*.

St. Thomas's solution to this problem rests upon his idea that God's knowledge is not temporal in the way that our knowledge is. God is outside of time, in eternity, and everything is eternally present to God. As a result, what God knows is the present-tense proposition that the man is doing *A*, and not the future-sense proposition, and there is no reason why it must be contingent. When a thing is, it need no longer have the contingency that the future must have in order for free will to be possible. Looking at the above argument, then, St. Thomas would deny (3).

This solution is not entirely satisfactory. To begin with, as Kenny and Prior point out, it really means a certain limitation on God's knowledge because he will not know the truth of tensed propositions. Secondly, there are difficulties in this idea of a timeless eternity that is simultaneous with all events in time.

So we must find some other alternative. Professor Kenny suggests that we ought to deny (a) and therefore (d). He argues that there really is no way in which what has occurred is now necessary, and that the whole problem rests upon this illusion. Professor Prior, in effect, suggests that we ought to deny (c). The trouble with this argument, he points out, is its assumption that if at some future time he does *A*, then it was already true that he will do *A* and that therefore God knows it. If we drop this assumption, as Pierce suggested, then (c) will not follow from (b) and the argument collapses.

It is clear that both of these possible solutions rest upon views about the relation between time, reality, and truth. One cannot simply adopt one of them without considering its implications for a whole host of related logical and metaphysical issues. The working out of all of these issues is left, therefore, for the reader as a task.

OMNIPOTENCE

ST. THOMAS AQUINAS

3.1 The Limits on God's Abilities

We proceed thus to the Third Article:—
Objection 1. It seems that God is not omnipotent. For movement and passiveness belong to everything. But this is impossible for God, since He is immovable, as was said above. Therefore He is not omnipotent.

Obj. 2. Further, sin is an act of some kind. But God cannot sin, nor *deny Himself,* as it is said 2 *Tim.* ii. 13. Therefore He is not omnipotent.

Obj. 3. Further, it is said of God that He manifests His omnipotence *especially by sparing and having mercy.* Therefore the greatest act possible to the divine power is to spare and have mercy. There are things much greater, however, than sparing and having mercy; for example, to create another world, and the like. Therefore God is not omnipotent.

Obj. 4. Further, upon the text, *God hath made foolish the wisdom of this world* (*I Cor.* i. 20), the *Gloss* says: *God hath made the wisdom of this world foolish* by showing those things to be possible which it judges to be impossible. Whence it seems that nothing is to be judged possible or impossible in reference to inferior causes, as the wisdom of this world judges them; but in reference to the divine power. If God, then were omnipotent, all things would be possible; nothing, therefore, impossible. But if we take away the impossible, then we destroy also the necessary; for what necessarily exists cannot possibly not exist. Therefore, there would be nothing at all that is necessary in things if God were omnipotent. But this is an impossibility. Therefore God is not omnipotent.

From *Summa Theologica*, Part I, trans. Dominican Fathers of English Province (New York: Benziger, Inc., 1947). Reprinted by permission of the publisher.

On the contrary, It is said: *No word shall be impossible with God* (*Luke* i. 37).

I answer that, All confess that God is omnipotent; but it seems difficult to explain in what His omnipotence precisely consists. For there may be a doubt as to the precise meaning of the word "all" when we say that God can do all things. If, however, we consider the matter aright, since power is said in reference to possible things, this phrase, *God can do all things*, is rightly understood to mean that God can do all things that are possible; and for this reason He is said to be omnipotent. Now according to the Philosopher a thing is said to be possible in two ways. First, in relation to some power; thus whatever is subject to human power is said to be possible to man. Now God cannot be said to be omnipotent through being able to do all things that are possible to created nature; for the divine power extends farther than that. If, however, we were to say that God is omnipotent because He can do all things that are possible to His power, there would be a vicious circle in explaining the nature of His power. For this would be saying nothing else but that God is omnipotent because He can do all that He is able to do.

It remains, therefore, that God is called omnipotent because he can do all things that are possible absolutely; which is the second way of saying a thing is possible. For a thing is said to be possible or impossible absolutely, according to the relation in which the very terms stand to one another: possible, if the predicate is not incompatible with the subject, as that Socrates sits; and absolutely impossible when the predicate is altogether incompatible with the subject, as, for instance, that a man is an ass.

It must, however, be remembered that since every agent produces an effect like itself, to each active power there corresponds a thing possible as its proper object according to the nature of that act on which its active power is founded; for instance, the power of giving warmth is related, as to its proper object, to the being capable of being warmed. The divine being, however, upon which the nature of power in God is founded, is infinite; it is not limited to any class of being, but possesses within itself the perfection of all being. Whence, whatsoever has or can have the nature of being is numbered among the absolute possibles, in respect of which God is called omnipotent.

Now nothing is opposed to the notion of being except non-being. Therefore, that which at the same time implies being and non-being is repugnant to the notion of an absolute possible, which is subject to the divine omnipotence. For such cannot come under the divine omnipotence; not indeed because of any defect in the power of God, but because it has not the nature of a feasible or possible thing. Therefore, everything that does not imply a contradiction in terms is numbered among those possibles in respect of which God is called omnipotent; whereas whatever implies contradiction does not come within the scope of divine omnipotence, because it cannot have the aspect of possibility. Hence it is more appropriate to say that such things cannot be done, than that God cannot do them. Nor is this contrary to the word of the angel, saying: *No word shall be impossible with God* (*Luke* i. 37). For whatever implies a contradiction cannot be a word, because no intellect can possibly conceive such a thing.

Reply Obj. 1. God is said to be omnipotent in respect to active power, not to passive power, as was shown above. Whence the fact that He is immovable or impassible is not repugnant to His omnipotence.

Reply Obj. 2. To sin is to fall short of a perfect action; hence to be able to sin is to be able to fall short in action, which is repugnant to omnipotence. Therefore it is that God cannot sin, because of His omnipotence. Now it is true that the Philosopher says that *God can deliberately do what is evil.* But this must be understood either on a condition, the antecedent of which is impossible—as, for instance, if we were to say that God can do evil things if He will. For there is no reason why a conditional proposition should not be true, though both the antecedent and consequent are impossible: as if one were to say: *If man is an ass, he has four feet.* Or he may be understood to mean that God can do some things which now seem to be evil: which, however, if He did them, would then be good. Or he is, perhaps, speaking after the common manner of the pagans, who thought that men became gods, like Jupiter or Mercury.

Reply Obj. 3. God's omnipotence is particularly shown in sharing and having mercy, because in this it is made manifest that God has supreme power, namely, that He freely forgives sins. For it is not for one who is bound by laws of a superior to forgive sins of his own free choice. Or, it is thus shown because by sparing and having mercy upon men, He leads them to the participation of an infinite good; which is the ultimate effect of the divine power. Or it is thus shown because, as was said above, the effect of the divine mercy is the foundation of all the divine works. For nothing is due anyone, except because of something already given him gratuitously by God. In this way the divine omnipotence is particularly made manifest, because to it pertains the first foundation of all good things.

Reply Obj. 4. The absolute possible is not so called in reference either to higher causes, or to inferior causes, but in reference to itself. But that which is called possible in reference to some power is named possible in reference to its proximate cause. Hence those things which it belongs to God alone to do immediately—as, for example, to create, to justify, and the like—are said to be possible in reference to a higher cause. Those things, however, which are such as to be done by inferior causes, are said to be possible in reference to those inferior causes. For it is according to the condition of the proximate cause that the effect has contingency or necessity, as was shown above. Thus it is that the wisdom of the world is deemed foolish, because what is impossible to nature it judges to be impossible to God. So it is clear that the omnipotence of God does not take away from things their impossibility and necessity.

GEORGE I. MAVRODES

3.2   *Some Puzzles*
        Concerning Omnipotence

The doctrine of God's omnipotence appears to claim that God can do anything. Consequently, there have been attempts to refute the doctrine by giving
examples of things which God cannot do; for example, He cannot draw a
square circle.

Responding to objections of this type, St. Thomas pointed out that "anything" should be here construed to refer only to objects, actions, or states of
affairs whose descriptions are not self-contradictory.[1] For it is only such
things whose nonexistence might plausibly be attributed to a lack of power
in some agent. My failure to draw a circle on the exam may indicate my lack
of geometrical skill, but my failure to draw a square circle does not indicate
any such lack. Therefore, the fact that it is false (or perhaps meaningless) to
say that God could draw one does no damage to the doctrine of His omnipotence.

A more involved problem, however, is posed by this type of question: can
God create a stone too heavy for Him to lift? This appears to be stronger
than the first problem, for it poses a dilemma. If we say that God can create
a stone, then it seems that there might be such a stone. And if there might
be a stone too heavy for Him to lift, then He is evidently not omnipotent.
But if we deny that God can create such a stone, we seem to have given up
His omnipotence already. Both answers lead us to the same conclusion.

Further, this problem does not seem obviously open to St. Thomas' solution. The form "*x* is able to draw a square circle" seems plainly to involve
a contradiction, while "*x* is able to make a thing too heavy for *x* to lift" does
not. For it may easily be true that I am able to make a boat too heavy for
me to lift. So why should it not be possible for God to make a stone too
heavy for Him to lift?

Despite this apparent difference, this second puzzle *is* open to essentially
the same answer as the first. The dilemma fails because it consists of asking
whether God can do a self-contradictory thing. And the reply that He cannot
does no damage to the doctrine of omnipotence.

The specious nature of the problem may be seen in this way. God is either

---

From *The Philosophical Review* 72 (1963): 221–23. Reprinted by permission of the author
and the editors.
[1]St. Thomas Aquinas, *Summa Theologiae*, Ia, q. 25, a. 3.

omnipotent or not.[2] Let us assume first that He is not. In that case the phrase "a stone too heavy for God to lift" may not be self-contradictory. And then, of course, if we assert either that God is able or that He is not able to create such a stone, we may conclude that He is not omnipotent. But this is no more than the assumption with which we began, meeting us again after our roundabout journey. If this were all that the dilemma could establish it would be trivial. To be significant it must derive this same conclusion *from the assumption that God is omnipotent*; that is, it must show that the assumption of the omnipotence of God leads to a *reductio*. But does it?

On the assumption that God is omnipotent, the phrase "a stone too heavy for God to lift" becomes self-contradictory. For it becomes "a stone which cannot be lifted by Him whose power is sufficient for lifting anything." But the "thing" described by a self-contradictory phrase is absolutely impossible and hence has nothing to do with the doctrine of omnipotence. Not being an object of power at all, its failure to exist cannot be the result of some lack in the power of God. And, interestingly, it is the very omnipotence of God which makes the existence of such a stone absolutely impossible, while it is the fact that I am finite in power which makes it possible for me to make a boat too heavy for me to lift.

But suppose that some die-hard objector takes the bit in his teeth and denies that the phrase "a stone too heavy for God to lift" is self-contradictory, even on the assumption that God is omnipotent. In other words, he contends that the description "a stone too heavy for an omnipotent God to lift" is self-coherent and therefore describes an absolutely possible object. Must I then attempt to prove the contradiction which I assume above as intuitively obvious? Not necessarily. Let me reply simply that if the objector is right in this contention, then the answer to the original question is "Yes, God can create such a stone." It may seem that this reply will force us into the original dilemma. But it does not. For now the objector can draw no damaging conclusion from this answer. And the reason is that he has just now contended that such a stone is compatible with the omnipotence of God. Therefore, from the possibility of God's creating such a stone it cannot be concluded that God is not omnipotent. The objector cannot have it both ways. The conclusion which he himself wishes to draw from an affirmative answer to the original question is itself the required proof that the descriptive phrase which appears there is self-contradictory. And "it is more appropriate to say that such things cannot be done, than that God cannot do them."[3]

The specious nature of this problem may also be seen in a somewhat different way.[4] Suppose that some theologian is convinced by this dilemma that he must give up the doctrine of omnipotence. But he resolves to give up

---

[2] I assume, of course, the existence of God, since that is not being brought in question here.

[3] St. Thomas, *loc. cit.*

[4] But this method rests finally on the same logical relations as the preceding one.

as little as possible, just enough to meet the argument. One way he can do so is by retaining the infinite power of God with regard to lifting, while placing a restriction on the sort of stone He is able to create. The only restriction required here, however, is that God must not be able to create a stone too heavy for Him to lift. Beyond that the dilemma has not even suggested any necessary restriction. Our theologian has, in effect, answered the original question in the negative, and he now regretfully supposes that this has required him to give up the full doctrine of omnipotence. He is now retaining what he supposes to be the more modest remnants which he has salvaged from that doctrine.

We must ask, however, what it is which he has in fact given up. Is it the unlimited power of God to create stones? No doubt. But what stone is it which God is now precluded from creating? The stone too heavy for Him to lift, of course. But we must remember that nothing in the argument required the theologian to admit any limit on God's power with regard to the lifting of stones. He still holds that to be unlimited. And if God's power to lift is infinite, then His power to create may run to infinity also without outstripping that first power. The supposed limitation turns out to be no limitation at all, since it is specified only by reference to another power which is itself infinite. Our theologian need have no regrets, for he has given up nothing. The doctrine of the power of God remains just what it was before.

Nothing I have said above, of course, goes to prove that God is, in fact, omnipotent. All I have intended to show is that certain arguments intended to prove that He is not omnipotent fail. They fail because they propose, as tests of God's power, putative tasks whose descriptions are self-contradictory. Such pseudo-tasks, not falling within the realm of possibility, are not objects of power at all. Hence the fact that they cannot be performed implies no limit on the power of God, and hence no defect in the doctrine of omnipotence.

HARRY G. FRANKFURT

3.3 *The Logic of Omnipotence*

George Mavrodes has recently presented an analysis designed to show that, despite some appearances to the contrary, a certain well-known puzzle actually raises no serious difficulties in the notion of divine omnipotence.[1] The puzzle suggests a test of God's power—can He create a stone too heavy for Him to lift?—which, it seems, cannot fail to reveal that His power is limited. For He must, it would appear, either show His limitations by being unable to create such a stone or by being unable to lift it once He had created it.

In dealing with this puzzle, Mavrodes points out that it involves the setting of a task whose description is self-contradictory—the task of creating a stone too heavy for an omnipotent being to lift. He calls such tasks "pseudo-tasks" and he says of them: "Such pseudo-tasks, not falling within the realm of possibility, are not objects of power at all. Hence the fact that they cannot be performed implies no limit on the power of God, and hence no defect in the doctrine of omnipotence."[2] Thus his way of dealing with the puzzle relies upon the principle that an omnipotent being need not be supposed capable of performing tasks whose descriptions are self-contradictory.

Now this principle is one which Mavrodes apparently regards as self-evident, since he offers no support for it whatever except some references which indicate that it was also accepted by Saint Thomas Aquinas. I do not wish to suggest that the principle is false. Indeed, for all I know it may even be self-evident. But it happens to be a principle which has been rejected by some important philosophers.[3] Accordingly, it might be preferable to have

From *The Philosophical Review* 73 (1964). Reprinted by permission of the author and the editors.

[1]George Mavrodes, "Some Puzzles Concerning Omnipotence," *Philosophical Review* 72 (1963), 221–23.[See selection 3.2 this volume—ED.]

[2]*Ibid.*, p. 223.

[3]Descartes, for instance, who in fact thought it blasphemous to maintain that God can do only what can be described in a logically coherent way: "The truths of mathematics . . . were established by God and entirely depend on Him, as much as do all the rest of His creatures. Actually, it would be to speak of God as a Jupiter or Saturn and to subject Him to the Styx and to the Fates, to say that these truths are independent of Him. . . . You will be told that if God established these truths He would be able to change them, as a king does his laws; to which it is necessary to reply that this is correct. . . . In general we can be quite certain that God can do whatever we are able to understand, but not that He cannot do what we are unable to understand. For it would be presumptuous to think that

an analysis of the puzzle in question which does not require the use of this principle. And in fact, such an analysis is easy to provide.

Suppose, then, that God's omnipotence enables Him to do even what is logically impossible and that He actually creates a stone too heavy for Him to lift. The critic of the notion of divine omnipotence is quite mistaken if he thinks that this supposition plays into his hands. What the critic wishes to claim, of course, is that when God has created a stone which He cannot lift He is then faced with a task beyond His ability and is therefore seen to be limited in power. But this claim is not justified.

For why should God not be able to perform the task in question? To be sure, it is a task—the task of lifting a stone which He cannot lift—whose description is self-contradictory. But if God is supposed capable of performing one task whose description is self-contradictory—that of creating the problematic stone in the first place—why should He not be supposed capable of performing another—that of lifting the stone? After all, is there any greater trick in performing two logically impossible tasks than there is in performing one?

If an omnipotent being can do what is logically impossible, then he can not only create situations which he cannot handle but also, since he is not bound by the limits of consistency, he can handle situations which he cannot handle.

---

our imagination extends as far as His power" (letter to Mersenne, 15 April 1630). "God was as free to make it false that all the radii of a circle are equal as to refrain from creating the world" (letter to Mersenne, 27 May 1630). "I would not even dare to say that God cannot arrange that a mountain should exist without a valley, or that one and two should not make three; but I only say that He has given me a mind of such a nature that I cannot conceive a mountain without a valley or a sum of one and two which would not be three, and so on, and that such things imply contraditions in my conception" (letter to Arnauld, 29 July 1648). "As for the difficulty in conceiving how it was a matter of freedom and indifference to God to make it true that the three angles of a triangle should equal two right angles, or generally that contradictions should not be able to be together, one can easily remove it by considering that the power of God can have no limit. . . . God cannot have been determined to make it true that contradictions cannot be together, and consequently He could have done the contrary" (letter to Mesland, 2 May 1644).

C. WADE SAVAGE

3.4   The Paradox of the Stone

A. (1) Either God can create a stone which He cannot lift, or He cannot create a stone which He cannot lift.
   (2) If God can create a stone which He cannot lift, then He is not omnipotent (since He cannot lift the stone in question).
   (3) If God cannot create a stone which He cannot lift, then He is not omnipotent (since He cannot create the stone in question).
   (4) Therefore, God is not omnipotent.

Mr. Mavrodes has offered a solution[1] to the familiar paradox above; but it is erroneous. Mavrodes states that he assumes the existence of God,[2] and then reasons (in pseudo-dilemma fashion) as follows. God is either omnipotent or He is not. If we assume that He is not omnipotent, the task of creating a stone which He cannot lift is not self-contradictory. And we can conclude that God is not omnipotent on the grounds that both His ability and His inability to perform this task imply that He is not omnipotent. But to prove His non-omnipotence in this way is trivial. "To be significant [the paradoxical argument] must derive this same conclusion *from the assumption that God is omnipotent*; that is, it must show that the assumption of the omnipotence of God leads to a *reductio*." However, on the assumption that God is omnipotent, the task of creating a stone which God cannot lift is self-contradictory. Since inability to perform a self-contradictory task does not imply a limitation on the agent, one of the premises of the paradoxical argument—premise A(3)—is false. The argument is, in consequence, either insignificant or unsound.

There are many objections to this solution. First, the paradoxical argument need not be represented as a *reductio*; in A it is a dilemma. Mavrodes' reasoning implies that the paradoxical argument must either assume that God is omnipotent or assume that He is not omnipotent. This is simply false: neither asusmption need be made, and neither is made in A. Second, "a stone which God cannot lift" is self-contradictory—on the assumption that God is omnipotent—only if "God is omnipotent" is necessarily true. "Russell can lift any

From *The Philosophical Review* 76 (1967): 74–79. Reprinted by permission of the author and the editors.
    [1][See Mavrodes, selection 3.2 this volume—ED.] The heart of his solution is contained in paragraphs 6, 7, and 11.
    [2]See n. 2, [p. 341 this volume—ED.]

stone" is a contingent statement. Consequently, if we assume that Russell can lift any stone we are thereby committed only to saying that creating a stone which Russell cannot lift is a task which *in fact* cannot be performed by Russell or anyone else. Third, if "God is omnipotent" is necessarily true—as Mavrodes must claim for his solution to work—then his assumption that God exists begs the question of the paradoxical argument. For what the argument really tries to establish is that the existence of an omnipotent being is logically impossible. Fourth, the claim that inability to perform a self-contradictory task is no limitation on the agent is not entirely uncontroversial. Descartes suggested that an omnipotent God must be able to perform such self-contradictory tasks as making a mountain without a valley and arranging that the sum of one and two is not three.[3] No doubt Mavrodes and Descartes have different theories about the nature of contradictions; but that is part of the controversy.

Mavrodes has been led astray by version A of the paradox, which apparently seeks to prove that *God is not omnipotent*. Concentration on this version, together with the inclination to say that God is by definition omnipotent, leads straight to the conclusion that the paradox is specious. For if God is by definition omnipotent, then, obviously, creating a stone which God (an omnipotent being who can lift any stone) cannot lift is a task whose description is self-contradictory. What the paradox of the stone really seeks to prove is that the notion of an omnipotent being is logically inconsistent—that is, that *the existence of an omnipotent being, God or any other, is logically impossible.* It tries to do this by focusing on the perfectly consistent task of creating a stone which the creator cannot lift. The essence of the argument is that an omnipotent being must be able to perform this task and yet cannot perform the task.

Stated in its clearest form, the paradoxical argument of the stone is as follows. Where x is any being:

> B. (1) Either x can create a stone which x cannot lift, or x cannot create a stone which x cannot lift.

---

[3]Harry G. Frankfurt, "The Logic of Omnipotence," *Philosophical Review*, 73 (1964), 262–63. [selection 3.3 this volume—ED.] The relevant passage from Descartes is quoted by Frankfurt in a long footnote. Mavrodes assumes (on his "significant" interpretation of the paradox) that creating a stone which God cannot lift is a self-contradictory task, and contends that God therefore cannot perform it. This forces him onto the second horn of dilemma A, which he tries to break by arguing that inability to perform a self-contradictory task does not imply a limitation on the agent. Frankfurt also assumes that creating a stone which God cannot lift is a self-contradictory task, but contends with Descartes (for the sake of the argument) that God can nevertheless perform it. This forces him onto the first horn of the dilemma, which he tries to break with the following argument. If God can perform the self-contradictory task of creating a stone which He cannot lift, then He can just as easily perform the additional self-contradictory task of lifting the stone which He (creates and) cannot lift. Frankfurt's fundamental error is the same as Mavrodes': both suppose that on any significant interpretation the paradox sets for God the self-contradictory task of creating a stone which God (an omnipotent being who can lift any stone) cannot lift.

(2) If x can create a stone which x cannot lift, then, necessarily, there is at least one task which x cannot perform (namely, lift the stone in question).

(3) If x cannot create a stone which x cannot lift, then, necessarily, there is at least one task which x cannot perform (namely, create the stone in question).

(4) Hence, there is at least one task which x cannot perform.

(5) If x is an omnipotent being, then x can perform any task.

(6) Therefore, x is not omnipotent.

Since x is any being, this argument proves that the existence of an omnipotent being, God or any other, is logically impossible.

It is immediately clear that Mavrodes' solution will not apply to this version of the paradox. B is obviously a significant, non-trivial argument. But since it does not contain the word "God," no critic can maintain that B assumes that God is omnipotent. For the same reason, the point that "a stone which God cannot lift" is self-contradictory is simply irrelevant. Notice also that B is neutral on the question of whether inability to perform a self-contradictory task is a limitation on the agent's power. We can, however, replace every occurrence of "task" with "task whose description is not self-contradictory" without damaging the argument in any way.

The paradox does have a correct solution, though a different one from that offered by Mavrodes. The two solutions are similar in that both consist in arguing that an agent's inability to create a stone which he cannot lift does not entail a limitation on his power. But here the similarity ends. For, as we shall see presently, the basis of the correct solution is not that creating a stone which the creator cannot lift is a self-contradictory task (which it is not). Consequently, the correct solution side-steps the question of whether an agent's inability to perform a self-contradictory task is a limitation on his power.

The fallacy in the paradox of the stone lies in the falsity of the second horn—B(3)—of its dilemma: "x can create a stone which x cannot lift" does indeed entail that there is a task which x cannot perform and, consequently, does entail that x is not omnipotent. However, "x cannot create a stone which x cannot lift" does not entail that there is a task which x cannot perform and, consequently, does not entail that x is not omnipotent. That the entailment *seems* to hold is explained by the misleading character of the statement "x cannot create a stone which x cannot lift." The phrase "cannot create a stone" seems to imply that there is a task which x cannot perform and, consequently, seems to imply that x is limited in power. But this illusion vanishes on analysis: "x cannot create a stone which x cannot lift" can only mean "If x can create a stone, then x can lift it." It is obvious that the latter statement does not entail that x is limited in power.

A schematic representation of B(1)–B(3) will bring our point into sharper focus. Let S = stone, C = can create, and L = can lift; let x be any being; and let the universe of discourse be conceivable entities. Then we obtain:

C. (1)   (∃y) (Sy · Cxy · −Lxy) v −(∃y) (Sy · Cxy · −Lxy).
   (2)   (∃y) (Sy · Cxy · −Lxy) ⊃ (∃y) (Sy · −Lxy).
   (3) −(∃y) (Sy · Cxy · −Lxy) ⊃ (∃y) (Sy · −Cxy).

That the second alternative in C(1) is equivalent to "(y) [(Sy · Cxy) ⊃ Lxy]" schematically explains our interpretation "x cannot create a stone which x cannot lift" as meaning "If x can create a stone, then x can lift it." It is now quite clear where the fallacy in the paradoxical argument lies. Although C(2) is logically true, C(3) is not. " ∃y (Sy · Cxy · −LXy)" logically implies "(∃y) (Sy · −Lxy)." But "−(∃y) (Sy · Cxy · −Lxy)" does not logically imply "(∃y) (Sy · −Cxy)"; nor does it logically imply "(∃y) (Sy · −Lxy)." In general, "x cannot create a stone which x cannot lift" does not logically imply "There is a task which x cannot perform."

For some reason the above analysis does not completely remove the inclination to think that an agent's inability to create a stone which he himself cannot lift does entail his inability to perform some task, does entail a limitation on his power. The reason becomes clear when we consider the task of creating a stone which someone *other than* the creator cannot lift. Suppose that y cannot lift any stone heavier than seventy pounds. Now if x cannot create a stone which y cannot lift, then x cannot create a stone heavier than seventy pounds, and is indeed limited in power. But suppose that y is omnipotent and can lift stones of any poundage. Then x's inability to create a stone which y cannot lift does not necessarily constitute a limitation on x's power. For x may be able to create stones of any poundage, although y can lift any stone which x creates. If y can lift stones of any poundage, and x cannot create a stone heavier than seventy pounds, then x cannot create a stone which y cannot lift, and x is limited in power. But if x can create stones of any poundage, and y can lift stones of any poundage, then x cannot create a stone which y cannot lift, and yet x is not thereby limited in power. Now it is easy to see that precisely parallel considerations obtain where x is both stone-creator and stone-lifter.

The logical facts above may be summarized as follows. Whether x = y or x ≠ y, x's inability to create a stone which y cannot lift constitutes a limitation on x's power only if (i) x is unable to create stones of any poundage, or (ii) y is unable to lift stones of any poundage. And since either (i) or (ii) may be false, "x cannot create a stone which y cannot lift" does not entail "x is limited in power." This logical point is obscured, however, by the normal context of our discussions of abilities and inabilities. Since such discussions are normally restricted to beings who are limited in their stone-creating, stone-lifting, and other abilities, the inability of a being to create a stone which he himself or some other being cannot lift *normally* constitutes a limitation on his power. And this produces the illusion that a being's inability to create a stone which he himself or some other being cannot lift *necessarily* constitutes a limitation on his power, the illusion that "x cannot create a stone which y

cannot lift" (where either $x = y$ or $x \neq y$) entails "x is limited in power."
Since our discussions normally concern beings of limited power, the erroneous belief that "x cannot create a stone which x cannot lift" entails "x is limited in power" will normally cause no difficulty. But we must beware when the discussion turns to God—a being who is presumably unlimited in power. God's inability to create a stone which He cannot lift is a limitation on His power only if (i) He is unable to create stones of any poundage, or (ii) He is unable to lift stones of any poundage—that is, only if He is limited in His power of stone-creating or His power of stone-lifting. But until it has been proved otherwise—and it is difficult to see how this could be done—we are free to suppose that God suffers neither of these limitations. On this supposition, God's inability to create a stone which He cannot lift is nothing more or less than a necessary consequence of two facets of His omnipotence.[4] For if God is omnipotent, then He can create stones of any poundage and lift stones of any poundage. And "God can create stones of any poundage, and God can lift stones of any poundage" entails "God cannot create a stone which He cannot lift."

---

[4]Mavrodes apparently sees this point in the last three paragraphs of his article. But his insight is vitiated by his earlier mistaken attempt to solve the paradox.

NELSON PIKE

3.5   Omnipotence and God's Ability to Sin

In the first chapter of the *Epistle of James* (verse 13) it is said that "God cannot be tempted by evil." This idea recurs in the confessional literature of the Christian tradition,[1] and is stated in its fullest form in the theological doctrine of God's *impeccability*.[2] God is not only free from sin, He is incapable of moral deviation. God not only does not sin, He *cannot* sin. This is generally held to be part of what is communicated in the claim that God is perfectly good. On the surface, at least, this doctrine appears to be in conflict with the traditional Christian doctrine of divine omnipotence. An omnipotent being is one that can do all things possible. But, surely, it is possible to sin. Men

---

From the *American Philosophical Quarterly* 6 (1969): 208–16. Reprinted by permission of the author and the editors.
[1]See, for example, the *Westminister Confession*, ch. V, sect IV and the *Longer Catechism of the Eastern Church*, sects. 156–57.
[2]See the *Catholic Encyclopedia* (New York, Robert Appleton Co., 1967).

do this sort of thing all the time. It would thus appear that if God is perfectly good (and thus impeccable), He cannot sin; and if God is omnipotent (and thus can do all things possible), He can sin.

This argument appears to be sophistical. We are tempted to dismiss it with a single comment, viz., it involves an equivocation on the model element in the statement "God can (cannot) sin." In the long run, I think (and shall try to show) that this single remark is correct. But that's in the long run; and in the interim there is a complicated and interesting terrain that has not yet been adequately explored. In this paper I shall discuss this matter in detail. After working through what I judge to be a number of conceptual tangles that have accumulated in this literature on this topic, I shall end by making a suggestion as to how the various senses of "God can (cannot) sin" ought to be sorted out.

I

I shall begin by identifying three assumptions that will work importantly in the discussion to follow.

First, I shall assume that within the discourse of the Christian religion, the term "God" is a descriptive expression having an identifiable meaning. It is not, e.g., a proper name. As part of this first assumption, I shall suppose, further, that "God" is a very special type of descriptive expression—what I shall call a *title*. A title is a term used to mark a certain position or value-status as does, e.g., "Caesar" in the sentence "Hadrian is Caesar." To say that Hadrian is Caesar is to say that Hadrian occupies a certain governmental position; more specifically, it is to say that Hadrian is Emperor of Rome. To affirm of some individual that He is God is to affirm that that individual occupies some special position (e.g., that He is Ruler of the Universe) or that that individual has some special value-status (e.g., that He is a being a greater than which cannot be conceived).

Secondly, I shall assume that whatever the particular semantical import of the term "God" may be (i.e., whether it means, for instance, "Ruler of the Universe," "a being than which no greater can be conceived," etc.), the attribute-terms "perfectly good," "omnipotent," "omniscient," and the like, attach to it in such a way as to make the functions "If x is God, then x is perfectly good," "If x is God, then x is omnipotent," etc., necessary truths. It is a logically necessary condition of bearing the title "God," that an individual be perfectly good, omnipotent, omniscient, and so on for all of the standard attributes traditionally assigned to the Christian God. If we could assume that in order to be Emperor (as opposed to Empress) of Rome one had to be male (rather than female), then if "x is Caesar" means "x is Emperor of Rome," then "If x is Caesar, then x is male" would have the same logical status as I am assuming for "If x is God, then x is perfectly good," "If x is God, then x is omnipotent," etc.

If there is an individual (e.g., Yahweh) who occupies the position or has the value-status marked by the term "God," then that individual is perfectly good, omnipotent, omniscient, etc. If He were not, then He could not (logically) occupy the position or have the value-status in question. However, with respect to the predicate "perfectly good," I shall assume that any individual possessing the attribute named by this phrase might not (logically) have possessed that attribute. This assumption entails that any individual who occupies the position or who has the value-status indicated by the term "God" might not (logically) have held that position or had that status. It should be noticed that this third assumption covers only a *logical* possibility. I am not assuming that there is any real (e.i., material) possibility that Yahweh (if He exists) is not perfectly good. I am assuming only that the hypothetical function "If *x* is *Yahweh*, then *x* is perfectly good" differs from the hypothetical function "If *x* is *God*, then *x* is perfectly good" in that the former, unlike the latter, does not formulate a necessary truth. With Job, one might at least *entertain* the idea that Yahweh is not perfectly good. This is at least a *consistent* conjecture even though to assert such a thing would be to deny a well-established part of the Faith.[3]

I now want to make two further preliminary comments—one about the predicate "omnipotent" and one about the concept of moral responsibility.

Pre-analytically, to say that a given individual is omnipotent is to say that that individual has unlimited power. This is usually expressed in religious discourse with the phrase "infinite power." St. Thomas explicated the intuitive content of this idea as follows: "God is called omnipotent because He can do all things that are possible absolutely.[4] As traditionally understood, St. Thomas' formula must be given a relatively restricted interpretation. The permissive verb "do" in "do all things possible" is usually replaced with one of a range of more specific verbs such as "create," "bring about," "effect," "make-to-be," "produce," etc.[5] God's omnipotence is thus to be thought of as creative-power only. It is not to be understood as the ability to *do* anything at all, e.g., it is not to be interpreted as including the ability to swim the English Channel or ride a bicycle. God is omnipotent in that He can create, bring about, effect, make-to-be, produce, etc., anything possible absolutely. For St. Thomas, something is "possible absolutely" when its description is logically consistent. Thus, on the finished analysis, God is omnipotent insofar as He can bring about any consistently describable object or state of affairs. In his article on "omnipotence" in the *Catholic Encyclopedia*,[6] J. A. McHugh analyzes the notion in this way. It seems clear from the context of

---

[3]The truth of this assumption is argued at some length by C. B. Martin in the fourth chapter of his *Religious Belief* (Ithaca, Cornell Press, 1964).

[4]*Summa Theologica*, Pt. I, Q. 25, a 3. This passage taken from *The Basic Writings of St. Thomas Aquinas*, ed. by Anton Pegis, p. 263.

[5]These verbs are sometimes called "factitive verbs."

[6]New York, Robert Appleton Co., 1911.

this piece that McHugh meant to be reformulating St. Thomas' view of the matter. I might add that I think this restricted interpretation of the pre-analytical notion of infinite power is an accurate portrayal of the way this concept works in the ordinary as well as in most of the technical (theological) discourse of the Christian religion.

Now, let us suppose that an innocent child suffers a slow and torturous death by starvation. Let it be true that this event was avoidable and that no greater good was served by its occurrence. Let it also be true that neither the child (or its parents) committed an offense for which it (or its parents) could be righteously punished. This is a consistently describable state of affairs (whether or not it ever occurred). I think it is clear that an individual that knowingly brought this state of affairs about would be morally reprehensible.

We can now formulate the problem under discussion in this paper more rigorously than above. God is omnipotent. When read hypothetically, this statement formulates a necessary truth. On the analysis of "omnipotent" with which we are working, it follows that God (if He exists) can bring about any consistently describable state of affairs. However, God is perfectly good. Again, when read hypothetically, this statement formulates a necessary truth. Further, an individual would not qualify as perfectly good if he were to act in a morally reprehensible way. Thus, the statement "God acts in a morally reprehensible way" is logically incoherent. This is to say that "God sins" is a logical contradiction.[7] Hence, some consistently describable states of affairs are such that God (being perfectly good) could not bring them about.[8] The problem, then, is this: If God is both omnipotent and perfectly good, there are at least some consistently describable states of affairs that He both can and cannot bring about. There would thus appear to be a logical conflict in the claim that God is both omnipotent and perfectly good.

I think it is worth noting that the problem just exposed is not the same as the classical theological problem of evil. The problem of evil is generally formulated as follows: Evil exists. If God exists and is omnipotent, He could have prevented evil if He had wanted to. If God exists and is perfectly good, He would have wanted to. Since evil in fact exists, it follows that God does not exist. This argument is supposed to point up a conflict between the attribute of perfect goodness and the attribute of omnipotence. But the conflict is not of a rigorous sort. So far as this argument goes, it is logically possible for there to exist a being who is both perfectly good and omnipotent. The argument is supposed to show only that since it is contingently true that evil exists, it is contingently false that omnipotence and perfect goodness are pos-

---

[7] There is probably some distinction to be made between acting in a morally reprehensible way and sinning. However, for purposes of this discussion, I shall treat these concepts as one.

[8] I am here assuming that if God brings about a given circumstance, He does so *knowingly*. God could not bring about a given circumstance by mistake. I think this follows from the idea that God is omniscient.

sessed by a single individual. However, the problem we are now discussing has a sharper report than this. The argument generating this latter is supposed to show that there is a direct logical conflict between the attribute of perfect goodness and the attribute of omnipotence. No contingent premiss is employed (such as, e.g., that evil exists) and the conclusion drawn is that it is logically impossible (not just contingently false) that there exists an individual who is both omnipotent and perfectly good.

II

In reply to objection 2, article 3, question 25, Part I of the *Summa Theologica*, St. Thomas Aquinas writes as follows[9]

> To sin is to fall short of a perfect action; hence to be able to sin is to be able to fall short in action, which is repugnant to omnipotence. Therefore, it is that God cannot sin, because of his omnipotence. Now, it is true that the philosopher says that *God can deliberately do what is evil*. But this must be understood either on condition, the antecedent of which is impossible—as, for instance, if we were to say that God can do evil things if He will. For there is no reason why a conditional proposition should not be true, though both the antecedent and the consequent are impossible; as if one were to say: *If a man is an ass, he has four feet.* Or, he may be understood to mean that God can do some things which now seem to be evil: which, however, if He did them, would then be good. Or he is, perhaps, speaking after the common manner of the pagans, who thought that men became gods, like Jupiter or Mercury.

In this passage St. Thomas offers three suggestions as to how the problem we are discussing might be solved. (I do not count the suggestion made in the last sentence of this passage because it is clear that St. Thomas is not here talking about *God* but about individuals such as Jupiter or Mercury who are mistakenly thought to be God by certain misguided pagans.) Let us look at these three suggestions:

(A) St. Thomas begins with the claim that "to sin is to fall short of a perfect action." He then says that an omnipotent being cannot fall short in action. The conclusion is that God cannot sin because He is omnipotent. Essentially this same reasoning is developed in slightly more detail in the seventh chapter of St. Anselm's *Proslogium*. Anselm says:[10]

> But how art Thou omnipotent, if Thou are not capable of all things? or, if Thou canst not be corrupted and canst not lie . . . how are Thou capable of all things? Or else to be capable of these things is not power but impotence. For he who is capable of these things is capable of what is not for his good, and of what he ought not to do and the more capable of them he is, the more

---

[9]This passage is taken from *The Basic Writings of St. Thomas Aquinas, op. cit.*, p. 264.
[10]This passage is taken from S. N. Deane, *St. Anselm* (LaSalle, Open Court, 1958), p. 14.

power have adversity and perversity against him; and the less has he himself against these.

Anselm concludes that since God is omnipotent, adversity and perversity have no power against Him and He is not capable of anything through impotence. Therefore, since God is omnipotent, He is not capable of performing morally reprehensible actions.

This argument is interesting. Both Thomas and Anselm agree that God is unable to sin. Their effort is to show that instead of being in conflict with the claim that God is omnipotent, the assignment of this inability is a direct consequence of this latter claim. However, I think that the reasoning fails. Let us agree that to the extent that an individual is such that "adversity and perversity" can prevail against him, to that extent is he weak—*morally* weak. He is then capable of "falling short in action," i.e., of doing "what he ought not to do." So far as I can see, an individual that is able to bring about any consistently describable state of affairs might well be morally weak. I can find no conceptual difficulty in the idea of a diabolical omnipotent being. Creative-power and moral strength are readily discernible concepts. If this is right, then it does not follow from the claim that God is omnipotent that He is unable to act in a morally reprehensible way. In fact, as was set out in the original statement of the problem, quite the opposite conclusion seems to be warranted. If a being is able to bring about *any* consistently describable state of affairs, it would seem that he should be able to bring about states of affairs the production of which would be morally reprehensible. St. Thomas' first suggestion thus seems to be ineffective as a solution to the problem we are confronting. (I shall have something more to say on this topic in the fourth section of this paper.)

(B) The Philosopher says that God can deliberately do what is evil. Looking for a way of understanding this remark whereby it can be squared with his own view on the matter, St. Thomas suggests that what Aristotle may have meant is that the individual that is God can do evil *if He wants to*. Thomas adds that this last statement might be true even if it is impossible that God should want to do evil and even if it is also impossible that He can do evil. The point seems to be that although the statements "The individual that is God wants to do evil" and "The individual that is God can do evil" are false (or impossible), the conditional statement containing the first of these statements as the antecedent and the second of these statements as the consequent, might nonetheless be true.

Consider the statement: "Jones has an ace in his hand if he wants to play it." This statement has the surface grammar of a conditional, but it is not a conditional. The item mentioned in the "if . . ." clause does not condition the item described in the rest of the statement. If Jones has an ace in his hand, he has an ace in his hand whether or not he wants to play it. What, then, does the "if . . ." clause do in this statement? I think that it serves as a way of recording a certain indeterminacy as to what will be done about (or, with respect to) the unconditional fact described in the rest of the statement. Whether or not this last remark is precisely right, the major point to be seen here is this: The statement "Jones has an ace in his hand if he wants to play it" is false if the statement "Jones has an ace in his hand" is false. We are here dealing with a use of "if . . ." that does not fit the analysis usually given conditional statements such as "I shall be nourished if I eat."

Now consider the statement: "Jones can wiggle his ear if he wants to." I think that this is another instance in which "if . . ." operates in a nonconditional capacity. If Jones has the ability to wiggle his ear, he has the ability whether or not he wants to wiggle his ear. The question of whether he wants to wiggle his ear is independent of whether he has the ability to do so. As in the case above, what the "if . . ." clause adds in this statement is not a condition on the claim that Jones has an ability. It serves as a way of recording the idea that there is some indeterminacy as to whether the ability that Jones has will be exercised. But again, I am less concerned with whether this last remark about the function of the "if . . ." clause is precisely right than I am with the relation between the truth values of "Jones can wiggle his ear if he wants to" and "Jones can wiggle his ear." In this case, as above, if Jones does not have the ability to wiggle his ear, then the statement "Jones can wiggle his ear if he wants to" is false. If the second of the above statements is false, then the first is false too.

St. Thomas says that the statement "God can sin if He wants to" is true. He adds that both the antecedent and the consequent of this conditional are "impossible." The trouble here, I think, is that "God can sin if He wants to" is not a conditional statement; and the most important point to be seen in this connection is that this statement is false if its component "God can sin" is false. But, St. Thomas clearly holds that "God can sin" is false (or impossible)—he says that God's inability to sin is a consequence of the fact that He is omnipotent. The conclusion must be that "God can sin if He wants to" is also false (or impossible). Thomas has not provided a way of understanding The Philosopher's claim that God can deliberately do what is evil. As long as St. Thomas insists that God does not have the ability to sin (which, he says, follows from the claim that God is omnipotent) he must deny that God can sin if He wants to. He must then reject The Philosopher's claim that God can deliberately do what is evil if this latter means that God can sin if He wants to.

(C) Still looking for a way of understanding the idea that God can deliberately do what is evil, St. Thomas' next suggestion is that God can do things which seem evil to us but which are such that if God did them, they would not be evil. I think that there are at least two ways of understanding this comment.

First, Thomas may be suggesting that God has the ability to bring about states of affairs that are, in fact, good, but which seem evil to us due to our limited knowledge, sympathy, moral insight, etc. However, even if we were to agree that this is true, Thomas could draw no conclusion as regards the starving-child situation described earlier. We have specified this situation in such a way that it not only *seems* evil to us, but *is* evil in fact. We have included in our description of this case that the child suffers intensely; that this suffering is not deserved and that it might have been avoided. We have added that the suffering does not contribute to a greater good. Thus, this line of reasoning does not really help with the major problem we are discussing in this paper. We still have a range of consistently describable states of affairs that God (being perfectly good) cannot bring about. We thus still have reason to think that God (being perfectly good) is not omnipotent.

Secondly, St. Thomas may be suggesting that God has the ability to bring about *any* consistently describable states of affairs (including the starving-child situation), but that if *He* were to bring about such a situation, it would no longer count as evil. Let "evil" cover any situation which is such that if one were to (knowingly) bring it about (though it is avoidable), that individual would be morally reprehensible. The view we are now considering requires that we append a special theory about the meanings of the *other* value-terms involved in our discussion. In particular, it requires that when applied to God, the expressions "not morally reprehensible" and "perfectly good" be assigned meanings other than the ones they have when used to characterize individuals other than God. If a man were knowingly to bring about the starving-child situation, he would be morally reprehensible. He could no longer be described as perfectly good. But (so the argument goes) if God were to bring about the same situation, He might still count as perfectly good (not morally reprehensible) in the special senses of "not morally reprehensible" and "perfectly good" that apply *only* to God.

I have two comments to make about this second way of understanding St. Thomas' claim that God can do things that seem evil to us but which are such that if He did them, they would not be evil.

First, in my opinion the view we are now entertaining about the theological use of "perfectly good" and "not morally reprehensible" is one that was decisively criticized by Duns Scotus, Bishop Berkeley, and John Stuart Mill.[11] If God were to bring about circumstances such as the starving-child situation, He would be morally reprehensible and thus not perfectly good in the ordinary senses of these phrases. If we now contrive some special phrases (retaining the tabletures "not morally reprehensible" and "perfectly good") that might apply to God though He produces the situation in question, this will be of no special interest. Whatever *else* can be said of God, if He were to bring about the starving-child situation, He would not be an appropriate object of

---

[11]See Scotus' *Oxford Commentary on the Sentences of Peter Lombard*, Q.II ("Man's Natural Knowledge of God"), second statement, argument IV; Berkeley's *Alcephron*, Dialogue IV, sects. 16–22 (especially sect. 17); and J. S. Mill's *An Examination of Sir William Hamilton's Philosophy*, ch. 6. What follows in this paragraph is what I think constitutes the center of these three discussions.

the *praise* we ordinarily convey with the phrase "perfectly good." He would be an appropriate object of the *blame* we ordinarily convey with the phrase "morally reprehensible." We might put this point as follows: If we deny that God is perfectly good in the ordinary sense of "perfectly good," and if we cover this move by introducing a technical, well-removed, sense of "perfectly good" that can apply to God though He brings about circumstances such as the starving-child situation, it may appear that we have solved the problem under discussion in this paper, but we haven't. We have eliminated conflict by agreeing that God lacks one of the "perfections," i.e., one of the qualities the possession of which makes an individual better (more praiseworthy) than he would otherwise be. Unless a being is perfectly good in the *ordinary* sense of "perfectly good," that being is not as praiseworthy as he might otherwise be. It was the sense of "perfectly good" that connects with the idea of being morally praiseworthy (in the ordinary sense) that gave rise to the problem in the first place. Surely, it is this sense of "perfectly good" that religious people have in mind when they characterize God as perfectly good.

The second remark I should like to make about this second interpretation of St. Thomas' third suggestion is that the view assigned to St. Thomas in this interpretation is one that he would most likely reject. I shall need a moment to develop this point.[12]

Consider the word "triangle" as it occurs in the discourse of geometry. Compare it with "triangle" as it is used in the discourse of carpentry or woodworking. Within the discourse of geometry, the criteria governing the use of this term are more strict than are the criteria governing its use in the discourse of carpentry. The geometrical figure is an exemplary (i.e., perfect) version of the shape embodied in the triangular block of wood. We reach an understanding of the geometrical shape by correcting imperfections (i.e., irregularities) in the shape of the triangular block. Now, let's ask whether "triangle" has the same meaning in the two cases. We might answer this question in either way. Once the relation between the criteria governing its use in the two cases is made clear, no one would be confused if we were to say that "triangle" has the same meaning in the two cases, and no one would be confused if we were to say that "triangle" has different meaning in the two cases. Regarding the relation between the criteria, the following point seems to me to be of considerable importance: If a block of wood is triangular, it has three angles that add up (roughly) to 180 degrees and its sides are (roughly) straight. *At least this much* is implied with respect to a geometrical figure when one characterizes it as a triangle. By this I mean that if one could find reasons sufficient for rejecting the claim that a given thing is a

---

[12]The next two paragraphs are taken almost without change from the Introduction to my book *God and Timelessness* (London, Routledge and Kegan-Paul, 1969). What I say here about the relation between "triangle" as used in the discourse of geometry and "triangle" as used in the discourse of carpentry is very much like a thesis developed by John Stuart Mill in the text mentioned above.

triangle as "triangle" is used in the discourse of carpentry (suppose that one of its sides is visibly curved or suppose it has four angles), these same reasons would be sufficient for rejecting the claim that the thing in question is a triangle as "triangle" is used in the discourse of geometry. In fact, more than this can be said. If one could find slight irregularities in the shape of a thing that would cause some hesitation or prompt some reservation about whether it is a triangle as "triangle" is used in the discourse of carpentry, such irregularities would be sufficient to establish that the thing in question is not a triangle as "triangle" is used in the discourse of geometry.

According to St. Thomas, finite things are caused by God. They thus bear a "likeness" to God. God's attributes are exemplary-versions of the attributes possessed by finite things. We reach whatever understanding we have of God's attributes, by removing "imperfections" that attend these qualities when possessed by finite things.[13] With respect to the predicate "good," St. Thomas writes as follows in the *Summa Theologica* (Pt. I, Q. 6, A. 4):[14]

> Each being is called good because of the divine goodness, the first exemplar principle as well as the efficient and telic cause of all goodness. Yet it is nonetheless the case that each being is called good because of a likeness of the divine goodness by which it is denominated.

Again, in *questiones disputatae de veritate* (XXI, 4), St. Thomas says:

> Every agent is found to produce effects which resemble it. Hence, if the first goodness is the efficient cause of all things, it must imprint its likeness upon things which it produces. Thus each thing is called good because of an intrinsic goodness impressed upon it, and yet is further denominated good because of the first goodness which is the exemplar and efficient cause of all created goodness.

Shall we say that "good" has the same meaning when applied to God as it has when applied to things other than God (e.g. Socrates)? As above, it seems to me that the answer we give to this question is unimportant once we get this far into the discussion. We might say that "good" has the same meaning

---

[13]In the *Summa Theologica* (Pt. I, Q. 14, a.1) St. Thomas says: "Because perfections flowing from God to creatures exist in a higher state in God Himself, whenever a name taken from any created perfection is attributed to God, there must be separated from its signification anything that belongs to the imperfect mode proper to creatures." (Quoted from *The Basic Writings of St. Thomas Aquinas, op. cit.*, p. 136.)

[14]Both of the following passages were translated by George P. Klubertanz, S. J., *Thomas Aquinas on Analogy* (Chicago, Loyola Press, 1960), p. 55. For a good analysis of St. Thomas' views on the topic of theological predication, see the whole of Klubertanz' discussion in ch. III. For an enlightening discussion of how poorly St. Thomas has been understood on this topic (even by his most illustrious interpreters) see Klubertanz' remarks in ch. I and Berkeley's discussion of St. Thomas in *Alcephron*, IV, sects. 20–22. According to Berkeley, St. Thomas' doctrine of "analogy by proportionality" is to be regarded as an expression of the view we are now discussing.

in the two cases, and we might say that it has different meanings in the two cases. We might even say (as St. Thomas sometimes says) that we are here dealing with a case in which "good" is "midway between" having the same meaning and having different meanings in the two cases. However, as above, the following point has importance regardless of how one answers the question about same or different meanings. When St. Thomas affirms that God is good, I think he means to be saying *at least as much* about God as one would say about, e.g., Socrates, if one were to affirm that Socrates is good. A study of "good" in nontheological contexts reveals at least the minimum implications of the corresponding predication statements relating to God. If we could find reasons sufficient for rejecting the claim that a given thing is good as "good" is used in discourse about finite agents, these same reasons would be sufficient for rejecting the claim that the thing in question is good as "good" is used in discourse about the nature of God. In fact, if we could find moral irregularities sufficient to cause hesitations or prompt reservations about whether a thing is good as "good" is used in discourse about finite agents, these irregularities would be sufficient to establish that the agent under consideration is not good as "good" is used in the discourse of theology.

So far as I can see, St. Thomas would not endorse a technical, well-removed sense of the phrase "perfectly good" that could apply to God even if God were to bring about circumstances or states of affairs the production of which would be morally reprehensible (in the ordinary sense of "morally reprehensible"). When St. Thomas says that God is good, he means to be saying that God possesses the exemplary version of the quality assigned to Socrates in the sentence "Socrates is good." This is to say that while Socrates is good, God is *perfectly* good. But on this understanding of the matter, God could not be perfectly good were He to bring about the starving-child situation described earlier. If Socrates were to bring about such a situation, we would probably refuse to describe him as "good." At the very least, we would surely have hesitations or reservations concerning his moral goodness. But if such an action would be sufficient to cause hesitations concerning an application of "good" in discourse about finite agents, this same action would be sufficient to *defeat* an application of "good" in discourse about the nature of God. In this latter context, "good" means "*perfectly* good." The logic of this phrase will not tolerate even a minor moral irregularity.

III

I want now to discuss an approach to our problem that is very different from any of those suggested by St. Thomas. It is an approach taken by J. A. McHugh in the *Encyclopedia* article mentioned above. I think we can best get at the center of McHugh's thinking if we start with a review of that side of the problem generated by the concept of perfect goodness.

God is perfectly good. This is a necessary statement. If a being is perfectly good, that being does not bring about objects or states of affairs the production of which would be morally reprehensible. This, too, is a necessary truth. Thus, the statement "God brings about objects or states of affairs the production of which would be morally reprehensible" is logically contradictory. It follows that God cannot bring about such states of affairs. But, McHugh argues, this should not be taken as a reason for denying God's omnipotence. As St. Thomas has pointed out, a being may be omnipotent and yet not be able to do an act whose description is logically contradictory. (A being may be omnipotent though he is not able to make a round-square.) Since the claim that God acts in a morally reprehensible way is logically contradictory, God's inability to perform such acts does not constitute a limitation of power.

Consider the following argument: The term "Gid" is the title held by the most efficient of those who make only leather sandals. "Gid makes leather belts" is thus a logical contradiction. It follows that the individual that is Gid cannot make leather belts. But Gid may still be omnipotent. Though He does not have the ability to make leather belts, our analysis of "omnipotence" requires only that an omnipotent being be able to do an act whose description is logically consistent and "Gid makes leather belts" is logically inconsistent. Thus, Gid's inability to make leather belts does not constitute a limitation on his power.

I think it is plain that this last argument is deficient since its conclusion is absurd. I think, too, that in this case, two difficulties are forced pretty close to the surface.

First, the description of the kind of object that Gid is (allegedly) unable to make (viz., leather belts) is not logically contradictory. What is contradictory is the claim that *Gid makes them.* But our definition of "omnipotent" requires only that the *state of affairs* brought about be consistently describable (excluding, therefore, round squares). It does not require that a statement in which it is claimed that a given individual brings it about be consistent. Thus, if Gid does not have the ability to produce leather belts, he is not omnipotent on St. Thomas' definition of "omnipotent." If it follows from the definition of "Gid" that the individual who bears this title cannot make leather belts; and if this entails that the individual in question does not have the creative-ability to make belts, the conclusion must be that, by definition, the individual who bears this title is a limited being. I think the same kind of conclusion must be drawn in the case of God's ability to sin. If it follows from the definition of "God" that the individual bearing this title cannot bring about objects or states of affairs the production of which would be morally reprehensible; and if it follows from this that the individual bearing this title does not have the creative power necessary to bring about such states of affairs though they are consistently desirable; the conclusion is that the individual who is God is not omnipotent on the analysis of "omnipotent" that we are supposing. The fact (if it is a fact) that this creative limitation is built into the definition of "God" making "God sins" a logical contradiction does not disturb this conclusion. The upshot is, simply, that the term "God" has been so specified that an individual qualifying for this title could not be omnipotent. (Of course, this is awkward because it is also a condition of bearing this title that the individual in question be omnipotent.)

The second difficulty in the argument about Gid is this: The term "Gid" has been defined in such a way that "Gid makes leather belts" is logically contradictory. The conclusion drawn is that Gid *cannot* make belts. What this means is that if some individual makes leather belts, this is logically sufficient to assure that the individual in question does not bear the title "Gid." But it does not follow from this (as is supposed in the argument) that the individual who is Gid does not have the *ability* to make leather belts. All we can conclude is that if he does have this ability, it is one that he does not *exercise*. Thus, as is affirmed in the argument, the individual who is Gid might be omnipotent though he cannot make leather belts (and be Gid). If we suppose that he is omnipotent, we must conclude that he has the ability to make belts; but since, by hypothesis, the individual in question is Gid, we know (analytically) that he does not exercise this ability. Again, I think the same is true with respect to the argument about God's inability to sin. The term "God" has been so specified that the individual who is God *cannot* sin and be God. But it will not follow from this that the individual who is God does not have the *ability* to sin. He might have the creative power necessary to bring about states of affairs the production of which would be morally reprehensible. He is perfectly good (and thus God) insofar as He does not exercise this power.

IV

If we collect together a number of threads developed in the preceding discussions, I think we shall have enough to provide at least a tentative solution to the problem we have been discussing. I shall proceed by distinguishing three ways in which the statement "God cannot sin" might be understood.

"God cannot sin" might mean: "If a given individual sins, it follows logically that the individual does not bear the title 'God'." In this case, the "cannot" in "cannot sin" expresses logical impossibility. The sentence as a whole might be rewritten as follows: $N(x)$ (If x is God then x does not sin.) On the assumptions we are making in this paper, this statement is true. We have supposed that the meaning of the title term "God" is such that it is a logically necessary condition of bearing this title that one be perfectly good and thus that one not perform actions that are morally reprehensible.

Secondly, "God cannot sin" might mean that if a given individual is God, that individual does not have the ability to sin, i.e., He does not have the creative power necessary to bring about states of affairs the production of which would be morally reprehensible, such as, e.g., the starving-child situation described earlier. In this case, the "cannot" in "cannot sin" does not express logical impossibility. It expresses a material concept—that of a limita-tion of creative-power (as in, e.g., "I cannot make leather sandals"). On St. Thomas' analysis of "omnipotence" if the individual who is God (Yahweh) cannot sin in this sense, He is not omnipotent. Further, I think there is strong reason to suspect that if the individual that is God (Yahweh) cannot sin in this sense, He is not perfectly good either. Insofar as the phrase "perfectly good" applies to the individual that is God (Yahweh) as an expression of praise—warranted by the fact that this individual does not sin—God could not be perfectly good if He does not have the ability to sin. If an individual does not have the creative-power necessary to bring about evil states of affairs, he cannot be praised (morally) for failing to bring them about. Insofar as I do not have the physical strength necessary to crush my next door neighbor with my bare hands, it is not to my credit (morally) that I do not perform this heinous act.

Thirdly, "God cannot sin" might mean that although the individual that is God (Yahweh) has the ability (i.e., the creative power necessary) to bring about states of affairs the production of which would be morally reprehensible, His nature or character is such as to provide material assurance that He will not act in this way. This is the sense in which one might say that Jones, hav-ing been reared to regard animals as sensitive and precious friends, just *cannot* be cruel to animals. Here "cannot" is not to be analyzed in terms of the notion of logical impossibility and it does not mark a limitation on Jones's physical power he may be physically able to kick the kitten). It is used to express the idea that Jones is *strongly disposed* to be kind to animals or at least to avoid actions that would be cruel. We have a special locution in Eng-lish that covers this idea. When we say that Jones cannot be cruel to animals, what we mean is that Jones cannot *bring himself* to be cruel to animals. On this third analysis of "God cannot sin," the claim conveyed in this form of words is that the individual that is God (Yahweh) is of such character that he cannot bring himself to act in a morally reprehensible way. God is strongly disposed to perform only morally acceptable actions.

Look back for a moment over the ground we have covered.

McHugh noticed that the statement "God sins" is logically incoherent. He thus (rightly) concluded that God cannot sin. He was here affirming that the semantical import of the title term "God" is such that an individual could not (logically) bear this title and be a sinner. McHugh's conclusion ("God cannot sin") was thus intended in the first sense just mentioned. But McHugh then went on to suppose that God cannot sin in a sense of this phrase that connects with the notion of omnipotence. This is the second sense mentioned above. This conclusion was not warranted. The individual who bears the title "God" (Yahweh) might have the creative power necessary to bring about objects or states of affairs the production of which would be morally repre-hensible even though "God sins" is logically contradictory. The conclusion is, simply, that if an individual bears the title "God," He does not exercise this creative-power.

St. Thomas and St. Anselm said that God cannot sin in that "adversity and perversity cannot prevail against Him." This appears to be the claim put forward in the *Epistle of James* 1:13—the claim embodied in the theological doctrine of God's impeccability—viz., "God cannot be tempted by evil." The individual that is God has a very special kind of strength—moral strength, or strength of character. He is, as we say, "above temptation." Both Thomas and Anselm concluded that God's inability to sin has a direct connection with the notion of omnipotence. It is because God is omnipotent that He is unable to sin. This line of reasoning confuses the second and third senses of the statement "God cannot sin." If we say that the individual who is God cannot sin in this second sense (i.e., in the sense that connects with the idea of creative power and thus with the standard notion of omnipotence) this is not to assign that individual strength. It is to assign Him a very definite limitation. The strength-concept in this cluster of ideas is the notion of not being able to *bring oneself* to sin. God has a special strength of character. But this latter concept is expressed in the third sense of "God cannot sin." As I argued earlier, this third sense appears to have no logical connection with the idea of having or lacking the creative power to bring about consistently describable states of affairs. It thus appears to have no logical connection to the notion of omnipotence as this latter concept is explicated by St. Thomas.

The individual that is God cannot sin and bear the title "God." The individual that is God cannot sin in that sinning would be contrary to a firm and stable feature of His nature. These claims are compatible with the idea that the individual that is God has the ability (i.e., the creative power necessary) to bring about states of affairs the production of which would be morally reprehensible. All we need add is that there is complete assurance that He will not exercise this ability and that if He did exercise this ability (which is logically possible but materially excluded), He would not bear the title "God." Further, if God is to be omnipotent in St. Thomas' sense of "omnipotent," and if God is to be perfectly good in a sense of this phrase that expresses praise for the fact that He refrains from sinful actions, this appears to be the conclusion that *must* be drawn.

ST. THOMAS AQUINAS

3.6   Knowledge and Change

We proceed thus to the Fifteenth Article:—
Objection 1. It seems that the knowledge of God is variable. For knowledge is related to what is knowable. But whatever imports relation to the creature is applied to God from time, and varies according to the variation of creatures. Therefore, the knowledge of God is variable according to the variation of creatures.

Obj. 2. Further, whatever God can make He can know. But God can make more things than He does. Therefore, He can know more than He knows. Thus, His knowledge can vary according to increase and diminution.

Obj. 3. Further, God knew that Christ would be born. But He does not know now that Christ will be born, because Christ is not to be born in the future. Therefore God does not know everything He once knew; and thus the knowledge of God is variable.

On the contrary, It is said, that in God *there is no change nor shadow of alteration* (*Jas.* i. 17).

I answer that, Since the knowledge of God is His substance, as is clear from the foregoing, just as His substance is altogether immutable, as was shown above, so His knowledge likewise must be altogether invariable.

Reply Obj. 1. Lord, Creator, and the like, import relations to creatures in so far as they are in themselves. But the knowledge of God imports relation to creatures in so far as they are in God; because everything is actually understood according as it is in the one who understands. Now created things are in God in an invariable manner; while they exist variably in themselves.—Or we may say that *Lord, Creator,* and the like, import the relations consequent upon the acts which are understood as terminating in the creatures themselves as they are in themselves; and thus these relations are attributed to God variously, according to the variation of creatures. But *knowledge* and *love,* and the like, import relations consequent upon the acts which are understood to be in God; and therefore these are predicated of God in an invariable manner.

Reply Obj. 2. God knows also what He can make, and does not make.

From *Summa Theologica,* Part I, trans. Dominican Fathers of English Province (New York: Benziger, Inc., 1947). Reprinted by permission of the publisher.

Hence from the fact that He can make more than He makes, it does not follow that He can know more than He knows, unless this be referred to the *knowledge of vision*, according to which He is said to know those things which actually exist in some period of time. But from the fact that He knows that some things can be which are not, or that some things can not-be which are, it does not follow that His knowledge is variable, but rather that He knows the variability of things. If, however, anything existed which God did not previously know, and afterwards knew, then His knowledge would be variable. But this is impossible, for whatever is, or can be in any period of time, is known by God in His eternity. Therefore, from the fact that a thing is said to exist in some period of time, we must say that it is known by God from all eternity. Therefore, it cannot be granted that God can know more than He knows; because such a proposition implies that first of all He did not know, and then afterwards knew.

Reply Obj. 3. The ancient Nominalists said that it was the same thing to say *Christ is born* and *will be born*, and *was born;* because the same thing is signified by these three—viz., the nativity of Christ. Therefore it follows, they said, that whatever God knew, He knows; because now He knows that Christ is born, which means the same thing as that Christ will be born. This opinion, however, is false both because the diversity in the parts of a sentence causes a diversity in enunciations, and because it would follow that a proposition which is true once would always be true; which is contrary to what the Philosopher lays down when he says that this sentence, *Socrates sits*, is true when he is sitting, and false when he stands up. Therefore, it must be conceded that this proposition, *Whatever God knew He knows*, is not true if referred to what is enunciated. But because of this, it does not follow that the knowledge of God is variable. For as it is without variation in the divine knowledge that God knows one and the same thing sometime to be, and sometime not, so it is without variation in the divine knowldge that God knows that an enunciation is sometime true, and sometime false. The knowledge of God, however, would be variable if He knew enunciations according to their own limitations, by comparison and division, as occurs in our intellect. Hence our knowledge varies either as regards truth and falsity, for example, if when a thing is changed we retained the same opinion about it; or as regards diverse opinions, as if we first thought that someone was sitting, and afterwards thought that he was not sitting; neither of which can be in God.

NORMAN KRETZMANN

3.7   *Omniscience and Immutability*

It is generally recognized that omniscience and immutability are necessary characteristics of an absolutely perfect being. The fact that they are also incompatible characteristics seems to have gone unnoticed. .

In the main body of this paper I will present first an argument that turns on the incompatability of omniscience and immutability and, secondly, several objections to that argument with my replies to the objections.

(1)   A perfect being is not subject to change.[1]

(2)   A perfect being knows everything.[2]

(3)   A being that knows everything always knows what time it is.[3]

(4)   A being that always knows what time it is is subject to change.[4]

From *The Journal of Philosophy* 63 (1966). Reprinted by permission of the author and the editors.

[1]This principle of immutability is regularly supported by one of two arguments. (I) *From Supreme Excellence:* A perfect being is a supremely excellent being; thus any change in such a being would constitute corruption, deterioration, loss of perfection. (See Plato, *Republic*, II, 381B.) (II) *From Complete Actualization:* A perfect being is a being whose capacities for development are all fully realized. A being subject to change, however, is in that respect and to that extent a being with an unrealized capacity for development, a being merely potential and not fully actualized, a being in a state of process and not complete; hence not perfect. (See Aristotle, *Metaphysics*, XII, 9 1074b26.) The principle of immutability is a thesis of orthodox Christian theology, drawn from Greek philosophy and having among its credentials such biblical passages as Malachi 3.6 and James 1.17. (See Aquinas, *Summa theologica*, I, Q. 9, art. 1.)

[2]Being incapable of knowing all there is to know or being capable of knowing all there is to know and knowing less than that are conditions evidently incompatible with absolute perfection. Hence (2), which seems even more familiar and less problematic than (1).

[3]Part of what is meant by premise (3) is, of course, that a being that knows everything always knows what time it is in every time zone on every planet in every galaxy; but it is not quite in that horological sense that its knowledge of what time it is is most plainly relevant to considerations of omniscience and immutability. The relevant sense can be brought out more easily in the consideration of objections against the argument.

[4]Adopting 'it is now t_n' as a convenient standard form for propositions as to what time it is, we may say of a being that always knows what time it is that the state of its knowledge changes incessantly with respect to propositions of the form 'it is now t_n'. First such a being knows that it is now t_1 (and that it is not now t_2), and then it knows that it is now t_2 (and that it is not now t_1). To say of any being that it knows something different from what it used to know is to say that it has changed; hence (4).

∴ (5) A perfect being is subject to change.

∴ (6) A perfect being is not a perfect being.

Finally, therefore,

(7) There is no perfect being.[5]

In discussing this argument with others[6] I have come across various objections against one or another of its premises. Considering such objections here helps to clarify the line taken in the argument and provides an opportunity to anticipate and turn aside natural criticisms of that line.

Because premises (1) and (2) present the widely accepted principles of immutability and omniscience, objections against them are not so much criticisms of the line taken in the argument as they are attempts to modify the concept of a perfect being in the light of the argument. And since premise (3) gives every impression of being an instance of a logical truth, premise (4) is apparently the one most vulnerable to attacks that are genuinely attacks on the argument. The first four of the following seven objections are all directed against premise (4), although Objection D raises a question relevant to premise (3) as well.

Objection A: It must be granted that a being that always knows what time it is knows something that is changing—say, the state of the universe. But change in the object of knowledge does not entail change in the knower.

The denial that a change in the object necessitates a change in the knower depends on imprecise characterizations of the object. For example, I know that the Chrysler Building in Manhattan is 1,046 feet tall. If it is said that the Chrysler Building is the object of my knowledge, then of course many changes in it—in its tenants or in its heating system, for example—do not necessitate changes in the state of my knowledge. If, however, it is more precisely

---

[5] [1f] (x) $(Px \supset \sim Cx)$; [2f] (x) $(Px \supset (p)$ $(p \equiv Kxp))$ [K: . . . knows that . . .]; [3f] (x) $((p)$ $(p \equiv Kxp) \supset (p)$ $(Tp \supset (p \equiv Kxp)))$ [T: . . . is of the form 'it is now t_n'] [4f] (x) $((p)$ $(Tp \supset (p \equiv Kxp)) \supset Cx]$; [5f] (x) $(Px \supset Cx)$ [entailed by 2f, 3f, 4f]; [6f] (x) $(Px \supset \sim Px)$ [entailed by 1f, 5f]; [7f] (x) $\sim Px$ [equivalent to 6f]. The formalization [3f] is an instance of a logical truth; nevertheless, premise (3) is not one of the established principles in philosophical or theological discussions of the nature of a perfect being. Not only is it not explicitly affirmed, but it seems often to be implicitly denied. This circumstance may arouse a suspicion that the formalization [3f] is inaccurate or question-begging. Any such suspicion will, I think, be dissipated in the course of considering the objections to the argument, but it may be helpful in the meantime to point out that the validity of the argument does not depend on this formalization. It is of course possible to adopt less detailed formalizations that would not disclose the special logical status of premise (3) and would nevertheless exhibit the validity of the argument. For example, [2f'] (x) $(Px \supset Ox)$; [3f'] (x) $(Ox \supset Nx)$ together with a similarly imprecise formalization of premise (4) would serve that purpose.

[6] I am indebted especially to Miss Marilyn McCord and to Professors H. N. Castañeda, H. G. Frankfurt, C. Ginet, G. B. Matthews, G. Nakhnikian, W. L. Rowe, S. Shoemaker, and W. Wainwright.

said that the object of my knowledge is the *height* of the Chrysler Building, then of course a change in the object of my knowledge does necessitate a change in me. If a 40-foot television antenna is extended from the present tip of the tower, either I will cease to know the height of the Chrysler Building or I will give up believing that its height is 1,046 feet and begin believing that its height is 1,086 feet. In the case of always knowing what time it is, if we are to speak of an object of knowledge at all it must be characterized not as the state of the universe (which might also be said to be the object of, for example, a cosmologist's knowledge), but as the *changing* of that state. To know the changing of anything is to know first that *p* and then that not-*p* (for some particular instance of *p*), and a knower that knows first one proposition and then another is a knower that changes.

Objection B: The beliefs of a being that always knows what time it is are subject to change, but a change in a being's beliefs need not constitute a change in the being itself. If last year Jones believed the platonic epistles to be genuine and this year he believes them to be spurious, then Jones has changed his mind; and that sort of change in beliefs may be considered a change in Jones. But if last year Jones believed that it was 1965 and this year he believes that it is 1966, he has not changed his mind, he has merely taken account of a calendar change; and that sort of change in beliefs should not be considered a change in Jones. The change in beliefs entailed by always knowing what time it is is that taking-account sort of change rather than a change of mind, the sort of change in beliefs that might reasonably be said to have been at least in part initiated by the believer and that might therefore be reasonably attributed to him.

It seems clear, first of all, that the sort of change in beliefs entailed by knowing the changing of anything is the taking-account sort of change rather than a change of mind. But once that much has been allowed, Objection B seems to consist in no more than an expression of disappointment in the *magnitude* of the change necessitated by always knowing what time it is. The entailed change in beliefs is not, it is true, sufficiently radical to qualify as a change of character or of attitude, but it is no less incompatible with immutability for all that. If Jones had been immutable from December 1965 through January 1966 he could no more have taken account of the calendar change than he could have changed his mind.

It may be worth noting that just such small-scale, taking-account changes in beliefs have sometimes been recognized by adherents of the principle of immutability as incompatible with immutability. Ockham, for example, argues at length against the possibility of a change in the state of God's foreknowledge just because God's changelessness could not be preserved through such a change. In Question Five of his *Tractatus de praedestinatione et de praescientia Dei et de futuris contingentibus* Ockham maintains that "if 'God knows that *A*' (where *A* is a future contingent proposition) and 'God does not know that *A'* could be true successively, it *would* follow that God was changeable," and the principle on which Ockham bases that claim is in no way restricted to future contingents. (As an adherent of the principle of immutability Ockham of course proceeds to deny that God could first know that *A* and then not know that *A*, but his reasons for doing so involve considerations peculiar to future contingent propositions and need not concern us here.)[7]

Objection C: For an omniscient being always to know what time it is is to know the state of the universe at every instant, but it is possible for an omniscient being to know the state of the universe at every instant all at once rather than successively. Consequently it is possible for an omniscient being always to know what time it is without being subject to change.

The superficial flaw in this objection is the ambiguity of the phrase 'to know the state of the universe at every instant', but the ambiguity is likely to be overlooked because the phrase is evidently an allusion to a familiar, widely accepted account of omniscience, according to which omniscience regarding contingent events is nothing more nor less than knowledge of the entire scheme of contingent events from beginning to end at once. I see no reason for quarreling here with the ascription of such knowledge to an omniscient being; but the underlying flaw in Objection C is the drastic *incompleteness* of this account of omniscience regarding contingent events.

The kind of knowledge ascribed to an omniscient being in this account is sometimes characterized as "seeing all time at a glance," which suggests that if one sees the entire scheme of contingent events from beginning to end at once one sees all there is to see of time. The totality of contingent events, we are to suppose, may be known either simultaneously or successively, and an omniscient being will of course know it not successively but simultaneously. In his *Summa contra gentiles* (Book I, Ch. 55, sects. [6]–[9]) Aquinas presents a concise version of what seems to be the standard exposition of this claim.

> . . . the intellect of one considering *successively* many things cannot have only one operation. For since operations differ according to their objects, the operation by which the first is considered must be different from the operation by which the second is considered. But the divine intellect has only one operation, namely, the divine essence, as we have proved. Therefore God con-

---

[7]The most interesting historical example of this sort that I have seen was called to my attention by Professor Hugh Chandler after I had submitted this paper for publication. It is Problem XIII in the *Tahdfut al-Faldsifah* of al-Ghazali (d. ea. 1111): "REFUTATION OF THEIR [i.e., the philosophers', but principally Avicenna's] DOCTRINE THAT GOD (MAY HE BE EXALTED ABOVE WHAT THEY SAY) DOES NOT KNOW THE PARTICULARS WHICH ARE DIVISIBLE IN ACCORDANCE WITH THE DIVISION OF TIME INTO 'WILL BE', 'WAS', AND 'IS' " (tr. S. A. Kamali; Lahore, Pakistan Philosophical Congress, 1963; pp. 153–162). This work was not known to medieval Christian philosophers. [See Etienne Gilson, *History of Christian Philosophy in the Middle Ages* (New York: Random House, 1955), p. 216.]

siders all that he knows not successively, but *together*. Moreover, succession cannot be understood without time nor time without motion . . . But there can be no motion in God, as may be inferred from what we have said. There is, therefore, no succession in the divine consideration . . . Every intellect, further-more, that understands one thing after another is at one time *potentially* understanding and at another time *actually* understanding. For while it under-stands the first thing actually it understands the second thing potentially. But the divine intellect is never potentially but always actually understanding. Therefore it does not understand things successively but rather understands them together.

On this view an omniscient being's knowledge of contingent events is the knowledge that event *e* occurs at time *t* (for every true instance of that form). Thus an omniscient being knows that my birth occurs at t_n, that my writing these words occurs at t_{n+x}, that my death occurs at t_{n+x+y}. This omniscient be-ing also knows what events occur simultaneously with each of those events— knows, for example, that while I am writing these words my desk calendar lies open at the page bearing the date "Friday, March 4, 1966," and the watch on my wrist shows 10:15. Moreover, since an omniscient being by any ac-count knows all necessary truths, including the truths of arithmetic, this omni-scient being knows how much time lapses between my birth and my writing these words and between these words and my death. But I *am* writing these words just *now*, and on this view of omniscience an omniscient being is in-capable of knowing that that is what I am now doing, and for all this omnis-cient being knows I might just as well be dead or as yet unborn. That is what knowing everything amounts to if knowing "everything" does not in-clude always knowing what time it is. Alternatively, that is what knowing the state of the universe at every instant comes to if that phrase is interpreted in the way required by the claim that it is possible to have that sort of knowl-edge all at once.

According to this familiar account of omniscience, the knowledge an omnis-cient being has of the entire scheme of contingent events is in many relevant respects exactly like the knowledge you might have of a movie you had writ-ten, directed, produced, starred in, and seen a thousand times. You would know its every scene in flawless detail, and you would have the length of each scene and the sequence of scenes perfectly in mind. You would know, too, that a clock pictured in the first scene shows the time to be 3:45, and that a clock pictured in the fourth scene shows 4:30, and so on. Suppose, however, that your movie is being shown in a distant theater today. You know the movie immeasurably better than do the people in the theater who are now seeing it for the first time, but they know one big thing about it you don't know, namely, what is now going on on the screen.

Thus the familiar account of omniscience regarding contingent events is drastically incomplete, An omniscient being must know not only the entire scheme of contingent events from beginning to end at once, but also *at what stage of realization that scheme now is.* It is in this sense of knowing what time it is that it is essential to claim in premise (3) that a being that knows everything always knows what time it is, and it is in this sense that always knowing what time it is entails incessant change in the knower, as is claimed in premise (4).

In orthodox Christianity the prevalence of the incomplete accounts of omniscience regarding contingent events effectively obscures the incompatilibity of omniscience and immutability. Aquinas, for example, is not content with proving merely that "it is impossible for God to change in any way." He goes on in the *Summa theologica* (Book I. Q. 14, art. 15) to argue that "since God's knowledge is his substance, as is clear from the foregoing, just as his substance is altogether immutable, as was shown above, so *his knowledge likewise must be altogether invariable.*" What Aquinas, Ockham, and others *have* recognized is that God's knowledge cannot be variable if God is to remain immutable. What has *not* been seen is that God's knowledge cannot be altogether invariable if it is to be perfect, if it is to be genuine omniscience.

Objection D: A perfect being transcends space and time. Such a being is therefore not subject to change, whether as a consequence of knowing what time it is or for any other reason.

The importance of this objection lies in its introduction of the pervasive, mysterious doctrine of the transcendence of space and time, a doctrine often cited by orthodox Christians as if it were both consistent with their theology and explanatory of the notion that God sees all time at a glance. It seems to me to be neither.

In *Proslogium* Chapters XIX and XX Anselm apostrophizes the being transcendent of space and time as follows:

> Thou wast not, then, yesterday, nor wilt thou be tomorrow; but yesterday and today and tomorrow thou art; or, rather, neither yesterday nor today nor tomorrow thou art, but simply *thou art, outside all time.* For yesterday and today and tomorrow have no existence except in time, but thou, although nothing exists without thee, nevertheless dost not exist in space or time, but all things exist in thee. For nothing contains thee, but thou containest all.

For present purposes the spatial aspect of this doctrine may be ignored. What is meant by the claim that an entity transcends time? The number 2 might, I suppose, be said to transcend time in the sense that it does not age, that it is no older now than it was a hundred years ago. I see no reason to quarrel with the doctrine that a perfect being transcends time in *that* sense, since under that interpretation the doctrine is no more than a gloss on the principle of immutability. But under that interpretation the doctrine begs the question of premise (4) rather than providing a basis for objecting to it.

Only one other interpretation of the doctrine of the transcendence of time suggests itself, and that is that from a God's-eye point of view there is no time, that the passage of time is a universal human illusion. (Whatever else may be said of this interpretation, it surely cannot be considered compatible with such essential theses of Christian doctrine as the Incarnation and the the Resurrection.) Under this interpretation the doctrine of the transcendence of time does have a devastating effect on the argument, since it implies either that there are no true propositions of the form 'it is now t_n' or that there is exactly one (eternally) true proposition of that form. Thus under this interpretation premise (3) either is vacuous or has a single trivializing instance, and premise (4) is false. But this interpretation preserves the immutability of a perfect being by imposing immutability on everything else, and that is surely an inconceivably high price to pay, in the view of Christians and non-Christians alike.

The remaining three objections are directed against premises (1) or (2) and may, therefore, be considered not so much criticisms of the argument as attempts to revise the principle of immutability or the principle of omniscience in the light of the argument. Objections E and F have to do with premise (2), Objection G with premise (1).

Objection E: Since a perfect being transcends time it is logically impossible that a perfect being know what time it is and hence logically impossible that such a being know everything. But it is no limitation on a perfect being that it cannot do what is logically impossible. Therefore, its not knowing absolutely everything (in virtue of not knowing what time it is) does not impair its perfection.

Objections E and F are attempts to hedge on omniscience as philosophers and theologians have long since learned to hedge on omnipotence. In Objection E this attempt depends on directly invoking one of the standard limitations on omnipotence, but the attempt does not succeed. Perhaps the easiest way of pointing up its failure is to produce analogous inferences of the same form, such as this: since I am a human being and a human being is a mortal rational animal, it is logically impossible that I should live forever: therefore it is no limitation on me that I must die—or this: since I am a creature of limited power, it is logically impossible that I be capable of doing whatever is logically possible; therefore it is no limitation on me that I cannot do whatever is logically possible. What is wrong with all these inferences is that the crucial limitation is introduced in the initial description of the being in question, after which it does of course make sense to deny that mere consequences of the limiting description are to be introduced as if they constituted additional limitations. It is not an *additional* limitation on a legless man that he cannot walk, or on a mortal being that it must die, or on a creature of limited power that it cannot do whatever it might choose to do. No more is it an *additional* limitation on a being that is *incapable* of knowing what time it is that it *does not* know what time it is. But any claim to perfection that might have been made on behalf of such a being has already been vitiated in the admission that its transcendence of time renders it incapable of omniscience.

Objection F: Just as in explicating the concept of omnipotence we have been forced to abandon the naive formula 'a perfect being can do anything' and replace it with 'a perfect being can do anything the doing of which does not impair its perfection', so the argument suggests that the naive formula 'a perfect being knows everything' must be revised to read 'a perfect being knows everything the knowing of which does not impair its perfection'. Thus, since the argument does show that knowing what time it is impairs the perfection of the knower, it cannot be a part of the newly explicated omniscience to know what time it is.

Even if Objection F could be sustained, this particular grasping of the nettle would surely impress many as just too painful to bear, for in deciding whether or not to try to evade the conclusion of the argument in this way it is important to remember that in the context of the argument 'knowing what time it is' means knowing *what is going on*. Objection F at best thus provides an exceptionally costly defense of absolute perfection, emptying it of much of its content in order to preserve it; for under the newly explicated notion of omniscience Objection F commits one to the view that it is impossible for a *perfect, omniscient* being to know what is going on.

Objection F attempts to draw an analogy between an explication of omnipotence and a proposed explication of omniscience, borrowing strength from the fact that in the case of omnipotence such an explication has long been recognized as a necessary condition of the coherence of the notion. In evaluating this attempt it is helpful to note that here are at least three types of provisos that may be inserted into formulas of omnipotence for that purpose. The first is relevant to omnipotence generally, the second specifically to eternal omnipotence, and the third specifically to eternal omnipotence as one perfect characteristic of a being possessed of certain other perfect characteristics. (For present purposes it is convenient to say simply that the third is relevant specifically to eternal omnipotence as one aspect of an absolutely perfect being.) These three types of provisos may be exemplified in the following three formulas of omnipotence.

I. A being that is omnipotent (regardless of its other characteristics) can do anything provided that (a) the description of what is to be done does not involve a logical inconsistency.

II. A being that is eternally omnipotent (regardless of its other characteristics) can do anything provided that (a) . . . and (b) the doing of it does not constitute or produce a limitation on its power.

III. A being that is absolutely perfect (hence eternally omnipotent) can do anything provided that (a) . . . and (b) . . . and (c) the doing of it does not constitute a violation of some aspects of its perfection other than its power.

Provisos of type (c) only are at issue in Objection F, no doubt because provisos of types (a) and (b) have no effective role to play in the explication of omniscience. No being knows anything that *is not* the case; *a fortiori* no omniscient being knows anything that *cannot be* the case. So much for type (a). As for type (b), since certain things the description of which involves no logical inconsistency would if done incapacitate the doer—committing suicide, for example, or creating another omnipotent being—there is good reason for such a proviso in the explication of eternal omnipotence. It might likewise be claimed that an omniscient being knows everything except things that would if known limit the being's *capacity for knowledge,* the formal justification for this claim being just the same as that for the corresponding omnipotence-claim. The significant difference between these two claims is that the omniscience-claim is evidently vacuous. There is no reason to suspect that there *are* things that would if known limit the knower's capacity for knowledge. More directly to the point at issue in the argument, there is no reason whatever to think that knowing what is going on is a kind of knowing that limits the knower's capacity for knowledge. Thus although a type (b) proviso is needed in the explication of eternal omnipotence in order to preserve the coherence of the notion of eternal omnipotence, no such proviso need be inserted into the formula of omniscience in order to preserve the coherence of that notion.

The putative analogy in Objection F presupposes that a proviso of type (c) will preserve omniscience as it preserves omnipotence in such a (Cartesian) argument as the following. It is impossible for an absolutely perfect being to lie, for although such a being, as omnipotent, has the power to lie, the exercise of that power would violate the perfect goodness of the being. To say that it is impossible for an absolutely perfect being to lie is not to say that it lacks the power to lie but rather that its absolute perfection in another aspect—perfect goodness—necessitates its refraining from the exercise of that power. Whether or not this line of argument succeeds in doing what it is designed to do, it seems clear that there is no genuine analogue for it in the case of omniscience. Consider the following candidate. It is impossible for an absolutely perfect being to know what is going on, for although such a being, as omniscient, has the power to know what is going on, the exercise of that power would violate the immutability of the being. To say that it is impossible for an absolutely perfect being to know what is going on is not to say that it lacks the power to know what is going on but rather that its absolute perfection in another aspect—immutability—necessitates its refraining from the exercise of that power. A being that has the power to do something that it refrains from doing may not thereby even jeopardize its omnipotence. All the same, a being that has the power to know something that it refrains from knowing does thereby forfeit its omniscience. Omniscience is not the *power to know* everything; it is the *condition of knowing* everything, and that condition cannot be preserved through even a single instance of omitting to exercise the power to know everything.

Therefore, whatever strength Objection F seems to derive from its appeal to the putative analogy between omnipotence and omniscience in this respect is illusory, and this attempted evasion of the argument's conclusion reduces to an arbitrary decision to sacrifice omniscience to immutability.

Objection G: The traditional view of philosophers and theologians that absolute perfection entails absolute immutability is mistaken, founded on the misconception that in a perfect being any change would have to be for the worse. In particular the kind of change entailed by always knowing what time it is is a kind of change that surely cannot be construed as deterioration, even when it is ascribed to an absolutely perfect being. No doubt an absolutely perfect being must be immutable in most and perhaps in all other respects, but the argument shows that absolute perfection *entails* mutability in at least this one respect.

Objection G proceeds on the assumption that immutability is ascribed to a perfect being for only one reason—namely, that all change in such a being must constitute deterioration. There is, however, a second reason, as has been indicated at several points in the discussion so far—namely, that any change in a "perfect" being must indicate that the being was in some respect not in the requisite state of completion, actualization, fixity. The aspect of absolute completion is no less essential an ingredient in the concept of absolute perfection than is the aspect of absolute excellence. Moreover, those such as Aquinas and Ockham who argue against the mutability of a perfect being's *knowledge* would surely agree that the change they are intent on ruling out would not constitute *deterioration*, since they regularly base their arguments on the inadmissibility of *process* in an absolutely perfect being.

An absolutely perfect being may be described as a being possessing all logically compossible perfections. Thus if the argument has shown that omniscience and immutability were logically incompossible, it would have called for no more than an adjustment in the concept of absolute perfection, an adjustment of the sort proposed in Objection G. The proposition 'things change' is, however, not necessarily but only contingently true. If as a matter of fact nothing else ever did change, an omniscient being could of course remain immutable. In Objection G, however, an absolutely perfect being has been confused with a being possessing all really compossible perfections, the best of all *really* possible beings. Perhaps, as the objection implies, the most *nearly* absolutely perfect being in the circumstances that happen to prevail *would* be mutable in the respect necessitated by always knowing what time it is. But that is of no consequence to the argument, which may be taken as showing that the prevailing circumstances do not admit of the existence of an absolutely perfect being.

This concluding section of the paper is in the nature of an appendix. It might be subtitled "Omniscience and Theism"; for it may be shown that the doctrine that God knows everything is incompatible also with theism, the doctrine of a personal God distinct from other persons.[8]

Consider these two statements:

S_1. Jones knows that he is in a hospital.

S_2. Jones knows that Jones is in a hospital.

S_1 and S_2 are logically independent. It may be that Jones is an amnesia case. He knows perfectly well that he is in a hospital, and after reading the morning papers he knows that Jones is in a hospital. An omniscient being surely must know all that Jones knows. Anyone can know what S_2 describes Jones as knowing, but no one other than Jones can know what S_1 describes Jones as knowing. (A case in point: Anyone could have proved that Descartes existed, but that is not what Descartes proved in the Cogito, and what he proved in the Cogito could not have been proved by anyone else.) The kind of knowledge S_1 ascribes to Jones is, moreover, the kind of knowledge characteristic of every self-conscious entity, of every person. Every person knows certain propositions that no *other* person *can* know. Therefore, if God is omniscient, theism is false; and if theism is true, God is not omniscient.

It may fairly be said of God, as it once was said of William Whewell, that "omniscience [is] his foible."

---

[8]The following argument was suggested to me by certain observations made by Professor Hector Castañeda in a paper entitled "He," presented at the Wayne State University philosophy colloquium in the fall of 1964.

HECTOR-NERI CASTAÑEDA

3.8   Omniscience and Indexical Reference*

In a very intriguing and exciting paper† Norman Kretzmann has argued for the thesis (A) that God's omniscience is incompatible with his immutability, and, in an appendix suggested by certain results of mine,[1] for the thesis (B) that omniscience is incompatible with theism, i.e., the doctrine that God is a person distinct from others. Kretzmann's arguments depend on certain features of indexical reference, i.e., reference to times, places, events, objects, or persons by means of demonstrative or personal pronouns or adverbs. The argument for (A) relies essentially on the fact that a person's indexical references to time, e.g., by means of the word 'now', are ephemeral: at different times of utterance 'now' refers to different times. The argument for (B) depends essentially on the fact that a person's indexical references to himself, e.g., by means of the first-person pronoun 'I', are intransferable: nobody can refer to another man by means of a genuine first-person reference. Thus, Kretzmann's arguments and conclusions suggest parallel arguments and conclusions for the other types of indexical reference. For example, I can imagine, in the spirit of Kretzmann's arguments, a reasoning intended to show that an omniscient being cannot exist at any place in space, and, hence, cannot be ubiquitous, as a Christian tradition conceives God to be, for an omniscient being knows the truth of every proposition expressible with the sentence 'I am here, but not there', regardless of who it is who says 'I'.

But Kretzmann's essay has an even more important value: through the two special cases, it raises the general question: How can a person whether omniscient or not, believe, know, consider, or, in general, apprehend and formulate for himself and by himself a proposition or statement (I will use these terms as having the same referent) that contains an indexical reference by another person? Kretzmann's arguments for (A) and (B) simply assume that the answer to this general question is: "In no way at all." This is the assump-

From *The Journal of Philosophy* 64 (1967): 203–10. Reprinted by permission of the author and the editors.

*This paper was written while the author was doing research on quasi-indicators under the National Science Foundation Grant No. GS-828.

†"Omniscience and Immutability," pp. 366–76 this volume—ED.

[1] In " 'He': A Study in the Logic of Self-consciousness," *Ratio*, VIII, 1 (February 1967); this article will be cited as *He*. See also my "On the Logic of Self-Knowledge," *Nous* I, 1 (March 1967).

tion behind his claim that "Every person knows certain propositions that no *other* person *can* know" (his italics). But it seems to me that there is a perfectly accessible way of, so to speak, capturing another person's indexical references intact, so that one can formulate another person's indexical statements qua indexical. This way consists in the use of what I have elsewhere called "quasi-indicators."[2]

Here I want: (i) to show how Kretzmann's arguments for (A) and (B) depend essentially on the assumption that a person's indexical statements cannot be known or formulated by another, (ii) to show the impact of quasi-indexical references on those arguments, and (iii) to explore the effect of indexical and quasi-indexical reference on omniscience.

I. KRETZMANN'S ARGUMENT AND QUASI-INDICATORS

Kretzmann's argument for (A) has the following relevant premise:

(4) A being that always knows what time it is is subject to change.
He supports (4) both by an argument and by replies to four objections to (4). His argument is worthy of careful examination; it is:

> Adopting 'it is now t_n' as a convenient standard form for propositions as to what time it is, we may say of a being that always knows what time it is that the state of its knowledge changes incessantly with respect to propositions of the form 'it is now t_n'. First such a being knows that it is now t_1 (and that it is not now t_2), and then it knows that it is now t_2 (and that it is not t_1). To say of a being that it knows something different from what it used to know is to say that it has changed; hence (4).

Kretzmann does not assign any special meaning to the word 'now'. Presumably his argument can be understood on the assumption that this word is used by him in its ordinary sense. Letting 'X' be the name of the being he is talking about, Kretzmann's crucial premise is:

(4a) First X knows that it is now t_1 and not t_2, and then X knows that it is now t_2 and not t_1.
(From now on I will use expressions like '(4a)' to refer either to the indented sentence they precede or to a given ordinary statement the sentence in question is supposed to express. The context should make clear which is meant. Double quotes around a sentence will name a statement made with it; single quotes will name the sentence.) From (4a) Kretzmann infers that X knows at t_2 something different from what he knew at t_1. The inference is persuasive, and its examination most instructive.

In ordinary usage an indicator like 'now' or 'I' or 'here' is used, even in *oratio obliqua* [as in (4a) above], to make indexical references by the speaker.

---

[2]In "Indicators and Quasi-indicators," *The American Philosophical Quarterly*, IV, 2 (April 1967). See also *He*.

Thus, in ordinary usage the occurrences of 'now' in (4a) formulate Kretzmann's own indexical references to times t_1 and t_2, respectively. But since the two occurrences of 'now' refer to two different times, the proposition or statement formulated by the occurrence of the clause 'it is now t_1' in sentence (4a) is different from, but not incompatible with, the statement formulated by the occurrence of the clause 'it is not now t_1' in (4a); and similarly for the statements expressed by 'it is not now t_2' and 'it is now t_2'. Hence, according to (4a), X knew at t_1 two propositions about time, and at t_2 he knew two other compatible propositions about time. Thus, if he knew all four propositions at t_1, X may very well have known at t_2 exactly the same propositions he knew at t_1, and Kretzmann would err in inferring from statements (4a) that X's knowledge, and *a fortiori* X himself, changed from t_1 to t_2. We must then investigate whether or not X can know at t_1 the proposition that Kretzmann expressed by his use of the clause 'it is now t_2' occurring in (4a). Indeed, can Kretzmann himself know at t_1 the very same proposition he expressed at t_2 by using 'it is now t_2' as part of (4a)? The rub lies here in the indexical reference of 'now'. Obviously, if the indexical reference of Kretzmann's statement at t_2 "it is now t_2" cannot be captured intact at time t_1, then at t_1 this statement cannot even be formulated, let alone be known by X or by Kretzmann himself. Hence, if this is the case, it would seem that Kretzmann is after all justified in deriving (4) from (4a). (I will not stop here to consider the very relevant view that X at any time, as well as Kretzmann at t_1, can apprehend and know the latter's indexical statement at t_2, without being able to formulate it.)

There is, however, a serious but subtle difficulty with Kretzmann's argument. As the preceding analysis shows, the argument relies heavily on the fact that the clause 'it is now t_2' in (4a) expresses an indexical proposition. But it is Kretzmann's own indexical proposition, since *indicators in oratio obliqua express indexical references by the speaker, and leave it open whether the person spoken about refers to the same objects indexically or not.*[3] Thus, when I say "Privatus believes that I (you, this) weigh (weighs) 150 pounds," I do not imply that Privatus has made an indexical reference to me (you, or this). Indeed, my sentences of the form 'Privatus believes that I . . .' have a certain misleadingness, since Privatus cannot refer to me in the first person! More strikingly, when Gaskon says "Yesterday Privatus thought (guessed, predicted, etc.) that it would be raining now (today)," Gaskon's statement both contains his own indexical uses of 'now' ('today') and fails to imply that Privatus referred indexically to the time at which Gaskon makes his statement. Likewise, Kretzmann's statement (4a) above both formulates Kretzmann's *own* indexical references to t_1 and t_2, and does *not* imply that X referred to t_1 or t_2 indexically. Thus my reason above for saying that it would

---

[3]For some problems about indicators in *oratio obliqua,* see "Indicators and Quasi-indicators," sec. 4.

seem that Kretzmann is after all justified in deriving (4) from (4a) is really irrelevant: for (4a) does not preclude the possibility that the four propositions that X is said to know may be nonindexical, i.e., contain no indexical references at all, so that he may know all four of them at t_1. We must, then, reformulate Kretzmann's argument without the word 'now'.

Furthermore, Kretzmann means to be making a general point that has nothing to do with him or his indexical references. His point is both that, to know what time it is at a given time, a person has to make some indexical references of *his own* that will put him into the stream of changes in the world, and that, thus, that person cannot be immutable. Hence, the very effectiveness of Kretzmann's argument requires that we be able to reformulate it without mentioning or alluding to Kretzmann's own indexical references, i.e., without using the word 'now'. We must, then, ask whether or not we can formulate a premise about another person's knowing a proposition that contains indexical references by that person. And the answer lies ready at hand. The crucial premise Kretzmann's argument needs can be formulated adequately and in full generality as follows:

(4b) At t_1 X knows [tenselessly] that it is [tenselessly] *then* t_1, but not t_2, and at t_2, later than t_1, X knows that it is *then* t_2, but not t_1.

The crucial difference between (4b) and (4a) is, phonetically, very simple: the word 'then' instead of the word 'now'. But semantically the difference is enormous: (a) 'now' does, while 'then' does not, express an indexical reference by the speaker; (b) 'then' does, while 'now' does not, attribute to X an indexical reference to time t_1 in the first and to time t_2 in the second conjunct; (c) whereas sentence (4a) cannot be used by Kretzmann or anybody else to make exactly the same statement at times other than t_1 and t_2, sentence (4b) can be used repeatedly at any time by anybody to make exactly the same statement on each occasion of its utterance. Thus, 'then' as used in (4b) is not an indicator: it is, in my terminology, a *quasi-indicator*. Among its syntacticosemantical characteristics are: (i) its appearing in *oratio obliqua,* i.e., in a clause subordinated to a verb expressing a propositional attitude; (ii) its having an antecedent not in the same oratio obliqua, which in (4b) is 't_1' for the first occurrence of 'then' and 't_2' for the second occurrence; (iii) its not being replaceable by its antecedent with preservation of the proposition or statement formulated with the whole sentence; in our example, sentence (4b) clearly formulates a different statement from that formulated by

(4c) At t_1 X knew that it was t_1 at t_1, but not t_2, and at t_2 he knew that it was t_2 at t_2, but not t_1.

The statement expressed by (4c) is true if X knows that t_1 is different from t_2, even if at t_1 or at t_2 he does not know what time it is then.

Again, according to (4b), X knows four propositions or statements to be true. Again, the issue is whether or not X can know all four statements to be true. Again, the issue is whether or not X can know all four statements to be true at t_1 as well as at t_2. If X can, then Kretzmann's argument for his premise (4) is invalid. Interestingly enough, the problem is now *not* that of reformulating a statement containing indexical references, but the different problem of reformulating a statement containing quasi-indexical references. And by characteristic (c) above, a statement containing quasi-indexical references is repeatable by different persons at different times by means of the very same sentence. Thus, there seems in principle to be no difficulty about finding a formulation of the quasi-indexical statement contained in (4b) and expressed by 'it was then t_2' so that at t_1 X could know it or have any other propositional attitude toward it. We need, however, an important, but perfectly trivial principle, to wit:

(P) If a sentence of the form 'X knows that a person Y knows that . . .' formulates a true statement, then the person X knows the statement formulated by the clause filling the blank '. . .'.

This principle must be carefully understood: it establishes a sort of transitivity of knowledge, but it does *not* say anything about detaching expressions of the form 'Y knows that'. Undoubtedly, in most cases such detachment is legitimate. For instance, "Jones knows that Smith knows that $2 + 5 = 7$" does entail "Jones knows that $2 + 5 = 7$." But if the very last subordinate clause of a sentence of the form "X knows that Y knows that — — —" contains quasi-indicators, such detachment may lead to absurdity or to a fallacy. For instance "Mary knows that George knows that he (himself) is in pain" does not entail (since there is no such proposition as) "Mary knows that he (himself) is in pain."[4] Yet, the former entails that Mary and George know the very same proposition about George's being in pain. For perspicuity I will write 'then$_A$' to represent an occurrence of the quasi-indicator 'then' having the expression A as antecedent.

Thus, (4b) is compatible with

(4d) Time t_2 is later than t_1, and at t_1 X knows both (1) that it is then$_{t1}$ t_1, but not t_2, and (2) that somebody knows (or would know) at t_2 that it is (would be) then$_{t2}$ t_2 but not t_1.

By (P), (4d) entails that at t_1 X knew not only the two propositions that according to (4b) he knew at t_1, but also the other two propositions that by

---

[4]For a discussion of the irreducibility of the quasi-indicator 'he (himself)' see *He*, sec. 2; see "Indicators and Quasi-indicators," for a total defense of the irreducibility of quasi-indexical reference.

(4b) he knew at t_2. Hence, it does not follow from (4b) and (4d), or from (4b) alone, that at t_2 X underwent a change in knowledge. Therefore, Kretzmann's argument for his premise (4) is really invalid.

II. KNOWLEDGE OF CHANGE

Kretzmann defends his thesis (4), that a being that always knows what time it is is subject to change, by replying to four objections. Both the objections and his replies raise very interesting issues, which I will simply not consider here, except for the first objection. An anonymous discussant objects to (4) by saying: A change in the object of knowledge does not entail a change in the knower. Kretzmann argues that sometimes a change in the object of knowledge requires a change of knowledge. He illustrates as follows:

> ... if the object of my knowledge is the *height* of the Chrysler Building, then of course a change in the object of my knowledge does necessitate a change in me. If a 40-foot television antenna is extended from the present tip of the tower, either I will cease to know the [present] height of the Chrysler Building or I will give up believing that its height is 1,046 feet and begin believing that it is 1,086 feet.

Again, the argument is based on indexical references, this time on those made by means of the present tense. And again, the question the argument raises is whether or not a person can know at time t_1 (prior to the extension of the antenna) a proposition that he would express at t_2 (after the extension) by uttering a sentence containing an indicator, e.g., "Now the Chrysler Building is 1,086 feet tall." Once again, the answer is "yes," and a way of finding one formulation of that proposition is the method illustrated above, in which we employed principle (P). Thus, suppose that

(5) Kretzmann knows at t_1 that: the Chrysler Building is 1,046 feet high at t_1, and at t_3 it will have a 40-foot antenna extended from its tip, and that the man who makes the extension knows at t_2 that the Chrysler Building is 1,086 feet high then.

Clearly, if (5) obtains, Kretzmann knows of the change in height without having to change his knowledge. Of course, at t_2 Kretzmann can use the words 'now' and 'present' to refer to the height of the Chrysler Building, words that were not available to him at t_1. But this is an entirely different issue.

III. SELF-KNOWLEDGE

Kretzmann argues that omniscience and theism are incompatible on the ground that there are certain propositions that only one person can know. His example is

(7) Jones knows that he (himself) is in the hospital.

Clearly, (7) is a statement quite different from "Jones knows that Jones is in the hospital." The statement that Jones knows by (7) is one that Jones would express by saying "I am in the hospital." That is, (7) attributes to Jones a first-person indexical reference. In short, the expression 'he (himself)' in sentence (7) is a quasi-indicator. It cannot be eliminated from (7) by any name or description of Jones that includes no first-person quasi-indicator. It is this fact that leads Kretzmann to say that the statement expressed by the occurrence of 'he (himself) is in the hospital' in (7) cannot be known by any other person. But this does not follow. If Kretzmann, or the reader, knows that Jones knows that he (himself) is in the hospital, then, by principle (P) above, Kretzmann or the reader knows the very same proposition that by (7) Jones knows to be true. Hence, theism is not, by the present route, incompatible with omniscience.

At this juncture one can, of course, raise the problem of other minds. If there is a sense of 'know' in which one cannot know facts of the form "*X*, different from me, knows that —— —," then there is a sense in which one cannot know another person's *oratio recta* indexical statements, *whether they are about himself or not, and whether they are about physical or psychological matters.* But this is another, though related, issue, which undoubtedly takes a different shape for the case of an omniscient God.

IV. OMNISCIENCE AND OMNIPOTENCE

The preceding discussion makes it clear, I hope, that neither theism nor immutability is incompatible with God on account of indexical references' being personal, intransferable, and ephemeral. We have indicated, via principle (P), a method for capturing indexical references intact, that is, for apprehending another person's indexical statements qua indexical statements, even though these are ephemeral and intransferable. Other methods can be devised by using other principles of epistemic logic. But all such methods are conceived on the principle that an indexical statement for one person cannot be the very same statement, indexical or otherwise, for another person. This principle has some theological consequences, although not so revolutionary as those which Kretzmann derived from the principle that a person's indexical statement cannot be known by another person. I think it is clear that from the preceding discussion it follows that:

First, the existence of an omniscient being is impossible, or an omniscient being does not know every proposition in *oratio recta:* indexical propositions he must know in *oratio obliqua,* in the form of quasi-indexical propositions.

Second, the existence of an omniscient and immutable being is impossible, or an omniscient immutable being knows the contents of other minds on grounds other than behavior and circumstances: for in order to know of changes in behavior or circumstances he must think of them, quasi-indexically, as known by other persons.

Third, an omniscient being cannot be omnipotent, or omnipotence does not include the ability to derive whatever proposition P a finite person X knows from the proposition "X" knows that — — —," where the blanks are occupied by a sentence S expressing P and nothing but P: if P is an indexical proposition, S will have quasi-indicators that cannot be used in *oratio recta*.[5]

Fourth, an omniscient being who is also immutable cannot be omnipotent, or omnipotence does not include the ability to formulate indexical propositions.

---

[5]For a detailed discussion of this type of inference, see *He*, sec. 4, and "Indicators and Quasi-indicators," sec. 5.

WILLIAM L. ROWE

3.9   *Augustine on Foreknowledge and Free Will*

The problem with which this paper is concerned is raised in the following passage in Book III of St. Augustine's treatise *On Free Will:*

> ii, 4. (Evodius) . . . I have a deep desire to know how it can be that God knows all things beforehand and that, nevertheless, we do not sin by necessity. . . . Since God knew that man would sin, that which God foreknew must necessarily come to pass. How then is the will free when there is apparently this unavoidable necessity?
> iii. 6 (Augustine) Your trouble is this. You wonder how it can be that these two propositions are not contradictory and incompatible, namely that God has foreknowledge of all future events, and that we sin voluntarily and not by necessity. For if, you say, God foreknew that a man will sin, he must necessarily sin. But if there is necessity there is no voluntary choice in sinning, but rather fixed and unavoidable necessity. You are afraid that by that reasoning the conclusion may be reached either that God's foreknowledge of all future events must be impiously denied, or, if that cannot be denied, that sin is committed not voluntarily but by necessity. Isn't that your difficulty? (Evodius) Exactly that.[1]

The problem, as Augustine sees it, is to show how it is possible both that we voluntarily (freely) will to perform certain actions and that God foreknows

---

From the *Review of Metaphysics* 18 (1964): 356–63. Reprinted by permission of the author and the editor.
[1]*On Free Will*, trans. by John H. S. Burleigh, in *Augustine: Earlier Writings*, The Library of Christian Classics, Vol. VI (Philadelphia, 1953), pp. 172–73.

that we shall will to perform these actions. The argument which gives rise to this problem may be expressed as follows:

(1)   God has foreknowledge of all future events.
(2)   Hence, if a man is going to sin, God foreknows that he will sin.
(3)   Whatever God foreknows must necessarily happen.
(4)   Hence, if God foreknows that a man will sin, he must necessarily sin.
(5)   But if such a man must necessarily sin, there is no voluntary choice in his sinning.
(6)   Therefore, such a man does not have free will.

I shall begin by examining Augustine's solution to this problem.

Augustine, if I understand him correctly, proposes to solve the problem by denying premiss (5). That is, he denies that if a man must necessarily sin, there is no voluntary choice in his sinning. Suppose that a man is going to sin and, hence, is going to will or choose to sin.[2] Given that God foreknows that a man is going to will to sin, it appears to follow from premiss (3) that it is necessary that the man is going to will or choose to sin. But if a man must necessarily will or choose to sin, how can we claim that he, nevertheless, voluntarily or freely wills to sin? It is this question that Augustine sets himself to answer.

Augustine's answer to the question just raised is that even though a man *necessarily* wills to sin he, nevertheless, freely wills to sin. The reason this is so is that the will is something that is always in our power, and whatever is in our power is *free*. The important passages in which he explains and argues this point are the following:

> But if he (a denier of free will) . . . says that, because he must necessarily so will, his will is not in his own power, he can be countered by the answer you gave me when I asked whether you could become happy against your will. You replied that you would be happy now if the matter were in your power; for you willed to be happy but could not achieve it . . . we cannot say we do not have the power unless we do not have what we will. If we do not have the will, we may think we will but in fact we do not. If we cannot will without willing those who will have will, and all that is in our power we have by willing. Our will would not be will unless it were in our power. Because it is in our power, it is free. We have nothing that is free which is not in our power, and if we have something it cannot be nothing. Hence it is not necessary to deny that God has foreknowledge of all things, while at the same time our wills are our own. God has foreknowledge of our will, so that of which he has foreknowledge must come to pass. In other words, we shall exercise our wills in the future because he has foreknowledge that we shall do so; and there can be no will or voluntary action unless it be in our power.[3]

---

[2] On Augustine's theory the essential elements in every sinful act is "a movement of the will away from unchangeable good to mutable good." (*Ibid.* (III. 1. 1), p. 170.)

[3] *Ibid.*, (III. 3. 8), pp. 175–76.

... there is nothing so much in our power as is the will itself. For as soon as we will (*volumus*) immediately will (*voluntas*) is there. We can say rightly that we do not grow old voluntarily but necessarily, or that we do not die voluntarily but from necessity, and so with other similar things. But who but a raving fool would say that it is not voluntarily that we will? Therefore though God knows how we are going to will in the future, it is not proved that we do not voluntarily will anything. [4]

For if that is to be called *our necessity* which is not in our power, but even though we be unwilling effects what it can effect—as, for instance, the necessity of death—it is manifest that our wills by which we live uprightly or wickedly are not under such a necessity; for we do many things which, if we were not willing, we should certainly not do. This is primarily true of the act of willing itself—for if we will, it *is*; if we will not, it *is* not—for we should not will if we were unwilling. But if we define necessity to be that according to which we say that it is necessary that anything be of such a nature, or be done in such and such a manner, I know not why we should have any dread of that necessity taking away the freedom of our will. [5]

Augustine's proposed solution, I believe, proceeds as follows. Granted that a man necessarily wills to sin, it does not follow that his will is not in his power, that he does not freely will to sin. To see that this is so we must first see what it means to say of something that it is not in a man's power. Augustine's view is that to say that x is not in a man's power is to say (roughly) that the presence or absence of x is not a result of the man's will. That is, x is not in a man's power if and only if either (1) x fails to occur even though the man wills to do x—for example, running a mile in four minutes is not in my power because the feat fails to be accomplished even though I will to accomplish it—or (2) x occurs even though the man does not will to do x—for example, my growing old is not in my power because it occurs even though I do not will it to occur. Thus where x is something that occurs, the question whether x is in our power reduces to the question whether x would occur even though we do not will it. This much granted, Augustine argues as follows. Even though a man necessarily wills to sin, we cannot say that this sinful act of will is not in the man's power. For clearly the act of will would not occur if the man did not will. To say that the man's willing to sin is not in his power is to say that the man wills to sin even though he does not will to sin—and this is impossible. Thus Augustine seems to hold that it is a necessary truth that the will is in our power and, therefore, free. As he puts it, "Our will would not be will unless it were in our power. Because it is in our power it is free." The fact that a man necessarily wills to sin does not conflict with his freely willing to sin because his willing to sin (although necessary) is still in his power—for it would not occur were he not to will to sin. In this way Augustine is led to reject premiss (5) in the argument under

---

[4]*Ibid.*, (III. 3. 7), pp. 174–75.

[5]Augustine, *The City of God*, Bk. V. Ch. X, trans. by J. J. Smith, in *Basic Writings of St. Augustine*, Vol. II (New York, 1948), p. 68.

consideration. That is, he rejects the claim that if a man must necessarily sin, there is no voluntary choice in his sinning.

There is, I believe, a mistake in Augustine's reasoning in support of the claim that even though a sinful act of will is necessary it is, nevertheless, in one's power. His analysis of "*x* is not in our power" is, in part, "*x* occurs even though we do not will *x*." Thus *my growing old* is not in my power because I grow old even though I do not will to grow old. He argues, as we saw, that to say *my willing to sin* is not in my power is to say that I will to sin even though I do not will to sin—which, of course, is impossible. But surely there is a mistake here. If the case of my willing to sin is to parallel the case of my growing old then to say that my willing to sin is not in my power is *not* to say that I will to sin even though I do not will to will to sin; rather, it is to say that I will to sin even though I do not will to sin. The point I am making can be expressed just as well by taking as an example an act of will that does not occur—say, the act of willing to refrain from sinning. This act of will which does not occur corresponds to my act of running a mile in four minutes, which does not occur either. Now on Augustine's analysis of "*x* is not in our power" it follows that *x* is not in my power if I fail to do *x* even though I will to do *x*. Thus it follows that running a mile in four minutes is not in my power if I fail to run such a mile even though I will to run a mile in four minutes. Consider now the case of my willing to refrain from sinning. Parallel to the case of running a four-minute mile, the proper analysis of "willing to refrain from sinning is not in my power" should be, on Augustine's view, the following:

(a)   I fail to will to refrain from sinning even though I will to will to refrain from sinning

rather than,

(b)   I fail to will to refrain from sinning even though I will to refrain from sinning.

(a) and (b) are not the same. (b) seems to express an impossibility—hence Augustine's conviction that the will would not be will unless it were in our power. About (a) I wish to make two comments. First it is not clear that the phrase "I will to will to refrain from sinning" makes any sense at all. G. E. Moore suggested that there is such a thing as ". . . making an effort to induce overselves to choose a particular course."[6] If there is such a thing as Moore suggested and if we take the phrase in question as expressing that thing, then per-

---

[6]*Ethics* (London, 1912), pp. 135–36.

haps we can interpret (a) in such a way that it expresses an intelligible proposition—namely, that I fail to will to refrain from sinning even though I make
an effort to will or choose to refrain from sinning. The second comment is
that if we so interpret (a) then it seems clear that (a) may be true and, consequently, we cannot conclude, in the simple way Augustine does, that it is in
a man's power to will to refrain from sinning, that the will is something that
is always in our power. Therefore, I conclude that Augustine has not made
good his claim that, even though a man necessarily wills to sin, his willing
or choosing to sin is voluntary or free. If this is so, it follows that Augustine
has not succeeded in showing that premiss (5) is not true, and, therefore, has
not succeeded in solving Evodius' problem of how God's foreknowledge is
compatible with the freedom of the will.

Returning to the argument that Augustine wishes to refute, it would seem
that there is a logical mistake either in the drawing of (4) from (3) *or* in the
interpretation of (3). Let's look at (3) for a moment. Let "*p*" pick out some
event. We must distinguish between interpreting (3) as (3a) "It is necessary
that if God foreknows *p, p* will happen"—here the necessity applies to the
conditional "If God foreknows *p, p* will happen"; and (3b) "If God foreknows
p, p will happen necessarily"—here the necessity applies not to the conditional
but to its consequent "*p* will happen." Since (4) is drawn from (3), and since
(5) presupposes that (4) is an instance of (3b) rather than of (3a)—otherwise
we have no reason for supposing in the antecedent of (5) that the man in
question must *necessarily* sin—it is clear that the inference from (3) to (4) is
valid only if (3) is interpreted as (3b) rather than (3a). But, although (3a) is
accepted as true within the context of classical theology, classical theology
need not—and to my knowledge does not—hold (3b) to be true.[7] Hence,

---

[7]Both Boethius (see *The Consolation of Philosophy*, Book V, 6) and Aquinas are clear
on this point. In considering a proposition similar to (3), Aquinas distinguishes between
taking it as (3a) and as (3b). He then claims, in effect, that (3a) is true but (3b) is false.
Thus he says: "Hence also this proposition, *Everything known by God must necessarily be*,
is usually distinguished, for it may refer to the thing or to the saying. If it refers to the
thing, it is divided and false; for the sense is, *Everything which God knows is necessary.*
If understood of the saying, it is composite and true, for the sense is, *This proposition,
'that which is known by God is' is necessary*" (*Summa Theologiae*, I, 14, 13, ad 3). Thus,
no problem arises in classical theology in connection with (3b)—for that proposition is
rejected as false. However, a problem does arise out of accepting (3a) and claiming, in
addition, that the *antecedent* of (3a) is itself necessary. Thus in discussing the necessarily
true conditional statement "If God knew that this thing will be, it will be" Aquinas explicitly points out concerning the antecedent "God knew this contingent to be future" that
"it must be said that this antecedent is absolutely necessary" (*ST.*, I, 14, 13, ad 2). In
order to avoid the conclusion that no future event is contingent, Aquinas distinguishes
between things as they exist in the knower (God) and as they exist in themselves. His
suggestion is that in saying that "this thing will be" is absolutely necessary we are speaking
of it only as it exists in God, and not as it exists in itself. As it exists in itself it is *contingent,*
as it exists in God it is *absolutely necessary.* It is interesting to note that this difficulty
does not arise in Aquinas' discussion of the divine *will*. ". . . But the divine knowledge has
a necessary relation to the thing known; not the divine will to the thing willed. The reason
for this is that knowledge is of things as they exist in the knower; but the will is directed

either the inference from (3) to (4) is valid but (3) (interpreted as (3b)) is not true *or* (3) (interpreted as (3a)) is true but the inference from (3) to (4) is invalid. On either account, we have sufficient grounds for rejecting the argument Augustine presents.[8]

In this paper I have (1) explained and criticized what I take to be Augustine's main reason for rejecting Evodius' argument that God's foreknowledge is incompatible with free will, and (2) suggested another way of rejecting the argument. Augustine does make, however, one further point which merits attention. He points out that the line of argument Evodius has taken implies not simply that *God's* foreknowledge is incompatible with free will but that anyone's foreknowledge is incompatible with free will. For he shows that on Evodius' reasoning it is foreknowledge generally and not God's foreknowledge specially that causes the events foreknown to happen by necessity. This creates a difficulty for Evodius since he believes that *we* sometimes foreknow the decisions and actions of men without thereby rendering those decisions and actions *involuntary*.

The importance of this *ad hominem* argument against Evodius must not be overlooked. For if we claim that there is a *special* problem for the theologian who believes in divine foreknowledge and human freedom then the reasons we give in support of that claim must at some point concern *God's* foreknowledge, rather than foreknowledge generally. Otherwise, the theologian is involved in no more or less a difficulty than anyone who believes that *we* sometimes foreknow the free decisions and actions of men.

---

to things as they exist in themselves. Since then all other things have necessary existence inasmuch as they exist in God; but no absolute necessity so as to be necessary in themselves, insofar as they exist in themselves; it follows that God knows necessarily whatever He knows, but does not will necessarily whatever He wills" (*ST.*, I, 19, 3, ad 6; Cf. *Summa contra Gentiles*, I, 81). Having admitted that God's willing *p* is not necessary, Aquinas is free to assert that *p* need not happen by necessity. He points out, of course, that the conditional proposition "If God wills *p*, *p* will happen" is necessary, but denies that any necessity need attach to the consequent "*p* will happen" (*CG.*, I, 85). Thus he is able to say, "Although the non-existence of an effect of the divine will is incompatible with the divine will, the possibility that the effect should be lacking is given simultaneously with the divine will. God's willing someone to be saved and the possibility that that person be damned are not incompatible; but God's willing him to be saved and his actually being damned are incompatible" (*De Veritate*, 23, 5, ad 3).

[8]This way of rejecting Augustine's argument was argued in some detail by C. E. Caton and myself in a joint paper, "Divine Foreknowledge and Contingent Events," presented at the meeting of the Western Division of the American Philosophical Association, May 1961.

ST. THOMAS AQUINAS

3.10 *God's Eternal Knowledge*

We proceed thus to the Thirteenth Article:—
Objection 1. It seems that the knowledge of God is not of future contingent things. For from a necessary cause proceeds a necessary effect. But the knowledge of God is the cause of things known, as was said above. Since therefore that knowledge is necessary, what He knows must also be necessary. Therefore the knowledge of God is not of contingent things.

Obj. 2. Further, every conditional proposition, of which the antecedent is absolutely necessary, must have an absolutely necessary consequent. For the antecedent is to the consequent as principles are to the conclusion: and from necessary principles only a necessary conclusion can follow, as is proved in *Poster.* i. But this is a true conditional proposition, *If God knew that this thing will be, it will be,* for the knowledge of God is only of true things. Now, the antecedent of this conditioned proposition is absolutely necessary, because it is eternal, and because it is signified as past. Therefore the consequent is also absolutely necessary. Therefore whatever God knows is necessary; and so the knowledge of God is not of contingent things.

Obj. 3. Further, everything known by God must necessarily be, because even what we ourselves know must necessarily be; and, of course, the knowledge of God is much more certain than ours. But no future contingent thing must necessarily be. Therefore no contingent future thing is known by God.

On the contrary, It is written (*Ps.* xxxii. 15), *He Who hath made the hearts of every one of them, Who understandeth all their works,* that is, of men. Now the works of men are contingent, being subject to free choice. Therefore God knows future contingent things.

I answer that, Since, as was shown above, God knows all things, not only things actual but also things possible to Him and to the creature, and since some of these are future contingent to us, it follows that God knows future contingent things.

In evidence of this, we must observe that a contingent thing can be considered in two ways. First, in itself, in so far as it is already in act, and in this sense it is not considered as future, but as present; neither is it considered

From *Summa Theologica*, Part I, trans. Dominican Fathers of English Province (New York: Benziger, Inc., 1947). Reprinted by permission of the publisher.

as contingent to one of two terms, but as determined to one; and because of this it can be infallibly the object of certain knowledge, for instance to the sense of sight, as when I see that Socrates is sitting down. In another way, a contingent thing can be considered as it is in its cause, and in this way it is considered as future, and as a contingent thing not yet determined to one; for a contingent cause has relation to opposite things: and in this sense a contingent thing is not subject to any certain knowledge. Hence, whoever knows a contingent effect in its cause only, has merely a conjectural knowledge of it. Now God knows all contingent things not only as they are in their causes, but also as each one of them is actually in itself. And although contingent things become actual successively, nevertheless God knows contingent things not successively, as they are in their own being, as we do, but simultaneously. The reason is because His knowledge is measured by eternity, as is also His being; and eternity, being simultaneously whole, comprises all time, as was said above. Hence, all things that are in time are present to God from eternity, not only because He has the essences of things present within Him, as some say, but because His glance is carried from eternity over all things as they are in their presentiality. Hence it is manifest that contingent things are infallibly known by God, inasmuch as they are subject to the divine sight in their presentiality; and yet they are future contingent things in relation to their own causes.

Reply Obj. 1. Although the supreme cause is necessary, the effect may be contingent by reason of the proximate contingent cause; just as the germination of a plant is contingent by reason of the proximate contingent cause, although the movement of the sun, which is the first cause, is necessary. So, likewise, things known by God are contingent because of their proximate causes, while the knowledge of God, which is the first cause, is necessary.

Reply Obj. 2. Some say that this antecedent, *God knew this contingent to be future*, is not necessary, but contingent; because, although it is past, still it imports a relation to the future. This, however, does not remove necessity from it, for whatever has had relation to the future, must have had it, even though the future sometimes is not realized. On the other hand, some say that this antecedent is contingent because it is a compound of the necessary and the contingent; as this saying is contingent, *Socrates is a white man*. But this also is to no purpose; for when we say, *God knew this contingent to be future*, contingent is used here only as the matter of the proposition, and not as its principal part. Hence its contingency or necessity has no reference to the necessity or contingency of the proposition, or to its being true or false. For it may be just as true that I said a man is an ass, as that I said Socrates runs, or God is: and the same applies to necessary and contingent.

Hence it must be said that this antecedent is absolutely necessary. Nor does it follow, as some say, that the consequent is absolutely necessary because the antecedent is the remote cause of the consequent, which is contingent by reason of the proximate cause. But this to no purpose. For the conditional would be false were its antecedent the remote necessary cause, and the consequent a contingent effect; as, for example, if I said, *if the sun moves, the grass will grow.*

Therefore we must reply otherwise: when the antecedent contains anything belonging to an act of the soul, the consequent must be taken, not as it is in itself, but as it is in the soul; for the being of a thing in itself is other than the being of a thing in the soul. For example, when I say, *What the soul understands is immaterial,* the meaning is that it is immaterial as it is in the intellect, not as it is in itself. Likewise if I say, *If God knew anything, it will be,* the consequent must be understood as it is subject to the divine knowledge, that is, as it is in its presentiality. And thus it is necessary, as is also the antecedent; *for everything that is, while it is, must necessarily be,* as the Philosopher says in *Periherm.* i.

Reply Obj. 3. Things reduced to actuality in time are known by us successively in time, but by God they are known in eternity, which is above time. Whence to us they cannot be certain, since we know future contingent things only as contingent futures; but they are certain to God alone, Whose understanding is in eternity above time. Just as he who goes along the road does not see those who come after him; whereas he who sees the whole road from a height sees at once all those traveling on it. Hence, what is known by us must be necessary, even as it is in itself; for what is in itself a future contingent cannot be known by us. But what is known by God must be necessary according to the mode in which it is subject to the divine knowledge, as we have already stated, but not absolutely as considered in its proper causes. Hence also this proposition, *Everything known by God must necessarily be,* is usually distinguished, for it may refer to the thing or to the saying. If it refers to the thing, it is divided and false; for the sense is, *Everything which God knows is necessary.* If understood of the saying, it is composite and true, for the sense is, *This proposition, 'that which is known by God is' is necessary.*

Now some urge an objection and say that this distinction holds good with regard to forms that are separable from a subject. Thus if I said, *It is possible for a white thing to be black,* it is false as applied to the saying, and true as applied to the thing: for a thing which is white can become black; whereas this saying, *a white thing is black,* can never be true. But in forms that are inseparable from a subject, this distinction does not hold: for instance, if I said, *A black crow can be white;* for in both senses it is false. Now to be known by God is inseparable from a thing; for what is known by God cannot be not known. This objection, however, would hold if these words *that which is known* implied any disposition inherent in the subject; but since they import an act of the knower, something can be attributed to the known thing in itself (even if it always be known) which is not attributed to it in so far as it falls under an act of knowledge. Thus, material being is attributed to a stone in itself, which is not attributed to it inasmuch as it is intelligible.

JONATHAN EDWARDS

3.11   *Foreknowledge Inconsistent with Contingency*

Having proved, that God has a certain and infallible prescience of the acts of the will of moral agents, I come now, in the *second* place, to shew the consequence; to shew how it follows from hence, that these events are *necessary*, with a necessity of connection or consequence.

The chief Arminian divines, so far as I have had opportunity to observe, deny this consequence; and affirm, that if such foreknowledge be allowed, 'tis no evidence of any necessity of the event foreknown. Now I desire, that this matter may be particularly and thoroughly enquired into. I cannot but think, that on particular and full consideration, it may be perfectly determined, whether it be indeed so, or not.

In order to ensure a proper consideration of this matter, I would observe the following things.

I. 'Tis very evident, with regard to a thing whose existence is infallibly and indissolubly connected with something which already hath, or has had existence, the existence of that thing is necessary. Here may be noted,

1. I observed before, in explaining the nature of necessity, that in things which are past, their past existence is now necessary: having already made sure of existence, 'tis too late for any possibility of alteration in that respect: 'tis now impossible, that it should be otherwise than true, that that thing has existed.

2. If there be any such thing as a divine foreknowledge of the volitions of free agents, that foreknowledge, by the supposition, is a thing which already *has*, and long ago *had* existence; and so, now its existence is necessary; it is now utterly impossible to be otherwise, than that this foreknowledge should be, or should have been.

3. 'Tis also very manifest, that those things which are indissolubly connected with other things that are necessary, are themselves necessary. As that proposition whose truth is necessarily connected with another proposition, which is necessarily true, is itself necessarily true. To say otherwise, would be a contradiction; it would be in effect to say, that the connection was indissoluble, and yet was not so, but might be broken. If that, whose existence is indissolubly connected with something whose existence is now necessary, is

---

From Jonathan Edwards, *Freedom of the Will* (1754), section 12.

itself not necessary, then it may *possibly not exist,* notwithstanding that indissoluble connection of its existence.—Whether the absurdity ben't glaring, let the reader judge.

4. 'Tis no less evident, that if there be a full, certain and infallible foreknowledge of the future existence of the volitions of moral agents, then there is a certain infallible and indissoluble connection between those events and that foreknowledge; and that therefore, by the preceeding observations, those events are necessary events; being infallibly and indissoluby connected with that whose existence already is, and so is now necessary, and can't but have been.

To say, the foreknowledge is certain and infallible, and yet the connection of the event with that foreknowledge is not indissoluble, but dissoluble and fallible, is very absurd. To affirm it, would be the same thing as to affirm, that there is no necessary connection between a proposition being infallibly known to be true, and its being true indeed. So that it is perfectly demonstrable, that if there be any infallible knowledge of future volitions, the event is *necessary;* or, in other words, that it is *impossible* but the event should come to pass. For if it ben't impossible but that it may be otherwise, then it is not impossible but that the proposition which affirms its future coming to pass, may not now be true. But how absurd is that, on the supposition that there is now an infallible knowledge (i.e knowledge which it is impossible should fail) that it is true. There is this absurdity in it, that it is not impossible but that there now should be no truth in that proposition, which is now infallibly known to be true.

II. That no future event can be certainly foreknown, whose existence is contingent, and without all necessity, may be proved thus; 'tis impossible for a thing to be certainly known to any intellect without *evidence.* To suppose otherwise, implies a contradiction: because for a thing to be certainly known to any understanding, is for it to be *evident* to that understanding; and for a thing to be *evident* to any understanding, is the same thing, as for that understanding to *see evidence* of it: but no understanding, created or increated, can *see evidence* where there is none: for that is the same thing, as to see that to be, which is not. And therefore, if there be any truth which is absolutely without evidence, that truth is absolutely unknowable, insomuch that it implies a contradiction to suppose that it is known.

But if there be any future event, whose existence is contingent, without all necessity, the future existence of that event is absolutely *without evidence.* If there be any evidence of it, it must be one of these two sorts, either *self-evidence,* or *proof;* for there can be no other sort of evidence but one of *these two;* an evident thing must be either evident *in itself,* or evident in *something else;* that is, evident by connection with something else. But a future thing, whose existence is without all necessity, can have neither of these sorts of evidence. It can't be *self-evident:* for if it be, it may be now known by what is now to be seen in the thing itself; either its present existence, or the necessity of its nature: but both these are contrary to the supposition. It is supposed, both that the thing has no present existence to be seen; and also that it is not of such a nature as to be necessarily existent for the future: so that its future existence is not self-evident. And *secondly*, neither is there any *proof*, or evidence in *anything else*, or evidence of connection with some thing else that is evident; for this also is contrary to the supposition. 'Tis supposed, that there is now nothing existent, with which the future existence of the *contingent* event is connected. For such a connection destroys its *contingence*, and supposes necessity. Thus 'tis demonstrated, that there is in the nature of things absolutely no evidence at all of the future existence of that event, which is contingent, without all necessity (if any such event there be) neither self-evidence nor proof. And therefore the thing in reality is not evident; and so can't be seen to be evident, or, which is the same thing, can't be known.

Let us consider this in an example. Suppose that five thousand seven hundred and sixty years ago, there was no other being but the divine being; and then this world, or some particular body or spirit, all at once starts out of nothing into being, and takes on itself a particular nature and form; all in *absolute contingence*, without any concern of God, or any other cause, in the matter; without any manner of ground or reason of its existence; or any dependence upon, or connection at all with anything foregoing; I say, that if this be supposed, there was no evidence of that event before hand. There was no evidence of it to be seen *in the thing itself;* for the thing itself, as yet, was not. And there was no evidence of it to be seen *in any* thing else; for *evidence* in something else, is *connection with* something else; but such connection is contrary to the supposition. There was no evidence before, that this thing *would happen;* for by the supposition, there was no reason why it *should happen*, rather than something else, or rather than nothing. And if so, then all things before were exactly equal, and the same, with respect to that and other possible things; there was no preponderation, no superior weight or value; and therefore nothing that could be of any weight or value to determine any understanding. The thing was absolutely without evidence, and absolutely unknowable. An increase of understanding, or of the capacity of discerning, has no tendency, and makes no advance, to a discerning any signs or evidences of it, let it be increased never so much; yea, if it be increased infinitely. The increase of the strength of sight may have a tendency to enable to discern the evidence which is far off, and very much hid, and deeply involved in clouds and darkness; but it has no tendency to enable to discern evidence where there is none. If the sight be infinitely strong, and the capacity of discerning infinitely great, it will enable to see all that there is, and to see it perfectly, and with ease; yet it has no tendency at all to enable a being to discern that evidence which is not; but on the contrary, it has a tendency to enable to discern with great certainty that there is none.

III. To suppose the future volitions of moral agents not to be necessary events; or, which is the same thing, events which it is not impossible but that they may not come to pass; and yet to suppose that God certainly foreknows them, and knows all things; is to suppose God's knowledge to be inconsistent with itself. For to say, that God certainly, and without all conjecture, knows that a thing will infallibly be, which at the same time he knows to be so *contingent*, that it may possibly not be, is to suppose his knowledge inconsistent with itself; or that one thing that he knows is utterly inconsistent with another thing that he knows; 'tis the same thing as to say, He now knows a proposition to be of certain infallible truth, which he knows to be of contingent uncertain truth. If a future volition is so without all necessity, that there is nothing hinders but that it may not be, then the proposition which asserts its future existence, is so uncertain, that there is nothing hinders but that the truth of it may entirely fail. And if God knows all things, he knows this proposition to be thus uncertain. And that is inconsistent with his knowing that it is infallibly true; and so inconsistent with this infallibly knowing that it is true. If the thing be indeed contingent, God views it so, and judges it to be contingent, if he views things as they are. If the event be not necessary, then it is possible it may never be: and if it be possible it may never be, God knows it may possibly never be; and that is to know that the proposition which affirms its existence, may possibly not be true; and that is to know that the truth of it is uncertain; which surely is inconsistent with his knowing it as a certain truth. If volitions are in themselves contingent events, without all necessity, then 'tis no argument of perfection of knowledge in any being to determine preemptorily that they will be; but on the contrary an argument of ignorance and mistake: because it would argue, that he supposes that proposition to be certain, which in its own nature, and all things considered, is uncertain and contingent. To say in such a case, that God may have ways of knowing contingent events which we can't conceive of, is ridiculous; as much so, as to say, that God may know contradictions to be true, for ought we know, or that he may know a thing to be certain, and at the same time know it not to be certain, though we can't conceive how; because he has ways of knowing, which we can't comprehend.

Corol. 1. From what has been observed it is evident, that the absolute *decrees* of God are no more inconsistent with human liberty, on account of any necessity of the event which follows from such decrees, than the absolute *foreknowledge* of God. Because the connection between the event and certain foreknowledge, is as infallible and indissoluble, as between the event and an absolute decree. That is, 'tis no more impossible that the event and decree should not agree together, than that the event and absolute knowledge should disagree. The connection between the event and foreknowledge is absolutely perfect, by the supposition, because it is supposed, that the certainty and infallibility of the knowledge is absolutely perfect. And it being so, the certainty can't be increased; and therefore the connection between the knowledge and thing known, can't be increased; so that if a decree be added to the foreknowledge, it don't at all increase the connection, or make it more infallible and indissoluble. If it were not so, the certainty of knowledge might be increased by the addition of a decree; which is contrary to the supposition, which is, that the knowledge is absolutely perfect, or perfect to the highest possible degree.

There is as much of an impossibility but that the things which are infallibly foreknown, should be, or (which is the same thing) as great a necessity of their future existence, as if the event were already written down, and was known and read by all mankind, through all preceeding ages, and there were the most indissoluble and perfect connection possible, between the writing, and the thing written. In such a case, it would be as impossible the event should fail of existence, as if it had existed already; and a decree can't make an event surer or more necessary than this.

And therefore, if there be any such foreknowledge, as it has been proved there is, then necessity of connection and consequence, is not at all *inconsistent* with any liberty which man, or any other creature enjoys. And from hence it may be inferred, that absolute decrees of God, which don't at all increase the necessity, are not at all inconsistent with the liberty which man enjoys, on any such account, as that they make the event decreed necessary, and render it utterly impossible but that it should come to pass. Therefore if absolute decrees are inconsistent with man's liberty as a moral agent, or his liberty in a state of probation, or any liberty whatsoever that he enjoys, it is not on account of any necessity which absolute decrees infer.

Dr. Whitby supposes, there is a great difference between God's foreknowledge, and his decrees, with regard to necessity of future events. In his discourse on the Five Points, p. 474, etc. he says, "God's prescience has no influence at all on our actions.—Should God (says he) by immediate revelation, give me the knowledge of the event of any man's state or actions, would my knowledge of them have any influence upon his actions? Surely none at all.—Our knowledge doth not affect the things we know, to make them more certain, or more future, then they would be without it. Now foreknowledge in God is knowledge. As therefore knowledge has no influence on things that are, so neither has foreknowledge on things that shall be. And consequently, the foreknowledge of any action that would otherwise free, cannot alter or diminish that freedom. Whereas God's decree of election is powerful and active, and comprehends the preparation and exhibition of such means, as shall unfrustrably produce the end.—Hence God's prescience renders no actions necessary." And to this purpose, p. 473, he cites Origen, where he says, *God's prescience is not the cause of things future, but their being future is the cause of God's prescience that they will be:* and Le Blanc, where he says, *This is the truest resolution of this difficulty, that prescience is not the cause that things are future; but their being future is the cause they are foreseen.* In like manner Dr. Clark, in his *Demonstration of the Being and Attributes of God,* p. 95–99. And the author of *The Freedom of the Will in God and the Crea-*

ture, speaking to the like purpose with Dr. Whitby, represents *foreknowledge as having no more influence on things known, to make them necessary*, than *after-knowledge*, or to that purpose.

To all which I would say; that what is said about knowledge, its not having influence on the thing known to make it necessary, is nothing to the purpose, nor does it in the least affect the foregoing reasoning. Whether prescience be the thing that *makes* the event necessary or no, it alters not the case. Infallible foreknowledge may *prove* the necessity of the event foreknown, and yet not be the thing which *causes* the necessity. If the foreknowledge be absolute, this *proves* the event known to be necessary, or proves that 'tis impossible but that the event should be, by some means or other, either by a decree, or some other way, if there be any other way: because, as was said before, 'tis absurd to say, that a proposition is known to be certainly and infallibly true, which may possibly prove not true.

The whole of the seeming force of this evasion lies in this; that, in as much as certain foreknowledge don't *cause* an event to be necessary, as a decree does; therefore it don't *prove* it to be necessary, as a decree does. But there is no force in this arguing. For it is built wholly on this supposition, that nothing can *prove*, or *be an evidence* of a thing's being necessary, but that which has a *causal influence to make it so*. But this can never be maintained. If certain foreknowledge of the future existing of an event, be not the thing which first makes it impossible that it should fail of existence; yet it may, and certainly does *demonstrate*, that it is impossible it should fail of it, however that impossibility comes. If foreknowledge be not the cause, but the effect of this impossibility, it may prove that there is such an impossibility, as much as if it were the cause. It is as strong arguing from the effect to the cause, as from the cause to the effect. 'Tis enough, that an existence which is infallibly foreknown, cannot fail, whether that impossibility arises from the foreknowledge, or is prior to it. 'Tis as evident, as 'tis possible anything should be, that it is impossible a thing which is infallibly known to be true; should prove not to be true; therefore there is a *necessity* that it should not be otherwise; whether the knowledge be the cause of this necessity, or the necessity the cause of the knowledge.

All certain knowledge, whether it be foreknowledge or after-knowledge, or concomitant knowledge, proves the thing known now to be necessary, by some means or other; or proves that it is impossible it should not be otherwise than true.—I freely allow, that foreknowledge don't prove a thing to be necessary any more than after-knowledge: but then after-knowledge which is certain and infallible, proves that 'tis now become impossible but that the proposition known should be true. Certain after-knowledge proves that it is now, in the time of the knowledge, by some means or other, become impossible but that the proposition which predicates past existence on the event, should be true. And so does certain foreknowledge prove, that now, in the time of the knowledge, it is by some means or other, become impossible but that the proposition which predicates *future* existence on the event, should be true. The necessity of the truth of the propositions, consisting in the present impossibility of the non-existence of the event affirmed, in both cases, is the immediate ground of the certainty of the knowledge; there can be no certainty of knowledge without it.

There must be a certainty in things themselves, before they are certainly known, or (which is the same thing) known to be certain. For certainty of knowledge is nothing else but knowing or discerning the certainty there is in the things themselves which are known. Therefore there must be a certainty in things to be a ground of certainty in knowledge, and to render things capable of being known to be certain. And this is nothing but the necessity of the truth known, or its being impossible that it should not be true; or, in other words, the firm and infallible connection between the subject and predicate of the proposition that contains that truth. All certainty of knowledge consists in the view of the firmness of that connection. So God's certain foreknowledge of the future existence of any event, is his view of the firm and indissoluble connection of the subject and predicate of the proposition that affirms its future existence. The subject is that possible event; the predicate is its future existing; But if future existence be firmly and indissolubly connected with that event, then the future existence of that event is necessary. If God certainly knows the future existence of an event which is wholly contingent, and may possibly never be, then he sees a firm connection between a subject and predicate that are not firmly connected, which is a contradiction.

I allow what Dr. Whitby says to be true, *that mere knowledge don't affect the thing known, to make it more certain or more future.* But yet, I say, it *supposes* and *proves* the thing to be *already*, both *future*, and *certain;* i.e necessarily future. Knowledge of *futurity*, supposes *futurity;* and *a certain knowledge* of futurity, supposes *certain futurity*, antecedent to that certain knowledge. But there is no other certain futurity of a thing, antecedent to certainty of knowledge, than a prior impossibility but that the thing should prove true; or (which is the same thing) the necessity of the event.

I would observe one thing further concerning this matter, and it is this: that if it be as those forementioned writers suppose, that God's foreknowledge is not the cause, but the effect of the existence of the event foreknown; this is so far from shewing that this foreknowledge don't infer the necessity of the existence of that event, that it rather shews the contrary the more plainly. Because it shews the existence of the event to be so settled and firm that it is as if it had already been; in as much as *in effect* it actually exists already; its future existence has already had actual *influence* and *efficiency*, and has *produced an effect*, viz. prescience: the effect exists already; and as the effect supposes the cause, is connected with the cause, and depends entirely upon it, therefore it is as if the future event, which is the cause, had existed already. The effect is firm as possible, it having already the possession of existence, and has made sure of it. But the effect can't be more firm and stable than its cause, ground and reason. The building can't be firmer than the foundation.

To illustrate this matter, let us suppose the appearance and images of things in a glass; for instance, a reflecting telescope to be the real effects of heavenly bodies (at a distance, and out of sight) which they resemble: if it be so, then, as these images in the telescope have had a past actual existence, and it is become utterly impossible now that it should be otherwise than that they have existed; so they being the true effects of the heavenly bodies they resemble, this proves the existing of those heavenly bodies to be as real, infallible, firm and necessary, as the existing of these effects; the one being connected with, and wholly depending on the other.—Now let us suppose future existence some way or other to have influence back, to produce effects beforehand, and cause exact and perfect images of themselves in a glass, a thousand years before they exist, yea, in all preceeding ages; but yet that these images are real effects of these future existences, perfectly dependent on, and connected with their cause; these effects and images, having already had actual existence, rendering that matter of their existing perfectly firm and stable, and utterly impossible to be otherwise; this proves in like manner as in the other instance, that the existence of the things which are their causes, is also equally sure, firm and necessary; and that it is alike impossible but that they should be, as if they had been already, as their effects have. And if instead of images in a glass, we suppose the antecedent effects to be perfect ideas of them in the divine mind, which have existed there from all eternity, which are as properly effects, as truly and properly connected with their cause, the case is not altered.

Another thing which has been said by some Arminians, to take off the force of what is urged from God's prescience, against the contingence of the volitions of moral agents, is to this purpose; "That when we talk of foreknowledge in God, there is no strict propriety in our so speaking; and that although it be true, that there is in God the most perfect knowledge of all events from eternity to eternity, yet there is no such thing as *before* and *after* in God, but he sees all things by one perfect unchangeable view, without any succession." To this I answer,

1. It has been already shewn, that all certain knowledge proves the necessity of the truth known; whether it be *before, after,* or *at the same time.*— Though it be true, that there is no succession in God's knowledge, and the manner of his knowledge is to us inconceivable, yet thus much we know concerning it, that there is no event, past, present, or to come, that God is ever uncertain of: he never is, never was, and never will be without infallible knowledge of it; he always sees the existence of it to be certain and infallible. And as he always sees things just as they are in truth; hence, there never is in reality anything contingent in such a sense, as that possibly it may happen never to exist. If strictly speaking, there is no foreknowledge in God, 'tis because those things which are future to us, are as present to God, as if they

already had existence: and that is as much as to say, that future events are always in God's view as evident, clear, sure and necessary, as if they already were. If there never is a time wherein the existence of the event is not present with God, then there never is a time wherein it is not as much impossible for it to fail of existence, as if its existence were present, and were already come to pass.

God's viewing things so perfectly and unchangeably as that there is no succession in his ideas or judgment, don't hinder it but that there is properly now, in the mind of God, a certain and perfect knowledge of the moral actions of men, which to us are an hundred years hence: yea the objection supposes this; and therefore it certainly don't hinder but that, by the foregoing arguments, it is now impossible these moral actions should not come to pass.

We know, that God knows the future voluntary actions of men in such a sense beforehand, as that he is able particularly to declare, and foretell them, and write them, or cause them to be written down in a book, as he often has done; and that therefore the necessary connection which there is between God's knowledge and the event known, does as much prove the event to be necessary beforehand, as if the divine knowledge were in the same sense before the event, as the prediction or writing is. If the knowledge be infallible, then the expression of it in the written prediction is infallible; that is, there is an infallible connection between that written prediction and the event. And if so, then it is impossible it should ever be otherwise, than that that prediction and the event should agree: and this is the same thing as to say, 'tis impossible but that the event should come to pass: and this is the same as to say, that its coming to pass is necessary—So that it is manifest, that there being no proper succession in God's mind, makes no alteration as to the necessity of the existence of the events which God knows. Yea,

2. This is so far from weakening the proof, which has been given of the impossibility of the not coming to pass of future events known, as that it establishes that wherein the strength of the foregoing arguments consists, and shews the clearness of the evidence. For,

(1) The very reason why God's knowledge is without succession, is, because it is absolutely perfect, to the highest possible degree of clearness and certainty: all things, whether past, present or to come, being viewed with equal evidence and fulness; future things being seen with as much clearness, as if they were present; the view is always in absolute perfection; and absolute constant perfection admits of no alteration, and so no succession; the actual existence of the thing known, don't at all increase, or add to the clearness or certainty of the thing known: God calls the things that are not, as though they were; they are all one to him as if they had already existed. But herein consists the strength of the demonstration before given, of the impossibility of the not existing of those things whose existence God knows; that it is as impossible they should fail of existence, as if they existed already.

This objection, instead of weakening this argument, sets it in the clearest and strongest light; for it supposes it to be so indeed, that the existence of future events is in God's view so much as if it already had been, that when they come actually to exist, it makes not the least alteration or variation in his view or knowledge of them.

(2) The objection is founded on the immutability of God's knowledge: for 'tis the immutability of knowledge makes his knowledge to be without succession. But this most directly and plainly demonstrates the thing I insist on, viz. that 'tis utterly impossible the known events should fail of existence. For if that were possible, then it would be possible for there to be a change in God's knowledge and view of things. For if the known event should fail of existence, and not come into being as God expected, then God would see it, and so would change his mind, and see his former mistake; and thus there would be change and succession in his knowledge. But as God is immutable, and so it is utterly and infinitely impossible that his view should be changed; so 'tis, for the same reason, just so impossible that the foreknown event should not exist: and that is to be impossible in the highest degree and therefore the contrary is necessary. Nothing is more impossible than that the immutable God should be changed, by the succession of time; who comprehends all things, from eternity to eternity; in one, most perfect, and unalterable view; so that his whole eternal duration is *vitae interminabilis, tota, simul,* and *perfecta possessio.*

On the whole, I need not fear to say, that there is no geometrical theorem or proposition whatsoever, more capable of strict demonstration, than that God's certain prescience of the volitions of moral agents is inconsistent with such a contingence of these events, as is without all necessity; and so is inconsistent with the Arminian notion of liberty.

Corol. 2. Hence the doctrine of the Calvinists, concerning the absolute decrees of God, does not at all infer any more *fatality* in things, than will demonstrably follow from the doctrine of most Arminian divines, who acknowledge God's omniscience, and universal prescience. Therefore all objections they make against the doctrine of the Calvinists, as implying Hobbes's doctrine of necessity, or the stoical doctrine of fate, lie no more against the doctrine of Calvinists, than their own doctrine: and therefore it don't become those divines, to raise such an outcry against the Calvinists, on this account.

Corol. 3. Hence all arguing from necessity, against the doctrine of the inability of unregenerate men to perform the conditions of salvation, and the commands of God requiring spiritual duties, and against the Calvinistic doctrine of efficacious grace; I say, all arguings of Arminians (such of 'em as own God's omniscience) against these things, on this ground, that these doctrines, though they don't suppose men to be under any constraint or coaction, yet suppose 'em under necessity, with respect to their moral actions, and those things which are required of 'em in order to their acceptance with God; and their arguing against the necessity of men's volitions, taken from the reasonableness of God's commands, promises, and threatenings, and the sincerity of his counsels and invitations; and all objections against any doctrines of the Calvinists as being inconsistent with human liberty, because they infer necessity; I say, all these arguments and objections must fall to the ground, and be justly esteemed vain and frivolous, as coming from them; being maintained in an inconsistence with themselves, and in like manner levelled against their own doctrine, as against the doctrine of the Calvinists.

ANTHONY KENNY

3.12 *Divine Foreknowledge and Human Freedom*

In this paper* I intend to discuss whether belief in God's foreknowledge of the future is compatible with belief in the freedom of human actions. Before stating the problem in further detail, I must make clear which problems I do *not* intend to consider. I shall not discuss whether there is a God, nor whether it is the case that some human actions are free. I shall not try to show that an action which is causally determined is not free, nor that God knows the future free actions of men. It might be thought, indeed, that this last at least needs no proving: surely, if there is a God at all, He knows all that is to come; a God who did not know the future would not be a real God. But this is not so. It is indeed the case that any God worthy of the name knows everything that there is to be known; but it does not follow from this alone that He knows the future free actions of men. For many philosophers have maintained, and some do maintain, that statements about as-yet-undecided free actions, such as the statement "The United States will declare war on China," are as yet neither true nor false. Since only what is true can be known, then if it is not yet true either that the United States will declare war on China or that the United States will not declare war on China, then not even God can know whether the United States will do so or not. Again, as a matter of history there have been philosophers who have believed that God was omniscient without thereby believing that God knew the future free actions of men. Indeed, as

From *Aquinas: A Collection of Critical Essays* by Anthony Kenny, copyright © 1969 by Anthony Kenny. Reprinted by permission of Doubleday & Company, Inc., New York, and of Macmillan & Company, Ltd., London and Basingstoke.

*Revised version of a paper read at Liverpool in 1960. In the original preparation of the paper I had the advantage of discussions with Miss G. E. M. Anscombe and Mr. A. N. Prior.

we shall see, even a philosopher so orthodox as St. Thomas Aquinas denied, in one important sense, that God knows the future when the future is not already determined by causal necessity. Even to theists, therefore, it needs to be proved that God knows what is going to take place through the free action of his creature. As I have said, I do not intend to argue for this. I intend merely to investigate whether there is or is not compatibility between two statements—namely, "God knows beforehand everything that men will do" and "Some actions of men are free." Even in this restricted area I intend to examine only two arguments which have been brought up to show that the statements are incompatible. The question of incompatibility retains its interest for philosophers even if both statements are in fact false.

It is necessary, as a final preamble, to insist that the problem to be discussed concerns only foreknowledge and not foreordaining. Just as people have believed that God knows beforehand all that happens in the world, so also they have believed that He ordains beforehand all that happens in the world. Just as no human action escapes God's prescience, so no human action escapes His providence. Accordingly, just as there is a problem how God's foreknowledge may be reconciled with human freedom, so also there is a problem how human freedom may be reconciled with God's providence. In particular, since, according to traditional Christian belief, no-one is saved who is not predestined by God to be saved, those who accept that belief have a special problem in reconciling it with the belief that those who are damned are damned through their own fault. These further problems are interesting, complicated, and difficult; but they will not be our concern in this paper.

The problem may be stated as follows. God's foreknowledge appears to be incompatible with human freedom. It does not seem to be possible both that God should know what I shall do in the future and that I shall do freely whatever it is that I shall do. For in order for me to be able to do an action freely, it is necessary that it should be within my power not to do that action. But if God knows what my action is going to be before I do it, then it does not seem to be within my power not to do it. For it cannot be the case both that God knows that I shall do such and such action and that I shall not in fact do it. For what God knows must be true: and indeed what anyone knows must be true, since it is impossible to know what is false. But if what God knows is true, and God knows that I will do such and such an action, then it must be true that I will do it. And if it is true that I will do it, then it seems that nothing I can do can prevent its coming true that I am doing it. And if nothing I can do can prevent its coming true that I am doing it, then I cannot prevent myself from doing it. And if I cannot prevent myself from doing a certain action, then that action cannot be free. Therefore, either God cannot know what I shall do tomorrow, or else whatever I shall do tomorrow will not be done freely.

For example: if God knows now that I will tell a lie this time tomorrow, then it seems that I cannot be free not to tell a lie this time tomorrow. For it cannot be the case both that God knows that I will tell a lie tomorrow and that I will not in fact tell a lie tomorrow. For what God knows must be true: so that if God knows that I will tell a lie tomorrow, it must be true that I will tell a lie tomorrow. But if it must be true that I will tell a lie tomorrow, then I cannot be free not to tell a lie tomorrow. But if I am not free not to tell a lie tomorrow, then when tomorrow I tell a lie, I shall not do so freely. A similar argument appears to hold, no matter what human action we consider instead of telling lies. Therefore it seems that if God foresees all human actions, no human action can be free.

This difficulty is a very old one. It is stated, for instance, in St. Thomas Aquinas' *Summa Theologiae*, Ia, 14, 3, 3. Aquinas' statement of the difficulty is as follows: "Whatever is known by God must be; for whatever is known by us must be, and God's knowledge is more certain than ours. But nothing which is future and contingent *must* be. Therefore, nothing which is future and contingent is known by God." This difficulty is recognizably the same as the one which I have just stated more verbosely. The only difference of importance is that while I spoke of future free actions, St. Thomas speaks of future contingent events. St. Thomas uses the word "contingent" as equivalent to "not causally determined." Assuming that no causally determined action is a free action, a free human action would be a contingent event within the meaning of St. Thomas' phrase. Indeed St. Thomas expressly states (ibid., *Sed contra*) that free human actions are contingent events. He thought also that there were other contingent events besides free human actions: the budding of a tree, for instance. Whether he was correct in thinking this is an interesting question, but not to our purpose.

To the difficulty which he has set, St. Thomas provides a long answer. Part of his answer runs as follows:

> The proposition "whatever is known by God must be" can be analysed in two ways. It may be taken as a proposition *de dicto* or as a proposition *de re;* in others words, it may be taken either *in sensu composito* or *in sensu diviso.* As a *de re* proposition, it means:
> Of everything which is known by God, it is true that that thing must be. So understood the proposition is false. As a proposition *de dicto* it means: The proposition "whatever God knows is the case" is necessarily true. So understood, the proposition is true.

There is much more in St. Thomas' answer than this paragraph, but this argument, as it stands, seems to me an adequate answer to the difficulty. In order to understand it one must know something about the medieval distinction between propositions *de dicto* and propositions *de re*. Consider the following proposition.

(1) If there is a University at Oxford, then necessarily there is a University at Oxford.

Someone who asserts that proposition may be taken to assert

(2) "If there is a University at Oxford, then there is a University at Oxford" is a necessary truth.

Or he may be taken to assert

(3) If there is a University at Oxford, then "there is a University at Oxford" is a necessary truth.

The medievals would have called proposition (1), if interpreted in the sense of proposition (2), a proposition *de dicto*; if interpreted in the sense of proposition (3) they would call it a proposition *de re*. The difference between the two interpretations is obviously of crucial importance. For (2), which merely states that a certain conditional—whose consequent is a repetition of its antecedent—is necessarily true, is itself true. But (3) is false, since its antecedent is true (there is a University at Oxford), and its consequent is false (it is not a necessary truth that there is a University at Oxford, since there has not always been a University at Oxford).

It is not difficult to see how to apply this to the problem in hand. The proposition "Whatever is known by God is necessarily true" if taken *de dicto* means

(4) "Whatever is known by God is true" is a necessary truth.
Interpreted *de re*, however, it means

(5) Whatever is known by God is a necessary truth.

Proposition (4) is true, but it has no tendency to show that acts foreseen by God are not free. For, it is equally a necessary truth that if I will tell a lie this time tomorrow, then I will tell a lie this time tomorrow: but this necessary truth has no tendency to show that my telling of a lie tomorrow will not be free. On the other hand, (5) if true would rule out the possibility of free action. If it is a necessary truth that I will tell a lie tomorrow, then I have no choice in the matter. But this need not trouble us; for proposition (5) is simply false. If God knows everything, then God knows that I am now writing this paper; but "I am writing this paper" is not a necessary truth, since it was in fact false ten days ago. We might bring out the difference between the two interpretations of "whatever is known by God is necessarily true" by punctuation, as follows:

(4a) Whatever is known by God is, necessarily, true.
(5a) Whatever is known by God is necessarily-true.

It seems to me, therefore, that St. Thomas' answer to this particular difficulty is entirely satisfactory. But he puts to himself a further, and more persuasive, difficulty; and his answer to this second difficulty does not appear satisfactory at all.

The further difficulty runs as follows. In any true conditional proposition whose antecedent is necessarily true, the consequent is also necessarily true. That is to say, whatever is implied by a necessary proposition is itself a necessary proposition. The following is clearly a true conditional proposition: "If it has come to God's knowledge that such and such a thing will happen, then such and such a thing will happen." The antecedent of the conditional, if it is true at all, appears to be necessarily true: for it is in the past tense, and what is past cannot be changed. What has been the case cannot now not have been the case. Therefore, the consequent is also necessarily true. Therefore, whatever is known by God is a necessary truth.

This is a powerful argument: it appears, at least at first sight, impossible to deny any of its premises. St. Thomas himself treated it with great respect: before putting forward his own solution he considered and rejected three attempts to deny one or other premise. In the end, he could find no alternative to accepting the argument, while trying to show that the conclusion is not, as it appears to be, incompatible with the occurrence of contingent events.

His solution runs as follows. God, he says, is outside time: God's life is measured not by time, but by eternity. Eternity, which has no parts, overlaps the whole of time; consequently, the things which happen at different times are all present together to God. An event is known *as future* only when there is a relation of future to past between the knowledge of the knower and the happening of the event. But there is no such relation between God's knowledge and any contingent event: the relation between God's knowledge and any event in time is always one of simultaneity. Consequently, a contingent event, as it comes to God's knowledge, is not future but present; and as present it is necessary; for what is the case, is the case, and is beyond anyone's power to alter. Hence, we can admit that what is known to God is a necessary truth; for as known by God it is no longer future but present. But this necessity does not destroy contingency: for the fact that an event is necessary when it happens does not mean that it was predetermined by its causes.

St. Thomas adds plausibility to his solution with a famous illustration.

> To us, because we know future contingent events as future, there can be no certainty about them; but only to God, whose knowing is in eternity, above time. A man who is walking along a road cannot see those who are coming after him; but a man who looks down from a hill upon the whole length of the road can see at the same time all those who are travelling along it. So it is with God. . . . Future events which are in themselves contingent cannot be known to us. What is known to God is necessary in the way in which it lies

open to God's knowledge [namely, in its presentness]; it is not necessary in regard to its own causes.[1]

This explanation of St. Thomas' has become the classic solution of the problem raised by God's foreknowledge. It is still sometimes presented in popular expositions of Christian theology, for instance in *Theology and Sanity* by F. J. Sheed.

> If God knew last Tuesday what you were going to do next Tuesday, what becomes of your free will? . . . God did *not* know *last* Tuesday. Tuesday is a period of time and part of the duration in which I act. But God acts in eternity which has no Tuesdays. God acts in the spacelessness of his immensity and the timelessness of his eternity: we receive the effects of his acts in space and time [p. 117].

Despite the authority of St. Thomas, the solution seems fundamentally misconceived. In the first place, it forces one to deny that it is true, in any strict sense, that God knows future free actions. St. Thomas insists repeatedly that no-one, not even God, can know contingent events *qua* future: he says of such events that we should rather say "if God knows something, then it *is*" than "if God knows something, then it *will be*" (*De Veritate* 2, 12 ad 7). Strictly speaking, then, God has no *fore*knowledge of contingent events: as He knows them, they are not still future but already present. A defender of St. Thomas might reply that this does not matter: when we say that God knows future events we mean merely that (*a*) God knows all events; (*b*) some events are future *to us*. Of any event which is future to us it will be true to say that God knows it, though He will not know *qua* future. Thus, let us suppose that at some future date a man will land on Mars. The event which is the landing on Mars is, as far as we are concerned, in the future; but to God it is already present. Thus, although we cannot say that God knows that a man *will* land on Mars (for this would be to make God know it *qua* future), we can say that God knows, timelessly, the event which is the landing on Mars. And this event is future to us—that is to say, it comes later in the time series than, e.g., your reading this.

But this reply does not meet the objection. If "to know the future" means to know more than "to know a fact which comes later in the time series than some other fact" then we, no less than God, can know the future. For we know about the Wars of the Roses which *were* future when Cleopatra was a girl. If we were to take St. Thomas' suggestion seriously, we should have to say that God knows that a man *is landing* on Mars; but we cannot say this, since the statement that a man is landing on Mars, being false, cannot be known, even by God, to be true.

St. Thomas' solution, then, is not so much a defence as a denial of God's foreknowledge. But it forces us to deny not only God's foreknowledge, but

---

[1]*Summa Theologiae*, Ia, 14, 13 ad 3 (words in brackets from the body of the article). The preceding paragraph is a mosaic of translations from *De Veritate* 2, 12.

also God's omniscience. For the statement that God's foreknowledge is outside time must mean, if anything, that no temporal qualifications can be attached to God's knowledge. Where God is the subject, verbs of knowing cannot have adverbs of time affixed to them. We cannot, therefore, say that God knows now that Brutus killed Caesar; or that God will know tomorrow what time I went to bed tonight. But as A. N. Prior has remarked, it seems an extraordinary way of affirming God's omniscience if a person, when asked what God knows *now*, must say "Nothing," and when asked what He knew *yesterday*, must again say "Nothing," and must yet again say "Nothing" when asked what God will know *tomorrow*.

An argument *ad hominem* against St. Thomas' position may be drawn from the notion of prophecy. St. Thomas believed that God could foretell, and had foretold, future contingent events. He believed, for example, that God, as the principal author of the Epistle to the Romans, had foretold the conversion of the Jewish people to Christianity. On the view that God's knowledge is timeless, such prediction becomes inexplicable. For, if God's knowledge is timeless, then we cannot attach to statements about God's knowledge such adverbial clauses as "at the time when the Epistle to the Romans was written." We cannot, for example, say "At the time when the Epistle to the Romans was written God already knew that the Jews would finally be converted." But if God did not then know it, how could He then foretell it? To put it bluntly: if God did not then *know* that the Jews would be converted, He had no right then to *say* that they would.

Indeed, the whole concept of a timeless eternity, the whole of which is simultaneous with every part of time, seems to be radically incoherent. For simultaneity as ordinarily understood is a transitive relation. If A happens at the same time as B, and B happens at the same time as C, then A happens at the same time as C. If the BBC programme and the ITV programme both start when Big Ben strikes ten, then they both start at the same time. But, on St. Thomas' view, my typing of this paper is simultaneous with the whole of eternity. Again, on his view, the great fire of Rome is simultaneous with the whole of eternity. Therefore, while I type these very words, Nero fiddles heartlessly on.

If St. Thomas' solution to the difficulty is unacceptable, is it possible to give a different one? The objection ran thus. What is implied by a necessary proposition is itself necessarily true. But from "it has come to God's knowledge that such and such will be the case" it follows that "such and such will be the case." But "it has come to God's knowledge that such and such will be the case" is necessarily true; therefore "such and such will be the case" is necessarily true. Therefore, if God knows the future, the future is not contingent.[2]

---

[2]Using "Lp" for "Necessarily p," "Gp" for "It has come to God's knowledge that p," and "Cpq" for "If p, then q," we could symbolise the argument thus: $LCLCGppLCLGpLp$; $LCGpp$; LGp; ergo, Lp.

The premises of the argument appear difficult to deny; yet if its conclusion is true, there is no freedom or else no foreknowledge. For if it must be the case that I will murder my grandfather, then I am not free not to murder my grandfather; and conversely, if I am free not to murder my grandfather, then God cannot know that I will murder him even if in fact I will do so.

Let us examine each premise in turn. It appears incontrovertible that what follows from a necessary proposition is itself necessary.[3] Moreover, it cannot be denied that "it is the case that p" follows from "It has come to God's knowledge that p": this is true *ex vi termini* "know." So, for any substitution for "p," if "It has come to God's knowledge that p" is necessarily true, then "it is the case that p" is also necessarily true.

But is it true, for all substitutions for "p," that it must be the case that it has come to God's knowledge that p? St. Thomas accepted it without question. "It has come to God's knowledge that p" is a proposition in the past tense, and for St. Thomas as for Aristotle all propositions in the past tense are necessary. Now let us first notice that even if this doctrine were true, there has occurred a significant change in the sense of "necessary." Hitherto, "necessarily" has been used in such a way that in every case it could have been replaced by "it is a logical truth that. . . ." But if an Aristotelian claims that "Cesare Borgia was a bad man" is now necessarily true, he must be using necessarily" in a different sense. For he cannot claim that it is a logical truth that Cesare Borgia was a bad man. Again, let us notice that the necessity of past propositions, if they are necessary, is not something that is *eo ipso* incompatible with freedom. If it is now necessary that Cesare Borgia was a bad man, it does not follow from this alone that it was, when he was born, necessary that he *would* be a bad man. For, according to Aristotle, necessity applies only to true past and present propositions, not to future propositions of contingent fact. But, when Cesare Borgia was born, the proposition "Cesare Borgia will be a bad man" was a future-tensed proposition of contingent fact —as indeed it still is.

It is clear, then, that if present- and past-tensed propositions are, as Aristotle thought, necessary in a way in which future-tensed propositions are not, they are not necessary in the way in which logical truths are necessary; and they are not necessary in a way which excludes the freedom of the action they report, if they report an action at all.

But is there any sense at all in which past- and present-tensed propositions have a necessity which is not shared by future-tensed propositions? The very least which seems to be demanded of a proposition if it is to be called "necessary" is that it is, always has been, and always will be, true. In this sense of "necessary" the proposition "there is a God" is necessarily true if it is true at all; but of course the proposition "there is a God" is not a logical truth, as critics of the ontological argument, from Gaunilo to Russell, have frequently pointed out. Now, the proposition "Queen Anne is dead," which is a true

---

[3]*LCLCpqLCLpLq* is a law in every standard modal system.

present-tensed proposition if ever there was one, is not a necessary truth in this sense at all, since before 1714 it was not true. The past-tensed proposition "Queen Anne has died" will indeed never cease to be true; but it *was* not true in King Alfred's day. So, even if "necessary" is given the weak interpretation of "true at all times," there seems no reason to believe the Aristotelian doctrine that past- and present-tensed propositions *in materia contingenti* are necessary.

Yet is it not true that what has happened cannot now not have happened, and that which is happening cannot now not be happening? We have a very strong inclination to think that there is some way in which we can change the future, in which we cannot change the past. But this inclination appears to be a delusion. There appears to be no sense in which we can change the future in which we cannot change the past. As A. N. Prior has pointed out, whatever changes of plan we may make, the future is whatever takes place after all the changes are made; what we alter is *not* the future, but our plans; the real future can no more be altered than the past. The sort of case which we have in mind when we are tempted to say that we can change the future is this: suppose that I have no intention of typing "elephant" backwards; then I decide I will do so; and finally I do so. Does not my decision change the future, since without my decision the word would never have been typed backwards? No, for even when I had no intention of doing so, e.g., ten years ago, it *was* true that I would, ten years later, type "elephant" backwards; and so my decision altered nothing except my own intentions. There is, indeed, a sense in which we can change the future: we can change the truth-value of a future-tensed proposition. Suppose that it is true that I will commit suicide: then the proposition "A. K. will commit suicide" now has the truth-value "true." I can change this truth-value by committing suicide; for, once I have committed suicide the proposition "A. K. will commit suicide" ceases to be true, and the quite different proposition "A. K. has committed suicide" becomes true instead. But if "to change the future" means merely "to change the truth-value of a future-tensed proposition" then in a corresponding sense I can change the past no less than the future. Nothing is easier. Tnahpele. The past-tensed proposition "A. K. has typed 'elephant' backwards" which *was* false, is now true; and so I have changed the past.

It seems, then, that there is no sense in which we can change the future in which we cannot change the past. Still, it does seem true that we can bring about the future, but cannot bring about the past; our present activity may have a causal effect on the future but cannot have a causal effect on the past. Consequently, deliberation about the future is sensible, deliberation about the past absurd; so if God's knowledge of what I will do tomorrow is already a thing of the past, deliberation about what I will do tomorrow appears already pointless, and once again there appears to be an incompatibility between foreknowledge and freedom.

However, in certain cases, it does seem that present actions can affect the past. By begetting a son, I make my grandfather, long dead, into a great-grandfather; by becoming Poet Laureate I make my late grandmother's belief that I would one day be Poet Laureate into a true belief. In such cases, of course, what we are doing is establishing new relations between past things and events and present or future things or events. But the truth of a belief, and the question of whether a certain belief does or does not constitute knowledge, involve relationships between those beliefs and the events they concern. So it is possible that it is precisely by telling a lie today that I bring it about that God knew yesterday that I would tell a lie today. Of course, I do not bring it about by today's lie that God yesterday *believed* that I would lie; but it is my current lie which makes His belief then true.

Even so, it might be retorted, this does not make it possible for God to have *known* yesterday without curtailment of my freedom; because knowledge is not true belief, but justified true belief; and the justification of a past belief would have to be past grounds for the belief; and nothing in the past could be adequate grounds for a belief about my current action unless it necessitated that action. To this the reply is open that even in non-theological contexts there seem to be cases in which true belief, without grounds, constitutes knowledge. One such case is our knowledge of our own actions. Commonly, we know what we are doing with our hands, and we do not know this on the basis of any evidence or grounds. Of course, we can be mistaken: I may think I am typing "piece" and in fact be typing "peice." But when I am not mistaken, my belief about what I am doing constitutes knowledge. It does not seem unreasonable to suggest that in this respect a Creator's knowledge of His creature's actions might resemble a human agent's knowledge of his own actions.

There seems, then, no reason to maintain that "It has come to God's knowledge that *p*" is a necessary truth, in any of the senses we have suggested, merely because it is past-tensed. Might it not be argued, however, that it is a necessary truth for a different reason: namely, that it is a truth about God's knowledge, which is the knowledge of a necessarily omniscient necessary being? If God is omniscient, it might be argued, then, whatever we substitute for "*p*," "it has come to God's knowledge that *p*" will be true. But "if it has come to God's knowledge that *p*" is true no matter what we substitute for "*p*," then it must be something like a logical truth, and so a necessary truth in the sense in which necessity is incompatible with freedom.

It does not take a moment to detect the fallacy in this argument. God's omniscience does not at all imply that whatever we substitute for "*p*" in "God knows that *p*" is true. For instance, if we substitute "$2+2=3$" we get not a necessary truth but the falsehood "God knows that $2+2=3$." It is indeed a logical truth that if *p* is true, then *p* is known by any omniscient being; but this is insufficient to provide the premise needed by St. Thomas' objector.[4] A sentence such as "God knows that I am sitting down" expresses not a neces-

---

[4]We have not LGp but $LCpGp$.

sary, but a contingent truth: it may be true now, but it was not true last night, and it will cease to be true as soon as I stand up. In fact, God's knowledge will only be necessary where what He knows is necessary: "$2+2=4$" is a necessary truth, so "God knows that $2+2=4$" is a necessary truth.[5] But, by definition, a contingent proposition—such as a proposition reporting or predicting a free action—is never a necessary truth. Hence, the argument which we have been considering has no tendency to show that human freedom and divine foreknowledge are incompatible.

There are other arguments to prove this incompatibility: Aquinas alone gives thirteen of which we have considered only two. None, however, are as initially plausible, or as complicated to unravel, as the two we have considered.

---

[5]We have not $LCpLGp$, but $LCLpLGp$.

A. N. PRIOR

3.13 The Formalities of Omniscience

What do we mean by saying that a being, God for example, is omniscient? One way of answering this question is to translate 'God is omniscient' into some slightly more formalised language than colloquial English, e.g. one with variables of a number of different types, including variables replaceable by statements, and quantifiers binding these. In such a language, the common form of the statements

God knows that $2+2=4$
God knows that $2+2=5$
God knows that God knows that $2+2=4$

can clearly be given as

God knows that p,

and this is going to be useful in answering our opening question.

If there is no God, it would seem that all statements of the form just given are false; but even if there is a God, it would seem that some of them are. For example, God doesn't know that 2 and 2 are 5, for the simple reason that 2 and 2 *aren't* 5.

This example is sufficient to show that one way in which we might be

---

From *Philosophy* (1962). Reprinted by permission of Mrs. Mary Prior and the editors of *Philosophy*.

tempted to translate 'God is omniscient' simply will not do. I mean the translation

(1) For every p, God knows that p.

At least, this won't do if we want to mean something *true* by 'God is omniscient'. For it is a general rule that we may pass from a universal proposition to any singular instantiation of it, and one instantiation of (1) would be the false proposition

God knows that $2 + 2 = 5$.

And we know this to be false, not by any subtle or dubious theologising, but simply by the logic of knowledge as such—if anyone thinks that $2 + 2 = 5$, his state of mind isn't knowledge but error.

Still, the correction required to this first effort seems simple and obvious. When we say that anyone knows everything, it is surely understood that what we mean is that he knows everything that's true. So, as a second attempted translation of 'God is omniscient' let us put

For every p, if it is *true* that p then God knows that p,

or more simply

(2) For every p, if p then God knows that p.

And it does seem that all the instantiations of *this* proposition are things which a believer in God's omniscience *would* wish to maintain. For example

If $2 + 2 = 4$ then God knows that $2 + 2 = 4$

If $2 + 2 = 5$ then God knows that $2 + 2 = 5$

If God knows everything then God knows that God knows everything.

These are 'instantiations' of (2) in the sense that they are formed by simply dropping the initial quantifier and putting some actual statement for the variable 'p' at the two places where it occurs, the same statement at each place. There are also 'instantiations' of (2) in a slightly more complicated sense, and all of these are, I think propositions which a believer in God's omniscience would wish to maintain. These more complicated instantiations of (2) are ones like

(3) For every x, if x $+ 2 = 4$ then God knows that $x + 2 = 4$.

It is easy to see how we get instantiations of (2) like this. In place of the two 'p's after the quantifier in (2) we put, not actual statements, but *forms* of statements still containing variables, and we replace the initial quantifier 'For every p' by another one containing whatever variables occur in the replacement for 'p.'

Here is another example of the same sort: Suppose we write 'fx' for any statement about x, e.g. 'f(Plato)' for any statement about Plato. Then the proposition

(4) For every f, if f(Plato) then God knows that f(Plato)

would mean that God knows everything there is to know about Plato, and this too would be an instantiation of (2). So also would

(5) For every f and x, if fx then God knows that fx,

which asserts in plain English that God knows everything about everything.

Again, suppose we introduce a variable d which stands for any expression which, attached to a statement, forms a statement, for example, 'It is not the case that————,' 'Johnny believes that————,' and so on. Thus a formula like 'd(2 + 2 = 5)' can stand indifferently for such statements as

It is not the case that 2 + 2 = 5
Johnny believes that 2 + 2 = 5
I wish it were the case that 2 + 2 = 5

and so on; and also for such statements as

1 + 1 = 3 *and* 2 + 2 = 5
Either my name is Percy or 2 + 2 = 5
If my name is not Percy then 2 + 2 = 5

and, for that matter, for such statements as

If 2 + 2 = 5 *then* 2 + 3 = 6
Either 2 + 2 = 5 *or my name is Percy*
That 2 + 2 = 5 *is less surprising than that my name is Percy,*

in which the expression substituted for 'd', and making a statement by being attached to '2 + 2 = 5', isn't attached to '2 + 2 = 5' by being *prefixed* to it but rather by being as it were wrapped around it. And among the instantiations of the proposition (2) is this:

(6) For all d, if d(2 + 2 = 5) then God knows that d(2 + 2 = 5).

This could be a way of translating something rather puzzling that some of the schoolmen used to say, namely that there *is* a sense in which God knows even false propositions,[1] for He *understands* them just as completely as He understands true propositions, and of course as part of this complete understanding He understands or knows that they are false. He knows, we might say, all truths into which the idea of 2 and 2 being 5 in any way enters, e.g. the truth that it is not the case that 2 + 2 = 5, that some idiotic boy believes that 2 + 2 = 5, and so on.

But now we must raise a deeply controversial point. In this statement that for every p, if p then God knows that p, are we to understand this verb 'knows' as a verb in the present tense, or are we not? Many very reputable philosophers, e.g. St Thomas Aquinas, have held that God's knowledge is in some way right outside of time, in which case presumably the verb 'knows' in our translation would have to be thought of as tenseless. I want to argue against this view, on the ground that its final effect is to restrict *what God knows* to those truths, if any, which are themselves timeless. For example, God could not, on the view I am considering, know that the 1960 final examinations at Manchester are now over; for this isn't something that He or anyone could know timelessly, because it just isn't true timelessly. It's true now, but it wasn't true a year ago (I write this on August 29th, 1960) and so far as I can see all that can be said on this subject timelessly is that the

---

[1]See, e.g., Ockham, *Tractatus de Praedestinatione*, etc., ed. P. Boehner (Franciscan Institute, 1954), pp. 56, 101B.

finishing-date of the 1960 final examinations is an earlier one than August 29th, and this is *not* the thing we know when we know that those exams are over. I cannot think of any better way of showing this than one I've used before,[2] namely, the argument that what we know when we know that the 1960 final examinations are over can't be just a timeless relation between dates because this isn't the thing we're *pleased* about when we're pleased that the exams are over. In any case it seems an extraordinary way of affirming God's omniscience if a person, when asked what God knows *now*, must say 'Nothing', and when asked what He knew yesterday, must again say 'Nothing', and must yet again say 'Nothing' when asked what God will know tomorrow.

Of course if we take the 'knows' in our translation to be the ordinary present-tense 'knows', then we must regard the 'is' in the thing it's a translation *of*, namely 'God is omniscient', as the ordinary present-tense 'is', and if we want to translate the belief that God's omniscience is a permanent and unalterable thing we must expand our (2) to this:

(7) It is, always has been, and always be the case that for all p, if p then God knows that p.

We may further note that even with respect to what God is said in both formula (2) and formula (7) to know *now*, the statements over which the variable 'p' may range include not only present-tense but past-tense and future-tense ones, and tenseless ones also, if any such there be. For example, we can infer by instantiation from both (2) and (7) the following propositions:

If there were living organisms a million years ago, God knows that there were living organisms a million years ago;

and

If there will be living organisms a million years hence, God knows that there will be living organisms a million years hence.

Omniscience as here defined, in other words, covers *fore*-knowledge of whatever will be, that is, *knowledge at every moment of whatever at that moment will be.*

But now I want to raise a subtler point. Is the believer in God's omniscience committed to the following proposition:

(8) For all p, if (it is the case that) p, God has always known that it would be the case that p,

(for example, if I now scratch my head, God has always known that I would scratch my head on this occasion)? The first thing to be said about this proposition is that it *isn't* a simple logical consequence of God's omniscience in the sense of our proposition (7). It does follow from proposition (7) that

(9) If, at any time, it was the case at that time that it would be the case that p, then God knew at that time that it would be the case that p.

But this is not enough to give us proposition (8), unless we supplement it by

[2]A. N. Prior, "Thank Goodness that's Over," *Philosophy*, Jan. 1959, p. 17. Cf. C. D. Broad, *Examination of McTaggart's Philosophy*, Vol. II, Part I, pp. 266–67.

(10) For all p, if (it is the case that) p then it has always been the case that it would be the case that p.

If (10) is true, and God is omniscient in the sense of proposition (7), then (8) is true. And contrariwise if (10) is false, then (8) must be false also. For if (10) is false, that means that in some cases in which it *is* the case that p, it nevertheless *hasn't* always been the case that p would be the case, and if this hasn't always *been* true, then clearly neither God nor anyone can have *known* it to be true. So that at this point everything really depends on whether for every p that *is* the case, it has always been the case that it would come to pass that p, or as I sometimes loosely put it, whether whatever *is* the case *has always been going to be* the case. This proposition, together with God's omniscience, *does* yield the conclusion that with respect to whatever is now the case, God has always known that it would be the case; but that conclusion, i.e. our proposition (8), does *not* follow from God's omniscience alone. And my own view would be that, whatever may be the case with the doctrine of God's omniscience itself, proposition (8) is not true, nor is proposition (10). And on both these points, I mean the denial of the logical proposition (10) and even of the theological proposition (8), I rather think that, for what this is worth, I have St. Thomas Aquinas on my side, though this involves some very tricky questions of exposition.

Let's look, anyhow, at a bit of what Thomas has to say about these matters in his *De Veritate*, Question 2, Article 12, 'Whether God knows singular future contingents'.[3] He begins by stating some twelve arguments for the negative, of which I think the most persuasive is the seventh, which begins like this: Given any true proposition of the form 'If p then q', if the antecedent p is absolutely necessary, then the consequent q must be absolutely necessary also. The point of this *necessarium absolute*, and the sort of necessity with which Thomas is contrasting it, is obvious enough. If I make a statement of the form 'If p then necessarily q', I may not mean that from the truth of p we can infer that q is in itself a *necessary truth*, i.e. I may not mean 'If p then necessarily-q'; I may only mean that the truth of q—it could quite well be the *contingent* truth of q—*necessarily follows* from the truth of p, i.e. I may only mean 'If p then—necessarily q'. This is not an absolute but a merely conditional necessity of q; in fact not really a necessity of q at all, but only a necessary connection between q and something else. Nevertheless we can legitimately infer the necessity of q in itself if we are given not only its necessary following from p, but also the necessity of p in itself. What necessarily follows from something necessary is itself necessary. That's the first premiss that Thomas's imaginary objector uses here, and Thomas himself, we shall find, quite explicitly assents to it.[4]

---

[3]Directly on the maxim that *id quod est verum in praesenti, semper fuit verum esse futurum*, it is worth also glancing at *Summa Theologica*, Part I, Question 16, Article 7, Obj. 3 and answer.

[4]Stock sources for this law in Aristotle are *An. Pr.* I, Ch. 15, 34a, 23, and *An. Post.* I, ch. 6, 75a, 1–11.

Now here, the objector goes on, is a true proposition of the form 'If p then q': 'If anything is known to God, then that thing will be'. This perhaps needs filling out a little; it is clear from the context that what the objector has in mind is any proposition of the general form 'If it has come to God's knowledge that X will happen, then X *will* happen'. But the antecedent of this, at least if it's true at all, is necessary, if only because it's *past*, and so beyond anyone's power to prevent—*quod fuit, non potest non fuisse*, 'What has been, cannot now not have been'.[5] So anything that follows from this necessary, i.e. now-unpreventable, truth, must itself be now-unpreventable. From this in turn it follows—the corollary is too obvious for Thomas to bother drawing it explicity—that whatever *isn't* now-unpreventable *hasn't* yet come to God's knowledge. That's against proposition (8); it is clear that a similar argument could be used to show, against proposition (10), that whatever *has already come to be* part of what is to come is now-unpreventable, and so whatever isn't yet unpreventable hasn't yet come to be part of what is to come.

The general point of this type of argument might be brought out by using a few symbols. Suppose we use 'X = Y' to assert that the propositions X and Y are logically equivalent, i.e. inferable from one another; this equivalence having the usual properties of symmetry (if $X = Y$, $Y = X$) and transitiveness (if $X = Y$ and $Y = Z$, $X = Z$) and also the property that if $X = Y$ then $f(X) = f(Y)$, where f is any logical function, e.g. 'Not'. Let us, further, include among logical functions of a proposition p the functions 'Necessarily p' (or 'Now-unpreventably p'), symbolised as 'Lp'; 'It was the case n time-units ago that p', written 'Pnp'; 'It will be the case n time-units hence that p', written 'Fnp'; and 'God knows that p', written 'Gp'. It is easy to show that if we have the logical equivalence

$$Pnp = LPnp$$

('It was the case that p if and only if it now-unpreventably was the case that p') and any logical equivalence of the form

(i) $X = PnY$,

we can prove

(ii) $X = LX$

for we have $X = PnY = LPnY = LX$. Thus if we have

(iii) $p = PnGFnp$

('p is the case if and only if God knew n time-units ago that p would be the case n time-units later'; i.e. approximately proposition (8)), then we have

$$p = PnGFnp = LPnGFnp = Lp;$$

while if we have

(iv) $p = PnFnp$

('p is the case if and only if God knew n time-units ago that p would be the the case n time-units later'; i.e. approximately proposition (10)), then we have

$$p = PnFnp = LPnFnp = Lp.$$

---

[5]The main stock source for this is the *Nicomachean Ethics*, VI, 1139 b. See also *De Caelo* I, 283 b 13.

And if we have

(v) $p = Gp$

('p if and only if God knows that p'), then we can derive (iii) from (iv) and *vice versa* (my earlier point about the deductive equivalence of (8) and (10), given God's omniscience); for by (v), $Fnp = GFnp$, and so $PnFnp = PnGFnp$.

I wish I knew where Thomas got his seventh objection from. It was developed very powerfully *after* Thomas by the fifteenth-century anti-Occamist Louvain philosopher Peter de Rivo;[6] and Peter de Rivo knew, but so far as I can discover Thomas did not know, Cicero's *De Fato*, in which a very similar argument is put into the mouth of Diodorus the Megarian.[7] In the absence of any better theory, I would suggest that perhaps Thomas himself constructed this argument against the theological proposition (8) on the pattern of the analogous argument against the logical proposition (10) which he found in Aristole's *De Interpretatione*, and enlarged upon (and so far as I can see accepted) in his commentary on that work, Book I, *Lectio* 13. But wherever Thomas got the argument from, it seems to me, with one slight modification that I'll discuss later, entirely conclusive. Thomas treats it, too, with the respect it deserves and brushes aside three ways of dealing with it which he considers inadequate before putting forward an answer of his own.

There are some, he tells us, who argue that the antecedent of this conditional, despite its expressing a truth about the past, is contingent. For, these people say, it has a reference to the future, and that sort of truth about the past isn't always unpreventable—we do sometimes say truly that a thing was going to happen, and then when the time comes it doesn't. Thomas admits this sense of 'going to happen'—we do sometimes say that a thing was going to happen when we mean that everything was so to speak pointing that way—but even in this sense of 'going to happen', Thomas points out, if it's ever true that a thing was going to happen, then it cannot by that time not have been going to happen in that sense, even though perhaps by this time it isn't happening and it's clear that it never will.

Others, again, say that the proposition 'It has come to God's knowledge that X will happen' is contingent because it's a compound proposition with a contingent component, like 'Peter is a white man'—Peter cannot but be a man, but he needn't be white, and so needn't be a white man. To this Thomas replies that the necessity or contingency of a proposition doesn't depend on the character of its subject-matter but on the nature of the main 'link' in its construction; e.g. 'I believe that man is an animal' and 'I believe that Peter is running' are equally contingent though the thing believed is necessary in the one case and contingent in the other. I'm not sure that this rule of Thomas's always works; with simple conjunctions like 'Peter is an animal and Peter is running' the modality of the whole *does* depend up

---

[6]See L. Baudry's excellent collection of texts, *La Querelle des Futurs Contingents* (*Louvain* 1465–1475), Vrin, 1950; e.g. p. 70.

[7]Cicero, *De Fato*, vii, 14.

to a point on the modality of the bits; but the point perhaps is that what we have here isn't that sort of combination but rather the sort in which there is definitely a principal clause ('It has come to God's knowledge—') and a subordinate one, and here the pastness and consequent 'necessity' of the principal clause does seem to settle the matter.[8]

While I think Thomas was right on the main point here, I ought to mention that this is what was called in question by most of the writers subsequent to him who considered this argument and were not satisfied with his handling of it; for example, the fifteenth-century Occamists. They held that an element of futurity even in a subordinate clause could destroy the sort of necessity which normally attaches to past-tense truths, and in fact made such truths essentially future in sense even if past in form.[9] If, to construct a new example, my own future choice and nothing else can cause me to start smoking tomorrow, then my own future choice and nothing else can cause it to *have been* the case yesterday that I would start smoking in two days' time from then; and this fact that is directly about yesterday and only indirectly about tomorrow, if it is a fact at all, is as much a contingent fact as the one that is directly about tomorrow. Nor have Occamists hesitated to ascribe a like contingency to God's foreknowledge. But I must confess to a difficulty here. I think I can attach intelligible senses to the phrases 'was *true* yesterday' and 'was *the case* yesterday' which give the Occamist results; but I cannot find any such sense for 'was *known* yesterday'. I can by my free choice, not exercised until tomorrow, cause a person's *guess*, made yesterday, to have been a correct one (I do this simply by deciding to do what he guessed I would); and I can by the same act convey the same retrospective verification to another person's guess, made right now, that the first person's guess *was* a correct one. It is so to speak still open to this latter guess, despite its past-tense subject matter, either to turn out to have been correct or to turn out not to have been correct; its present correctness, if it does turn out to have been correct, is thus entirely contingent. But while contingent futures, and contingent future-infected pasts, can in this way be correctly or incorrectly guessed, I cannot see in what way they can be 'known'; or to put it another way, I cannot see in what way the alleged knowledge, even if it were God's, could be more than correct guessing. For there would be *ex hypothesi* nothing that could *make* it knowledge, no present *ground* for the guess's correctness which a specially penetrating person might perceive.[10] So if we talk this way, while

---

[8]On these two very different ways in which a proposition may be compounded out of past-tense and future-tense elements, see Peter de Rivo in Baudry, *op. cit.*, p. 339.

[9]See Ockham himself on this, *op. cit.*, pp. 5–6, C, and Ferdinand of Cordova in Baudry, *op. cit.*, p. 159. For what seems to be a very similar view, see Ryle's *Dilemmas*, "It Was to Be."

[10]I owe much in this paragraph to Professor J. M. Shorter. Cf. also, on the negative point, Jonathan Edwards on the Will, Part II, Sect. XII, Observation II. But this is a frequently repeated Thomist point too—that there can logically be no *knowledge* of the future, for one who is still awaiting its actualisation, but what he can gather from its already present causes. (See, e.g., *De Malo*, XVI, 7.)

we do get my proposition (10) in a rather trivial way, I don't think we get my proposition (8), because I don't think we get the thing that ties the two together, namely God's omniscience, except in the weak sense that He *knows whatever is knowable*, this being no longer co-extensive with what is true. This conclusion (that you don't get omniscience this way) seems confirmed by the fact that Ockham, who I suppose was the classical exponent of the point of view I've just been sketching, was driven to assert that 'it is impossible to express clearly the manner in which God knows future contingencies'.[11]

Returning now to Thomas: he goes on to consider a third way of answering this 'seventh objection', namely by arguing that a necessary antecedent of a true conditional *can* have a contingent consequent, as in, for example, 'If the sun shines this tree will flower'. The sun cannot but shine; but something *could* interfere with its influence on the tree so that it doesn't flower after all. Only where the connection between antecedent and consequent is immediate, without the possibility of anything intervening to frustrate it, does the rule really hold. So it is argued; but Thomas argues on the contrary that it is only where there is no possibility of frustration that the conditional is strictly true. 'If the sun shines the tree will flower' is for this reason *not* true; if it *were true*, the necessity of its antecedent *would* be conveyed to its consequent.

Once again I think Thomas is right, but there is something that ought to be added here to obviate a misunderstanding. Some writers on these topics have thought it important to insist that no sort of knowledge, not knowledge of what is to come any more than knowledge of what has been, actually *causes* the truth of that which is known. Thomas doesn't insist on this, I think because in the case of divine knowledge he doesn't believe it is true. Personally I do think it is true, but not very relevant to the argument we are considering. For a conditional proposition such as 'If it has come to God's knowledge that X will be, then X will be', doesn't require for its truth, or for its conveying necessity from its antecedent to its consequent, that its antecedent should *causally bring about* its consequent. It is enough that the former cannot be the case without the latter being the case, regardless of why this is so. And in fact if we like to say that it is because X will be that it can be known that it will be, rather than *vice versa*, this means more than ever that X's future coming to pass is beyond prevention, since it has already *had consequences* which its opposite could not have (I take this point from Jonathan Edwards,[12] who reproduced this Objection 7 in the eighteenth century for a different purpose—not to show that God cannot know future contingencies, but to show that, just because God does know all the future, none of it can *be* contingent).

11Ockham, *op. cit.*, p. 15.
12Edwards, *op. cit.*, Observation III, Corollary I, discussion of Whitby. My attention was first drawn to this Section in Edwards, and the resemblances between its opening argument and Thomas's Objection 7, by Mr J. C. Thornton.

What, then, with all these lines of escape stopped up, are we left with? Nothing, Thomas thinks, but to accept the objector's conclusion; only with a careful elucidation of the exact sense in which it is true. Here I must do a little re-translating of his Latin. Above, I have used the phrase 'has come to God's knowledge' to render Thomas's *est scitum a Deo*, because this translation brings out the pastness of the *scitum*, on which the objection as stated so heavily depends. But in fact what is *scitum a Deo* is necessarily so whether this *scitum* expresses a *past* fact or an *eternal* one, and this point is explicitly admitted by Thomas when he restates this objection in the *Summa Theologica*, Part I, Question 14, Article 13 (Objection 2). His answer to the argument, however, requires him to insist that what *is* in fact expressed, so far as we may suppose the antecedent to be true at all, is not proper pastness but eternity. And his answer consists in simply admitting that what is known to God *is* unalterable in the form in which God knows it; for God does not see the future contingent fact as future but as present. It is, he says, nearer the truth to say that if God knows a thing it *is*, than that if He knows it, it *will be*. At an earlier point, where he is neither stating nor answering an objection but simply setting out his own view, he argues thus: The contingent, considered as future (*ut futurum est*) cannot be the object of any sort of knowledge which cannot fall into falsehood; so since the divine knowledge neither does nor can fall into falsehood, God could not possibly have any knowledge of future contingencies if He knows them *as* future. Divine *fore*knowledge of such events is, in fact, out; as He knows them, they are not still to come, but already there. This (which is what I had in mind when I said earlier that Thomas denies not only the logical proposition (10) but even in a way the theological proposition (8)) is a doctrine taken over from Boethius; its import is perhaps illuminated by the comment of an earlier follower of Boethius, namely Anselm, who observes that the unchanging 'presence' which on this view all things have to God, is in some ways less like our own present than our past. Looking back over what *has* happened, we can distinguish what was bound to happen as it did from what could have happened otherwise, though of course none of it *can now*, by the time we look back on it, have happened otherwise. It is in some such way as this that God distinguishes necessities and contingencies even though there is no contingency left in the latter in the form in which they reach His gaze.

For myself, I cannot wholly agree either with the objection or with Thomas's answer to it. I do agree with both that in some sense in which we *can* alter the future we *cannot* alter the past. But there is an objection to this that the future is precisely whatever it is that does come to pass after our alleged alteration has taken place, so what we alter *isn't* the future after all, and the real future can no more be altered than the past can. What I want to say to this—and as far as it goes I think it is Thomist doctrine too—is that nothing can be said to be truly 'going-to-happen' (*futurum*) until it is so 'present in its causes' as to be beyond stopping; until that happens, neither

'It will be the case that p' nor 'It will be the case that not p' is strictly speaking true. What Thomas says is that neither of them is true *determinate*; and what this appears to mean is that though they somehow share truth and falsehood between them, neither is as yet definitely attached to either proposition rather than the other.[13] I don't myself now think—though I once did—that this complication is necessary; it is enough to distinguish (as Thomas did not) between the form 'It will be that it is not the case that p' (which commits one to the futurition of Not-p) and the form 'It is not the case that it will be that p' (which could also be true if it is simply as yet undetermined whether it is p or not-p that the future holds). Writing 'F' for the simple 'It will be that', 'N' for 'Not', and 'AXY' for 'Either X or Y', I would say that we have at this stage

NAFpFNp

('Neither it-will-be-that p nor it-will-be-that not-p'). And this state of affairs we can alter, changing it to

AFpFNp

when it is in our power to decide one way or the other and we do so. But what is past cannot be thus altered, for it is *always* the case that either p *has been* the case or Not-p has, i.e. we always have

APpPNp,

and there can be no question of changing from this to its opposite or *vice versa*. Moreover, with respect to any specific past time, say n time-units ago, we have

APnpPnNp,

but for some future times we have, on the contrary,

NAFnpFnNp.

Let us now put 'MFnp' for the assertion that p is one of the things that *can* happen n time-units hence, and take this to mean that it *isn't* yet settled that p will *not* be the case at that time; i.e.

(vi) MFnp = NFnNp.

We can similarly define 'It can be that p *has* happened n time-units ago', MPnp, as NPnNp; but there is a very big difference between this case and the preceding. For 'It *isn't* the case that p was then *not* the case' is true only of those times of which it *is* the case that p then *was* the case,[14] i.e. we have

(vii) MPnp = Pnp,

whereas 'It isn't (yet) the case that p will then not be the case' can be true of 'thens' of which it isn't yet the case, either, that p will then *be* the case, i.e. we do *not* have as a law

MFnp = Fnp.

---

[13]See, especially, the latter part of Part I, *Lectio* 13, in his *Peri Hermeneias* commentary.

[14]At least the theory of future contingencies provides no exceptions to this. For the possibility of other exceptions, see *Summa Theologica*, Part I, Question 16, Article 7, Objection 4 and answer; and my own *Time and Modality*, Ch. 4, and "Identifiable Individuals," *Review of Metaphysics*, June 1960, pp. 692, 695–96.

So I want to say that 'It can be that X' is logically equivalent to the simple X where X is a past-tense proposition, but not where it is a future-tense. Thomas and his objector would, I think, agree with this, but they say, further, that 'It *must* be that X' is equivalent to the simple X where X is in the past tense and not where it is future; and this difference I cannot myself obtain in any straightforward way.[15] What I have succeeded in formalising is in fact not quite the Aristotelian-Thomist account of this whole situation, but a slight modification of it that you get in C. S. Peirce, who says that the past is the region of 'brute fact', while the future divides into the necessitated, for which alone we have either Fnp or FnNp, and the merely possible, for which we have neither.[16]

Still, with this position also the proposed distinction between past and future can be shown to break down if we equate p either with PnFnp or with PnGFnp, at least if we also admit (as all writers that I know of do) that

(viii) $p = FnPnp$,

i.e. a proposition *is* true if and only if it *will* be the case at any given time hence that it *was* the case that interval of time before. For on these assumptions we have

$$MFnp = NFnNp \text{ (vi)}$$
$$= FnPnNFnNp \text{ (viii)}$$
$$= FnNPnNNFnNp \text{ (vii)}$$
$$= FnNPnFnNp \text{ (NNp} = p)$$
$$= FnNNp \text{ (iv)}$$
$$= Fnp \text{ (NNp} = p)$$

('$= FnNPnGFnNP$' may be inserted after the 4th line by (v) and removed by (iii)). Intuitively, the argument proceeds thus: Suppose it is now possible that a certain thing, say p, should come to pass n time-units hence. Then it *will* be true when that time comes (whatever actually happens then) that this thing *was* possible now. That is, it *will* be false then that the thing *was* at this present time booked to fail to come to pass. But if this will be false then, it will also be false then that it *is* failing to come to pass (for on the hypothesis that we are considering, if it were then failing to come to pass, it *would* now have been going to fail). But if it will then be *false* that it *isn't* coming to pass, it will be *true* that it *is* coming to pass. That is, from the mere possibility of a future event we can by these steps infer that it will actually occur. On this view also, then, the reality of future contingency is incompatible with our proposition (10), and by the same type of argument with proposition (8).

There is an interesting, and formally rather beautiful, relation between the 'tense-logic' here advocated and the 'Occamist' tense-logic mentioned earlier as an alternative to Thomas's. We can formalise the Occamist system by having one set of variables, say 'p', 'q', 'r', etc., for statements generally, and a special

[15]For the difficulty here, see my *Time and Modality*, p. 97.
[16]Collected Papers of C. S. Peirce, 5, 459.

further set, say 'a', 'b', 'c', etc., restricted to statements with no trace of futurity in them. We might then have 'a = La' as a law but not the more general 'p = Lp' and not even 'Pnp = LPnp', though we would have 'Pna = LPna'. Certain functions of the 'A-variables' would be substitutable for them in laws (would constitute 'A-formulae'), others not. For example, 'Pna' as well as the plain 'a' (and 'Na') would count as an A-formula, and be substitutable for 'a' in laws, but 'Fna' would not, nor would 'PmFna', though both of these would be substitutable for 'p'. ('Pna' would be an A-formula because formed by prefixing 'Pn' to an A-formula, but 'PmFna' would not, because the formula to which the 'Pm' is here prefixed isn't one.) 'LFna' and 'LPmFna' are of course wellformed, and propositions of this form could some-times be true; and there is a case for counting as an 'A-formula', i.e. as not having *proper* futurity, any formula at all that begins with 'L', even ones like 'LFna'. (Such assertions 'haven't proper futurity' because whether it is or is not necessary that Fna must depend solely on factors now in being, which either do or do not now leave open an alternative future, n time-units hence, to a.) And earlier I have in effect sketched a case for taking the same line with 'G', and for having in this sort of system the law 'a = Ga', but not 'p = GP'.

The laws of this system would include both 'NPnp = PnNp' ('It is not the case that p was then so, if and only if it was then the case that not-p') and 'NFnp = FnNp' ('It is not the case that p will then be, if and only if it will then be that not p'), and of course the substitutions of 'a' for 'p' in these. But whereas they will include 'NLPna = LPnNa' (by the law 'a = La', the fact that 'Pna' and 'PnNa' are A-formulae, and a preceding equivalence, these giving us the chain 'NLPna = NPna = PnNa = LPnNa'), they will not include 'NLFna = LFnNa' (the chain breaks because 'Fna' and 'FnNa' are not substitutable for 'a' in 'a = La').

Suppose now we remove the Occamist's functor 'F' from the system and replace it by another 'F' equivalent to the Occamist's 'LF'. Assuming that there is no way of forming 'non-A' propositions out of the A ones except by the use of the Occamist 'F', in this new system none but A-propositions will be formulable, so no variables need be used but A-variables; or if you like, the P-variables can be treated as A-variables. Because we had 'a = La' in the old system, we will have 'p = Lp' in the new one; in fact there will be no use in it for the operator 'L'. And we will have 'NPnp = PnNp' in the new system as in the old; but we will *not* have 'NFnp = FnNp', for the new 'F' is the old 'LF', and we didn't have 'NLFna = LFnNa'. We will, though, now have 'p = Gp', since we had 'a = Ga' in the old.

This "new" system is in fact precisely the "Peircean" or near-Aristotelian system advocated above. So it could be said, and indeed it has been said (e.g. by Professor Shorter), that the system advocated is merely the Occamist one robbed of its means of expressing contingent truths. I would reply that in an important sense of 'truths' there are no contingent truths; once a thing reaches the status of a 'truth' there can be no going back on it; though there are 'contingencies', i.e. matters of which it is not yet true either that they will be the case or that they will fail to be the case. This is of course a terminological difference rather than one of substance, but being a difference as to what we shall count as a 'truth', it affects what we mean by 'God knows all truths', and so could (and in my view should) affect what truth-value we attach to this statement.

There is, we may observe at this point, an even more direct way of getting 'p = Lp' than the method of Thomas's Objection 7. For the schoolmen commonly contrasted the contingency of the future with the necessity not only of the past but also of the present—not only what *has been* the case cannot now not have been the case, but what *is* the case cannot now not *be* the case. But it is plausible to say that the functor 'It is the case that———' makes no difference to the truth or falsehood of *anything* to which it is prefixed, so that *all* propositions are equivalent to ones which are of the present tense in their principal clause. Thomas seems to admit this when, commenting on *De Interpretatione* 16 b 17–19, he equates *est praeteritum* and *fuit praesens*, and *est futurum* and *erit praesens*—putting 'Sp' for 'It is the case that p', we have 'Sp = p' and in particular 'SPp = Pp = PSp' and 'SFp = Fp = FSp'. And this, given 'Sp = LSp', gives 'Fp = SFp = LSFp = LFp', thus breaking down the above difference between future and present. The Occamist answer to this is presumably to replace 'p' by 'a' in the new 'Sp = LSp' (there is then no need for him to alter 'p = Sp'); the Peircean admits the conclusion but gets the reality of future and unreality of present and past contingency in another way.

As to Thomas's own answer to his real or imaginary objector, I can only say this: I simply cannot see how the presentness, pastness or futurity of any state of affairs can be in any way relative to the *persons to whom* this state of affairs is known.[17] What makes this quite impossible to stomach is precisely the truth that both Thomas and his objector insist on, namely that the future has an openness to alternatives which the past has not; such openness is just not the sort of thing that can be present for one observer and absent for another—either it exists or it doesn't, and there's an end to it; and so either a thing has already occurred or it hasn't, and there's an end to *that*. But the presentness, pastness or futurity of states of affairs does of course vary with *time*, i.e. it is itself a tensed matter—what *was* future or present, *is* now and *will be* past, and so on.[18] So I don't understand what is meant by saying that contingent future occurrences are neither contingent nor future *as* God sees them, though I do understand what would be meant if it were said that they are neither contingent nor future *when* God sees them. How, in fact, could God *know* a state of affairs to be present and beyond alteration,

---

[17]Cf. Scotus, as given in Ockham, *op. cit.*, p. 53 and n.
[18]Cf. McTaggart, *The Nature of Existence*, Ch. XXXIII, Sects. 305, 330; and my own "Time after Time," *Mind*, April 1958, pp. 244–46.

until it *is* present and beyond alteration (for if He sees it as present when it is not, surely He is in error)? But to know that something is so when it is so, is surely not *fore*knowledge. So when I try to set out to myself what Boethius and Thomas—and later on, Peter de Rivo (and even Peirce[19])—are saying here, I find that either I cannot understand what I am saying, or I slip into something which I certainly *can* understand, but which is surely too trivial altogether to express the intention of these writers. Still, with this trivial thing, so far as it goes, I do agree; I agree that is, that God, or let us say any omniscient being, knows what is happening when it is happening; and of course I agree also with the negative admission of Thomas and of Peter de Rivo that God *doesn't* know future contingencies literally *when* they are still future and contingent, and that it is impossible that He or anyone else should know them in this way. But (and this is what Thomas himself says[20]) this is only because there is not then any truth of the form 'It will be the case that p' (or 'It will be the case that not p'), with respect to this future contingency p, for Him to know; and *nihil potest sciri nisi verum*.

---

[19]C. S. Peirce, *op. cit.*, 4, 67.
[20]*De Veritate*, Question 2, Article 13, Objection 1 and answer.

∾ PART FOUR

GOD'S RELATION
TO THE WORLD

INTRODUCTION

Many religious people want to claim that there is a special relationship between God and the world, the relationship of creator to created. Although they may disagree as to whether God created the world from nothing (creation *ex nihilo*) or whether he molded, shaped, and gave order to preexisting matter, they all agree that the universe, as we know it now, governed by the laws that it is governed by, is a product of the creative activity of God. With this belief comes the additional belief that God can then intervene so as to ensure that a particular result will come about and that these acts of intervention may result in an event whose occurrence violates the laws of nature (God can perform miracles).

Both the doctrine of creation and the doctrine of miracles raise a variety of philosophical problems, some of which are examined in this section. We begin with a variety of problems raised by the idea that, at some given point in time, God created the universe. Stated simply, these problems arise out of the question, "Why did God create the universe when he did rather than at some other time?"

St. Augustine raises one version of the problem as follows: if God is eternal and immutable, then his creative activity must be so as well (or else, it would involve a change in him). But if it is, then why hasn't the universe existed eternally?—how could it come about that it only came into existence at a given moment in time? Leibniz raises another version of the problem as follows: there must be a reason why a given event occurs rather than some other event. Now suppose that God created the universe at some given time. Why did that event occur rather than the other event of his having created it a year earlier? Given empty time without anything in it, there could, says Leibniz, be no reason why the one event should occur rather than the other.

In attempting to deal with these problems, both Augustine and Leibniz are forced into adopting certain theories about the nature of time. For St. Augustine, time is a created entity which was created, like all other such entities, by God. There was then no time before God's creative activity, and so it is true that the universe has existed for all time. But that does not mean, of course, that the universe is eternal like God. God's eternity involves his not being in time at all, and not his existing successively at all times.

Leibniz adopts, instead, a very different theory about the nature of time. According to his theory, time is not an entity at all. Instead, it is a series of relations (the relations we call the temporal relations) between entities. And if these relations remain the same, there is no change in the time in question. Consequently, if the temporal relations among the events in the history of the universe remain the same, it is meaningless to talk of the possibility of God's having created the universe a year earlier.

Leibniz offers this solution to his problem as an alternative to the solution proposed by Samuel Clarke. Clarke can not see why there is a problem; after all, he argues, God might have his reasons as to why he created the universe at some given time rather than at some earlier time. Clarke, it should be noted, was forced into adopting this position since, as a good Newtonian, he wanted to insist that space and time were things (contra Leibniz) that were infinite in extension no matter what is the extension of the universe (contra Augustine). But, of course, Clarke's position will not do. As Leibniz points out, given the homogeneity of empty time, what reason could God have?

It should be noted that, even on Leibniz's position, the universe could have existed longer than it has. But this would require there existing things and events that preceded all that has actually existed. And, of course, there would then be no problem about God's having his reasons why he created the actual universe rather than any of these possible universes; his reasons could be based upon merits of having these additional things and events.

So much for the problem about creation. We turn now to a consideration of problems that arise in connection with the idea of God's performing miracles. There are several different, although related, problems about miracles that are discussed in the selections: What exactly is a miracle? Can we explain any event by saying that it is a miracle? Can we ever know that a miracle has occurred? If we can, would this serve as a justification for holding a particular religious belief? We shall look at each of these questions separately.

It is normal to think of a miracle as an event that occurs in violation of the laws of nature by virtue of the activity of God. There is, however, a very important objection that can be raised against this conception of a miracle. While there is no doubt that the laws of the state can be violated, does it even make sense to talk of the laws of nature being violated? The laws of nature are, after all, descriptions of the types of things that can happen; therefore, if some other type of thing happens, then doesn't that just mean that we have a wrong account of the laws of nature?

There are two ways to meet this objection, and both are discussed in the article by Professor Holland. The first is to introduce a different conception of a miracle. According to this other conception of a miracle, a miracle is an extraordinary coincidence brought about by the activity of God. The occurrence of each part of the coincidence has a natural cause, and their joint occurrence, while not having a natural cause, is not in violation of any law of nature. The miracle is simply that these parts occurred together in this remarkable coincidence. According to this conception of a miracle, then, a miracle involves no violations of the laws of nature, so the objection to miracles fails. The other way is to press the idea that laws of nature are prescriptive in a way analogous to the laws of the state, and therefore there can be miracles in the sense of events that actually violate the prescriptions of the laws of nature. Professor Holland actually adopts both of these ways of meeting the objection, and claims that there are two types of miracles.

Whichever of these conceptions of a miracle one adopts, one will still be committed to the idea that a miracle is due to the activity of God. And with this idea comes another that religious people have often expressed, viz., that miraculous events are explained when one sees them as being miraculous, as being the result of God's activity. Professor Nowell-Smith argues that this additional aspect of the concept of a miracle is mistaken. Explanations, he says, involve laws governing the phenomenon in question, laws that can be used as the basis for predictions about new phenomena. But the explanation of miraculous events as being due to the activity of God does not involve any such laws that can be used to predict new phenomena. Religious people do not, after all, want to say that God's interventions are governed by laws. Therefore, concludes Nowell-Smith, to say that an event is a miracle is to classify it as inexplicable and not to explain it in terms of the activity of the Deity.

Professor Dietl, in his article, claims that this objection is fallacious because it rests upon the assumption that all explanations must involve laws that can be used as a basis for prediction. According to Dietl, even if we forget about miracles, that assumption is not true when we consider the actions of intelligent beings. Their actions can be explained by simply showing the point of them. And, presumably, the same thing could be done for miracles, for they too are the actions of an (admittedly special) intelligent being. Dietl's response rests, of course, upon his assumption about the way in which we explain the actions of intelligent beings, and that assumption needs much further debate and discussion.

We turn then to a consideration of our third question. Can we ever know that a miracle has occurred? This question divides itself, of course, into two parts: can we know that the extraordinary event in question has occurred?—and can we know that it is due to the activity of God?

David Hume offered a classical argument to prove that the answer to both questions is no. In any case in which we receive a report of a miracle, says

Hume, we have to evaluate the reliability of the testimony as to its occurrence. In evaluating testimony, says Hume, there are many factors to take into account, but one of the most important of them is the intrinsic probability of the event. The more unusual and unlikely the event that is reported, the less credible is the testimony. Now consider a case in which what is reported is the occurrence of a violation of the laws of nature. Then it is such an extremely improbable event that no testimony is going to establish its occurrence, or, at least, no testimony will do so unless its falsehood would be more miraculous than the event in question.

It should be noted that Hume, in pressing his objection, is really challenging our accepting the occurrence of these extraordinary events. But there is another challenge raised by our question. Couldn't one also grant that the event in question has occurred, but claim that we have not shown that it is a miracle for we have not proved, and it really is impossible to prove, that the event in question has no natural cause.

Both Professor Holland and Professor Dietl claim that these challenges can be met. They construct examples in which, it seems to them, we really cannot say either that the event has not occurred or that it can be explained as anything other than the result of the intervention of a Divine Agent. What the reader will have to decide for himself is whether or not it really is true that we can say neither of those things in the cases in question, and if that is the case, why is that so? After all, the skeptical arguments, at least as stated in the abstract, seem perfectly plausible.

The final point that should be noted is in connection with the last of our original questions. All of our authors who discuss the question seem to agree that, even if we knew of the occurrence of a miracle, we could not use miracles as a basis for a particular set of religious beliefs. To begin with, they don't even tell us what is the nature of the intelligent person whose activity produced the miracle. They certainly do not indicate, for instance, that the entity in question is Anselm's all-perfect God. Secondly, it does not seem that there is one religion, and only one, with miracles that could meet the skeptical challenge. Many different religions, with conflicting religious claims, have miracles that seem equally well authenticated; and if any of their miracles meet the skeptical challenge, so too will the miracles of the others. Which, then, would be the correct religion? It is not clear how this final challenge could be met.

CREATION

ST. AUGUSTINE

4.1 God's Will and the Beginning of the Universe

In this Beginning, O God, hast Thou made heaven and earth, in Thy Word, in Thy Son, in Thy Power, in Thy Wisdom, in Thy Truth; wondrously speaking, and wondrously making. Who shall comprehend? Who declare it? What is that which gleams through me, and strikes my heart without hurting it; and I shudder and kindle? I shudder, inasmuch as I am unlike it; I kindle, inasmuch as I am like it. It is Wisdom, Wisdom's self which gleameth through me; severing my cloudiness which yet again mantles over me, fainting from it, through the darkness which for my punishment gathers upon me. For my strength is brought down in need, so that I cannot support my blessings, till Thou, Lord, Who hast been gracious to all mine iniquities, shalt heal all my infirmities. For Thou shalt also redeem my life from corruption, and crown me with loving kindness and tender mercies, and shalt satisfy my desire with good things, because my youth shall be renewed like an eagle's. For in hope we are saved, wherefore we through patience wait for Thy promises. Let him that is able hear Thee inwardly discoursing out of Thy oracle: I will boldly cry out. How wonderful are Thy works, O Lord, in Wisdom hast Thou made them all; and this Wisdom is the Beginning, and in that Beginning didst Thou make heaven and earth.

Lo, are they not full of their old leaven who say to us, "What was God doing before He made heaven and earth? For if (say they) He were unem-

---

From St. Augustine's *Confessions* (397–401), Book XI.

ployed and wrought not, why does He not also henceforth, and for ever, as He did heretofore? For did any new motion arise in God, and a new will to make a creature which He had never before made, how then would that be a true eternity, where there ariseth a will which was not? For the will of God is not a creature, but before the creature; seeing nothing could be created, unless the will of the Creator had preceded. The will of God then belongeth to His very Substance. And if aught have arisen in God's Substance which before was not, that Substance cannot be truly called eternal. But if the will of God has been from eternity that the creature should be, why was not the creature also from eternity?"

Who speak thus, do not yet understand Thee, O Wisdom of God, Light of souls, understand not yet how the things be made, which by Thee and in Thee are made; yet they strive to comprehend things eternal, whilst their heart fluttereth between the motions of things past and to come, and is still unstable. Who shall hold it, and fix it, that it be settled awhile, and awhile catch the glory of that ever-fixed Eternity, and compare it with the times which are never fixed, and see that it cannot be compared; and that a long time cannot become long, but out of many motions passing by, which cannot be prolonged altogether; but that in the Eternal nothing passeth, but the whole is present; whereas no time is all at once present; and that all time past is driven on by time to come, and all to come followeth upon the past; and all past and to come is created, and flows out of that which is ever present? Who shall hold the heart of man, that it may stand still, and see how eternity, ever still-standing, neither past nor to come, uttereth the times past and to come? Can my hand do this, or the hand of my mouth by speech bring about a thing so great?

See, I answer him that asketh, "What did God before He made heaven and earth?" I answer not as one is said to have done merrily (eluding the pressure of the question): "He was preparing hell (saith he) for pryers into mysteries." It is one thing to answer enquiries, another to make sport of enquirers. So I answer not; for rather had I answer, "I know not" what I know not, than so as to raise a laugh at him who asketh deep things and gain praise for one who answereth false things. But I say that Thou, our God, art the Creator of every creature; and, if by the name "heaven and earth" every creature be understood, I boldly say, "that before God made heaven and earth, He did not make anything. For if He made, what did He make but a creature?" And would I knew whatsoever I desire to know to my profit, as I know that no creature was made before there was made any creature.

But if any excursive brain rove over the images of forepassed times, and wonder that Thou the God Almighty and All-creating and All-supporting, Maker of heaven and earth, didst for innumerable ages forbear from so great a work, before Thou wouldest make it; let him awake and consider that he wonders at false conceits. For whence could innumerable ages pass by, which Thou madest not, Thou the Author and Creator of all ages? or what times should there be, which were not made by Thee? or how should they pass by, if they never were? Seeing then Thou art the Creator of all times, if any time was before Thou madest heaven and earth, why say they that Thou didst forego working? For that very time didst Thou make, nor could times pass by before thou madest those times. But if before heaven and earth there was no time, why is it demanded what Thou then didst? For there was no "then," when there was no time.

Nor dost Thou by time precede time; else shouldest Thou not precede all times. But Thou precedest all things past, by the sublimity of an ever-present eternity; and surpassest all future because they are future, and when they come, they shall be past; but "Thou art the Same, and Thy years fail not." Thy years neither come nor go; whereas ours both come and go, that they all may come. Thy years stand together, because they do stand; nor are departing thrust out by coming years, for they pass not away; but ours shall all be, when they shall no more be. Thy years are one day; and Thy day is not daily, but Today, seeing Thy Today gives not place unto tomorrow, for neither doth it replace yesterday. Thy Today is Eternity; therefore didst Thou beget the Coeternal, to whom Thou saidst, "This day have I begotten Thee." Thou hast made all things; and before all times Thou art; neither in any time was time not.

LEIBNIZ AND CLARKE

4.2 Controversy on Time and Creation

G. W. LEIBNIZ:

3. These gentlemen maintain therefore, that space is a real absolute being. But this involves them in great difficulties; for such a being must needs be eternal and infinite. Hence some have believed it to be God himself, or, one of his attributes, his immensity. But since space consists of parts, it is not a thing which can belong to God.

4. As for my own opinion, I have said more than once, that I hold space to be something merely relative, as time is; that I hold it to be an order of co-existences, as time is an order of successions. For space denotes, in terms of possibility, an order of things which exist at the same time, considered as existing together; without enquiring into their manner of existing. And when many things are seen together, one perceives that order of things among themselves.

From the Leibniz–Clarke Correspondence, published 1717.

5. I have many demonstrations, to confute the fancy of those who take space to be a substance, or at least an absolute being. But I shall only use, at the present, one demonstration, which the author here gives me occasion to insist upon. I say then, that if space was an absolute being, there would something happen for which it would be impossible there should be a sufficient reason. Which is against my axiom. And I prove it thus. Space is something absolutely uniform; and, without the things placed in it, one point of space does not absolutely differ in any respect whatsoever from another point of space. Now from hence it follows, (supposing space to be something in itself, besides the order of bodies among themselves,) that 'tis impossible there should be a reason, why God, preserving the same situations of bodies among themselves, should have placed them in space after one certain particular manner, and not otherwise; why every thing was not placed the quite contrary way, for instance, by changing East into West. But if space is nothing else, but that order or relation; and is nothing at all without bodies, but the possibility of placing them; then those two states, the one such as it now is, the other supposed to be the quite contrary way, would not at all differ from one another. Their difference therefore is only to be found in our chimerical supposition of the reality of space in itself. But in truth the one would exactly be the same thing as the other, they being absolutely indiscernible; and consequently there is no room to enquire after a reason of the preference of the one to the other.

6. The case is the same with respect to time. Supposing any one should ask, why God did not create every thing a year sooner; and the same person should infer from thence, that God has done something, concerning which 'tis not possible there should be a reason, why he did it so, and not otherwise: the answer is, that his inference would be right, if time was any thing distinct from things existing in time. For it would be impossible there should be any reason, why things should be applied to such particular instants, rather than to others, their succession continuing the same. But then the same argument proves, that instants, consider'd without the things, are nothing at all; and that they consist only in the successive order of things: which order remaining the same, one of the two states, viz. that of a supposed anticipation, would not at all differ, nor could be discerned from, the other which now is.

7. It appears from what I have said, that my axiom has not been well understood; and that the author denies it, tho' he seems to grant it. 'Tis true, says he, that there is nothing without a sufficient reason why it is, and why it is thus, rather than otherwise: but he adds, that this sufficient reason, is often the simple or mere will of God: as, when it is asked why matter was not placed otherwhere in space; the same situations of bodies among themselves being preserved. But this is plainly maintaining, that God wills something, without any sufficient reason for his will: against the axiom, or the general rule of whatever happens. This is falling back into the loose indifference, which I have confuted at large, and showed to be absolutely chi-

merical even in creatures, and contrary to the wisdom of God, as if he could operate without acting by reason.

8. The author objects against me, that if we don't admit this simple and mere will, we take away from God the power of choosing, and bring in a fatality. But the quite contrary is true. I maintain that God has the power of choosing, since I ground that power upon the reason of a choice agreeable to his wisdom. And 'tis not this fatality, (which is only the wisest order of providence) but a blind fatality or necessity, void of all wisdom and choice, which we ought to avoid.

SAMUEL CLARKE:

4. If space was nothing but the order of things coexisting; it would follow, that if God should remove in a straight line the whole material world entire, with any swiftness whatsoever; yet it would still always continue in the same place: and that nothing would receive any shock upon the most sudden stopping of that motion. And if time was nothing but the order of succession of created things; it would follow, that if God had created the world millions of ages sooner than he did, yet it would not have been created at all the sooner. Further: space and time are quantities; which situation and order are not.

5. The argument in this paragraph, is; that because space is uniform or alike, and one part does not differ from another; therefore the bodies created in one place, if they had been created in another place, (supposing them to keep the same situation with regard to each other,) would still have been created in the same place as before: which is a manifest contradiction. The uniformity of space, does indeed prove, that there could be no (external) reason why God should create things in one place rather than in another: but does that hinder his own will, from being to itself a sufficient reason of acting in any place, when all places are indifferent or alike, and there be good reason to act in some place?

6. The same reasoning takes place here, as in the foregoing.

7 and 8. Where there is any difference in the nature of things, there the consideration of that difference always determines an intelligent and perfectly wise agent. But when two ways of acting are equally and alike good, (as in the instances before mentioned;) to affirm in such case, that God cannot act at all, or that 'tis no perfection in him to be able to act, because he can have no external reason to move him to act one way rather than the other, seems to be a denying God to have in himself any original principle or power of beginning to act, but that he must needs (as it were mechanically) be always determined by things extrinsic.

DAVID HUME

4.3   *Skeptical Challenge to the Belief in Miracles*

There is, in Dr. Tillotson's writings, an argument against the *real presence* which is as concise and elegant and strong as any argument can possibly be supposed against a doctrine so little worthy of a serious refutation. It is acknowledged on all hands, says that learned prelate, that the authority either of the Scripture or of tradition is founded merely on the testimony of the Apostles, who were eyewitnesses to those miracles of our Saviour by which he proved his divine mission. Our evidence, then, for the truth of the *Christian* religion is less than the evidence for the truth of our senses, because, even in the first authors of our religion, it was no greater; and it is evident it must diminish in passing from them to their disciples, nor can anyone rest such confidence in their testimony as in the immediate object of his senses. But a weaker evidence can never destroy a stronger; and therefore, were the doctrine of the real presence ever so clearly revealed in Scripture, it were directly contrary to the rules of just reasoning to give our assent to it. It contradicts sense, though both the Scripture and tradition, on which it is supposed to be built, carry not such evidence with them as sense when they are considered merely as external evidences, and are not brought home to everyone's breast by the immediate operation of the Holy Spirit.

Nothing is so convenient as a decisive argument of this kind, which must at least *silence* the most arrogant bigotry and superstition and free us from their impertinent solicitations. I flatter myself that I have discovered an argument of a like nature which, if just, will, with the wise and learned, be an everlasting check to all kinds of superstitious delusion, and consequently will be useful as long as the world endures; for so long, I presume, will the accounts of miracles and prodigies be found in all history, sacred and profane.

Though experience be our only guide in reasoning concerning matters of fact, it must be acknowledged that this guide is not altogether infallible, but in some cases is apt to lead us into errors. One who in our climate should expect better weather in any week of June than in one of December would reason justly and conformably to experience, but it is certain that he may happen, in the event, to find himself mistaken. However, we may observe that in such a case he would have no cause to complain of experience, be-

---

From David Hume, *An Inquiry Concerning Human Understanding* (1748), section X.

cause it commonly informs us beforehand of the uncertainty by that contrariety of events which we may learn from a diligent observation. All effects follow not with like certainty from their supposed causes. Some events are found, in all countries and all ages, to have been constantly conjoined together; others are found to have been more variable, and sometimes to disappoint our expectations, so that in our reasonings concerning matter of fact there are all imaginable degrees of assurance, from the highest certainty to the lowest species of moral evidence.

A wise man, therefore, proportions his belief to the evidence. In such conclusions as are founded on an infallible experience, he expects the event with the last degree of assurance and regards his past experience as a full *proof* of the future existence of that event. In other cases he proceeds with more caution: he weighs the opposite experiments; he considers which side is supported by the greater number of experiments—to that side he inclines with doubt and hesitation; and when at last he fixes his judgment, the evidence exceeds not what we properly call "probability." All probability, then, supposes an opposition of experiments and observations where the one side is found to overbalance the other and to produce a degree of evidence proportioned to the superiority. A hundred instances or experiments on one side, and fifty on another, afford a doubtful expectation of any event, though a hundred uniform experiments, with only one that is contradictory, reasonably beget a pretty strong degree of assurance. In all cases we must balance the opposite experiments where they are opposite, and deduct the smaller number from the greater in order to know the exact force of the superior evidence.

To apply these principles to a particular instance, we may observe that there is no species of reasoning more common, more useful, and even necessary to human life than that which is derived from the testimony of men and the reports of eyewitnesses and spectators. This species of reasoning, perhaps, one may deny to be founded on the relation of cause and effect. I shall not dispute about a word. It will be sufficient to observe that our assurance in any argument of this kind is derived from no other principle than our observation of the veracity of human testimony and of the usual conformity of facts to the report of witnesses. It being a general maxim that no objects have any discoverable connection together, and that all the inferences which we can draw from one to another are founded merely on our experience of their constant and regular conjunction, it is evident that we ought not to make an exception to this maxim in favor of human testimony whose connection with any event seems in itself as little necessary as any other. Were not the memory tenacious to a certain degree, had not men commonly an inclination to truth and a principle of probity, were they not sensible to shame when detected in a falsehood—were not these, I say, discovered by *experience* to be qualities inherent in human nature, we should never repose the least confidence in human testimony. A man delirious or noted for falsehood and villainy has no manner of authority with us.

And as the evidence derived from witnesses and human testimony is founded on past experience, so it varies with the experience and is regarded either as a *proof* or a *probability*, according as the conjunction between any particular kind of report and any kind of object has been found to be constant or variable. There are a number of circumstances to be taken into consideration in all judgments of this kind; and the ultimate standard by which we determine all disputes that may arise concerning them is always derived from experience and observation. Where this experience is not entirely uniform on any side, it is attended with an unavoidable contrariety in our judgments and with the same opposition and mutual destruction of argument as in every other kind of evidence. We frequently hesitate concerning the reports of others. We balance the opposite circumstances which cause any doubt or uncertainty; and when we discover a superiority on any side, we incline to it, but still with a diminution of assurance, in proportion to the force of its antagonist.

This contrariety of evidence, in the present case, may be derived from several different causes: from the opposition of contrary testimony, from the character or number of the witnesses, from the manner of their delivering their testimony, or from the union of all these circumstances. We entertain a suspicion concerning any matter of fact when the witnesses contradict each other, when they are but few or of a doubtful character, when they have an interest in what they affirm, when they deliver their testimony with hesitation or, on the contrary, with too violent asseverations. There are many other particulars of the same kind which may diminish or destroy the force of any argument derived from human testimony.

Suppose, for instance, that the fact which the testimony endeavors to establish partakes of the extraordinary and the marvelous—in that case the evidence resulting from the testimony admits of a diminution, greater or less in proportion as the fact is more or less unusual. The reason why we place any credit in witnesses and historians is not derived from any *connection* which we perceive *a priori* between testimony and reality, but because we are accustomed to find a conformity between them. But when the fact attested is such a one as has seldom fallen under our observation, here is a contest of two opposite experiences, of which the one destroys the other as far as its force goes, and the superior can only operate on the mind by the force which remains. The very same principle of experience which gives us a certain degree of assurance in the testimony of witnesses gives us also, in this case, another degree of assurance against the fact which they endeavor to establish; from which contradiction there necessarily arises a counterpoise and mutual destruction of belief and authority.

"I should not believe such a story were it told me by Cato" was a proverbial saying in Rome, even during the lifetime of that philosophical patriot. The incredibility of a fact, it was allowed, might invalidate so great an authority.

The Indian prince who refused to believe the first relations concerning the effects of frost reasoned justly, and it naturally required very strong testimony to engage his assent to facts that arose from a state of nature with which he was unacquainted, and which bore so little analogy to those events of which he had had constant and uniform experience. Though they were not contrary to his experience, they were not conformable to it.

But in order to increase the probability against the testimony of witnesses, let us suppose that the fact which they affirm, instead of being only marvelous, is really miraculous; and suppose also that the testimony, considered apart and in itself, amounts to an entire proof—in that case there is proof against proof, of which the strongest must prevail, but still with a diminution of its force, in proportion to that of its antagonist.

A miracle is a violation of the laws of nature; and as a firm and unalterable experience has established these laws, the proof against a miracle, from the very nature of the fact, is as entire as any argument from experience can possibly be imagined. Why is it more than probable that all men must die, that lead cannot of itself remain suspended in the air, that fire consumes wood and is extinguished by water, unless it be that these events are found agreeable to the laws of nature, and there is required a violation of these laws, or, in other words, a miracle to prevent them? Nothing is esteemed a miracle if it ever happen in the common course of nature. It is no miracle that a man, seemingly in good health, should die on a sudden, because such a kind of death, though more unusual than any other, has yet been frequently observed to happen. But it is a miracle that a dead man should come to life, because that has never been observed in any age or country. There must, therefore, be a uniform experience against every miraculous event, otherwise the event would not merit that appellation. And as a uniform experience amounts to a proof, there is here a direct and full *proof*, from the nature of the fact, against the existence of any miracle, nor can such a proof be destroyed or the miracle rendered credible but by an opposite proof which is superior.

The plain consequence is (and it is a general maxim worthy of our attention) that no testimony is sufficient to establish a miracle unless the testimony be of such a kind that its falsehood would be more miraculous than the fact which it endeavors to establish. And even in that case there is a mutual destruction of arguments, and the superior only gives us an assurance suitable to that degree of force which remains after deducting the inferior. When anyone tells me that he saw a dead man restored to life, I immediately consider with myself whether it be more probable that this person should either deceive or be deceived, or that the fact which he relates should really have happened. I weigh the one miracle against the other, and according to the superiority which I discover I pronounce my decision, and always reject the greater miracle. If the falsehood of his testimony would be more miraculous than the event which he relates, then, and not till then, can he pretend to command my belief or opinion.

PATRICK NOWELL-SMITH

4.4   *Miracles*[1]

I

Mr. Lunn throws down the gauntlet, several gauntlets, to the 'modernist'; but it is not on behalf of modernism that I intend to take up his challenge. I shall confine myself solely to the question of miracles, and to one aspect only of this many-sided problem. First let me indicate the extent of my agreement with Mr. Lunn:

(*a*) I am in full agreement with him about the value of controversy and about the need, in controversy, for sticking to accepted definitions. One can prove anything with sufficient elasticity or watering down of terms.

(*b*) The problem must be attacked with an open mind, that is to say, with a mind not disposed to reject evidence because it conflicts with some preconceived theory. I have known a very distinguished physicist to explain that Dr. Rhine's experimental results in 'parapsychology' must be false because such things just cannot happen. The parallel which Mr. Lunn adduces between this attitude and that of the Church towards Galileo is apt.

(*c*) I hold no brief for the Euhemerizing attitude of some modernists. I do not altogether agree that it is illogical to accept what seems credible in the gospel stories and to reject the miracles, when the evidence is the same for both. It seems to me that we are sometimes entitled to accept part of a witness's story and reject another part. But I will not quarrel with Mr. Lunn over this, since I reject Euhemerism myself for other reasons. Nevertheless, I must protest that to reject the thesis that Jesus was a man on to whom fabulous stories have been foisted is not to prove the Christian view that he was a Man-God. As Mr. Lunn knows, there is the alternative theory that he was always a God and that the growth of the gospel stories is not the progressive deification of a man but the progressive humanization of a God. However, Mr. Lunn was explicitly attacking the modernist view, and it is not fair to

---

From *New Essays in Philosophical Theology*, ed. Antony Flew and Alastair MacIntyre (1955). Reprinted by permission of the Macmillan Company (New York) and the Student Christian Movement Press Ltd. (London).

[1]This was originally written as a reply to Mr. (now Sir) Arnold Lunn's article "Miracles —The Scientific Approach," *Hibbert Journal*, April 1950, itself a reply to an article by Professor H. Dubs in the same journal, January 1950.

criticize him for not fighting his battle on two fronts at once. I mention this point solely as an illustration of Mr. Lunn's tendency to treat a convincing refutation of one view as a proof of another which is not the only possible alternative, a tendency of which I shall produce a more important example later.

So much for my agreement with Mr. Lunn. Whether modernists commit the fallacies of bad definition, the closed mind and Euhemerism I shall not presume to say. Let it suffice that they are fallacies; and now let us turn to miracles.

To put my cards on the table at once, I have no intention of trying to refute Mr. Lunn's explanation of miracles, since he has put it beyond the bounds of possible refutation. But I do not think that it *explains* and I am at a loss to understand it. In particular, I am at a loss to understand the distinction of the 'natural' and the 'supernatural' of which he makes so much in his explanation of miracles, but which he does not explain in its turn. But before coming to my main point I shall first summarize Mr. Lunn's argument and put out of the way two minor points. Mr. Lunn's main argument is as follows:

(*a*) A miracle is defined as 'an event above or contrary to or exceeding nature which is explicable only as a direct act of God'.

(*b*) Miracles certainly occur. (There is plenty of evidence for them, if only people will bother to investigate it instead of rejecting miracles out of hand.)

(*c*) Miracles are 'evidence provided by God to demonstrate the existence of a divine order'.

(*d*) Therefore we must believe that reality is not 'co-terminous with the natural order' and must answer in the negative the momentous question 'whether all phenomena recorded and witnessed by man are due to purely natural causes, such as the actions of the human will or physical causes'. Moreover, it is on the authority of the scientists themselves 'that we declare that a particular phenomenon is inexplicable as the effect of natural agents and must therefore be ascribed to supernatural agents'.

Before coming to my main point, I have two objections to make to this thesis: the first will certainly be familiar to Mr. Lunn and he has probably answered it elsewhere; the second is more important. In the first place, every religion has its own stock of miracles, some of which are as well-attested as the Christian miracles. Would Mr. Lunn deny that these miracles occurred? And, if he does, must it not be from some arbitrary standpoint such as he himself condemns? If he is willing to accept them, must there not be some flaw in the argument by which the devotees of other religions prove the existence of their Gods from such evidence? And might not this flaw appear also in the Christian case? Or are we to accept the God of Muhammad and the whole Greek and Hindu Pantheons?

My second and more serious, point is that Mr. Lunn *defines* 'miracle' in such a way that, whatever scientists may say, it can well be doubted whether miracles have in fact occurred. If any scientist has said that a certain phenomenon 'is inexplicable as the effect of natural agents and must *therefore* be ascribed to supernatural agents', he is not speaking as a scientist, but as a philosopher; and whatever authority he may have in his own scientific field he is by no means a safe guide here. We may trust him, as a trained observer, accurately to describe the phenomenon; we may believe him when he says that no scientific method or hypothesis known to him will explain it. But to say that it is inexplicable as a result of natural agents is already beyond his competence as a scientist, and to say that it must be ascribed to supernatural agents is to say something that no one could possibly have the right to affirm on the evidence alone. Mr. Lunn defines a miracle, not merely as an event 'exceeding nature', but also as one *which is explicable only as a direct Act of God.* But to say that a phenomenon is a direct act of God is to offer an explanation, not to report its occurrence. Let us accept all the evidence for miracles; what this evidence shows is that extraordinary phenomena occur, and it is only in this sense that the evidence forces us to admit that miracles occur. If we define 'miracle' in the way that Mr. Lunn does, we could only be forced to admit the occurrence of miracles by means of some *argument,* such as Mr. Lunn himself offers. Mr. Lunn has, in short, smuggled his explanation of these phenomena into the evidence for them, and this he has no right to do. Evidence must be kept distinct from explanatory theory; otherwise, in accepting the evidence, we are already committed to accepting the theory. But, no matter how strange an event someone reports, the statement that it must have been due to a supernatural agent cannot be a part of that report.

II

As I have said, my main difficulty is to understand Mr. Lunn's distinction between the 'natural' and the 'supernatural'. There is, first, a certain inconsistency in his use of these terms. At one point he regards God's intervention as analogous to that of human beings. It 'does not violate the laws of nature but modifies some of the laws of nature by a process analogous to that by which the human will influences nature'. Here the human will is held to be, in some sense 'non-natural', if not supernatural. (Otherwise the analogy has no point). 'Natural' comes near to meaning 'physical' or even 'material'. But in the next paragraph the actions of the human will are treated, along with 'physical causes' as natural; so that the phrase 'natural order' cannot be regarded as co-terminous with the domain of physical science.

It is true that some scientists claim that, in the end, all explanation will turn out to be physical. I do not propose to examine this claim, as it is irrelevant. Mr. Lunn must be intending to attack a different thesis, namely, that all phenomena will ultimately admit of a natural explanation. It is vital, therefore, that he should let us clearly understand what he means by this phrase.

Mr. Lunn's belief that 'natural' explanations cannot be given seems to me to rest on an unstated, and therefore unexamined assumption as to the nature of natural science. He seems to believe that science is committed to certain definite *theories* and to the use of certain definite *concepts*—for instance, the concepts of matter and motion. But surely this is a mistake. Scientific theories are continually being overthrown; the scientific vocabulary is continually being revised and enriched. For example, 'Energy' does not mean for a scientist today what it meant for Newton; still less what it meant for Aristotle. In addition to explaining more and more with its existing battery of concepts and theories, science may advance by developing radically new concepts. The concept of gravity was unknown to Galileo and that of an electric charge unknown to Newton; and it is for this reason that if Newton himself said that such and such an event was inexplicable I should take leave to doubt him. Let us grant that Mr. Lunn has a right to say, on the authority of 'scientists', that no scientist can at present explain certain phenomena. It does not follow that the phenomena are inexplicable by scientific methods, still less that they must be attributed to supernatural agents.

It might be argued that I am cheating here by using the term "science" in such a loose way that it can be used to cover any type of explanation. But this is not so. Science is committed, not to definite theories or concepts, but to a certain *method* of explanation. I do not say that this must be the only method; but I do not see what other there can be.

I may be doing Mr. Lunn an injustice in saying that he regards science as committed to definite theories and concepts rather than committed to a certain method. But so many of his points, both good and bad, seem to me to follow from this assumption that I cannot but attribute it to him. In the first place, his strictures on the absence of *Zetesis* in the attitude of some scientists seem to me to presuppose this view (as does the absence of *Zetesis* itself). It is true that some scientists refuse to admit any explanations that are not couched in terms of the orthodox scientific concepts of today; and it is also true that this is a mistake, a blindness fitly compared with that of Galileo's opponents. Mr. Lunn says: 'All evidence for such (i.e. supernatural) agencies must, on modernist assumptions, either be explained here and now as the result of natural causes or be referred to the science of the future to interpret in accordance with modernist preconceptions.' But there is an ambiguity here that must, I think, arise from the mistaken view of science that I have attributed to Mr. Lunn. If he means that, according to the modernist, science must either be able to explain everything here and now or be able, in the future, to explain everything *in terms now current*, he is right to object. But there is still the possibility that science may be able, in the future, to offer an explanation which, though couched in quite new terms, remains strictly scientific. And I shall try to show later that this is the only possible alternative to saying that *no* explanation is possible. Thus the breakdown of all explanations in terms of present-day science does not, as Mr. Lunn thinks, immediately force us outside the realm of the 'natural'; and we can only think that it does so if we make the mistake of equating 'science' with a certain set of theories. An explanation would still be 'natural' if it made use of quite different terms, provided that its method was scientific. If this be conceded, it is difficult to understand Mr. Lunn's distinction between the 'natural' and the 'supernatural'. For the problem is not whether science can explain everything in current terms, but whether the explanation of miracles requires a method quite different from that of science. Unless this latter thesis is proved, it is hard to see why miracles should be called 'supernatural'.

III

If the notion of the 'natural' is unclear, that of a 'miracle' is no less so; and that in spite of Mr. Lunn's explicit definition, At times he holds that a miracle is 'above, contrary to or exceeding nature'; at others he holds that, in performing miracles, God does not violate natural law. I find it hard to reconcile these two views; at least the words 'contrary to' must go; and with them the analogy between Acts of God and human actions. Mr. Lunn sees that a fieldsman who catches a cricket ball is not violating or suspending—he is not even modifying—the law of gravity. And if God's interventions are analogous to those of human agents, they conform to natural laws. In this case they are in principle predictable (however great the difficulties may be in practice); and the word 'supernatural' loses its force.

It might be argued that God's interventions are indeed 'lawful'; but that they proceed according to laws which are not 'natural laws'; but at this point the difference between a 'natural' and a 'supernatural' law cries out for explanation. There are many different kinds of scientific law—physical, chemical, biological, psychological and so on. If supernatural law is another group alongside these, it is not necessarily unscientific. But in calling it 'supernatural' Mr. Lunn evidently means to imply that it is different, for example, from physical law in a way in which a physical law is not different from a biological law. Yet I cannot imagine what this difference would be. If it is a law, it must (*a*) be based on evidence; (*b*) be of a general type 'Under such and such conditions, so and so will happens'; (*c*) be capable of testing in experience. And if it conforms to this specification, how does it differ from a natural law? The supernatural seems to dissolve on the one hand into the natural and on the other into the inexplicable.

And this is no *a priori* dogma; it follows from the nature of explanation. It is, I think, a failure to investigate what is involved in the notion of an explanation that leads Mr. Lunn to leap at once into the supernatural. A scientific explanation is an hypothesis from which predictions can be made, which can afterwards be verified. It is of the essence of such an hypothesis—a 'law' is but a well-confirmed hypothesis—that it should be capable of such predictive expansion. This is, incidentally, the burden of the old attack on *virtus dormitiva* and Bacon's '*tamquam virgo intacta, nihil parit*'. The type of explanation satirized by Molière and Bacon is futile because it merely repeats in learned jargon what has already been said in plain language in stating the phenomenon to be explained. A scientific explanation—any explanation— must do more than this. It must be capable of application to new phenomena. Now, Mr. Lunn's explanations are inevitably *ex post facto*; we can only recognize a miracle after it has occurred. Mr. Lunn may reply that it is 'illogical to exploit against an hypothesis consequences which are inevitable if that hypothesis is correct'. Certainly; but my argument is not intended to show that Mr. Lunn's hypothesis is false; it is intended to show that it is not an hypothesis at all. It is as if one were to say: 'Certain events in the past were caused by boojums; but I cannot tell you on what principles boojums operate or what they will do in the future; my hypothesis inevitably involves this consequence.' If anyone said this, we should have to treat his phrase 'caused by boojums' as simply a special way of describing the phenomena, moreover a misleading way, since it looks like an explanatory hypothesis. But in fact it is not. In the same way, to say that God's interventions in the natural order are 'lawful', but that we cannot use these laws for prediction is to retreat into an asylum of ignorance and to use the word 'law' in a most paradoxical sense.

To illustrate this let me turn to the example of Leverrier, which Mr. Lunn cites: 'If Leverrier had assumed that the planetary order is a closed system he would never have discovered Neptune.' True; and a valid argument against the exaggerated orthodoxy which Mr. Lunn and I both condemn and also against *a priori* proofs in the Hegelian manner of the number of planets that there must be. But the analogy with explanations in supernatural terms is invalid. For Leverrier discovered Neptune, not merely by saying: 'The planetary system is not closed; there is something outside.' He showed how the aberrations in the orbits of other planets could be accounted for; and his explanation involved a prediction that if astronomers examined a certain quarter of the sky they would find a new planet. And lo! it was so. It is here that the analogy breaks down; for Mr. Lunn's 'explanation' involves saying: 'Known laws and factors will not explain this phenomenon; there must be something outside; but I cannot tell you what this is or how it operates.' An explanation must explain *how* an event comes about; otherwise it is simply a learned (or a tendentious) name for the phenomenon to be explained.

Moreover, the entity postulated by Leverrier was not of an altogether unknown type; it was another planet assumed to obey the known laws. I am prepared to allow Mr. Lunn much more than this (at least for the purpose of this discussion), and to admit that the present hypotheses of science can never be expanded to cover miraculous phenomena; that we may require new concepts and new laws. What I reject is the theory of science which makes it possible to claim that any phenomenon is essentially inexplicable, the leap to 'supernatural agencies', and the view that such agencies in fact explain the phenomena. If miracles are 'lawful' it should be possible to state the laws; if not, the alleged explanation amounts to a confession that they are inexplicable.

IV

Having said that miracles must be attributed to supernatural agencies, Mr. Lunn goes on to claim that they are 'evidence provided by God to demonstrate the existence of the divine order'. But what, in detail, can they prove? If we can detect any order in God's interventions it should be possible to extrapolate in the usual way and to predict when and how a miracle will occur. To expect accurate and detailed predictions would be to expect too much. But we must be able to make some predictions, however vague. Otherwise the hypothesis is not open either to confirmation or refutation. As far as I can see, we are limited to saying that God has in the past intervened in such a way. If Mr. Lunn would say more than this, I would ask how his method differs from that of a scientist. We would be faced, not with the supernatural, but with a new department of the natural, a department that might be as strange as electrical phenomena once were. But if he confesses that no predictions can be made, is not the phrase 'Act of God', which is introduced in order to explain miracles, in fact but a synonym for 'the miraculous'? We are back at the *virtus dormitiva* type of explanation. If 'Christ is risen' implies 'Christ is supernatural', we are entitled to ask what *other* attributes, besides rising from the dead, 'supernatural' connotes. We shall then be in a position to see whether a being that rises from the dead necessarily or probably has those attributes. Mr. Lunn passes from unusual or abnormal events (for which there is evidence) to the miraculous, from the miraculous to the supernatural and from the supernatural to God. He cannot mean each successive phrase to be a mere synonym for the previous one; each step in the argument is intended to explain the last and to add something more. But, to make use of an old-fashioned way of putting this, we have no right to postulate in the cause any power greater than what is necessary to produce the effect. The difficulty with the argument from miracles, as with other arguments for the existence of God, is that it is first claimed that certain evidence requires us to postulate an unknown X; we then call this X 'God', and we then claim to have proved the existence of a being endowed with characteristics by no means warranted by the original evidence. Now science too does this. The gravitational theory says much more than is necessary to describe the fall of an apple. But we can test the truth of this 'more' by predicting how other bodies will behave. It is the absence of such a test for supernatural explanations that makes them at once unscientific and also non-explanatory.

It might be argued that I am in effect begging the question because my thesis amounts to saying that the phrase 'supernatural explanation' is a contradiction in terms. To assume this is tantamount to assuming that all explanation must be scientific. Now I certainly would not claim to be able to prove this dogma. To do so I should have to appeal to some premiss that would be equally unacceptable. All I can do is offer Mr. Lunn a challenge. Let him consider the meaning of the word 'explanation' and let him ask himself whether this notion does not involve that of a law or hypothesis capable of predictive expansion. And then let him ask himself whether such an explanation would not be natural, in whatever terms it was couched, and how the notion of 'the supernatural' could play any part in it. If he objects that I am in effect conceding his point by offering so very wide a definition of 'natural,' my reply would be:

> By all means; I do not wish to quarrel about words. I will concede your supernatural, if this is all that it means. For the supernatural will be nothing but a new field for scientific inquiry, a field as different from physics as physics is from psychology, but not differing in principle or requiring any non-scientific method.

The supernatural is either so different from the natural that we are unable to investigate it at all or it is not. If it is not, then it can hardly have the momentous significance that Mr. Lunn claims for it; and if it is it cannot be invoked as an explanation of the unusual.

R. F. HOLLAND

4.5 The Miraculous

Most people think of a miracle as a violation of natural law; and a good many of those who regard the miraculous in this way incline to the idea that miracles are impossible and that "science" tells us this (the more sophisticated might say that what tells us this is an unconfused *conception* of science). I shall argue that the conception of the miraculous as a violation of natural

From the *American Philosophical Quarterly* 2 (1965). Reprinted by permission of the author and the editor.

law is an inadequate conception because it is unduly restrictive, though there is also a sense in which it is not restrictive enough. To qualify for being accounted a miracle, an occurrence does not have to be characterizable as a violation of natural law. However, though I do not take the conception of miracles as violations of natural law to be an adequate conception of the miraculous, I shall maintain that occurrences are conceivable in respect to which it could be said that some law or laws of nature had been violated—or it could be said equally that there was a contradiction in our experience: and if the surrounding circumstances were appropriate it would be possible for such occurrences to have a kind of human significance and hence intelligible for them to be hailed as miracles. I see no philosophical reason against this.

But consider first the following example. A child riding his toy motor-car strays on to an unguarded railway crossing near his house and a wheel of his car gets stuck down the side of one of the rails. An express train is due to pass with the signals in its favor and a curve in the track makes its impossible for the driver to stop his train in time to avoid any obstruction he might encounter on the crossing. The mother coming out of the house to look for her child sees him on the crossing and hears the train approaching. She runs forward shouting and waving. The little boy remains seated in his car, looking downward, engrossed in the task of pedaling it free. The brakes of the train are applied and it comes to rest a few feet from the child. The mother thanks God for the miracle; which she never ceases to think of as such, although, as she in due course learns, there was nothing supernatural about the manner in which the brakes of the train came to be applied. The driver had fainted, for a reason which had nothing to do with the presence of the child on the line, and the brakes were applied automatically as his hand ceased to exert pressure on the control lever. He fainted on this particular afternoon because his blood pressure had risen after an exceptionally heavy lunch during which he had quarrelled with a colleague, and the change in blood pressure caused a clot of blood to be dislodged and circulate. He fainted at the time when he did on the afternoon in question because this was the time at which the coagulation in his blood stream reached the brain.

Thus the stopping of the train and the fact that it stopped when it did have a natural explanation. I do not say a *scientific* explanation, for it does not seem to me that the explanation here as a whole is of this kind (in order for something to be unsusceptible of scientific explanation it does not have to be anything so queer and grandiose as a miracle). The form of explanation in the present case, I would say, is *historical*; and the considerations which enter into it are various. They include medical factors, for instance, and had these constituted the whole extent of the matter the explanation could have been called scientific. But as it is, the medical considerations, though obviously important, are only one aspect of a complex story, alongside other considerations of a practical and social kind; and in addition there is a reference to mechanical considerations. All of these enter into the explanation of, or story behind, the stopping of the train. And just as there is an explanatory story behind the train's stopping when and where it did, so there is an explanatory story behind the presence of the child on the line at the time when, and in the place where, he was. But these two explanations or histories are independent of each other. They are about as disconnected as the history of the steam loom is from the history of the Ming dynasty. The spatio-temporal coincidence, I mean the fact that the child was on the line at the time when the train approached and the train stopped a few feet short of the place where he was, is exactly what I have just called it, a coincidence—something which a chronicle of events can merely record, like the fact that the Ming dynasty was in power at the same time as the house of Lancaster.

But unlike the coincidence between the rise of the Ming dynasty and the arrival of the dynasty of Lancaster, the coincidence of the child's presence on the line with the arrival and then the stopping of the train is impressive, significant; not because it is very unusual for trains to be halted in the way this one was, but because the life of a child was imperiled and then, against expectation, preserved. The significance of some coincidences as opposed to others arises from their relation to human needs and hopes and fears, their effects for good or ill upon our lives. So we speak of our luck (fortune, fate, etc.). And the kind of thing which, outside religion, we call luck is in religious parlance the grace of God or a miracle of God. But while the reference here is the same, the meaning is different. The meaning is different in that whatever happens by God's grace or by a miracle is something for which God is thanked or thankable, something which has been or could have been prayed for, something which can be regarded with awe and be taken as a sign or made the subject of a vow (e.g., to go on a pilgrimage), all of which can only take place against the background of a religious tradition. Whereas what happens by a stroke of luck is something in regard to which one just seizes one's opportunity or feels glad about or feels relieved about, something for which one may thank one's lucky stars. To say that one thanks one's lucky stars is simply to express one's relief or to emphasize the intensity of the relief: if it signifies anything more than this it signifies a superstition (*cf.* touching wood).

But although a coincidence can be taken religiously as a sign and called a miracle and made the subject of a vow, it cannot without confusion be taken as a sign of divine interference with the natural order. If someone protests that it is no part of the natural order that an express train should stop for a child on the line whom the driver cannot see, then in *protesting* this he misses the point. What he says has been agreed to be perfectly true in the sense that there is no natural order relating the train's motion to the child which could be either preserved or interfered with. The concept of the miraculous which we have so far been considering is distinct therefore from the concept exemplified in the Biblical stories of the turning of water into wine and the feeding of five thousand people on a very few loaves and fishes. Let us call the former the contingency concept and the latter the violation concept. To establish the contingency concept of the miraculous as a possible concept it seems to me enough to point out (1) that *pace* Spinoza, Leibniz, and others, there are genuine contingencies in the world, and (2) that certain of these contingencies can be, and are in fact, regarded religiously in the manner I have indicated. If you assent to this and still express a doubt—"But are they really miracles?"—then you must now be questioning whether people are right to react to contingencies in this way, questioning whether you ought yourself to go along with them. Why not just stick to talking of luck? When you think this you are somewhat in the position of one who watches others fall in love and as an outsider thinks it unreasonable, hyperbolical, ridiculous (surely friendship should suffice).

To turn now to the concept of the miraculous as a violation of natural law: I am aware of two arguments which, if they were correct, would show that this concept were not a possible concept. The first can be found in chapter ten of Hume's *Enquiry Concerning Human Understanding:*

> Nothing is esteemed a miracle, if it ever happen in the common course of nature. It is no miracle that a man, seemingly in good health, should die on a sudden: because such a kind of death, though more unusual than any other, has yet been frequently observed to happen. But it is a miracle, that a dead man should come to life; because that has never been observed in any age or country. There must, therefore, be a uniform experience against every miraculous event, otherwise the event would not merit that appellation. And as a uniform experience amounts to a proof, there is here a direct and full *proof,* from the nature of the fact, against the existence of any miracle; nor can such a proof be destroyed, or the miracle rendered credible, but by an opposite proof, which is superior.

> The plain consequence is (and it is a general maxim worthy of our attention), "That no testimony is sufficient to establish a miracle, unless the testimony be of such a kind, that its falsehood would be more miraculous, than the fact, which it endeavours to establish; and even in that case there is a mutual destruction of arguments, and the superior only gives us an assurance suitable to that degree of force, which remains, after deducting the inferior." When anyone tells me, that he saw a dead man restored to life, I immediately consider with myself, whether it be more probable, that this person should either deceive or be deceived, or that the fact, which he relates, should really have happened. I weigh the one miracle against the other; and according to the superiority, which I discover, I pronounce my decision, and always reject the greater miracle. If the falsehood of his testimony would be more miraculous, than the event which he relates; then, and not till then, can he pretend to command my belief or opinion.

Hume's concern in the chapter from which I have just quoted is ostensibly with the problem of assessing the *testimony of others* in regard to the allegedly miraculous. This is not the same problem as that which arises for the man who has to decide whether or not he himself has witnessed a miracle. Hume gives an inadequate account of the considerations which would influence one's decision to accept or reject the insistence of another person that something has happened which one finds it extremely hard to believe could have happened. The character and temperament of the witness, the kind of person he is and the kind of understanding one has of him, the closeness or distance of one's personal relationship with him are obviously important here, whereas Hume suggests that if we give credence to some witnesses rather than others the reason must be simply that we are accustomed to find in their case a conformity between testimony and reality (§ 89). Maybe the weakness of Hume's account of the nature of our trust or lack of trust in witnesses is connected with the fact that in some way he intended his treatment of the problem of witness concerning the miraculous to have a more general application —as if he were trying to cut across the distinction between the case in which we are ourselves confronted with a miracle (or something we may be inclined to call one) and the case in which other people intervene, and wanting us to consider it all as fundamentally a single problem of evidence, a problem of witness in which it would make no difference whether what were doing the witnessing were a person other than oneself, or oneself in the role of a witness to oneself, or one's senses as witnesses to oneself. This, anyway, is the view I am going to take of his intention here.

I can imagine it being contended that, while Hume has produced a strong argument against the possibility of our ever having certitude or even very good evidence that a miracle has occurred, his thesis does not amount to an argument against the possibility of miracles as such. But I think that this would be a misunderstanding. For if Hume is right, the situation is not just that we do not happen as a matter of fact to have certitude or even good evidence for the occurrence of any miracle, but rather that *nothing can count* as good evidence: the logic of testimony precludes this. And in precluding this it must, as far as I can see, preclude equally our having *poor* evidence for the occurrence of any miracle, since a contrast between good evidence and poor evidence is necessary if there is to be sense in speaking of either. Equally it must follow that there can be no such thing as (because nothing is being allowed to count as) discovering, recognizing, becoming aware, etc., that a miracle has occurred; and if there be no such thing as finding out or being aware (etc.) that a miracle has occurred, there can be no such thing as failing to find out or failing to be aware that a miracle has occurred either; no such thing as a discovered or an undiscovered miracle . . . *en fin*, no such thing as a miracle. So Hume's argument is, after all, an argument against the very possibility of miracles. I do not think that his argument is cogent either on the interpretation I have just put upon it or on the interpretation according to which it would be an argument merely against the possibility of our having good evidence for a miracle. But before giving my reason I would like first to mention the only other line of argument which I can at present envisage against the conception of the miraculous as a violation of natural law.

Consider the proposition that a criminal is a violator of the laws of the state. With this proposition in mind you will start to wonder, when someone says that a miracle is a violation of the laws of nature, if he is not confusing a law of nature with a judical law as laid down by some legal authority. A judicial law is obviously something which can be violated. The laws of the state prescribe and their prescriptions can be flouted. But are the laws of nature in any sense prescriptions? Maybe they are, in the sense that they prescribe to us what we are to expect; but since *we* formulated the laws, this is really a matter of our offering prescriptions or recipes to ourselves. And we can certainly fail to act on these prescriptions. But the occurrences which the laws are about are not prescribed to: they are simply *de*scribed. And if anything should happen of which we are inclined to say that it goes counter to a law of nature, what this must mean is that the description we have framed has been, not flouted or violated, but falsified. We have encountered something which the description does not fit, and we must therefore withdraw or modify our description. The law was wrong; we framed it wrongly: or rather what we framed has turned out not to have been a law. The relation between an occurrence and a law of nature is different, then, from a man's relations to a law of the state, for when the latter is deviated from, we do not, save in exceptional circumstances, say that the law is wrong but rather that the man is wrong—he is a criminal. To suggest that an occurrence which has falsified a law of nature is *wrong* would be an absurdity: and it would be just as absurd to suggest that the law has been violated. Nothing can be conceived to be a violation of natural law, and if that is how the miraculous is conceived, there can be no such thing as the miraculous. Laws of nature can be formulated or reformulated to cope with any eventuality, and would-be miracles are transformed automatically into natural occurrences the moment science gets on the track of them.

But there is an objection to this line of argument. If we say that a law of nature is a description, what exactly are we taking it to be a description of? A description of what has happened up to now or is actually happening now? Suppose that we have a law to the effect that all unsupported bodies fall. From this I can deduce that if the pen now in my hand were unsupported it *would* fall and that when in a moment I withdraw from it the support it now has it *will* fall. But if the law were simply a description of what has happened up to now or is happening now and no more, these deductions would be impossible. So it looks as if the law must somehow describe the future as well as the past and present. "A description of the future." But what on earth is that? For, until the future ceases to be the future and becomes actual, there are no events for the description to describe—over and above those which either have already taken place or are at this moment taking place.

It seems that if we are to continue to maintain that a natural law is nothing but a description, then we must say that the description covers not only the actual but also the possible and is every bit as much a description of the one as it is of the other. And this only amounts to a pleonastic way of saying that the law tells us, defines for us, what is and is not *possible* in regard to the behavior of unsupported bodies. At this point we might just as well drop the talk about describing altogether and admit that the law does not just describe—it stipulates: stipulates that it is impossible for an unsupported body to do anything other than fall. Laws of nature and legal laws, though they may not resemble each other in other respects, are at least alike in this: that they both stipulate something. Moreover the stipulations which we call laws of nature are in many cases so solidly founded and knitted together with other stipulations, other laws, that they come to be something in the nature of a framework through which we look at the world and which to a considerable degree dictates our ways of describing phenomena.

Notice, however, that insofar as we resist in this way the second of the two arguments for the impossibility of the violation concept of the miraculous, and insofar as we object to the suggestion that it is possible for our laws of nature to be dropped or reformulated in a sort of *ad hoc* manner to accommodate any would-be miracle, we seem to be making the first argument— the Humean argument against the miraculous—all the stronger. For, if we take a law of nature to be more than a generalized description of what has happened up to now, and if at the same time we upgrade the mere probability or belief to which Hume thought we were confined here into certainty and real knowledge, then surely it must seem that our reluctance to throw overboard a whole nexus of well-established, mutually-supporting laws and theories must be so great as to justify us in rejecting out of hand, and not being prepared to assign even a degree of probability to, any testimony to an occurrence which our system of natural law decisively rules out; and surely we shall be justified in classifying as illusory any experience which purports to be the experience of such an occurrence.

The truth is that this position is not at all justified, and we should only be landed in inconsistency if we adopted it. For if it were granted that there can be no certainty in regard to the individual case, if there can be no real knowledge that a particular event has occurred in exactly the way in which it has, how could our system of laws have been established in the first place?

On Hume's view, the empirical in general was synonymous with the probable. No law of nature could have more than a degree of probability, and neither for that matter could the occurrence of any particular event. This is what gave point to the idea of a balance of probabilities and hence to his thesis about the impossibility of ever establishing a miracle. But while in the one case, that of the general law, he was prepared (in the passage from which I quoted) to allow that the probability could have the status of a proof, in the other case he was curiously reluctant to allow this.

Now, if in the interest of good conceptual sense we upgrade the probability of natural laws into certainty, so as to be able to distinguish a well-established law from a more or less tenable hypothesis, it is equally in the interest of good conceptual sense that we should upgrade in a comparable fashion the probability attaching to particular events and states of affairs, so as to allow that some of these, as opposed to others, can be certain and really known to be what they are. Otherwise a distinction gets blurred which is at least as important as the distinction between a law and a hypothesis—namely the distinction between a hypothesis and a fact. The distinction between a hypothesis and a fact is, for instance, the distinction between my saying when I come upon an infant who is screaming and writhing and holding his ear "he's got an abscess" and my making this statement again after looking into the ear, whether by means of an instrument or without, and actually seeing, coming upon, the abscess. Or again it is the difference between the statement "it is snowing" when made by me now as I sit here and the same statement uttered as I go outside the building into the snow and get snowed on. The second statement, unlike the first, is uttered directly in the face of the circumstance which makes it true. I can be as certain in that situation that it is snowing as I can be of anything. And if there were not things of this kind of which we can be certain, we would not be able to be uncertain of anything either.

If it were remarked here that our senses are capable of deceiving us, I should reply that it does not follow from this that there are not occasions when we know perfectly well that we are not being deceived. And this is one of them. I submit that nothing would persuade you—or if it would it should not—that you are not at this moment in the familiar surroundings of your university and that in what you see as you look around this room you are subject to an illusion. And if something very strange were to happen, such as one of us bursting into flame, you would soon know it for what it was; and of course you would expect the natural cause to be duly discovered (the smoldering pipe which set fire to the matches or whatever it might be).

But then suppose that you failed to discover any cause. Or suppose that something happened which was truly bizarre, like my rising slowly and steadily three feet into the air and staying there. You could *know* that this happened if it did, and probably you would laugh and presume that there must be some natural explanation: a rod behind, a disguised support beneath, a thin wire above. Or could it even be done by air pressure in some way? Or by a tremendously powerful magnet on the next floor, attracting metal in my clothing? Or if not by magnetic attraction then by magnetic repulsion? I rise in the air, then, and since it is no magician's demonstration you can and do search under me, over me, and around me. But suppose that you find nothing, nothing on me and nothing in the room or above, below, or around it. You cannot think that it is the effect of an anti-gravity device (even if there be sense in that idea) because there just is no device. And you know that, excluding phenomena like tornadoes, it is impossible for a physical body in free air to behave thus in the absence of a special device. So does it not come to this: that if I were to rise in the air now, you could be completely certain of two incompatible things: (1) that it is impossible, and (2) that it has happened?

Now, against what I have just said I envisage two objections. The first is that my rising three feet into the air in the absence of some special cause can only be held to be an impossibility by someone who is ignorant of the statistical basis of modern physics. For example, the water in a kettle comprises a vast number of atoms in motion, and anything I do to the kettle, such as tilting it or heating it, will affect the movements of these atoms. But there is no way of determining what the effect will be in the case of any single atom. It is no more within the power of physicists to predict that a particular atom will change its position in such and such a way, or even at all, than it is within the power of insurance actuaries to predict that a certain man will die next week in a road accident, or die at all. However, reliable statistical statements can be made by actuaries about the life prospects of large numbers of people taken together, and, somewhat similarly, statistical laws are framed by physicists about the behavior of atoms in large numbers. Statistical laws are laws of probability, and it gets argued that, since this is the kind of law on which the behavior of water in a heated vessel ultimately rests, there can be no *certainty* that the kettle on the hob will boil however fierce the fire, no certainty that it will boil absolutely *every* time, because there is always the probability —infinitesimally small, admittedly, but still a definite probability—that enough of the constituent atoms in their molecules will move in a way which is incompatible with its doing so. Vessels of water and rubber balls seem to be the most frequently used examples when this argument is deployed, but the suggestion has been made to me that it (or some similar argument) could be applied to the behavior of an unsupported body near the surface of the earth, in respect of which it could be maintained that there is a certain probability, albeit a very low one, in favor of the body's having its state of rest three feet above the ground.

However, it seems to me that any such argument must rest on the kind of confusion which Eddington fell into when he said, mentioning facts about atoms as the reason, that his table was not solid but consisted largely of empty space. If you add to this that your table is in a continuous vibratory motion and that the laws governing its behavior are laws of probability only, you are continuing in the same vein. To make the confusion more symmetrical you might perhaps go on to say that the movements of tables in space are only predictable even with probability when tables get together in large numbers (which accounts for the existence of warehouses). Anyway, my point is that, using words in their ordinary senses, it is about as certain and as much a matter of common understanding that my kettle, when put on a fierce fire, will boil or that I shall not next moment float three feet in the air as it is certain and a matter of common understanding that my desk is solid and will continue for some time to be so. The validity of my statement about the desk is not impugned by any assertion about the behavior of atoms whether singly or in the aggregate; neither is the validity of the corresponding statements about the kettle and my inability to float in the air impugned by any assertion about the statistical basis of modern science.

The second objection grants the impossibility of a body's rising three feet into the air in the absence of a special cause and grants my certitude of this. But what I can never be certain of, the objection runs, is that all the special causes and devices which accomplish this are absent. So I am entirely unjustified in asserting the outright impossibility of the phenomenon—especially when I think to do so in the very teeth of its occurrence. My saying that it is impossible could only have the force here of an ejaculation like " 'struth" *Ab esse ad posse valet consequentia.* Supposing the thing to have occurred, we as ungullible people should respond by maintaining confidence in the existence of a natural cause, by persisting indefinitely in searching for one, and by classifying the occurrence in the meantime as an unsolved problem. So runs the second objection.

However, the idea that one cannot establish the absence of a natural cause is not to my mind the unassailable piece of logic it might seem at first glance to be. Both our common understanding and our scientific understanding include conceptions of the sort of thing which can and cannot happen, and of the sort of thing which has to take place to bring about some other sort of thing. These conceptions are presupposed to our arguing in such patterns as "*A* will do such and such unless *Y*," or "If *Z* happens it can only be from this, that or the other (kind of) cause," or "If *W* cannot be done in this way or that way it cannot be done at all." An example of the first pattern is "The horse will die if it gets no food." My rising steadily three feet in the air is a subject for argument according to the second pattern. The second pattern presents the surface appearance of being more complicated than the first, but logically it is not. Let us turn our attention to the example of the first pattern.

Suppose that a horse, which has been normally born and reared, and is now deprived of all nourishment (we could be completely certain of this), instead of dying, goes on thriving (which again is something we could be completely certain about). A series of thorough examinations reveals no abnormality in the horse's condition: its digestive system is always found to be working and to be at every moment in more or less the state it would have been in if the horse had eaten a meal an hour or two before. This is utterly inconsistent with our whole conception of the needs and capacities of horses; and because it is an impossibility in the light of our prevailing conception, my objector, in the event of its happening, would expect us to abandon the conception—as though we had to have consistency at any price. Whereas the position I advocate is that the price is too high and that it would be better to be left with the inconsistency; and that in any event the prevailing conception has a logical status not altogether unlike that of a necessary truth and cannot be simply thrown away as a mistake—not when it rests on the experience of generations, not when all the other horses in the world are continuing to behave as horses have always done, and especially not when one considers the way our conception of the needs and capacities of horses interlocks with conceptions of the needs and capacities of other living things and with a conception of the difference between animate and inanimate behavior quite generally. These conceptions form part of a common understanding which is well-established and with us to stay. Any number of discoveries remain to be made by zoologists, and plenty of scope exists for conceptual revision in biological theory, but it is a confusion to think that it follows from this that we are less than well enough acquainted with, and might have serious misconceptions about, what is and is not possible in the behavior under familiar conditions of common objects with which we have a long history of practical dealings. Similarly with the relation between common understanding and physical discoveries, physical theories: what has been said about the self-sustaining horse seems to me applicable *mutatis mutandis* to the levitation example also. Not that my thesis about the miraculous rests on the acceptance of this particular example. The objector who thinks that there is a loophole in it for natural explanation strikes me as lacking a sense of the absurd but can keep his opinion for the moment, since he will (I hope) be shown the loophole being closed in a further example with which I shall conclude.

I did not in any case mean to suggest that if I rose in the air now in the absence of any device it would be at all proper for a religious person to hail this as a miracle. Far from it. From a religious point of view it would either signify nothing at all or else be regarded as a sign of devilry; and if the phenomenon persisted I should think that a religious person might well have recourse to exorcism, if that figured among the institutions of his religion. Suppose, however, that by rising into the air I were to avoid an otherwise certain death: then it would (against a religious background) become possible to speak of a miracle, just as it would in what I called the contingency case. Or the phenomenon could be a miracle although nothing at all were achieved by it, provided that I were a religiously significant figure, one of whom prophets had spoken, or at least an exceptionally holy man.

My thesis, then, in regard to the violation concept of the miraculous, by contrast with the contingency concept, which we have seen to be also a possible concept, is that a conflict of certainties is a necessary though not a sufficient condition of the miraculous. In other words, a miracle, though it cannot only be this, must at least be something the occurrence of which can be categorized at one and the same time as empirically certain and conceptually impossible. If it were less than conceptually impossible, it would reduce merely to a very unusual occurrence such as could be treated (because of the empirical certainty) in the manner of a decisive experiment and result in a modification to the prevailing conception of natural law; while if it were less than empirically certain, nothing more would be called for in regard to it than a suspension of judgment. So if there is to be a type of the miraculous other than the contingency kind, it must offend against the principle *ab esse ad posse valet consequentia*. And since the violation concept of the miraculous does seem to me to be a possible concept, I therefore reject that time-honored logical principle.

I know that my suggestion that something could be at one and the same time empirically certain and conceptually impossible will sound to many people ridiculous. Must not the actual occurrence of something show that it *was* conceptually possible after all? And if I contend, as I do, that the fact that something has occurred might *not* necessarily show that it was conceptually possible, or—to put it the other way round—if I contend, as I do, that the fact that something is conceptually impossible does not necessarily preclude its occurrence, then am I not opening the door to the instantiation of round squares, female fathers, and similar paradigms of senselessness? The answer is that the door is being opened only as far as is needed and no farther; certainly not to instantiations of the *self*-contradictory. There is more than one kind of conceptual impossibility.

Let me illustrate my meaning finally by reference to the New Testament story of the turning of water into wine. I am not assuming that this story is true, but I think that it logically could be. Hence if anyone chooses to maintain its truth as a matter of faith I see no philosophical objection to his doing so. A number of people could have been quite sure, could have had the fullest empirical certainty, that a vessel contained water at one moment and wine a moment later—good wine, as St. John says—without any device having been applied to it in the intervening time. Not that this last really needs to be added; for that any device should have existed *then* at least is inconceivable, even if it might just be argued to be a conceptual possibility now. I have in mind the very remote possibility of a liquid chemically indistinguishable from, say, mature claret being produced by means of atomic and molecular transformations. The device would have to be conceived as something enormously complicated, requiring a large supply of power. Anything less thorough-going would hardly meet the case, for those who are alleged to have drunk the wine were practiced wine-bibbers, capable of detecting at once the difference between a true wine and a concocted variety in the "British Wine, Ruby Type" category. However, that water could conceivably have been turned into wine in the first century A.D. by means of a device is ruled out of court at once by common understanding; and though the verdict is supported by scientific knowledge, common understanding has no need of this support.

In the case of my previous example of a man, myself for instance, rising three feet into the air and remaining there unsupported, it was difficult to deal with the objection that we could not be certain that there was not some special cause operating, *some* explanation even though we had searched to the utmost of our ability and had found none. And I imagined the objector trying to lay it down as axiomatic that, while there is such a thing as not knowing what the cause or explanation of a phenomenon might be, there can be no such thing as establishing the absence of a cause. The example of water being turned into wine is stronger, and I would think decisive, here. At one moment, let us suppose, there was water and at another moment wine, in the same vessel, although no one had emptied out the water and poured in the wine. This is something which could conceivably have been established with certainty. What is not conceivable is that it could have been done by a device. Nor is it conceivable that there could have been a natural cause of it. For this would have had to be the natural cause of the water's becoming wine. And water's becoming wine is not the description of any conceivable natural process. It is conceptually impossible that the wine could have been gotten naturally from water, save in the very strained sense that moisture is needed to nourish the vines from which the grapes are taken, and this very strained sense is irrelevant here.

"But can we not still escape from the necessity to assert that one and the same thing is both empirically certain and conceptually impossible? For what has been said to be conceptually impossible is the turning of water into wine. However, when allusion is made to the alleged miracle, all the expression 'turned into' can signify is that at one moment there was water and at a moment later wine. This is what could have been empirically certain: whereas what is conceptually impossible is that water should have been turned into wine if one really *means* turned into. It is not conceptually impossible that at one moment water should have been found and at another moment wine in the same vessel, even though no one had emptied out the water and poured in the wine." So someone might try to argue. But I cannot see that it does any good. To the suggestion that the thing is conceivable so long as we refrain from saying that the water *turned into the wine* I would reply: either the water turns into the wine or else it disappears and wine springs into existence in its place. But water cannot *conceivably* disappear like that without going anywhere, and wine cannot *conceivably* spring into existence from nowhere. Look at it in terms of transformation, or look at it in terms of "coming into being and passing away"—or just look at it. Whatever you do, you cannot make sense of it: on all accounts it is inconceivable. So I keep to the position that the New Testament story of the turning of water into wine is the story of something which could have been known empirically to have occurred, and it is also the story of the occurrence of something which is conceptually impossible. It has to be both in order to be the miracle-story which, whether true or false, it is.

That expression "the occurrence of something which is conceptually impossible" was used deliberately just then. And it will be objected, no doubt, that to speak of something which is conceptually impossible is to speak of a nullity. To ask for an example of something which is conceptually impossible is not (I shall be told) like asking for a sample of a substance, and you cannot in order to comply with this request produce anything visible or tangible, you cannot point to an occurrence. Indeed you cannot, strictly speaking, offer a description either: you can only utter a form of words. What I have been arguing in effect is that there is a contradiction in St. John's "description" of the water-into-wine episode. But if so, then nothing has really been described; or alternatively something has been—one should not say misdescribed but rather garbled—since a conceptual impossibility is *ex vi termini* one of which sense cannot be made.

I would reply to this that sense can certainly be made of a conceptual impossibility in the respect that one can see often enough that there *is* a conceptual impossibility there and also, often enough, what kind of a conceptual impossibility it is and how it arises. We can see that there is an inconsistency; and words, moreover, are not the only things in which we can see inconsistency. Human actions can be pointed to here quite obviously. And I am maintaining that there is also such a thing as making sense, and failing to make sense, of *events*. If the objector holds that in the case of events, unlike the case of human actions, sense must always be there although one perhaps fails to find it, I ask: how does he know? Why the *must*? It is not part of my case that to regard a sequence of events as senseless or miraculous is to construe it as if it were a sort of action, or to see the invisible hand of a superperson at work in it. I have contended that there are circumstances in respect to which the expression "occurrence of something which is conceptually impossible" would have a natural enough use, and I have offered three examples. I think that the expression "violation of a law of nature" could also be introduced quite naturally in this connection, or we could speak of a contradiction in our experience.

PAUL J. DIETL

4.6 On Miracles

Some of the most remarkable turns in recent philosophical discussion have been the resurrection of issues original readers of *Language, Truth, and Logic* would have thought forever dead. "Freewill" is no longer considered a pseudoproblem. There is serious controversy concerning the existence of God. Ethics

From the *American Philosophical Quarterly* 5 (1968): 130–34. Reprinted by permission of Mrs. Jane Dietl and the editors.

is considered cognitively significant in respectable circles. In fact the concept of a miracle is probably the only concept left for resurrection. Here there is a general agreement—among sophisticated theologians as well as militant atheists—that *a priori* rejection of claims is justified. Miracle claims, it is generally believed, could not be true because of the very nature of the concept of a miracle. Nonetheless I should like to argue for its vindication. The crucial issue is whether conditions could ever obtain which would justify one in applying "miracle" in any way resembling its standard historical use. I shall argue that there could be such conditions, that we could very well recognize them, so that we do know what miracles are, and therefore that miracle claims are at worst false.

Here as elsewhere Hume anticipated much later opinion, so it is reasonable to begin with his contribution. The difficulty is that in much of what he wrote on the subject Hume seemed to be arguing that the event which is supposed to have been an exception to a law of nature could not happen. The laws themselves are based on "a firm and unalterable experience" and "as a uniform experience amounts to a proof, there is here a direct and full proof, from the nature of the fact, against the existence of any miracle. . . ."[1] In at least one place, though, Hume does admit that bizarre events could occur.

> Suppose all authors, in all languages, agree that from the first of January, 1600, there was total darkness over the whole earth for eight days; suppose that the tradition of this extraordinary event is still strong and lively among the people; that all travelers who return from foreign countries, bring us accounts of the same tradition without the least variation or contradiction—it is evident that our present philosophers, instead of doubting the fact, ought to receive it as certain and ought to search for the causes from whence it might be derived.[2]

Apparently the bizarre cannot be ruled out on the grounds that it is bizarre. Indeed, given the right circumstances, even the second-hand *reports* of bizarre events are immune to the criticism that the claim must be false on the grounds that it goes against laws of nature. Nevertheless, even though it is possible that exceptions to established laws should occur, apparently we are never justified in describing the events as miraculous. One looks in vain for Hume's reasons for this latter thesis.

P. H. Nowell-Smith has tried to defend this second view.[3] Nowell-Smith repudiates the view that miracle-claims can be refuted on the grounds that they are exceptions to laws of nature, but he cannot understand the difference between the natural and the supernatural upon which the interpretation or

---

[1]David Hume, *An Enquiry Concerning Human Understanding*, sect. 10, pt. 1, p. 115 (references are to the L. A. Selby-Bigge edition entitled *Enquiries*).

[2]*Ibid.*, p. 128.

[3]In "Miracles," reprinted in *New Essays in Philosophical Theology*, ed. A. Flew and A. MacIntyre (London, 1955), pp. 243–53.

explanation of a bizarre event as miraculous depends.[4] Science, he reminds us, has come to explain things which at an earlier date were beyond its very concepts. He claims that no matter what happens, if it is explained at all, that explanation will take its place in some department of the university. Perhaps a new department will have to be created to accommodate it but that the new department will be among the natural-science faculties Nowell-Smith has no doubt. The point is that to describe an event as miraculous is to say that it could never be explained in any natural science whatsoever, and we can never say that. Not even science itself could show it.

> To say that it is inexplicable as a result of natural agents is already beyond the competence of any scientist as a scientist, and to say that it must be ascribed to supernatural agents is to say something that no one could possibly have the right to affirm on the evidence alone.[5]

Some would answer this charge by attempting to reconcile an event's being miraculous with its eventually being naturally explainable but, say, highly coincidental. That there is such a usage for "miracle" I do not contest, but I am interested in defending the concept Nowell-Smith is attacking. That there is also a usage of "miracle" according to which to call an event a miracle is to attribute it to the will of a supernatural agent and to claim that if the supernatural agent had not intervened that event would not have taken place is, I think, equally clear. Indeed this latter usage is unquestionably more frequent in the history of religion.

It follows that in the way in which I am using "miracle" miracle-claims do have the implications Nowell-Smith envisages. "Supernatural" implies that the agent be able to bring about events which are exceptions to physical laws. Nothing else about the agent is at issue, however. For example, we are not concerned with questions of whether he is all-good or all-powerful or eternal or even with the question of whether there is more than one such being. But he must be a being who can control the laws of nature. The question is whether or not any event would ever be rationally described as a manifestation of power of such a being. It will only be such if all causes other than such a being can be ruled out—which is precisely what Nowell-Smith denied could be done.

Before I construct what I think is a counterexample to Nowell-Smith's thesis, I want to call attention to two features of miracles. The first is simply that there is nothing amiss in one person having several miracles he can perform. In the Book of Exodus, for example, Moses is given more than a dozen miracles with which he attempts to melt the Pharaoh's heart. He brings on several miraculous catastrophes and then stops them. The Pharaoh's heart remains hard, and so Moses brings about several more. The second

---

[4]*Ibid.*, p. 244.
[5]*Ibid.*, pp. 246–47.

feature of historical accounts to which I wish to call attention is the rather elaborate circumstances in which they may take place. The people who wrote the Old Testament quite obviously had some notion of how to tell the real thing from a fake. Take the story about Elijah at Carmel (I Kings 18). Controversy had arisen whether prayer should be directed to the Lord God of the Jews or to Baal. Elijah took the people to Mt. Carmel and said: "Let them . . . give us two bullocks; and let them choose one bullock for themselves, and cut it to pieces, and lay it on wood." The ministers of Baal took the meat from one animal and made a pile, and Elijah called upon the ministers of Baal to ask Baal to cook their meat. "But there was no voice, nor any that answered. And they leaped upon the altar which was made. And it came to pass at noon, that Elijah mocked them, and said, Cry aloud; for he is a god; either he is talking, or he is pursuing, or he is on a journey, or peradventure he sleepeth, and must be awakened. And they cried aloud, and cut themselves after their manner with knives and lances, till the blood gushed out upon them." But all this to no avail. Then Elijah stepped up and said: "Fill four barrels with water, and pour it on the burnt sacrifice, and on the wood." And he said, Do it the second time. And they did it the second time. And he said, Do it the third time. And they did it the third time. And the water ran round about the altar; and he filled the trench also with water. Then he called on God for fire and "Then the fire of the Lord fell, and consumed the burnt sacrifice, and the wood, and the stones, and the dust, and licked up the water that was in the trench."

We are given here, first of all, about as artificial a setting as any laboratory affords. The account also involves a random sampling of the material to be set on fire, a prediction that one pile will burn up and one will not, a prediction when the fire will start, and twelve barrels of precaution against earthly independent variables. There is obviously nothing wrong with applying somewhat sophisticated experimental design to miracles.

Now for the example. Its essential ingredients are simply a bundle of miracles no larger than Moses had and a randomizing technique just a little more complicated than Elijah's. Let us assume that a local prophet opens, or appears with the help of God to open, the mighty Schuylkill River. Two possibilities arise. The first is that the prophet does not figure causally in the natural explanation but that he notices a cue in the physical situation which indicates natural sufficient conditions. This is especially tempting because he might not be consciously aware of the cue and so might himself honestly believe in the miracle. This sort of explanation can be ruled out, however, if he is required to do miracles at random. Say he allows non-believers to pick twelve miracles and number them. Which one he will do will be determined by the roll of a pair of unloaded dice, and the hour of the day at which it will occur will be determined by a second roll. Rolling the dice without his prediction could establish that the dice had no efficacy and using the dice to randomize the predictions proves that the prophet does not predict on the basis of a natural cue.[6]

This randomizing also establishes that there is a cause at work other than would have operated if the prophet had not been there. But perhaps there is still some law covering the events. To see how vastly different this would be from an ordinary scientific law, however, one has only to realize that there would be no new scientific department on a par with, say, physics or chemistry, which included such laws. This would be a department which dealt with all the other sciences and had no laws of its own, except that when this prophet spoke, all laws, or any one of an indefinitely large number, are broken.

Odd, you might say, but not yet miraculous. Such a prophet might require a new metascientific department, but we still have not been forced to admit supernatural explanation. But this is so only because we have not yet looked at the *explanans* in these supposed scientific explanations. What could possibly be the natural conditions which this new department will ascertain to be necessary and sufficient for the unexpected events?

If the prophet prayed we might think that the prayer was connected in some curious way with the exceptions. But what if he does not pray? What if he just requests? Could it be the sounds of his words which have the extraordinary effect? Then let him predict in different languages. Might we mention language-independent brain processes as the sufficient conditions? Let him predict what will happen later when he is asleep—even drugged, or dead.

But surely it has become obvious that there is nothing which could be pinned down as the independent variable in a scientific explanation; for no conceivable candidate is necessary. The prophet asks God to do miracle No. 4 at midnight and then goes to sleep. Or he asks God to do whatever miracle turns up at whatever hour turns up and then dies. We are dealing with requests and answers—that is, thoughts, and thoughts not as psychological occurrences but as understood.

No natural law will do because only vehicles of thought could function as the natural *explanans* and no such vehicle is necessary. There would have to be one law connecting the acoustics of English with general law-breaking, another for French, and so on indefinitely—and when the prophet asks that whatever miracle turns upon the dice be performed and then goes to sleep before the dice are thrown, there just is not anything left except his request as understood.[7]

What is needed here is not a law but an understanding which can grasp the request and then bring it about that a physical law be broken. But an

---

[6]One might object to "proves," but such procedures eliminate candidates with as much certainty as any non-logical procedures ever could.

[7]Since in this case the prophet does not know what miracle will be asked for, precognition is also ruled out.

understanding physical-law breaker is a supernatural being, and that is why if a new department is set up it will not be with the science faculties at all. It will be a department of religion.

I should like here to attempt to forestall some foreseeable objections. The first one is that even if what I have said is all true, that still does not prove that there ever has been a miracle. Of course I agree with this objection. The sophistication of the experimental design of the Elijah account may be the progressive result of centuries of anxious parents' trying to convince doubting children of false stories. The point is that the concept of miracle allowed such sophistication. What they *meant* to say was ascertainable, or at least they meant to *say* that it was ascertainable, in principle. Whether or not their claims were actually true is another question.

A second criticism shows a hankering after a simple *a priori* disproof. Believing in miracles, it will be said, inevitably involves believing in the suspension of some physical law. We can always avoid this by doubting the data. Hallucinations do not rest on the suspension of such laws. The trouble with this sort of objection to the miraculous is that it can quickly be pushed to the point at which the very distinction between hallucinatory and veridical experiences breaks down. Faith, it has been said, can move mountains. Suppose that someone moved the Poconos to northern Minnesota. Thousands saw them flying through the air. Old maps showed them in Pennsylvania where we all remembered them to have been, and a thriving ski industry grows up where there had only been the exhausted open mines of the Mesabi Range. If that is a hallucination then everything is.

A third criticism is that the account of physical laws in this paper is hopelessly over-simple and crude. I agree. One must show, however, that the crudity and simplicity make a difference to the general thesis about miracles. As far as I can see, the introduction of statistics and probability, or the ideal nature of some or all laws, or of accounts of laws as models or inference tickets or as the designation of patterns we find intelligible, makes no difference. Specifically, the account offered here does not rest on belief in metaphysical connections between causes and effects. Of course, physical laws are only descriptive. But I take it that they do serve as bases for predictions and also for contrary-to-fact conditionals. They are not ontological, but they must be nomological. As long as according to the natural laws operative (e.g., gravity) and the state of the world at one time (e.g., including a free body) another state can be predicted to occur (e.g., the body's fall), then, even though there may never have been an exactly true formulation of the law or a perfect instantiation of the initial conditions (no body ever quite free), as long as the denial of the predicted event is internally coherent, to speak of exceptions is meaningful.

A fourth rejoinder to my arguments might be that even if I have proved that there could be conditions which, if you experienced them, would justify your belief in a miracle, and even though we might have reason to believe second-hand reports of bizarre phenomena, we could still never have better reasons to believe a second-hand miracle claim than to doubt the veracity of the man reporting it; and surely this is really all that Hume, if not Nowell-Smith, set out to prove. In answer let me say first that if you had good reason to believe that what the report describes as happening really did happen—and happened as the reports describe, viz., with randomizing and predictions—then it seems to me that you have good reasons to believe in supernatural intervention as an explanation of the events. But in any case remember Exodus once more. Moses had brought several miraculous plagues, then called them off, then brought down a new batch. Now say that you happened into Egypt during the second batch of catastrophes. Could you rule out *a priori* the possibility that there had been an earlier set? I think not.

Fifthly, one might object that even if I have shown that there could be evidence for miracles and even in the sense in which "miracle" implies supernatural intervention, this is still of no religious significance unless "miracle" also implies *divine* intervention. Miracles, as defined here, in short, do not tend to prove the existence of God. My only answer is that to prove the existence of a being who deserves some of the predicates which "God" normally gets would be to go some way toward proving the existence of *God*. The question whether the comprehensibility of miracle claims strengthens the position of the theologians or whether the paucity of latter-day evidence has the opposite effect, I leave to the theologians and more militant atheists.

A final criticism might be that calling an event a miracle appears to be offering an explanation for it, but is really not an explanation at all since explanations must always rest on laws. In fact, it might be held, this is the real dilemma behind miracle hypotheses. Either there are laws covering miracles or not. If there are no laws then miracles cannot be explanations: they are not hypotheses at all. But if there are laws, then there is no difference between natural and supernatural explanations. Nowell-Smith's argument goes:

(A) Calling an event a miracle is apparently to explain it.
(B) Explanations must rest on laws.
(C) If one has laws one can predict the events they explain.
(D) We cannot predict miracles, therefore calling an event a miracle has no (explanatory) meaning over and above a mere (descriptive) statement of the phenomena to be explained.[8]

Now, a prediction was involved in the Elijah story, and I do not see how one could pin down God as the independent variable unless predictions like those were possible. These predictions, however, were not made possible by anything Nowell-Smith would call a law. Indeed, that the prediction did not rest on the knowledge of a regularity between initial conditions and effect was the reason for looking to the supernatural. In other words, it cannot be objected

---

°Nowell-Smith, p. 250.

that miracles are not explanations because miracles are not lawful until it has been proved that all explanations are lawful. This is all the more pressing since part of the point of interpreting an event as a miracle is to see it not as a natural event but as an action, or the result of an action, of an intelligent being.[9] That all intelligible *actions* are subsumable under laws is even less credible than that all *events* are. An action can be made intelligible by showing its *point* (for example, to bring wayward children back to the truth, to reward the holy, to save the chosen people, etc.), and showing the good of an action is not automatically to subsume it under a law.

I conclude that "miracle" is perfectly meaningful. To call an event a miracle is to claim that it is the result of supernatural intervention into the natural course of events. We could know that the supernatural agent was intelligent, but little else (though when and for whom he did miracles would be evidence about his character).[10]

---

[9]This is the point of drawing an analogy between explanations in terms of miracles and human intervention into the course of nature. Whether or not such divine intervention would have to be in conformity to the laws of nature because human intervention apparently is would be a further question. Nowell-Smith seems to think that anyone who draws the analogy at all must admit that divine intervention would have to be in accordance with laws (p. 249).

[10]This paper has profited from criticisms by Professors William Wisdom and Michael Scriven.

PART FIVE

MAN'S RELATION
TO GOD

INTRODUCTION

In this section of the book, we will consider a variety of philosophical issues that arise in connection with three of the ways in which human beings who hold religious beliefs relate to their Deity. To begin with, some such people actually claim to have experienced the Deity in their mystical experiences. Philosophers have naturally been concerned with understanding the nature of these experiences, seeing whether they can be understood in other ways, and deciding on the basis of their investigations whether these experiences shed any light upon the issue of the existence of God. Secondly, most religious people claim that God can be worshipped in prayer and in acts of ritual. Philosophers have been concerned with the rationale for these acts—are they merely arbitrarily chosen or are there reasons for them?—and with the more general question why religious worship has to be performed in actions and not merely in feelings and thoughts. Finally, many religious people claim that moral codes are imposed upon us by God and that his will is the basis for morality. In acting morally, we are, according to these people, following the will of God. Once more, philosophers have been concerned with the question whether or not morality could have such a religious basis. In Part 5 we will consider all of these philosophical issues, beginning with the issues surrounding mystical experiences.

As James and Stace point out, mystical experiences are a very special type of experience. According to those who have had them, they do not in any way resemble sensuous experiences, and they are not describable in terms of our concepts and language. It is for this reason that mystics talk of their experiences as being ineffable. It is for this reason, also, that mystics differentiate mystical experiences from visions, etc. Those visionary experiences are sensuous experiences, although with most unusual objects, and they can be described using our concepts and language.

While mystics do say that their experiences are in this way ineffable, they want to say that these experiences also involve a deep insight into the nature of things. Naturally, different mystics disagree about what exactly this insight is. But, on the whole, there seems to be at least some agreement about it. For Professor Stace, the crucial apprehension is that of an ultimate unity of things. For William James, the crucial point is that the apprehension is antinaturalistic and otherworldly. But, it would appear, there is no disagreement here, since the mystical teaching as James describes it involves a claim that, behind the pluralistic natural universe, there is another more fundamental unity.

One further characteristic of mystical experiences should be noted. The mystic typically claims that, in these experiences, the distinction disappears between the subject who has the experience and the object that is experienced. But at the same time, the mystic wants to talk of his experience as being of the individual self although as part of the undifferentiated unity. How he is to maintain both of these claims is not entirely clear.

Having described the nature of the mystical experience, both James and Stace go on to consider the question whether it does provide us with some knowledge of how the world really is. James's attitude is rather complicated. On the one hand, he wants to say that the mystic, who has had the experience, has as much right as the ordinary individual to suppose that whatever he has experienced exists. On the other hand, he wants to claim that, despite the impressive agreement among mystics about what they have experienced, the nonmystic is not compelled to admit the reality of what is experienced. The reader will have to (a) see what his reasons are for this claim, and (b) decide whether or not the two claims really are compatible.

Stace is concerned with a different aspect of this issue. As he points out, the religious mystic, for a variety of reasons, tends to identify the undifferentiated unity that he experiences with the Deity. On the basis of this identification, the mystic claims to have experienced God and to know therefore that God exists. It is this part of the mystic's claim that Stace wants to challenge. While he is inclined to believe (without, it should be noted, offering any arguments for this inclination) that the mystic has come to know, through his experience, some reality that we could not know through our ordinary experiences, he does not see any basis for justifying the identification of this reality with some Deity.

It is obvious that the crucial and fundamental epistemological question is the one that James was concerned with, viz., whether mystical experiences provide the mystics or anyone else with knowledge of some objective reality (regardless of whether or not it is to be identified with a particular Deity). To be sure, the mystic claims that he knows of its existence through his experience, but is that experience of the type that generates knowledge of some reality other than the subjective states of the mystic? It is just this issue that is discussed in Professor Martin's article.

Martin's main reason for differentiating between the claims of the mystic and the claims of the ordinary perceiver is that the latter, but not the former, lend themselves to checking and testing by the perceiver and by others. It might well be suggested that it is just this intersubjective testing that lends credence to the ordinary perceiver's claim that what he has experienced really exists. The fact that such testing is not present in the case of the mystic's experience must certainly cast doubt upon his claim. More fundamentally, however, it means that his claim really resembles, in these important respects, normal claims about one's subjective states. And this naturally raises the question whether it is possible for the mystic to avoid the assimilation of his claim into the latter class of claims, something he surely wants to avoid.

We turn now to a consideration of the philosophical issues surrounding ritual and prayer. In order to understand these issues it is important to keep in mind that most classical religions embody a variety of claims about the sorts of actions that people should and should not do. Some of these claims seem to be straightforward moral claims having to do with relations between people, and it is indeed an open question (some aspects of which will be discussed below) whether or not these claims are really dependent upon the theological presuppositions of that particular religion. Others, however, are very different. Some of them deal with the relationship between man and God; they call upon man, for example, to thank God in prayer, and to show the proper respect for him in a variety of ways. Some of them call upon men to perform a variety of actions whose purpose is unclear or to desist from certain actions where the purpose of this desisting is unclear. In these cases, the claim is that one should do so because that is what God commanded. It is clear that these claims really are dependent upon the theological presuppositions of the particular religion.

The Talmudic scholar Saadya ben Joseph (882–942), in the excerpt from his *Book of Beliefs and Opinions*, is concerned with this last set of claims—religious claims about ritual actions. There are two issues that he considers: (a) why should God impose any ritual observances on mankind? (b) does God have any reasons at all for imposing the ones that He does, or is it all a matter of arbitrary choice? Saadya's answer to the first question is that God has imposed these commandments upon mankind so that He can reward man for obeying them. This answer clearly presupposes, of course, that there are goods that God can legitimately give man as a reward for obedience but which He could not otherwise legitimately give to man. Whether this presupposition is correct is something that the reader will have to decide for himself. Saadya's answer to the second question is that each of the particular ritual observances does produce some benefit for the observer, so it would be wrong to think of God as having arbitrarily chosen just any observance at all.

St. Thomas discusses many of these same issues, but the results that he comes to are different in many ways from Saadya's. He finds a different reason for the imposition of ritual commandments and offers a different account of why God chose the particular ritual commandments that he did choose.

For St. Thomas, the ritual actions are all to be thought of as acts of worship of God (ones performed by use of the body) or as aids to worship, and the reason for their existence is that men should worship God. While, no doubt, men will be rewarded for their performance, that reward is not part of the reason for the imposition of the commandments. Secondly, unlike Saadya, he emphasizes the figurative (symbolic) reason for God's having chosen the particular rituals that he did assign, although, it should be noted, he does not want thereby to exclude their also having literal reasons pertaining to the worship of God.

It is clear that at least some ritual actions like prayer are acts of worship, and, if St. Thomas is right, perhaps we should view all ritual actions that way. Both Saadya and St. Thomas find no difficulty with the idea that there are commandments about worshiping God, for they see the worship of God as showing honor and reverence to him who deserves it. But there is a problem about these acts of worship that is raised by St. Thomas and discussed more fully by Professor Matthews. God knows, after all, what we think and feel, so why do we have to worship him in some external action? Why isn't it enough that we worship him in our thoughts and feelings? This problem, as St. Thomas notes, is really a problem only for individual worship and prayer; there is no problem in the case of common worship. St. Thomas finds three purposes for external acts of worship such as vocal prayer: (a) they excite internal devotion; (b) when we have a great deal of interior devotion, it inevitably spills over into external worship; and (c) they enable man to worship God with his body as well as his mind, and this is fitting since both come from God. It is important to keep in mind, in connection with this third point, that it is still man, and not his body, who is worshiping God. Otherwise, the third point would be in conceptual trouble.

The first of these three Thomistic answers is already to be found in St. Augustine, and Professor Matthews begins his article by criticizing this Augustinian approach. It rests, he feels, on the mistaken conception that mere bodily motions in acts of ritual can have an effect on our feelings and thoughts. Instead, he claims, this can only come about by the sincere and understanding performance of the ritual. So why do we need the bodily motions? Matthews feels that the whole problem rests upon another mistaken idea, viz., that the performance of the bodily act of worship has as its function the informing of God of one's thoughts and feelings toward Him, a function that is obviously inappropriate in light of the fact that God already knows about them. Once one recognizes that an actual acknowledgment in words or actions of one's feeling that one has done wrong, or of one's feeling of gratitude, can serve other functions as well (functions that Matthews spells out), the problem disappears. The bodily performance of these acts of ritual are intended to fulfill these other functions.

We turn now to the third way in which religious people relate to their

Deity, the fulfillment of those moral codes that he has laid down for man-kind. The crucial philosophical question that arises here is a very simple one: are those moral codes mere reflections of the will of God (in which case it would seem that the actions in question are right or wrong only because God has willed us to do, or to refrain from doing, them) or are they reflections of God's knowledge that these actions really are right or wrong (in which case it would seem that they would be right or wrong independently of God)?

This issue was first raised by Plato in the *Euthyphro*. Euthyphro defines a holy action like the one he proposes doing as an action loved by the Gods. Socrates tries to get Euthyphro to adopt the alternative view that the Gods love certain actions because they are holy, that the moral value of the action, in other words, is independent of, and the cause of, the attitude of the Gods to it. The argument presented by Socrates is a tricky one, and the reader will have to work very hard on it. A modernized version of an argument like it is found in the beginning of Professor Brody's paper.

The reader might well wonder which of the two alternatives is adopted in the theoretical portions of classical religious moralities. As one looks, for ex-ample, through St. Thomas's presentation of just such a theoretical basis, one finds an interesting answer to this question. St. Thomas supposes that there is an eternal law promulgated by God which governs human actions. God has implanted in us a natural ability to discern this law, to discern what is right or wrong (as natural law), but, for a variety of reasons, he has also re-vealed the eternal law to us (as divine law). Now insofar as St. Thomas talks of the eternal law as presupposing a promulgation by God, he would seem to be supposing that its moral dictates are not independent of God. But in-sofar as he talks of the eternal law as coming from God's practical reason, he would seem to be supposing that its moral dictates are not mere arbitrary acts of willing. For a religious person, St. Thomas's approach seems like a desirable middle ground between the two earlier positions. Morality is more than the mere arbitrary will of God but it is still dependent upon the existence of God and his promulgating it. But St. Thomas's middle ground rests, un-fortunately, on the difficult assumption that a moral principle exists only in-sofar as it is promulgated, and if one cannot support that assumption, then the religious person seems forced back into choosing between the two alterna-tives sketched above.

It is pretty clear that religious people have reasons for being dissatisfied with the idea that the moral codes revealed by God are based upon his recog-nition of the independent rightness and wrongness of the actions in question. This would mean, in effect, that these codes ultimately are independent of any religious basis, that they could equally well be accepted on a nonreligious level. In short, it would mean that they are not really religious codes of mo-rality, just codes of morality held by a particular religious group. What rea-sons have religious people, however, for being dissatisfied with the idea that these codes represent God's arbitrary acts of will as to how people should behave?

There seem to be two answers to this question. The first, which forms the basis for the discussion in Professor Brody's paper, is that the postulation of such arbitrary acts of willing seem, at least to many religious people, to introduce an imperfection into the conception of God. The second, which is introduced at the very beginning of Professor Nowell-Smith's article, is that this view would not leave us with any moral reason for obeying the will of God. We have a moral reason (as opposed to a prudential reason, e.g. obeying Him so He will not punish us) for obeying the will of God only if we are already convinced of its independent goodness, and that presupposes a morality that is independent of the will of God.

Professor Brody attempts to show that it is possible to say that God's will is not arbitrary, is based upon reasons, while still claiming that the actions in question are right or wrong only because God has willed us to do or refrain from doing them. The crucial idea is that we have to take into account the additional fact that God is the creator, and therefore has special rights vis-à-vis the world and everything in it, including us. It is shown that, if we keep that fact in mind, it is possible for us to see why certain actions are right or wrong because God has willed us to do them or to refrain from doing them, but would not be right or wrong otherwise, even though God's willings were not arbitrary. Adopting this approach, we can avoid the impropriety of attributing to a perfect being arbitrary acts of willing while still claiming that the rightness or wrongness of the actions in question depend upon the will of God. The reader should ask himself whether adopting this approach also meets Professor Nowell-Smith's objections.

Another type of objection to religious moralities that is raised by Professor Nowell-Smith has to do not with their source but with their form. Religious moralities tend to be deontological moralities, moralities which emphasize the following of certain rules no matter what the circumstances. Professor Nowell-Smith finds this feature of religious moralities childlike and wants to claim that a properly mature moral code would emphasize instead the particular circumstances and people concerned. Many religious people accept the claim that a religious morality does have this deontological feature, but they insist, contra Nowell-Smith, that this is a desirable feature. Indeed, they say, it is just this feature that is the distinctive contribution of religion to morality. There are, then, two final questions about religious morality that the reader has to consider: (a) is this feature desirable?—and (b) if it is, can it be maintained in a nonreligious moral system?

RELIGIOUS EXPERIENCE

WILLIAM JAMES

5.1   Mysticism

Over and over again in these lectures I have raised points and left them open and unfinished until we should have come to the subject of Mysticism. Some of you, I fear, may have smiled as you noted my reiterated postponements. But now the hour has come when mysticism must be faced in good earnest, and those broken threads wound up together. One may say truly, I think, that personal religious experience has its root and centre in mystical states of consciousness; so for us, who in these lectures are treating personal experience as the exclusive subject of our study, such states of consciousness ought to form the vital chapter from which the other chapters get their light. Whether my treatment of mystical states will shed more light or darkness, I do not know, for my own constitution shuts me out from their enjoyment almost entirely, and I can speak of them only at second hand. But though forced to look upon the subject so externally, I will be as objective and receptive as I can; and I think I shall at least succeed in convincing you of the reality of the states in question, and of the paramount importance of their function.

First of all, then, I ask, What does the expression "mystical states of consciousness" mean? How do we part off mystical states from other states?

The words "mysticism" and "mystical" are often used as terms of mere reproach, to throw at any opinion which we regard as vague and vast and sentimental, and without a base in either facts or logic. For some writers a "mystic" is any person who believes in thought-transference, or spirit-return.

From William James, *The Varieties of Religious Experience* (1902).

Employed in this way the word has little value: there are too many less ambiguous synonyms. So, to keep it useful by restricting it, I will do what I did in the case of the word "religion," and simply propose to you four marks which, when an experience has them, may justify us in calling it mystical for the purpose of the present lectures. In this way we shall save verbal disputation, and the recriminations that generally go therewith.

1. *Ineffability.*—The handiest of the marks by which I classify a state of mind as mystical is negative. The subject of it immediately says that it defies expression, that no adequate report of its contents can be given in words. It follows from this that its quality must be directly experienced; it cannot be imparted or transferred to others. In this peculiarity mystical states are more like states of feeling than like states of intellect. No one can make clear to another who has never had a certain feeling, in what the quality or worth of it consists. One must have musical ears to know the value of a symphony; one must have been in love one's self to understand a lover's state of mind. Lacking the heart or ear, we cannot interpret the musician or the lover justly, and are even likely to consider him weak-minded or absurd. The mystic finds that most of us accord to his experiences an equally incompetent treatment.

2. *Noetic quality.*—Although so similar to states of feeling, mystical states seem to those who experience them to be also states of knowledge. They are states of insight into depths of truth unplumbed by the discursive intellect. They are illuminations, revelations, full of significance and importance, all inarticulate though they remain; and as a rule they carry with them a curious sense of authority for aftertime.

These two characters will entitle any state to be called mystical, in the sense in which I use the word. Two other qualities are less sharply marked, but are usually found. These are:—

3. *Transiency.*—Mystical states cannot be sustained for long. Except in rare instances, half an hour, or at most an hour or two, seems to be the limit beyond which they fade into the light of common day. Often, when faded, their quality can but imperfectly be reproduced in memory; but when they recur it is recognized; and from one recurrence to another it is susceptible of continuous development in what is felt as inner richness and importance.

4. *Passivity.*—Although the oncoming of mystical states may be facilitated by preliminary voluntary operations, as by fixing the attention, or going through certain bodily performances, or in other ways which manuals of mysticism prescribe; yet when the characteristic sort of consciousness once has set in, the mystic feels as if his own will were in abeyance, and indeed sometimes as if he were grasped and held by a superior power. This latter peculiarity connects mystical states with certain definite phenomena of secondary or alternative personality, such as prophetic speech, automatic writing, or the mediumistic trance. When these latter conditions are well pronounced, however, there may be no recollection whatever of the phe-

nomenon, and it may have no significance for the subject's usual inner life, to which, as it were, it makes a mere interruption. Mystical states, strictly so-called, are never merely interruptive. Some memory of their content always remains, and a profound sense of their importance. They modify the inner life of the subject between the times of their recurrence. Sharp divisions in this region are, however, difficult to make, and we find all sorts of gradations and mixtures.

These four characteristics are sufficient to mark out a group of states of consciousness peculiar enough to deserve a special name and to call for careful study. Let it then be called the mystical group.

Our next step should be to gain acquaintance with some typical examples. Professional mystics at the height of their development have often elaborately organized experiences and a philosophy based thereupon. But you remember what I said in my first lecture: phenomena are best understood when placed within their series, studied in their germ and in their over-ripe decay, and compared with their exaggerated and degenerated kindred. The range of mystical experience is very wide, much too wide for us to cover in the time at our disposal. Yet the method of serial study is so essential for interpretation that if we really wish to reach conclusions we must use it. I will begin, therefore, with phenomena which claim no special religious significance, and end with those of which the religious pretensions are extreme.

The simplest rudiment of mystical experience would seem to be that deepened sense of the significance of a maxim or formula which occasionally sweeps over one. "I've heard that said all my life," we exclaim, "but I never realized its full meaning until now." "When a fellow-monk," said Luther, "one day repeated the words of the Creed: 'I believe in the forgiveness of sins,' I saw the Scripture in an entirely new light; and straightway I felt as if I were born anew. It was as if I had found the door of paradise thrown wide open." This sense of deeper significance is not confined to rational propositions. Single words, and conjunctions of words, effects of light on land and sea, odors and musical sounds, all bring it when the mind is tuned aright. Most of us can remember the strangely moving power of passages in certain poems read when we were young, irrational doorways as they were through which the mystery of fact, the wildness and the pang of life, stole into our hearts and thrilled them. The words have now perhaps become mere polished surfaces for us; but lyric poetry and music are alive and significant only in proportion as they fetch these vague vistas of a life continuous with our own, beckoning and inviting, yet ever eluding our pursuit. We are alive or dead to the eternal inner message of the arts according as we have kept or lost this mystical susceptibility.

A more pronounced step forward on the mystical ladder is found in an extremely frequent phenomenon, that sudden feeling, namely, which sometimes sweeps over us, of having "been here before," as if at some indefinite past time, in just this place, with just these people, we were already saying just these things. As Tennyson writes:

> Moreover, something is or seems
> That touches me with mystic gleams,
> Like glimpses of forgotten dreams—
>
> Of something felt, like something here;
> Of something done, I know not where;
> Such as no language may declare.

Sir James Crichton-Browne has given the technical name of "dreamy states" to these sudden invasions of vaguely reminiscent consciousness. They bring a sense of mystery and of the metaphysical duality of things, and the feeling of an enlargement of perception which seems imminent but which never completes itself. In Dr. Crichton-Browne's opinion they connect themselves with the perplexed and scared disturbances of self-consciousness which occasionally precede epileptic attacks. I think that this learned alienist takes a rather absurdly alarmist view of an intrinsically insignificant phenomenon. He follows it along the downward ladder, to insanity; our path pursues the upward ladder chiefly. The divergence shows how important it is to neglect no part of a phenomenon's connections, for we make it appear admirable or dreadful according to the context by which we set it off.

Somewhat deeper plunges into mystical consciousness are met with in yet other dreamy states. Such feelings as these which Charles Kingsley describes are surely far from being uncommon, especially in youth:—

> When I walk the fields, I am oppressed now and then with an innate feeling that everything I see has a meaning, if I could but understand it. And this feeling of being surrounded with truths which I cannot grasp amounts to indescribable awe sometimes. . . . Have you not felt that your real soul was imperceptible to your mental vision, except in a few hallowed moments?

A much more extreme state of mystical consciousness is described by J. A. Symonds; and probably more persons than we suspect could give parallels to it from their own experience.

> Suddenly (writes Symonds) at church, or in company, or when I was reading, and always, I think, when my muscles were at rest, I felt the approach of the mood. Irresistibly it took possession of my mind and will, lasted what seemed an eternity, and disappeared in a series of rapid sensations which resembled the awakening from anaesthetic influence. One reason why I disliked this kind of trance was that I could not describe it to myself. I cannot even now find words to render it intelligible. It consisted in a gradual but swiftly progressive obliteration of space, time, sensation, and the multitudinous factors of experience which seem to qualify what we are pleased to call our Self. In proportion as these conditions of ordinary consciousness were subtracted, the sense of an

underlying or essential consciousness acquired intensity. At last nothing remained but a pure, absolute, abstract Self. The universe became without form
and void of content. But Self persisted, formidable in its vivid keenness, feeling
the most poignant doubt about reality, ready, as it seemed, to find existence
break as breaks a bubble round about it. And what then? The apprehension
of a coming dissolution, the grim conviction that this state was the last state of
the conscious Self, the sense that I had followed the last thread of being to the
verge of the abyss, and had arrived at demonstration of eternal Maya or illusion, stirred or seemed to stir me up again. The return to ordinary conditions
of sentient existence began by my first recovering the power of touch, and
then by the gradual though rapid influx of familiar impressions and diurnal
interests. At last I felt myself once more a human being; and though the riddle
of what is meant by life remained unsolved, I was thankful for this return
from the abyss—this deliverance from so awful an initiation into the mysteries
of skepticism.

This trance recurred with diminishing frequency until I reached the age of
twenty-eight. It served to impress upon my growing nature the phantasmal
unreality of all the circumstances which contribute to a merely phenomenal
consciousness. Often have I asked myself with anguish, on waking from that
formless state of denuded, keenly sentient being, Which is the unreality—the
trance of fiery, vacant, apprehensive, skeptical Self from which I issue, or these
surrounding phenomena and habits which veil that inner Self and build a self
of flesh-and-blood conventionality? Again, are men the factors of some dream,
the dream-like unsubstantiality of which they comprehend at such eventful
moments? What would happen if the final stage of the trance were reached?

In a recital like this there is certainly something suggestive of pathology.
The next step into mystical states carries us into a realm that public opinion
and ethical philosophy have long since branded as pathological, though private practice and certain lyric strains of poetry seem still to bear witness to
its ideality. I refer to the consciousness produced by intoxicants and anaesthetics, especially by alcohol. The sway of alcohol over mankind is unquestionably due to its power to stimulate the mystical faculties of human nature,
usually crushed to earth by the cold facts and dry criticism of the sober hour.
Sobriety diminishes, discriminates, and says no; drunkenness expands, unites,
and says yes. It is in fact the greater exciter of the *Yes* function in man. It
brings its votary from the chill periphery of things to the radiant core. It makes
him for the moment one with truth. Not through mere perversity do men
run after it. To the poor and the unlettered it stands in the place of symphony
concerts and of literature; and it is part of the deeper mystery and tragedy
of life that whiffs and gleams of something that we immediately recognize as
excellent should be vouchsafed to so many of us only in the fleeting earlier
phases of what in its totality is so degrading a poisoning. The drunken consciousness is one bit of the mystic consciousness, and our total opinion of it
must find its place in our opinion of that larger whole.

Nitrous oxide and ether, especially nitrous oxide, when sufficiently diluted
with air, stimulate the mystical consciousness in an extraordinary degree.
Depth beyond depth of truth seems revealed to the inhaler. This truth fades
out, however, or escapes, at the moment of coming to; and if any words re-

main over in which it seemed to clothe itself, they prove to be the veriest nonsense. Nevertheless, the sense of a profound meaning having been there persists; and I know more than one person who is persuaded that in the nitrous oxide trance we have a genuine metaphysical revelation.

Some years ago I myself made some observations on this aspect of nitrous oxide intoxication, and reported them in print. One conclusion was forced upon my mind at that time, and my impression of its truth has ever since remained unshaken. It is that our normal waking consciousness, rational consciousness as we call it, is but one special type of consciousness, whilst all about it, parted from it by the filmiest of screens, there lie potential forms of consciousness entirely different. We may go through life without suspecting their existence; but apply the requisite stimulus, and at a touch they are there in all their completeness, definite types of mentality which probably somewhere have their field of application and adaptation. No account of the universe in its totality can be final which leaves these other forms of consciousness quite disregarded. How to regard them is the question—for they are so discontinuous with ordinary consciousness. Yet they may determine attitudes though they cannot furnish formulas, and open a region though they fail to give a map. At any rate, they forbid a premature closing of our accounts with reality. Looking back on my own experiences, they all converge towards a kind of insight to which I cannot help ascribing some metaphysical significance. The keynote of it is invariably a reconciliation. It is as if the opposites of the world, whose contradictoriness and conflict make all our difficulties and troubles, were melted into unity. Not only do they, as contrasted species, belong to one and the same genus, but *one of the species*, the nobler and better one, *is itself the genus, and so soaks up and absorbs its opposite into itself*. This is a dark saying, I know, when thus expressed in terms of common logic, but I cannot wholly escape from its authority. I feel as if it must mean something, something like what the Hegelian philosophy means, if one could only lay hold of it more clearly. Those who have ears to hear, let them hear; to me the living sense of its reality only comes in the artificial mystic state of mind.

I just now spoke of friends who believe in the anaesthetic revelation. For them too it is a monistic insight, in which the *other* in its various forms appears absorbed into the One.

> Into this pervading genius (writes one of them) we pass, forgetting and forgotten, and thenceforth each is all, in God. There is no higher, no deeper, no other, than the life in which we are founded. "The One remains, the many change and pass;" and each and every one of us *is* the One that remains. . . . This is the ultimatum. . . . As sure as being—whence is all our care—so sure is content, beyond duplexity, antithesis, or trouble, where I have triumphed in a solitude that God is not above.

This has the genuine religious mystic ring! I just now quoted J. A. Symonds. He also records a mystical experience with chloroform, as follows:—

After the choking and stifling had passed away, I seemed at first in a state of utter blankness; then came flashes of intense light, alternating with blackness, and with a keen vision of what was going on in the room around me, but no sensation of touch. I thought that I was near death; when, suddenly, my soul became aware of God, who was manifestly dealing with me, handling me, so to speak, in an intense personal present reality. I felt him streaming in like light upon me. . . . I cannot describe the ecstasy I felt. Then, as I gradually awoke from the influence of the anaesthetics, the old sense of my relation to the world began to return, the new sense of my relation to God began to fade. I suddenly leapt to my feet on the chair where I was sitting, and shrieked out, "It is too horrible, it is too horrible, it is too horrible," meaning that I could not bear this disillusionment. Then I flung myself on the ground, and at last awoke covered with blood, calling to the two surgeons (who were frightened), "Why did you not kill me? Why would you not let me die?" Only think of it. To have felt for that long dateless ecstasy of vision the very God, in all purity and tenderness and truth and absolute love, and then to find that I had after all had no revelation, but that I had been tricked by the abnormal excitement of my brain.

Yet, this question remains, Is it possible that the inner sense of reality which succeeded, when my flesh was dead to impressions from without, to the ordinary sense of physical relations, was not a delusion but an actual experience? Is it possible that I, in that moment, felt what some of the saints have said they always felt, the undemonstrable but irrefragable certainty of God?

With this we make connection with religious mysticism pure and simple. Symonds's question takes us back to those examples which you will remember my quoting in the lecture on the Reality of the Unseen, of sudden realization of the immediate presence of God. The phenomenon in one shape or another is not uncommon.

I know (writes Mr. Trine) an officer on our police force who has told me that many times when off duty, and on his way home in the evening, there comes to him such a vivid and vital realization of his oneness with this Infinite Power, and this Spirit of Infinite Peace so takes hold of and so fills him, that it seems as if his feet could hardly keep to the pavement, so buoyant and so exhilarated does he become by reason of this inflowing tide.

Certain aspects of nature seem to have a peculiar power of awakening such mystical moods. Most of the striking cases which I have collected have occurred out of doors. Literature has commemorated this fact in many passages of great beauty—this extract, for example, from Amiel's Journal Intime:—

Shall I ever again have any of those prodigious reveries which sometimes came to me in former days? One day, in youth, at sunrise, sitting in the ruins of the castle of Faucigny; and again in the mountains, under the noonday sun, above Lavey, lying at the foot of a tree and visited by three butterflies; once more at night upon the shingly shore of the Northern Ocean, my back upon the sand and my vision ranging through the milky way;—such grand and spacious, immortal, cosmogonic reveries, when one reaches to the stars, when one owns the infinite! Moments divine, ecstatic hours; in which our thought flies from world to world, pierces the great enigma, breathes with a respiration broad, tranquil, and deep as the respiration of the ocean, serene and limitless as the blue firmament; . . . instants of irresistible intuition in which one feels one's self great as the universe, and calm as a god. . . . What hours, what memories! The vestiges they leave behind are enough to fill us with belief and enthusiasm, as if they were visits of the Holy Ghost.

Here is a similar record from the memoirs of that interesting German idealist, Malwida von Meysenbug:—

> I was alone upon the seashore as all these thoughts flowed over me, liberating and reconciling; and now again, as once before in distant days in the Alps of Dauphiné, I was impelled to kneel down, this time before the illimitable ocean, symbol of the Infinite. I felt that I prayed as I had never prayed before, and knew now what prayer really is: to return from the solitude of individuation into the consciousness of unity with all that is, to kneel down as one that passes away, and to rise up as one imperishable. Earth, heaven, and sea resounded as in one vast world-encircling harmony. It was as if the chorus of all the great who had ever lived were about me. I felt myself one with them, and it appeared as if I heard their greeting: "Thou too belongest to the company of those who overcome."

This well known passage from Walt Whitman is a classical expression of this sporadic type of mystical experience.

> I believe in you, my Soul . . .
> Loaf with me on the grass, loose the stop from your throat; . . .
> Only the lull I like, the hum of your valved voice.
> I mind how once we lay, such a transparent summer morning.
> Swiftly arose and spread around me the peace and knowledge that pass all the
>   argument of the earth,
> And I know that the hand of God is the promise of my own,
> And I know that the spirit of God is the brother of my own,
> And that all the men ever born are also my brothers and the women my
>   sisters and lovers,
> And that a kelson of the creation is love.

I could easily give more instances, but one will suffice. I take it from the Autobiography of J. Trevor.

> One brilliant Sunday morning, my wife and boys went to the Unitarian Chapel in Macclesfield. I felt it impossible to accompany them—as though to leave the sunshine on the hills, and go down there to the chapel, would be for the time an act of spiritual suicide. And I felt such need for new inspiration and expansion in my life. So, very reluctantly and sadly, I left my wife and boys to go down into the town, while I went further up into the hills with my stick and my dog. In the loveliness of the morning, and the beauty of the hills and valleys, I soon lost my sense of sadness and regret. For nearly an hour I walked along the road to the "Cat and Fiddle," and then returned. On the way back, suddenly, without warning, I felt that I was in Heaven—an inward state

of peace and joy and assurance indescribably intense, accompanied with a
sense of being bathed in a warm glow of light, as though the external condition
had brought about the internal effect—a feeling of having passed beyond the
body, though the scene around me stood out more clearly and as if nearer to
me than before, by reason of the illumination in the midst of which I seemed
to be placed. This deep emotion lasted, though with decreasing strength, until
I reached home, and for some time after, only gradually passing away.

The writer adds that having had further experiences of a similar sort, he
now knows them well.

The spiritual life (he writes) justifies itself to those who live it; but what can
we say to those who do not understand? This, at least, we can say, that it is a
life whose experiences are proved real to their possessor, because they remain
with him when brought closest into contact with the objective realities of life.
Dreams cannot stand this test. We wake from them to find that they are but
dreams. Wanderings of an overwrought brain do not stand this test. These
highest experiences that I have had of God's presence have been rare and
brief—flashes of consciousness which have compelled me to exclaim with
surprise—God is *here!*—or conditions of exaltation and insight, less intense,
and only gradually passing away. I have severely questioned the worth of these
moments. To no soul have I named them, lest I should be building my life and
work on mere phantasies of the brain. But I find that, after every questioning
and test, they stand out to-day as the most real experiences of my life, and
experiences which have explained and justified and unified all past experiences
and all past growth. Indeed, their reality and their far-reaching significance
are ever becoming more clear and evident. When they came, I was living the
fullest, strongest, sanest, deepest life. I was not seeking them. What I was
seeking, with resolute determination, was to live more intensely my own life,
as against what I knew would be the adverse judgment of the world. It was in
the most real seasons that the Real Presence came, and I was aware that I
was immersed in the infinite ocean of God.

Even the least mystical of you must by this time be convinced of the existence of mystical moments as states of consciousness of an entirely specific
quality, and of the deep impression which they make on those who have
them. A Canadian psychiatrist. Dr. R. M. Bucke, gives to the more distinctly
characterized of these phenomena the name of cosmic consciousness. "Cosmic consciousness in its more striking instances is not," Dr. Bucke says, "simply an expansion or extension of the self-conscious mind with which we are
all familiar, but the superaddition of a function as distinct from any possessed
by the average man as *self*-consciousness is distinct from any function possessed by one of the higher animals."

The prime characteristic of cosmic consciousness is a consciousness of the
cosmos, that is, of the life and order of the universe. Along with the consciousness of the cosmos there occurs an intellectual enlightenment which alone
would place the individual on a new plane of existence—would make him
almost a member of a new species. To this is added a state of moral exaltation,

an indescribable feeling of elevation, elation, and joyousness, and a quickening of the moral sense, which is fully as striking, and more important than is the enhanced intellectual power. With these come what may be called a sense of immortality, a consciousness of eternal life, not a conviction that he shall have this, but the consciousness that he has it already.

It was Dr. Bucke's own experience of a typical onset of cosmic consciousness in his own person which led him to investigate it in others. He has printed his conclusions in a highly interesting volume, from which I take the following account of what occurred to him:—

> I had spent the evening in a great city, with two friends, reading and discussing poetry and philosophy. We parted at midnight. I had a long drive in a hansom to my lodging. My mind, deeply under the influence of the ideas, images, and emotions called up by the reading and talk, was calm and peaceful. I was in a state of quiet, almost passive enjoyment, not actually thinking, but letting ideas, images, and emotions flow of themselves, as it were, through my mind. All at once, without warning of any kind, I found myself wrapped in a flame-colored cloud. For an instant I thought of fire, an immense conflagration somewhere close by in that great city; the next, I knew that the fire was within myself. Directly afterward there came upon me a sense of exultation, of immense joyousness accompanied or immediately followed by an intellectual illumination impossible to describe. Among other things, I did not merely come to believe, but I saw that the universe is not composed of dead matter, but is, on the contrary, a living Presence; I became conscious in myself of eternal life. It was not a conviction that I would have eternal life, but a consciousness that I possessed eternal life then; I saw that all men are immortal; that the cosmic order is such that without any peradventure all things work together for the good of each and all; that the foundation principle of the world, of all the worlds, is what we call love, and that the happiness of each and all is in the long run absolutely certain. The vision lasted a few seconds and was gone; but the memory of it and the sense of the reality of what it taught has remained during the quarter of a century which has since elapsed. I knew that what the vision showed was true. I had attained to a point of view from which I saw that it must be true. That view, that conviction, I may say that consciousness, has never, even during periods of the deepest depression, been lost.

We have now seen enough of this cosmic or mystic consciousness, as it comes sporadically. We must next pass to its methodical cultivation as an element of the religious life. Hindus, Buddhists, Mohammedans, and Christians all have cultivated it methodically.

In India, training in mystical insight has been known from time immemorial under the name of yoga. Yoga means the experimental union of the individual with the divine. It is based on persevering exercise; and the diet, posture, breathing, intellectual concentration, and moral discipline vary slightly in the different systems which teach it. The yogi, or disciple, who has by these means overcome the obscurations of his lower nature sufficiently, enters into the condition termed *samâdhi*, "and comes face to face with facts which no instinct or reason can ever know." He learns—

That the mind itself has a higher state of existence, beyond reason, a super-conscious state, and that when the mind gets to that higher state, then this knowledge beyond reasoning comes. . . . All the different steps in yoga are intended to bring us scientifically to the superconscious state or Samâdhi. . . . Just as unconscious work is beneath consciousness, so there is another work which is above consciousness, and which, also, is not accompanied with the feeling of egoism. . . . There is no feeling of *I*, and yet the mind works, desire-less, free from restlessness, objectless, bodiless. Then the Truth shines in its full effulgence, and we know ourselves—for Samâdhi lies potential in us all—for what we truly are, free, immortal, omnipotent, loosed from the finite, and its contrasts of good and evil altogether, and identical with the Atman or Universal Soul.

The Vedantists say that one may stumble into superconsciousness sporad-ically, without the previous discipline, but it is then impure. Their tests of its purity, like our test of religion's value, is empirical: its fruits must be good for life. When a man comes out of Samâdhi, they assure us that he remains "enlightened, a sage, a prophet, a saint, his whole character changed, his life changed, illumined."

The Buddhists used the word "samâdhi" as well as the Hindus; but "dhyâna" is their special word for higher states of contemplation. There seem to be four stages recognized in dyhâna. The first stage comes through con-centration of the mind upon one point. It excludes desire, but not discern-ment or judgment: it is still intellectual. In the second stage the intellectual functions drop off, and the satisfied sense of unity remains. In the third stage the satisfaction departs, and indifference begins, along with memory and self-consciousness. In the fourth stage the indifference, memory, and self-con-sciousness are perfected. [Just what "memory" and "self-consciousness" mean in this connection is doubtful. They cannot be the faculties familiar to us in the lower life.] Higher stages still of contemplation are mentioned—a region where there exists nothing, and where the mediator says: "There exists ab-solutely nothing," and stops. Then he reaches another region where he says: "There are neither ideas nor absence of ideas," and stops again. Then an-other region where, "having reached the end of both idea and perception, he stops finally." This would seem to be, not yet Nirvâna, but as close an ap-proach to it as this life affords.

In the Mohammedan world the Sufi sect and various dervish bodies are the possessors of the mystical tradition. The Sufis have existed in Persia from the earliest times, and as their pantheism is so at variance with the hot and rigid monotheism of the Arab mind, it has been suggested that Sufism must have been inoculated into Islam by Hindu influences. We Christians know little of Sufism, for its secrets are disclosed only to those initiated. To give its existence a certain liveliness in your minds, I will quote a Moslem document, and pass away from the subject.

Al-Ghazzali, a Persian philosopher and theologian, who flourished in the eleventh century, and ranks as one of the greatest doctors of the Moslem church, has left us one of the few autobiographies to be found outside of Christian literature. Strange that a species of book so abundant among ourselves should be so little represented elsewhere—the absence of strictly personal confessions is the chief difficulty to the purely literary student who would like to become acquainted with the inwardness of religions other than the Christian.

M. Schmölders has translated a part of Al-Ghazzali's autobiography into French:—

> The Science of the Sufis (says the Moslem author) aims at detaching the heart from all that is not God, and at giving to it for sole occupation the meditation of the divine being. Theory being more easy for me than practice, I read [certain books] until I understood all that can be learned by study and hearsay. Then I recognized that what pertains most exclusively to their method is just what no study can grasp, but only transport, ecstasy, and the transformation of the soul. How great, for example, is the difference between knowing the definitions of health, of satiety, with their causes and conditions, and being really healthy or filled. How different to know in what drunkenness consists—as being a state occasioned by a vapor that rises from the stomach—and *being* drunk effectively. Without doubt, the drunken man knows neither the definition of drunkenness nor what makes it interesting for science. Being drunk, he knows nothing; whilst the physician, although not drunk, knows well in what drunkenness consists, and what are its pre-disposing conditions. Similarly there is a difference between knowing the nature of abstinence, and *being* abstinent or having one's soul detached from the world.—Thus I had learned what words could teach of Sufism, but what was left could be learned neither by study nor through the ears, but solely by giving one's self up to ecstasy and leading a pious life.
>
> Reflecting on my situation, I found myself tied down by a multitude of bonds—temptations on every side. Considering my teaching, I found it was impure before God. I saw myself struggling with all my might to achieve glory and to spread my name. [Here follows an account of his six months' hesitation to break away from the conditions of his life at Bagdad, at the end of which he fell ill with a paralysis of the tongue.] Then, feeling my own weakness, and having entirely given up my own will, I repaired to God like a man in distress who has no more resources. He answered, as he answers the wretch who invokes him. My heart no longer felt any difficulty in renouncing glory, wealth, and my children. So I quitted Bagdad, and reserving from my fortune only what was indispensable for my subsistence, I distributed the rest. I went to Syria, where I remained about two years, with no other occupation than living in retreat and solitude, conquering my desires, combating my passions, training myself to purify my soul, to make my character perfect, to prepare my heart for meditating on God—all according to the methods of the Sufis, as I had read of them.
>
> This retreat only increased my desire to live in solitude, and to complete the purification of my heart and fit it for meditation. But the vicissitudes of the times, the affairs of the family, the need of subsistence, changed in some respects my primitive resolve, and interfered with my plans for a purely solitary life. I had never yet found myself completely in ecstasy, save in a few single hours; nevertheless, I kept the hope of attaining this state. Every time that the accidents led me astray, I sought to return; and in this situation I spent ten

years. During this solitary state things were revealed to me which it is impossible either to describe or to point out. I recognized for certain that the Sufis are assuredly walking in the path of God. Both in their acts and their inaction, whether internal or external, they are illumined by the light which proceeds from the prophetic source. The first condition for a Sufi is to purge his heart entirely of all that is not God. The next key of the contemplative life consists in the humble prayers which escape from the fervent soul, and in the meditations on God in which the heart is swallowed up entirely. But in reality this is only the beginning of the Sufi life, the end of Sufism being total absorption in God. The intuitions and all that precede are, so to speak, only the threshold for those who enter. From the beginning, revelations take place in so flagrant a shape that the Sufis see before them, whilst wide awake, the angels and the souls of the prophets. They hear their voices and obtain their favors. Then the transport rises from the perception of forms and figures to a degree which escapes all expression, and which no man may seek to give an account of without his words involving sin.

Whosoever has had no experience of the transport knows of the true nature of prophetism nothing but the name. He may meanwhile be sure of its existence, both by experience and by what he hears the Sufis say. As there are men endowed only with the sensitive faculty who reject what is offered them in the way of objects of the pure understanding, so there are intellectual men who reject and avoid the things perceived by the prophetic faculty. A blind man can understand nothing of colors save what he has learned by narration and hearsay. Yet God has brought prophetism near to men in giving them all a state analogous to it in its principal characters. This state is sleep. If you were to tell a man who was himself without experience of such a phenomenon that there are people who at times swoon away so as to resemble dead men, and who [in dreams] yet perceive things that are hidden, he would deny it [and give his reasons]. Nevertheless, his arguments would be refuted by actual experience. Wherefore, just as the understanding is a stage of human life in which an eye opens to discern various intellectual objects uncomprehended by sensation; just so in the prophetic the sight is illumined by a light which uncovers hidden things and objects which the intellect fails to reach. The chief properties of prophetism are perceptible only during the transport, by those who embrace the Sufi life. The prophet is endowed with qualities to which you possess nothing analogous, and which consequently you cannot possibly understand. How should you know their true nature, since one knows only what one can comprehend? But the transport which one attains by the method of the Sufis is like an immediate perception, as if one touched the objects with one's hand.

This incommunicableness of the transport is the keynote of all mysticism. Mystical truth exists for the individual who has the transport, but for no one else. In this, as I have said, it resembles the knowledge given to us in sensations more than that given by conceptual thought. Thought, with its remoteness and abstractness, has often enough in the history of philosophy been contrasted unfavorably with sensation. It is a commonplace of metaphysics that God's knowledge cannot be discursive but must be intuitive, that is, must be constructed more after the pattern of what in ourselves is called immediate feeling, that after that of proposition and judgment. But *our* immediate feelings have no content but what the five senses supply; and we have seen and shall see again that mystics may emphatically deny that the senses play any part in the very highest type of knowledge which their transports yield.

In the Christian church there have always been mystics. Although many of them have been viewed with suspicion, some have gained favor in the eyes of the authorities. The experiences of these have been treated as precedents, and a codified system of mystical theology has been based upon them, in which everything legitimate finds its place. The basis of the system is "orison" or meditation, the methodical elevation of the soul towards God. Through the practice of orison the higher levels of mystical experience may be attained. It is odd that Protestantism, especially evangelical Protestantism, should seemingly have abandoned everything methodical in this line. Apart from what prayer may lead to, Protestant mystical experience appears to have been almost exclusively sporadic. It has been left to our mindcurers to reintroduce methodical meditation into our religious life.

The first thing to be aimed at in orison is the mind's detachment from outer sensations for these interfere with its concentration upon ideal things. Such manuals as Saint Ignatius's Spiritual Exercises recommend the disciple to expel sensation by a graduated series of efforts to imagine holy scenes. The acme of this kind of discipline would be a semi-hallucinatory mono-ideism—an imaginary figure of Christ, for example, coming fully to occupy the mind. Sensorial images of this sort, whether literal or symbolic, play an enormous part in mysticism. But in certain cases imagery may fall away entirely, and in the very highest raptures it ends to do so. The state of consciousness becomes then insusceptible of any verbal description. Mystical teachers are unanimous as to this. Saint John of the Cross, for instance, one of the best of them, thus describes the condition called the "union of love," which, he says, is reached by "dark contemplation." In this the Deity compenetrates the soul, but in such a hidden way that the soul—

> finds no terms, no means, no comparison whereby to render the sublimity of the wisdom and the delicacy of the spiritual feeling with which she is filled. . . . We receive this mystical knowledge of God clothed in none of the kinds of images, in none of the sensible representations, which our mind makes use of in other circumstances. Accordingly in this knowledge, since the senses and the imagination are not employed, we get neither form nor impression, nor can we give any account or furnish any likeness, although the mysterious and sweet-tasting wisdom comes home so clearly to the inmost parts of our soul. Fancy a man seeing a certain kind of thing for the first time in his life. He can understand it, use and enjoy it, but he cannot apply a name to it, nor communicate any idea of it, even though all the while it be a mere thing of sense. How much greater will be his powerlessness when it goes beyond the senses! This is the peculiarity of the divine language. The more infused, intimate, spiritual, and supersensible it is, the more does it exceed the senses, both inner and outer, and impose silence upon them. . . . The soul then feels as if placed in a vast and profound solitude, to which no created thing has access, in an

immense and boundless desert, desert the more delicious the more solitary it is. There, in this abyss of wisdom, the soul grows by what it drinks in from the well-springs of the comprehension of love, . . . and recognizes, however sublime and learned may be the terms we employ, how utterly vile, insignificant, and improper they are, when we seek to discourse of divine things by their means.

I cannot pretend to detail to you the sundry stages of the Christian mystical life. Our time would not suffice, for one thing; and moreover, I confess that the subdivisions and names which we find in the Catholic books seem to me to represent nothing objectively distinct. So many men, so many minds; I imagine that these experiences can be as infinitely varied as are the idiosyncrasies of individuals.

The cognitive aspects of them, their value in the way of revelation, is what we are directly concerned with, and it is easy to show by citation how strong an impression they leave of being revelations of new depths of truth. Saint Teresa is the expert of experts in describing such conditions, so I will turn immediately to what she says of one of the highest of them, the "orison of union."

In the orison of union (says Saint Teresa) the soul is fully awake as regards God, but wholly asleep as regards things of this world and in respect of herself. During the short time the union lasts, she is as it were deprived of every feeling, and even if she would, she could not think of any single thing. Thus she needs to employ no artifice in order to arrest the use of her understanding: it remains so stricken with inactivity that she neither knows what she loves, nor in what manner she loves, nor what she wills. In short, she is utterly dead to the things of the world and lives solely in God. . . . I do not even know whether in this state she has enough life left to breathe. It seems to me she has not; or at least that if she does breathe, she is unaware of it. Her intellect would fain understand something of what is going on within her, but it has so little force now that it can act in no way whatsoever. So a person who falls into a deep faint appears as if dead. . . .

Thus does God, when he raises a soul to union with himself, suspend the natural action of all her faculties. She neither sees, hears, nor understands, so long as she is united with God. But this time is always short, and it seems even shorter than it is. God establishes himself in the interior of this soul in such a way, that when she returns to herself, it is wholly impossible for her to doubt that she has been in God, and God in her. This truth remains so strongly impressed on her that, even though many years should pass without the condition returning, she can neither forget the favor she received, nor doubt of its reality. If you, nevertheless, ask how it is possible that the soul can see and understand that she has been in God, since during the union she has neither sight nor understanding, I reply that she does not see it then, but that she sees it clearly later, after she has returned to herself, not by any vision, but by a certitude which abides with her and which God alone can give her. I knew a person who was ignorant of the truth that God's mode of being in everything must be either by presence, by power, or by essence, but who, after having received the grace of which I am speaking, believed this truth in the most unshakable manner. So much so that, having consulted a half-learned man who was as ignorant on this point as she had been before she was enlightened, when he replied that God is in us only by "grace," she disbelieved his reply, so sure she was of the true answer; and when she came to ask wiser doctors, they confirmed her in her belief, which much consoled her. . . .

But how, you will repeat, *can* one have such certainty in respect to what one does not see? This question, I am powerless to answer. These are secrets of God's omnipotence which it does not appertain to me to penetrate. All that I know is that I tell the truth; and I shall never believe that any soul who does not possess this certainty has ever been really united to God.

The kinds of truth communicable in mystical ways, whether these be sensible or supersensible, are various. Some of them relate to this world—visions of the future, the reading of hearts, the sudden understanding of texts, the knowledge of distant events, for example; but the most important revelations are theological or metaphysical.

Saint Ignatius confessed one day to Father Laynez that a single hour of meditation at Manresa had taught him more truths about heavenly things than all the teachings of all the doctors put together could have taught him. . . . One day in orison, on the steps of the choir of the Dominican church, he saw in a distinct manner the plan of divine wisdom in the creation of the world. On another occasion, during a procession, his spirit was ravished in God, and it was given him to contemplate, in a form and images fitted to the weak understanding of a dweller on the earth, the deep mystery of the holy Trinity. This last vision flooded his heart with such sweetness, that the mere memory of it in after times made him shed abundant tears.

Similarly with Saint Teresa.

One day, being in orison (she writes), it was granted me to perceive in one instant how all things are seen and contained in God. I did not perceive them in their proper form, and nevertheless the view I had of them was of a sovereign clearness, and has remained vividly impressed upon my soul. It is one of the most signal of all the graces which the Lord has granted me. . . . The view was so subtle and delicate that the understanding cannot grasp it.

She goes on to tell how it was as if the Deity were an enormous and sovereignly limpid diamond, in which all our actions were contained in such a way their their full sinfulness appeared evident as never before. On another day, she relates, while she was reciting the Athanasian Creed—

Our Lord made me comprehend in what way it is that one God can be in three persons. He made me see it so clearly that I remained as extremely surprised as I was comforted, . . . and now, when I think of the holy Trinity, or hear It spoken of, I understand how the three adorable Persons form only one God and I experience an unspeakable happiness.

On still another occasion, it was given to Saint Teresa to see and understand in what wise the Mother of God had been assumed into her place in Heaven.

The deliciousness of some of these states seems to be beyond anything known in ordinary consciousness. It evidently involves organic sensibilities, for it is spoken of as something too extreme to be borne, and as verging on bodily pain. But it is too subtle and piercing a delight for ordinary words to denote. God's touches, the wounds of his spear, references to ebriety and to nuptial union have to figure in the phraseology by which it is shadowed forth. Intellect and senses both swoon away in these highest states of ecstasy. "If our understanding comprehends," says Saint Teresa, "it is in a mode which remains unknown to it, and it can understand nothing of what it comprehends. For my own part, I do not believe that it does comprehend, because, as I said, it does not understand itself to do so. I confess that it is all a mystery in which I am lost." In the condition called *raptus* or ravishment by theologians, breathing and circulation are so depressed that it is a question among the doctors whether the soul be or be not temporarily dissevered from the body. One must read Saint Teresa's descriptions and the very exact distinctions which she makes, to persuade one's self that one is dealing, not with imaginary experiences, but with phenomena which, however rare, follow perfectly definite psychological types.

To the medical mind these ecstasies signify nothing but suggested and imitated hypnoid states, on an intellectual basis of superstition, and a corporeal one of degeneration and hysteria. Undoubtedly these pathological conditions have existed in many and possibly in all the cases, but that fact tells us nothing about the value for knowledge of the consciousness which they induce. To pass a spiritual judgment upon these states, we must not content ourselves with superficial medical talk, but inquire into their fruits for life.

Their fruits appear to have been various. Stupefaction, for one thing, seems not to have been altogether absent as a result. You may remember the helplessness in the kitchen and schoolroom of poor Margaret Mary Alacoque. Many other ecstatics would have perished but for the care taken of them by admiring followers. The "other-worldliness" encouraged by the mystical consciousness makes this over-abstraction from practical life peculiarly liable to befall mystics in whom the character is naturally passive and the intellect feeble; but in natively strong minds and characters we find quite opposite results. The great Spanish mystics, who carried the habit of ecstasy as far as it has often been carried, appear for the most part to have shown indomitable spirit and energy, and all the more so for the trances in which they indulged.

Saint Ignatius was a mystic, but his mysticism made him assuredly one of the most powerfully practical human engines that ever lived. Saint John of the Cross, writing of the intuitions and "touches" by which God reaches the substance of the soul, tells us that—

> They enrich it marvelously. A single one of them may be sufficient to abolish at a stroke certain imperfections of which the soul during its whole life had vainly tried to rid itself, and to leave it adorned with virtues and

loaded with supernatural gifts. A single one of these intoxicating consolations may reward it for all the labors undergone in its life—even were they numberless. Invested with an invincible courage, filled with an impassioned desire to suffer for its God, the soul then is seized with a strange torment—that of not being allowed to suffer enough.

Saint Teresa is as emphatic, and much more detailed. You may perhaps remember a passage I quoted from her in my first lecture. There are many similar pages in her autobiography. Where in literature is a more evidently veracious account of the formation of a new centre of spiritual energy, than is given in her description of the effects of certain ecstasies which in departing leave the soul upon a higher level of emotional excitement?

Often, infirm and wrought upon with dreadful pains before the ecstasy, the soul emerges from it full of health and admirably disposed for action . . . as if God had willed that the body itself, already obedient to the soul's desires, should share in the soul's happiness. . . . The soul after such a favor is animated with a degree of courage so great that if at that moment its body should be torn to pieces for the cause of God, it would feel nothing but the liveliest comfort. Then it is that promises and heroic resolutions spring up in profusion in us, soaring desires, horror of the world, and the clear perception of our proper nothingness. . . . What empire is comparable to that of a soul who, from this sublime summit to which God has raised her, sees all the things of earth beneath her feet, and is captivated by no one of them? How ashamed she is of her former attachments! How amazed at her blindness! What lively pity she feels for those whom she recognizes still shrouded in the darkness! . . . She groans at having ever been sensitive to points of honor, at the illusion that made her ever see as honor what the world calls by that name. Now she sees in this name nothing more than an immense lie of which the world remains a victim. She discovers, in the new light from above, that in genuine honor there is nothing spurious, that to be faithful to this honor is to give our respect to what deserves to be respected really, and to consider as nothing, or as less than nothing, whatsoever perishes and is not agreeable to God. . . . She laughs when she sees grave persons, persons of orison, caring for points of honor for which she now feels profoundest contempt. It is suitable to the dignity of their rank to act thus, they pretend, and it makes them more useful to others. But she knows that in despising the dignity of their rank for the pure love of God they would do more good in a single day than they would effect in ten years by preserving it. . . . She laughs at herself that there should ever have been a time in her life when she made any case of money, when she ever desired it. . . . Oh! if human beings might only agree together to regard it as so much useless mud, what harmony would then reign in the world! With what friendship we would all treat each other if our interest in honor and in money could but disappear from earth! For my own part, I feel as if it would be a remedy for all our ills.

Mystical conditions may, therefore, render the soul more energetic in the lines which their inspiration favors. But this could be reckoned an advantage only in case the inspiration were a true one. If the inspiration were erroneous, the energy would be all the more mistaken and misbegotten. So we stand once more before the problem of truth which confronted us at the end of the lectures on saintliness. You will remember that we turned to mysticism precisely to get some light on truth. Do mystical states establish the truth of those theological affections in which the saintly life has its root?

In spite of their repudiation of articulate self-description, mystical states in general assert a pretty distinct theoretic drift. It is possible to give the outcome of the majority of them in terms that point in definite philosophical directions. One of these directions is optimism, and the other is monism. We pass into mystical states from out of ordinary consciousness as from a less into a more, as from a smallness into a vastness, and at the same time as from an unrest to a rest. We feel them as reconciling, unifying states. They appeal to the yes-function more than to the no-function in us. In them the unlimited absorbs the limits and peacefully closes the account. Their very denial of every adjective you may propose as applicable to the ultimate truth —He, the Self, the Atman, is to be described by "No! no!" only, say the Upanishads—though it seems on the surface to be a no-function, is a denial made on behalf of a deeper yes. Whoso calls the Absolute anything in particular, or says that it is *this,* seems implicitly to shut it off from being *that—* it is as if he lessened it. So we deny the "this," negating the negation which it seems to us to imply, in the interests of the higher affirmative attitude by which we are possessed. The fountainhead of Christian mysticism is Dionysius the Areopagite. He describes the absolute truth by negatives exclusively.

> The cause of all things is neither soul nor intellect; nor has it imagination, opinion, or reason, or intelligence; nor is it reason or intelligence; nor is it spoken or thought. It is neither number, nor order, nor magnitude, nor littleness, nor equality, nor inequality, nor similarity, nor dissimilarity. It neither stands, nor moves, nor rests. . . . It is neither essence, nor eternity, nor time. Even intellectual contact does not belong to it. It is neither science nor truth. It is not even royalty or wisdom; not one; not unity; not divinity or goodness; nor even spirit as we know it (etc., *ad libitum*).

But these qualifications are denied by Dionysius, not because the truth falls short of them, but because it so infinitely excels them. It is above them. It is *super-*lucent, *super-*splendent, *super-*essential, *super-*sublime, *super every-thing* that can be named. Like Hegel in his logic, mystics journey towards the positive pole of truth only by the "Methode der Absoluten Negativität."

Thus comes the paradoxical expressions that so abound in mystical writings. As when Eckhart tells of the still desert of the Godhead, "where never was seen difference, neither Father, Son, nor Holy Ghost, where there is no one at home, yet where the spark of the soul is more at peace than in itself." As when Boehme writes of the Primal Love, that "it may fitly be compared to Nothing, for it is deeper than any Thing, and is as nothing with respect to all things, forasmuch as it is not comprehensible by any of them. And because it is nothing respectively, it is therefore free from all things, and is that only good, which a man cannot express or utter what it is, there being nothing to which it may be compared, to express it by." Or as when Angelus Silesius sings:—

> Gott ist ein lauter Nichts, ihn rührt kein Nun noch Hier;
> Je mehr du nach ihm greiffst, je mehr entwind er dir.

To this dialectical use, by the intellect, of negation as a mode of passage towards a higher kind of affirmation, there is correlated the subtlest of moral counterparts in the sphere of the personal will. Since denial of the finite self and its wants, since asceticism of some sort, is found in religious experience to be the only doorway to the larger and more blessed life, this moral mystery intertwines and combines with the intellectual mystery in all mystical writings.

> Love (continues Behmen) [is Nothing, for] when thou art gone forth wholly from the Creature and from that which is visible, and art become Nothing to all that is Nature and Creature, then thou art in that eternal One, which is God himself, and then thou shalt feel within thee the highest virtue of Love. . . . The treasure of treasures for the soul is where she goeth out of the Somewhat into that Nothing out of which all things may be made. The soul here saith, *I have nothing*, for I am utterly stripped and naked; *I can do nothing*, for I have no manner of power, but am as water poured out; *I am nothing*, for all that I am is no more than an image of Being, and only God is to me I AM; and so, sitting down in my own Nothingness, I give glory to the eternal Being, and *will nothing* of myself, that so God may will all in me, being unto me my God and all things.

In Paul's language, I live, yet not I, but Christ liveth in me. Only when I become as nothing can God enter in and no difference between his life and mine remain outstanding.

This overcoming of all the usual barriers between the individual and the Absolute is the great mystic achievement. In mystic states we both become one with the Absolute and we become aware of our oneness. This is the everlasting and triumphant mystical tradition, hardly altered by differences of clime or creed. In Hinduism, in Neoplatonism, in Sufism, in Christian mysticism, in Whitmanism, we find the same recurring note, so that there is about mystical utterances an eternal unanimity which ought to make a critic stop and think, and which brings it about that the mystical classics have, as has been said, neither birthday nor native land. Perpetually telling of the unity of man with God, their speech antedates languages, and they do not grow old.

"That are Thou!" says the Upanishads, and the Vedantists add: "Not a part, not a mode of That, but identically That, that absolute Spirit of the World." "As pure water poured into pure water remains the same, thus, O Gautama, is the Self of a thinker who knows. Water in water, fire in fire,

ether in ether, no one can distinguish them: likewise a man whose mind has
entered into the self." 'Everyman,' says the Sufi Gulshan-Râz, whose heart
is no longer shaken by any doubts, knows with certainty that there is no being save only One. . . . In his divine majesty the *me*, and *we*, the *thou*, are
not found, for in the One there can be no distinction. Every being who is
annulled and entirely separated from himself, hears resound outside of him
this voice and this echo: *I am God*: he has an eternal way of existing, and is
no longer subject to death.' " In the vision of God, says Plotinus, "what sees
is not our reason, but something prior and superior to our reason. . . . He who
thus sees does not properly see, does not distinguish or imagine two things.
He changes, he ceases to be himself, preserves nothing of himself. Absorbed
in God, he makes but one with him, like a centre of a circle coinciding with
another centre." "Here," writes Suso, "the spirit dies, and yet is all alive in
the marvels of the Godhead . . . and is lost in the stillness of the glorious dazzling obscurity and of the naked simple unity. It is in this modeless *where*
that the highest bliss is to be found." "Ich bin so gross als Gott," sings Angelus
Silesius again, "Er ist als ich so klein; Er kann nich über mich, ich unter
ihm nicht sein."

In mystical literature such self-contradictory phrases as "dazzling obscurity," "whispering silence," "teeming desert," are continually met with. They
prove that not conceptual speech, but music rather, is the element through
which we are best spoken to by mystical truth. Many mystical scriptures are
indeed little more than musical compositions.

> He who would hear the voice of Nada, "the Soundless Sound," and com-
> prehend it, he has to learn the nature of Dhâranâ. . . . When to himself his
> form appears unreal, as do on waking all the forms he sees in dreams; when
> he has ceased to hear the many, he may discern the ONE—the inner sound
> which kills the outer. . . . For then the soul will hear, and will remember. And
> then to the inner ear will speak THE VOICE OF THE SILENCE. . . . And now thy
> *Self* is lost in SELF, *thyself* unto THYSELF, merged in that SELF from which
> thou first didst radiate. . . . Behold! thou hast become the Light, thou hast
> become the Sound, thou art thy Master and thy God. Thou art THYSELF the
> object of thy search: the VOICE unbroken, that resounds throughout eternities,
> exempt from change, from sin exempt, the seven sounds in one, the VOICE
> OF THE SILENCE. *Om tat Sat.*

These words, if they do not awaken laughter as you receive them, probably
stir chords within you which music and language touch in common. Music
gives us ontological messages which non-musical criticism is unable to contradict, though it may laugh at our foolishness in minding them. There is a verge
of the mind which these things haunt; and whispers therefrom mingle with
the operations of our understanding, even as the waters of the infinite ocean
send their waves to break among the pebbles that lie upon our shores.

> Here begins the sea that ends not till the world's end. Where we stand,
> Could we know the next high sea-mark set beyond these waves that gleam,
> We should know what never man hath known, nor eye of man hath scanned. . . .

Ah, but here man's heart leaps, yearning towards the gloom with venturous
   glee,
From the shore that hath no shore beyond it, set in all the sea.

That doctrine, for example, that eternity is timeless, that our "immortality,"
if we live in the eternal, is not so much future as already now and here, which
we find so often expressed to-day in certain philosophical circles, finds its
support in a "hear, hear!" or an "amen," which floats up from that mys-
teriously deeper level. We recognize the passwords to the mystical region as
we hear them, but we cannot use them ourselves; it alone has the keeping of
"the password primeval."

I have now sketched with extreme brevity and insufficiency, but as fairly
as I am able in the time allowed, the general traits of the mystic range of
consciousness. *It is on the whole pantheistic and optimistic, or at least the
opposite of pessimistic. It is anti-naturalistic, and harmonizes best with twice-
bornness and so-called other-worldly states of mind.*

My next task is to inquire whether we can invoke it as authoritative. Does
it furnish any *warrant for the truth* of the twice-bornness and supernaturality
and pantheism which it favors? I must give my answer to this question as
concisely as I can.

In brief my answer is this—and I will divide it into three parts:—

(1) Mystical states, when well developed, usually are, and have the right to
be, absolutely authoritative over the individuals to whom they come.

(2) No authority emanates from them which should make it a duty for those
who stand outside of them to accept their revelations uncritically.

(3) They break down the authority of the non-mystical or rationalistic consciousness, based upon the understanding and the senses alone. They show it
to be only one kind of consciousness. They open out the possibility of other
orders of truth, in which, so far as anything in us vitally responds to them,
we may freely continue to have faith.

I will take up these points one by one.

1. As a matter of psychological fact, mystical states of a well-pronounced
and emphatic sort *are* usually authoritative over those who have them.
They have been "there," and know. It is vain for rationalism to grumble about
this. If the mystical truth that comes to a man proves to be a force that he
can live by, what mandate have we of the majority to order him to live in another way? We can throw him into a prison or a madhouse, but we cannot
change his mind— we commonly attach it only the more stubbornly to its beliefs.
It mocks our utmost efforts, as a matter of fact, and in point of logic it absolutely escapes our jurisdiction. Our own more "rational" beliefs are based
on evidence exactly similar in nature to that which mystics quote for theirs.
Our senses, namely, have assured us of certain states of fact; but mystical
experiences are as direct perceptions of fact for those who have them as any
sensations ever were for us. The records show that even though the five senses

be in abeyance in them, they are absolutely sensational in their epistemological quality, if I may be pardoned the barbarous expression—that is, they are face to face presentations of what seems immediately to exist.

The mystic is, in short, *invulnerable*, and must be left, whether we relish it or not, in undisturbed enjoyment of his creed. Faith, says Tolstoy, is that by which men live. And faith-state and mystic state are practically convertible terms.

2. But I now proceed to add that mystics have no right to claim that we ought to accept the deliverance of their peculiar experiences, if we are ourselves outsiders and feel no private call thereto. The utmost they can ever ask of us in this life is to admit that they establish a presumption. They form a consensus and have an unequivocal outcome; and it would be odd, mystics might say, if such a unanimous type of experience should prove to be altogether wrong. At bottom, however, this would only be an appeal to numbers, like the appeal of rationalism the other way; and the appeal to numbers has no logical force. If we acknowledge it, it is for "suggestive," not for logical reasons: we follow the majority because to do so suits our life.

But even this presumption from the unanimity of mystics is far from being strong. In characterizing mystic states as pantheistic, optimistic, etc., I am afraid I over-simplified the truth. I did so for expository reasons, and to keep the closer to the classic mystical tradition. The classic religious mysticism, it now must be confessed, is only a "privileged case." It is an *extract*, kept true to type by the selection of the fittest specimens and their preservation in "schools." It is carved out from a much larger mass; and if we take the larger mass as seriously as religious mysticism has historically taken itself, we find that the supposed unanimity largely disappears. To begin with, even religious mysticism itself, the kind that accumulates traditions and makes schools, is much less unanimous than I have allowed. It has been both ascetic and antinomianly self-indulgent within the Christian church. It is dualistic in Sankhya, and monistic in Vedanta philosophy. I called it pantheistic; but the great Spanish mystics are anything but pantheists. They are with few exceptions non-metaphysical minds, for whom "the category of personality" is absolute. The "union" of man with God is for them much more like an occasional miracle than like an original identity. How different again, apart from the happiness common to all, is the mysticism of Walt Whitman, Edward Carpenter, Richard Jefferies, and other naturalistic pantheists, from the more distinctively Christian sort. The fact is that the mystical feeling of enlargement, union, and emancipation has no specific intellectual content whatever of its own. It is capable of forming matrimonial alliances with material furnished by the most diverse philosophies and theologies, provided only they can find a place in their framework for its peculiar emotional mood. We have no right, therefore, to invoke its prestige as distinctively in favor of any special belief, such as that in absolute idealism, or in the absolute monistic identity, or in the absolute goodness, of the world. It is only relatively in favor of all these things—it passes out of common human consciousness in the direction in which they lie.

So much for religious mysticism proper. But more remains to be told, for religious mysticism is only one half of mysticism. The other half has no accumulated traditions except those which the text-books on insanity supply. Open any one of these, and you will find abundant cases in which "mystical ideas" are cited as characteristic symptoms of enfeebled or deluded states of mind. In delusional insanity, paranoia, as they sometimes call it, we may have a *diabolical* mysticism, a sort of religious mysticism turned upside down. The same sense of ineffable importance in the smallest events, the same texts and words coming with new meanings, the same voices and visions and leadings and missions, the same controlling by extraneous powers; only this time the emotion is pessimistic: instead of consolations we have desolations; the meanings are dreadful; and the powers are enemies to life. It is evident from the point of view of their psychological mechanism, the classic mysticism and these lower mysticisms spring from the same mental level, from that great subliminal or transmarginal region of which science is beginning to admit the existence, but of which so little is really known. That region contains every kind of matter: "seraph and snake" abide there side by side. To come from thence is no infallible credential. What comes must be sifted and tested, and run the gauntlet of confrontation with the total context of experience, just like what comes from the outer world of sense. Its value must be ascertained by empirical methods, so long as we are not mystics ourselves.

Once more, then, I repeat that non-mystics are under no obligation to acknowledge in mystical states a superior authority conferred on them by their intrinsic nature.

3. Yet, I repeat once more, the existence of mystical states absolutely overthrows the pretension of non-mystical states to be the sole and ultimate dictators of what we may believe. As a rule, mystical states merely add a supersensuous meaning to the ordinary outward data of consciousness. They are excitements like the emotions of love or ambition, gifts to our spirit by means of which facts already objectively before us fall into a new expressiveness and make a new connection with our active life. They do not contradict these facts as such, or deny anything that our senses have immediately seized. It is the rationalistic critic rather who plays the part of denier in the controversy, and his denials have no strength, for there never can be a state of facts to which new meaning may not truthfully be added, provided the mind ascend to a more enveloping point of view. It must always remain an open question whether mystical states may not possibly be such superior points of view, windows through which the mind looks out upon a more extensive and inclusive world. The difference of the views seen from the different mystical windows need not prevent us from entertaining this supposition. The wider world would

in that case prove to have a mixed constitution like that of this world, that is all. It would have its celestial and its infernal regions, its tempting and its saving moments, its valid experiences and its counterfeit ones, just as our world has them; but it would be a wider world all the same. We should have to use its experiences by selecting and subordinating and substituting just as is our custom in this ordinary naturalistic world; we should be liable to error just as we are now; yet the counting in of that wider world of meanings, and the serious dealing with it, might, in spite of all the perplexity, be indispensable stages in our approach to the final fullness of the truth.

In this shape, I think, we have to leave the subject. Mystical states indeed wield no authority due simply to their being mystical states. But the higher ones among them point in directions to which the religious sentiments even of non-mystical men incline. They tell of the supremacy of the ideal, of vastness, of union, of safety, and of rest. They offer us *hypotheses*, hypotheses which we may voluntarily ignore, but which as thinkers we cannot possibly upset. The supernaturalism and optimism to which they would persuade us may, interpreted in one way or another, be after all the truest of insights into the meaning of this life.

"Oh, the little more, and how much it is; and the little less, and what worlds away!" It may be that possibility and permission of this sort are all that our religious consciousness requires to live on. In my last lecture I shall have to try to persuade you that this is the case. Meanwhile, however, I am sure that for many of my readers this diet is too slender. If supernaturalism and inner union with the divine are true, you think, then not so much permission, as compulsion to believe, ought to be found. Philosophy has always professed to prove religious truth by coercive argument; and the construction of philosophies of this kind has always been one favorite function of the religious life, if we use this term in the large historic sense. But religious philosophy is an enormous subject, and in my next lecture I can only give that brief glance at it which my limits will allow.

W. T. STACE

5.2 The Teachings of the Mystics

(4) *A New Kind of Consciousness.* In his book *The Varieties of Religious Experience* William James suggests, as a result of his psychological researches, that "our normal consciousness, rational consciousness as we call it, is but one special type of consciousness, whilst all about it, parted from it by the filmiest of screens, there lie potential forms of consciousness entirely different." This statement exactly fits mystical consciousness. It is entirely unlike our everyday consciousness and is wholly incommensurable with it. What are the fundamental characteristics or elements of our ordinary consciousness? We may think of it as being like a building with three floors. The ground floor consists of physical sensations—sights, sounds, smells, tastes, touch sensations, and organic sensations. The second floor consists of images, which we tend to think of as mental copies of sensations. The third floor is the level of the intellect, which is the faculty of concepts. On this floor we find abstract thinking and reasoning processes. This account of the mind may be open to cavil. Some philosophers think that colors, sounds, and so on, are not properly called "sensations"; others that images are not "copies" of sensations. These fine points, however, need not seriously concern us. Our account is sufficiently clear to indicate what we are referring to when we speak of sensations, images, and concepts as being the fundamental elements of the cognitive aspects of our ordinary consciousness. Arising out of these basic cognitive elements and dependent upon them are emotions, desires, and volitions. In order to have a name for it we may call this whole structure—including sensations, images, concepts, and their attendant desires, emotions, and volitions—our *sensory-intellectual consciousness.*

Now the mystical consciousness is quite different from this. It is not merely that it involves different kinds of sensation, thought, or feeling. We are told that some insects or animals can perceive ultraviolet color and infrared color; and that some animals can hear sounds which are inaudible to us; even that some creatures may have a sixth sense quite different from any of our five senses. These are all, no doubt, kinds of sensations different from any we have. But they are still sensations. And the mystical consciousness is destitute

From W. T. Stace, ed., *The Teachings of the Mystics* (New York: New American Library of World Literature, 1960). Reprinted by permission of Mrs. Blanche Stace.

of any sensations at all. Nor does it contain any concepts or thoughts. It is not a sensory-intellectual consciousness at all. Accordingly, it cannot be described or analyzed in terms of any of the elements of the sensory-intellectual consciousness, with which it is wholly incommensurable.

This is the reason why mystics always say that their experiences are "ineffable." All words in all languages are the products of our sensory-intellectual consciousness and express or describe its elements or some combination of them. But as these elements (with the doubtful exception of emotions) are not found in the mystical consciousness, it is felt to be impossible to describe it in any words whatever. In spite of this the mystics do describe their experiences in roundabout ways, at the same time telling us that the words they use are inadequate. This raises a serious problem for the philosophy of mysticism, but it is not possible for us to dwell on it here.

The incommensurability of the mystical with the sensory-intellectual consciousness is also the ultimate reason why we have to exclude visions and voices, telepathy, precognition, and clairvoyance from the category of the mystical. Suppose someone sees a vision of the Virgin Mary. What he sees has shape, the shape of a woman, and color—white skin, blue raiment, a golden halo, and so on. But these are all images or sensations. They are therefore composed of elements of our sensory-intellectual consciousness. The same is true of voices. Or suppose one has a precognition of a neighbor's death. The components one is aware of—a dead man, a coffin, etc.—are composed of elements of our sensory-intellectual consciousness. The only difference is that these ordinary elements are arranged in unfamiliar patterns which we have come to think cannot occur, so that if they do occur they seem supernormal. Or the fact that such elements are combined in an unusual way so as to constitute the figure of a woman up in the clouds, perhaps surrounded by other humanlike figures with wings added to them—all this does not constitute a different *kind* of consciousness at all. And just as sensory elements of any sort are excluded from the mystical consciousness, so are conceptual elements. It is not that the thoughts in the mystical consciousness are different from those we are accustomed to. It does not include any thoughts at all. The mystic, of course, expresses thoughts about his experience after that experience is over, and he remembers it when he is back again in his sensory-intellectual consciousness. But there are no thoughts *in* the experience itself.

If anyone thinks that a kind of consciousness without either sensations, images, or thoughts, because it is totally unimaginable and inconceivable to most of us, cannot exist, he is surely being very stupid. He supposes that the possibilities of this vast universe are confined to what can be imagined and understood by the brains of average human insects who crawl on a minute speck of dust floating in illimitable space.

On the other hand, there is not the least reason to suppose that the mystical consciousness is miraculous or supernatural. No doubt it has, like our ordinary consciousness, been produced by the natural processes of evolution. Its existence in a few rare men is a psychological fact of which there is abundant evidence. To deny or doubt that it exists as a psychological fact is not a reputable opinion. It is ignorance. Whether it has any value or significance beyond itself, and if so what—these, of course, are matters regarding which there can be legitimate differences of opinion. Owing to the comparative rarity of this kind of consciousness, it should no doubt be assigned to the sphere of abnormal psychology.

(5) *The Core of Mysticism.* I shall, for the present, treat it as an hypothesis that although mystical experiences may in certain respects have different characteristics in different parts of the world, in different ages, and in different cultures, there are nevertheless a number of fundamental common characteristics. I shall also assume that the agreements are more basic and important, the differences more superficial and relatively less important. This hypothesis can only be fully justified by an elaborate empirical survey of the descriptions of their experiences given by mystics and collected from all over the world. But I believe that enough of the evidence for it will appear in the following pages to convince any reasonable person.

The most important, the central characteristics in which all *fully developed* mystical experiences agree, and which in the last analysis is definitive of them and serves to mark them off from other kinds of experiences, is that they involve the apprehension of *an ultimate nonsensuous unity in all things,* a oneness or a One to which neither the senses nor the reason can penetrate. In other words, it entirely transcends our sensory-intellectual consciousness.

It should be carefully noted that only fully developed mystical experiences are necessarily apprehensive of the One. Many experiences have been recorded which lack this central feature but yet possess other mystical characteristics. These are borderline cases, which may be said to shade off from the central core of cases. They have to the central core the relation which some philosophers like to call "family resemblance."

We should also note that although at this stage of our exposition we speak of mystical experience as an apprehension *of* the Unity, the mystics of the Hindu and Buddhist cultures, as well as Plotinus and many others, generally insist that this is incorrect since it supposes a division between subject and object. We should rather say that the experience *is* the One. Thus Plotinus writes: "We should not speak of seeing, but instead of seen and seer, speak boldly of a simple Unity for in this seeing we neither distinguish nor are there two." But we will leave the development of this point till later. And often for convenience' sake we shall speak of the experience *of* the unity.

(6) *Extrovertive Mysticism.* There appear to be two main distinguishable types of mystical experience, both of which may be found in all the higher cultures. One may be called extrovertive mystical experience, the other introvertive mystical experience. Both are apprehensions of the One, but they reach it in different ways. The extrovertive way looks outward and through

the physical senses into the external world and finds the One there. The introvertive way turns inward, introspectively, and finds the One at the bottom of the self, at the bottom of the human personality. The latter far outweighs the former in importance both in the history of mysticism and in the history of human thought generally. The introvertive way is the major strand in the history of mysticism, the extrovertive way a minor strand. I shall only briefly refer to extrovertive mysticism and then pass on, and shall take introvertive mysticism as the main subject of this book.

The extrovertive mystic with his physical senses continues to perceive the same world of trees and hills and tables and chairs as the rest of us. But he sees these objects transfigured in such manner that the Unity shines through them. Because it includes ordinary sense perceptions, it only partially realizes the description given in section (4). For the full realization of this we have to wait for the introvertive experience. I will give two brief historical instances of extrovertive experience. The great Catholic mystic Meister Eckhart (circa 1260–1329) wrote as follows: "Here [i.e., in this experience] all blades of grass, wood, and stone, all things are One. . . . When is a man in mere understanding? When he sees one thing separated from another. And when is he above mere understanding? When he sees all in all, then a man stands above mere understanding."

In this quotation we note that according to Eckhart seeing a number of things as separate and distinct, seeing the grass and the wood and the stone as three different things, is the mark of the sensory-intellectual consciousness. For Eckhart's word "understanding" means the conceptual intellect. But if one passes beyond the sensory-intellectual consciousness into the mystical consciousness, then one sees these three things as being "all one." However, it is evident that in this extrovertive experience the distinctions between things have not wholly disappeared. There is no doubt that what Eckhart means is that he sees the three things as distinct and separate and yet at the same time as not distinct but identical. The grass is identical with the stone, and the stone with the wood, although they are all different. Rudolph Otto, commenting on this, observes that it is as if one said that black is the same as white, white the same as black, although at the same time white remains white and black remains black. Of course this is a complete paradox. It is in fact contradictory. But we shall find that paradoxicality is one of the common characteristics of all mysticism. And it is no use saying that this is all logically impossible, and that no consciousness of this kind can exist, unless we wish, on these a priori grounds, to refuse to study the evidence—which is overwhelming.

What some mystics simply call the One other mystics often identify with God. Hence we find Jakob Böhme (1575–1624) saying much the same thing about the grass and the trees and the stones as Eckhart does, but saying that they are all God instead of just all One. The following is a statement of one of his experiences: "In this light my spirit saw through all things and into all creatures and I recognized God in grass and plants."

It is suggested that the extrovertive type of experience is a kind of halfway house to the introvertive. For the introvertive experience is wholly nonsensuous and nonintellectual. But the extrovertive experience is sensory-intellectual in so far as it still perceives physical objects but is nonsensuous and nonintellectual in so far as it perceives them as "all one."

We may sum up this short account of the extrovertive consciousness by saying that it is a perception of the world as transfigured and unified in one ultimate being. In some cultures the one being is identified with God; and since God is then perceived as the inner essence of all objects, this type of experience tends toward pantheism. But in some cultures—for example, Buddhism—the unity is not interpreted as God at all.

(7) *Introvertive Mysticism.* Suppose that one could shut all physical sensations out of one's consciousness. It may be thought that this would be easy as regards some of the senses, namely sight, hearing, taste, and smell. One can shut one's eyes, stop up one's ears, and hold one's nose. One can avoid taste sensations by keeping one's mouth empty. But one cannot shut off tactual sensations in any simple way of this kind. And it would be even more difficult to get rid of organic sensations. However, one can perhaps suppose it possible somehow to thrust tactual and organic sensations out of conscious awareness—perhaps into the unconscious. Mystics do not, as far as I know, descend to the ignominious level of holding their noses and stopping their ears. My only point is that it is possible to conceive of getting rid of all sensations, and in one way or other mystics claim that they do this.

Suppose now, after this has been done, we next try to get rid of all sensuous *images* from our minds. This is very difficult. Most people, try as they will not to picture anything at all, will find vague images floating about in consciousness. Suppose, however, that it is possible to suppress all images. And suppose finally that we manage to stop all thinking and reasoning. Having got rid of the whole empirical content of sensations, images, and thoughts, presumably all emotions and desires and volitions would also disappear, since they normally exist only as attachments to the cognitive content. What, then, would be left of consciousness? What would happen? It is natural to suppose that with all the elements of consciousness gone consciousness itself would lapse and the subject would fall asleep or become *un*conscious.

Now it happens to be the case that this total suppression of the whole empirical content of consciousness is precisely what the introvertive mystic claims to achieve. And he claims that what happens is not that all consciousness disappears but that only the ordinary sensory-intellectual consciousness disappears and is replaced by an entirely new kind of consciousness, the mystical consciousness. Naturally we now ask whether any description of this new consciousness can be given. But before trying to answer that difficult question,

I propose to turn aside for a brief space to speak about the methods which mystics use to suppress sensuous images, and thinking, so as to get rid of their sensory-intellectual consciousness. There are the Yoga techniques of India; and Christian mystics in Catholic monasteries also evolved their own methods. The latter usually call their techniques "prayers," but they are not prayers in the vulgar sense of asking God for things; they are much more like the "meditation" and "concentration" of Yogis than may be commonly supposed. This is too vast a subject to be discussed in detail here. But I will give two elementary illustrations.

Everyone has heard of the breathing exercises undertaken by the yogins of India seeking samadhi—samadhi being the Indian name for mystical consciousness. What is this special method of breathing, and what is it supposed to accomplish? The theory of the matter is, I understand, something like this: It is practically impossible, or at least very difficult, to stop all sensing, imaging, and thinking by a forcible act of the will. What comes very near to it, however, is to concentrate one's attention on some single point or object so that all other mental content falls away and there is left nothing but the single point of consciousness. If this can be done, then ultimately that single point will itself disappear because contrast is necessary for our ordinary consciousness, and if there is only one point of consciousness left, there is nothing to form a contrast to it.

The question then is: On what single thing should one concentrate? A simple way is to concentrate on the stream of one's own breath. Simple instructions which I have heard given are these. One first adopts a suitable physical position with spine and neck perfectly erect. Then breathe in and out slowly, evenly, and smoothly. Concentrate your attention on this and nothing else. Some aspirants, I believe, count their breaths, 1, 2, 3, . . . up to 10, and then begin the count again. Continue this procedure till you attain the desired results.

A second method is to keep repeating in one's mind some short formula of words over and over again till the words lose all meaning. So long as they carry meaning, of course, the mind is still occupied with the thought of this meaning. But when the words become meaningless there is nothing left of consciousness except the monotonous sound-image, and that too, like the consciousness of one's breath, will in the end disappear. There is an interesting connection between this method and a remark made by the poet Tennyson. From childhood up Tennyson had frequent mystical experiences. They came to him spontaneously, without effort, and unsought. But he mentions the curious fact that he could induce them at will by the odd procedure of repeating his own name over and over again to himself. I know of no evidence that he studied mysticism enough to understand the theory of his own procedure, which would presumably be that the constantly repeated sound image served as the focus of the required one-pointed attention.

This leads to another curious reflection. Mystics who follow the procedure of constantly repeating a verbal formula often, I believe, tend to choose some religious set of words, for instance a part of the Lord's Prayer or a psalm. They probably imagine that these uplifting and inspirational words will carry them upwards toward the divine. But Tennyson's procedure suggests that any nonsense words would probably do as well. And this seems to agree with the general theory of concentration. It doesn't seem to matter what is chosen as the single point of concentration, whether it be one's breathing, or the sound of one's own name, or one's navel, or anything else, provided only it serves to shut off all other mental content.

Another point on which mystics usually insist in regard to spiritual training is what they call "detachment." Emphasis on this is found just as much in Hinduism and Buddhism as in Christianity. What is sought is detachment from desire, the uprooting of desire, or at any rate of all self-centered desires. The exact psychology of the matter presents great difficulties. In Christian mysticism the idea of detachment is usually given a religious and moral twist by insisting that it means the destruction of self-will or any kind of self-assertiveness, especially the rooting out of pride and the attainment of absolute humility. In non-Christian mysticism detachment does not usually get this special slant. But in the mysticism of all cultures detachment from desires for sensations and sensory images is emphasized.

We will now return to the main question. Supposing that the sensory-intellectual consciousness has been successfully supplanted by the mystical consciousness, can we find in the literatures of the subject any descriptions of this consciousness that will give us any idea of what it is like? The answer is that although mystics frequently say that their experiences are ineffable and indescribable, they nevertheless do often in fact describe them, and one can find plenty of such descriptive statements in the literature. They are usually extremely short—perhaps only three or four lines. And frequently they are indirect and not in the first person singular. Mystics more often than not avoid direct references to themselves.

I will give here a famous description which occurs in the Mandukya Upanishad. The Upanishads are supposed to have been the work of anonymous forest seers in India who lived between three thousand and twenty-five hundred years ago. They are among the oldest records of mysticism in the world. But they are of an unsurpassable depth of spirituality. For long ages and for countless millions of men in the East they have been, and they remain, the supreme source of the spiritual life. Of the introvertive mystical consciousness the Mandukya says that it is "beyond the senses, beyond the understanding, beyond all expression. . . . It is the pure unitary consciousness, wherein awareness of the world and of multiplicity is completely obliterated. It is ineffable peace. It is the Supreme Good. It is One without a second. It is the Self."

It will repay us, not to just slur over this passage, but to examine it carefully clause by clause. The first sentence is negative, telling us only what the experience is *not*. It is "beyond the senses, beyond the understanding." That is to say, it is beyond the sensory-intellectual consciousness; and there are in it no elements of sensation or sensuous imagery and no elements of conceptual thought. After these negatives there comes the statement that "it is the unitary consciousness, wherein all awareness of multiplicity has been obliterated." The core of the experience is thus described as an undifferentiated unity—a oneness or unity in which there is no internal division, no multiplicity.

I happen to have quoted a Hindu source. But one can find exactly the same thing in Christian mysticism. For instance the great Flemish mystic Jan van Ruysbroeck (1293–1381) says of what he calls "the God-seeing man" that "his spirit is undifferentiated and without distinction, and therefore it feels nothing but the unity." We see that the very words of the faithful Catholic are almost identical with those of the ancient Hindu, and I do not see how it can be doubted that they are describing the same experience. Not only in Christianity and Hinduism but everywhere else we find that the essence of the experience is that it is an *undifferentiated unity*, though each culture and each religion interprets this undifferentiated unity in terms of its own creeds or dogmas.

It may be objected that "undifferentiated unity" is a conceptual thought, and this is inconsistent with our statement that the experience is wholly nonintellectual. The answer is that concepts such as "one," "unity," "undifferentiated," "God," "Nirvana," etc., are only applied to the experience *after* it has passed and when it is being *remembered*. None can be applied during the experience itself.

The passage of the Upanishad goes on to say that the undifferentiated unity "is the Self." Why is this? Why is the unity now identified with the Self? The answer is plain. We started with the full self or mind of our ordinary everyday consciousness. What was it full of? It was full of the multiplicity of sensations, thoughts, desires, and the rest. But the mind was not merely this multiplicity. These disparate elements were held together in a unity, the unity of the single mind or self. A multiplicity without a unity in which the multiple elements are together is inconceivable—e.g., many objects in one space. Now when we emptied all the multiple contents out of this unity of the self what is left, according to the Upanishad, is the unity of the self, the original unity minus its contents. And this is the self. The Upanishads go further than this. They always identify this individual self with the Universal Self, the soul of the world. [. . . But] for the moment we may continue to think in terms of the individual self, the pure ego of you or me. The undifferentiated unity is thought to be the pure ego.

I must draw the reader's attention to several facts about this situation. In the first place it flatly contradicts what David Hume said in a famous passage about the self. He said that when he looked introspectively into himself and searched for the I, the self, the ego, all he could ever introspect was the multiplicity of the sensations, images, thoughts, and feelings. He could never observe any I, any pure self apart from its contents, and he inferred that the I is a fiction and does not really exist. But now a vast body of empirical evidence, that of the mystics from all over the world, affirms that Hume was simply mistaken on a question of psychological fact, and that it is possible to get rid of all the mental contents and find the pure self left over and to experience this. This evidence need not mean that the self is a thing or a "substance," but can be taken as implying that it is a pure unity, the sort of being which Kant called the "transcendental unity" of the self.

The next thing to note is that the assertion of this new kind of consciousness is completely paradoxical. One way of bringing out the paradox is to point out that what we are left with here, when the contents of consciousness are gone, is a kind of consciousness which has no objects. It is not a consciousness *of* anything, but yet it is still consciousness. For the contents of our ordinary daily consciousness, the colors, sounds, wishes, thoughts are the same as the objects of consciousness, so that when the contents are gone the objects are gone. This consciousness of the mystics is not even a consciousness of consciousness, for then there would be a duality which is incompatible with the idea of an undifferentiated unity. In India it is called *pure* consciousness. The word "pure" is used in somewhat the same sense as Kant used it—meaning "without any empirical contents."

Another aspect of the paradox is that this pure consciousness is simultaneously both positive and negative, something and nothing, a fullness and an emptiness. The positive side is that it is an actual and positive consciousness. Moreover, all mystics affirm that it is pure peace, beatitude, joy, bliss, so that it has a positive affective tone. The Christians call it "the peace of God which passeth all understanding." The Buddhists call it Nirvana. But although it has this positive character, it is quite correct to say also that when we empty out all objects and contents of the mind *there is nothing whatever left*. That is the negative side of the paradox. What is left is sheer Emptiness. This is fully recognized in all mystical literature. In Mahayan Buddhism this total emptiness of the mystical consciousness is called the Void. In Christian mysticism the experience is identified with God. And this causes Eckhart and others to say that God, or the Godhead, is pure Nothingness, is a "desert," or "wilderness," and so on. Usually the two sides of the paradox are expressed in metaphors. The commonest metaphor for the positive side is light and for the negative side darkness. This is the darkness of God. It is called darkness because all distinctions disappear in it just as all distinctions disappear in a physical darkness.

We must not say that what we have here is a light *in* the darkness. For that would be no paradox. The paradox is that the light *is* the darkness, and the darkness *is* the light. This statement can be well documented from the literature of different cultures. I will give two examples, one from Christianity, one from Buddhism—and from the Buddhism of Tibet of all places in the world. Dionysius the Areopagite, a Christian, speaks of God as "the dazzling obscurity which outshines all brilliance with the intensity of its darkness." And the Tibetan book of the Dead puts the same paradox in the words, "the clear light of the Void." In Dionysius we see that the obscurity, or the darkness, *is* the brilliance, and in the Tibetan book we see that the Void itself *is* a clear light.

(8) *Mysticism and Religion.* Most writers on mysticism seem to take it for granted that mystical experience is a religious experience, and that mysticism is necessarily a religious phenomenon. They seem to think that mysticism and religious mysticism are one and the same thing. But this is far from being correct. It is true that there is an important connection between mysticism and religion, but it is not nearly so direct and immediate as most writers have seemed to think, nor can it be simply taken for granted as an obvious fact.

There are several grounds for insisting that intrinsically and in itself mystical experience is not a religious phenomenon at all and that its connection with religions is subsequent and even adventitious. In the first place, it seems to be clear that if we strip the mystical experience of all intellectual interpretation such as that which identifies it with God, or with the Absolute, or with the soul of the world, what is left is simply the undifferentiated unity. Now what is there that is religious about an undifferentiated unity? The answer seems to be, in the first instance, "Nothing at all." There seems to be nothing religious about an undifferentiated unity as such.

In the theistic religions of the West, in Christianity, Judaism, and Islam, the experience of the undifferentiated unity is interpreted as "union with God." But this is an interpretation and is not the experience itself. It is true that some Christian mystics, such as St. Teresa of Avila, invariably speak simply of having experienced "union with God," and do not talk about an undifferentiated unity. St. Teresa did not have a sufficiently analytical mind to distinguish between the experience and its interpretation. But other Christian mystics who are more analytically minded, such as Eckhart and Ruysbroeck, do speak of the undifferentiated unity.

These considerations are further underlined by the fact that quite different interpretations of the same experience are given in different cultures. The undifferentiated unity is interpreted by Eckhart and Ruysbroeck in terms of the Trinitarian conception of God, but by Islamic mystics as the unitarian God of Islam, and by the leading school of the Vedantists as a more impersonal Absolute. And when we come to Buddhism we find that the experience is not interpreted as any kind of God at all. For the Buddhist it becomes the Void or Nirvana. Buddha denied the existence of a Supreme Being altogether. It is often said that Buddhism is atheistic. And whether this description of Buddhism is true or not, it is certainly the case that there can exist an atheistic mysticism, a mystical experience naked and not clothed in any religious garb.

In view of these facts, we have a problem on our hands. Why is it that, in spite of exceptions, mysticism *usually* takes on some religious form and is usually found in connection with a definitely religious culture and as being a part of some definite religion? The following are, I think, the main reasons.

First, there is a very important feature of the introvertive mystical experience which I have not mentioned yet. I refer to the experience of the "melting away" into the Infinite of one's own individuality. Such phrases as "melting away," "fading away," "passing away" are found in the mystical literature of Christianity, Islam, Hinduism, and Buddhism. Among the Sufis of Islam there is a special technical term for it. It is called fanā. It must be insisted that this is not an inference or an interpretation or a theory or a speculation. It is an actual experience. The individual, as it were, directly experiences the disappearance of his own individuality, its fading away into the Infinite. To document this, one could quote from Eckhart, or from the Upanishads or the Sufis. But I believe I can bring home the point to a modern reader better by quoting a modern author. I referred earlier to the fact that Tennyson had frequent mystical experiences. His account of them is quoted by William James in his *The Varieties of Religious Experience.* Tennyson wrote, "All at once, as it were out of the intensity of the consciousness of individuality, individuality itself seemed to dissolve and fade away into boundless being. . . . the loss of personality, if such it were, seeming no extinction but the only true life." "Boundless being" seems to have the same meaning as "the Infinite." The Infinite is in most minds identified with the idea of God. We are finite beings, God is the only Infinite Being. One can see at once, therefore, how this experience of the dissolution of one's own individuality, its being merged into the Infinite, takes on a religious meaning. In theistic cultures the experience of melting away into boundless being is interpreted as union with God.

A second reason for the connection between mysticism and religion is that the undifferentiated unity is necessarily thought of by the mystics as being *beyond space and beyond time.* For it is without any internal division or multiplicity of parts, whereas the essence of time is its division into an endless multitude of successive parts, and the essence of space is its division into a multitude of parts lying side by side. Therefore the undifferentiated unity, being without any multiplicity of parts, is necessarily spaceless and timeless. Being timeless is the same as being eternal. Hence Eckhart is constantly telling us that the mystical experience transcends time and is an experience of "the Eternal Now." But in religious minds the Eternal, like the Infinite, is another name for God. Hence the mystical experience is thought of as an experience of God.

A third reason for this identification of the undifferentiated unity with God lies in the emotional side of the experience. It is the universal testimony of the mystics that their kind of consciousness brings feelings of an exalted peace, blessedness, and joy. It becomes identified with the peace of God, the gateway of the Divine, the gateway of salvation. This is also why in Buddhism, though the experience is not personified or called God, it nevertheless becomes Nirvana which is the supreme goal of the Buddhist religious life.

Thus we see that mysticism naturally, though not necessarily, becomes intimately associated with whatever is the religion of the culture in which it appears. It is, however, important to realize that it does not favor any particular religion. Mystical experience in itself does not have any tendency to make a man a Christian or a Buddhist. Into the framework of what creed he will fit his experience will tend to depend mostly on the culture in which he lives. In a Buddhist country the mystic interprets his experience as a glimpse of Nirvana, in a Christian country he may interpret it as union with God or even (as in Eckhart) as penetrating into the Godhead which is beyond God. Or if he is a highly sophisticated modern individual, who has been turned by his education into a religious skeptic, he may remain a skeptic as regards the dogmas of the different religions; he may allow his mystical experience to remain naked without any clothing of creeds or dogmas; but he is likely at the same time to feel that in that experience he has found something *sacred*. And this feeling of the sacred may quite properly be called "religious" feeling though it does not clothe itself in any dogmas. And this alone may be enough to uplift his ideals and to revolutionize his life and to give it meaning and purpose.

(9) *The Ethical Aspects of Mysticism.* It is sometimes asserted that mysticism is merely an escape from life and from its duties and responsibilities. The mystic, it is said, retreats into a private ecstasy of bliss, turns his back on the world, and forgets not only his own sorrows but the needs and sorrows of his fellow-men. In short, his life is essentially selfish.

It is possible that there have been mystics who deserved this kind of condemnation. To treat the bliss of the mystical consciousness as an end in itself is certainly a psychological possibility. And no doubt there have been men who have succumbed to this temptation. But this attitude is not the mystic ideal, and it is severely condemned by those who are most representative of the mystics themselves. For instance, St. John of the Cross condemns it as "spiritual gluttony." Eckhart tells us that if a man were in mystical ecstasy and knew of a poor man who needed his help, he should leave his ecstasy in order to go and serve the poor man. The Christian mystics especially have always emphasized that mystical union with God brings with it an intense and burning love of God which must needs overflow into the world in the form of love for our fellow-men; and that this must show itself in deeds of charity, mercy, and self-sacrifice, and not merely in words.

Some mystics have gone beyond this and have insisted that the mystical consciousness is the secret fountain of all love, human as well as divine; and that since love in the end is the only source of true moral activity, therefore mysticism is the source from which ethical values ultimately flow. For all selfishness and cruelty and evil result from the separateness of one human being from another. This separateness of individuals breeds egoism and the war of all against all. But in the mystical consciousness all distinctions disappear and therefore the distinction between "I" and "you" and "he" and "she." This is the mystical and metaphysical basis of love, namely the realization that my brother and I are one, and that therefore his sufferings are my sufferings and his happiness is my happiness. This reveals itself dimly in the psychological phenomena of sympathy and more positively in actual love. For one who had no touch of the mystical vision all men would be islands. And in the end it is because of mysticism that it is possible to say that "no man is an island" and that on the contrary every man is "a part of the main."

(10) *Alternative Interpretations of Mysticism*. We have seen that the same experience may be interpreted in terms of different religious creeds. There is also another set of alternative interpretations which we ought to mention. We may believe that the mystic really is in touch, as he usually claims, with some being greater than himself, some spiritual Infinite which transcends the temporal flux of things. Or we may, on the other hand, adopt the alternative solution of the skeptic who will think that the mystical consciousness is entirely subjective and imports nothing outside itself. My own vote would be cast for the former solution. I would agree with the words of Arthur Koestler [. . . when] he speaks of a higher order of reality which for us is like a text written in invisible ink. "I also liked to think," he says, "that the founders of religions, prophets, saints and seers had at moments been able to read a fragment of the invisible text; after which they had so much padded, dramatised and ornamented it, that they themselves could no longer tell what parts of it were authentic."

But I wish to point out that even if one should choose the skeptical alternative and suppose that the mystical consciousness reveals no reality outside its owner's brain, one is far from having disposed of mysticism as some worthless delusion which ought to be got rid of. Even if it is wholly subjective, it still reveals something which is supremely great in human life. It is still the peace which passeth all understanding. It is still the gateway to salvation—not, I mean, in a future life, but as the highest beatitude that a man can reach in this life, and out of which the greatest deeds of love can flow. But it must be added, of course, that it belongs among those things of which Spinoza wrote in those famous words: "If the road which I have shown is very difficult, it yet can be discovered. And clearly it must be very hard if it is so rarely found. For how could it be that it is neglected by practically all, if salvation . . . could be found without difficulty. But all excellent things are as difficult as they are rare."

C. B. MARTIN

5.3   *A Religious Way of Knowing*

I

Some theologians support their claim to knowledge of the existence of God on the basis of direct experience of God. I shall attempt to point out some of the eccentricities of this alleged way of knowing. The two main sources which I shall use are Professor J. Baillie's *Our Knowledge of God* and Professor H. H. Farmer's *Towards Belief in God*.

> We are rejecting logical argument of any kind as the first chapter of our theology or as representing the process by which God comes to be known. We are holding that our knowledge of God rests rather on the revelation of His personal Presence as Father, Son, and Holy Spirit. . . . Of such a Presence it must be true that to those who have never been confronted with it argument is useless, while to those who have it is superfluous. [BAILLIE, p. 132.]
>
> It is not as the result of an inference of any kind, whether explicit or implicit, whether laboriously excogitated or swiftly intuited, that the knowledge of God's reality comes to us. It comes rather through our direct, personal encounter with Him in the Person of Jesus Christ His Son our Lord. [*Ibid.,* p. 143.]
>
> If now we ask how we would expect such a reality (God) to disclose itself to us, the answer can only be that we can have no expectancy about the matter at all; for in the nature of the case there are no parallels, no analogies on which expectancy may be based. The divine reality is, by definition, unique. Or, in other words, we would expect that if we know the reality of God in respect of this fundamental aspect of His being at all, we shall just know that we are dealing with God, the ultimate source and disposer of all things, including ourselves, and there will be nothing more to be said. It will not be possible to describe the compelling touch of God otherwise than as the compelling touch of God. To anyone who has no such awareness of God, leading as it does to the typically religious attitudes of obeisance and worship, it will be quite impossible to indicate what is meant; one can only hope to evoke it, on the assumption that the capacity to become aware of God is part of normal human nature like the capacity to see light or to hear sound. [FARMER, p. 40.]

The arguments of the theologians quoted have been taken out of context. I do not want to suggest that the quotations give a faithful or complete im-

From *Mind* 61 (1952). Reprinted by permission of the author and Basil Blackwell (London), publisher.

pression of their total argument. The following quotations from Professor Farmer indicate two further lines of argument which cannot be discussed here.

Reflection

For what we have now in mind is no demonstrative proofs *from* the world, but rather confirmatory considerations which present themselves to us when we bring belief in God with us *to* the world. It is a matter of the coherence of the belief with other facts. If we find that the religious intuition which has arisen from other sources provides the mind with a thought in terms of which much else can without forcing be construed, then that is an intellectual satisfaction, and a legitimate confirmation of belief, which it would be absurd to despise. [FARMER, p. 113.]

Pragmatic Element

We shall first speak in general terms of what may be called the human situation and need, and thereafter we shall try to show how belief in God, as particularized in its Christian form (though still broadly set forth), fits on to this situation and need. [*Ibid.*, p. 62.]

II

The alleged theological way of knowing may be described as follows:

"I have direct experience (knowledge, acquaintance, apprehension) of God, therefore I have valid reason to believe that God exists."

A. By this it may be meant that the statement "I have had direct experience of God, but God does not exist" is contradictory. Thus, the assertion that "I have had direct experience of God" commits one to the assertion that God exists. From this it follows that "I have had direct experience of God" is more than a psychological statement, because it claims more than the fact that I have certain sensations—it claims that God exists. Thus as it stands this is a correct form of deductive argument. The assertion "I have direct experience of God" includes the assertion "God exists" thus, the conclusion "therefore, God exists" follows tautologically.

B. Unfortunately, this deduction is useless. The addition of the existential claim "God exists" to the psychological claim of having religious experiences must be shown to be warrantable. It cannot be shown to be warrantable by any deductive argument, because psychological statements of the form:

(1) I feel as if an unseen person were interested in (willed) my welfare.

(2) I feel an elation quite unlike any I have ever felt before.

(3) I have feelings of guilt and shame at my sinfulness.

(4) I feel as if I were committed to bending all of my efforts to living in a certain way,

etc., etc.

can make the claim only that I have these complex feelings and sensations. Nothing else follows deductively. No matter what the existential statement might be that is added to the psychological statement, it is always logically possible for future psychological statements to call this existential claim in doubt. The only thing that I can establish beyond correction on the basis of having certain feelings and sensations is that I have these feelings and sensations. No matter how unique an experience may be claimed to be, it cannot do the impossible.

There is an influential and subtle group of religious thinkers who would not insist upon any existential claim. My remarks are largely irrelevant to this group. It would be hasty to describe their religious belief as "psychological" or employ any other such general descriptive term. For example, the "call," in even the most liberal and "subjective" Quaker sects, could not be reduced to feeling statements, etc. The "call," among other things, implies a mission or intricate programme of behaviour. The non-subjective element of the "call" is evident because in so far as one failed to live in accordance with a mission just so far would the genuineness of the "call" be questioned. It will be seen that this verification procedure is necessarily not available in the religious way of knowing to be examined.

C. Neither is the addition of the existential claim "God exists" to the psychological claim made good by any inductive argument. There are no tests agreed upon to establish genuine experience of God and distinguish it decisively from the ungenuine. Indeed, many theologians deny the possibility of any such test or set of tests. Nor is there any increased capacity for prediction produced in the Christian believer which we cannot explain on a secular basis. However, just such a capacity is implied by those who talk of religious experience as if it were due to some kind of sixth sense.

(1) The believer may persuade us that something extraordinary has happened by saying, "I am a changed man since 6.37 p.m., 6th May, 1939." This is a straightforward empirical statement. We can test this by noticing whether or not he has given up bad habits, etc. We may allow the truth of the statement, even if he has not given up bad habits, etc. because we may find evidence of bad conscience, self-searchings and remorse that had not been present before that date.

(2) However, if the believer says, "I had a direct experience of God at 6.37 p.m., 6th May, 1939," this is not an empirical statement in the way that the other statement is. The checking procedure is very far from clear. No matter how much or how little his subsequent behaviour such as giving up bad habits, etc., is affected, it could never prove or disprove his statement.

An important point to note is that the theologian discourages any detailed description of the required experience ("apprehension of God"). The more naturalistic and detailed the description of the required experience became, the easier would it become to deny the existential claim. One could say, "Yes, I had those very experiences, but they certainly did not convince me of God's existence." The only sure defence here would be for the theologian to make the claim analytic—"You *couldn't* have those experiences and at the same time sincerely deny God's existence."

D. The way in which many theologians talk would seem to show that they think of knowing God as something requiring a kind of sixth sense.

(1) The Divine Light is not merely of a colour usually visible only to eagles and the Voice of God is not merely of a pitch usually audible only to dogs. No matter how much more keen our senses became, we should be no better off than before. This sixth sense, therefore, must be very different from the other five.

(*a*) This supposed religious sense has no vocabulary of its own, but depends upon metaphors drawn from the other senses. There are no terms which apply to it and it alone. There is a vocabulary for what is sensed but not for the sense. We "see" the Holy, the Numinous, the Divine, etc. This linguistic predicament may be compared with the similar one of the intuitionists when they talk of "seeing" a logical connection. It also may be compared with "hearing" the Voice of Conscience.

(*b*) The intuitionists seldom differ from the rest of us in the number of facts referred to in describing how we come to understand logical statements and their relations. The intuitionist, however, emphasizes the fact that often we come to understand the point of an argument or problem in logic very suddenly. We mark this occurrence by such phrases as "the light dawned," "understood it in a flash." Such events are usually described in terms of a complete assurance that one's interpretation is correct and a confidence that one will tend to be able to reproduce or recognize the argument or problem in various contexts in the future. A vitally important distinction between this "seeing" and the religious "seeing" is that there is checking procedure for the former, but not for, the latter. If the intuitionist finds that his boasted insight was wrong, then he says, "I couldn't really have 'seen' it." No matter how passionate his claims he cannot have "seen" that $2 + 2 = 5$.

III

The religious way of knowing is described as being unique.

A. No one can deny the existence of feelings and experiences which the believer calls "religious" and no one can deny their power. Because of this and because the way of knowing by direct experience is neither inductive nor deductive, theologians have tried to give this way of knowing a special status. One way in which this has been done has been to claim that religious experience is unique and incommunicable. There is a sense in which this is true. This sense may be brought out by a list such as the following:

(1) You don't know what the experience of God is until you have had it.

(2) You don't know what a blue sky is until you have been to Naples.

(3) You don't know what poverty is until you have been poor.

(4) "We can only know a person by the direct communion of sympathetic intercourse." (William Temple).

Professor Baillie, in likening our knowledge of God to our knowledge of other minds, says that it is

> like our knowledge of tridimensional space and all other primary modes of knowledge, something that cannot be imagined by one who does not already possess it, since it cannot be described to him in terms of anything else than itself. [BAILLIE, p. 217.]

What Professor Baillie does not see is that according to his criteria anything can qualify as a primary mode of knowledge. Each one of the statements in the above list is unique and incommunicable in just this way. You must go to Naples and not just to Venice. A postcard is no substitute.

B. That this sort of uniqueness is not to the point in supporting the existential claim "God exists" can be seen by examining the following two samples:

(1) You don't know what the experience of God is until you have had it.

(2) You don't know what the colour blue is until you have seen it.

Professor Farmer says,

> All the basic elements in our experience are incommunicable. Who could describe light and colour to one who has known nothing but darkness? [FARMER, p. 41.]

Just in so far as the experience of God is unique and incommunicable in this way, then just so far is it not to the point in supporting the existential claim "God exists."

All that this proves is that a description of one group of sensations A in terms of another set of sensations B is never sufficient for knowing group A. According to this definition of "know," in order to know one must have those sensations. Thus, all that is proved is that in order to know what religious experience is one must have a religious experience. This helps in no way at all to prove that such experience is direct apprehension of God and helps in no way to support the existential claim "God exists."

C. Professor Farmer makes the point that describing the experience of God to an unbeliever is like describing colour to a blind man. So it is, in the sense that the believer has usually had experiences which the unbeliever has not. However, it is also very much unlike. The analogy breaks down at some vital points.

(1) The blind man may have genuine though incomplete knowledge of colour. He may have an instrument for detecting wave lengths, etc. Indeed, he may even increase our knowledge of colour. More important still, the blind man may realize the differences in powers of prediction between himself and the man of normal eyesight. He is well aware of the fact, unlike himself, the man of normal eyesight does not have to wait to hear the rush of the bull in order to be warned.

(2) This point is connected with the problem of how we are to know when someone has the direct experience of God or even when we ourselves have the direct experience of God. It was shown above how the situation is easier in the case of the blind man. It is easy also, in the case of knowing a blue sky in Naples. One can look at street signs and maps in order to be sure that this is the really blue sky in question. It is only when one comes to such a case as knowing God that the society of tests and check-up procedures that surround other instances of knowing, completely vanishes. What is put in the place of these tests and checking procedures is an immediacy of knowledge that is supposed to carry its own guarantee. This feature will be examined later.

D. It is true that the man of normal vision has a way of knowing colour which the blind man does not have. Namely, he can see coloured objects. However, as we have seen, it would be wrong to insist that this is the only way of knowing colour and that the blind man has *no* way of knowing colour. There is a tendency to deny this and to maintain that having colour sensations is *the* way of knowing colour. Perhaps Professor Farmer has this in mind when he tries to make an analogy between the incommunicability of the believer's direct knowledge of God to the unbeliever and the incommunicability of the normal man's knowledge of colour to the blind man. The analogy is justified if "knowing colour" is made synonymous with "having colour sensations."

(1) On this account, no matter how good his hearing and reliable his colour-detecting instruments, etc., the blind man could not know colour and the man of normal vision could not communicate to him just what this knowledge would be like.

(2) The believer has had certain unusual experiences which, presumably, the unbeliever has not had. If "having direct experience of God" is made synonymous with "having certain religious experiences," and the believer has had these and the unbeliever has not, then we may say that the believer's knowledge is incommunicable to the unbeliever in that it has already been legislated that in order to know what the direct experience of God is one must have had certain religious experiences.

> To anyone who has no such awareness of God, leading as it does to the typically religious attitudes of obeisance and worship, it will be quite impossible to indicate what is meant; one can only hope to evoke it. . . . [FARMER, p. 40.]

Reading theological text-books and watching the behaviour of believers is not sufficient.

E. The theologian has made the above analogy hold at the cost of endangering the existential claim about God which he hoped to establish.

(1) If "knowing colour" is made synonymous with "having colour sensa-

tions" and "having direct experience of God" is made synonymous with "having certain religious experiences," then it is certainly true that a blind man cannot "know colour" and that a non-religious man cannot "have direct experience of God." By definition, also, it is true that the blind man and the non-religious man cannot know the meaning of the phrases "knowing colour" and "having direct experience of God," because it has been previously legislated that one cannot know their meaning without having the relevant experiences.

(2) If this analogy is kept then the phrases "knowing colour" and "having direct experience of God" seem to make no claim beyond the psychological claims about one's colour sensations and religious feelings.

(3) If this analogy is not kept then there is no sense in the comparison between the incommunicability between the man of normal vision and the blind man and the incommunicability between the believer and the unbeliever.

(4) If "knowing colour" is to be shaken loose from its purely psychological implications and made to have an existential reference concerning certain features of the world then a whole society of tests and check-up procedures which would be wholly irrelevant to the support of the psychological claim about one's own colour sensations become relevant. E.g. what other people see and the existence of light waves and the description of their characteristics needing the testimony of research workers and scientific instruments.

F. Because "having direct experience of God" does not admit the relevance of a society of tests and checking procedures it places itself in the company of the other ways of knowing which preserve their self-sufficiency, "uniqueness" and "incommunicability" by making a psychological and not an existential claim. E.g. "I seem to see a blue piece of paper." This statement requires no further test or checking procedure in order to be considered true. Indeed, if A makes the statement "I seem to see a blue piece of paper," then not only does A need no further corroboration, but there could be no disproof of his statement for him, for, if B says to A, "It does not seem to me as if I were now seeing a blue piece of paper," then B's statement does *not* call A's statement in doubt for A though it does for B. However, if A makes the statement, "I see a piece of blue paper," and B says in the same place and at the same time, "I do not see a piece of blue paper," then B's statement *does* call A's statement in doubt for A. Further investigation will then be proper and if no piece of paper can be felt and other investigators cannot see or feel the paper and photographs reveal nothing, then A's statement will be shown to have been false. A's only refuge will be to say, "Well, I certainly seem to see a piece of blue paper." This is a perfect refuge because no one can prove him wrong, but its unassailability has been bought at the price of making no claim about the world beyond the claim about his own state of mind.

G. Another way of bringing out the closeness of the religious statement to the psychological statement is the following.

(1) When A wishes to support the assertion that a certain physical object

exists, the tests and checking procedures made by A himself are not the only things relevant to the truth of his assertion. Testimony of what B, C, D, etc. see, hear, etc. is also relevant. That is, if A wanted to know whether it was really a star that he saw, he could not only take photographs, look through a telescope, etc., but also ask others if they saw the star. If a large proportion of a large number of people denied seeing the star, A's claim about the star's existence would be weakened. Of course, he might still trust his telescope. However, let us now imagine that A does not make use of the tests and checking procedures (photographs and telescopes) but is left with the testimony of what he sees and the testimony of others concerning what they see. In this case, it is so much to the point if a large number of people deny seeing the star, that A will be considered irrational or mad if he goes on asserting its existence. His only irrefutable position is to reduce his physical object claim to an announcement concerning his own sensations. Then the testimony of men and angels cannot disturb his certitude. These sensations of the moment he knows directly and immediately and the indirect and non-immediate testimony of men and angels is irrelevant. Absolute confidence, and absolute indifference to the majority judgment, is bought at the price of reducing the existential to the psychological.

(2) The religious claim is similar to, though not identical with, the above case in certain important features. We have seen that there are no tests or checking procedures open to the believer to support his existential claim about God. Thus, he is left with the testimony of his own experience and the similar testimony of the experience of others. And, of course, he is not left wanting for such testimony, for religious communities seem to fulfil just this sort of need.

(3) Let us imagine a case comparable to the one concerning the existence of a physical object. In this case A is a professor of Divinity and he believes that he has come to know of the existence of God through direct experience of God. In order to understand the intricate character of what Professor A is asserting we must imagine a highly unusual situation. The other members of the faculty and the members of Professor A's religious community suddenly begin sincerely to deny his and what has been their assertion. Perhaps they still attend church services and pray as often as they used to, and perhaps they claim to have the same sort of experiences as they had when they were believers, but they refuse to accept the conclusion that God exists. Whether they give a Freudian explanation or some other explanation or no explanation of their experiences, they are agreed in refusing to accept the existential claim (about God) made by Professor A. How does this affect Professor A and his claim? It may affect Professor A very deeply—indeed, he may die of broken-hearted disappointment at the loss of his fellow-believers. However, the loss of fellow-believers may not weaken his confidence in the truth of his assertion or in the testimony of his experience. In this matter his experience may be all that ultimately counts for him in establishing his con-

fidence in the truth of his claim about the existence of God. It has been said that religious experience carries its own guarantee and perhaps the above account describes what is meant by this.

H. It is quite obvious from the examples given above that the religious statement ("I have direct experience of God") is of a different status from the physical object statement ("I can see a star") and shows a distressing similarity to the psychological statement (I seem to see a star"). The bulk of this paper has been devoted to showing some of the many forms this similarity takes. Does this mean then that the religious statement and its existential claim concerning God amount to no more than a reference to the complex feelings and sensations of the believer?

I. Perhaps the best way to answer this last question is to take a typical psychological statement and see if there is anything which must be said of it and all other psychological statements which cannot be said of the religious statement.

(1) One way of differentiating a physical object statement from a psychological statement is by means of prefixing the phrase "I seem. . . .". For instance, the statement "I can see a star" may be transformed from a statement concerning the existence of a certain physical object to a statement concerning my sensations by translating it into the form "I seem to see a star." The first statement involves a claim about the existence of an object as well as an announcement concerning my sensations and therefore subjects itself to the risk of being wrong concerning that further claim. Being wrong in this case is determined by a society of tests and checking procedures such as taking photographs and looking through telescopes, and by the testimony of others that they see or do not see a star. The second statement involves no claim about the existence of an object and so requires no such tests and no testimony of others; indeed, the sole judge of the truth of the statement is the person making it. If no existential claim is lost by the addition of this phrase to a statement then the statement is psychological. For instance, the statement "I feel pain" loses nothing by the addition of "I seem to feel pain."

(2) In the case of the religious statement "I have direct experience of God" the addition of the phrase is fatal to all that the believer wants to assert. "I seem to be having direct experience of God" is a statement concerning my feelings and sensations of the moment and as such it makes no claim about the existence of God. Thus, the original statement "I have direct experience of God" is not a psychological statement. This should not surprise us. We should have known it all along, for isn't it an assertion that one comes to know something, namely God, by means of one's feelings and sensations and this something is not reducible to them? The statement is not a psychological one just because it is used to assert the existence of something. Whether this assertion is warranted and what exactly it amounts to is quite another question.

We are tempted to think that the religious statement *must* be of one sort or another. The truth is that *per impossibile* it is both at once. The theologian must use it in both ways and which way he is to emphasize at a particular time depends upon the circumstances of its use; and most particularly upon the direction of our probings.

(3) The statement "I seem to be having direct experience of God" is an eccentric one. It is eccentric not only because introspective announcements are unusual and because statements about God have a peculiar obscurity, but for a further and more important reason. This pecularity may be brought out by comparing this statement with others having the same form. A first formulation of this may be put in the following way. In reference to things other than our sensations of the moment knowledge is prior to seeming as if.

The statement "I seem to be looking directly at a chair" has a meaning only in so far as I already *know* what it is like to look directly at a chair. The statement "I seem to be listening to a choir" has a meaning only in so far as I already *know* what it is like to be listening to a choir. The assumption of knowledge in both of these cases is one which all normal people are expected to make or do in fact make.

The statement "I seem to be having direct experience of God" does not lend itself so easily to the criterion for meaning exemplified in the above, because if this statement has meaning only in so far as one already *knows* what it is like to have direct experience of God, then the assumption of such knowledge is certainly not one which all normal people may be expected to be able or do in fact make.

However, it may be said that the assumption of such knowledge as knowledge of what it is like to see a gorgon may not be assumed of all normal people and, therefore, the case of religious knowledge is in no peculiar position.

The answer to this objection and the discovery of the peculiarity of the religious statement may come about by asking the question "How do we come to learn what it would be like to look directly at a chair, hear a choir, see a gorgon, have direct experience of God?"

It is not that there are no answers to the question concerning how we come to learn what it would be like to have direct experience of God. We are not left completely in the dark. Instead, the point is that the answers to this question are quite different from those referring to the questions concerning how we come to learn what it would be like to look directly at a chair, hear a choir, and see a gorgon.

No one has ever seen a gorgon, yet there certainly are people who, by means of their specialized knowledge of mythical literature, may claim in a perfectly meaningful manner that it now seems to them as if they were seeing a gorgon.

Let us imagine a society in which there are no chairs and no one knows anything at all about chairs. If we were to try to teach one of the members of this society what it would be like to see a chair and if we were not allowed to construct a chair, what sort of thing might we do? We might look around at the furniture and say, "A chair is a kind of narrow settee. It is used to sit on." This would be a beginning. Then we might compare different settees as to which are more chair-like. We might draw pictures of chairs, make gestures with our hands showing the general shape and size of different sorts of chairs. If, on the following day, he said, "I had a most unusual dream last night. I seemed to be looking directly at a chair," we should admit that his statement was closer in meaning to a similar one which we who have seen chairs might make than it would be to a similar one which another member might make who had no information or instruction or experience of chairs. We would insist that we had better knowledge of what it is to see a chair than does the instructed member of society who has still actually to see a chair. However, to know pictures of chairs is to know chairs in a legitimate sense.

But let us now imagine a utopian society in which none of the members has ever been in the least sad or unhappy. If we were to try to teach one of the members of this society what it would be like to feel sad, how would we go about it? It can be said that giving definitions, no matter how ingenious, would be no help, drawing pictures of unhappy faces, no matter how well drawn, would be no help, so long as these measures failed to evoke a feeling of sadness in this person. Comparing the emotion of sadness with other emotions would be no help, because no matter how like other emotions (weariness, etc.) are to sadness they fail just because they are not sadness. No, sadness is unique and incomparable.

To anyone who has no such awareness of sadness, leading as it does to the typically unhappy behaviour of tears and drawn faces, it will be quite impossible to indicate what is meant, one can only hope to evoke it, on the assumption that the capacity to become aware of sadness is part of normal human nature like the capacity to see light or to hear sound.

This last paragraph is a play upon a quotation given at the very beginning of the paper. The following is the original version.

> To anyone who has no such awareness of God, leading as it does to the typically religious attitudes of obeisance and worship, it will be quite impossible to indicate what is meant; one can only hope to evoke it, on the assumption that the capacity to become aware of God is part of normal human nature like the capacity to see light or to hear sound. [FARMER, p. 40.]

(4)

> We are rejecting logical argument of any kind as the first chapter of our epistemology of aesthetics, or as representing the process by which beauty comes to be known. . . .
>
> It is not as the result of an inference of any kind, whether explicit or implicit, whether laboriously excogitated or swiftly intuited, that the knowledge of beauty comes to us.

... to those who have never been confronted with the experience of seeing the beauty of something, argument is useless.

As these statements stand they are plainly false. Professors of aesthetics and professional art critics often do help us to come to "knowledge of beauty" by all kinds of inference and arguments. They may, and often do, help us to come to a finer appreciation of beautiful things. Knowledge of the rules of perspective and understanding of an artist's departure from them is relevant to an aesthetic appreciation of his work.

However, it is possible to interpret these statements as true and this is more important for our purpose.

There is sense in saying that an art critic, who has vastly increased our aesthetic sensitivity and whose books of art criticism are the very best, may never have known beauty. If there are no signs of this critic ever having been stirred by any work of art, then no matter how subtle his analyses, there is sense in claiming that he has never been confronted with the experience of seeing the beauty of something. This sense just is that we are determined not to say that a person has seen the beauty of something or has knowledge of beauty if he does not at some time have certain complex emotions and feelings which are typically associated with looking at paintings, hearing music and reading poetry. To "know beauty" or to "see beauty of something" means, among other things, to have certain sorts of emotions and feelings.

The quotation given above was a play on a quotation given at the beginning of the paper. The following is the original version with the appropriate cuts.

> We are rejecting logical argument of any kind as the first chapter of our theology or as representing the process by which God comes to be known. . . .
> It is not as the result of an inference of any kind, whether explicit or implicit, whether laboriously excogitated or swiftly intuited, that the knowledge of God comes to us.
> . . . to those who have never been confronted with it [direct, personal encounter with God] argument is useless.

As these statements stand they are plainly false. Professors of divinity and clergymen are expected to do what Professor Baillie claims cannot be done.

However, it is possible to interpret these statements as true and this is more important for our purpose.

There is sense in saying that a theologian (who has vastly increased our religious sensitivity and whose books of theology are the very best) may never have known God. If there are no signs of this theologian ever having been stirred by any religious ritual or act of worship, then no matter how subtle his analyses, there is sense in claiming that he has never been confronted with God's personal Presence. This sense just *is* that we are determined not to say that a person has knowledge of God if he does not at some time have certain complex emotions and feelings which are associated with attending religious services, praying and reading the Bible. To "know God" or to be confronted with God's "personal Presence" means, of necessity, having certain sorts of emotions and feelings.

(5) The analogy suggested above between aesthetic experience and religious experience and between aesthetic knowledge and religious knowledge cannot be examined further in this paper. However, certain preliminary suggestions may be made. The following quotations set the problem.

> In it [art] also there is an awareness, however unformulated and inarticulate, of a world of beauty which can be grasped and actualized in creative activity, yet it will never be possible fully to grasp it and actualize it in all its infinite reach and depth. In the appreciation of beauty in artistic products something of the same sense of an "infinite beyond" disclosing itself through, yet transcending, what is contemplated and enjoyed, is present. It is precisely this that marks the difference between, say, a Beethoven symphony and a shallow and "tinny" jazz-dance. [FARMER, *Towards Belief in God*, p. 56.]

After quoting Santayana's remark, "Religions are better or worse, never true or false," Professor Farmer says:

> It is sufficient answer to this suggestion to say that it is utterly false both to art and to religion. It is a central element in the artistic consciousness that it is, in its work, seeking to grasp and express an ideal world which in spite of its ideality is real and in some sense stands objectively over against the artist; it is never apprehended as merely a source of internal satisfaction and delights. Without this neither the work of artistic production nor its product would internally satisfy or delight. This is even more obviously true of religion. In religion the reality-interest is paramount. Once persuade the religious man that the reality with which he supposes himself to be dealing is not "there" in the sense in which he supposes it to be "there" and his religion vanishes away. [FARMER, *Towards Belief in God*, p. 176.]

One may select a group of statements to compare and analyse. The following would be samples of such statements.

"The Believer experiences God."

"The Sensitive Listener experiences Beauty in the music."

"The Believer experiences something of the infinite goodness of God."

"The Sensitive Listener experiences the subtlety, sadness, colour, etc., of the music as part of what is the Beauty in the music."

"One may hear God through prayer."

"One may hear the Beautiful above or in the voices of the actors and the instruments of the orchestra."

"What the artist experiences and knows, namely Beauty, is ultimately incommunicable."

"What the Believer experiences and knows, namely God, is ultimately incommunicable."

"One may learn to come to know God."

"One may learn to come to know Beauty."

"One may learn to come to know one's wife."

Going over the complex uses of such statements may help one to discover something of the intricate logic of certain kinds of religious statements.

In this paper the analogy between seeing blue and experiencing God has been examined and found to be misleading. The suggested analogy between experiencing the Beautiful and experiencing God has further complexities and requires another examination which, among other things, would show how religious experience is and is not another experience in the way in which seeing red may be said to be another experience to seeing blue or hearing a nightingale.

Another important subject with which this paper has not dealt is the connection between what the believer expects from immortality and his religious belief. This peculiar kind of test or verification has special difficulties which cannot be treated here.

IV

Conclusion

It must be made clear in conclusion that the lack of tests and checking procedures which has been noted is not merely an unfortunate result of human frailty. It is necessarily the nature of the case. If tests and checking procedures were devised they would not, could not, support the claim of the believer. They may do for the detection of saints and perhaps even angels, but never of God. Of course, in a way theologians know this.

This paper has been an attempt to indicate how statements concerning a certain alleged religious way of knowing betray a logic extraordinarily like that of statements concerning introspective and subjective ways of knowing. It is not my wish to go from a correct suggestion that the logic is *very, very* like to an incorrect suggestion that the logic is *just* like.

PRAYER AND RITUAL

SAADYA

5.4 *The Types of Commandments*

CHAPTER I

Now that I have made this preliminary observation, let me state by way of introduction that our Lord, exalted and magnified be He, has informed us by the speech of His prophets that He has assigned to us a religion whereby we are to serve Him. It embraces laws prescribed for us by Him which we must observe and carry out with sincerity. That is the import of the statement of Scripture: *This day the Lord thy God commandeth thee to do these statutes and ordinances; thou shalt, therefore, observe and do them with all thy heart, and with all thy soul* (Deut. 26:16).

Moreover, in support of the validity of these laws, His messengers executed certain signs and wondrous miracles, with the result that we observed and carried out these laws immediately. Afterwards we discovered the rational basis for the necessity of their prescriptions so that we might not be left to roam at large without guidance.

Certain matters and classifications relative to this subject that reason makes imperative must now be explained by me. I say, then, that logic demands that whoever does something good be compensated either by means of a favor shown to him, if he is in need of it, or by means of thanks, if he does not require any reward. Since, therefore, this is one of the general demands of reason, it would not have been seemly for the Creator, exalted and magnified be He, to neglect it in His own case. It was, on the contrary, necessary for

From Saadya, *The Book of Beliefs and Opinions*, trans. Samuel Rosenblatt (New Haven: Yale University Press, 1948), pp. 138–45. Reprinted by permission of the publisher.

Him to command His creatures to serve Him and thank Him for having created them. Reason also demands that he that is wise do not permit himself to be treated with contempt or to be insulted. It was, therefore, likewise necessary for the Creator to forbid His servants to conduct themselves in such a way toward Him.

Furthermore, reason demands that the creatures be prevented from wronging each other in all sorts of ways. Hence it was also necessary for the All-Wise not to permit them to do such a thing. Reason also deems it proper for a wise man to give employment to an individual who performs a certain function and to pay him a wage for it, merely in order to confer a benefit upon him, since this is something that redounds to the benefit of the worker without hurting the employer.

If, now, we were to combine these four classes of requirements, their sumtotal would make up all the laws prescribed for us by our Lord. For example, He made it obligatory upon us to learn to know Him, to worship Him, and to dedicate ourselves wholeheartedly to Him, as the saint has said: *And thou, Solomon my son, know thou the God of thy father, and serve Him with a whole heart and with a willing mind* (I Chron. 28:9). Next he forbade us to conduct ourselves in an ugly insulting fashion toward Him, even though it could not hurt Him, because it is not the way of divine Wisdom to permit it, as Scripture says: *Whosoever curseth his God shall bear his sin* (Lev. 24:15). Nor would He permit one of us to wrong the other or commit violence against him, as Scripture says: *Ye shall not steal; neither shall ye deal falsely, nor lie to one another* (Lev. 19:11). These three classes of injunctions and whatever might be included in them constitute, then, the first of the two divisions of the laws of the Torah.

Now in the first of the [three] categories [we have mentioned above] there are to be included such acts as humble submission to God and serving Him and standing before Him and whatever resembles these, all of which are found in the text of Holy Writ. In the second class are to be included such injunctions as the one not to associate anyone else with God, nor to swear falsely in His name, nor to describe Him with mundane attributes and whatever resembles these, all of which are [also] found in the text of Holy Writ. To the third division, again, are to be added the practice of justice, truth, fairness, and righteousness, and the avoidance of the killing of human beings, and [the observance of] the prohibition of fornication and theft and deception and usury. [There is to be appended] also the duty devolving upon the believer to love his brother like himself and whatever else is embraced in these paragraphs, all of which is found in the text of Holy Writ.

Now the approval of each of these classes of acts that we have been commanded to carry out is implanted in our minds just as is the disapproval of each of the classes of acts that we are forbidden to commit. Thus has Wisdom, which is identical with reason, said: *For my mouth shall utter truth, and wickedness is an abomination to my lips* (Prov. 8:7).

The second [general] division [of the precepts of the Torah, on the other hand,] consists of things neither the approval nor the disapproval of which is decreed by reason, on account of their own character, but in regard to which our Lord has imposed upon us a profusion of commandments and prohibitions in order thereby to increase our reward and happiness. This is borne out by the remark of Scripture: *The Lord was pleased, for His righteousness' sake, to make the Torah great and glorious* (Isa. 42:21).

What is commanded of this group of acts is, consequently, [to be considered as] good, and what is prohibited as reprehensible; because the fulfillment of the former and the avoidance of the latter implies submissiveness to God. From this standpoint they might be attached secondarily to the first [general] division [of the laws of the Torah]. Nevertheless one cannot help noting, upon deeper reflection, that they have some partial uses as well as a certain slight justification from the point of view of reason, just as those belonging to the first [general] division have important uses and great justification from the point of view of reason.

CHAPTER II

Now it is fitting that I proceed first to the discussion of the rational precepts of the Torah. I say, then, that divine Wisdom imposed a restraint upon bloodshed among men, because if license were to prevail in this matter, they would cause each other to disappear. The consequence would be, in addition to the pain experienced by the victims, a frustration of the purpose that the All-Wise had in mind with regard to them. For their murder would cut them off from the fulfillment of the function for which He had created them and in the execution of which He had employed them.

Furthermore [divine] Wisdom forbade fornication in order that men might not become like the beasts with the result that no one would know his father so as to show him reverence in return for having raised him. [Another reason for this prohibition was] that the father might bequeath unto his son his possessions just as the son had received from his father the gift of existence. [A further reason was] that a human being might know the rest of his relatives, such as his paternal and maternal uncles, and show them whatever tenderness he was capable of.

Theft was forbidden by [divine] Wisdom because, if it were permitted, some men would rely on stealing the others' wealth, and they would neither till the soil nor engage in any other lucrative occupation. And if all were to rely on this source of livelihood, even stealing would become impossible, because, with the disappearance of all property, there would be absolutely nothing in existence that might be stolen.

Finally, [divine] Wisdom has made it one of its first injunctions that we speak the truth and desist from lying. For the truth is an assertion about a thing as it really is and in accordance with its actual character, whereas telling a lie is making an assertion about a thing that does not correspond to what it really is or to its actual character. Then when the senses, perceiving it, find it to be constituted in one form whilst the soul, reasoning about it, asserts that it is constituted otherwise, these two contrary views set up in the soul will oppose each other, and, on account of their mutual exclusion, the thing will be regarded by the soul as something grotesque.

Let me say next that I have seen some people who are of the opinion that these four principal vices that have been listed above are not at all objectionable. Only that is objectionable in their view which causes them pain and worry and grief, whilst the good is what affords them pleasure and rest. This thesis will be refuted by me at considerable length in the fourth treatise of this book, in the chapter on "justice." I shall, however, cite a portion of that refutation here, and say that whoever entertains such an opinion leaves out of account all the arguments we have produced here, and whoever leaves such matters out of account is an ignoramus about whom we need not trouble ourselves. Nevertheless I shall not be content until I have convinced him of the contradiction and the conflict inherent in his views.

I say, then, that the slaying of an enemy is an act that gives pleasure to the slayer but pain to the slain. Likewise the taking of another man's possessions or his wife gives pleasure to the robber but pain to the robbed. In the opinion of those who hold this view, however, each of these two acts would have to be regarded as wisdom and folly at one and the same time—as wisdom because it affords pleasure to the murderer or the thief or the adulterer, and as folly because it inflicts pain on his opponent. Now any theory that leads to such internal contradiction and mutual exclusion must be false. In fact, there are instances in which two such contrary things can both befall one and the same person, as when he eats honey into which some poison has fallen. This is something that gives pleasure and also causes death, and would consequently, according to their theory, have to be considered as wisdom and folly at one and the same time.

Let me proceed further now and discourse about the second general division of the laws of the Torah. This division consists of acts which from the standpoint of reason are optional. Yet the Law has made some of them obligatory and others forbidden, and left the rest optional as they had been. They include such matters as the consecration of certain days from among others, like the Sabbath and the festivals, and the consecration of certain human beings from among others, such as the prophet and the priest, and refraining from eating certain foods, and the avoidance of cohabitation with certain persons, and going into isolation immediately upon the occurrence of certain accidents because of defilement.

But even though the chief reason for the fulfillment of these principal precepts and their derivatives and whatever is connected with them is the fact that they represent the command of our Lord and enable us to reap a special advantage, yet I find that most of them have as their basis partially useful purposes. I see fit, therefore, to note some of these motivations and discuss them, although the wisdom of God, blessed and exalted be He, is above all that.

Now among the benefits accruing from the consecration of certain seasons, by desisting from work on them, there is first of all that of obtaining relaxation from much exertion. Furthermore it presents the opportunity for the attainment of a little bit of knowledge and a little additional praying. It also affords men leisure to meet each other at gatherings where they can confer about matters of their religion and make public announcements about them, and perform other functions of the same order.

Some of the benefits accruing from consecrating a particular person from among others are that it makes it possible to obtain more knowledge from him and to secure his services as an intercessor. [It] also [enables him] to imbue his fellow-men with the desire for righteousness so that they might thereby attain something like his own eminence. Finally [it permits him] to concern himself with the moral improvement of humanity, since he is qualified for such a task, and other things of this nature.

Among the advantages, again, that result from the prohibition against the eating of [only] certain animals is the prevention of any comparison between them and the Creator. For it is inconceivable that God would permit anything resembling Him to be eaten or, on the other hand, that [the eating of such a being] could cause defilement to man. This precept also serves to keep man from worshiping any of these animals, since it is not seemly for him to worship what has been given to him for food, nor what has been declared unclean for him.

As for the advantages accruing from the avoidance of cohabitation with certain women, those derived from observing this ruling in regard to a *married woman*, are such as we have stated previously. As far as the mother, sister, and daughter are concerned, since the relationship with them is necessarily intimate, the license to marry them would encourage dissoluteness on their part. There exists also the danger, if this were permitted, that men would be fascinated by those of their female relatives who have a beautiful figure, while those possessing homely features would be spurned even by strangers, since the latter would see that the male relatives [of these women] do not desire them.

Some of the benefits accruing from the observance of the laws of uncleanliness and cleanliness are that man is thereby led to think humbly of his flesh, that it enhances for him the value of prayer by virtue of his being cut off therefrom for a while during the period of defilement, that it endears to him the Temple which he was prevented from entering in the state of impurity, and finally that it causes him to dedicate his heart to the fear of God.

Similarly, if one were to follow up most of these revealed precepts, one would discover that they are, to a large extent at least, partially justified and possess much utilitarian value, although the wisdom and the view that the Creator had in mind in decreeing them is far above anything that man can grasp, as Scripture says: *For as the heavens are higher than the earth, so are My ways higher than your ways* (Isa. 55:9).

ST. THOMAS AQUINAS

5.5 The Ceremonial Laws

WHETHER THE OLD LAW COMPRISES CEREMONIAL, BESIDES MORAL, PRECEPTS

We proceed thus to the Third Article:—

Objection 1. It would seem that the Old Law does not comprise ceremonial, besides moral, precepts. For every law that is given to man is for the purpose of directing human actions. Now human actions are called moral, as stated above (Q. 1, A. 3). Therefore it seems that the Old Law given to men should not comprise other than moral precepts.

Obj. 2. Further, those precepts that are styled ceremonial seem to refer to the Divine worship. But Divine worship is the act of a virtue, viz., religion, which, as Tully says (*De Invent.* ii) *offers worship and ceremony to the Godhead.* Since, then, the moral precepts are about acts of virtue, as stated above (A. 2), it seems that the ceremonial precepts should not be distinct from the moral.

Obj. 3. Further, the ceremonial precepts seem to be those which signify something figuratively. But, as Augustine observes (*De Doctr. Christ.* ii. 3, 4), *of all signs employed by men words hold the first place.* Therefore there was no need for the Law to contain ceremonial precepts about certain figurative actions.

On the contrary, It is written (Deut. iv 13, 14): *Ten words . . . He wrote in two tables of stone; and He commanded me at that time that I should teach you the ceremonies and judgments which you shall do.* But the ten commandments of the Law are moral precepts. Therefore besides the moral precepts there are others which are ceremonial.

I answer that, As stated above (A. 2), the Divine law is instituted chiefly in order to direct men to God; while human law is instituted chiefly in order to direct men in relation to one another. Hence human laws have not concerned themselves with the institution of anything relating to Divine worship except as affecting the common good of mankind: and for this reason they

From *Summa Theologica*, Parts I–II, trans. Dominican Fathers of English Province (New York: Benziger, Inc., 1947). Reprinted by permission of the publisher.

have devised many institutions relating to Divine matters, according as it seemed expedient for the formation of human morals; as may be seen in the rites of the Gentiles. On the other hand the Divine law directed men to one another according to the demands of that order whereby man is directed to God, which order was the chief aim of that law. Now man is directed to God not only by the interior acts of the mind, which are faith, hope, and love, but also by certain external works, whereby man makes profession of his subjection to God: and it is these works that are said to belong to the Divine worship. This worship is called *ceremony*,—the *munia*, i.e., gifts, of *Ceres* (who was the goddess of fruits), as some say: because, at first, offerings were made to God from the fruits:—or because, as Valerius Maximus states, the word *ceremony* was introduced among the Latins, to signify the Divine worship, being derived from a town near Rome called *Caere:* since, when Rome was taken by the Gauls, the sacred chattels of the Romans were taken thither and most carefully preserved. Accordingly those precepts of the Law which refer to the Divine worship are specially called ceremonial.

Reply Obj. 1. Human acts extend also to the Divine worship: and therefore the Old Law given to man contains precepts about these matters also.

Reply Obj. 2. As stated above (Q. 91, A. 3), the precepts of the natural law are general, and require to be determined: and they are determined both by human law and by Divine law. And just as these very determinations which are made by human law are said to be, not of natural, but of positive law; so the determinations of the precepts of the natural law, effected by the Divine law, are distinct from the moral precepts which belong to the natural law. Wherefore to worship God, since it is an act of virtue, belongs to a moral precept; but the determination of this precept, namely that He is to be worshipped by such and such sacrifices, and such and such offerings, belongs to the ceremonial precepts. Consequently the ceremonial precepts are distinct from the moral precepts.

Reply Obj. 3. As Dionysius says (*Cœl. Hier.* i), the things of God cannot be manifested to men except by means of sensible similitudes. Now these similitudes move the soul more when they are not only expressed in words, but also offered to the senses. Wherefore the things of God are set forth in the Scriptures not only by similitudes expressed in words, as in the case of metaphorical expressions; but also by similitudes of things set before the eyes, which pertains to the ceremonial precepts.

OF THE CEREMONIAL PRECEPTS IN THEMSELVES

We must now consider the ceremonial precepts: and first we must consider them in themselves; secondly, their cause; thirdly, their duration. Under the first head there are four points of inquiry: (1) The nature of the ceremonial precepts: (2) Whether they are figurative? (3) Whether there should have been many of them? (4) Of their various kinds.

WHETHER THE NATURE OF THE CEREMONIAL PRECEPTS CONSISTS IN THEIR PERTAINING TO THE WORSHIP OF GOD

We proceed thus to the First Article:—

Objection 1. It would seem that the nature of the ceremonial precepts does not consist in their pertaining to the worship of God. Because, in the Old Law, the Jews were given certain precepts about abstinence from food (Levit. xi); and about refraining from certain kinds of clothes, *e.g.* (Levit. xix. 19): *Thou shalt not wear a garment that is woven of two sorts; and again* (Num. xv. 38): *To make to themselves fringes in the corners of their garments.* But these are not moral precepts; since they do not remain in the New Law. Nor are they judicial precepts; since they do not pertain to the pronouncing of judgment between man and man. Therefore they are ceremonial precepts. Yet they seem in no way to pertain to the worship of God. Therefore the nature of the ceremonial precepts does not consist in their pertaining to Divine Worship.

Obj. 2. Further, some state that the ceremonial precepts are those which pertain to solemnities; as though they were so called from the *cerei* (candles) which are lit up on those occasions. But many other things besides solemnities pertain to the worship of God. Therefore it does not seem that the ceremonial precepts are so called from their pertaining to the Divine worship.

Obj. 3. Further, some say that the ceremonial precepts are patterns, i.e., rules, of salvation: because the Greek καιoε is the same as the Latin *salve*. But all the precepts of the Law are rules of salvation, and not only those that pertain to the worship of God. Therefore not only those precepts which pertain to the Divine worship are called ceremonial.

Obj. 4. Further, Rabbi Moses says (*Doct. Perplex.* iii) that the ceremonial precepts are those for which there is no evident reason. But there is evident reason for many things pertaining to the worship of God; such as the observance of the Sabbath, the feasts of the Passover and of the Tabernacles, and many other things, the reason for which is set down in the Law. Therefore the ceremonial precepts are not those which pertain to the worship of God.

On the contrary, It is written (Exod. xvii. 19, 20): *Be thou to the people in those things that pertain to God . . . and . . . shew the people the ceremonies and the manner of worshipping.*

I answer that, As stated above (Q. 99, A. 4), the ceremonial precepts are determinations of the moral precepts whereby man is directed to God, just as the judicial precepts are determinations of the moral precepts whereby he is directed to his neighbor. Now man is directed to God by the worship due to Him. Wherefore those precepts are properly called ceremonial, which pertain to the Divine worship.—The reason for their being so called was given above (*ibid.,* A. 3), when we established the distinction between the ceremonial and the other precepts.

Reply Obj. 1. The Divine worship includes not only sacrifices and the like, which seem to be directed to God immediately, but also those things whereby His worshippers are duly prepared to worship Him: thus too in other matters, whatever is preparatory to the end comes under the science whose object is the end. Accordingly those precepts of the Law which regard the clothing and food of God's worshippers, and other such matters, pertain to a certain preparation of the ministers, with the view of fitting them for the Divine worship: just as those who administer to a king make use of certain special observances. Consequently such are contained under the ceremonial precepts.

Reply Obj. 2. The alleged explanation of the name does not seem very probable: especially as the Law does not contain many instances of the lighting of candles in solemnities; since, even the lamps of the Candlestick were furnished with *oil of olives*, as stated in Levit. xxiv. 2. Nevertheless we may say that all things pertaining to the Divine worship were more carefully observed on solemn festivals: so that all ceremonial precepts may be included under the observance of solemnities.

Reply Obj. 3. Neither does this explanation of the name appear to be very much to the point, since the word *ceremony* is not Greek but Latin. We may say, however, that, since man's salvation is from God, those precepts above all seem to be rules of salvation, which direct man to God: and accordingly those which refer to Divine worship are called ceremonial precepts.

Reply Obj. 4. This explanation of the ceremonial precepts has a certain amount of probability: not that they are called ceremonial precisely because there is no evident reason for them; this is a kind of consequence. For, since the precepts referring to the Divine worship must needs be figurative, as we shall state further on (A. 2), the consequence is that the reason for them is not so very evident.

WHETHER THE CEREMONIAL PRECEPTS ARE FIGURATIVE

We proceed thus to the Second Article:—

Objection 1. It would seem that the ceremonial precepts are not figurative. For it is the duty of every teacher to express himself in such a way as to be easily understood, as Augustine states (*De Doctr. Christ.* iv. 4, 10) and this seems very necessary in the framing of a law: because precepts of law are proposed to the populace; for which reason a law should be manifest, as Isidore declares (*Etym.* v. 21). If therefore the precepts of the Law were given as figures of something, it seems unbecoming that Moses should have delivered these precepts without explaining what they signified.

Obj. 2. Further, whatever is done for the worship of God, should be entirely free from unfittingness. But the performance of actions in representation of others, seems to savor of the theatre or of the drama: because formerly the actions performed in theatres were done to represent the actions of others. Therefore it seems that such things should not be done for the worship of

God. But the ceremonial precepts are ordained to the Divine worship, as stated above (A. 1). Therefore they should not be figurative.

Obj. 3. Further, Augustine says (*Enchirid.* iii., iv) that *God is worshipped chiefly by faith, hope, and charity.* But the precepts of faith, hope, and charity are not figurative. Therefore the ceremonial precepts should not be figurative.

Obj. 4. Further, Our Lord said (Jo. iv. 24): *God is a spirit, and they that adore Him, must adore Him in spirit and in truth.* But a figure is not the very truth: in fact one is condivided with the other. Therefore the ceremonial precepts, which refer to the Divine worship, should not be figurative.

On the contrary, The Apostle says (Coloss. ii, 16, 17): *Let no man . . . judge you in meat or in drink, or in respect of a festival day, or of the new moon, or of the sabbaths, which are a shadow of things to come.*

I answer that, As stated above (A. 1. Q. 99, AA. 3, 4), the ceremonial precepts are those which refer to the worship of God. Now the Divine worship is twofold: internal, and external. For since man is composed of soul and body, each of these should be applied to the worship of God; the soul by an interior worship; the body by an outward worship: hence it is written (Ps. lxxxiii. 3): *My heart and my flesh have rejoiced in the living God.* And as the body is ordained to God through the soul, so the outward worship is ordained to the internal worship. Now interior worship consists in the soul being united to God by the intellect and affections. Wherefore according to the various ways in which the intellect and affections of the man who worships God are rightly united to God, his external actions are applied in various ways to the Divine worship.

For in the state of future bliss, the human intellect will gaze on the Divine Truth in Itself. Wherefore the external worship will not consist in anything figurative, but solely in the praise of God, proceeding from the inward knowledge and affection, according to Isa. li. 3: *Joy and gladness shall be found therein, thanksgiving and the voice of praise.*

But in the present state of life, we are unable to gaze upon the Divine Truth in Itself, and we need the ray of Divine light to shine upon us under the form of certain sensible figures, as Dionysius states (*Cœl. Hier.* i); in various ways, however, according to the various states of human knowledge. For under the Old Law, neither was the Divine Truth manifest in Itself, nor was the way leading to that manifestation as yet opened out, as the Apostle declares (Heb. ix. 8). Hence the external worship of the Old Law needed to be figurative not only of the future truth to be manifested in our heavenly country, but also of Christ, Who is the way leading to that heavenly manifestation. But under the New Law this way is already revealed: and therefore it needs no longer to be foreshadowed as something future, but to be brought to our minds as something past or present: and the truth of the glory to come, which is not yet revealed, alone needs to be foreshadowed. This is what the Apostle says (Heb. xi. 1): *The Law has* (Vulg.,—*having*) *a shadow of the good things to come, not the very image of the things:* for a shadow is less than an image; so that the image belongs to the New Law, but the shadow to the Old.

Reply Obj. 1. The things of God are not to be revealed to man except in proportion to his capacity: else he would be in danger of downfall, were he to despise what he cannot grasp. Hence it was more beneficial that the Divine mysteries should be revealed to uncultured people under a veil of figures, that thus they might know them at least implicitly by using those figures to the honor of God.

Reply Obj. 2. Just as human reason fails to grasp poetical expressions on account of their being lacking in truth, so does it fail to grasp Divine things perfectly, on account of the sublimity of the truth they contain: and therefore in both cases there is need of signs by means of sensible figures.

Reply Obj. 3. Augustine is speaking there of internal worship; to which, however, external worship should be ordained, as stated above.

The same answer applies to the Fourth Objection: because men were taught by Him to practice more perfectly the spiritual worship of God.

WHETHER THERE SHOULD HAVE BEEN MANY CEREMONIAL PRECEPTS

We proceed thus to the Third Article:—

Objection 1. It would seem that there should not have been many ceremonial precepts. For those things which conduce to an end should be proportionate to that end. But the ceremonial precepts, as stated above (AA. 1, 2), are ordained to the worship of God, and to the foreshadowing of Christ. Now *there is but one God, of Whom are all things, . . . and one Lord Jesus Christ, by Whom are all things* (1 Cor. viii. 6). Therefore there should not have been many ceremonial precepts.

Obj. 2. Further, the great number of the ceremonial precepts was an occasion of transgression, according to the words of Peter (Acts xv. 10): *Why tempt you God, to put a yoke upon the necks of the disciples, which neither our fathers nor we have been able to bear?* Now the transgression of the Divine precepts is an obstacle to man's salvation. Since, therefore, every law should conduce to man's salvation, as Isidore says (*Etym.* v. 3), it seems that the ceremonial precepts should not have been given in great number.

Obj. 3. Further, the ceremonial precepts referred to the outward and bodily worship of God, as stated above (A. 2). But the Law should have lessened this bodily worship: since it directed men to Christ, Who taught them to worship God *in spirit and in truth*, as stated in John iv. 23. Therefore there should not have been many ceremonial precepts.

On the contrary, It is written (Osee viii. 12): *I shall write to them* (Vulg.,— him) *My manifold laws*; and (Job. xi. 6): *That He might show thee the secrets of His wisdom, and that His Law is manifold.*

I answer that, As stated above (Q. 96, A. 1), every law is given to a people. Now a people contains two kinds of men: some, prone to evil, who have to be coerced by the precepts of the law, as stated above (Q. 95, A. 1); some, inclined to good, either from nature or from custom, or rather from grace; and the like have to be taught and improved by means of the precepts of the law. Accordingly, with regard to both kinds of men it was expedient that the Old Law should contain many ceremonial precepts. For in that people there were many prone to idolatry; wherefore it was necessary to recall them by means of ceremonial precepts from the worship of idols to the worship of God. And since men served idols in many ways, it was necessary on the other hand to devise many means of repressing every single one: and again, to lay many obligations on such like men, in order that being burdened, as it were, by their duties to the Divine worship, they might have no time for the service of idols. As to those who were inclined to good, it was again necessary that there should be many ceremonial precepts; both because thus their mind was turned to God in many ways, and more continually; and because the mystery of Christ, which was foreshadowed by these ceremonial precepts, brought many boons to the world, and afforded men many considerations, which needed to be signified by various ceremonies.

Reply Obj. 1. When that which conduces to an end is sufficient to conduce thereto, then one such thing suffices for one end: thus one remedy, if it be efficacious, suffices sometimes to restore man to health, and then the remedy needs not to be repeated. But when that which conduces to an end is weak and imperfect, it needs to be multiplied: thus many remedies are given to a sick man, when one is not enough to heal him. Now the ceremonies of the Old Law were weak and imperfect, both for representing the mystery of Christ, on acount of its surpassing excellence; and for subjugating men's minds to God. Hence the Apostle says (Heb. vii. 18, 19): *There is a setting aside of the former commandment because of the weakness and unprofitableness thereof, for the law brought nothing to perfection.* Consequently these ceremonies needed to be in great number.

Reply Obj. 2. A wise lawgiver should suffer lesser transgressions, that the greater may be avoided. And therefore, in order to avoid the sin of idolatry, and the pride which would arise in the hearts of the Jews, were they to fulfil all the precepts of the Law, the fact that they would in consequence find many occasions of disobedience did not prevent God from giving them many ceremonial precepts.

Reply Obj. 3. The Old Law lessened bodily worship in many ways. Thus it forbade sacrifices to be offered in every place and by any person. Many such like things did it enact for the lessening of bodily worship; as Rabbi Moses the Egyptian testifies (*Doct. Perplex.* iii). Nevertheless it behooved not to attenuate the bodily worship of God so much as to allow men to fall away into the worship of idols.

OF THE CAUSES OF THE CEREMONIAL PRECEPTS

We must now consider the causes of the ceremonial precepts: under which head there are six points of inquiry: (1) Whether there was any cause for the ceremonial precepts? (2) Whether the cause of the ceremonial precepts was literal or figurative? (3) The causes of the sacrifices; (4) The causes of the sacraments; (5) The causes of the sacred things; (6) The causes of the observances.

WHETHER THERE WAS ANY CAUSE FOR THE CEREMONIAL PRECEPTS

We proceed thus to the First Article:—

Objection 1. It would seem that there was no cause for the ceremonial precepts. Because on Ephes. ii. 15, *Making void the law of the commandments*, the gloss says, i.e., *making void the Old Law as to the carnal observances, by substituting decrees*, i.e., *evangelical precepts, which are based on reason*. But if the observances of the Old Law were based on reason, it would have been useless to void them by the reasonable decrees of the New Law. Therefore there was no reason for the ceremonial observances of the Old Law.

Obj. 2. Further, the Old Law succeeded the law of nature. But in the law of nature there was a precept for which there was no reason save that man's obedience might be tested; as Augustine says (*Gen. ad lit.* viii. 6, 13), concerning the prohibition about the tree of life. Therefore in the Old Law there should have been some precepts for the purpose of testing man's obedience, having no reason in themselves.

Obj. 3. Further, man's works are called moral according as they proceed from reason. If therefore there is any reason for the ceremonial precepts, they would not differ from the moral precepts. It seems therefore that there was no cause for the ceremonial precepts: for the reason of a precept is taken from some cause.

On the contrary, It is written (Ps. xviii. 9): *The commandment of the Lord is lightsome, enlightening the eyes.* But the ceremonial precepts are commandments of God. Therefore they are lightsome: and yet they would not be so, if they had no reasonable cause. Therefore the ceremonial precepts have a reasonable cause.

I answer that, Since, according to the Philosopher (*Metaph.* i. 2), it is the function of a *wise man to do everything in order*, those things which proceed from the Divine wisdom must needs be well ordered, as the Apostle states (Rom. xiii. 1). Now there are two conditions required for things to be well ordered. First, that they be ordained to their due end, which is the principle of the whole order in matters of action: since those things that happen by chance outside the intention of the end, or which are not done seriously but for fun, are said to be inordinate. Secondly, that which is done in view of the end should be proportionate to the end. From this it follows that the reason for whatever conduces to the end is taken from the end: thus the reason for the disposition of a saw is taken from cutting, which is its end, as stated in *Phys.* ii. 9. Now it is evident that the ceremonial precepts, like all the other precepts of the Law, were institutions of Divine wisdom: hence it is written (Deut. iv. 6): *This is your wisdom and understanding in the sight of nations.* Consequently we must needs say that the ceremonial precepts were ordained to a certain end, wherefrom their reasonable causes can be gathered.

Reply Obj. 1. It may be said that there was no reason for the observances of the Old Law, in the sense that there was no reason in the very nature of the thing done: for instance that a garment should not be made of wool and linen. But there could be a reason for them in relation to something else: namely, in so far as something was signified or excluded thereby. On the other hand, the decrees of the New Law, which refer chiefly to faith and the love of God, are reasonable from the very nature of the act.

Reply Obj. 2. The reason for the prohibition concerning the tree of knowledge of good and evil was not that this tree was naturally evil: and yet this prohibition was reasonable in its relation to something else, in as much as it signified something. And so also the ceremonial precepts of the Old Law were reasonable on account of their relation to something else.

Reply Obj. 3. The moral precepts in their very nature have reasonable causes: as for instance, *Thou shalt not kill, Thou shalt not steal.* But the ceremonial precepts have a reasonable cause in their relation to something else, as stated above.

WHETHER THE CEREMONIAL PRECEPTS HAVE A LITERAL CAUSE OR MERELY A FIGURATIVE CAUSE

We proceed thus to the Second Article:—

Objection 1. It would seem that the ceremonial precepts have not a literal, but merely a figurative, cause. For among the ceremonial precepts, the chief was circumcision and the sacrifice of the paschal lamb. But neither of these had any but a figurative cause: because each was given as a sign. For it is written (Gen. xvii. 11): *You shall circumcise the flesh of your foreskin, that it may be for a sign of the covenant between Me and you:* and of the celebration of the Passover it is written (Exod. xiii. 9): *It shall be as a sign in thy hand, and as a memorial before thy eyes.* Therefore much more did the other ceremonial precepts have none but a figurative reason.

Obj. 2. Further, an effect is proportionate to its cause. But all the ceremoniel precepts are figurative, as stated above (Q. 101, A. 2). Therefore they have no other than a figurative cause.

Obj. 3. Further, if it be a matter of indifference whether a certain thing, considered in itself, be done in a particular way or not, it seems that it has not a literal cause. Now there are certain points in the ceremonial precepts, which appear to be a matter of indifference, as to whether they be done in one way or in another: for instance, the number of animals to be offered, and other such particular circumstances. Therefore there is no literal cause for the precepts of the Old Law.

On the contrary, Just as the ceremonial precepts foreshadowed Christ, so did the stories of the Old Testament: for it is written (1 Cor. x. 11) that *all (these things) happened to them in figure.* Now in the stories of the Old Testament, besides the mystical or figurative, there is the literal sense. Therefore the ceremonial precepts had also literal, besides their figurative causes.

I answer that, As stated above (A. 1), the reason for whatever conduces to an end must be taken from that end. Now the end of the ceremonial precepts was twofold: for they were ordained to the Divine worship, for that particular time, and to the foreshadowing of Christ; just as the words of the prophets regarded the time being in such a way as to be utterances figurative of the time to come, as Jerome says on Osee i. 3. Accordingly the reasons for the ceremonial precepts of the Old Law can be taken in two ways. First, in respect of the Divine worship which was to be observed for that particular time: and these reasons are literal: whether they refer to the shunning of idolatry; or recall certain Divine benefits; or remind men of the Divine excellence; or point out the disposition of mind which was then required in those who worshipped God.—Secondly, their reasons can be gathered from the point of view of their being ordained to foreshadow Christ: and thus their reasons are figurative and mystical: whether they be taken from Christ Himself and the Church, which pertains to the allegorical sense; or to the morals of the Christian people, which pertains to the moral sense; or to the state of future glory, in as much as we are brought thereto by Christ, which refers to the anagogical sense.

Reply Obj. 1. Just as the use of metaphorical expressions in Scripture belongs to the literal sense, because the words are employed in order to convey that particular meaning; so also the meaning of those legal ceremonies which commemorated certain Divine benefits on account of which they were instituted, and of others similar which belonged to that time, does not go beyond the order of literal causes. Consequently when we assert that the cause of the celebration of the Passover was its signification of the delivery from Egypt, or that circumcision was a sign of God's covenant with Abraham, we assign the literal cause.

Reply Obj. 2. This argument would avail, if the ceremonial precepts had been given merely as figures of things to come, and not for the purpose of worshipping God then and there.

Reply Obj. 3. As we stated when speaking of human laws (Q. 96, AA. 1, 6), there is a reason for them in the abstract, but not in regard to particular conditions, which depend on the judgment of those who frame them; so also many particular determinations in the ceremonies of the Old Law have no literal cause, but only a figurative cause; whereas in the abstract they have a literal cause.

PRAYER
WHETHER IT IS BECOMING TO PRAY

We proceed thus to the Second Article:—

Objection 1. It would seem that is unbecoming to pray. Prayer seems to be necessary in order that we may make our needs known to the person to whom we pray. But according to Matth. vi. 32, *Your Father knoweth that you have need of all these things.* Therefore it is not becoming to pray to God.

Obj. 2. Further, by prayer we bend the mind of the person to whom we pray, so that he may do what is asked of him. But God's mind is unchangeable and inflexible, according to 1 Kings xv. 29, *But the Triumpher in Israel will not spare, and will not be moved to repentance.* Therefore it is not fitting that we should pray to God.

Obj. 3. Further, it is more liberal to give to one that asks not, than to one who asks, because, according to Seneca (*De Benefic.* ii), *nothing is bought more dearly than what is bought with prayers.* But God is supremely liberal. Therefore it would seem unbecoming to pray to God.

On the contrary, It is written (Luke xvii. 1): *We ought always to pray, and not to faint.*

I answer that, Among the ancients there was a threefold error concerning prayer. Some held that human affairs are not ruled by Divine providence; whence it would follow that it is useless to pray and to worship God at all: of these it is written (Malach. iii. 14): *You have said: He laboreth in vain that serveth God.* Another opinion held that all things even in human affairs, happen of necessity, whether by reason of the unchangeableness of Divine providence, or through the compelling influence of the stars, or on account of the connection of causes: and this opinion also excluded the utility of prayer. There was a third opinion of those who held that human affairs are indeed ruled by Divine providence, and that they do not happen of necessity; yet they deemed the disposition of Divine providence to be changeable, and that it is changed by prayers and other things pertaining to the worship of God. All these opinions were disproved in the First Part (Q. 19, AA. 7, 8; Q. 22, AA. 2, 4; Q. 115, A. 6; Q. 116). Wherefore it behooves us so to account for the utility of prayer as neither to impose necessity on human affairs subject to Divine providence, nor to imply changeableness on the part of the Divine disposition.

In order to throw light on this question we must consider that Divine providence disposes not only what effects shall take place, but also from what causes and in what order these effects shall proceed. Now among other causes human acts are the causes of certain effects. Wherefore it must be that men do certain actions, not that thereby they may change the Divine disposition, but that by those actions they may achieve certain effects according to the order of the Divine disposition: and the same is to be said of natural causes. And so is it with regard to prayer. For we pray, not that we may change the Divine disposition, but that we may impetrate that which God has disposed to be fulfilled by our prayers, in other words *that by asking, men may deserve to receive what Almighty God from eternity has disposed to give,* as Gregory says (*Dial.* i. 8).

Reply Obj. 1. We need to pray to God, not in order to make known to Him our needs or desires, but that we ourselves may be reminded of the necessity of having recourse to God's help in these matters.

Reply Obj. 2. As stated above, our motive in praying is, not that we may change the Divine disposition, but that, by our prayers, we may obtain what God has appointed.

Reply Obj. 3. God bestows many things on us out of His liberality, even without our asking for them: but that He wishes to bestow certain things on us at our asking, is for the sake of our good, namely, that we may acquire confidence in having recourse to God, and that we may recognize in Him the Author of our goods. Hence Chrysostom says: *Think what happiness is granted thee, what honor bestowed on thee, when thou conversest with God in prayer, when thou talkest with Christ, when thou askest what thou wilt, whatever thou desirest.*

WHETHER PRAYER IS AN ACT OF RELIGION

We proceed thus to the Third Article:—

Objection 1. It would seem that prayer is not an act of religion. Since religion is a part of justice, it resides in the will as in its subject. But prayer belongs to the intellective part, as stated above (A. 1). Therefore prayer seems to be an act, not of religion, but of the gift of understanding whereby the mind ascends to God.

Obj. 2. Further, the act of *latria* falls under a necessity of precept. But prayer does not seem to come under a necessity of precept, but to come from the mere will, since it is nothing else than a petition for what we will. Therefore prayer seemingly is not an act of religion.

Obj. 3. Further, it seems to belong to religion that one *offers worship and ceremonial rites to the Godhead.* But prayer seems not to offer anything to God, but to ask to obtain something from Him. Therefore prayer is not an act of religion.

On the contrary, It is written (Ps. cxl. 2: *Let my prayer be directed as incense in Thy sight:* and a gloss on the passage says that *it was to signify this that under the Old Law incense was said to be offered for a sweet smell to the Lord.* Now this belongs to religion. Therefore prayer is an act of religion.

I answer that, As stated above (Q. 81, AA. 2, 4), it belongs properly to religion to show honor to God, wherefore all those things through which reverence is shown to God, belong to religion. Now man shows reverence to God by means of prayer, in so far as he subjects himself to Him, and by praying confesses that he needs Him as the Author of his goods. Hence it is evident that prayer is properly an act of religion.

Reply Obj. 1. The will moves the other powers of the soul to its end, as stated above (Q. 82, A. 1, *ad* 1), and therefore religion, which is in the will, directs the acts of the other powers to the reverence of God. Now among the other powers of the soul the intellect is the highest, and the nearest to the will; and consequently after devotion which belongs to the will, prayer which belongs to the intellective part is the chief of the acts of religion, since by it religion directs man's intellect to God.

Reply Obj. 2. It is a matter of precept not only that we should ask for what we desire, but also that we should desire aright. But to desire comes under a precept of charity, whereas to ask comes under a precept of religion, which precept is expressed in Matth. vii. 7, where it is said: *Ask and ye shall receive.*

Reply Obj. 3. By praying man surrenders his mind to God, since he subjects it to Him with reverence and, so to speak, presents it to Him, as appears from the words of Dionysius quoted above (A. 1, *Obj.* 2). Wherefore just as the human mind excels exterior things, whether bodily members, or those external things that are employed for God's service, so too, prayer surpasses other acts of religion.

WHETHER WE OUGHT TO ASK FOR SOMETHING DEFINITE WHEN WE PRAY

We proceed thus to the Fifth Article:—

Objection 1. It would seem that we ought not to ask for anything definite when we pray to God. According to Damascene (*De Fide Orthod.* iii. 24), *to pray is to ask becoming things of God*; wherefore it is useless to pray for what is inexpedient, according to James iv. 3, *You ask, and receive not: because you ask amiss.* Now according to Rom. viii. 26, *we know not what we should pray for as we ought.* Therefore we ought not to ask for anything definite when we pray.

Obj. 2. Further, those who ask another person for something definite strive to incline his will to do what they wish themselves. But we ought not to endeavor to make God will what we will; on the contrary, we ought to strive to will what He wills, according to a gloss on Ps. xxxii. 1, *Rejoice in the Lord, O ye just.* Therefore we ought not to ask God for anything definite when we pray.

Obj. 3. Further, evil things are not to be sought from God; and as to good things, God Himself invites us to take them. Now it is useless to ask a person to give you what he invites you to take. Therefore we ought not to ask God for anything definite in our prayers.

On the contrary, Our Lord (Matth. vi and Luke xi) taught His disciples to ask definitely for those things which are contained in the petitions of the Lord's Prayer.

I answer that, According to Valerius Maximus, *Socrates deemed that we should ask the immortal gods for nothing else but that they should grant us good things, because they at any rate know what is good for each one, whereas when we pray we frequently ask for what it had been better for us not to obtain.* This opinion is true to a certain extent, as to those things which may have an evil result, and which man may use ill or well, such as *riches, by which,* as stated by the same authority (*ibid.*), *many have come to an evil end; honors, which have ruined many; power, of which we frequently witness the unhappy results; splendid marriages, which sometimes bring about the total wreck of a family.* Nevertheless there are certain goods which man cannot ill use, because they cannot have an evil result. Such are those which are the object of beatitude and whereby we merit it: and these the saints seek absolutely when they pray, as in Ps. lxxix. 4, *Show us Thy face, and we shall be saved,* and again in Ps. cxviii. 35, *Lead me into the path of Thy commandments.*

Reply Obj. 1. Although man cannot by himself know what he ought to pray for, *the Spirit,* as stated in the same passage, *helpeth our infirmity,* since by inspiring us with holy desires. He makes us ask for what is right. Hence our Lord said (Jo. iv. 24) that true adorers *must adore . . . in spirit and in truth.*

Reply Obj. 2. When in our prayers we ask for things concerning our salvation, we conform our will to God's, of Whom it is written (1 Tim. ii. 4) that *He will have all men to be saved.*

Reply Obj. 3. God so invites us to take good things, that we may approach to them not by the steps of the body, but by pious desires and devout prayers.

WHETHER MAN OUGHT TO ASK GOD FOR TEMPORAL THINGS WHEN HE PRAYS

We proceed thus to the Sixth Article:—

Objection 1. It would seem that man ought not to ask God for temporal things when he prays. We seek what we ask for in prayer. But we should not seek for temporal things, for it is written (Matth. vi. 33): *Seek ye . . . first the kingdom of God, and His justice: and all these things shall be added unto you,* that is to say, temporal things, which, says He, we are not to seek, but they will be added to what we seek. Therefore temporal things are not to be asked of God in prayer.

Obj. 2. Further, no one asks save for that which he is solicitous about. Now we ought not to have solicitude for temporal things, according to the saying of Matth. vi. 25, *Be not solicitous for your life, what you shall eat.* Therefore we ought not to ask for temporal things when we pray.

Obj. 3. Further, by prayer our mind should be raised up to God. But by asking for temporal things, it descends to things beneath it, against the saying of the Apostle (2 Cor. iv. 18), *While we look not at the things which are seen, but at the things which are not seen. For the things which are seen are temporal, but the things which are not seen are eternal.* Therefore man ought not to ask God for temporal things when he prays.

Obj. 4. Further, man ought not to ask of God other than good and useful things. But sometimes temporal things, when we have them, are harmful, not only in a spiritual sense, but also in a material sense. Therefore we should not ask God for them in our prayers.

On the contrary, It is written (Prov. xxx. 8): *Give me only the necessaries of life.*

I answer that, As Augustine says (*ad Probam, de orando Deum, Ep.* cxxx. 12): *It is lawful to pray for what it is lawful to desire.* Now it is lawful to desire temporal things, not indeed principally, by placing our end therein, but as helps whereby we are assisted in tending towards beatitude, in so far, to wit, as they are the means of supporting the life of the body, and are of service to us as instruments in performing acts of virtue, as also the Philosopher states (*Ethic.* i. 8). Augustine too says the same to Proba (*ibid.* 6. 7) when he states that *it is not unbecoming for anyone to desire enough for a livelihood, and no more; for this sufficiency is desired, not for its own sake, but for the welfare of the body, or that we should desire to be clothed in a way befitting one's station, so as not to be out of keeping with those among whom we have to live. Accordingly we ought to pray that we may keep these things if we have them, and if we have them not, that we may gain possession of them.*

Reply Obj. 1. We should seek temporal things not in the first but in the second place. Hence Augustine says (*De Serm. Dom. in Monte* ii. 16): *When He says that this* (i. e., the kingdom of God) *is to be sought first, He implies that the other* (i.e., temporal goods) *is to be sought afterwards, not in time but in importance, this as being our good, the other as our need.*

Reply Obj. 2. Not all solicitude about temporal things is forbidden, but that which is superfluous and inordinate, as stated above (Q. 55, A. 6).

Reply Obj. 3. When our mind is intent on temporal things in order that it may rest in them, it remains immersed therein; but when it is intent on them in relation to the acquisition of beatitude, it is not lowered by them, but raises them to a higher level.

Reply Obj. 4. From the very fact that we ask for temporal things not as the principal object of our petition, but as subordinate to something else, we ask God for them in the sense that they may be granted to us in so far as they are expedient for salvation.

WHETHER PRAYER SHOULD BE VOCAL

We proceed thus to the Twelfth Article:—

Objection 1. It would seem that prayer ought not to be vocal. As stated above (A. 4), prayer is addressed chiefly to God. Now God knows the language of the heart. Therefore it is useless to employ vocal prayer.

Obj. 2. Further, prayer should lift man's mind to God, as stated above (A. 1, *ad* 2). But words, like other sensible objects, prevent man from ascending to God by contemplation. Therefore we should not use words in our prayers.

Obj. 3. Further, prayer should be offered to God in secret, according to Matth. vi. 6, *But thou, when thou shalt pray, enter into thy chamber, and having shut the door, pray to thy Father in secret.* But prayer loses its secrecy by being expressed vocally. Therefore prayer should not be vocal.

On the contrary, It is written (Ps. cxli. 2): *I cried to the Lord with my voice, with my voice I made supplication to the Lord.*

I answer that, Prayer is twofold, common and individual. Common prayer is that which is offered to God by the ministers of the Church representing the body of the faithful: wherefore such like prayer should come to the knowledge of the whole people for whom it is offered: and this would not be possible unless it were vocal prayer. Therefore it is reasonably ordained that the ministers of the Church should say these prayers even in a loud voice, so that they may come to the knowledge of all!

On the other hand individual prayer is that which is offered by any single person, whether he pray for himself or for others; and it is not essential to such a prayer as this that it be vocal. And yet the voice is employed in such like prayers for three reasons. First, in order to excite interior devotion, whereby the mind of the person praying is raised to God, because by means of external signs, whether of words or of deeds, the human mind is moved as regards apprehension, and consequently also as regards the affections. Hence Augustine says (*ad Probam, Ep.* cxxx. 9) that *by means of words and other signs we arouse ourselves more effectively to an increase of holy desires.* Hence then alone should we use words and such like signs when they help to excite the mind internally. But if they distract or in any way impede the mind we should abstain from them; and this happens chiefly to those whose mind is sufficiently prepared for devotion without having recourse to those signs. Wherefore the Psalmist (Ps. xxvi. 8) said: *My heart hath said to Thee: "My face hath sought Thee,"* and we read of Anna (1 Kings i. 13) that *she spoke in her heart.* Secondly, the voice is used in praying as though to pay a debt, so that man may serve God with all that he has from God, that is to say, not only with his mind, but also with his body: and this applies to prayer considered especially as satisfactory. Hence it is written (Osee xiv. 3): *Take away all iniquity, and receive the good: and we will render the calves of our lips.* Thirdly, we have recourse to vocal prayer, through a certain overflow from the soul into the body, through excess of feeling, according to Ps. xv. 9, *My heart hath been glad, and my tongue hath rejoiced.*

Reply Obj. 1. Vocal prayer is employed, not in order to tell God something

He does not know, but in order to lift up the mind of the person praying or of other persons to God.

Reply Obj. 2. Words about other matters distract the mind and hinder the devotion of those who pray: but words signifying some object of devotion lift up the mind, especially one that is less devout.

Reply Obj. 3. As Chrysostom says, *our Lord forbids one to pray in presence of others in order that one may be seen by others. Hence when you pray, do nothing strange to draw men's attention, either by shouting so as to be heard by others, or by openly striking the heart, or extending the hands, so as to be seen by many. And yet, according* to Augustine (*De Serm. Dom in Monte* ii. 3), *it is not wrong to be seen by men, but to do this or that in order to be seen by men.*

GARETH B. MATTHEWS

5.6 Bodily Motions and Religious Feelings

For when men pray they do with the members of their bodies what befits suppliants—when they bend their knees and stretch out their hands, or even prostrate themselves, and whatever else they do visibly, although their invisible will and the intention of their heart is known to God. Nor does He need these signs for the human mind to be laid bare to Him. But in this way a man excites himself to pray more and to groan more humbly and more fervently. I do not know how it is that, although these motions of the body cannot come to be without a motion of the mind preceding them, when they have been made, visibly and externally, that invisible inner motion which caused them is itself strengthened. And in this manner the disposition of the heart which preceded them in order that they might be made, grows stronger because they are made. Of course if someone is constrained or even bound, so that he cannot do these things with his limbs, it does not follow that, when he is stricken with remorse, the inner man does not pray and prostrate himself before the eyes of God in his most secret chamber.

(Augustine: *De cura pro mortuis* 5.7)

One smiles and tells the expert chef how good the sauce béarnaise is, not so much to inform him about the sauce (he knows better than we do how good it is) as to assure him that we are enjoying it and that we appreciate his ef-

From the *Canadian Journal of Philosophy* 1 (1971): 75–86. Reprinted by permission of the Canadian Association for Publishing in Philosophy.

forts. But when a man kneels in his pew and repeats a litany of thanksgiving it is not, it seems, that he means to be informing God of anything—not even of his thankfulness. For God, unlike the chef, has no need of information.

So why do religious men do all the things they do in prayer "with the members of their bodies"?

The answer Augustine gives in the above passage from his treatise, "On the Care of the Dead," is that the bodily performance of ritual has the effect of intensifying appropriate religious attitudes and affections. (". . . in this way a man excites himself to pray more and to groan more humbly and more fervently.") Yet Augustine is puzzled by his answer. "I do not know how it is," he says.[1]

And he should be puzzled. For, as Augustine conceives it, the intensification of a religious attitude or feeling by the performance of a ritualistic act is a case of movements of the body having the effect of moving the soul. (". . . when [these motions of the body] have been made, visibly and externally, that invisible inner motion which caused them is itself strengthened.") And this never happens—it cannot happen. For, according to Augustine, the soul, any soul, is superior to the body, any body (*Enarrationes in psalmos* 145.3 and *De musica* 6.5.8); and that which is inferior can never move that which is superior (*De genesi ad litteram* 12.16.33).

There would have been an even better reason for Augustinian puzzlement. Augustine, like Descartes, conceives the soul and the body as two different things of such disparate sorts that the idea of interaction between a body and a soul becomes incomprehensible. Augustine is presumably led to overlook this incomprehensibility by the (to him) very obvious fact that the soul *does* affect the body (c.f., e.g., *De genesi ad litteram* 12.19.41). Perhaps a similarity robust sense of fact leads him to throw out his metaphysical principle about the superior and the inferior and to concede that the actual performance of ritual often does intensify the attitudes and feelings that give rise to it.

Sometimes, of course, the reverse is true. A child who is made to say "Thank

---

[1]In a passage somewhat reminiscent of Augustine, Jonathan Edwards says this: "To instance in the duty of prayer: it is manifest that we are not appointed in this duty to declare God's perfections. His majesty, holiness, goodness, and all-sufficiency, and our meanness, emptiness, dependence, and unworthiness, and our wants and desires, to inform God of these things, or to incline His heart, and prevail with Him to be willing to show us mercy; but suitably to affect our own hearts with the things we express, and so to prepare us to receive the blessings we ask. And such gestures and manner of external behaviour in the worship of God, which custom has made to be significations of humility and reverence, can be of no further use than as they have some tendency to affect our own hearts, or the hearts of others." (*The Religious Affections* 2.9) Edwards's suggestion that one reason for gesticulation is to affect the hearts of others seems a natural addition to what Augustine says. It is noteworthy, however, that Edwards, unlike Augustine, shows no puzzlement over the idea that "external behaviour" might have "some tendency to affect our own hearts."

you" upon receipt of any and every benefaction may thereby be made more thankful; he may also be made more resentful. It all depends.

Some people are annoyed and offended by ritual. Even those for whom characteristically religious attitudes are enormously important may abhor ritual; indeed they may abhor ritual precisely because they feel it encourages the wrong feelings and attitudes.

Augustine can hardly have forgotten that it was Jesus who condemned the Pharisee's energetic recitation of a public prayer. Jesus advised praying in secret, where concern with externals could be eliminated or at least minimized. Perhaps this is a second reason for Augustine's embarrassment and puzzlement in the passage above. Aware that Jesus criticized ritualizers (cf. Augustine's *De sermone domini in monte* 1.3) Augustine nevertheless finds himself somewhat uneasily suggesting that the behavior of the outer man often intensifies the spiritual motions of the inner man.

II

Metaphysics and theology aside, it seems obviously true that sometimes and for some people participation in a liturgical rite nurtures certain religious attitudes and affections. But why? Well, if I refer to myself as a poor and miserable sinner often enough, I may come finally to believe that this is what I am. Is this not an honored truth of both pedagogy and propaganda?

Now suppose I bow or kneel. This in itself may have an important effect upon my attitudes (the primary meaning of 'attitude' is relevant to the point), even though it does not involve making an assertion.

I suppose we might try to understand the effect of non-verbal gestures and ritualistic movements in terms of what they symbolize—what they "say."[2] Kneeling, e.g., "says": "I am a suppliant."[3] Then we could add that the performance of these ritualistic acts, like the repetition of a statement, encourages one to believe what is thereby "said."

Yet this is all much too easy. Not just any old repetition of a statement encourages belief. Not just any old performance of a ritual instills the appropriate attitudes. The mocking repetition of a statement may undermine its credibility. And the pharasical performance of a ritual may discourage the favored attitudes. At most it is sincere, or at least apparently sincere, repetition that instills belief.

Now, however, we have torn ourselves loose from the terms of Augustine's

---

[2]"No less than words, actions or gestures are also a type of language; they too hold a message for us. They have a meaning which the person who sincerely wishes to pray the Liturgy must get to know. Whether used by man for practical or symbolical reasons, gestures or ceremonies help man to express himself better, make his thought and intent clearer and more vivid." *Fundamentals of the Liturgy* by John H. Miller C.S.C. (Notre Dame: Fides, 1959), p. 188.

[3]"In the Liturgy . . . kneeling was usually associated with fasting and was a penitential and suppliant posture." *op. cit.* p. 192.

problem. His problem is how what the outer man does can affect the inner man—how the mere "motions of the body," motions that "cannot come to be without a motion of the mind preceding them," can affect the mind itself. That Augustine identifies the outer man with the body, something merely physical, that "part" of a man buried at death, is shown in this passage from *The City of God*:

> . . . a man is not just a body, or just a soul, but a being made up of body and soul. . . . The soul is not the whole man, but the better part of a man; the body is not the whole, but the inferior part of a man. When both are joined together they have the name "man," which, however, they do not either one lose when we speak of them singly. For who is prohibited from saying, in ordinary language, "That man is dead and is now in peace or in torment," though this can be said only of the soul; or "That man is buried in that place or in that," though this cannot be understood except as referring to the body alone? Will they say that Holy Scripture follows no such usage? On the contrary, it so thoroughly adopts it that even when a man is alive and his body and soul are joined together it calls each of them singly by the name "man", speaking of the soul as the "inner man" and the body as the "outer man"— as if there were two men, although both together are one man. [*De civitate dei* 13.24.2]

Now clearly a motion of the outer man (or body), so understood, cannot be either sincere or insincere, mocking or serious. It takes the action of the whole man—body and mind (or soul)—to be insincere. According to Augustine its insincerity will lie in a certain discrepancy between what the *outer* man does and what the *inner* man does.

This means that our effort to understand a physical motion as "saying" something (e.g., "I am a suppliant") is misplaced. For a mere motion of an Augustinian body could not by itself have meaning in the way required.

Thus we cannot explain how the mere motion of the body in ritual inculcates religious attitudes and intensifies religious feelings because it is not the mere motion of the body that has this effect. What has this effect, or may have it, is the (more or less) sincere understanding performance of ritual.

III

So the puzzle Augustine leaves himself and us with is a specious puzzle. What about the puzzle Augustine starts with? That is, what about the worry as to why one need pray outwardly when God knows already what is in a man's heart? Augustine's answer to this worry—that the bodily performance of ritual may have the effect of intensifying appropriate religious attitudes and affections—suggests that Augustine's question ("Why need one pray outwardly?") is really two questions. One question is "Why pray, when God knows already everything one could possibly tell him?" and the other is "Why pray *outwardly*, with 'the members of the body', when God knows already one's 'invisible will' and the intention of one's heart?"

It seems perverse to run these two questions together. Surely one can't make a good judgment as to whether what Augustine offers us is a good reason for praying *outwardly* until one is reasonably clear about what a good reason for *praying* might be. And there is a further point. Suppose the reason for praying were Q. It might actually follow from Q (or perhaps from Q together with certain natural assumptions) that one ought often to pray *outwardly*. So an answer to the first question might actually be all, or most, of an answer to the second.

Perhaps Augustine tends to conceive praying inwardly as simply *having* certain feelings and attitudes without expressing them, much as one might conceive giving alms inwardly as simply having feelings of charity. If this is the way Augustine conceives, or tends to conceive, inward praying, then the question "Why pray, when God knows already?" easily becomes the question "Why pray *outwardly*, when God knows already?"

I think that such is, in fact, the way Augustine conceives inward, versus outward, praying. That this is so can be seen at once from his use of the Biblical locution "inner man" to mean simply *mind* or *soul*[4] and "outer man" to mean simply *body*—as in the quotation from *The City of God* in the last section.

Augustine therefore looks upon inner acts and speeches as making up the authentic mental and spiritual life of a man. Outer acts and speeches, only contingently related to inner acts and speeches, may sometimes manifest the inner ones with a modest degree of accuracy; but they need not do even that. In any case, psychological descriptions of a man (descriptions of his thoughts, desires, intentions, attitudes, feelings, etc.) are really descriptions of the independent and self-sufficient inner man.

With this sort of picture before us it is natural to suppose that the body's only functions are to manifest the soul's thoughts, to help gratify the soul's desires, and to help execute decisions made by the soul. And since ritual serves neither to advance practical ends nor to pass on information to God, the question arises, why engage in ritual?

That Augustine's dualism, so expressed, affords a mistaken basis for interpreting the Biblical inner-outer contrast could be shown in detail; but I shall not attempt that here. Instead I shall just say, rather dogmatically, that when (to pick just one example) the psalmist speaks of someone as blessing outwardly and cursing inwardly[5] he is describing the mock piety of an insincere man, not a merely physical movement of a body. As we have already noted, a merely physical movement is not either sincere or insincere.

Moreover, the inner-outer contrast one finds in the Bible, far from rendering problematic the importance of ritual to one's devotional life, in fact underlines its central significance. Corresponding to each inner act or gesture that

---

[4]Augustine identifies the inner man indifferently as the soul (*anima*), rational soul (*animus*) and the mind (*mens*).

[5]"They bless with their mouth, but they curse inwardly." (Ps. 62:4)

one may be said to perform there is a state, attitude or feeling that all and only those who perform the inner act may be said to have. Thus, "He kneels inwardly" corresponds to the claim that he has contrition, or is contrite, or does something contritely, and "He gives alms inwardly" corresponds to the claim that he has charity, or is charitable, or does something charitably. In making use of an inner-man locution rather than the corresponding abstract substantive, adejective or adverb, Biblical writers remind us of the way of life in which typically religious attitudes and feelings take form.

Two caveats are in order. First, the believer's participation in this life of worship may be insincere. His actions may then be said to be merely outward. (But that doesn't, of course, mean that they are merely physical.) Second, a man may be faithful and God-fearing though he is either physically or psychologically unable to worship in the standard ritualistic ways. This inability may be only momentary, or it may be long-term. But in saying that one kneels (etc.) inwardly, the Biblical writer reveals that it is by reference to the standard ritualistic case that he conceives and understands piety.

IV

Augustine is puzzled about why prostrating oneself outwardly before God is important. Surely inward prostration is what counts. In the last section we saw that, for Augustine, the contrast between doing something inwardly and doing it outwardly is pretty much the contrast between having certain feelings or attitudes and giving them expression. So Augustine's puzzle comes to this: Why is it important to tip God off concerning one's feelings and attitudes? Surely God, being omniscient, has no need of the information.

The grip that this puzzle may have upon us has, I think, two distinct sources. The first source is an overly simple contrast between dealing with an omniscient being and dealing with men. And the second source is a misunderstanding as to what it is to give one's feelings and attitudes expression, which misunderstanding is intimately connected with Augustine's dualistic way of conceiving the inner-outer contrast. (As we shall see, these two sources are themselves inter-connected.)

It is very easy to overdraw the contrast between being sorry for one's sins before God and being sorry that one has wronged another person.[6] Of course no human being is omniscient. But sometimes a human being knows as much about the feelings of another human being as is relevant to an apology. And then the fact that an omniscient being would know infinitely more is not important to the apology.

Suppose I have wronged you, and I am sorry for what I have done. I may want to bring it about that you know I have the feelings that I in fact have. In order to achieve this result I may apologize by saying, "I'm sorry."

---

[6] I owe the idea developed in this section and the next to discussions with Stanley Cavell.

But of course you may already know that I am sorry. You may know by the sound of my voice, by the look on my face. Furthermore, I may know that you know I am sorry. In such a case I do not need to bring about the result that you know I have the feelings of sorrow I have. I do not need to bring about this result because it is already achieved. In such a case you are like God insofar as He, too, already knows; and I know that he knows.

Still, there may be a place for me to tell you what you already know, viz., that I am sorry. That is, there may yet be a place for apology. Here are some reasons why an apology may yet be important.

1. I need to *acknowledge* my wrong-doing. I have done you wrong. I know it. You know it. But unless and until I acknowledge my guilt, there is something important to us both that has gone unsaid. It needs to be said. Our relationship cannot be put right until I have "owned up" to what I have done.

2. I need to *ask for* forgiveness. And I cannot ask for forgiveness without owning up to what I need to be forgiven for. Of course you may be able and willing to forgive me without an apology. "He didn't know what he was doing," you may say; or, "He is not aware how his actions strike others." But you cannot excuse me like this as a general thing. Or at least if you do, you will not be treating me as a moral agent, responsible for what I do; you will be treating me as a child, or perhaps as a case-study.

3. I may want to *commiserate* with you. You have been hurt by my misdeed. As your friend, I want to express sympathy for your hurt. But, since it was I who wronged you, I cannot commiserate sincerely, or successfuly, without apologizing.

4. I may need to *share the burden* of my guilt. To apologize is to invite a response from you. By responding in a forgiving way you accept me, wrongdoing and all, and so relieve me of some of the burden of my guilt.

I think it is clear that there are theological analogues to most, if not all, these four points. I shall try to bring them out by references to the Prayer of General Confession from the Episcopalian Book of Common Prayer. This is the way the prayer goes:

> Almighty God, Father of our Lord Jesus Christ,
> Maker of all things, Judge of all men;
> We acknowledge and bewail our manifold sins and wickedness,
> Which we, from time to time, most grievously have committed,
> By thought, word, and deed,
> Against thy Divine Majesty,
> Provoking most justly thy wrath and indignation against us.
> We do earnestly repent,
> And are heartily sorry for these our misdoings;
> The remembrance of them is grievous unto us;
> The burden of them is intolerable.
> Have mercy upon us.
> Have mercy upon us, most merciful Father;
> For thy Son our Lord Jesus Christ's sake,

Forgive us all that is past;
And grant that we may ever hereafter
Serve and please thee
In newness of life,
To the honour and glory of thy Name;
Through Jesus Christ our Lord. Amen.

1. The importance of acknowledging one's sins is made clear in the opening statement, "We acknowledge and bewail our manifold sins and wickedness...." It is not enough to be sorry. One must acknowledge one's sins.

2. The connection between being sorry, acknowledging one's sins and asking for forgiveness is brought out in this sequence: "We do earnestly repent, And are heartily sorry for these our misdoings... Have mercy upon us... Forgive us all that is past; And grant that we may ever hereafter Serve and please thee In newness of life...."

3. One might question whether there is any place in the believer's relations with God for commiserating with God. To attempt to commiserate with God might seem to be attempting something presumptuous and inappropriate. Still, there is a recognition in the Prayer of General Confession that one's misdeeds are an affront to the Divine Majesty ("... our manifold sins and wickedness. Which we, from time to time, most grievously have committed... Against thy Divine Majesty....") And to recognize that affront is, perhaps, to offer a kind of commiseration.

4. Finally, the request to share one's burdens is suggested in the lines, "The remembrance of [our misdeeds] is grievous unto us; The burden of them is intolerable." God is conceived as not merely lifting the burden of one's guilt, but sharing it. This is the point of the doctrine of the atonement. ("Surely he hath borne our griefs, and carried our sorrows."—Isaiah 53.4)

It is clear now that our Augustinian puzzle—Why is it necessary to *express* sorrow for one's sins, when God knows already? Why isn't it enough to *have* feelings of sorrow?—arises from an oversimplified picture of what it is to say that one is sorry for having done wrong. It is not, or anyhow not merely, to do something to bring about the result that another knows what feelings one has. For there may be point in saying that one is sorry for a misdeed even when one's hearer already knows how one feels, and one knows that he knows. One may need to say one is sorry, to acknowledge guilt, to ask for forgiveness, to commiserate with him whom one has wronged, and to share the burden of one's guilt.

v

In the last section I concentrated on one kind of religious feeling, viz., sorrow for one's sins. I chose that particular feeling because of its great importance in Western religious thought. The question now arises whether the conclusion of the last section can be generalized to cover other religious feelings as well.

I suspect it can. But I know of no way to establish this besides considering each kind of religious feeling one at a time. I shall not attempt, however, to discuss in this paper all the various religious feelings. Instead I shall confine my discussion to a brief consideration of two additional religious feelings.

I should point out, however, that the conclusion of the last section is already enough to dissolve the puzzle with which we have been mainly concerned—at least in its perfectly general form. If it is clear why it might be important to "acknowledge and bewail our manifold sins," as well as feel sorry for having committed them, then there is no longer any general puzzle as to why it should be thought important to express, rather than simply have, religious feelings.

Still, there may be some interest in seeing how the reasoning of the last section could be adapted to a discussion of other religious feelings besides sorrow for one's sins.

First I shall consider gratitude to God for one's blessings.

Here, as before, it is easy to overdraw the contrast between relations with God and relations with a human being. If A has done a favour to B, other things being equal, this fact needs to be acknowledged by B. It will not, in general, be enough that B is grateful, even if A knows he is grateful and B knows that A knows. B needs to say, "Thank you."

To get an idea of the importance of B's saying "Thank you" we might think of possible explanations for his failing to do so.

One explanation might be that B, though grateful, is too proud to admit his indebtedness to A. Another possible explanation would be the opposite, viz., that B lacks sufficient self-respect to be able to admit his gratitude to A. Saying "Thank you" may threaten the little self-esteem B has. In both these situations it will be important to B himself, and to his relationship to A, that he come to be able to say "Thank you."

There are, of course, all sorts of ways that saying "Thank you" may go wrong. The "Thank you" may be grudging, servile, resentful, patronizing or automatic. But it may be appropriately spoken and appropriately received. My point is that saying "Thank you" is not simply doing something to bring about the result that another person knows one has feelings of gratitude. It is acting in a way appropriate to the receipt of a gift or favour.

Most of this carries over to the theological case. The believer needs to acknowledge God's blessings. It may be hard for him to do this, and especially hard to do this in the right spirit. But to do so is to offer a kind of return gift; it is to *give* thanks, which is itself an act of worship.

I turn now to feelings of joy. "My soul shall be joyful in the Lord," says the psalmist. One religious feeling of joy is joy *in* God. We do not ordinarily think of ourselves as rejoicing or being joyful *in* other people (though we certainly delight in our children, or take delight in them); but we do rejoice *in* the good fortune, success or happiness of other people. Perhaps an interhuman analogue to being joyful in God is therefore being joyful in the success, happiness or good fortune of another person.

We often express joy in the good fortune of another person by a celebration. We throw a party. Suppose I have a friend who has just passed a difficult examination. I have sweated out his ordeal with him. I am overjoyed with his success. Since he is a good friend of mine, he can easily tell how elated I am. And I know he can tell. Yet it would be ridiculous to say there is no need for me to throw a party for him, since he knows already how happy I am at his success, perhaps even how pleased everyone else is who would come to the party. The role of the celebration is in no way usurped by anyone's prior knowledge of the feelings of joy it is meant to express.

So it is also with joy in God. The Bible enjoins us to be joyful in God. We are to "make a joyful noise unto the Lord," to "make a loud noise, and rejoice, and sing praise." (Ps. 98:4) Among the many recommended noise-makers are the harp, the voice, trumpets and a cornet. (Ps. 98:5-6) The role of such a celebration is in no way usurped by a prior knowledge—whether Divine or human—of the feelings of joy it is meant to express.

I said at the beginning of section IV that the two sources of the Augustinian puzzle about why one need pray outwardly (first, an overly simple contrast between dealing with God and dealing with men and, second, a misunderstanding of what the point might be in giving one's feelings and attitudes expression) are interconnected. The interconnection should now be clear. The idea that the point of expressing a feeling or attitude (sorrow, say, or joy) must be simply, even mainly, to convey information, to tip someone off as to what things are like "inside," reinforces the tendency to think that dealings with God must be radically unlike dealings with men—for God, surely, has no need of being tipped off about anything ("Nor does He need these signs for the human mind to be laid bare to Him"). Moreover, coming to a better understanding of what the various reasons might actually be for expressing one's feelings and attitudes to others should help dispel the notion that, just because God is omniscient, dealings with him have to be radically unlike dealings with men.

VI

Both the puzzle Augustine begins within the passage cited from his treatise "On the Care of the Dead" and the puzzle he ends up with have turned out to be specious. The puzzle he ends up with is this: How can the mere motions of the body in ritual intensify religious feelings and attitudes? This puzzle is specious because it is not the mere motions of the body that have such an effect; what has (or may have) such an effect is (among other things) the more or less sincere and understanding performance of ritual. (The fact that this puzzle is specious does not, of course, mean that the solution Augustine offers to the puzzle he begins with is better even than Augustine had thought; in fact it is worse. But, since the puzzle Augustine begins with is also specious, the fact that his solution to it is no good does not really matter.)

The puzzle Augustine begins with is then this: Why need one express, as well as simply have, feelings such as sorrow for one's sins, since God knows already what feelings one has? This puzzle is specious because it presupposes that the only (or at least the primary) reason for saying (e.g.) that I am sorry for having done something wrong, is to bring about the result that someone else knows (or thinks) that I have certain feelings. But this is not so. An apology may have real point even when the person it is directed toward already knows, and I know that he knows, what is in my heart. And so, for that matter, may a banquet. And so may a liturgical service in which, as Augustine says, mean "do with the members of their bodies what benefits suppliants— when they bend their knees and stretch out their hands, or even prostrate themselves. . . ."

MORALITY AND RELIGION

5.7 Why Are Holy Actions Holy

Socrates. But shall we . . . say that whatever all the gods hate is unholy, and whatever they all love is holy: while whatever some of them love, and others hate, is either both or neither? Do you wish us now to define holiness and unholiness in this manner?

Euthyphro. Why not, Socrates?

Socr. There is no reason why I should not, Euthyphro. It is for you to consider whether that definition will help you to instruct me as you promised.

Euth. Well, I should say that holiness is what all the gods love, and that unholiness is what they all hate.

Socr. Are we to examine this definition, Euthyphro, and see if it is a good one? or are we to be content to accept the bare assertions of other men, or of ourselves, without asking any questions? Or must we examine the assertions?

Euth. We must examine them. But for my part I think that the definition is right this time.

Socr. We shall know that better in a little while, my good friend. Now consider this question. Do the gods love holiness because it is holy, or is it holy because they love it?

Euth. I do not understand you, Socrates.

Socr. I will try to explain myself: we speak of a thing being carried and carrying, and begin led and leading, and being seen and seeing; and you understand that all such expressions mean different things, and what the difference is.

Euth. Yes, I think I understand.

From Plato's *Euthyphro.*

Socr. And we talk of a thing being loved, and, which is different, of a thing loving?

Euth. Of course.

Socr. Now tell me: is a thing which is being carried in a state of being carried, because it is carried, or for some other reason?

Euth. No, because it is carried.

Socr. And a thing is in a state of being led, because it is led, and of being seen, because it is seen?

Euth. Certainly.

Soc. Then a thing is not seen because it is in a state of being seen; it is in a state of being seen because it is seen: and a thing is not led because it is in a state of being led; it is in a state of being led because it is led: and a thing is not carried because it is in a state of being carried; it is in a state of being carried because it is carried. Is my meaning clear now, Euthyphro? I mean this: if anything becomes, or is affected, it does not become because it is in a state of becoming; it is in a state of becoming because it becomes; and it is not affected because it is in a state of being affected: it is in a state of being affected because it is affected. Do you not agree?

Euth. I do.

Socr. Is not that which is being loved in a state, either of becoming, or of being affected in some way by something?

Euth. Certainly.

Socr. Then the same is true here as in the former cases. A thing is not loved by those who love it because it is in a state of being loved. It is in a state of being loved because they love it.

Euth. Necessarily.

Socr. Well, then, Euthyphro, what do we say about holiness? Is it not loved by all the gods, according to your definition?

Euth. Yes.

Socr. Because it is holy, or for some other reason?

Euth. No, because it is holy.

Socr. Then it is loved by the gods because it is holy: it is not holy because it is loved by them?

Euth. It seems so.

Socr. But then what is pleasing to the gods is pleasing to them, and is in a state of being loved by them, because they love it?

Euth. Of course.

Socr. Then holiness is not what is pleasing to the gods, and what is pleasing to the gods is not holy, as you say, Euthyphro. They are different things.

Euth. And why, Socrates?

Socr. Because we are agreed that the gods love holiness because it is holy: and that it is not holy because they love it. Is not this so?

Euth. Yes.

Socr. And that what is pleasing to the gods because they love it, is pleasing to them by reason of this same love: and that they do not love it because it is pleasing to them.

Euth. True.

Socr. Then, my dear Euthyphro, holiness, and what is pleasing to the gods, are different things. If the gods had loved holiness because it is holy, they would also have loved what is pleasing to them because it is pleasing to them; but if what is pleasing to them had been pleasing to them because they loved it, then holiness too would have been holiness, because they loved it. But now you see that they are opposite things, and wholly different from each other. For the one is of a sort to be loved because it is loved: while the other is loved, because it is of a sort to be loved. My question, Euthyphro, was, What is holiness? But it turns out that you have not explained to me the essence of holiness; you have been content to mention an attribute which belongs to it, namely, that all the gods love it. You have not yet told me what is its essence. Do not, if you please, keep from me what holiness is; begin again and tell me that. Never mind whether the gods love it, or whether is has other attributes: we shall not differ on that point. Do your best to make it clear to me what is holiness and what is unholiness.

ST. THOMAS AQUINAS

5.8   *The Eternal Law and the Natural Law*

We must now consider the various kinds of law, under which head there are six points of inquiry: (1) Whether there is an eternal law? (2) Whether there is a natural law? (3) Whether there is a human law? (4) Whether there is a divine law? (5) Whether there is one divine law, or several? (6) Whether there is a law of sin?

WHETHER THERE IS AN ETERNAL LAW

We proceed thus to the First Article:—

Objection 1. It would seem that there is no eternal law. For every law is imposed on someone. But there was not someone from eternity on whom a law could be imposed, since God alone was from eternity. Therefore no law is eternal.

From *Summa Theologica*, Part I, trans. Dominican Fathers of English Province (New York: Benziger, Inc., 1947). Reprinted by permission of the publisher.

Obj. 2. Further, promulgation is essential to law. But promulgation could not be from eternity, because there was no one to whom it could be promulgated from eternity. Therefore no law can be eternal.

Obj. 3. Further, law implies order to an end. But nothing ordained to an end is eternal, for the last end alone is eternal. Therefore no law is eternal.

On the contrary, Augustine says: *That Law which is the Supreme Reason cannot be understood to be otherwise than unchangeable and eternal.*

I answer that, As we have stated above, law is nothing else but a dictate of practical reason emanating from the ruler who governs a perfect community. Now it is evident, granted that the world is ruled by divine providence, as was stated in the First Part, that the whole community of the universe is governed by the divine reason. Therefore the very notion of the government of things in God, the ruler of the universe, has the nature of a law. And since the divine reason's conception of things is not subject to time, but is eternal, according to *Prov.* viii, 23, therefore it is that this kind of law must be called eternal.

Reply Obj. 1. Those things that do not exist in themselves exist in God, inasmuch as they are known and preordained by Him, according to *Rom.* iv. 17: *Who calls those things that are not as those that are.* Accordingly, the eternal concept of the divine law bears the character of an eternal law in so far as it is ordained by God to the government of things foreknown by Him.

Reply Obj. 2. Promulgation is made by word of mouth or in writing, and in both ways the eternal law is promulgated, because both the divine Word and the writing of the Book of Life are eternal. But the promulgation cannot be from eternity on the part of the creature that hears or reads.

Reply Obj. 3. Law implies order to the end actively, namely, in so far as it directs certain things to the end; but not passively,—that is to say, the law itself is not ordained to the end, except accidentally, in a governor whose end is extrinsic to him, and to which end his law must needs be ordained. But the end of the divine government is God Himself, and His law is not something other than Himself. Therefore the eternal law is not ordained to another end.

WHETHER THERE IS IN US A NATURAL LAW

We proceed thus to the Second Article:—

Objection 1. It would seem that there is no natural law in us. For man is governed sufficiently by the eternal law, since Augustine says that *the eternal law is that by which it is right that all things should be most orderly.* But nature does not abound in superfluities as neither does she fail in necessaries. Therefore man has no natural law.

Obj. 2. Further, by the law man is directed, in his acts, to the end, as was stated above. But the directing of human acts to their end is not a function of nature, as is the case in irrational creatures, which act for an end solely by their

natural appetite; whereas man acts for an end by his reason and will. Therefore man has no natural law.

Obj. 3. Further, the more a man is free, the less is he under the law. But
man is freer than all the animals because of his free choice, with which he
is endowed in distinction from all other animals. Since, therefore, other animals are not subject to a natural law, neither is man subject to a natural law.

On the contrary, The *Gloss* on *Rom.* ii. 14 (*When the Gentiles, who have
not the law, do by nature those things that are of the law*) comments as follows: *Although they have no written law, yet they have the natural law,
whereby each one knows, and is conscious of, what is good and what is evil.*

I answer that, As we have stated above, law, being a rule and measure,
can be in a person in two ways: in one way, as in him that rules and measures; in another way, as in that which is ruled and measured, since a thing
is ruled and measured in so far as it partakes of the rule or measure. Therefore, since all things subject to divine providence are ruled and measured by
the eternal law, as was stated above, it is evident that all things partake in
some way in the eternal law, in so far as, namely, from its being imprinted
on them, they derive their respective inclinations to their proper acts and
ends. Now among all others, the rational creature is subject to divine providence in a more excellent way, in so far as it itself partakes of a share of
providence, by being provident both for itself and for others. Therefore it has
a share of the eternal reason, whereby it has a natural inclination to its proper
act and end; and this participation of the eternal law in the rational creature
is called the natural law. Hence the Psalmist, after saying (*Ps.* iv. 6): *Offer
up the sacrifice of justice,* as though someone asked what the works of justice
are, adds: *Many say, Who showeth us good things?* in answer to which question he says: *The light of Thy countenance, O Lord, is signed upon us.* He
thus implies that the light of natural reason, whereby we discern what is good
and what is evil, which is the function of the natural law, is nothing else
than an imprint on us of the divine light. It is therefore evident that the natural
law is nothing else than the rational creature's participation of the eternal law.

Reply Obj. 1. This argument would hold if the natural law were something
different from the eternal law; whereas it is nothing but a participation thereof,
as we have stated above.

Reply Obj. 2. Every act of reason and will in us is based on that which is
according to nature, as was stated above. For every act of reasoning is based
on principles that are known naturally, and every act of appetite in respect of
the means is derived from the natural appetite in respect of the last end. Accordingly, the first direction of our acts to their end must needs be through
the natural law.

Reply Obj. 3. Even irrational animals partake in their own way of the
eternal reason, just as the rational creature does. But because the rational
creature partakes thereof in an intellectual and rational manner, therefore
the participation of the eternal law in the rational creature is properly called

a law, since a law is something pertaining to reason, as was stated above. Irrational creatures, however, do not partake thereof in a rational manner, and therefore there is no participation of the eternal law in them, except by way of likeness.

WHETHER THERE IS A HUMAN LAW

We proceed thus to the Third Article:—

Objection 1. It would seem that there is not a human law. For the natural law is a participation of the eternal law, as was stated above. Now through the eternal law *all things are most orderly*, as Augustine states. Therefore the natural law suffices for the ordering of all human affairs. Consequently there is no need for a human law.

Obj. 2. Further, law has the character of a measure, as was stated above. But human reason is not a measure of things, but *vice versa*, as is stated in *Metaph.* x. Therefore no law can emanate from the human reason.

Obj. 3. Further, a measure should be most certain, as is stated in *Metaph.* x. But the dictates of the human reason in matters of conduct are uncertain, according to *Wis.* ix. 14: *The thoughts of mortal men are fearful, and our counsels uncertain.* Therefore no law can emanate from the human reason.

On the contrary, Augustine distinguishes two kinds of law, the one eternal, the other temporal, which he calls human.

I answer that, As we have stated above, a law is a dictate of the practical reason. Now it is to be observed that the same procedure takes places in the practical and in the speculative reason, for each proceeds from principles to conclusions, as was stated above. Accordingly, we conclude that, just as in the speculative reason, from naturally known indemonstrable principles we draw the conclusions of the various sciences, the knowledge of which is not imparted to us by nature, but acquired by the efforts of reason, so too it is that from the precepts of the natural law, as from common and indemonstrable principles, the human reason needs to proceed to the more particular determination of certain matters. These particular determinations, devised by human reason, are called human laws, provided that the other essential conditions of law be observed, as was stated above. Therefore Tully says in his *Rhetoric* that *justice has its source in nature; thence certain things came into custom by reason of their utility; afterwards these things which emanated from nature, and were approved by custom, were sanctioned by fear and reverence for the law.*

Reply Obj. 1. The human reason cannot have a full participation of the dictate of the divine reason, but according to its own mode, and imperfectly. Consequently, just as on the part of the speculative reason, by a natural participation of divine wisdom, there is in us the knowledge of certain common principles, but not a proper knowledge of each single truth, such as that contained in the divine wisdom, so, too, on the part of the practical reason, man has a natural participation of the eternal law, according to certain common principles, but not as regards the particular determinations of individual cases, which are, however, contained in the eternal law. Hence the need for human reason to proceed further to sanction them by law.

Reply Obj. 2. Human reason is not, of itself, the rule of things. But the principles impressed on it by nature are the general rules and measures of all things relating to human conduct, of which the natural reason is the rule and measure, although it is not the measure of things that are from nature.

Reply Obj. 3. The practical reason is concerned with operable matters, which are singular and contingent, but not with necessary things, with which the speculative reason is concerned. Therefore human laws cannot have that inerrancy that belongs to the demonstrated conclusions of the sciences. Nor it is necessary for every measure to be altogether unerring and certain, but according as it is possible in its own particular genus.

WHETHER THERE WAS ANY NEED FOR A DIVINE LAW

We proceed thus to the Fourth Article:—

Objection 1. It would seem that there was no need for a divine law. For, as was stated above, the natural law is a participation in us of the eternal law. But the eternal law is the divine law, as stated above. Therefore there is no need for divine law in addition to the natural law and to human laws derived therefrom.

Obj. 2. Further, it is written (*Ecclus.* xv. 14) that *God left man in the hand of his own counsel.* Now counsel is an act of reason, as was stated above. Therefore man was left to the direction of his reason. But a dictate of human reason is a human law, as stated above. Therefore there is no need for man to be governed also by a divine law.

Obj. 3. Further, human nature is more self-sufficing than irrational creatures. But irrational creatures have no divine law besides the natural inclination impressed on them. Much less, therefore, should the rational creature have a divine law in addition to the natural law.

On the contrary, David prayed God to set His law before him, saying (*Ps.* cxviii. 33): *Set before me for a law the way of Thy justifications, O Lord.*

I answer that, Besides the natural and the human law it was necessary for the directing of human conduct to have a divine law. And this for four reasons. First, because it is by law that man is directed how to perform his proper acts in view of his last end. Now if man were ordained to no other end than that which is proportionate to his natural ability, there would be no need for man to have any further direction, on the part of his reason, in addition to the natural law and humanly devised law which is derived from it. But since man is ordained to an end of eternal happiness which exceeds man's natural ability, as we have stated above, therefore it was necessary that, in addition to the natural and the human law, man should be directed to his end by a law given by God.

Secondly, because, by reason of the uncertainty of human judgment, especially on contingent and particular matters, different people form different judgments on human acts; whence also different and contrary laws result. In order, therefore, that man may know without any doubt what he ought to do and what he ought to avoid, it was necessary for man to be directed in his proper acts by a law given by God, for it is certain that such a law cannot err.

Thirdly, because man can make laws in those matters of which he is competent to judge. But man is not competent to judge of interior movements, that are hidden, but only of exterior acts which are observable; and yet for the perfection of virtue it is necessary for man to conduct himself rightly in both kinds of acts. Consequently, human law could not sufficiently curb and direct interior acts, and it was necessary for this purpose that a divine law should supervene.

Fourthly, because, as Augustine says, human law cannot punish or forbid all evil deeds, since, while aiming at doing away with all evils, it would do away with many good things, and would hinder the advance of the common good, which is necessary for human living. In order, therefore, that no evil might remain unforbidden and unpunished, it was necessary for the divine law to supervene, whereby all sins are forbidden.

And these four cases are touched upon in *Ps.* cxviii, 8, where it is said: *The law of the Lord is unspotted, i.e.,* allowing no foulness of sin; *converting souls,* because it directs not only exterior, but also interior, acts; *the testimony of the Lord is faithful,* because of the certainty of what is true and right; *giving wisdom to little ones,* by directing man to an end supernatural and divine.

Reply Obj. 1. By the natural law the eternal law is participated proportionately to the capacity of human nature. But to his supernatural end man needs to be directed in a yet higher way. Hence the additional law given by God, whereby man shares more perfectly in the eternal law.

Reply Obj. 2. Counsel is a kind of inquiry, and hence must proceed from some principles. Nor is it enough for it to proceed from principles imparted by nature, which are the precepts of the natural law, for the reasons given above; but there is need for certain additional principles, namely, the precepts of the divine law.

Reply Obj. 3. Irrational creatures are not ordained to an end higher than that which is proportionate to their natural powers. Consequently the comparison fails.

. . .

We must now consider the natural law, concerning which there are six points of inquiry: (1) What is the natural law? (2) What are the precepts of the natural law? (3) Whether all the acts of the virtues are prescribed by the natural law? (4) Whether the natural law is the same in all? (5) Whether it is changeable? (6) Whether it can be abolished from the mind of man?

WHETHER THE NATURAL LAW IS A HABIT

We proceed thus to the First Article:—

Objection 1. It would seem that the natural law is a habit. For, as the Philosopher says, *there are three things in the soul, power, habit and passion.* But the natural law is not one of the soul's powers, nor is it one of the passions, as we may see by going through them one by one. Therefore the natural law is a habit.

Obj. 2. Further, Basil says that the *conscience or synderesis is the law of our mind*, which can apply only to the natural law. But *synderesis* is a habit, as was shown in the First Part. Therefore the natural law is a habit.

Obj. 3. Further, the natural law abides in man always, as will be shown further on. But man's reason, which the law regards, does not always think about the natural law. Therefore the natural law is not an act, but a habit.

On the contrary, Augustine says that *a habit is that whereby something is done when necessary.* But such is not the natural law, since it is in infants and in the damned who cannot act by it. Therefore the natural law is not a habit.

I answer that, A thing may be called a habit in two ways. First, properly and essentially, and thus the natural law is not a habit. For it has been stated above that the natural law is something appointed by reason, just as a proposition is a work of reason. Now that which a man does is not the same as that whereby he does it, for he makes a becoming speech by the habit of grammar. Since, then, a habit is that by which we act, a law cannot be a habit properly and essentially.

Secondly, the term habit may be applied to that which we hold by a habit. Thus *faith* may mean *that which we hold by faith.* Accordingly, since the precepts of the natural law are sometimes considered by reason actually, while sometimes they are in the reason only habitually, in this way the natural law may be called a habit. So, too, in speculative matters, the indemonstrable principles are not the habit itself whereby we hold these principles; they are rather the principles of which we possess the habit.

Reply Obj. 1. The Philosopher proposes there to discover the genus of virtue; and since it is evident that virtue is a principle of action, he mentions only those things which are principles of human acts, viz., powers, habits and passions. But there are other things in the soul besides these three: *e.g.*, acts, as *to will* is in the one that wills; again, there are things known in the knower; moreover its own natural properties are in the soul, such as immortality and the like.

Reply Obj. 2. *Synderesis* is said to be the law of our intellect because it is a habit containing the precepts of the natural law, which are the first principles of human actions.

Reply Obj. 3. This argument proves that the natural law is held habitually; and this is granted.

To the argument advanced in the contrary sense we reply that sometimes a man is unable to make use of that which is in him habitually, because of some impediment. Thus, because of sleep, a man is unable to use the habit of science. In like manner, through the deficiency of his age, a child cannot use the habit of the understanding of principles, or the natural law, which is in him habitually.

WHETHER THE NATURAL LAW CONTAINS SEVERAL PRECEPTS, OR ONLY ONE

We proceed thus to the Second Article:—

Objection 1. It would seem that the natural law contains not several precepts, but only one. For law is a kind of precept, as was stated above. If therefore there were many precepts of the natural law, it would follow that there are also many natural laws.

Obj. 2. Further, the natural law is consequent upon human nature. But human nature, as a whole, is one, though, as to its parts, it is manifold. Therefore, either there is but one precept of the law of nature because of the unity of nature as a whole, or there are many by reason of the number of parts of human nature. The result would be that even things relating to the inclination of the concupiscible power would belong to the natural law.

Obj. 3. Further, law is something pertaining to reason, as was stated above. Now reason is but one in man. Therefore there is only one precept of the natural law.

On the contrary, The precepts of the natural law in man stand in relation to operable matters as first principles do to matters of demonstration. But there are several first indemonstrable principles. Therefore there are also several precepts of the natural law.

I answer that, As was stated above, the precepts of the natural law are to the practical reason what the first principles of demonstrations are to the speculative reason, because both are self-evident principles. Now a thing is said to be self-evident in two ways: first, in itself: secondly, in relation to us. Any proposition is said to be self-evident in itself; if its predicate is contained in the notion of the subject; even though it may happen that to one who does not know the definition of the subject, such a proposition is not self-evident. For instance, this proposition, *Man is a rational being*, is, in its very nature, self-evident, since he who says *man*, says *a rational being*; and yet to one who does not know what a man is, this proposition is not self-evident. Hence it is that, as Boethius says, certain axioms or propositions are universally self-evident to all; and such are the propositions whose terms are known to all, as, *Every whole is greater than its part*, and, *Things equal to one and the same are equal to another*. But some propositions are self-evident only to the wise, who understand the meaning of the terms of such propositions. Thus to one who understands that an angel is not a body, it is self-evident that an angel is not circumscriptively in a place. But this is not evident to the unlearned, for they cannot grasp it.

Now a certain order is to be found in those things that are apprehended by men. For that which first falls under apprehension is *being*, the understanding of which is included in all things whatsoever a man apprehends. Therefore the first indemonstrable principle is that *the same thing cannot be affirmed and denied at the same time*, which is based on the notion of *being* and *not-being*: and on this principle all others are based, as is stated in *Metaph*. iv. Now as *being* is the first thing that falls under the apprehension absolutely, so *good* is the first thing that falls under the apprehension of the practical reason, which is directed to action (since every agent acts for an end, which has the nature of good.) Consequently, the first principle in the practical reason is one founded on the nature of good, viz., that *good is that which all things seek after*. Hence this is the first precept of law, that *good is to be done and promoted, and evil is to be avoided*. All other precepts of the natural law are based upon this; so that all the things which the practical reason naturally apprehends as man's good belong to the precepts of the natural law under the form of things to be done or avoided.

Since, however, good has the nature of an end, and evil, the nature of the contrary, hence it is that all those things to which man has a natural inclination are naturally apprehended by reason as being good, and consequently as objects of pursuit, and their contraries as evil, and objects of avoidance. Therefore, the order of the precepts of the natural law is according to the order of natural inclinations. For there is in man, first of all, an inclination to good in accordance with the nature which he has in common with all substances, inasmuch, namely, as every substance seeks the preservation of its own being, according to its nature; and by reason of this inclination, whatever is a means of preserving human life, and of warding off its obstacles, belongs to the natural law. Secondly, there is in man an inclination to things that pertain to him more specially, according to that nature which he has in common with other animals; and in virtue of this inclination, those things are said to belong to the natural law *which nature has taught to all animals*, such as sexual intercourse, the education of offspring and so forth. Thirdly, there is in man an inclination to good according to the nature of his reason, which nature is proper to him. Thus man has a natural inclination to know the truth about God, and to live in society; and in this respect, whatever pertains to this inclination belongs to the natural law: *e.g.*, to shun ignorance, to avoid offending those among whom one has to live, and other such things regarding the above inclination.

Reply Obj. 1. All these precepts of the law of nature have the character of one natural law, inasmuch as they flow from one first precept.

Reply Obj. 2. All the inclinations of any parts whatsoever of human nature, *e.g.*, of the concupiscible and irascible parts, in so far as they are ruled by reason, belong to the natural law, and are reduced to one first precept, as was stated above. And thus the precepts of the natural law are many in themselves, but they are based on one common foundation.

Reply Obj. 3. Although reason is one in itself, yet it directs all things regarding man; so that whatever can be ruled by reason is contained under the law of reason.

WHETHER ALL THE ACTS OF THE VIRTUES ARE PRESCRIBED BY THE NATURAL LAW

We proceed thus to the Third Article:—

Objection 1. It would seem that not all the acts of the virtues are prescribed by the natural law. For, as was stated above, it is of the nature of law that it be ordained to the common good. But some acts of the virtues are ordained to the private good of the individual, as is evident especially in regard to acts of temperance. Therefore, not all the acts of the virtues are the subject of natural law.

Obj. 2. Further, every sin is opposed to some virtuous act. If therefore all the acts of the virtues are prescribed by the natural law, it seems to follow that sins are against nature; whereas this applies to certain special sins.

Obj. 3. Further, those things which are according to nature are common to all. But the acts of the virtues are not common at all, since a thing is virtuous in one, and vicious in another. Therefore, not all the acts of the virtues are prescribed by the natural law.

On the contrary. Damascene says that *virtues are natural.* Therefore virtuous acts also are subject to the natural law.

I answer that, We may speak of virtuous acts in two ways: first, in so far as they are virtuous; secondly, as such and such acts considered in their proper species. If, then, we are speaking of the acts of the virtues in so far as they are virtuous, thus all virtuous acts belong to the natural law. For it has been stated that to the natural law belongs everything to which a man is inclined according to his nature. Now each thing is inclined naturally to an operation that is suitable to it according to its form: *e.g.*, fire is inclined to give heat. Therefore, since the rational soul is the proper form of man, there is in every man a natural inclination to act according to reason; and this is to act according to virtue. Consequently, considered thus, all the acts of the virtues are prescribed by the natural law, since each one's reason naturally dictates to him to act virtuously. But if we speak of virtuous acts, considered in themselves, *i.e.*, in their proper species, thus not all virtuous acts are prescribed by the natural law. For many things are done virtuously, to which nature does not primarily incline, but which, through the inquiry of reason, have been found by men to be conducive to well-living.

Reply Obj. 1. Temperance is about the natural concupiscences of food, drink and sexual matters, which are indeed ordained to the common good of nature, just as other matters of law ordained to the moral common good.

Reply Obj. 2. By human nature we may mean either that which is proper to man, and in this sense all sins, as being against reason, are also against nature, as Damascene states; or we may mean that nature which is common to man and other animals, and in this sense, certain special sins are said to be against nature: *e.g.*, contrary to sexual intercourse, which is natural to all animals, is unisexual lust, which has received the special name of the unnatural crime.

Reply Obj. 3. This argument considers acts in themselves. For it is owing to the various conditions of men that certain acts are virtuous for some, as being proportioned and becoming to them, while they are vicious for others, as not being proportioned to them.

WHETHER THE NATURAL LAW IS THE SAME IN ALL MEN

We proceed thus to the Fourth Article:—

Objection 1. It would seem that the natural law is not the same in all. For it is stated in the *Decretals* that *the natural law is that which is contained in the Law and the Gospel*. But this is not common to all men, because as it is written (*Rom.* x. 16), *all do not obey the gospel*. Therefore the natural law is not the same in all men.

Obj. 2. Further, *Things which are according to the law are said to be just*, as is stated in *Ethics* v. But it is stated in the same book that nothing is so just for all as not to be subject to change in regard to some men. Therefore even the natural law is not the same in all men.

Obj. 3. Further, as was stated above, to the natural law belongs everything to which a man is inclined according to his nature. Now different men are naturally inclined to different things,—some to the desire of pleasures, others to the desire of honors, and other men to other things. Therefore, there is not one natural law for all.

On the contrary, Isidore says: *The natural law is common to all nations.*

I answer that, As we have stated above, to the natural law belong those things to which a man is inclined naturally; and among these it is proper to man to be inclined to act according to reason. Now it belongs to the reason to proceed from what is common to what is proper, as is stated in *Physics* i. The speculative reason, however, is differently situated, in this matter, from the practical reason. For, since the speculative reason is concerned chiefly with necessary things, which cannot be otherwise than they are, its proper conclusions, like the universal principles, contain the truth without fail. The practical reason, on the other hand, is concerned with contingent matters, which is the domain of human actions; and, consequently, although there is necessity in the common principles, the more we descend towards the particular, the more frequently we encounter defects. Accordingly, then, in speculative matters truth is the same in all men, both as to principles and as to conclusions; although the truth is not known to all as regards the conclusions, but only as regards the principles which are called *common notions*. But in matters of action, truth or practical rectitude is not the same for all as to what particular, but only as to the common principles; and where there is the same rectitude in relation to particulars, it is not equally known to all.

It is therefore evident that, as regards the common principles whether of speculative or of practical reason, truth or rectitude is the same for all, and is equally known by all. But as to the proper conclusions of the speculative reason, the truth is the same for all, but it is not equally known to all. Thus, it is true for all that the three angles of a triangle are together equal to two right angles, although it is not known to all. But as to the proper conclusions of the practical reason, neither is the truth or rectitude the same for all, nor, where it is the same, is it equally known by all. Thus, it is right and true for all to act according to reason, and from this principle it follows, as a proper conclusion, that goods entrusted to another should be restored to their owner. Now this is true for the majority of cases. But it may happen in a particular case that it would be injurious, and therefore unreasonable, to restore goods held in trust; for instance, if they are claimed for the purpose of fighting against one's country. And this principle will be found to fail the more, according as we descend further towards the particular, *e.g.*, if one were to say that goods held in trust should be restored with such and such a guarantee, or in such and such a way; because the greater the number of conditions added, the greater the number of ways in which the principle may fail, so that it be not right to restore or not to restore.

Consequently, we must say that the natural law, as to the first common principles, it is the same for all, both as to rectitude and as to knowledge. But as to certain more particular aspects, which are conclusions, as it were, of those common principles, it is the same for all in the majority of cases, both as to rectitude and as to knowledge; and yet in some few cases it may fail, both as to rectitude, by reason of certain obstacles (just as natures subject to generation and corruption fail in some cases because of some obstacle), and as to knowledge, since in some the reason is perverted by passion, or evil habit, or an evil disposition of nature. Thus at one time theft, although it is expressly contrary to the natural law, was not considered wrong among the Germans, as Julius Caesar relates.

Reply Obj. 1. The meaning of the sentence quoted is not that whatever is contained in the Law and the Gospel belongs to the natural law, since they contain many things that are above nature; but that whatever belongs to the natural law is fully contained in them. Therefore Gratian, after saying that *the natural law is what is contained in the Law and the Gospel*, adds at once, by way of example, *by which everyone is commanded to do to others as he would be done by.*

Reply Obj. 2. The saying of the Philosopher is to be understood of things that are naturally just, not as common principles, but as conclusions drawn from them, having rectitude in the majority of cases, but failing in a few.

Reply Obj. 3. Just as in man reason rules and commands the other powers, so all the natural inclinations belonging to the other powers must needs be directed according to reason. Therefore it is universally right for all men that all their inclinations should be directed according to reason.

WHETHER THE NATURAL LAW CAN BE CHANGED

We proceed thus to the Fifth Article:—

Objection 1. It would seem that the natural law can be changed. For on *Ecclus.* xvii. 9 (*He gave them instructions, and the law of life*) the *Gloss* says: *He wished the law of the letter to be written, in order to correct the law of nature.* But that which is corrected is changed. Therefore the natural law can be changed.

Obj. 2. Further, the slaying of the innocent, adultery and theft are against the natural law. But we find these things changed by God: as when God commanded Abraham to slay his innocent son (*Gen.* xxii. 2); and when He ordered the Jews to borrow and purloin the vessels of the Egyptians (*Exod.* xii. 35); and when He commanded Osee to take to himself *a wife of fornications* (*Osee* i. 2). Therefore the natural law can be changed.

Obj. 3. Further, Isidore says that *the possession of all things in common, and universal freedom, are matters of natural law.* But these things are seen to be changed by human laws. Therefore it seems that the natural law is subject to change.

On the contrary, It is said in the *Decretals: The natural law dates from the creation of the rational creature. It does not vary according to time, but remains unchangeable.*

I answer that, A change in the natural law may be understood in two ways. First, by way of addition. In this sense, nothing hinders the natural law from being changed, since many things for the benefit of human life have been added over and above the natural law, both by the divine law and by human laws.

Secondly, a change in the natural law may be understood by way of subtraction, so that what previously was according to the natural law, ceases to be so. In this sense, the natural law is altogether unchangeable in its first principles. But in its secondary principles, which, as we have said, are certain detailed proximate conclusions drawn from the first principles, the natural law is not changed so that what it prescribes be not right in most cases. But it may be changed in some particular cases of rare occurrence, through some special causes hindering the observance of such precepts, as was stated above.

Reply Obj. 1. The written law is said to be given for the correction of the natural law, either because it supplies what was wanting to the natural law, or because the natural law was so perverted in the hearts of some men, as to certain matters, that they esteemed those things good which are naturally evil; which perversion stood in need of correction.

Reply Obj. 2. All men alike, both guilty and innocent, die the death of nature; which death of nature is inflicted by the power of God because of original sin, according to I *Kings* ii. 6: *The Lord killeth and maketh alive.* Consequently, by the command of God, death can be inflicted on any man, guilty or innocent, without any injustice whatever.—In like manner, adultery is intercourse with another's wife; who is allotted to him by the law emanating from God. Consequently intercourse with any woman, by the command of God, is neither adultery nor fornication.—The same applies to theft, which is the taking of another's property. For whatever is taken by the command of God, to Whom all things belong, is not taken against the will of its owner, whereas it is in this that theft consists.—Nor it is only in human things that whatever is commanded by God is right; but also in natural things, whatever is done by God is, in some way, natural, as was stated in the First Part.

Reply Obj. 3. A thing is said to belong to the natural law in two ways. First, because nature inclines thereto: *e.g.*, that one should not do harm to another. Secondly, because nature did not bring with it the contrary. Thus, we might say that for man to be naked is of the natural law, because nature did not give him clothes, but art invented them. In this sense, *the possession of all things in common and universal freedom* are said to be of the natural law, because, namely, the distinction of possessions and slavery were not brought in by nature, but devised by human reason for the benefit of human life. Accordingly, the law of nature was not changed in this respect, except by addition.

PATRICK NOWELL-SMITH

5.9 Morality:
Religious and Secular

The central thesis of this paper is that religious morality is infantile. I am well aware that this will sound absurd. To suggest that Aquinas and Kant—to say nothing of millions of Christians of lesser genius—never grew up is surely to put oneself out of court as a philosopher to be taken seriously. My thesis is not so crude as that; I shall try to show that, in the moralities of adult

From *The Rationalist Annual*, 1961 (London: Pemberton Publishing Co. Ltd.). Reprinted by permission of the publisher.

Christians, there are elements which can be set apart from the rest and are, indeed, inconsistent with them, that these elements can properly be called "religious" and that just these elements are infantile.

I shall start by making some assumptions that I take to be common ground between Christians and secular humanists. I propose to say almost nothing about the *content* of morality; that love, sympathy, loyalty, and consideration are virtues, and that their opposites, malice, cruelty, treachery, and callousness, are vices, are propositions that I shall assume without proof. One can't do everything at the same time, and my job now is not to refute Thrasymachus. Secondly, I propose to occupy, as common ground, some much more debatable territory; I shall assume in broad outline the metaphysical view of the nature of man that we have inherited from Plato and Aristotle. The basis of this tradition is that there is something called "Eudaimonia" or "The Good Life," that this consists in fulfilling to the highest possible degree the nature of Man, and that the nature of Man is to be a rational, social animal. Love, I shall assume, is the supreme virtue because the life of love is, in the end, the only life that is fully rational and fully social. My concern will be, not with the content of morality, but with its form or structure, with the ways in which the manifold concepts and affirmations of which a moral system is composed hang together; not with rival views of what conduct is moral and what is immoral, but with rival views of what morality *is*.

This contrast between form and content is not difficult to grasp, but experience has taught me that it is often ignored. When they discover that I have moral views but no religious beliefs, people often ask me this question: "Where do you get your moral ideas from?" Faced with this question, my habit is to take it literally and to answer it truthfully. "From my father and mother," I say, "from the companions of my boyhood and manhood, from teachers and from books, from my own reflections on the experience I have had of the sayings and doings of myself and others, an experience similar in countless ways to that of other people born of middle-class English parents some forty-five years ago, but in its totality unique." This boring and autobiographical answer never satisfies the questioner; for, though it is the right answer to the question he actually asked, it is not, as I very well knew, the answer to the question he really had in mind. He did not want to know *from whom* I learnt my moral views; he wanted to know what *authority* I have for holding them. But why, if this is what he wanted to know, did he not ask me? He has confused two different questions; and it is natural enough that he should have confused them, since it is often the case that to point to the source of an opinion or claim is to show the authority on which it is based. We appeal to the dictionary to vindicate an assertion about the spelling of a word, and the policeman's production of a warrant signed by a magistrate is a necessary and sufficient condition of his authority to enter my house. But even a dictionary can make mistakes, and one may doubt whether one *ought* to admit the policeman even after his legal title to enter has been satisfactorily made out. "He certainly has a legal right," one might say, "but even so, things being as they are, ought I to admit him?"

Those who put this question to me have made an assumption that they have not examined because they have not reflected sufficiently on the form of morality. They have simply assumed that just as the legal propriety of an action is established by showing it to emanate from an authoritative source, so also the moral propriety of an action must be established in the same way; that legal rightness has the same form as moral rightness, and may therefore be used to shed light on it. This assumption made, they naturally suppose that, even when I agree with them—for example, about the immorality of murder—I have no right to hold this impeccable view unless I can show that I have received it from an authoritative source. My autobiographical answer clearly fails to do this. My parents may have had a right to my obedience, but no right to make the moral law. Morality, on this view, is an affair of being commanded to behave in certain ways by some person who has a right to issue such commands; and, once this premise is granted, it is said with some reason that only God has such a right. Morality must be based on religion, and a morality not so based, or one based on the wrong religion, lacks all validity.

It is this premise, that being moral consists in obedience to commands, that I deny. There is an argument, familiar to philosophers but of which the force is not always appreciated, which shows that this premise cannot be right. Suppose that I have satisfied myself that God has commanded me to do this or that thing—in itself a large supposition, but I will waive objections on this score in order to come quickly to the main point—it still makes *sense* for me to ask whether or not I *ought* to do it. God, let us say, is an omnipotent, omniscient creator of the universe. Such a creator might have evil intentions and might command me to do wrong; and if that were the case though it would be imprudent to disobey, it would not be wrong. There is nothing in the idea of an omnipotent, omniscient creator which, by itself, entails his goodness or his right to command, unless we are prepared to assent to Hobbes' phrase, "God, who by right, *that is by irresistible power*, commandeth all things." Unless we accept Hobbes' consistent but repugnant equation of God's right with his might, we must be persuaded *independently* of his goodness before we admit his right to command. We must judge for ourselves whether the Bible is the inspired word of a just and benevolent God or a curious amalgam of profound wisdom and gross superstition. To judge this is to make a moral decision, so that in the end, so far from morality being based on religion, religion is based on morality.

Before passing to my main theme, I must add two cautions about what this argument does *not* prove. It does not prove that we should in no case take authority as a guide. Suppose that a man's aim is to make money on the Stock Exchange. He decides that it would be most profitable to invest his money in company A; but his broker prefers company B. He will usually be well advised to accept the verdict of his broker, even if the broker is, as they often are, inarticulate in giving his reasons. He might decide to put all his financial affairs in the hands of a broker, and to do nothing but what the broker tells him to do. But *this* decision, even if it is the only financial decision he ever makes in his life, is still his own. In much the same way, a man might decide to put his conscience wholly into the hands of a priest or a Church, to make no moral decisions of his own but always to do what the priest tells him. Even he, though he makes but one moral decision in his life, must make and continually renew that one. Those who accept the authority of a priest or a Church on what to do are, in accepting that authority, deciding for themselves. They may not fully comprehend that this is so; but that is another matter.

Secondly, to deny that morality need or can have an external nonmoral basis on which to stand is by no means to deny that it can have an internal basis, in the sense of one or a few moral beliefs that are fundamental to the other beliefs of the system. A man's views on gambling or sex or business ethics may (though they need not) form a coherent system in which some views are held *because* certain others views are held. Utilitarianism is an example of such a system in which all moral rules are to be judged by their tendency to promote human happiness. A moral system of this kind is like a system of geometry in which some propositions appear as axioms, others as theorems owing their place in the system to their derivability from the axioms. Few of us are so rationalistic as to hold all our moral beliefs in this way, but to move towards this goal is to begin to think seriously about morals.

2. In any system of morality we can distinguish between its content and its form. By its "content" I mean the actual commands and prohibitions it contains, the characteristics it lists as virtues and as vices; by its "form" I mean the sort of propositions it contains and the ways in which these are thought of as connected with each other. The basic distinction here is between a teleological morality in which moral rules are considered to be subordinate to ends, to be rules *for* achieving ends and consequently to be judged by their tendency to promote those ends, and a deontological system in which moral rules are thought of as absolute, as categorical imperatives in no way depending for their validity on the good or bad consequences of obedience, and in which moral goodness is thought to lie in conformity to these rules for their own sake. The first of these ways of looking at morality as a whole derives from the Greeks, so I shall call it the Greek view of morality; it can be summed up in the slogan "the Sabbath was made for man, not man for the Sabbath." The second, deriving from Jewish sources, I shall call the Hebrew view. This involves a serious oversimplification, since we find deontological elements in the Greek New Testament and teleological elements in the Hebrew Old Testament; but, taken broadly, the contrast between the deontological character of the Old and the teleological character of the New Testaments is as striking as the difference of language. I shall also indulge in

another serious oversimplification in speaking of Christianity as a morality of the Hebrew type while it is, of course, an amalgam of both with different elements predominating in different versions. This oversimplification would be quite unjustifiable if my task were to give an account of Christian morality; but it is legitimate here because my task is to contrast those elements in the Christian tradition which secular humanists accept with those which they reject, and these are broadly coterminous with the Greek and the Hebrew elements in Christianity respectively.

How there can be these two radically different ways of looking at morality, one which sees it as a set of recipes to be followed for the achievement of ends, the other which sees it as a set of commands to be obeyed, can best be understood if we consider the way in which we learn what it is to be moral. For a man's morality is a set of habits of choice, of characteristic responses to his environment, in particular to his social environment, the people among whom he lives; and habits are learnt in childhood. Growing up morally is learning to cope with the world into which we find ourselves pitched, and especially to cope with our relations with other human beings. In the course of living we learn to reflect on our responses, to find in some of them sources of satisfaction, in others of regret, and "coping with the world" means coping with it in a manner ultimately satisfactory to ourselves. Philosophers such as Aristotle and Hobbes who boldly and crudely identified "good" with "object of desire" may have made a technical mistake; but they were certainly on the right lines. If men had no desires and aversions, if they felt no joy and no remorse, if they were totally indifferent to everything in the universe, there would be no such thing as choice and we should have no concept of morality, of good and evil.

The baby is born with some desires, not many; others it acquires as time goes on. Learning to cope with the world is learning how to satisfy and to modify these desires in a world that is partly propitious and partly hostile. For the world does not leap to gratify my desires like an assiduous flunkey; I do not get fed by being hungry. My desires are incompatible with each other and they come into conflict with those of other people. We have to learn both to bend the world to our wills and to bend our wills to the world. A man's morality is the way in which, in important matters, he does this.

Men are by nature rational and social animals, but only potentially so; they become actually rational and social only in a suitable environment, an environment in which they learn to speak a language. Learning how to cope with one's environment goes on side by side with learning to talk. The child's concepts, the meanings which, at every stage, words have for him, change as his horizon becomes wider, as he learns to grasp ideas that are more and more complicated, more and more remote from the primitive actions and passions that initially constitute his entire conscious life. It is not therefore surprising that the *form* of his morality, the meanings which moral words have and the ways in which they hang together, reflect at each stage the kind of experience he has. To babies who cannot yet talk we cannot, without serious error, attribute any thoughts at all; but though they cannot think, they can certainly feel, experience pleasure and pain, satisfaction and frustration. It is in these preverbal experiences that the origin of the ideas of "good" and "bad," even of "right" and "wrong," must be found; for their later development I turn to Piaget. My case for saying that religious morality is infantile cannot be conclusively made out without a much more detailed study of Piaget's researches than I have space for; I shall concentrate on a few points that seem to me to bear directly on the issue between the religious morality of law and the secular morality of purpose.

Piaget made a detailed study of the attitudes of children of different ages to the game of marbles, and he found three distinct stages. A very small child handles the marbles and throws them about as his humor takes him; he is playing, but not playing a *game*; for there are no rules governing his actions, no question of anything being done right or wrong. Towards the end of this stage he will, to some extent, be playing according to rules; for he will imitate older children who are playing a rule-governed game. But the child himself is not conscious of obeying rules; he has not yet grasped the concept of a "rule," of what a rule *is*. We may call this the premoral attitude to rules.

The second type of attitude is exhibited by children from five to nine. During this stage, says Piaget, "the rules are regarded as sacred and inviolable, emanating from adults and lasting for ever. Every suggested alteration in the rules strikes the child as a transgression." Piaget calls this attitude to rules "heteronomous" to mark the fact that the children regard the rules as coming, as indeed they do, from the outside, as being imposed on them by others. We might also call this the "deontological stage," to mark the fact that the rules are not questioned; they just *are* the rules of marbles, and that's that. At this stage the child has the concept of a rule, he knows what a rule is; but he has not yet asked what a rule is *for*. This deontological character is obviously connected with the unchangeability of the rules. Like laws in a primitive society, they are thought of as having been handed down from time immemorial, as much a part of the natural order of things as sunrise and sunset. The child may chafe at obedience and may sometimes disobey; but he does not question the authority of the rules.

Finally, at the third stage, the child begins to learn what the rules are for, what the point of having any rules is, and why it is better to have this rule rather than that. "The rule," says Piaget, "is now looked upon as a law due to mutual consent, which you must respect if you want to be loyal, but which it is permissible to alter on condition of enlisting the general opinion on your side." He calls this type of attitude "autonomous" to mark the fact that the children now regard themselves, collectively, as the authors of the rules. This is not to say that they falsely suppose themselves to have invented them; they know well enough that they received them from older children. But they are the authors in the sense of being the final authorities; what tradition gave them they can change; from "this is how we learnt to play" they no longer pass unquestioningly to "this is how we ought to play." We might also call this stage "teleological" to mark the fact that the rules are no longer regarded as sacred, as worthy of obedience simply because they are what they are, but as serving a purpose, as rules for playing a game that they want to play. Rules there must certainly be; and in one sense they are sacred enough. Every player must abide by them; he cannot pick and choose. But in another sense there is nothing sacred about them; they are, and are known to be, a *mere* device, to be molded and adapted in the light of the purpose which they are understood by all the players to serve.

To illustrate the transition between the second and the third stages I should like to refer to a case from my own experience. Last summer I was with one other adult and four children on a picnic, and the children wanted to play rounders. We had to play according to the rules they had learnt at school because those just were the rules of rounders. This involved having two teams, and you can well imagine that, with only three players in each team, the game quickly ran on the rocks. When I suggested adapting the rules to our circumstances all the children were scandalized at first. But the two older children soon came round to the idea that, situated as we were, we should have to change the rules or not play at all and to the idea that it would not be wicked to change the rules. The two younger children were troubled, one might say, in their consciences about the idea of changing the rules. In Piaget's words, they thought of an alteration of rules as a transgression against them, having as yet no grasp of the distinction between an alteration of the rules by common consent to achieve a common purpose and the unilateral breach or defiance of them. In the eyes of these younger children we were not proposing to play a slightly different game, one better adapted to our situation; we were proposing to play the old game, but to play it wrong, almost dishonestly.

In another of Piaget's researches, this time directly concerned with moral attitudes, he told the children pairs of stories in each of which a child does something in some sense "bad" and asked which of the children was naughtier, which deserved most punishment. In one such story a child accidently breaks fifteen cups while opening a door, and in the companion story breaks one cup while stealing jam. The replies of the very young children are mixed, some saying that the first child was naughtier; older children are unanimous in calling the second child naughtier. They have got beyond the primitive level of assessing moral guilt by the extent of the damage done.

Some of the youngest children do not recognize an act as wrong unless it is actually found out and punished, and we may call these last two points taken together "moral realism," because they display an attitude of mind that makes questions of morality questions of external fact. The inner state of the culprit —his motives and intentions—have nothing to do with it. To break crockery is wrong; therefore to break more crockery is more wrong. Moral laws are like laws of Nature, and Nature gives no marks for good or bad intentions and accepts no excuses. The fire will burn you if you touch it, however careful you were to avoid it. But if you are careless and, by good luck, avoid it, you will not be burnt; for Nature gives no bad marks for carelessness either. In the same way, if you lie and are punished, that is bad; but if you lie and are not punished, that is not bad at all. The fact that retribution did not follow *shows* that the lie was not, in this case, wrong.

3. I want now to compare the religious with the secular attitude towards the moral system which, in its content, both Christians and Humanists accept. I shall try to show that the religious attitude retains these characteristics of deontology, heteronomy and realism which are proper and indeed necessary in the development of a child, but not proper to an adult: But I must repeat the caution with which I began. The views which I called "moral realism," which make intentions irrelevant, were expressed by very young children. No doubt many of these children were Christians and I do not wish to suggest that they never grew up, that they never adopted a more mature and enlightened attitude. This would be absurd. My thesis is rather that these childish attitudes survive in the moral attitudes of adult Christians—and of some secular moralists—as an alien element, like an outcrop of igneous rock in an alluvial plain. When Freud says of someone that he is fixated at the oral stage of sexuality he does not mean that he still sucks his thumb; he means rather that some of his characteristic attitudes and behavior patterns can be seen as an adult substitute for thumb sucking. In the same way, I suggest that some elements characteristic of Christian morality are substitutes for childish attitudes. In the course of this comparison I shall try to show how these infantile attitudes belong to a stage that is a *necessary* stage on the way to the fully adult, a stage which we must have passed through in order to reach maturity.

It needs little reflection to see that deontology and heteronomy are strongly marked features of all religious moralities. First for deontology. For some Christians the fundamental sin, the fount and origin of all sin, is disobedience to God. It is not the nature of the act of murder or of perjury that makes it wrong; it is the fact that such acts are transgressions of God's commands. On the other hand, good acts are not good in themselves, good in their own nature, but good only *as* acts of obedience to God. "I give no alms only to satisfy the hunger of my brother, but to accomplish the will and command of my God; I draw not my purse for his sake that demands it, but his that enjoined it" (Sir Thomas Browne, *Religio Medici* II, 2). Here charity itself is held to be good *only because* God has told us to be charitable. It is difficult not to see in this a reflection of the small child's attitude towards his parents and the other authorities from whom he learns what it is right to do. In the first instance little Tommy learns that it is wrong to pull his sister's hair, not because it hurts her, but because Mummy forbids it.

The idea of heteronomy is also strongly marked in Christian morality. "Not as I will, but as thou wilt." The demand made by Christianity is that of surrendering self, not in the ordinary sense of being unselfish, of loving our neighbor and even our enemy. It is the total surrender of the *will* that is required; Abraham must be prepared to sacrifice Isaac at God's command, and I take this to mean that we must be prepared to sacrifice our most deeply felt moral concerns if God should require us to do so. If we dare to ask why, the only answer is "Have faith"; and faith is an essentially heteronomous idea; for it is not a reasoned trust in someone in whom we have good grounds for reposing trust; it is blind faith, utter submission of our own reason and will.

Now, to the small child morality is necessarily deontological and heteronomous in form; he must learn *that* certain actions are right and others wrong before he can begin to ask *why* they are, and he learns this from other people. The child has his own spontaneous springs of action; there are things he wants to do off his own bat; morality is a curb, at first nothing but a curb on his own volition. He comes up against parental discipline, even if only in the form of the giving and withdrawing of love, long before he can have any compassion, long before he has any conception of others as sentient beings. When he begins to learn language, words like "bad" must mean simply "what hurts me; what I don't like"; through the mechanism of parental discipline they come to mean "what adults forbid and punish me for." It is only because actions which cause suffering to others figure so largely among parental prohibitions that the child learns to connect the word "bad" with them at all.

If we consider the foundations of Christian ethics in more detail we shall find in them moral realism as well. Christianity makes much of charity and the love of our neighbor; but it does not say, as the Greeks did, that this is good because it is what befits the social animal, Man. We ought to be charitable because this is laid on us as a duty and because this state of the soul is the proper state for it during its transient mortal life. We must be charitable because (we are told) only so can we arrive at the soul's goal, the right relation to God. This fundamental isolation of the individual soul with God seems clearly to reflect what one supposes must be the state of mind of the small baby for whom, at the dawn of consciousness, there is only himself on the one side and the collective world of adults, represented largely by his parents, on the other, for whom the idea of others as individuals, as beings like himself, does not yet exist.

This impression is increased when we consider some accounts of what this right relationship between the soul and God is. Granted that to achieve this is the object of right living, just *what* relationship is it that we are to try to achieve? The terms of the relation are an omnipotent creator and his impotent creature, and between such terms the only relation possible is one of utter one-sided dependence, in which the only attitude proper to the creature must be one of adoration, a blend of love and fear. Surely this is just how the world must appear to the young child; for he really *is* impotent, wholly dependent on beings whose ways he cannot understand, beings sometimes loving, some-times angry, but always omnipotent, always capricious—in short, gods. "As for Dr. Wulicke himself personally, he had all the awful mystery, duplicity, obstinacy, and jealousy of the Old Testament God. He was as frightful in his smiles as in his anger."[1]

Consider in this connection the ideas of original sin and grace. Every son of Adam is, of his own nature, utterly corrupt, redeemable only by divine grace. Once more, the conditions in which the child learns morality provide an obvious source for this remarkable conception. Parents are not only omniscient and omnipotent; they are also necessarily and always morally in the right. This must be so, since they are, as the child sees it, the authors of the moral law. Morality, the idea of something being right or wrong, enters the horizon of the child only at those points at which he has, so to speak, a dispute with authority, only on those occasions on which he is told or made to do something that he does not spontaneously want to do. From these premises that, at the time when the meanings of "right" and "wrong" are being learnt, the child must disagree with its parents and that they must be right he naturally passes to the conclusion that he must always be wrong. To have the sense of actual sin is to have the sense that one has, on this occasion, done wrong; to have the sense of original sin is simply to feel that one must be always and inevitably wrong. This sense of sin has often been deliberately and cruelly fostered; John Bunyan is not the only man to have left on record the agony of his childhood; but the point I wish to make is that the infantile counterpart of the sense of sin is a necessity at a certain stage of moral de-velopment, the stage at which moral words are being learnt and moral rules accepted as necessarily what parents say they are.

On the other side of the picture there is the doctrine of grace. Each in-dividual soul is either saved or damned; but its fate, at least according to some versions, is wholly out of its own control. In these extreme versions, grace is absolutely necessary and wholly sufficient for salvation; and grace is the *free* gift of God. As far as the creature is concerned, there is absolutely nothing that he can do or even try to do either to merit or to obtain it.[2] From his point of view the giving or withholding of the means of salvation must be wholly capricious.

Once more, this is how parental discipline must seem to the child who cannot yet understand its aims and motives. Consider, for example, how even the most careful and consistent parents react towards what they call the clumsiness of a child. He knocks things over; he fumbles with his buttons.

---

[1]Thomas Mann, *Buddenbrooks*, referring to the headmaster whom Hanno and Kai nicknamed "The Lord God." The whole chapter, Part XI, ch. 2, illustrates this point.

[2]This is, I know, heretical; yet I cannot see in the subtle palliatives offered by Catholic theologians anything but evasions, vain attempts to graft a more enlightened moral outlook on to a theological tree which will not bear them. The reformers seem to me to have been right in the sense that they were restoring the original doctrine of the Church.

Though most parents do not think of themselves as punishing a child for such things, their behavior is, from the child's point of view, indistinguishable from punishment. They display more irritation when the child knocks over a valuable vase than when he knocks over a cheap cup, when the button-fumbling happens to occur at a moment when they are in a hurry than when it does not. If a father takes from a small child something that is dangerous to play with or stops him hurting himself by a movement necessarily rough, that to the child is indistinguishable from punishment; it is a thwarting of his inclination for no reason that he can see. Children often say things that they know to be untrue; sometimes they are reprimanded for lying, sometimes complimented on their imagination. How can the child know under which heading, the good or the bad, a piece of invention will come, except by observing whether it is punished or rewarded? The child, by this time, is beginning to make efforts to try to please his parents, to do what, in his childish mind, he thinks right. The parents, not being expert child psychologists, will often fail to notice this; more often they will disregard it. To the child, therefore, there is little correlation between his own intentions and the reactions he evokes from the adult world. Salvation in the form of parental smiles and damnation in the form of parental frowns will come to him, like grace, in a manner that both seems and is wholly unconnected with any inwardly felt guilt. The mystery of God's ways to Man is the mystery of a father's ways to his children.

This characterization of religious morality as essentially infantile may seem to be unnecessary; for do not Christians themselves liken their relationship to God as that of child to father? In so doing they do not seem to me always to realize how incompatible this father-child relationship is with the Greek conception of the good life which they recognize as one of the sources of their moral doctrine. Aristotle says that children, like animals, have no share in the good life (a remark which always sounds so odd when people translate it as "children have no share in happiness"), and the reason he gives is that children do not *act*. This is a deep furrow to begin to plough at this stage— what is meant by "action"; but briefly it is motion that is self-initiated and responsible. The prime difference between the adult and the child is that the adult has freedom to choose for himself and has, what goes with freedom, responsibility for his actions. In the life of a child there is always, in the last resort, the parent or some substitute for a parent to turn to. The father is responsible at law for the actions of his child; he will undo what harm the child has done; he will put things right, will save the child from the consequences of his mistakes. To pass from childhood into adulthood is essentially to pass from dependence into freedom, and the price we pay is responsibility. As adults we make our own choices and must accept their consequences; the shield that in our childish petulance we once thought so irksome is no longer there to protect us. To many of us this is a matter of life-long regret, and we search endlessly for a father substitute. Surely "they" will get us out of the mess; there ought to be a law; why doesn't somebody. . . .

These, in this godless age, are the common secular substitutes; religion, when it is not a patent substitute, is only a more profound, a more insinuating one.

4. The postulation of a god as the author of the moral law solves no more problems in ethics than the postulation of a god as first cause solves problems in metaphysics. Nor need we base morality, as I have done, on the metaphysical conception of Man as a rational, social animal, though we shall do so if we care to maintain the link with the old meaning of the word "humanist." To me, as a philosopher, some systematic view of the whole of my experience, some metaphysic, is essential, and this conception of the nature of Man makes more sense of my experience than any other I know. But I certainly should not argue that *because* the species Man has such and such a nature, *therefore* each and every man ought to act in such and such ways. In trying to sketch a humanist morality I shall start simply with the idea that a morality is a set of habits of choice ultimately determined by the question "What life is most satisfactory to me as a whole?" and I start with this because I simply do not *understand* the suggestion that I ought to do anything that does not fit into this conception. Outside this context the word "ought" has for me no meaning; and here at least I should expect Christians to agree with me.

If we start in this way, inquiries into my own nature and into the nature of Man at once become relevant. For my nature is such that there are some things that are impossible for me to do. Some hopes must be illusory, and nothing but frustration could come of indulging them. I could not, for example, become an operatic tenor or a test cricketer. Inquiries into the nature of Man are relevant in two ways; first, because I have to live as a man among men, secondly, because all men are to some degree alike and some of my limitations are common to us all. None of us can fly or witness past events. It is only insofar as men are alike that we can even begin to lay down rules as to how they should (all) behave; for it is only insofar as they are alike that they will find satisfaction and frustration in the same things. Prominent among the similarities among men are the animal appetites, the desire for the love and companionship of their own species, and the ability to think; and it is these three similarities that make us all "moral" beings. Morality consists largely, if not quite wholly, in the attempt to realize these common elements in our nature in a coherent way, and we have found that this cannot be done without adopting moral rules and codes of law. Humanism does not imply the rejection of all moral rules, but it does imply the rejection of a deontological attitude towards them. Even Piaget's older children could not have played marbles without rules; but they treated them as adaptable, as subservient to the purpose of playing a game, which is what they wanted to do. They treated the rules as a wise man treats his motor car, not as an object of veneration but as a convenience.

This, I suggest, is how we, as adults, should regard moral rules. They are necessary, in the first place, because one man's aim in life often conflicts with the aims of others and because most of our aims involve the cooperation of others, so that, even for purely selfish reasons, we must conform to rules to which others also conform. Most moral rules, from that prohibiting murder to that enjoining punctuality, exist for this purpose. But morality is not wholly an affair of regulating our dealings with others; each man has within himself desires of many different kinds which cannot all be fully satisfied; he must establish an order of priorities. Here I think almost all moralists, from Plato to D. H. Lawrence, have gone astray; for they have overemphasized the extent to which men are like each other and consequently been led to embrace the illusory concept of a "best life" that is the same for all of us. Plato thought this was a life dominated by the pursuit of knowledge, Lawrence one dominated by the pursuit of sensual experience and animal activity. I do not happen to enjoy lying naked on the grass; but I should not wish to force my preference for intellectual endeavor on anyone who did. Why should we not, within the framework of uniformity required for any life to be satisfactory to anyone at all, seek satisfaction in our own different ways?

The word "morality" is usually understood in a sense narrower than that in which I have been using it, to refer to just this necessary framework, to the rules to which we must all conform in order to make our aims, however diverse, realizable in a world which we all have to share. In Hobbes' words, the sphere of morality is limited to "those qualities of mankind that concern their living together in peace and unity" (*Leviathan*, ch. xi). If this is the purpose of moral rules, we must be willing to keep them under review and to discard or modify those that, in the light of experience, we find unnecessary or obstructive. But they must retain a certain inflexibility, since, in our casual contacts, it is important that people should be reliable, should conform so closely to a publicly agreed code that, even if we do not know them as individuals, we know what to expect of them. "That men perform their covenants made" is an adequate summary of morality in this limited sense.

But, though morality in this sense is necessary, it is not all. Rules belong to the superficial periphery of life. Like the multiplication table and other thought-saving dodges, they exist to free us for more important activities. It is beyond the power of any man to regulate all his dealings with all the people with whom he comes in casual contact by love; for love requires a depth of understanding that cannot be achieved except in close intimacy. Rules have no place in marriage or in friendship. This does not mean that a man must keep his word in business but may break promises made to his wife or to a friend; it is rather that the notion of keeping a promise made to a wife or friend from a sense of duty is utterly out of place, utterly foreign to the spirit of their mutual relationship. For what the sense of duty requires of us is always the commission or omission of specific acts.

That friends should be loyal to one another I take for granted; but we cannot set out a list of acts that they should avoid as disloyal with the sort of precision (itself none too great) with which we could list the things a man should not do in business. Too much will depend on the particular circumstances and the particular natures of the people concerned. Rules must, of their very nature, be general; that is their virtue and their defect. They lay down what is to be done or not done in *all* situations of a certain general kind, and they do this because their function is to ensure reliability in the absence of personal knowledge. But however large we make the book of rules, however detailed we try to make its provisions, its complexity cannot reach to that of a close personal relationship. Here what matters is not the commission or omission of specific acts but the spirit of the relationship as a whole. A man thinks, not of what his obligation to his wife or his friend requires of him, but of what it is best for his wife or his friend that he should do. A personal relationship does indeed consist of specific acts; the spirit that exists between husband and wife or between friends is nothing over and above the specific things they do together. But each specific act, like each brush stroke in a picture or each note in a symphony, is good or bad only as it affects the quality of the relationship as a whole. The life of love is, like a work of art, not a means to an end, but an end in itself. For this reason in all close human relationships there should be a flexibility in our attitude to rules characteristic to the expert artist, craftsman, or games player.

The expert moves quickly, deftly, and, to the untutored eye, even carelessly. It takes me hours to prune an apple tree, and I have to do it book in hand; the expert goes over the tree in a few minutes, snipping here and slashing there, with the abandonment of a small boy who has neither knowledge of pruning nor intention to prune. Indeed, to someone who does not know what he is about, his movements must seem more like those of Piaget's youngest children who just threw the marbles about. But the similarity is superficial. For one thing, the master craftsman's movements do mostly follow the book for all that he never refers to it; and for another he does know what he is about and it is just this knowledge that entitles him to flout the rules when it is suitable to do so. No apple tree is exactly like the drawing in the book, and expertise lies in knowing when and how to deviate from its instructions.

This analogy must not be pressed too far. The conduct of life is more complicated and more difficult than any such task as pruning a tree and few of us could claim, without improper pride, the master craftsman's licence. But I should like to press it some way, to suggest that, in all important matters, our chief consideration should be, not to conform to any code of rules, but simply how we can produce the best results; that we should so act that we can say in retrospect, not "I did right," but "I did what befitted the pattern of life I have set myself as a goal."

As a philosopher, I cannot but speak in abstract generalities, and it is central to my thesis that at this point the philosopher must give way to the novelist. Tolstoy, Thomas Mann, and Forster have given us many examples of the contrast between the rule-bound and the teleological attitudes to life. But I should like to end by descending one level, not to the particular, but to the relatively specific, and to consider as an example one moral rule, the prohibition of adultery.

By "adultery" I understand the act of sexual intercourse with someone other than one's spouse. It is expressly forbidden in the Bible, absolutely and without regard to circumstances; it is a crime in some countries and many would make it a crime in this. Until very recently it was almost the only ground for civil divorce. A marriage is supposed to be a life-long union. It could be entirely devoid of love—some married couples have not spoken to each other for years, communicating by means of a blackboard; yet no grounds for divorce existed. Or the husband might insist on sexual intercourse with his wife against her will and yet commit no sin. But let him once go out, get drunk, and have a prostitute and the whole scene changes. He has sinned; his wife has a legal remedy and, in the eyes of many who are not Christians but have been brought up in a vaguely Christian tradition, he has now done a serious wrong. This is a rule-and-act morality according to which what is wrong is a specific act; and it is wrong in all circumstances even, for example, if the wife is devoid of jealousy or so devoid of love that she would rather have her husband lie in any bed but hers.

If we look at this rule against adultery from a teleological standpoint it must appear wholly different. A humanist may, of course, reject the whole conception of monogamy; but if, like myself, he retains it, he will do so only because he believes that the life-long union of a man and a woman in the intimacy of marriage is a supreme form of love. Copulation has its part to play in such a union; but, for the species Man, it cannot be its essence. If someone who holds this view still thinks adultery is wrong, he will do so because it appears to him to be an act of disloyalty, an act likely to break the union which he values. Two consequences follow from this. The first is that if a marriage is, for whatever reason, devoid of love, there is now no union to break; so neither adultery nor any other act can break it. The second is that since adultery is now held to be wrong, not in itself, but only *as* an act of disloyalty, it will not *be* wrong when it is *not* an act of disloyalty. An adultery committed with the full knowledge and consent of the spouse will not be wrong at all. A so-called "platonic" friendship, even too assiduous an attendance at the local pub or sewing circle, anything that tends to weaken the bonds of love between the partners will be far more damaging to the marriage and consequently far more deeply immoral. Just *what* specific acts are immoral must, on this view, depend on the particular circumstances and the particular people concerned. Christians also insist on the uniqueness of individual people; but since law is, of its nature, general, this insistence seems wholly incompatible with the morality of law to which they are also committed.

BARUCH A. BRODY

5.10   Morality and Religion Reconsidered[1]

There are many people who believe that, in one way or another, morality needs a religious backing. One of the many things that might be meant by this vague and ambiguous claim[2] is the following: there are certain moral truths that are true only because of the truth of certain religious truths. In particular, the truth of certain claims about the rightness (wrongness) of a given action is dependent upon the truth of certain religious claims to the effect that God wants us to do (refrain from doing) that action. This belief, in effect, bases certain parts of morality upon the will of God.

Philosophers have not commonly agreed with such claims. And there is an argument, whose ancestor is an argument in the *Euthyphro*,[3] that is supposed to show that such claims are false. It runs as follows: the proponents of the claim in question have reversed the order of things. Doing a given action *A* is not right (wrong) because God wants us to do (refrain from doing) *A*; rather, God wants us to do (refrain from doing) *A* because of some other reason which is the real reason why *A* is right (wrong) for us to do. For, if the situation were the way it is depicted by the proponents of the claim in question, we would have moral truths based upon the arbitrary desires of God as to what we should do (refrain from doing), and this is objectionable.

I would like to reexamine this issue and to show that the situation is far more complicated than philosophers normally imagine it to be. I should like to show (a) that the general argument suggested by the *Euthyphro* is not as persuasive as it is ordinarily thought to be, and (b) that it is even less persuasive when we see the religious claim applied to specific moral issues, and that this is so because the claims about the will of God can be supplemented by additional theological claims.

---

[1]I should like to thank David Rosenthal for his many insightful comments on an earlier version of this paper.

[2]Other things that might be meant are: (a) we know that certain moral truths are true because we know the truth of certain religious truths (perhaps, that God has revealed to us that the action is right), and (b) we have a reason to do what is right because of the truth of certain religious truths (perhaps, that God will reward us if we do). We will not discuss these claims in this paper.

[3]We leave aside, for this paper, the question as to exactly what was the argument in the *Euthyphro*. On that issue, see R. Sharvy's "Euthyphro 9d–11b", *Nous* (1972) which influenced the way I constructed the argument to be considered below.

I

Let us begin by looking at the argument more carefully. We shall formulate it as follows:

(1) Let us suppose that it is the case that there is some action A that is right (wrong) only because God wants us to do (refrain from doing) it.

(2) There must be some reason for God's wanting us to do (refrain from doing) A, some reason that does not involve God's wanting us to do (refrain from doing) it.

(3) Therefore, that reason must also be a reason why A is right (wrong).

(4) So we have a contradiction, (1) is false, and either there are no actions that are right (wrong) because God wants us to do (refrain from doing) them or, if there are such actions, that is not the only reason why those actions are right (wrong).

What can be said by way of defense on (2)? The basic idea behind it seems to be the following: if God wanted us to do (refrain from doing) A, but he had no reason for that want that was independent of his act of wanting, then his act of wanting would be an arbitrary act, one that entails some imperfection in him. But God is a perfect being. Therefore, he must have some reason for wanting us to do (refrain from doing) A, some reason that is, of course, independent of that want of his. Now it is not entirely clear that this argument is sound, for it is not clear that the performance by an agent of an arbitrary act (even an arbitrary act of willing) entails some imperfection in the agent.[4] But we shall let that issue pass for now and focus, for the moment, on the crucial step (3).

It is clear that step (3) must rest upon some principle like the following:[5]

(Trans.) If p because of q and q because of r, then p because of r.

There are two things that should be noted about this principle. The first is that if we are to use it in our context we will have to take it as ranging over different types of cases in which we say "because." After all, there are significant differences between cases in which we make claims of the form "A is right (wrong) because God wants us to do (refrain from doing) A" and

---

[4]This is a claim that would certainly be denied by writers in the Calvinist tradition. Thus, Jonathan Edwards, writes as follows in connection with the question of salvation and damnation:

It is meet that God should order all these things according to his own pleasure. By reason of his greatness and glory, by which he is infinitely above all, he is worthy to be sovereign, and that his pleasure should in all things take place. [*Jonathan Edwards* (Hill and Wang: 1935) p. 119]

[5]It could, of course, rest upon the weaker principle, that only held in cases where q was some agent's wanting something. But all of the points we will make are equally applicable to this weaker principle.

cases in which we make claims of the form "God wants us to do (refrain from doing) A because r," for it is only in the latter type of case that we have the reason-for-wanting, "because." The second point is that there are real problems with this principle. While Joe may go home because his wife wants him to do so, and she may want him to do so because she wants to have it out with him, it may well not be the case that he goes home because she wants to have it out with him. So the principle is going to need some modifying, and it is not clear how one is to do this while still preserving the inference from (1) and (2) to (3).

Still, let us suppose that this can be done. Our argument faces the following further objection: God's wanting us to do (refrain from doing) A is not the whole of the reason why the action is right (wrong); the additional part of the reason is that he is our creator to whom we owe obedience. And when we take into account the full reason, the argument collapses. After all, the *Euthyphro* argument would then run as follows:

(1') Let us suppose that there is some action A that is right (wrong) only because God wants us to do (refrain from doing) A and he is our creator to whom we owe obedience.

(2') There must be some reason for God's wanting us to do (refrain from doing) A, some reason that does not involve God's wanting us to do (refrain from doing) A.

(3') Therefore, that reason must also be a reason why A is right (wrong).

(4') So we have a contradiction, (1') is false, and either there are no actions that are right (wrong) because God, who is our creator and to whom we owe obedience, wants us to do (refrain from doing) them, or, if there are such actions, that is not the only reason why those actions are right (wrong).

And, even supposing that (Trans.) is true, (3') would not follow from (1') and (2').

It is clear that the proponents of the *Euthyphro* argument have got to block this move. How might they do so? The most straightforward move is to deny the moral relevance of the fact that God is our creator, to claim that even if he is, we have no obligation to obey his wishes and that, therefore, the reason advanced in (1') cannot be a reason why A is right (wrong).

Is this move acceptable? Consider, for a moment, our special obligation to obey the wishes of our parents.[6] Why do we have that obligation? Isn't it because they created us? And since this is so, we seem to have an obligation, in at least some cases, to follow their wishes. So, x's being our creator can be part of a reason for doing (refraining from doing) an action A if the other

---

[6]This analogy between our obeying the will of God and the will of our parents is based upon the Talmudic discussion (in *Tractate Kedushin*, 30ᵇ) of the obligation to honor one's parents.

part is that that is *x*'s wish. And if this is so in the case of our parents, why shouldn't it also be so in the case of God? How then can the defendents of the *Euthyphro* argument say that the fact that God created us cannot, together with some facts about his wishes, be a reason for doing (refraining from doing) some action *A*?

The proponents of the *Euthyphro* argument have a variety of ways, of differing plausibilities, of objecting to this defense of (1'). They might claim: (a) that we have no special obligations at all to our parents; (b) that it is no part of the special obligations that we have to our parents to do (refrain from doing) what they want us to do (refrain from doing); (c) that our special obligations to our parents are due to something that they do other than merely creating us, something that God does not do, so the whole question of our special obligations to our parents has nothing to do with the truth of (1').[7]

But there is another move open to the proponents of the *Euthyphro* argument. Rather than attempting to object to (1'), they might construct the following alternative argument against it, one that has the additional merit of not depending upon (Trans.):

(1') Let us suppose that there is some action *A* that is right (wrong) only because God wants us to do (refrain from doing) *A* and he is our creator to whom we owe obedience.

(2'*) There must be some reason for God's wanting us to do (refrain from doing) *A*, some reason that does not involve God's wanting us to do (refrain from doing) *A*, and some reason that is, by itself, a reason why *A* is right (wrong).

(4') So we have a contradiction, (1') is false, and either there are no actions that are right (wrong) because God, who is our creator and to whom we owe obedience, wants us to do (refrain from doing) them, or, if there are such actions, that is not the only reason why those actions are right (wrong).

The trouble with this move, of course, is that it rests upon the extremely strong assumption (2'*), and even if, to avoid the problem with arbitrary acts of willing, we are prepared to grant (2'), there seems to be little reason to grant this stronger (2'*) with its extra assumption about what are the types of reasons that God has for his acts of willing.

In short, then, the traditional argument that the rightness or wrongness of an action cannot depend upon the will of God rests upon some dubious premises, and things get worse when we add the idea that we have an obligation to follow God's wishes because he is our creator. There is, however,

---

[7] Of the three moves, the third seems most plausible. But religious people might well respond to it as follows: let us grant that our special obligations to our parents are due to additional facts about the parent-child relationship (e.g., the way parents raise and sustain their children, etc.). God has those additional relations to all of his creations, and they therefore still have to him the special obligation of obedience.

more to say about this issue, for there are reasons to suppose that some particular moral truths may depend in a special way upon the idea that God is the creator. We turn, therefore, to a consideration of these special cases.

II

Let us begin by considering a set of issues surrounding the idea of property rights. What is involved in one's owning a piece of property, in one's having a right to it? It seems to mean, in part, that while one may not use that property so as to infringe upon the rights of others, one may, if one wants, use it in such a way as to benefit while others lose. No doubt this distinction is unclear for there are cases in which it is difficult to say whether someone's rights have been infringed upon or whether he has simply lost out.[8] But the distinction is clear enough for our purposes.

How does one come to own a piece of property? One intuitively attractive picture runs as follows: if there is a physical object that belongs to no one, and if some person comes along and does something with it (mixes his labor with it), then the object in question belongs to that person.[9] He may then, in one way or another, transfer that property to someone else, who then has property rights in that object. Indeed, transference is now the most prevalent way of acquiring property. But all property rights are ultimately based, in this picture, upon these initial acts of acquisition through the mixing of one's labor with unowned objects. This picture certainly faces some familiar objections.[10] To begin with, what right does a person have to appropriate the ownerless piece of property for himself, thereby depriving all of us of the right to use it? And secondly, does the act of mixing his labor with it give him ownership rights over the initial, ownerless object or simply over the products (if any) of his interaction with it? But we shall leave aside these worries for now and suppose that something like this account is correct, for the question that we want to consider is whether or not it would have to be modified in light of any theological truths.

This picture clearly presupposes that, if there is such a thing as property owned by human beings, then there was, at least at one point in human history, such a thing as ownerless property, property that one could acquire if one mixed one's labor with it. But suppose that the universe was created by a personal God. Then, it might well be argued, he owns the whole universe, and there is not, and never has been, such a thing as ownerless property. Now suppose further that this creator allows men to use for their purposes the property that they mix their labor with, but he does so with the restriction

---

[8]Here is just one: let us suppose that I build a high wall at the back of my property, thereby depriving your yard of sunlight. There is no doubt that you have suffered a loss, but have I deprived you of any of your rights?

[9]See, for example, chapter 5 of Locke's *Second Treatise of Civil Government*.

[10]See, for example, chapter 3 of the First Memoir of Proudhon's *What is Property?*

that they must not use it in such a way as to cause a great loss to other people (even though the rights of these people are not infringed upon). That is to say, suppose that this creator allows people to take his property only if they follow certain of his wishes. Then, don't they have an obligation to do so, or, at least, an obligation to either return the property or to do so?[11] So, in short, if God, the creator, does wish us not to use the things of the world in certain ways, this will entail certain moral restrictions on property rights that might not be present otherwise.

Let us, at this point, introduce the idea of stewardship over property. We shall say that someone has stewardship over a piece of property just in case they own that piece of property subject to certain restrictions as to how they may use it and/or subject to certain requirements as to how they must use it, restrictions and/or requirements that were laid down by some previous owner of that piece of property. Now, what I have been arguing for is the idea that, if certain theological beliefs (that God created the universe but allows man to appropriate the property in it subject to certain restrictions and requirements that he lays down) are true, then men will have rights of stewardship, and not property rights, over the property that they possess. And if this is so, then there will be moral truths (about restrictions and requirements that property-possessors must follow)[12] that might not be true if these theological beliefs were false. So we have here a set of moral claims whose truth or falsehood might depend upon the truth or falsehood of certain theological claims.

The question that we must now consider is whether or not the *Euthyphro* argument, even if sound in general, could be used against the claim we are now considering. How would it run in this context? Presumably, it would run as follows:

(1′′) Let us suppose that there are certain restrictions on property rights and that they exist only because God, from whom we get our stewardship over the earth, has imposed them.

(2′′) There must be some reason why God has imposed these restrictions, a reason that does not involve his wanting us to follow them.

(3′′) Therefore, that reason must also be a reason why we should follow those restrictions.

(4′′) So we have a contradiction, (1′′) is false, and either there are

---

[11]If the individual was aware of what these wishes are before he takes the property, then it would seem that he has the obligation to follow them. But if he was not, and if they turn out to be strange and/or arbitrary, then perhaps he only has the weaker obligation, and then only from that time at which he becomes aware of what the wishes are.

[12]It goes without saying that what exactly these restrictions are will vary from one theological system to another. The cases that are of the most interest for current discussions of property rights have to do, of course, with those systems in which the restrictions require one, in effect, at least to take into account the interests of other people and not merely their rights.

598 PART FIVE: MAN'S RELATION TO GOD

no such restrictions or there is some additional reason as to why they exist

As we saw in the last section, when we considered (1')–(4'), even if we grant (2'') and (Trans.), (3'') doesn't follow from (1'') and (2''). Now even if we grant what we are reluctant to grant in the last section, viz., that (1') is objectionable because the mere fact that someone created us gives us no moral reason for following his wishes, we would still have no reason for independently objecting to (1''). For if we have mere stewardship over the property we possess, then surely we do have an obligation to follow the wishes of him from whom we got our stewardship, and if God did create the world, then it certainly looks as though our property possession is a property stewardship gotten ultimately from God.

This point can also be put as follows. Neither (3') nor (3'') follows from the previous steps in their respective arguments, even if we grant the truth of (Trans.), because the reasons they provide for the moral claims in question involve some other theological facts besides God's willing certain things. Now the defenders of the *Euthyphro* argument may try to attack (1'') on independent grounds, but it is difficult to see the grounds that they would have. So it looks then as though certain theological claims are relevant to certain moral truths having to do with the existence and extent of rights over property.

To be sure, the defenders of the *Euthyphro* argument might, in desperation, trot out the following argument:

(1'') Let us suppose that there are certain restrictions on property rights and that they exist only because God, from whom we get our stewardship over the earth, has imposed them.

(2''*) There must be some reason why God has imposed these restrictions, a reason that does not involve his wanting us to follow them, and one that is, by itself, a reason why we should follow these restrictions.

(4'') So we have a contradiction, (1'') is false, and either there are no such restrictions or there is some additional reason as to why they exist.

But like step (2'*) of the previous section, step (2''*) has little to recommend it. Even if a perfect God has to have reasons for wanting us to behave in certain ways, and, a fortiori, for imposing restrictions on our behavior, it is unclear why they must meet the very strong final requirement laid down by (2''*).

III

In the previous section, we have discussed the implications of the theological idea that God, the creator, owns the universe for the issue of property rights. It is sometimes felt that this idea also has implications for the moral issue of the permissibility of suicide.[13] We will, in this section, explore that possibility.

The liberal argument for the permissibility of suicide is stated very clearly early on in the *Phaedo:*

> ... sometimes and for some people death is better than life. And it probably seems strange to you that it should not be right for those to whom death would be an advantage to benefit themselves, but that they should have to await the services of someone else. [62A]

It will do no good, of course, to object that the person might have some extremely important obligations that he would leave unfulfilled if he committed suicide, and this is why it is wrong for him to do so, because we could easily confine the discussions to cases in which he has no such obligations or to cases in which he could arrange for the executors of his estate to fulfill them. And moreover, such an argument would really only show that one should not be remiss in fulfilling one's obligations, it would not really show that there was something particularly wrong with the way the person who committed suicide did that.

Plato himself does not accept this argument for suicide (although he does think one can accede in being condemned to death), and he is opposed to suicide on the grounds that we are the possessions of the gods. His argument runs as follows:

> If one of your possessions were to destroy itself without intimation from you that you wanted it to die, wouldn't you be angry with it and punish it, if you had any means of doing so ... so if you look at it this way, I suppose it is not unreasonable to say that we must not put an end to ourselves until God sends more compulsions like the one we are facing now. [62C]

Leaving aside the peculiarity of the idea that one ought, if one can, to punish those who succeed in destroying themselves—as opposed to the more reasonable idea that one ought to punish those who merely try,—the idea that Plato is advancing is that the gods' property rights extend to us, and that we therefore have no right to destroy ourselves unless they give their permission.[14]

There are cases in which many religious people want to allow that suicide is permissible. One such case[15] is that of the person who commits suicide rather than face being compelled to do some very evil act. Thus, in a great

---

13R. F. Holland, in "Suicide" in Rachels's *Moral Problems* (Harper and Row: 1971) discusses other ways in which the moral issues surrounding suicide are intertwined with theological questions.

14Plato here is assuming the overly strong thesis that we never have a right to destroy someone else's property without their permission. Whether and how he could get a weaker thesis that would still leave the argument intact is something that cannot be considered here.

15For a discussion of such cases, see the opinion of Rabenu Tam mentioned in the Tosafot glosses to *Talmud, Tractate Avodat Zarah,* 18a.

many religious traditions, it would even be thought to be a meritorious act to commit suicide rather than face being tortured into committing acts of apostasy. Another such case is that of the person who commits suicide rather than reveal under torture secrets that would lead to the destruction of many innocent people. Can these exceptions be reconciled with the argument against suicide that we have been considering? It seems to me that they can. After all, the crucial objection to our destroying ourselves is that we have no right to do so without the permission of our owner, God, and the religious person might well add the additional claim that God has (perhaps in a revelation) already given his permission in these cases.

Obviously, the *Euthyphro* argument cannot be raised against the claim that we are considering. After all, the crucial first premise[16] would be the claim that

(1′′′) Let us suppose that we cannot take our own lives only because we are the property of God, who created us, and he does not want us to destroy this piece of his property.

Then even if we add

(2′′′) There must be some reason why he doesn't want us to do so, some reason that does not involve this want of his.

we will not, even assuming (Trans.), get the crucial

(3′′′) Therefore, that reason must also be a reason why we should not take our own lives.

We can, no doubt, consider using

(2′′′*) There must be some reason why he doesn't want us to do so, some reason that does not involve this want of his, and which is, by itself, a reason why we should not take our own lives.

instead of (2′′′), but it is no more plausible than (2′*) and (2′′*). Nor can we easily object to (1′′′) in the way that we did to (1′). Even if we have no obligation to listen to the wishes of him who has created us, just because he has created us, we do have an obligation not to destroy someone else's property, and, if God created us, then perhaps we are God's property.

Having said this, we can now see that more is at stake here than a mere

---

[16]Notice that the obligation to listen to the wishes of the property owner is stronger here than in the previous case. Even if his wishes are strange and/or arbitrary, that does not give us a right to disregard them and destroy the property.

prohibition of suicide. For if we are the property of God, then perhaps we just have an obligation to do whatever he says, and then perhaps we can return to our initial general claims about morality and consider the possible claim that

(1'#) actions are right (wrong) for us to do just in case and only because God, who has created us and owns us and whom we therefore have an obligation to follow, wants us to do (refrain from doing) them.

So a great deal hinges on this point.

Despite all that we have seen, it is unclear that this argument against suicide (and, a fortiori, the more general claim just considered) will do. In the case of property rights, the crucial idea was that God, who created the world, owns all property, and this claim seemed a coherent one. But here, in (1'''), the crucial idea is that God, because he created us, owns us. And perhaps one can object directly to (1''') that it is incoherent. Does it make sense, after all, to talk of an all-just being owning or possessing a human being? Isn't doing that an unjust act, one that cannot meaningfully be ascribed to an all-just being?

It is difficult to assess this objection. There is no doubt that the objection to the institution of slavery is exactly that we think it unjust for one human being to own another human being, to have another human being as his possession. But is it unjust for God, who is vastly superior to us and is our creator, to possess human beings? To put this question another way, is slavery unjust because it is wrong for one human being to possess another (in which case, both the argument against suicide and the general claim, with their supposition that we are the possessions of God, can stand) or because it is wrong that a human being be a possession, a piece of property (in which case, both collapse on the grounds of incoherence)? Religious people have, very often, opted for the former alternative,[17] and as it is difficult to see an argument to disprove their contentions; we have, probably, to conclude that theological claims might make a difference to the truth or falsity of moral claims concerning suicide, and perhaps to a great many other issues as well.

IV

There is still one final issue about which it is often claimed that theological beliefs about the will of a God who created the world are relevant to the truth of moral beliefs about that issue. This is the moral issue raised by vegetarians. At least some vegetarians argue as follows: we normally suppose that it is wrong, except in certain very special cases, to take the life of an innocent human being. But we normally have no objections to taking the life

---

[17]This is evidenced in the Talmudic idea (*Kedushin*, 22ᵇ) that it is wrong for man to sell himself into slavery because God would object on the grounds that "they are my slaves, and not the slaves of slaves."

of members of many other species to obtain from their bodies food, clothing, etc. Let us call these normal moral views the conventional consciousness. Now, argues the vegetarian, it is difficult to defend the conventional consciousness. What characteristics are possessed by all human beings, but by no members of any other species, and are such as to justify such a sharp moral distinction as the one drawn by the conventional consciousness?

I think that no one would deny that there is a gradation of development between different species, and most would concede that this gives rise to a gradation of rights. While few would object to killing a mosquito if it is being a minor nuisance, many would object to killing a dog on the same grounds. The interesting point, says the vegetarian, is that when we get to the case of human beings, the conventional consciousness accords to them many rights (including the strong right to life) even though there is not a sufficiently dramatic biological difference between these species to justify such a sharp moral difference. Therefore, concludes the vegetarian, we should reject the conventional consciousness and accord more of these rights (especially the right to life) to members of more species of animals.

This vegetarian argument draws further support from the fact that the intuitions embedded in the conventional consciousness are about species. After all, there are a variety of extreme cases (newly born infants, severely retarded individuals, people who are near death) in which many of the subtler features of human beings are not present but in which the conventional consciousness accords to the people in question far more rights than those normally accorded to animals. This makes it far more difficult to believe that there are some characteristics (a) possessed by all human beings, (b) not possessed by all animals, and (c) which justify the moral distinctions drawn by the conventional consciousness. So, the vegetarian concludes, we must reject the conventional consciousness.

There is a religious response to this vegetarian argument which runs as follows: when God created the world, he intended that man should use certain other species for food, clothing, etc. God did not, of course, give man complete freedom to do what he wants with these creatures. They are not, for example, to be treated cruelly. But, because that was God's intention, man can, and should use these creatures to provide him with food, clothing, etc. This view is embodied in the following Talmudic story:[18]

> A calf was being taken to the slaughter, when it broke away, hid his head under Rabbi's skirts, and lowed in terror. *Go, said he, for this wast thou created.* [B. Metzia, 85a]

It is pretty clear, once more, that the *Euthyphro* argument will not do against the claim we are considering. It is

---

[18]To be sure, Rabbi is punished for his answer, but only, as the text makes clear, because he fails to show compassion, not because his answer is unacceptable.

(1′′′′) Man can take the lives of animals so that he can obtain from their bodies food, clothing, etc., only because God, who created the world and owns everything in it, intended that he do so.

and even if we grant

(2′′′′) There is some reason why he intended things that way, some reason that does not involve that intention.

and (Trans.), we do not get the crucial

(3′′′′) This must also be a reason why it is permissible for us to take the lives of animals for the sake of obtaining food, clothing, etc.

The crucial objection to this claim has to do with the coherency of (1′′′′). Let us suppose that we are not troubled by the religious claims discussed in the previous section; let us suppose that we find nothing objectionable with the idea that God owns us. Then, presumably, even if we are impressed with the vegetarian argument, we will still find nothing objectionable with the idea that God owns animals as well. But we may still find (1′′′′) objectionable. For it, in effect, supposes that God's property rights extend so far as to allow the life of the piece of property in question to be taken by others, indeed, to so order things that this is done. And is this compatible with the idea of an all-just being? After all, even enlightened systems of slavery did not allow the slave-owner to take (or to have taken) the life of his slave. Does God's majesty really mean then that he can do even this?

We are straining here with the limits of the idea that everything is God's property because he is the creator of everything. When we applied the idea to inanimate objects, we saw that it could have important implications for the question of property rights. If we didn't object to applying it to human beings, we saw that it could (at least) have important applications for the question of the permissibility of suicide. If we are now prepared to take it to further extremes, it could serve as a response to the vegetarian's argument about animals and their right to life.

V

In a way, this essay can be seen as a gloss on the Psalmist's remarks that "the earth and all that fill it belong to God." We have tried to show that this idea may have important moral implications, and that it would therefore be wrong to suppose that there are no moral claims whose truth or falsehood may depend upon the truth or falsehood of theological claims. But it is, of course, clear that this is not the only theological belief that may have moral consequences. On other occasions, we shall look at other such theological beliefs.

PART SIX

THE END
OF THINGS

INTRODUCTION

An integral part of a great many religious systems is the belief in the immortality of the soul and the resurrection of the body. What exactly are these beliefs? The former is the belief that the person continues to exist forever, in a disembodied fashion, after his death and after the destruction of his body. The latter is the belief that, at some point after his death, the person resumes existence in an embodied fashion. These two beliefs are often combined in the following fashion: after his death, the person exists in a disembodied fashion. Eventually, however, the person resumes existence in an embodied fashion.

One finds connected with these beliefs additional beliefs about rewards and punishments after death for what one has done before one's death. And it is this additional feature that helps us understand the roles that these beliefs have within the religious approach. First, the religious person often wants to claim that God created the world and man so as to provide man with a period of trial and testing. Those who do the right things during this period are rewarded after their death by God for what they have done. Naturally, this whole view of the purpose of creation presupposes that the person survives his death. Second, given that the distribution of goods and evils in this life do not seem to be in proportion to moral worth, religious people want to claim that things will be balanced out and justice restored after the death of the individuals involved. This whole view also presupposes that the person survives his death.

It is important to keep in mind that it is not enough, for these purposes, that something that is merely in some way connected with the person survive his death. Both of the roles mentioned above presuppose that it is the person himself that exists after his death, for rewards and punishments must be given—if justice is to be preserved—to the person who has done the actions and acquired the degree of moral worth.

It is this point that raises the crucial philosophical issue in connection with these beliefs. Does it make any sense to suppose that a person could exist after his death and after the destruction of his body? There is, after all, one account of personal identity that rules this possibility out entirely. According to this account, a necessary condition for a person p_2 at time t_2 being identical with a person p_1 that existed at time t_1 is that p_2's body must be identical with p_1's body. If this is true, then it is obvious that no disembodied entity can be identical with some earlier embodied person, and that the embodied person cannot therefore continue to exist after his death in a disembodied form. Similarly, given any normal account of bodily identity, a body that came into existence many years after your death would not be identical with your body, and therefore, given this condition, it would follow that you could not be identical with some embodied person whose body came into existence many years after your death, and that you cannot therefore be resurrected many years after your death.

In order to meet this challenge, the religious person would have to construct some account of personal identity from which it would not follow that the condition of bodily identity is a necessary condition for personal identity. One of the most famous attempts to construct such a theory is to be found in the selection from Locke reprinted below. Locke's theory of personal identity, the so-called memory theory of personal identity, allows for p_2 at t_2 to be identical with p_1 at t_1 just in case p_2 at t_2 can remember some of what p_1 experienced and felt at t_1. None of this seems to imply that p_2 has a body at t_2, and, a fortiori, that p_2's body at t_2 is identical with p_1's body at t_1. So if Locke's theory is satisfactory, then it would seem that this challenge to the doctrines of the immortality of the soul and the resurrection of the body can be met.

There are, unfortunately, several grave difficulties with Locke's theory, difficulties that are developed at some length in Professor Flew's attack on it. To begin with, as Reid had already pointed out in his famous gallant-officer objection, Locke's theory does not even preserve the transitivity of personal identity. According to it, some p_3 at t_3 might be identical with some p_2 at t_2 (because of p_3's memories), that p_2 might be identical with some p_1 at t_1 (because of p_2's memories), but that p_3 is not identical with that p_1 (because p_3 remembers nothing that p_1 experienced and felt at t_1). Flew considers various ways of understanding "remembers" and "can" and concludes that this, or some other, objection will remain no matter what understanding of these terms we adopt. Secondly, argues Flew following Bishop Butler, the definition in question is really circular because it presupposes the notion of personal identity. Finally, argues Flew, Locke will be in trouble in certain of the problem cases that have came to be called splitting cases. Imagine a case in which, at t_2, there are two different persons who have the appropriate memories vis a vis the experiences of some p_1 at t_1. Then, according to Locke's theory, they will both be identical with p_1 although they are not identical with each other.

Flew himself feels that one of the basic troubles with Locke's whole approach was his failure to see that a person is not some special nonbodily entity that controls and inhabits a body but which might well survive the destruction of that body. The question that we have to consider is whether or not there can be a theory of personhood that can avoid these objections to Locke's theory and still provide us with a notion of personal identity that would make it possible for a person to survive the destruction of his body. It should be noted that that is all that we require; it is no requirement of the religious approach that the embodied person be, as Flew puts it, some non-bodily entity that controls or inhabits the body (although it should be noted that, in attempting to allow for the possibility of survival, most theologians have thought of persons that way).

Professor Quinton attempts to develop a theory of personal identity that would allow personal identity even when there is no identity of body. The theory is based upon the idea of the continuity of memory and character: p_2 at t_2 is identical with p_1 at t_1 just in case they are connected, directly or indirectly, by a continuous character and memory path. This immediately solves the gallant-officer type of objection because the persons at t_3 and t_1 are connected indirectly by a continuous character and memory path. Similarly, the circularity type of objection doesn't seem to arise. Unfortunately, Professor Quinton does not really deal with the third splitting-person objection.

Quinton, it should be noted, does not think that his theory really substantiates the possibility of disembodied survival, since he feels that it is physically necessary for memories and character possession that one have a body. It is surprising that he actually grants this point. At best, we have reasons for supposing that this is true in connection with embodied creatures. In any case, Quinton does want to conclude that there remains the possibility of survival in an embodied form. The reader is referred to the end of his article for further details on this point.

Professor Geach, in contrast to Professor Quinton, does want to maintain that the very meaning of so many of our mental terms requires that they be predicated only of embodied creatures, although he insists that this thesis does not in any way commit him to behaviorism. As a result, disembodied existence, while perhaps possible, cannot be the survival of a person. The only possible way in which we can survive is if we are resurrected. The belief in resurrection, claims Geach, must be distinguished from the belief in reincarnation in that in the former, but not in the latter, there must be a material continuity between the former body and the new body. And this, claims Geach, is why the former theory is preferable to the latter, because some sort of material continuity is necessary for personal identity.

As our survey of the selections indicates, the doctrines of the immortality of the soul and the resurrection of the body presuppose, for their very intelligibility, certain very controversial theses about the nature of mental acts and of personal identity. Naturally, then, it will be impossible to come to any final conclusions until these theses can be fully evaluated. That is, of course, the task of the reader.

IMMORTALITY AND RESURRECTION

JOHN LOCKE

6.1   On Personal Identity

Another occasion the mind often takes of comparing, is the very being of things, when, considering *anything as existing at any determined time and place*, we compare it with *itself existing at another time*, and thereon form the ideas of *identity* and *diversity*. When we see anything to be in any place in any instant of time, we are sure (be it what it will) that it is that very thing, and not another which at that same time exists in another place, how like and undistinguishable soever it may be in all other respects: and in this consists *identity*, when the ideas it is attributed to vary not at all from what they were that moment wherein we consider their former existence, and to which we compare the present. For we never finding, nor conceiving it possible, that two things of the same kind should exist in the same place at the same time, we rightly conclude, that, whatever exists anywhere at any time, excludes all of the same kind, and is there itself alone. When therefore we demand whether anything be the *same* or no, it refers always to something that existed such a time in such a place, which it was certain, at that instant, was the same with itself, and no other. From whence it follows, that one thing cannot have two beginnings of existence, nor two things one beginning; it being impossible for two things of the same kind to be or exist in the same instant, in the very same place; or one and the same thing in different places. That, therefore, that which had one beginning, is the same thing; and that which had a different beginning in time and place from that, is not the same, but diverse.

From John Locke, *An Essay Concerning Human Understanding* (1690), Book II, Chap. 27.

That which has made the difficulty about this relation has been the little care and attention used in having precise notions of the things to which it is attributed.

We have the ideas but of three sorts of substances: (*1*) *God*. (*2*) *Finite intelligences*. (*3*) *Bodies*.

First, *God* is without beginning, eternal, unalterable, and everywhere, and therefore concerning his identity there can be no doubt.

Second, *Finite spirits* having had each its determinate time and place of beginning to exist, the relation to that time and place will always determine to each of them its identity, as long as it exists.

Thirdly, The same will hold of every *particle of matter*, to which no addition or subtraction of matter being made, it is the same. For, though these three sorts of substances, as we term them, do not exclude one another out of the same place, yet we cannot conceive but that they must necessarily each of them exclude any of the same kind out of the same place: or else the notions and names of identity and diversity would be in vain, and there could be no such distinctions of substances, or anything else from one another. For example: could two bodies be in the same place at the same time; then those two parcels of matter must be one and the same, take them great or little; nay, all bodies must be one and the same. For, by the same reason that two particles of matter may be in one place, all bodies may be in one place: which, when it can be supposed, takes away the distinction of identity and diversity of one and more, renders it ridiculous. But it being a contradiction that two or more should be one, identity and diversity are relations and ways of comparing well founded, and of use to the understanding.

All other things being but modes or relations ultimately terminated in substances, the identity and diversity of each particular existence of them too will be by the same way determined: only as to things whose existence is in succession, such as are the actions of finite beings, v.g. *motion* and *thought*, both which consist in a continued train of succession, concerning *their* diversity there can be no question: because each perishing the moment it begins, they cannot exist in different times, or in different places, as permanent beings can at different times exist in distant places; and therefore no motion or thought, considered as at different times, can be the same, each part thereof having a different beginning of existence.

From what has been said, it is easy to discover what is so much inquired after, the *principium individuationis*; and that, it is plain, is existence itself; which determines a being of any sort to a particular time and place, incommunicable to two beings of the same kind. This, though it seems easier to conceive in simple substances or modes; yet, when reflected on, is not more difficult in compound ones, if care be taken to what is applied: v.g. let us suppose an atom, i.e. a continued body under one immutable superficies, existing in a determined time and place; it is evident, that, considered in any instant of its existence, it is in that instant the same with itself. For, being at that instant what it is, and nothing else, it is the same, and so must continue as long as its existence is continued; for so long it will be the same, and no other. In like manner, if two or more atoms be joined together into the same mass, every one of those atoms will be the same, by the foregoing rule: and whilst they exist united together, the mass, consisting of the same atoms, must be the same mass, or the same body, let the parts be ever so differently jumbled. But if one of these atoms be taken away, or one new one added, it is no longer the same mass or the same body. In the state of living creatures, their identity depends not on a mass of the same particles, but on something else. For in them the variation of great parcels of matter alters not the identity: an oak growing from a plant to a great tree, and then lopped, is still the same oak; and a colt grown up to a horse, sometimes fat, sometimes lean, is all the while the same horse: though, in both these cases, there may be a manifest change of the parts; so that truly they are not either of them the same masses of matter, though they be truly one of them the same oak, and the other the same horse. The reason whereof is, that, in these two cases—a *mass of matter* and a *living body*—identity is not applied to the same thing.

We must therefore consider wherein an oak differs from a mass of matter, and that seems to me to be in this, that the one is only the cohesion of particles of matter any how united, the other such a disposition of them as constitutes the parts of an oak; and such an organization of those parts as is fit to receive and distribute nourishment, so as to continue and frame the wood, bark, and leaves, &c., of an oak, in which consists the vegetable life. That being then one plant which has such an organization of parts in one coherent body, partaking of one common life, it continues to be the same plant as long as it partakes of the same life, though that life be communicated to new particles of matter vitally united to the living plant, in a like continued organization conformable to that sort of plants. For this organization, being at any one instant in any one collection of matter, is in that particular concrete distinguished from all other, and *is* that individual life, which existing constantly from that moment both forwards and backwards, in the same continuity of insensibly succeeding parts united to the living body of the plant, it has that identity which makes the same plant, and all the parts of it, parts of the same plant, during all the time that they exist united in that continued organization, which is fit to convey that common life to all parts so united.

The case is not so much different in *brutes* but that any one may hence see what makes an animal and continues it the same. Something we have like this in machines, and may serve to illustrate it. For example, what is a watch? It is plain it is nothing but a fit organization or construction of parts to a certain end, which, when a sufficient force is added to it, it is capable to attain. If we would suppose this machine one continued body, all whose organized parts were repaired, increased, or diminished by a constant addition or separation of insensible parts, with one common life, we should have something very much like the body of an animal; with this difference, That, in an ani-

mal the fitness of the organization, and the motion wherein life consists, begin together, the motion coming from within; but in machines the force coming sensibly from without, is often away when the organ is in order, and well
fitted to receive it.

This also shows wherein the identity of the same *man* consists; viz. in nothing but a participation of the same continued life, by constantly fleeting particles of matter, in succession vitally united to the same organized body.
He that shall place the identity of man in anything else, but, like that of other
animals, in one fitly organized body, taken in any one instant, and from thence
continued, under one organization of life, in several successively fleeting particles of matter united to it, will find it hard to make an embryo, one of years,
mad and sober, the *same* man, by any supposition, that will not make it possible for Seth, Ismael, Socrates, Pilate, St. Austin, and Caesar Borgia, to be
the same man. For if the identity of *soul alone* makes the same *man*; and there
be nothing in the nature of matter why the same individual spirit may not
be united to different bodies, it will be possible that those men, living in distant ages, and of different tempers, may have been the same man: which way
of speaking must be from a very strange use of the word man, applied to an
idea out of which body and shape are excluded. And that way of speaking
would agree yet worse with the notions of those philosophers who allow of
transmigration, and are of opinion that the souls of men may, for their mis-
carriages, be detruded into the bodies of beasts, as fit habitations, with organs suited to the satisfaction of their brutal inclinations. But yet I think nobody, could he be sure that the *soul* of Heliogabalus were in one of his hogs,
would yet say that hog were a *man* or *Heliogabalus*.

It is not therefore unity of substance that comprehends all sorts of identity,
or will determine it in every case; but to conceive and judge of it aright, we
must consider what idea the word it is applied to stands for: it being one
thing to be the same *substance*, another the same *man*, and the third the same
person, if *person, man*, and *substance*, are three names standing for three different ideas—for such as is the idea belonging to that name, such must be the
identity; which, if it had been a little more carefully attended to, would possibly have prevented a great deal of that confusion which often occurs about
this matter, with no small seeming difficulties, especially concerning *personal*
identity, which therefore we shall in the next place a little consider.

An animal is a living organized body; and consequently the same animal,
as we have observed, is the same continued *life* communicated to different
particles of matter, as they happen successively to be united to that organized
living body. And whatever is talked of other definitions, ingenious observation
puts it past doubt, that the idea in our minds, of which the sound man in
our mouths is the sign, is nothing else but of an animal of such a certain form.
Since I think I may be confident, that, whoever should see a creature of his
own shape or make, though it had no more reason all its life than a cat or a
parrot, would call him still a *man*; or whoever should hear a cat or a parrot
discourse, reason, and philosophize, would call or think it nothing but a *cat* or

a *parrot*; and say, the one was a dull irrational man, and the other a very intelligent rational parrot. A relation we have in an author of great note, is sufficient to countenance the supposition of a rational parrot. He words are:

"I had a mind to know, from Prince Maurice's own mouth, the account of a common, but much credited story, that I had heard so often from many others, of an old parrot he had in Brazil, during his government there, that spoke, and asked, and answered common questions, like a reasonable creature: so that those of his train there generally concluded it to be witchery or possession; and one of his chaplains, who lived long afterwards in Holland, would never from that time endure a parrot, but said they all had a devil in them. I had heard many particulars of this story, and assevered by people hard to be discredited, which made me ask Prince Maurice what there was of it. He said, with his usual plainness and dryness in talk, there was something true, but a great deal false of what had been reported. I desired to know of him what there was of the first. He told me short and coldly, that he had heard of such an old parrot when he had been at Brazil; and though he believed nothing of it, and it was a good way off, yet he had so much curiosity as to send for it: that it was a very great and a very old one; and when it came first into the room where the prince was, with a great many Dutchmen about him, it said presently *What a company of white man are here!* They asked it, what it thought that man was, pointing to the prince. It answered, *Some General or other.* When they brought it close to him, he asked it, *D'où venez-vous?* It answered, *De Marinnan.* The Prince, *À qui estes-vous?* The parrot, *À un Portugais.* The Prince, *Que fais-tu là?* Parrot, *Je garde les poulles.* The Prince laughed, and said, *Vous gardez les poulles?* The parrot answered, *Oui, moi; et je sçai bien faire*;[1] and made the chuck four or five times that people make to chickens when they call them. I set down the words of this worthy dialogue in French, just as Prince Maurice said them to me. I asked him in what language the parrot spoke, and he said in Brazilian. I asked whether he understood Brazilian; he said No, but he had taken care to have two interpreters by him, the one a Dutchman that spoke Brazilian and the other a Brazilian that spoke Dutch; that he asked them separately and privately, and both of them agreed in telling him just the same thing that the parrot had said. I could not but tell this odd story, because it is so much out of the way, and from the first hand, and what may pass for a good one; for I dare say this Prince at least believed himself in all he told me, having ever passed for a very honest and pious man: I leave it to naturalists to reason, and to other men to believe, as they please upon it; however, it is not, perhaps, amiss to relieve or enliven a busy scene sometimes with such degressions, whether to the purpose or no."

I have taken care that the reader should have the story at large in the au-

---

[1]*'Where do you come from?' 'From Marinnan.' 'To whom do you belong?' 'To a Portuguese.' 'What do you do there' 'I look after the chickens.' 'You look after the chickens?' 'Yes, I; and I know well enough how to do it.'*

thor's own words, because he seems to me not to have thought it incredible; for it cannot be imagined that so able a man as he, who had sufficiency enough to warrant all the testimonies he gives of himself, should take so much pains, in a place where it had nothing to do, to pin so close, not only a man whom he mentions as his friend, but on a Prince in whom he acknowledges very great honesty and piety, a story which, if he himself thought incredible, he could not but also think ridiculous. The Prince, it is plain, who vouches this story, and our author, who relates it from him, both of them call this talker a parrot: and I ask any one else who thinks such a story fit to be told, whether, if this parrot, and all of its kind, had always talked, as we have a prince's word for it this one did,—whether, I say, they would not have passed for a race of *rational animals*; but yet, whether, for all that, they would have been allowed to be men, and not *parrots*? For I presume it not the idea of a thinking or rational being alone that makes the *idea of a man* in most people's sense: but of a body, so and so shaped, joined to it, and if that be the idea of a man, the same successive body not shifted all at once, must, as well as the same immaterial spirit, go to the making of the same man.

This being premised, to find wherein personal identity consists, we must consider what *person* stands for;— which, I think, is a thinking intelligent being, that has reason and reflection, and can consider itself as itself, the same thinking thing, in different times and places; which it does only by that consciousness which is inseparable from thinking, and, as it seems to me, essential to it: it being impossible for any one to perceive without *perceiving* that he does perceive. When we see, hear, smell, taste, feel, meditate, or will anything, we know that we do so. Thus it is always as to our present sensations and perceptions: and by this every one is to himself that which he calls *self*:— it not being considered, in this case, whether the same self be continued in the same or divers substances. For, since consciousness always accompanies thinking, and it is that which makes every one to be what he calls self, and thereby distinguishes himself from all other thinking things, in this alone consists personal identity, i.e. the sameness of a rational being; and as far as this consciousness can be extended backwards to any past action or thought, so far reaches the identity of that person; it is the same self now it was then; and it is by the same self with this present one that now reflects on it, that that action was done.

But it is further inquired, whether it be the same identical substance. This few would think they had reason to doubt of, if these perceptions, with their consciousness, always remained present in the mind, whereby the same thinking thing would be always consciously present, and, as would be thought, evidently the same to itself. But that which seems to make the difficulty is this, that this consciousness being interrupted always by forgetfulness, there being no moment of our lives wherein we have the whole train of all our past actions before our eyes in one view, but even that best memories losing the sight of one part whilst they are viewing another; and we sometimes, and that the greatest part of our lives, not reflecting on our past selves, being intent on our present thoughts, and in sound sleep having no thoughts at all, or at least none with that consciousness which remarks our waking thoughts, —I say, in all these cases, our consciousness being interrupted, and we losing the sight of our past selves, doubts are raised whether we are the same thinking thing, i.e. the same *substance* or no. Which, however reasonable or unreasonable, concerns not *personal* identity at all. The question being what makes the same person; and not whether it be the same identical substance, which always thinks in the same person, which, in this case, matters not at all: different substances, by the same consciousness (where they do partake in it) being united into one person, as well as different bodies by the same life are united into one animal, whose identity is preserved in that change of substances by the unity of one continued life. For, it being the same consciousness that makes a man be himself to himself, personal identity depends on that only, whether it be annexed solely to one individual substance, or can be continued in a succession of several substances. For as far as any intelligent being *can* repeat the idea of any past action with the same consciousness it had of it at first, and with the same consciousness it has of any present action: so far it is the same personal self. For it is by the consciousness it has of its present thoughts and actions, that it is *self to itself* now, and so will be the same self, as far as the same consciousness can extend to actions past or to come; and would be by distance of time, or change of substance, no more two persons, then a man be two men by wearing other clothes today that he did yesterday, with a long or a short sleep between: the same consciousness uniting those distant actions into the same person, whatever substances contributed to their production.

That this is so, we have some kind of evidence in our very bodies, all whose particles, whilst vitally united to this same thinking conscious self, so that *we feel* when they are touched, and are affected by, and conscious of good or harm that happens to them, are a part of ourselves; i.e. of our thinking conscious self. Thus, the limbs of his body are to every one a part of himself; he sympathizes and is concerned for them. Cut off a hand, and thereby separate it from that consciousness he had of its heat, cold, and other affections, and it is then no longer a part of that which is himself, any more than the remotest part of matter. Thus, we see the *substance* whereof personal self consisted at one time may be varied at another, without the change of personal identity; there being no question about the same person, though the limbs which but now were a part of it, be cut off.

But the question is, Whether if the same substance which thinks be changed, it can be the same person; or, remaining the same, it can be different persons?

And to this I answer: First, This can be no question at all to those who place thought in a purely material animal constitution, void of an immaterial substance. For, whether their supposition be true or no, it is plain they conceive personal identity preserved in something else than identity of substance;

as animal identity is preserved in identity of life, and not of substance. And therefore those who place thinking in an immaterial substance only, before they can come to deal with these men, must show why personal identity cannot be preserved in the change of immaterial substances, or variety of particular immaterial substances, as well as animal identity is preserved in the change of material substances, or variety of particular bodies: unless they will say, it is one immaterial spirit that makes the same life in brutes, as it is one immaterial spirit that makes the same person in men; which the Cartesians at least will not admit, for fear of making brutes thinking things too.

But next, as to the first part of the question, Whether, if the same thinking substance (supposing immaterial substances only to think) be changed, it can be the same person? I answer, that cannot be resolved but by those who know what kind of substances they are that do think; and whether the consciousness of past actions can be transferred from one thinking substance to another. I grant were the same consciousness the same individual action it could not: but it being a present representation of a past action, why it may not be possible, that that may be represented to the mind to have been which really never was, will remain to be shown. And therefore how far the consciousness of last actions is annexed to any individual agent, so that another cannot possibly have it, will be hard for us to determine, till we know what kind of action it is that cannot be done without a reflex act of perception accompanying it, and how performed by thinking substances, who cannot think without being conscious of it. But that which we call the same consciousness, not being the same individual act, why one intellectual substance may not have represented to it, as done by itself, what *it* never did, and was perhaps done by some other agent—why, I say, such a representation may not possibly be without reality of matter of fact, as well as several representations in dreams are, which yet whilst dreaming we take for true—will be difficult to conclude from the nature of things. And that it never is so, will by us, till we have clearer views of the nature of thinking substances, be best resolved into the goodness of God; who, as far as the happiness or misery of any of his sensible creatures is concerned in it, will not, by a fatal error of theirs, transfer from one to another that consciousness which draws reward or punishment with it. How far this may be an argument against those would place thinking in a system of fleeting animal spirits, I leave to be considered. But yet, to return to the question before us, it must be allowed, that, if the same consciousness (which, as has been shown, is quite a different thing from the same numerical figure or motion in body) can be transferred from one thinking substance to another, it will be possible that two thinking substances may make but one person. For the same consciousness being preserved, whether in the same or different substances, the personal identity is preserved.

As to the second part of the question, Whether the same immaterial substance remaining, there may be two distinct persons; which question seems to me to be built on this,—Whether the same immaterial being, being conscious of the action of its past duration, may be wholly stripped of all the consciousness of its past existence, and lose it beyond the power of ever retrieving it again: and so as it were beginning a new account from a new period, have a consciousness that *cannot* reach beyond this new state. All those who hold pre-existence are evidently of this mind; since they allow the soul to have no remaining consciousness of what it did in that pre-existent state, either wholly separate from body, or informing any other body; and if they should not, it is plain experience would be against them. So that personal identity, reaching no further than consciousness reaches, a pre-existent spirit not having continued so many ages in a state of silence, must needs make different persons. Suppose a Christian Platonist or a Pythagorean should, upon God's having ended all his works of creation the seventh day, think his soul hath existed ever since; and should imagine it has revolved in several human bodies; as I once met with one, who was persuaded his had been the *soul* of Socrates (how reasonably I will not dispute; this I know, that in the post he filled, which was no inconsiderable one, he passed for a very rational man, and the press has shown that he wanted not parts or learning;)—would any one say, that he, being not conscious of any of Socrates' actions or thoughts, could be the same *person* with Socrates? Let any one reflect upon himself, and conclude that he has in himself an immaterial spirit, which is that which thinks in him, and, in the constant change of his body keeps him the same: and is that which he calls *himself*: let him also suppose it to be the same soul that was in Nestor or Thersites, at the siege of Troy, (for souls being, as far as we know anything of them, in their nature indifferent to any parcel of matter, the supposition has no apparent absurdity in it,) which it may have been, as well as it is now the soul of any other man: but he now having no consciousness of any of the actions either of Nestor or Thersites, does or can he conceive himself the same person with either of them? Can he be concerned in either of their actions? attribute them to himself, or think them his own, more than the actions of any other men that ever existed? So that this consciousness, not reaching to any of the actions of either of those men, he is no more one *self* with either of them than if the soul or immaterial spirit that now informs him had been created, and began to exist, when it began to inform his present body; though it were never so true, that the same *spirit* that informed Nestor's or Thersites' body were numerically the same that now informs his. For this would no more make him the same person with Nestor, than if some of the particles of matter that were once a part of Nestor were now a part of this man; the same immaterial substance, without the same consciousness, no more making the same person, by being united to any body, than the same particle of matter, without consciousness, united to any body, makes the same person. But let him once find himself conscious of any of the actions of Nestor, he then finds himself the same person with Nestor.

And thus may we be able, without any difficulty, to conceive the same person at the resurrection, though in a body not exactly in make or parts the same which he had here,—the same consciousness going along with the soul that inhabits it. But yet the soul alone, in the change of bodies, would scarce to any one but to him that makes the soul the man, be enough to make the same man. For should the soul of a prince, carrying with it the consciousness of the prince's past life, enter and inform the body of a cobbler, as soon as deserted by his own soul, every one sees he would be the same *person* with the prince, accountable only for the prince's actions: but who would say it was the same *man*? The body too goes to the making the man, and would, I guess, to everybody determine the man in this case, wherein the soul, with all its princely thoughts about it, would not make another man: but he would be the same cobbler to every one besides himself. I know that, in the ordinary way of speaking, the same person, and the same man, stand for one and the same thing. And indeed every one will always have a liberty to speak as he pleases, and to apply what articulate sounds to what ideas he thinks fit, and change them as often as he pleases. But yet, when we will inquire what makes the same *spirit, man,* or *person,* we must fix the ideas of spirit, man, or person in our minds; and having resolved with ourselves what we mean by them, it will not be hard to determine, in either of them, or the like, when it is the same, and when not.

But though the same immaterial substance or soul does not alone, wherever it be, and in whatsoever state, make the same *man*; yet it is plain, consciousness, as far as ever it can be extended—should it be to ages past— unites existences and actions very remote in time into the same *person*, as well as it does the existences and actions of the immediately preceding moment: so that whatever has the consciousness of present and past actions, is the same person to whom they both belong. Had I the same consciousness that I saw the ark and Noah's flood, as that I saw an overflowing of the Thames last winter, or as that I write now, I could no more doubt that I who write this now, that saw the Thames overflowed last winter, and that viewed the flood at the general deluge, was the same *self,*—place that self in what *substance* you please—than that I who write this am the same *myself* now whilst I write (whether I consist of all the same substance, material or immaterial, or no) that I was yesterday. For as to this point of being the same self, it matters not whether this present self be made up of the same or other substances—I being as much concerned, and as justly accountable for any action that was done a thousand years since, appropriated to me now by this self-consciousness, as I am for what I did the last moment.

Self is that conscious thinking thing,—whatever substance made up of, (whether spiritual or material, simple or compounded, it matters not)—which is sensible or conscious of pleasure and pain, capable of happiness or misery, and so is concerned for itself, as far as that consciousness extends. Thus every one finds that, whilst comprehended under that consciousness, the little finger is as much a part of himself as what is most so. Upon separation of this little finger, should this consciousness go along with the little finger, and leave the rest of the body, it is evident the little finger would be the person, the same person; and self then would have nothing to do with the rest of the body. As in this case it is the consciousness that goes along with the substance, when one part is separate from another, which makes the same person, and constitutes this inseparable self: so it is in reference to substances remote in time. That with which the consciousness of this present thinking thing *can* join itself, makes the same person, and is one self with it, and with nothing else; and so attributes to itself, and owns all the actions of that thing, as its own, as far as that consciousness reaches, and no further; as every one who reflects will perceive.

In this personal identity is founded all the right and justice of reward and punishment; happiness and misery being that for which every one is concerned for *himself,* and not mattering what becomes of any *substance,* not joined to, or affected with that consciousness. For, as it is evident in the instance I gave but now, if the consciousness went along with the little finger when it was cut off, that would be the same self which was concerned for the whole body yesterday, as making part of itself, whose actions then it cannot but admit as its own new. Though, if the same body should still live, and immediately from the separation of the little finger have its own peculiar consciousness, whereof the little finger knew nothing, it would not all be concerned for it, as a part of itself, or could own any of its actions, or have any of them imputed to him.

This may show us wherein personal identity consists: not in the identity of substance, but, as I have said, in the identity of consciousness, wherein if Socrates and the present mayor of Queensborough agree, they are the same person: if the same Socrates waking and sleeping do not partake of the same consciousness, Socrates waking and sleeping is not the same person. And to punish Socrates waking for what sleeping Socrates thought, and waking Socrates was never conscious of, would be no more of right, than to punish one twin for what his brother-twin did, where of he knew nothing, because their outsides were so like, that they could not be distinguished; for such twins have been seen.

But yet possibly it will still be objected,—Suppose I wholly lose the memory of some parts of my life, beyond a possibility of retrieving them, so that perhaps I shall never be conscious of them again; yet am I not the same person that did those actions, had those thoughts that I once was conscious of, though I have now forgot them? To which I answer, that we must here take notice what the word *I* is applied to; which, in this case, is the *man* only. And the same man being presumed to be the same person, I is easily here supposed to stand also for the same person. But if it be possible for the same man to have distinct incommunicable consciousness at different times, it is past doubt the same man would at different times make different persons; which, we see, is the sense of mankind in the solemnist declaration of their opinions, human laws not punishing the mad man for the sober man's actions, nor the sober man for what the mad man did,—thereby making them two persons: which is somewhat explained by our way of speaking in English when we say such an one is "not himself," or is "beside himself"; in which phrases it is insinuated, as if those who now, or at least first used them, thought that self was changed; the self-same person was no longer in that man.

But yet it is hard to conceive that Socrates, the same individual man, should be two persons. To help us a little in this, we must consider what is meant by Socrates, or the same individual *man.*

First, it must be either the same individual, immaterial, thinking substance; in short, the same numerical soul, and nothing else.

Secondly, or the same animal, without any regard to an immaterial soul.

Thirdly, or the same immaterial spirit united to the same animal.

Now, take which of these suppositions you please, it is impossible to make personal identity to consist in anything but consciousness; or reach any further than that does.

For, by the first of them, it must be allowed possible that a man born of different women, and in distant times, may be the same man. A way of speaking which, whoever admits, must allow it possible for the same man to be two distinct persons, as any two that have lived in different ages without the knowledge of one another's thoughts.

By the second and third, Socrates, in this life and after it, cannot be the same man any way, but by the same consciousness; and so making human identity to consist in the same thing wherein we place personal identity, there will be no difficulty to allow the same man to be the same person. But then they who place human identity in consciousness only, and not in something else, must consider how they will make the infant Socrates the same man with Socrates after the resurrection. But whatsoever to some men makes a man, and consequently the same individual man, wherein perhaps few are agreed, personal identity can by us be placed in nothing but consciousness, (which is that alone which makes what we call *self,*) without involving us in great absurdities.

But is not a man drunk and sober the same person? why else is he punished for the act he commits when drunk, though he be never afterwards conscious of it? Just as much the same person as a man that walks, and does other things in his sleep, is the same person, and is answerable for any mischief he shall do in it. Human laws punish both, with a justice suitable to *their* way of knowledge;—because, in these cases, they cannot distinguish certainly what is real, what counterfeit: and so the ignorance in drunkenness or sleep is not admitted as a plea. For, though punishment be annexed to personality, and personality to consciousness, and the drunkard perhaps be not conscious of what he did, yet human judicatures justly punish him; because the fact is proved against him, but want of consciousness cannot be proved for him. But in the Great Day, wherein the secrets of all hearts shall be laid open, it may be reasonable to think, no one shall be made to answer for what he knows nothing of; but shall receive his doom, his conscience accusing or excusing him.

Nothing but consciousness can unite remote existences into the same person: the identity of substance will not do it; for whatever substance there is, however framed, without consciousness there is no person: and a carcass may be a person, as well as any sort of substance be so, without consciousness.

Could we suppose two distinct incommunicable consciousnesses acting in the same body, the one constantly by day, the other by night; and, on the other side, the same consciousness, acting by intervals, in two distinct bodies: I ask, in the first case, whether the day- and the night-man would not be two as distinct persons as Socrates and Plato? And whether, in the second case, there would not be one person in two distinct bodies, as much as one man is the same in two distinct clothings? Nor is it at all material to say, that this same, and this distinct consciousness, in the cases above mentioned, is owing to the same and distinct immaterial substances, bringing it with them to those bodies; which, whether true or no, alters not the case: since it is evident the personal identity would equally be determined by the consciousness, whether that consciousness were annexed to some individual immaterial substance or no. For, granting that the thinking substance in man must be necessarily supposed immaterial, it is evident that immaterial thinking thing may sometimes part with its past consciousness, and be restored to it again: as appears in the forgetfulness men often have of their past actions; and the mind many times recovers the memory of a past consciousness, which it had lost for twenty years together. Make these intervals of memory and forgetfulness to take their turns regularly by day and night, and you have two persons with the same immaterial spirit, as much as in the former instance two persons with the same body. So that self is not determined by identity or diversity of substance, which it cannot be sure of, but only by identity of consciousness.

Indeed it may conceive the substance whereof it is now made up to have existed formerly, united in the same conscious being: but, consciousness removed, that substance is no more itself, or makes no more a part of it, than any other substance; as is evident in the instance we have already given of a limb cut off, of whose heat, or cold, or other affections, having no longer any consciousness, it is no more of a man's self than any other matter of the universe. In like manner it will be in reference to any immaterial substance, which is void of that consciousness whereby I am myself to myself: if there be any part of its existence which I cannot upon recollection join with that present consciousness whereby I am now myself, it is, in that part of its existence, no more *myself* than any other immaterial being. For, whatsoever any substance has thought or done, which I cannot recollect, and by my consciousness make my own thought and action, it will no more belong to me, whether a part of me thought or did it, than if it had been thought or done by any other immaterial being anywhere existing.

I agree, the more probable opinion is, that this consciousness is annexed to, and the affection of, one individual immaterial substance.

But let men, according to their diverse hypotheses, resolve of that as they please, This every intelligent being, sensible of happiness or misery, must grant—that there is something that is *himself*, that he is concerned for, and would have happy; that this self has existed in a continued duration more than one instant, and therefore it is possible may exist, as it has done, months and years to come, without any certain bounds to be set to its duration; and may be the same self, by the same consciousness continued on for the future. And thus, by this consciousness he finds himself to be the same self which did such and such an action some years since, by which he comes to be happy or miserable now. In all which account of self, the same numerical *substance* is not considered as making the same self; but the same contined *consciousness*, in which several substances may have been united, and again separated from it, which, whilst they continued in a vital union with that wherein this consciousness then resided, made a part of that same self. Thus any part of our bodies, vitally united to that which is conscious in us, makes a part of ourselves: but upon separation from the vital union by which that consciousness is communicated, that which a moment since was part of ourselves, is now no more so than a part of another man's self is a part of me: and it is not impossible but in a little time may become a real part of another person. And so we have the same numerical substance become a part of two different persons; and the same person preserved under the change of various substances. Could we suppose any spirit wholly stripped of all its memory or consciousness of past actions, as we find our minds always are of a great part of ours, and sometimes of them all; the union or separation of such a spiritual substance would make no variation of personal identity, any more than that of any particle of matter does. Any substance vitally united to the present thinking being is a part of that very same self which now is; anything united to it by a consciousness of former actions, makes also a part of the same self, which is the same both then and now.

Person, as I take it, is the name for this self. Wherever a man finds what he calls himself, there, I think, another may say is the same person. It is a forensic term, appropriating actions and their merit; and so belongs only to intelligent agents, capable of a law, and happiness, and misery. This personality extends itself beyond present existence to what is past, only by consciousness,—whereby it becomes concerned and accountable; owns and imputes to itself past actions, just upon the same ground and for the same reason as it does the present. All which is founded in a concern for happiness, the unavoidable concomitant of consciousness; that which is conscious of pleasure and pain, desiring that that self that is conscious should be happy. And therefore whatever past actions it cannot reconcile or *appropriate* to that present self by consciousness, it can be no more concerned in than if they had never been done: and to receive pleasure or pain, i.e. reward or punishment, on the account of any such action, is all one as to be made happy or miserable in its first being, without any demerit at all. For, supposing a *man* punished now for what he had done in another life, whereof he could be made to have no consciousness at all, what difference is there between that punishment and being *created* miserable? And therefore, conformable to this, the apostle tells us, that, at the great day, when every one shall "receive according to his doings, the secrets of all hearts shall be laid open." The sentence shall be justified by the consciousness all persons shall have, that *they themselves*, in what bodies soever they appear, or what substances soever that consciousness adheres to, are the *same* that committed those actions, and deserve that punishment for them.

I am apt enough to think I have, in treating of this subject, made some suppositions that will look strange to some readers, and possibly they are so in themselves. But yet, I think they are such as are pardonable, in this ignorance we are in of the nature of that thinking thing that is in us, and which we look on as *ourselves*. Did we know what it was; or how it was tied to a certain system of fleeting animal spirits; or whether it could or could not perform its operations of thinking and memory out of a body organized as ours is; and whether it has pleased God that no one such spirit shall ever be united to any but one such body, upon the right constitution of whose organs its memory should depend; we might see the absurdity of some of those suppositions I have made. But taking, as were ordinarily now do (in the dark concerning these matters,) the soul of a man for an immaterial substance, independent from matter, and indifferent alike to it all; there can, from the nature of things, be no absurdity at all to suppose that the same *soul* may at different times be united to different *bodies*, and with them make up for that time one *man*: as well as we suppose a part of a sheep's body yesterday should be a part of a man's body to-morrow, and in that union make a vital part of Meliboesus himself, as well as it did of his ram.

To conclude: Whatever substance begins to exist, it must, during its existence, necessarily be the same: whatever compositions of substances begin to exist, during the union of those substances, the concrete must be the same: whatsoever mode begins to exist, during its existence it is the same: and so if the composition be of distinct substances and different modes, the same rule holds. Whereby it will appear, that the difficulty or obscurity that has been about this matter rather rises from the names ill-used, than from any obscurity in things themselves. For whatever makes the specific idea to which the name is applied, if that idea be steadily kept to, the distinction of anything into the same and divers will easily be conceived, and there can arise no doubt about it.

For, supposing a rational spirit be the idea of a *man's*, it is easy to know what is the same man, viz. the same spirit—whether separate or in a body— will be the *same man*. Supposing a rational spirit vitally united to a body of a certain conformation of parts to make a man; whilst that rational spirit, with that vital conformation of parts, though continued in a fleeting successive body, remains, it will be the *same man*. But if to any one the idea of a man be but the vital union of parts in a certain shape; as long as that vital union and shape remain in a concrete, no otherwise the same but by a continued succession of fleeting particles, it will be the *same man*. For, whatever be the composition whereof the complex idea is made, whenever existence makes it one particular thing under any denomination, *the same existence continued* preserves it the *same* individual under the same denomination.

ANTONY FLEW

**6.2   Locke and the Problem
of Personal Identity**

I. PREAMBLE

This paper attempts to do three main things. First, it outlines Locke's contribution to the discussion of the problem of personal identity, that it, the philosophical problem of what is meant by the expression "same person." Second, it attacks Locke's proposed solution, showing that it is quite irreparably wrong. Third, it enquires how Locke was misled into offering this mistaken yet perennially seductive answer.

II. LOCKE'S CONTRIBUTION

Locke's contribution to the discussion was fourfold. First, he saw the importance of the problem. Second, he realized that the puzzle cases, the "strange suppositions," were relevant. Third, he maintained that "same" had a different meaning when applied to the noun "person" from its meaning in other applications. And, fourth, he offered his own answer to the main question of the meaning of "same person."

1. Locke saw the importance of the problem. It is important because, "In this personal identity is founded all the right and justice of reward and punishment" (*Essay*, II, xxvii, 18). That is to say, it is never fair to blame not just to punish the prisoner in the dock for murdering his bride in her bath unless the prisoner is the same person as he who did the deed. The same is equally true of the ascription of responsibility at the Last Judgment. Furthermore and even more fundamentally, as Locke clearly saw but never so clearly stated, all questions of survival, preexistence, and immortality, are questions of personal identity. The question "Is Cesare Borgia still alive, surviving bodily death?" is equivalent to "Is there a person now alive, surviving bodily death, who is the same person as Cesare Borgia?"

From *Philosophy* 26 (1951). Reprinted by permission of the author and *Philosophy*.

But it might still be argued (and certainly would be argued, by those numerous contemporary philosophers who pray, with the Trinity mathematicians, that their subject may never be of any use to anybody) that all that has been proved is that some important questions are or involve questions of personal identity, and that it has not been shown that these questions demand a solution of the philosophical problem of personal identity. Perhaps psychical research can proceed without benefit of any philosophical analysis of "same person" just as many other sciences proceed satisfactorily with the study of so-and-so's without feeling handicapped by the lack of philosophical analyses of the expression "so-and-so's." This analogy is misleading here. For it is precisely the cases studied by psychical researchers and parapsychologists, which raise, both in them and in everyone who reads of their work, exactly those questions of meaning which it is the proper business of analytical philosophy to answer.

When we are presented with stories like that of the Watseka Wonder, recorded by William James in Chapter x of *The Principles of Psychology*, we ask whether the patient Lurancy Vennum really was or became the same person as Mary Roff. Someone then is bound to ask what we mean by "same person," for this is pre-eminently the sort of question where, to coin a phrase, "It all depends what you mean." Or take an example from Locke: "I once met with one, who was persuaded that his had been the *soul* of Socrates (how reasonably I will not dispute; this I know, that in the post he filled, which was no inconsiderable one, he passed for a very rational man, and the press has shown that he wanted not parts or learning; . . ." (*Essay*, II, xxvii, 14: italics original). Perhaps this was a case which set Locke himself enquiring about personal identity. But for us it is sufficient if we have shown that the puzzle cases which are so characteristic of certain investigations inevitably and rightly raise philosophical questions about the meaning of "same person."

2. Locke seems to have been the first to appreciate the relevance of such puzzle cases. They present a challenge. Any solution to the problem must be able to do one of two things. Either it must consist in some sort of definition or set of rules, which will enable us to deal with all possible puzzles; either by telling us that "same person" is or is not correctly applicable; or by hinting to us what further factual information we require before we can know. Or else the solution must explain why the questions raised by the puzzle cases cannot be so definitively answered. Locke himself chose the first alternative, and answered all the puzzles he had invented in the light of this talismanic definition. For instance, he tells us what would decide the puzzle of the man who claimed to have the same soul as Socrates (*Essay*, II, xxvii, 19).

3. Locke maintained that "same" is systematically ambiguous: "It is not therefore unity of substance that comprehends all sorts of identity or will determine it in every case; but to conceive and judge of it aright, we must consider what idea the word it is applied to stands for" (*Essay*, II, xxvii, 8). It would not be relevant to discuss this general claim. It is enough to show

that Locke is right at least in so far as he is maintaining that there are special and peculiar problems about "same" as applied to persons. And this can be seen to be the case by the example of Hume, who thought he could solve the problem of the identity of things, but confessed himself completely at a loss as to "the nature of the bond which unites a person."

4. Locke proposed a solution to the philosophical problem. It is that X at time two is the same person as Y at time one if and only if X and Y are both persons and X can remember at time two (his doing) what Y did, or felt, or what have you, at time one. The parenthetical "his doing" has to go in since, as Professor Bernard Williams has pointed out, "we constantly say things like 'I remember my brother joining the army' without implying that I and my brother are the same person"; though it is worth stressing, as Williams does not, that all such utterances do still carry an implicit personal identity claim about the speaker—the claim that he was himself around and acquiring the information at the time in question. Certainly by making this insertion our reformulation becomes even more obviously exposed to "Butler's famous objection that memory, so far from constituting personal identity, presupposed it." Yet this is not a fault in the reformulation, considered as a representation of Locke's position. For that position actually is wide open to that objection. It is not, as Williams seems to be suggesting, only our present belated insertion which lends colour to it.[1]

A person is for Locke "a thinking intelligent being, that has reason and reflection, and can consider itself as itself, the same thinking thing, in different times and places" (*Essay*, II, xxvii, 11). This is distinguished from the idea of man since, "ingenious observation [*sic!*] puts it past doubt", that "the idea in our minds, of which the sound *man* in our mouths is the sign, is nothing else but of an animal of such certain form" (*Essay*, II, xxvii, 9; italics supplied); although a very little later we are told that the same idea consists "in most people's sense" of the idea of "a body, so and so shaped, joined to" that of "*a thinking or rational being*" (*Essay*, II, xxvii, 10: italics supplied).

Locke's proposed solution, in his own words, is that: "That with which the consciousness of this present thinking thing *can* join itself, makes the same person, and is one self with it, and with nothing else; and so attributes to itself and owns all the actions of that thing, as its own, as far as that consciousness reaches, and no further: as everyone who reflects will perceive" (*Essay*, II, xxvii, 17: italics original). One must here point out that the word "consciousness" is not used by Locke clearly and consistently. Sometimes it seems to mean self-conscious, in the tricky and curious sense in which to say that someone is self-conscious is not to say that he is embarrassed: for instance, we read that "a being that . . . can consider itself as itself . . . does so only by that consciousness which is inseparable from thinking . . ." (*Essay*, II, xxvii, 11).

---

[1]B. A. O. Williams, "Personal Identity and Individuation" in *Proceedings of the Aristotelian Society* 1956–57, p. 233: the objection itself is considered more fully in III (1), below.

Sometimes it seems to be more straightforwardly the consciousness which is the opposite of anaesthesia: for instance, when "self" is defined as "a conscious thinking thing . . . which is sensible or conscious of pleasure or pain, capable of happiness or misery . . ." (*Essay*, II, xxvii, 17). But in his main statements of his position "consciousness" is simply equivalent to "memory," as can be seen from the words, "Could we suppose any spirit wholly stripped of all its memory or consciousness of past actions; as we find our minds always are of a great part of ours, and sometimes of them all . . ." (*Essay*, II, xxvii, 25). In the interests of both clarity and brevity we have used "remember" instead of "be conscious of" in our restatements of Locke's central thesis.

III. OBJECTIONS TO LOCKE'S SOLUTION

There are two lines of attack.

1. The first and simpler was classically taken by Bishop Butler in his dissertation *Of Personal Identity*: "And one should really think it self-evident, that consciousness of personal identity presupposes, and therefore cannot constitute, personal identity; any more than knowledge, in any other case, can constitute truth, which it presupposes" (§ 3).[2] It is absurd to say that "he is the same person" *means* that "he can remember that he is the same person." The absurdity is usually slightly masked, since expressions such as "I remember doing, feeling, seeing something" do not refer explicity to the fact that what is remembered is that the speaker is the same person as did, felt, or saw whatever it was.

2. The second line of attack is much more intricate, demanding very careful generalship. The crux is that Locke's criterion is at the same time both too strict in blackballing and too lenient in admitting candidates. Often his definition would not allow us to apply the expression "same person," where we certainly should think it properly applicable; whereas in other cases Locke's ruling would be that it did apply, when we should certainly judge it not correctly applicable.

Before developing this second attack two distinctions have to be made. Two of the terms in Locke's definition are relevantly ambiguous. "Can" may be either "can as a matter of fact" (hereafter referred to as "can [factual]") or it may be "can without self-contradiction be said to" (hereafter referred to as "can [logical]"). There is also a more subtle ambiguity in "remember," which is best brought out by symbolic examples. "I know p" entails "p," whereas "He said that he knew p, and he was not lying" does not entail "p." Similarly, "I remember p" entails "p," but "He said that he remembered p, and he was not lying" does not entail "p." For, just as it is possible to be honestly mistaken in a claim to know something, so it is possible to be honestly mistaken in making a claim to remember something. When someone challenges a knowledge claim or a memory claim he is not necessarily, or even usually, chal-

---

[2]*Works*, ed. W. E. Gladstone, Oxford University Press, 1897.

lenging the claimant's integrity. He is much more likely to be merely questioning the truth of the proposition said to be known or remembered. And, of course, if the proposition is in fact false this is sufficient to defeat the claim really to know or truly to remember. (Another possibility, mentioned only to be dismissed as here irrelevant, is that the critic is either challenging the adequacy of the grounds available to support the knowledge claim or challenging the implicit claim to have been in the past in a position which qualifies the claimant to be remembering now.) We have, therefore, to distinguish between genuine remembering, which necessarily involves the truth of the proposition said to be remembered, and making honest memory claims, which does not.

It is now time and possible to ring the changes on these alternative interpretations of "can" and "remember."

(a) First, taking "can" as logical and "remember" as entailing the truth of what is remembered, Locke's definition could be made into a necessary truth, albeit a futile necessary truth. For it is manifestly true, though not an helpful definition of "same person," that X at time two is the same person as Y at time one if and only if X and Y are both persons and X can (logically) remember at time two (his doing) what Y did, or what have you, at time one. It is manifestly true since for it to be genuine memory the person remembering must necessarily be the same person as the person whose experience or activity he claims to be remembering as his own. On this interpretation what we have is of course not open to attack on the ground that it is too exclusive or too inclusive, only that it is an otiose only too truism.

(b) Second, taking "remember" in the same way as referring to genuine remembering and "can" as can (factual), Locke's definition is open to two objections. First, it excludes too much; for we often and rightly want to say that we must have done something or other though we cannot for the life of us remember doing it. We are even prepared to accept full responsibility for such forgotten actions, at any rate provided that they are not too important. Even if they are important, and even if we want to disown or diminish our moral or legal responsibility for them, we are prepared to concede that we are the same persons as did them, unless, mistakenly, we think that personal identity is not merely the necessary but also the sufficient condition of full moral and legal responsibility.

The second objection to the second interpretation is the famous paradox, The Case of the Gallant Officer. This objection seems to have been made first, but in a monochrome version, by Berkeley in the eighth section of *Alciphron* VII. Later it was reproduced by Reid in glorious Technicolor: "Suppose a brave officer to have been flogged when a boy at school, for robbing an orchard, to have taken a standard from the enemy in his first campaign, and also to have been made a general in advanced life."[3] Then, if the young of-

---

[3]*Essays on the Intellectual Powers of Man*, ed. A. D. Woozley, London, 1941, III, 6.

ficer could remember the flogging, and the general could remember taking the standard but not being flogged as a boy, on Locke's principles we should have to say that the general both is and is not the same person as the orchard robber. He is not the same (because he cannot now remember the robbery), and yet he is the same (because he is the same as the young officer who was in turn the same as the boy thief).

(c) The third possibility is to take "can" as can (logical) and "remember" as involving only the making of an honest memory claim. The objection to this is that it will let too much in. This point too was, it seems, first made by Berkeley in the private *Philosophical Commentaries:* "Wherein consists identity of person? Not in actual consciousness; for then I'm not the same person I was this day twelvemonth, but while I think of what I then did. Not in potential; for then all persons may be the same, for aught we know. *Mem:* story of Mr. Deering's aunt. Two sorts of potential consciousness—natural and preternatural. In the last section but one I mean the latter."[4]

It is surely our present point which Berkeley is making, since his preternatural potential consciousness is obviously equivalent to ability to remember in the present interpretations of "can" and "remember". No one seems able to provide any informative gloss on his note: "*Mem:* story of Mr. Deering's aunt." But presumably Berkeley is thinking of something which we should count as a puzzle case, and it looks as if he—unilke Locke's early critics—appreciated the relevance of such cases.

(d) The fourth possible combination, that of "can" as can (factual) with "remember" as involving only the making of an honest memory claim, yields an interpretation open to all three objections made against the thesis in interpretations two and three. First, it leaves too much out, ignoring amnesia. Second, it lets too much in, ignoring paramnesia. Third it is internally inconsistent, being exposed to the paradox of The Case of the Gallant Officer. Since people seem more familiar with amnesia than with paramnesia it is just worth remarking that paramnesia is not just a logical possibility but a real phenomenon. The stock and pathetic example is the British King George IV, who in his declining and demented years "remembered" his dashing leadership at the Battle of Waterloo; notwithstanding that only a devoutly Lockean, or an unscrupulously flattering, courtier could have pretended that the King must therefore have been present on that decisive field. Vulgar cases are provided daily by those who press forward to claim sincerely but without factual foundation the discredit for committing the latest newsy murder.

3. This completes our direct case against Locke's proposed solution of the main philosophical problem. But here, as in the political trials in less happier lands, the direct case can be rounded off with a sort of confession. For despite his insistence that, "the same consciousness being preserved, whether in

---

[4]*Works*, ed. A. A. Luce & T. E. Jessop, Edinburgh, 1948–57, Vol. I, p. 26, Entries 200–2: spelling and punctuation slightly modified.

the same or different substances, the personal identity is preserved" Locke is nevertheless, reasonably but inconsistently, anxious lest "one intellectual substance may not have represented to it, as done by itself, what *it* never did, and was perhaps done by some other agent . . ." (*Essay* II, xxvii, 13: italics original).

Locke's anxiety is indeed very reasonable, and, as F. H. Bradley said in a slightly different connection: "it may help us to perceive, what was evident before, that a self is not thought to be the same because of bare memory, but only so when the memory is considered not to be defective."[5] But, though reasonable, Locke's anxiety is entirely inconsistent with his official account of personal identity, which requires him to deny that there can (logical) be honest but falsidical memory claims. For if "being the same person as did that" *means* "being a person able to remember (his) doing, or being able to be conscious of (his) doing, that", then you cannot consistently say that a person may both be able to remember doing and yet not actually have done some particular thing. (Or, rather, to be absolutely strict, this can be made consistent only by interpreting "remember" to refer exclusively to genuine verdical memory; thus reducing this whole account of personal identity to vacuity.)

In his desperation Locke falls on his knees: "And that it never is so, will by us, till we have clearer views of the nature of thinking substances, be best resolved in the goodness of God; who as far as the happiness or misery of any of his sensible creatures is concerned will not, by a fatal error of theirs, transfer from one to another that consciousness which draws reward or punishment with it" (*Essay*, II, xxvii, 13). But the assistance for which Locke supplicates is beyond the resources even of Omnipotence. For on Locke's view there could be no sense in his own fear that people might lose or escape their deserts because they remembered doing what they had not in fact done. If anyone can remember doing something then necessarily—according to Locke's account—he is in fact the same person as did that deed. By making this desperate appeal, Locke both tacitly confesses the inadequacy of his own account of personal identity and provides one more example of phenomenon already all too familiar to the student of religious apologetic—the hope that the sheer physical power of a postulated God can make contradictions consistent or by itself make utterances to which no sense has been given sensible.

IV. SOURCES OF TROUBLE

The question now arises how Locke managed to get himself into this confused and catastrophic position. This is a question of very much more than merely antiquarian interest, since in one form or another both that position itself and the mistakes which misled Locke into it seem to have a perennial appeal. One first part of the answer lies in those possibilities of confusion

[5]*Appearance and Reality*, London and New York, 1893, p. 85.

about memory, which we have examined already. (See III, especially III (2), above.)

Second, as we have also seen, Locke uses the word "conscious" and its associates in several ways. He seems to slide from his definition of "person" as "a thinking intelligent being, that . . . can consider itself as itself, the same thinking thing, in different times and places," by way of talk of "that consciousness which is inseparable from thinking, and as it seems to me, essential to it," to the eventual conclusion that "and as far as this consciousness can be extended backwards to any past action or thought, so far reaches the identity of that person" (*Essay*, II, xxvii, 11). Here we seem in the first passage to be dealing with the sort of consciousness of self which is not the self-consciousness of embarrassment, in the second with that consciousness which is contrasted with complete unconsciousness, and in the concluding third with a conciousness which is identified with memory.

Third, Locke seems sometimes—like many others since—to have confused the epistemological questions, "How can we know, what good evidence can we have for, propositions about personal identity?" with the inseparable but not identical enquiry, "What do such propositions mean?" It is the latter which he is supposed to be pursuing. But what he offers would provide a partial answer to the former. Thus when he tells us that on the "Great Day" everyone will "receive his doom, his conscience accusing or excusing him," or that if he could remember "Noah's flood" as clearly as last winter's "overflowing of the Thames" he could no more doubt "that he was the same *self*" who saw both floods, he is clearly answering a question of the first sort; or perhaps one of the subtly but important different "How can we convince ourselves" sort (*Essay*, II, xxvii, 22 and 16). But neither sort of question can be identified with that to which Locke's main problem belongs: "in this doctrine not only is consciousness confounded with memory but, which is still more strange, personal identity is confounded with the evidence which we have of our personal identity."[6]

Fourth, as we have seen, Locke defined "person" as "a thinking intelligent being, that has reason and reflection, and can consider itself as itself, the same thinking thing, in different times and places." Ignoring the possible danger of circularity which lurks in this talk of "the same thinking thing," the more radical objection must be made that this definition misses the ordinary meaning and use of the term "person." We learn the world "people," by being shown people, by meeting them and shaking hands with them. They may be intelligent or unintelligent, introspective or extraverted, black, white, red, or brown, but what they cannot be is disembodied or in the shape of elephants. Locke's definition would make it a contingent truth about people that some or all of them are either embodied in, or are of, human form. But in the ordinary use of the word "people," we do actually meet people and shake

---

[6]Reid, *op. cit.*, III, 6.

hands with them; we do not meet the fleshy houses in which they are living or the containers in which they are kept. Nor is it logically possible for cougars (or parrots!) to be people. It is in short a necessary truth that people are of human shapes and sizes; and, not a contingent fact that some or all people inhabit human bodies or are of human form.

This is not to say that all talk of disembodied people (or even parrot people) must always and necessarily be self-contradictory. It may perhaps be that the word "people" is being used in a radically unusual sense by those who wish to point out an analogy between the behaviour of people and some situations in which no people are present. This is a perfectly respectable method of adding to our language, a method which only becomes dangerous when it is not understood, when it is thought that "person" in the new sense has the same meaning, the same logical liaisons, as "person" in the old, familiar sense. Locke himself admitted that his distinction between "man," which he used in substantially its ordinary sense, and "person," which he wants to use in a sense which would allow the possibility of disembodiment or embodiment, in different (or even non-human) bodies, is not made in ordinary language: "I know that, in the ordinary way of speaking, the same person, and the same man stand for one and the same thing" (*Essay*, II, xxvii, 15).

But though Locke did unguardedly admit this, he failed to realize how important this admission was and what its implications are. If you use "person" in a new sense, in a way other than the ordinary, then you wreck your chances of producing a descriptive analysis of "same person." And it was this which, most of the time, Locke has to be construed as trying to do: "we must consider what *person* stands for" he tells us, in introducing his definition of "person"; and he rounds off his account of the meaning of "same person" with the comment, "as everyone who reflects will perceive" (*Essay*, II, xxvii, 11 and 17).

V. PERSONS, UNLIKE MEN, THOUGHT OF AS INCORPOREAL

This attempt to make a fundamental distinction between "same man" and "same person" demands investigation. Why does Locke want to do it?

1. First, we can find certain nuances of English idiom which might suggest a distinction of this kind. For instance it would be slightly more natural to use "man" when referring to physical characteristics and "person" when referring to psychological ones: Charles Atlas and the Army offer to make a new man of you; the Pelman Institute, or your psychoanalyst, are more likely to promise that you would be an altogether different person after a course of their treatment. But this is the merest nuance. For, when Robert Browning wrote:

> There they are, my fifty men and women
> Naming me my fifty poems finished!

he was dedicating a collection of character sketches. A slightly more promising temptation lies in phrases like "Our Claude is quite a different person since he went away to school." As we are quite sure that he is really the same boy, the same person, as in fact we should only say someone was quite a different person (in this sense) if we were sure he was the same person (in the ordinary sense), we may become inclined to make our point by saying that the same man may or may not be the same person.

Then again there are in our language, and in many others, the embedded traces of what was once a scientific hypothesis, the hypothesis of possession. This degenerated into a mere alternative idiom through the addition of so many qualifications ("But it is an *invisible* spirit," and so on) that it no longer risked falsification. It thus ceased to be an hypothesis at all. Instead of saying, "He drove wildly," or "Why on earth did he do it?" we can say "He drove like a man possessed" or "Whatever possessed him to do it?" And this sometime hypothesis and present dead metaphor has even now perhaps not altogether lost its seductive power. Certainly it had not when Locke wrote. For, noticing that we do not punish "the mad man for the sober man's actions" he thought that this, "is somewhat explained by our way of speaking in English when we say such an one is 'not himself', or is 'beside himself'; in which phrases it is insinuated, as if those who now, or at least first used them, thought that self was changed; the self-same person was no longer in that man" (*Essay*, II, xxvii, 20).

2. This suggests a second reason for Locke's distinction between a man and a person. Locke seems to have assumed that there is one single necessary and sufficient condition of moral and legal responsibility. But he notices cases where he does not want to blame or punish someone who in some sense seems to have been the agent who did the wrong or criminal action. For instance, he does not want a madman to be punished for what he did before he went mad; and he does not want to blame people for actions which they simply cannot remember having done. So then, instead of saying that the person in question did do whatever it was but he is not to be held responsible, or at least not fully responsible, because he is now amnesic or insane, Locke distinguishes the man from the person, announcing that the word "person" is a "forensic term, appropriating actions and their merit" (*Essay*, II, xxvii, 26). This opens up for him the possibility of saying in some troubling case that blame or punishment would be here improper because we have before us only the same man and not the same person as did the deed.

3. The third basis for Locke's distinction between the man and the person was his Platonic-Cartesian conviction that people essentially are incorporeal spirits, and that human bodies in fact are controlled by internal shadow beings in ways similar to, but much less intelligible than, that in which ships are directed by their captains or vehicles by their drivers: "For I presume it is not the idea of a thinking or rational being alone that makes the *idea of man* in most people's sense; but of a body so and so shaped joined to it . . ."; but, though the idea of man thus involves the body as well, the essential person is the thinking or rational being which is not necessarily of human shape or even corporeal (*Essay*, II, xxvii, 10: italics original). Or, again, "if the identity

of soul alone makes the same man; and there be nothing in the nature of matter why the same individual spirit may not be united to different bodies, it will be possible that . . . men living in distant ages . . . may have been the same man; which way of speaking must be from a very strange use of the word *man*, applied to an idea out of which body and shape are excluded" (*Essay*, II, xxvii, 7: italics supplied). Which is all very well, but still takes for granted that people are souls; which, presumably, conceivably could thus transmigrate.

This is not the place either fully to characterize or generally to assail the Platonic-Cartesian view of man.[7] But it is worthwhile to devote some space to showing how fundamental and how important this view was for Locke, and how little inclined he was seriously to question it. For it is a view presupposed by his whole account of personal identity; while the impossibility of that account should itself in turn be seen as one of the most powerful objections against that view of the nature of man.[8]

Locke's first concern in the *Essay* is to prove that we have no surrepetitious access to black-market ideas, but are properly confined to getting our supplies through the official channels of post-natal waking experience. He claims at one point: "We know certainly, by experience, that we *sometimes* think; and thence draw this infallible consequence—that there is something in us which has the power to think" (*Essay*, II, i, 10; italics original). The conclusion of this lamentable argument opens up precisely the possibility which Locke is most concerned to close. For the word "thinking" is being used in the Cartesian sense, in which to think is to have any sort of conscious experience. Now, if our thinking is done by some possibly incorporeal internal thinking thing, then it becomes natural to ask whether perhaps it may not sometimes slip out to have some experiences on its own, maybe taking up station for the purpose inside some alien body. All of which suggestions, colourfully presented as the hypothetical doings of Socrates, Castor, Pollux or their several souls are then duly considered by Locke (II, xxvii, 13–15).

Yet the "infallible consequence" which here sets off these bizarre speculations is not validly drawn. For though we do undoubtedly know that "we sometimes think" this has not the slightest tendency to show that this thinking is done by "something in us which has the power to think." Quite the reverse. The argument derives what little plausibility it has from the tacit assumption that everything we do is done with some special organ. But this is false. We write with our hands, certainly. But we do not decide, or sleep, or fret with special organs of deciding, sleeping, or fretting. It is the same with thinking, both in the ordinary and in the wide Cartesian sense. Thinking, like sleeping and deciding, is an "affection of the whole man." It would be pleasant to believe that Locke was beginning to realize this when he wrote: "But

---

[7]For such more thorough treatment see G. Ryle, *The Concept of Mind*, London, 1949, perhaps comparing Antony Flew (editor), *Body, Mind, and Death*, New York, 1964.

[8]Compare A. M. Quinton "The Soul," *The Journal of Philosophy*, 1962, and Antony Flew " 'The Soul' of Mr. A. M. Quinton," *The Journal of Philosophy*, 1963.

whether sleeping without dreaming be not an affection of the whole man, mind as well as body, may be worth a waking man's consideration . . ." (*Essay*, II, i, 11).

4. One aspect of the Platonic-Cartesian view of man deserves special separate mention. It is that it provides something which may plausibly be held both to survive a man's death and to be accountable, on the "Great Day," for his deeds upon earth. Now to be justly accountable, here or hereafter for a murder you have to be the same person as the villain who did the murder. That is the necessary, though by no means the sufficient, condition of full responsibility. But if you attach the customary sense to "person", this necessary condition can never be satisfied by anyone who died before the "Great Day." For he will simply not exist to be to any degree responsible. He will have died and been buried. Nor can the situation be saved merely by producing an indistinguishable person to stand his trial. For "one thing cannot have two beginnings of existence, nor two things one beginning . . . That, therefore, that had one beginning, is the same thing; and that which had a different beginning in time and place from that, is not the same, but diverse" (*Essay*, II, xxvii, 1).

Locke therefore, committed as he was to beliefs both in immortality and in just reckoning on "that Great Day," had a very strong reason—or perhaps it should be called a motive, for insisting that "person" unlike "man" may refer to something incorporeal. For while it is immediately obvious that a person in the everyday sense, a person such as we can meet face to face in the streets, (logically) cannot survive bodily death and dissolution, it may perhaps seem at first sight conceivable that a person, in the sense of a series of experiences linked together in some subtle "gap-indifferent way," or in the sense of a "thing which is sensible or conscious of pleasure and pain, capable of happiness or misery," might survive, and be the bearer of responsibility for what that same person (in a new, and rather peculiar sense) did "in the body." There are appalling difficulties in the logic of such new senses of "person" and "same person," which we do not have to discuss here.[9]

Yet it is both relevant and worthwhile to draw attention to Locke's achievement in uncovering some of these difficulties. He himself did not see clearly what, or how great, or how numerous they are. This was partly because he thought he was defining the ordinary sense of "person". He therefore saw no difficulty in making a "disembodied person" (that is a person in some new sense) the same as (and thus possibly accountable for the actions of) some person who had lived at a previous date (some person, that is, in the old sense). Partly again it was because, since he thought he had successfully found in memory what Hume called the "uniting principle, which constitutes a person", he could scarcely be expected simultaneously to realize that memory can only discover and not constitute personal identity (in any sense of "person"). Partly, finally, it was for the simple reason that this territory Locke

---

[9]But see Quinton and Flew, *op. cit.*

had entered was too vast and too difficult for any single explorer to open up immediately.

Locke had to struggle to his insights through a rank growth of baffling terms, such as, "immaterial substances," "selves," "thinking substances," "rational souls." The insights which he did achieve are the more remarkable inasmuch as a critic of the calibre of Bishop Butler failed to see that the subject presented difficulties, complaining of the "strange perplexities" that had been raised: "Whether we are to live in a future state, as it is the most important question which can possibly be asked, so it is the most intelligible one which can be expressed in language" (§ 1). Locke, had he lived to read the dissertation *Of Personal Identity* would have agreed about the supreme importance of the question. But he might, very reasonably, have asked for some solution of those "strange perplexities" of the puzzle cases before being prepared to concede that things really were all quite so straightforward as Butler thought.

5. A fifth source of Locke's unhappy analysis of personal identity lies in his un-Lockean assumption that we can find a definition such that, granted we are provided with all the relevant factual data, we shall be able to say in every actual or imaginable case whether or not the expression "same person" can correctly be applied. This assumption is mistaken.

(a) Doubt may be thrown upon it in three ways. First, it is unsettling to see the troubles of those who have tried to fulfil such a requirement. Locke offered one such candidate definition, with the unfortunate results already examined. Berkeley, more prudently, refrained deliberately from the attempt. In the *Philosophical Commentaries* he reminds himself "carefully to omit defining of Person, or making much mention of it." This good advice he resolutely follows throughout his published works with the significant exception of a passage in the eighth section of Book VII of the *Alciphron*. There he challenges the minute philosophers to, "untie the knots and answer the questions which may be raised even about human personal identity" before requiring, "a clear and distinct idea of *person* in relation to the Trinity": a very typical piece of Berkeleian intellectual judo.

(b) Second, this assumption overlooks the possibilities of vagueness, of the marginal cases in which we do not quite know where to draw the line. Most words referring to physical objects are vague in some direction, somewhere there is an undemarcated frontier; somewhere there is a no man's land of indeterminacy; often there is a complete encircling penumbra of perplexity. And this is and must be so because nature has no natural kinds. God made the spectrum, man makes the pigeonholes. It was Locke himself who launched attack after attack on the superstitions of real essences and natural kinds. It is he himself who points again and again to the specimens which will not fit properly into any available category. It is he who points to the vagueness even of the term "man." It is he who draws attention to the changelings who are "something between a man and a beast," he too who tells us the story of the Abbot Malotru who was so monstrous at his birth that "he was baptized and declared a man provisionally," and Locke again who insists that "There are creatures . . . that, with language and reason and a shape in other things agreeing with ours, have hairy tails; others where the males have no beards, and others where the females have" (*Essay*, IV, iv, 13 and III, vi, 26 and 22).

Nevertheless, despite all this, Locke never seems to entertain the possibility that "person," "rational being," "soul," "Immaterial spirit," "self," and the rest of the words and expressions alleged to refer to the putative and elusive internal population of the body, may be affected in the same way. This failure shows up most strikingly when he argues that no external shape is an infallible sign that there is a rational soul inside: "Where now (I ask) shall be the just measure; which is the utmost bounds of that shape which carries with it a rational soul?" He points out once again "all the several degrees of mixture of the likeness of a man or a brute," and demands: "What sort of outside is the certain sign that there is or is not such an inhabitant within?" Finally he complains: "we talk at random of *man*; and shall always, I fear, do so, as long as we give ourselves up to certain sounds, and the imaginations of settled and fixed species in nature, we know not what . . . So necessary is it to quit the common notion of species and essences, if we will truly look into the nature of things . . ." (*Essay*, IV, iv, 16). Yet he himself is all the while assuming as it were a real essence of the rational souls, a fixed species or natural kind of the people who inhabit some, though we cannot always tell which, of these men and near men whom we meet.

(c) Third, since our ordinary language, and the concepts of ordinary language, have been evolved or introduced to deal with the situations which are ordinarily met with, and not with the extraordinary, we may reasonably expect some failures of adaptation when new and unexpected situations arise. And these do in fact occur. The old conceptual machinery breaks down. The old terminological tools fail to cope with the new tasks. These breakdowns are different from the cases in which indecision arises from the vagueness of a term. "Ship" is perhaps a vague term, in that a whole spectrum of similarity stretches between things which are certainly ships, via the things which provoke linguistic hesitation, to other things which are undoubtedly boats. But when a court has to decide whether the word "ship" in a statute covers flying boats, the difficulty arises: not so much from the vagueness of the term "ship" (that would imply that the drafting of the statute was bad and could perfectly well have been improved); but from what has been called its open-texture. The concept which we have has in fact evolved to cover the situations that have arisen before or were thought likely to arise, and not the situations which have not arisen and could not have been foreseen. Vagueness could have been removed by prescribing that nothing under so many tons was to count as a ship within the meaning of the act: "To remove vagueness is to outline the penumbra of a shadow. The line is there after we have drawn it and not before." But it is not possible "to define a concept like *gold* with absolute precision, i.e. in such a way that every nook and cranny is blocked against the entry of doubt. That is what is meant by *'open texture'* of a concept."[10] It is this open texture much more than any actual vagueness in use which prevents the definition of "person."

By imagining, fully two centuries before the foundation of the Society for Psychical Research, a series of puzzle cases which leave us at a loss as to whether or not to apply the expression "same person," Locke revealed what he did not himself see, that it is not possible to define the meaning of "same person" descriptively and at the same time give a definition which will answer all possible problems of application. This is not possible because there is no usage established for many of these unforeseen situations. Therefore no such proper usage can be described. In cases such as Locke produces we can only admit that we don't know what to say; and then perhaps prescribe what is to be the proper usage if such cases do occur or recur. It is not possible to produce even a prescriptive definition which will give absolute security against all possibility of surprise and indecision. Locke produced a definition of "same person" which enabled him to give an answer to all the puzzle cases which he imagined. Let someone appear who seemed to remember the Noah's flood as clearly and accurately as he remembered last year's overflowing of the Thames. If we accepted Locke's definition, then clearly we could and should say without hesitation that he had been present at Noah's flood: and answer which, assuming that he had been born in this century, would be false. But no prescription can give absolute determinacy. Locke did not, and could not, imagine all the possibilities. Suppose, what is not merely conceivable but imaginable, that a person splits like an amoeba—first into two Siamese twins—then separating into two identical twins. And suppose both twins, call them A_1 and A_2, can remember all that the original person, call him A, could remember before his unfortunate and disruptive experience. On Locke's definition A_1 and A_2 will both be the same person as A, and yet they will obviously be different people, just as are identical twins. Clearly we should not know what to say. This preposterous supposition will serve to show that it is not possible to produce either a descriptive or a prescriptive definition of "same person" which shall remove every possibility of linguistic perplexity. We can prescribe against vagueness. But then there is always the open texture through which forever threatens the insidious infiltration of the unforeseeable and the unforeseen.

VI. CONCLUSIONS

The search for the talismanic definition which shall solve all possible problems, the search for the real essence of personal identity, was therefore a

---

[10]F. Waismann, "Verfiability" in *Logic and Language* (First Series), ed. Antony Flew, Blackwell (London) 1951.

mistake. Why did Locke make it? It involved, as we have seen, an abandonment of his greatest insight and a betrayal of the glorious revolution he was leading against the superstition of real essences and natural kinds. However, it is just as easy to fail to apply a new discovery consistently as it is to push it to absurd extremes. We smile at the man who tells us: "I'm an atheist now, thank God!" But we all fall into similar inconsistencies. So there is every reason to expect with the notoriously inconsistent Locke, what we do in fact find, a failure to see all the implications of, and to apply thoroughly and systematically, his own discoveries.

Then we remember those long struggles that had to be fought, and which still drag on in some intellectual backwoods, before the doctrine of evolution was allowed to include, without reservation, our own species. We remember the bitter rear-guard actions, arguing for a special creation for this one most favoured species. We can see still in Rome the final forlorn hope to save the special creation of souls to inhabit the bodies which have at last been conceded to be the most recent results of the evolutionary process. In the light of all this, it no longer seems surprising that Locke, living two centuries before the famous Victorian battles over the origin of species, failed to take his great insight into the enclosure reserved for the ghostly company of "rational souls," "persons," and "thinking substances."

Another source of the inability to see that questions may be asked about personal identity to which there can be no true or false answer (until and unless a new decision, which may be wise or unwise, is made about what is to be proper usage) lies in the familiar fact that people often know things about their pasts which they conceal from other people. We tend, being aware of his familiar truth, to assume that all questions about the identity of persons are always wholly factual, susceptible of straight true or false answers, long after we have realized that questions as to whether this is or is not the same thing may sometimes not be so straightforward. We feel that the person in question must himself always know—yes or no—whether he is the same person as the man who broke the bank at Monte Carlo. Even if we cannot discover the answer because he will not tell us or because we do not trust him, even if he protests that he does not know, still we assume that if he could (seem to himself to) remember that would settle the issue definitively.

We are not, obviously, inclined to think that the thing could tell us if it wanted to: but we do tend to think that the person could, and, if he did, that would be that: "Whenever a man finds what he calls himself, there, I think, another may say is the same person" (*Essay*, II, xxvii, 26). And "should the soul of a prince, carrying with it the consciousness of the prince's past life, enter and inform the body of a cobbler . . . everyone sees he would be the same person with the prince . . ." (*Essay*, II, xxvii, 15). And so, confident that the subject must always know whether or not he is the same person, just as he always has the last word as to whether or not he is in pain, Locke proceeds to give his disastrous definition of personal identity; quite overlooking the facts of amnesia and paramnesia which show decisively that personal identity is in this respect not like pain. The honest testimony of the subject is not with personal identity as it is with pain the last word. But the fact that it is such very good evidence, combined with the fact that we are all too familiar with human reticence and deceit, misleads us into thinking that it is.

To sum up. We outlined Locke's contribution to the study of the philosophic problem of personal identity, and showed that his central answer was wrong. We then enquired at length into the sources of his mistakes, finding five; first, a series of confusions about memory; second, his muddled and slippery use of the term "consciousness"; third, the failure rigidly to distinguish the meaning of statements from, what is so inseparably connected with it, their methods of verification; fourth, the view that "person" refers to some bodies and intangible inhabitant of the dark room of the understanding (*Essay*, II, xi, 17) rather than to people like those we meet in everyday life; and, fifth, the assumption that there is some real essence of personal identity, that it is possible to produce a definition and a definition furthermore which can guard us against every threat of future linguistic indecision. We neither began nor intended to begin to tackle the problem itself; it was a sufficient, and very Lockean, task to clear the ground of a few obstructions and to point out some of the dangers which beset the road.

ANTHONY QUINTON

6.3   The Soul

1. THE SOUL AND SPIRITUAL SUBSTANCE

Philosophers in recent times have had very little to say about the soul. The word, perhaps, has uncomfortably ecclesiastical associations, and the idea seems to be bound up with a number of discredited or at any rate generally disregarded theories. In the history of philosophy the soul has been used for two distinct purposes: first, as an explanation of the vitality that distinguishes human beings, and also animals and plants, from the broad mass of material objects, and, secondly, as the seat of consciousness. The first of these, which sees the soul as an ethereal but nonetheless physical entity, a volatile collection of fire-atoms or a stream of animal spirits, on some views dissipated with the dissolution of the body, on others absorbed at death into the cosmic soul,

From *The Journal of Philosophy* 59 (1962): 393–409. Reprinted by permission of the author and the editors.

and on others again as capable of independent existence, need not detain us. The second, however, the soul of Plato and Descartes, deserves a closer examination than it now usually receives. For it tends to be identified with the view that in each person there is to be found a spiritual substance which is the subject of his mental states and the bearer of his personal identity. But on its widest interpretation, as the nonphysical aspect of a person, its acceptance need not involve either the existence of a spiritual substance over and above the mental states that make up a person's inner, conscious life or the proposition that this spiritual substance is what ultimately determines a person's identity through time. When philosophers dismiss the soul it is usually because they reject one or both of these supposed consequences of belief in it.

It is worth insisting, furthermore, that the existence of a spiritual substance is logically distinct from its being the criterion of personal identity. So the strong, and indeed fatal, arguments against the substance theory of personal identity do not at the same time refute the proposition, self-evident to Berkeley and many others, that there can be no conscious state that is not the state of some subject.

As a criterion of identity spiritual substance has three main weaknesses. First, it is regressive in just the same way as is an account of the identity of a material object through time in terms of its physical components. No general account of the identity of a kind of individual thing can be given which finds that identity in the presence of another individual thing within it. For the question immediately arises, how is the identity through time of the supposed identifier to be established? It, like the thing it is supposed to identify, can present itself at any one time only as it is at that time. However alike its temporally separate phases may be, they still require to be identified as parts of the same, continuing thing. In practice we do identify some wholes through their parts, normally where the parts are more stable and persistent unities than the wholes they compose and where, in consequence, the parts are more readily identifiable, as, for example, when we pick out one person's bundle of laundry from the bundles of others after the labels have been lost. But this can be only a practical expedient, not a theoretical solution.

A second difficulty is to find any observable mental entity that can effectively serve as a criterion in this case. The only plausible candidate is that dim, inchoate background, largely composed of organic sensations, which envelops the mental states occupying the focus of attention. This organic background is a relatively unchanging environment for the more dramatic episodes of conscious life to stand out against. But both the fixity and the peripheral status of this background are only relative. It does change, and it, or its parts, can come or be brought into the focus of attention. Even if its comparatively undisturbed persistence of character suggests it as a criterion, its vagueness makes it even less accessible to public application than the general run of mental criteria and leaves it with little power to distinguish between one person and another. The organic background is, of course, as regressive a criterion as any other part of a person's mental life. Its only virtues are that it is observable and that it does seem to be a universal constituent of the momentary cross sections of a person's experience. In this last respect it is preferable to most distinguishable features of a person's mental life. For, generally speaking, the parts of a complex and enduring thing are not necessary to the identity of that thing. Just as a cathedral is still the same cathedral if a piece has been knocked off it, whatever the piece may be, so a person is the same person if he ceases to have a particular belief or emotion, whatever that belief or emotion may be.

Finally, if it is held that the spiritual substance is nevertheless a permanent and unaltering constituent of a person's conscious life, it follows that it must be unobservable and so useless for purposes of identification. Suppose that from its very first stirrings my consciousness has contained a continuous whistling sound of wholly unvarying character. I should clearly never notice it, for I can only notice what varies independently of my consciousness—the whistles that start and stop at times other than those at which I wake up and fall asleep. It is this fact that ensured from the outset that Hume's search for a self over and above his particular perceptions was bound to fail. The unobservability of spiritual substance, and its consequent inapplicability as a criterion, can also be held to follow directly from taking its status as substance seriously, as an uncharacterized substratum for qualities and relations to inhere in with no recognizable features of its own.

But to admit that spiritual substance cannot possibly be the criterion of a person's identity and that it cannot be identified with any straightforwardly observable part of a person's mental life does not mean that it does not exist. It has seemed self-evident to many philosophers that every mental state must have an owner. To believe this is not to commit oneself to the existence of something utterly unobservable. If it is true, although both subjects and mental states are unobservable in isolation, each can be observed in conjunction with the other. There is a comparison here with the relations and observability of the positions and qualities of material things. One cannot be aware of a color except as present at some place and at some time or of a position except as the place and time where some discernible characteristics are manifested. So it might be argued that one can be aware of a conscious subject only as in some mental state or other and of a mental state only as belonging to some subject or other. Critics of the Berkeleyan principle sometimes suggest that it is no more than a faulty inference from the subject-object structure of the sentences in which mental facts are reported. It would certainly be a mistake to infer that a conscious subject is something entirely distinct from all its states from the linguistic fact that we commonly assign mental states to owners. We say of a chair that it has a back, a seat, arms, and legs, but this should not and does not lead us to conclude that the chair is something over and above the parts that it has, appropriately arranged. A more usual argument for the principle starts from the premise that mental states are acts that cannot be conceived without an agent in the same way as there cannot be a blow without a striker or a journey without a traveler. The premise of this argument has been much criticized by recent philosophers. A feeling of depression or a belief in the trustworthiness of a friend is not a precisely datable occurrence but a more or less persisting dispositional state. Nor is it an instance of agency in the sense of being the intentional execution of a decision. But these mistaken implications do not affect the validity of the argument under consideration. A disposition requires a possessor as much as an act requires an agent, and the blow I get from a swinging door still presupposes the existence of the door even though it did not mean to hit me.

The strength of the argument lies in the fact that we can assert the existence of some mental state, a feeling of anger let us say, only when we are in a position to assert either that we ourselves are angry or that somebody else is. We have given no sense to the words "discovering the existence of a mental state that is not my own or anyone else's." The nearest we come to speaking in this way is when we say, for example, "there is a sadness about the place," when walking about some ruins in a contemplative frame of mind. What we mean in this case is that the place inclines us to feel sad and might well give rise to the same inclination in others. And this capacity for producing sad feelings in myself and others, as a disposition, has its own substance, so to speak: the broken columns and collapsed walls with which it is bound up.

The subject in this rather thin and formal sense is not borne down in the ruin of that concept of spiritual substance in which it is proposed as the determinant of personal identity. It could be argued that it is a loose way of referring to the related series of other mental states or to the body or both with which any given mental state is universally associated by our manner of reporting such states. If it is something distinct from both of these, as it has traditionally been believed to be, it is not properly to be called the soul. It could not exist without any states at all, and even if it could it would be an emotionally useless form of survival of bodily death. Its existence, in fact, is irrelevant to the problem of the soul, which is that of whether a person is essentially mental in character and so distinct from his body, a connected sequence of mental states and not a physical object. It is irrelevant whether the sequence of mental states composing a person on this theory presupposes a distinguishable subject or not.

Spiritual substance cannot be the criterion of personal identity, and it may or may not be presupposed by the existence of conscious mental states. Whether as part or presupposition of our mental life, it should not be identified with the soul when this is conceived as the nonbodily aspect of a person. The well-founded conviction that there is no spiritual substance in the first sense and widespread doubts as to its existence in the second should not be allowed to obscure the issue of whether there is a unitary nonbodily aspect to a person and, if there is, whether it is the fundamental and more important aspect. Locke saw that spiritual substance could not account for personal

identity and, although he believed in its existence, speculated whether it might
not have been possible for God to endow a material substance with the
power of thinking. Yet he clearly believed in the soul as the connected sequence of a person's conscious states, regarded this sequence as what a person
essentially was, and held it to be capable of existing independently of the
body. I want to consider whether an empirical concept of the soul, which,
like Locke's, interprets it as a sequence of mental states logically distinct from
the body and is neutral with regard to the problem of the subject, can be
constructed.

2. THE EMPIRICAL CONCEPT OF THE SOUL

It will be admitted that among all the facts that involve a person there is a
class that can be described as mental in some sense or other. Is it enough to
define the soul as the temporally extended totality of mental states and events
that belong to a person? It will not be enough to provide a concept of the
soul as something logically distinct from the body if the idea of the series of
a person's mental states involves some reference to the particular human
body that he possesses. In the first place, therefore a nonbodily criterion of
personal identity must be produced. For if the soul were the series of mental
states associated with a given body, in the sense of being publicly reported by
it and being manifested by its behavior, two temporally separate mental states
could belong to the history of the same soul only if they were in fact associated with one and the same human body. This notion of the soul could
have no application to mental states that were not associated with bodies.
The soul must, then, be a series of mental states that is identified through
time in virtue of the properties and relations of these mental states themselves. Both the elements of the complex and the relations that make an
identifiable persisting thing out of them must be mental. To establish the
possibility of such a mental criterion of identity will be the hardest part of
the undertaking.

Locke's criterion of memory has been much criticized, and it is certainly
untenable in some of the interpretations it has been given. It will not do to
say that two mental states belong to the same soul if and only if whoever
has the later one can recollect the earlier one if the possibility of recollection
involved is factual and not formal. For people forget things, and the paradox
of the gallant officer is generated in which he is revealed as identical with both
his childish and his senile selves while these are not identical with each other.
However, a more plausible criterion can be offered in terms of continuity of
character and memory. Two soul-phases belong to the same soul, on this
view, if they are connected by a continuous character and memory path. A
soul-phase is a set of contemporaneous mental states belonging to the same
momentary consciousness. Two soul-phases are directly continuous if they
are temporally juxtaposed, if the character revealed by the constituents of

each is closely similar, and if the later contains recollections of some elements of the earlier. Two soul-phases are indirectly continuous and connected by a continuous character and memory path if there is a series of soul-phases all of whose members are directly continuous with their immediate predecessors and successors in the series and if the original soul-phases are the two end points of the series. There is a clear analogy between this criterion and the one by means of which material objects, including human bodies, are identified. Two object-phases belong to the same object if they are connected by a continuous quality and position path. Direct continuity in this case obtains between two temporally juxtaposed object-phases which are closely similar in qualities and are in the same position or in closely neighboring positions. Indirect continuity is once again the ancestral of direct continuity. There is no limit to the amount of difference in position allowed by the criterion to two indirectly continuous object-phases, but in normal discourse a limit is set to the amount of qualitative difference allowed by the requirement that the two phases be of objects of the same kind. Character in the mental case corresponds to quality in the physical and memory to spatial position. The soul, then, can be defined empirically as a series of mental states connected by continuity of character and memory.

Now there is an objection to the idea that memory can be any sort of fundamental criterion of identity which rests on the view that a memory criterion presupposes a bodily criterion. I shall defer the consideration of this issue, however, until two less serious difficulties have been met. These are that the construction suggested requires an exploded Cartesian dualism about the nature of mental states and, arising out of this, that a person's character is not clearly distinguishable from his body. The former, Rylean, objection can be met without difficulty. Even if the most extreme and reductive version of logical behaviorism were correct, even if a person's mental states were simply and solely behavioral dispositions, actual or potential, his character a complex property of these dispositions, and his memory a particular disposition to make first-person statements in the past tense without inference or reliance on testimony, the empirical concept of the soul would still apply to something distinct from any particular human body, though some body or other, not necessarily human perhaps, would be required to manifest the appropriate dispositions in its behavior and speech. In other words, an extreme, reductive, logical behaviorism is perfectly compatible with reincarnation, with the manifestation by one body of the character and memories that were previously manifested by another body that no longer exists. The second objection is that the soul as here defined and the body cannot be clearly distinguished, since the possession of some sorts of character trait requires the possession of an appropriate sort of body. I do not see that there is much empirical foundation for this to start with. It would be odd for a six-year-old girl to display the character of Winston Churchill, odd indeed to the point of outrageousness, but it is not utterly inconceivable. At first, no doubt, the girl's display of dogged endurance, a world-historical comprehensiveness of outlook, and so forth, would strike one as distasteful and pretentious in so young a child. But if she kept it up the impression would wear off. We do not, after all, find the story of Christ disputing with the doctors in the temple literally unintelligible. And a very large number of character traits seem to presume nothing about the age, sex, build, and general physical condition of their host. However, even if this were an empirically well-founded point, it would not be a relevant one. It would merely show that the possession of a given trait of character required the possession of an appropriate *kind* of body, a large one or a male one or an old one, and not the possession of a *particular* body. As things are, characters can survive large and even emotionally disastrous alterations to the physical type of a person's body, and these changes may have the effect of making it hard to others to recognize the continuity of character that there is. But courage, for example, can perfectly well persist even though the bodily conditions for its more obvious manifestations do not.

3. MENTAL AND BODILY CRITERIA OF IDENTITY

In recent philosophy there have been two apparently independent aspects to the view that the mind is logically dependent on the body. On the one hand, there are the doctrines that hold mental states either to be or necessarily to involve bodily states, whether bodily movement and dispositions thereto or neural events and configurations. With these doctrines, I have argued, the empirical concept of the soul can be reconciled. On the other hand, many philosophers have insisted that the basic and indispensable criterion of personal identity is bodily. Even mind-body dualists like Ayer, who have accepted the existence of a categorically clear-cut class of mental events, have sometimes taken this position. In his first treatment of the problem he appears at first to give a mental account of the concept of a person as being a series of experiences. But the relation that connects them in his theory involves an indispensable reference to a particular persisting human body. A person is made up of those total mental states which contain organic sensations belonging to one particular human body, presumably to be identical itself in terms of continuity of qualities and spatial position. Ayer draws the conclusion that properly follows from this and from any other account of personal identity that involves reference to a particular human body, namely that the notion of a person's disembodied existence is a self-contradictory one and, further, that even the association of a personality with different bodies at different times is inconceivable. These conclusions may well seem to constitute a reductio ad absurdum of the bodily criterion of personal identity rather than a disproof of the possibility of a person's survival of death. To explore them a little further will help to present the claims of mental as against bodily criteria in a clearer light.

At the outset it must be admitted that the theory of a bodily criterion has a number of virtues. It has, first, the theoretical attraction of simplicity, in that it requires only one mode of treatment for the identification through time of all enduring things, treating human beings as just one variety of concrete objects. Second, it has a practical appeal, in that its application yields uncontentiously correct answers in the very great majority of the actual cases of personal identification with which we are called upon to deal. Finally, it has the merit of realism, for it is, in fact, the procedure of identification that we do most commonly apply. Even where, for lack of relevant evidence, it is inapplicable, as in the case of the Tichborne claimant, it would not be supposed that the result of applying other criteria such as memory would conflict with what the bodily evidence would have shown if it had been forthcoming. Is there anything better to set against these powerful recommendations in favor of a bodily criterion than that it entails that things many people have wanted very deeply to say about the survival of death are inconsistent? A supporter of the bodily criterion might argue that it was so much the worse for them, that their inconsistent assertions arose from attempting to assert and deny at the same time that a person no longer existed.

It does seem strange, all the same, to say that all statements about disembodied or reincarnated persons are self-contradictory. Is it really at all plausible to say this about such familiar things as the simpler type of classical ghost story? It may be argued that there are plenty of stories which are really self-contradictory and yet which can be, in a way, understood and enjoyed, stories about time machines, for example. To try to settle the case we had better consider some concrete instances. Suppose I am walking on the beach with my friend *A*. He walks off a fair distance, treads on a large mine that someone has forgotten to remove, and is physically demolished in front of my eyes. Others, attracted by the noise, draw near and help to collect the scattered remains of *A* for burial. That night, alone in my room, I hear *A*'s voice and see a luminous but intangible object, of very much the shape and size of *A*, standing in the corner. The remarks that come from it are in *A*'s characteristic style and refer to matters that only *A* could have known about. Suspecting a hallucination, I photograph it and call in witnesses who hear and see what I do. The apparition returns afterwards and tells of where it has been and what it has seen. It would be very peculiar to insist, in these circumstances, that *A* no longer existed, even though his body no longer exists except as stains on the rocks and in a small box in the mortuary. It is not essential for the argument that the luminous object look like *A* or that it speak in *A*'s voice. If it were a featureless cylinder and spoke like a talking weighing machine we should simply take longer becoming convinced that it really was *A*. But if continuity of character and memory were manifested with normal amplitude, we surely should be convinced.

Consider a slightly different case. I know two men *B* and *C*. *B* is a dark, tall, thin, puritanical Scotsman of sardonic temperament with whom I have gone on bird-watching expeditions. C is a fair, short, plump, apolaustic Pole of indestructible enterprise and optimism with whom I have made a number of more urban outings. One day I come into a room where both appear to be, and the dark, tall, thin man suggests that he and I pursue tonight some acquaintances I made with C, though he says it was with him, a couple of nights ago. The short, fair, plump, cheerful-looking man reminds me in a strong Polish accent of a promise I had made to B, though he says it was to him, and which I had forgotten about, to go in search of owls on this very night. At first I suspect a conspiracy, but the thing continues far beyond any sort of joke, for good perhaps, and is accompanied by suitable amazement on their part at each other's appearance, their own reflections in the mirror, and so forth.

Now what would it be reasonable to say in these circumstances: that B and C have changed bodies (the consequence of a mental criterion), that they have switched character and memories (the consequence of a bodily criterion), or neither? It seems to me quite clear that we should not say that B and C had switched characters and memories. And if this is correct, it follows that bodily identity is not a logically complete criterion of personal identity; at best it could be a necessary condition of personal identity. Of the other alternatives, that of refusing to identify either of the psychophysical hybrids before us with B or C may seem the most scrupulous and proper. But the refusal might take a number of different forms. It might be a categorical denial that either of the hybrids is B or C. It might, more sophisticatedly be an assertion that the concept of personal identity had broken down and that there was no correct answer, affirmative or negative, to the question: which of these two is B and which C? It might, uninterestingly, be a state of amazed and inarticulate confusion.

What support is there for the conclusion required by the empirical concept of the soul, that B and C have substituted bodies? First of all, the rather weak evidence of imaginative literature. In F. Anstey's story *Vice Versa* the corpulent and repressive Mr. Bultitude and his athletic and impulsive school-boy son are the victims of a similar rearrangement. The author shows not the smallest trace of hesitation in calling the thing with the father's character and memories the father and the thing with the father's body the son. (Cf. also Conan Doyle's *Keinplatz Experiment.*) A solider support is to be found by reflecting on the probable attitude after the switch of those who are most concerned with our original pair, B and C, as persons, those who have the greatest interest in answering the question of their personal identity: their parents, their wives, their children, their closest friends. Would they say that B and C had ceased to exist, that they had exchanged characters and memories or that they had exchanged bodies? It is surely plain that if the character and memories of B and C really survived intact in their new bodily surroundings those closely concerned with them would say that the two had exchanged bodies, that the original persons were where the characters and memories were. For why, after all, do we bother to identify people so carefully? What is unique about individual people that is important enough for us to call them by individual proper names? In our general relations with other human beings their bodies are for the most part intrinsically unimportant. We use them as convenient recognition devices enabling us to locate without difficulty the persisting character and memory complexes in which we are interested, which we love or like. It would be upsetting if a complex with which we were emotionally involved came to have a monstrous or repulsive physical appearance, it would be socially embarrassing if it kept shifting from body to body while most such complexes stayed put, and it would be confusing and tiresome if such shifting around were generally widespread, for it would be a laborious business finding out where one's friends and family were. But that our concern and affection would follow the character and memory complex and not its original bodily associate is surely clear. In the case of general shifting about we should be in the position of people trying to find their intimates in the dark. If the shifts were both frequent and spatially radical we should no doubt give up the attempt to identify individual people, the whole character of relations between people would change, and human life would be like an unending sequence of shortish ocean trips. But, as long as the transfers did not involve large movements in space, the character and memory complexes we are concerned with could be kept track of through their audible identification of themselves. And there is no reason to doubt that the victim of such a bodily transfer would regard himself as the person whom he seems to remember himself as being. I conclude, then, that although, as things stand, our concept of a person is not called upon to withstand these strains and, therefore, that in the face of a psychophysical transfer we might at first not know what to say, we should not identify the people in question as those who now have the bodies they used to have and that it would be the natural thing to extend our concept of a person, given the purposes for which it has been constructed, so as to identify anyone present to us now with whoever it was who used to have the same character and memories as he has. In other words the soul, defined as a series of mental states connected by continuity of character and memory, is the essential constituent of personality. The soul, therefore, is not only logically distinct from any particular human body with which it is associated; it is also what a person fundamentally is.

It may be objected to the extension of the concept of personal identity that I have argued for that it rests on an incorrect and even sentimental view of the nature of personal relations. There are, it may be said, personal relationships which are of an exclusively bodily character and which would not survive a change of body but which would perfectly well survive a change of soul. Relations of a rather unmitigatedly sexual type might be instanced and also those where the first party to the relationship has violent racial feelings. It can easily be shown that these objections are without substance. In the first place, even the most tired of entrepreneurs is going to take some note of the character and memories of the companion of his later nights at work. He will want her to be docile and quiet, perhaps, and to remember that he takes two parts of water to one of scotch, and no ice. If she ceases to be plump and red-headed and vigorous he may lose interest in and abandon her, but he would have done so anyway in response to the analogous effects of the aging process. If he has any idea of her as a person at all, it will be as a unique cluster of character traits and recollections. As a body, she is simply an instrument of a particular type, no more and no less interesting to him than a physically identical twin. In the case of a purely sexual relationship no particular human body is required, only one of a more or less precisely demarcated kind. Where concern with the soul is wholly absent there is no interest in individual identity at all, only in identity of type. It may be said that this argument cuts both ways: that parents and children are concerned only that they should have round them children and parents with the same sort of character and memories as the children and parents they were with yesterday. But this is doubly incorrect. First, the memories of individual persons cannot be exactly similar, since even the closest of identical twins must see things from slightly different angles; they cannot be in the same place at the same time. More seriously, if more contingently, individual memories, even of identical twins, are seldom, if ever, closely similar. To put the point crudely, the people I want to be with are the people who remember me and the experiences we have shared, not those who remember someone more or less like me with whom they have shared more or less similar experiences. The relevant complexity of the memories of an individual person is of an altogether different order of magnitude from that of the bodily properties of an entrepreneur's lady friend. The lady friend's bodily type is simply enough defined for it to have a large number of instances. It is barely conceivable that two individual memories should be similar enough to be emotionally adequate substitutes for each other. There is the case of the absolutely identical twins who go everywhere together, side by side, and always have done so. Our tendency here would be to treat the pair as a physically dual single person. There would be no point in distinguishing one from the other. As soon as their ways parted sufficiently for the question of which was which to arise, the condition of different memories required for individuation would be satisfied.

It may be felt that the absolutely identical twins present a certain difficulty for the empirical concept of the soul. For suppose their characters and memories to be totally indistinguishable and their thoughts and feelings to have been precisely the same since the first dawning of consciousness in them. Won't the later phases of one of the twins be as continuous in respect of character and memory with the earlier phases of the other as they are with his own earlier phases? Should we even say that there are two persons there at all? The positional difference of the two bodies provides an answer to the second question. Although they are always excited and gloomy together, the thrills and pangs are manifested in distinct bodies and are conceivable as existing separately. We might ignore the duality of their mental states, but we should be able in principle to assert it. As to the matter of continuity, the environment of the two will be inevitably asymmetrical, each will at various times be nearer something than the other, each will block some things from the other's field of vision or touch; so there will always be some, perhaps trivial, difference in the memories of the two. But even if trivial, the difference will be enough to allow the application in this special case of a criterion that normally relies on radical and serious differences. However alike the character and memories of twin no. 1 on Tuesday and twin no. 2 on Wednesday, they will inevitably be less continuous than those of twin no. 2 on the two days.

4. MEMORY AND BODILY IDENTITY

I must now return to the serious objection to the use of memory as a criterion of personal identity whose consideration was postponed earlier. This has been advanced in an original and interesting article on personal identity recently published by Sydney S. Shoemaker in *The Journal of Philosophy*.[1] He argues that memory could not be the sole or fundamental criterion for the identity of other people, because in order to establish what the memories of other people are I have to be able to identify them in a bodily way. I cannot accept sentences offered by other people beginning with the words "I remember" quite uncritically. I must be assured, first, that these utterances really are memory claims, that the speaker understands the meaning of the sentences he is using, and, secondly, that his memory claims are reliable. Mr. Shoemaker contends that it is essential, if either of these requirements is to be satisfied, for me to be able to identify the maker of the apparent memory claims in an independent, bodily way. In order to be sure that his remarks really are intended as memory claims, I have to see that he generally uses the form of words in question in connection with antecedent states of affairs of which he has been a witness. And to do this I must be assured that he is at one time uttering a memory sentence and at another, earlier, time is a witness of the event he purports to describe; in other words I must be able to identify him at different times without taking his apparent memories into account. The point is enforced by the second requirement about the conditions under which I can take his memory claims as trustworthy. To do this I must be able to establish at least that he was physically present at and, thus, in a position to observe the state of affairs he now claims to recollect.

There is a good deal of force in these arguments, but I do not think they are sufficient to prove that the soul is not logically distinct from the particular body with which it happens to be associated at any given time. In the first place, the doubt about the significance of someone's current memory

---

[1]"Personal Identity and Memory." 56, 22 (Oct. 22, 1959): 868.

claims is not one that I must positively have laid to rest before taking these claims as evidence of his identity. The doubt could seriously arise only in very special and singular circumstances. If someone now says to me, "I remember the battle of Hastings," I will presume him to be slightly misusing the words, since I have good reasons for thinking that no one now alive was present at that remote event. I shall probably take him to be saying that he remembers that there was such a thing as the battle of Hastings, having learnt of it at school, or that it took place in 1066, that Harold was killed at it, that it was the crucial military factor in the Norman conquest, and so forth. But if, on being questioned, he says that these reinterpretations distort the meaning he intended, that he remembers the battle of Hastings in the same way as he remembers having breakfast this morning, if perhaps a little more dimly, then I cannot reasonably suppose that he doesn't understand the meaning of his remark though I may well think that it is false, whether deliberately or not. Mr. Shoemaker admits that in a case of apparent bodily transfer the significance of a person's memory claims could be established by considering the way in which he used memory sentences after the transfer had taken place. So at best this part of his argument could prove that in order to identify people we need to be able to make at least local applications of the criterion of bodily identity. They must be continuous in a bodily way for a period of time sufficient to enable us to establish that they are using memory sentences correctly. But in view of the somewhat strained and artificial character of the doubt in question, I am inclined to reject even this modest conclusion. At best it is a practical requirement: people must be sufficiently stable in a bodily way for me to be able to accumulate a large enough mass of apparent memory claims that are prima facie there to infer from the coherence of these apparent claims that they really are memory claims and not senseless noises.

The reliability of the memory claims of others is a more substantial issue. For, unlike significance, it is a feature of apparent memory claims that we commonly do have serious reason to doubt. It must be admitted, further, that if I have independent reasons for believing that Jones's body was physically present at an event that Jones now claims to remember, I have a piece of strong evidence in support of the correctness of his claim. It is not, of course, conclusive. Even if he were looking in the direction at the time, he might have been in a condition of day-dreaming inattentiveness. The question is, however: is it in any sense a necessary condition for the correctness of my acceptance of a man's present memory claim that I should be able, in principle, to discover that the very same body from which the claim under examination now emerges was actually present at the event now purportedly remembered? I cannot see that it is. To revert to the example of a radical psychophysical exchange between B and C. Suppose that from B's body memory claims emerge about a lot of what I have hitherto confidently taken to be C's experiences. I may have good reason to believe that C's body was present at the events apparently recalled. If the claims are very numerous and detailed, if they involve the recollection of things I didn't know *B* had seen although I can now establish that they were really present for *C* to observe, and if the emission of apparent *C* memories from *B*'s body and vice versa keeps up for a fair period, it would be unreasonable not to conclude that the memory claims emerging from *B*'s body were in fact correct, that they were the memory claims of *C* not of *B*, and that therefore the person with *B*'s body was in fact not now *B* but *C*. Here again a measure of local bodily continuity seems required. I shall not say that *C* inhabits *B*'s body at all unless he seems to do so in a fairly substantial way and over a fair period of time. But as long as the possibility of psychophysical exchange is established by some salient cases in which the requirement of local bodily continuity is satisfied I can reasonably conjecture that such exchange has taken place in other cases where the translocation of memory claims is pretty short-lived. At any rate it is only the necessity of local bodily continuity that is established, not the necessary association of a person with one particular body for the whole duration of either. Bodily continuity with a witness is a test of the reliability of someone's memory claims, and it is an important one, but it is not a logically indispensable one.

5. THE PROBLEM OF DISEMBODIMENT

Nothing that I have said so far has any direct bearing on the question whether the soul can exist in an entirely disembodied state. All I have tried to show is that there is no necessary connection between the soul as a series of mental states linked by character and memory and any particular continuing human body. The question now arises: must the soul be associated with some human body? The apparent intelligibility of my crude ghost story might seem to suggest that not even a body is required, let alone a human one. And the same point appears to be made by the intelligibility of stories in which trees, toadstools, pieces of furniture, and so on are endowed with personal characteristics. But a good deal of caution is needed here. In the first place, even where these personal characteristics are not associated with any sort of body in the physiological sense, they are associated with a body in the epistemological sense; in other words, it is an essential part of the story that the soul in question have physical manifestations. Only in our own case does it seem that strictly disembodied existence is conceivable, in the sense that we can conceive circumstances in which there would be some good reason to claim that a soul existed in a disembodied state. Now how tenuous and nonhuman could these physical manifestations be? To take a fairly mild example, discussed by Professor Malcolm, could we regard a tree as another person? He maintains with great firmness that we could not, on the rather flimsy ground that trees haven't got mouths and, therefore, could not be said to speak or communicate with us or make memory claims. But if a knothole in a tree trunk physically emitted sounds in the form of speech, why should we not call it a mouth? We may presume that ventriloquism, hidden record-players and microphones, dwarfs concealed in the foliage, and so forth have all been ruled out. If the remarks of the tree were coherent and appropriate to its situation and exhibited the type of continuity that the remarks of persons normally do exhibit, why shouldn't we regard the tree as a person? The point is that we might, by a serious conceptual effort, allow this in the case of one tree or even several trees or even a great many nonhuman physical things. But the sense of our attribution of personality to them would be logically parasitic on our attributions of personality to ordinary human bodies. It is from their utterances and behavior that we derive our concept of personality, and this concept would be applicable to nonhuman things only by more or less far-fetched analogy. That trees should be personal presupposes, then, the personality of human beings. The same considerations hold in the extreme case of absolutely minimal embodiment, as when a recurrent and localized voice of a recognizable tone is heard to make publicly audible remarks. The voice might give evidence of qualitative and positional continuity sufficient to treat it as an identifiable body, even if of an excessively diaphanous kind. The possibility of this procedure, however, is contingent on there being persons in the standard, humanly embodied sense to provide a clear basis for the acquisition of the concept that is being more or less speculatively applied to the voice.

Whatever the logic of the matter, it might be argued, the causal facts of the situation make the whole inquiry into the possibility of a soul's humanly or totally disembodied existence an entirely fantastic one. That people have the memories and characters that they do, that they have memories and characters at all, has as its causally necessary condition the relatively undisturbed persistence of a particular bit of physiological apparatus. One can admit this without concluding that the inquiry is altogether without practical point. For the bit of physiological apparatus in question is not the human body as a whole, but the brain. Certainly lavish changes in the noncerebral parts of the human body often affect the character and perhaps even to some extent the memories of the person whose body it is. But there is no strict relationship here. Now it is sometimes said that the last bit of the body to wear out is the brain, that the brain takes the first and lion's share of the body's nourishment, and that the brains of people who have starved to death are often found in perfectly good structural order. It is already possible to graft bits of one human body on to another, corneas, fingers, and even, I believe, legs. Might it not be possible to remove the brain from an otherwise worn-out human body and replace it either in a manufactured human body or in a cerebrally untenanted one? In this case we should have a causally conceivable analogue of reincarnation. If this were to become possible and if the resultant creatures appeared in a coherent way to exhibit the character and memories previously associated with the brain that had been fitted into them, we could say that the original person was still in existence even though only a relatively minute part of its original mass and volume was present in the new physical whole. Yet if strict bodily identity is a necessary condition of personal identity, such a description of the outcome would be ruled out as self-contradictory. I conclude, therefore, not only that a logically adequate concept of the soul is constructible but that the construction has some possible utility even in the light of our knowledge of the causal conditions of human life.

PETER GEACH

6.4   *Immortality*

Everybody knows that men die, and though most of us have read the advertisement 'Millions now living will never die', it is commonly believed that every man born will some day die; yet historically many men have believed that there is a life after death, and indeed that this after-life will never end. That is: there has been a common belief both in *survival* of bodily death and in *immortality*. Now a philosopher might interest himself specially in immortality, as opposed to survival; conceding survival for the sake of argument, he might raise and examine conceptual difficulties about *endless* survival. But the question of immortality cannot even arise unless men do survive bodily death; and, as we shall see, there are formidable difficulties even about survival. It is these difficulties I shall be discussing, not the special ones about endless survival.

There are various views as to the character of the after-life. One view is that man has a subtle, ordinarily invisible, body which survives the death of the ordinary gross body. This view has a long history, and seems to be quite popular in England at the moment. So far as I can see, the view is open to no philosophical objection, but likewise wholly devoid of philosophical interest; the mind-body problem must after all be just the same for an ethereal body as for a gross one. There could clearly be no philosophical reasons for belief in such subtle bodies, but only empirical ones; such reasons are in fact alleged, and we are urged to study the evidence.

Philosophy can at this point say something: about what sort of evidence would be required. The existence of subtle bodies is a matter within the

From Peter Geach, *God and the Soul* (1969), chap. 2. Reprinted by permission of Schocken Books Inc., New York, and Routledge & Kegan Paul Ltd., London.

purview of physical science; evidence for it should satisfy such criteria of existence as physicists use, and should refer not only to what people say they have seen, heard, and felt, but also to effects produced by subtle bodies on physicists' apparatus. The believer in 'subtle bodies' must, I think, accept the physicist's criteria of existence; there would surely be a conceptual muddle in speaking of 'bodies' but saying they might be incapable of affecting any physical apparatus. For what distinguishes real physical objects from hallucinations, even collective hallucinations, is that physical objects act on one another, and do so in just the same way whether they are being observed or not; this is the point, I think, at which a phenomenalist account of physical objects breaks down. If, therefore, 'subtle bodies' produce no physical effects, they are not bodies at all.

How is it, then, that 'subtle bodies' have never forced themselves upon the attention of physicists, as X-rays did, by spontaneous interference with physical apparatus? There are supposed to be a lot of 'subtle bodies' around, and physicists have a lot of delicate apparatus; yet physicists not engaged in psychical research are never bothered by the interference of 'subtle bodies'. In the circumstances I think it wholly irrational to believe in 'subtle bodies'. Moreover, when I who am no physicist am invited to study the evidence for 'subtle bodies', I find that very fact suspicious. The discoveries of X-rays and electrons did not appeal to the lay public, but to physicists, to study the evidence; and so long as physicists (at least in general) refuse to take 'subtle bodies' seriously, a study of evidence for them by a layman like myself would be a waste of time.

When *philosophers* talk of life after death, what they mostly have in mind is a doctrine that may be called Platonic—it is found in its essentials in the *Phaedo*. It may be briefly stated thus: Each man's make-up includes a wholly immaterial thing, his mind and soul. It is the mind that sees and hears and feels and thinks and chooses—in a word, is conscious. The mind is the person; the body is extrinsic to the person, like a suit of clothes. Though body and mind affect one another, the mind's existence is quite independent of the body's; and there is thus no reason why the mind should not go on being conscious indefinitely after the death of the body, and even if it never again has with any body that sort of connexion which it now has.

This Platonic doctrine has a strong appeal, and there are plausible arguments in its favour. It appears a clearly intelligible supposition that I should go on after death having the same sorts of experience as I now have, even if I then have no body at all. For although these experiences are connected with processes in the body—sight, for example, with processes in the eyes, optic nerves, and brain—nevertheless there is no necessity of thought about the connexion—it is easy to conceive of someone who has no eyes having the experience called sight. He would be having the same experience as I who have eyes do, and I know what sort of experience that is because I have the experience.

Let us now examine these arguments. When a word can be used to stand for a private experience, like the words 'seeing' or 'pain', it is certainly tempting to suppose that the giving these words a meaning is itself a private experience—indeed that they get their meaning just from the experiences they stand for. But this is really nonsense: if a sentence I hear or utter contains the word 'pain', do I help myself to grasp its sense by giving myself a pain? Might not this be, on the contrary, rather distracting? As Wittgenstein said, to think you get the concept of pain by having a pain is like thinking you get the concept of a minus quantity by running up an overdraft. Our concepts of seeing, hearing, pain, anger, etc., apply in the first instance to human beings; we willingly extend them (say) to cats, dogs, and horses, but we rightly feel uncomfortable about extending them to very alien creatures and speaking of a slug's hearing or an angry ant. Do we know at all what it would be to apply such concepts to an immaterial being? I think not.

One may indeed be tempted to evade difficulties by saying: 'An immaterial spirit is angry or in pain if it feels *the same way* as I do when I am angry or in pain'. But, as Wittgenstein remarked, this is just like saying: 'Of course I know what it is for the time on the Sun to be five o'clock: it's five o'clock on the Sun at the very moment when it's five o'clock here!'—which plainly gets us no further. If there is a difficulty in passing from 'I am in pain' or 'Smith is in pain' to 'an immaterial spirit is in pain', there is equally a difficulty in passing from 'Smith feels the same way as I do' to 'an immaterial spirit feels the same way as I do'.

In fact, the question is, whether a private experience does suffice, as is here supposed, to give a meaning to a psychological verb like 'to see'. I am not trying to throw doubt on there being private experiences; of course men have thoughts they do not utter and pains they do not show; of course I may see something without any behaviour to show I see it; nor do I mean to emasculate these propositions with neo-behaviourist dialectics. But it is not a question of whether seeing is (sometimes) a private experience, but whether one can attach meaning to the verb 'to see' by a private uncheckable performance; and this is what I maintain one cannot do to any word at all.

One way to show that a word's being given a meaning cannot be a private uncheckable performance is the following: We can take a man's word for it that a linguistic expression has given him some private experience—e.g. has revived a painful memory, evoked a visual image, or given him a thrill in the pit of the stomach. But we cannot take his word for it that he attached a sense to the expression, even if we accept his *bona fides*; for later events may convince us that in fact he attached no sense to the expression. Attaching sense to an expression is thus not to be identified with any private experience that accompanies the expression; and I have argued this, not by attacking the idea of private experiences, but by contrasting the attaching of sense to an expression with some typical private experiences that may be connected with the expression.

We give words a sense—whether they are psychological words like 'seeing' and 'pain', or other words—by getting into a way of using them; and though a man can invent for himself a way of using a word, it must be a way that other people *could* follow—otherwise we are back to the idea of conferring meaning by a private uncheckable performance. Well, how do we eventually use such words as 'see', 'hear', 'feel', when we have got into the way of using them? We do not exercise these concepts only so as to pick our cases of seeing and the rest in our separate worlds of sense-experience; on the contrary, these concepts are used in association with a host of other concepts relating, e.g., to the physical characteristics of what is seen and the behaviour of those who do see. In saying this I am not putting forward a theory, but just reminding you of very familiar features in the everyday use of the verb 'to see' and related expressions; our ordinary talk about seeing would cease to be intelligible if there were cut out of it such expressions as 'I can't see, it's too far off', 'I caught his eye', 'Don't look round', etc. Do not let the bogy of behaviourism scare you off observing these features; I am not asking you to believe that 'to see' is itself a word for a kind of behaviour. But the concept of seeing can be maintained only because it has threads of connexion with these other non-psychological concepts; break enough threads, and the concept of seeing collapses.

We can now see the sort of difficulties that arise if we try to apply concepts like *seeing* and *feeling* to disembodied spirits. Let me give an actual case of a psychological concept's collapsing when its connexions were broken. Certain hysterics claimed to have a magnetic sense; it was discovered, however, that their claim to be having magnetic sensations did not go with the actual presence of a magnet in their environment, but only with their belief that a magnet was present. Psychologists did not now take the line: We may take the patients' word for it that they have peculiar sensations—only the term 'magnetic sensations' has proved inappropriate, as having been based on a wrong causal hypothesis. On the contrary, patients' reports of magnetic sensations were thenceforward written off as being among the odd things that hysterical patients sometimes say. Now far fewer of the ordinary connexions of a sensation-concept were broken here than would be broken if we tried to apply a sensation-concept like seeing to a disembodied spirit.

If we conclude that the ascription of sensations and feelings to a disembodied spirit does not make sense, it does not obviously follow, as you might think, that we must deny the possibility of disembodied spirits altogether. Aquinas for example was convinced that there are disembodied spirits but ones that cannot see or hear or feel pain or fear or anger; he allowed them no mental operations except those of thought and will. Damned spirits would suffer from frustration of their evil will, but not from aches and pains or foul odours or the like. It would take me too far to discuss whether his reasons for thinking this were good; I want to show what follows from this view. In our human life thinking and choosing are intricately bound up with a play of sensations and mental images and emotions; if after a lifetime of thinking and choosing in this human way there is left only a disembodied mind whose thought is wholly nonsensuous and whose rational choices are unaccompanied by any human feelings—can we still say there remains the same person? Surely not: such a soul is not the person who died but a mere remnant of him. And this is just what Aquinas says (in his commentary on I Corinthians 15): *anima mea non est ego*, my soul is not I; and if only souls are saved, *I* am not saved, nor is any man. If some time after Peter Geach's death there is again a man identifiable as Peter Geach, then Peter Geach again, or still, lives: otherwise not.

Through a surviving mental remnant of a person, preserving some sort of physical continuity with the man you knew, would not be Peter Geach, this does not show that such a measure of survival is not possible; but its possibility does raise serious difficulties, even if such dehumanized thinking and willing is really conceivable at all. For *whose* thinking would this be? Could we tell whether *one* or *many* disembodied spirits thought the thoughts in question? We touch here on the old problem: what constitutes there being two disembodied minds (at the same time, that is)? Well, what constitutes there being two pennies? It may happen that one penny is bent and corroded while another is in mint condition; but such differences cannot be what make the two pennies to be two—the two pennies could not have these varied fortunes if they were not already distinct. In the same way, differences of memories or of aims could not constitute the difference between two disembodied minds, but could only supervene upon a difference already existing. What does constitute the difference between two disembodied human minds? If we could find no ground of differentiation, then not only would that which survived be a mere remnant of a person—there would not even be a surviving individuality.

Could we say that souls are different because in the first instance they were souls of different bodies, and then remain different on that account when they are no longer embodied? I do not think this solution would do at all if differentiation by reference to different bodies were merely retrospective. It might be otherwise if we held, with Aquinas, that the relation to a body was not merely retrospective—that each disembodied human soul permanently retained a capacity for reunion to such a body as would reconstitute a man identifiable with the man who died. This might satisfactorily account for the individuation of disembodied human souls; they would differ by being fitted for reunion to different bodies; but it would entail that the possibility of disembodied human souls stood or fell with the *possibility* of a dead man's living again *as a man*.

Some Scholastics held that just as two pennies or two cats differ by being different bits of matter, so human souls differ by containing different 'spiritual matter'. Aquinas regarded this idea as self-contradictory; it is at any rate much too obscure to count as establishing a possibility of distinct disembodied souls. Now this recourse to 'spiritual matter' might well strike us merely as the filling of a conceptual lacuna with a nonsensical piece of jargon. But it is not only Scholastic philosophers who assimilate mental processes to physical ones, only thinking of mental processes as taking place in an *immaterial* medium; and many people think it easy to conceive of distinct disembodied souls because they are illegitimately ascribing to souls a sort of differentiation —say, by existing *side by side*—that can be significantly ascribed only to bodies. The same goes for people who talk about souls as being 'fused' or 'merged' in a Great Soul; they are imagining some such change in the world of souls as occurs to a drop of water falling into a pool or to a small lump of wax that is rubbed into a big one. Now if only people *talked* about 'spiritual matter', instead of just thinking in terms of it unawares, their muddle could be more easily detected and treated.

To sum up what I have said so far: The possibility of life after death for Peter Geach appears to stand or fall with the possibility of there being once again a man identifiable as Peter Geach. The existence of a disembodied soul would not be a survival of the person Peter Geach; and even in such a truncated form, individual existence seems to require at least a persistent possibility of the soul's again entering into the make-up of a man who is identifiably Peter Geach.

This suggests a form of belief in survival that seems to have become quite popular of late in the West—at any rate as a half-belief—namely, the belief in reincarnation. Could it in fact have a clear sense to say that a baby born in Oxford this year is Hitler living again?

How could it be shown that the Oxford baby was Hitler? Presumably by memories and similarities of character. I maintain that no amount of such evidence would make it reasonable to identify the baby as Hitler. Similarities of character are of themselves obviously insufficient. As regards memories: If on growing up the Oxford baby reveals knowledge of what we should ordinarily say only Hitler can have known, does this establish a presumption that the child is Hitler? Not at all. In normal circumstances we know when to say 'only he can have known that'; when queer things start happening, we have no right to stick to our ordinary assumptions as to what can be known. And suppose that for some time the child 'is' Hitler by our criteria, and later on 'is' Goering? or might not several children simultaneously satisfy the criteria for 'being' Hitler?

These are not merely captious theoretical objections. Spirit-mediums, we are told, will in trance convincingly enact the part of various people: sometimes of fictitious characters, like Martians, or Red Indians ignorant of Red Indian languages, or the departed 'spirits' of Johnny Walker and John Jamieson; there are even stories of mediums' giving convincing 'messages' from people who were alive and normally conscious at the time of the 'message'. Now a medium giving messages from the dead is not said to be the dead man, but rather to be controlled by his spirit. What then can show whether the

Oxford child 'is' Hitler or is merely 'controlled' by Hitler's spirit? For all these reasons the appearance that there might be good evidence for reincarnation dissolves on a closer view.

Nor do I see, for that matter, how the mental phenomena of mediumship could ever make it reasonable to believe that a human soul survived and communicated. For someone to carry on in a dramatic way quite out of his normal character is a common hysterical symptom; so if a medium does this in a trance, it is no evidence of anything except an abnormal condition of the medium's own mind. As for the medium's telling us things that 'only the dead can have known', I repeat that in these queer cases we have no right to stick to our ordinary assumptions about what can be known. Moreover, as I said, there are cases, as well-authenticated as any, in which the medium convincingly enacted the part of X and told things that 'Only X could have known' when X was in fact alive and normally conscious, so that his soul was certainly not trying to communicate by way of the medium! Even if we accept all the queer stories of spirit-messages, the result is only to open up a vast field of queer possibilities—not in the least to force us to say that mediums were possessed by such-and-such souls. This was argued by Bradley long ago in his essay 'The Evidences of Spiritualism', and he has never been answered.

How could a living man be rightly identifiable with a man who previously died? Let us first consider our normal criteria of personal identity. When we say an old man is the same person as the baby born seventy years before, we believe that the old man has material continuity with the baby. Of course this is not a criterion in the sense of being what we judge identity by; for the old man will not have been watched for seventy years continuously, even by rota! But something we regarded as disproving the material continuity (e.g. absence of a birthmark, different fingerprints) would disprove personal identity. Further, we believe that material continuity establishes a one-one relation: one baby grows up into one old man, and one old man has grown out of one baby. (Otherwise there would have to be at some stage a drastic change, a fusion or fission, which we should regard as destroying personal identity.) Moreover, the baby-body never coexists with the aged body, but develops into it.

Now it seems to me that we cannot rightly identify a man living 'again' with a man who died unless *material* conditions of identity are fulfilled. There must be some one-one relation of material continuity between the old body and the new. I am not saying that the new body need be even in part materially *identical* with the old; this, unlike material continuity, is not required for personal identity, for the old man need not have kept even a grain of matter from the baby of seventy years ago.

We must here notice an important fallacy. I was indicating just now that I favour Aquinas's doctrine that two coexisting souls differ by being related to two different bodies and that two coexisting human bodies, like two pennies or two cats, differ by being different bits of matter. Well, if it is difference of matter that makes two bodies different, it may seem to follow that a body can maintain its identity only if at least some identifiable matter remains in it all the time; otherwise it is no more the same body than the wine in a cask that is continuously emptied and refilled is the same wine. But just this is the fallacy: it does not follow, if difference in a certain respect at a certain time suffices to show non-identity, that sameness in that respect over a period of time is necessary to identify. Thus, Sir John Cutler's famous pair of stockings were the same pair all the time, although they started as silk and by much mending ended as worsted; people have found it hard to see this, because if at a given time there is a silk pair and also a worsted pair then there are two pairs. Again, it is clear that the same man may be in Birmingham at noon and in Oxford at 7 p.m., even though a man in Birmingham and a man in Oxford at a given time must be two different men. Once formulated, the fallacy is obvious, but it might be deceptive if not formulated.

'Why worry even about material continuity? Would not mental continuity be both necessary and sufficient?' Necessary, but not sufficient. Imagine a new 'Tichborne' trial. The claimant knows all the things he ought to know, and talks convincingly to the long-lost heir's friends. But medical evidence about scars and old fractures and so on indicates that he cannot be the man; moreover, the long-lost heir's corpse is decisively identified at an exhumation. Such a case would bewilder us, particularly if the claimant's *bona fides* were manifest. (He might, for example, voluntarily take a lie-detecting test.) But we should certainly not allow the evidence of mental connexions with the long-lost heir to settle the matter in the claimant's favour: the claimant cannot be the long-lost heir, whose body we know lies buried in Australia, and if he honestly thinks he is then we must try to cure him of a delusion.

'But if I went on being conscious, why should I worry which body I have?' To use the repeated 'I' prejudges the issue; a fairer way of putting the point would be: If there is going to be a consciousness that includes ostensible memories of my life, why should I worry about which body this consciousness goes with? When we put it that way, it is quite easy to imagine circumstances in which one would worry—particularly if the ostensible memories of my life were to be produced by processes that can produce entirely spurious memories.

If, however, memory is not enough for personal identity; if a man's living again does involve some bodily as well as mental continuity with the man who lived formerly; then we might fairly call his new bodily life a resurrection. So the upshot of our whole argument is that unless a man comes to life again by resurrection, he does not live again after death. At best some mental remnant of him would survive death; and I should hold that the possibility even of such survival involves at least a permanent *capacity* for renewed human life; if reincarnation is excluded, this means: a capacity for resurrection. It may be hard to believe in the resurrection of the body: but Aquinas argued in his commentary on I Corinthians 15, which I have already cited, that it is much harder to believe in an immortal but permanently disembodied human soul; for that would mean believing that a soul, whose very identity depends on the capacity for reunion with one human body rather than another, will continue to exist for ever with this capacity unrealized.

Speaking of the resurrection, St. Paul used the simile of a seed that is planted and grows into an ear of corn, to show the relation between the corpse and the body that rises again from the dead. This simile fits in well enough with our discussion. In this life, the bodily aspect of personal identity requires a one-one relationship and material continuity; one baby body grows into one old man's body by a continuous process. Now similarly there is a one-one relationship between the buried seed and the ear that grows out of it; one seed grows into one ear, one ear comes from one seed; and the ear of corn is materially continuous with the seed but need not have any material identity with it.

There is of course no philosophical reason to expect that from a human corpse there will arise at some future date a new human body, continuous in some way with the corpse; and in some particular cases there appear strong empirical objections. But apart from the *possibility* of resurrection, it seems to me a mere illusion to have any hope for life after death. I am of the mind of Judas Maccabeus: if there is no resurrection, it is superfluous and vain to pray for the dead.

The traditional faith of Christianity, inherited from Judaism, is that at the end of this age Messiah will come and men rise from their graves to die no more. That faith is not going to be shaken by inquiries about bodies burned to ashes or eaten by beasts; those who might well suffer just such death in martyrdom were those who were most confident of a glorious reward in the resurrection. One who shares that hope will hardly wish to take out an occultistic or philosophical insurance policy, to guarantee some sort of survival as an annuity, in case God's promise of resurrection should fail.

BIBLIOGRAPHICAL ESSAY

Literature on the philosophy of religion is so vast that it would be almost impossible to offer a complete bibliography. Moreover, for lack of selectivity, such a bibliography would be useless to the ordinary student. What follows is therefore merely a selected introduction to the great body of literature.

Among the recent texts on the philosophy of religion, the reader might consult T. Penelhum, *Religion and Rationality* (New York: Random House, 1971). Several anthologies, notably J. Hick, *Classical and Contemporary Readings in the Philosophy of Religion*, 2nd ed. (Englewood Cliffs, N.J.: Prentice-Hall, 1969) and W. P. Alston, *Religious Belief and Philosophical Thought* (New York: Harcourt Brace, 1963) present good selections from the more classical literature, while S. Cahn, *Philosophy of Religion* (New York: Harper & Row, 1970), J. Donnelly, *Logical Analysis and Contemporary Theism* (New York: Fordham University Press, 1972), and B. Mitchell, *The Philosophy of Religion* (London: Oxford University Press, 1971) are good collections of more recent material. There are two philosophical journals, *Religious Studies* and *Sophia*, that are devoted exclusively to the philosophy of religion.

A very extensive literature, both classical and contemporary, is available on the ontological argument. Two fine anthologies are A. Plantinga, *The Ontological Argument* (Garden City, N.Y.: Doubleday, Anchor Books, 1965), and J. Hick and A. McGill, *The Many-Faced Argument* (New York: Macmillan, 1965). More recently, two extremely important treatments of the argument have appeared, R. Adams, "The Logical Structure of Anselm's Argument" in *Philosophical Review* (1971), and chapters 2 and 3 of A. Plantinga, *God and Other Minds* (Ithaca, N.Y.: Cornell University Press, 1967).

R. Burrill's anthology, *The Cosmological Arguments* (Garden City, N.Y.: Doubleday, Anchor Books, 1967) collects some of the material on the cosmological and teleological arguments not included in this volume. Several recent defenses of the cosmological argument that the reader might consult include chapter 3 of F. C. Copleston, *Aquinas* (Baltimore: Penguin, 1955) and chapter 7 of R. Taylor, *Metaphysics* (Englewood Cliffs, N.J.: Prentice-Hall, 1963). Plantinga, in the above-mentioned *God and Other Minds*, offers an unusual defense of the teleological argument. James Ross, *Philosophical Theology* (New York: Bobbs-Merrill, 1969) offers a defense of some medieval versions of these arguments.

More traditional philosophers of religion were very interested in the so-called moral argument, which is not included in our anthology. The interested reader might consult H. J. Paton, *The Modern Predicament* (New York: Macmillan, 1955) and A. E. Taylor, *The Faith of a Moralist* (New York: Macmillan, 1930).

The problem of evil has received considerable attention. For further discussion of the issues and possible solutions, the reader might consult J. Hick, *Evil and the God of Love* (New York: Macmillan, 1966) and M. B. Ahern, *The Problem of Evil* (London: Routledge & Kegan Paul, 1971), and the extensive literature cited there. One solution not discussed in our anthology involves modifying the conception of God so that he is thought of as a limited creature. First advocated by J. S. Mill in his essay "Nature," it has been revised in our times by E. S. Brightman in *The Problem of God* (Nashville, Tenn.: Abingdon Press, 1930).

H. H. Price, "Belief in and Belief that" in *Religious Studies* (1965), is an important analysis of what it is to believe in God. D. Z. Phillips, "Religious Belief and Language-Games," in *Ratio* (1970) defends religious faith and challenges the very possibility of a rational proof of religious claims. His position, sometimes called "Wittgensteinian Fideism," has been extensively criticized, and in this paper he refers to earlier versions of that thesis and to critics of it. Many important essays on this issue of religious belief may be found in J. Hick, *Faith and the Philosophers* (New York: Macmillan, 1964).

St. Thomas's theory of analogical predication is discussed in such works as E. L. Mascall, *Existence and Analogy* (London: Longmans, Green, 1949) and parts of D. M. High, *New Essays on Religious Language* (London: Oxford, Clarendon Press, 1969). More information about some aspects of the medieval discussion can be found in M. Menges, *The Concept of Univocity* (St. Bonaventure, Franciscan Institute, 1952) and Cardinal Cajetan, *The Analogy of Names* (Pittsburgh: Duquesne University Press, 1959). There is an extensive literature on the contemporary version of the problem. It is surveyed in F. Ferré, *Language, Logic, and God* (New York: Harper & Row, 1961) and W. T. Blackstone, *The Problem of Religious Knowledge* (Englewood Cliffs, N.J.: Prentice-Hall, 1963). Also devoted to that issue are most of the papers in S. Hook, *Religious Experience and Truth* (New York University Press, 1961) and J. Hick, *Philosophers and Faith* (New York: Macmillan, 1964), as well as some of the Royal Institute of Philosophy lectures in *Talk of God* (New York: St. Martin's Press, 1969). An important critique of Professor

Hick's position, not included in any of the above anthologies, is K. Nielsen's "Eschatological Verification" in *Canadian Journal of Theology* (1963).

The only issue in Part 3 on which there is an extensive literature is the problem of God's foreknowledge and human freedom. That and the related issue of God's timelessness is discussed in N. Pike, *God and Timelessness* (New York: Schocken Books, 1970). James Ross, *Philosophical Theology* (Bobbs, Merrill, 1969) has an extensive discussion of the analysis of omnipotence.

Among the recent analyses of the concept of creation are P. Geach's "Causality and Creation" in *Sophia* (1962) and "God's Relation to the World" in *Sophia* (1969), and J. Donnelly's "Creation ex nihilo" in *Proceedings of the American Catholic Philosophical Association* (1970). The problems connected with the idea of a miracle are explored in R. G. Swinburne, *The Concept of a Miracle* (New York: St. Martin's Press, 1970) and in the literature cited there. C. S. Lewis, *Miracles* (Centenary Press, 1947) contains a famous defense of the miracle doctrine.

There is an extensive literature surrounding mystical experiences. In addition to the selections included here from William James, *Variety of Religious Experiences* (1902) and W. T. Stace, *The Teachings of the Mystics* (New American Library, 1960), the reader might consult E. Underhill, *Mysticism* (New York: Macmillan, 1930), W. R. Inge, *Mysticism in Religion* (University of Chicago Press, 1948), and W. T. Stace, *Time and Eternity* (Princeton University Press, 1952) and *Mysticism and Philosophy* (New York: Macmillan, 1961). Positive treatments of the significance of these experiences can be found in J. Baillie, *Our Knowledge of God* (New York: Scribner's, 1962) and H. D. Lewis, *Our Experience of God* (New York: Macmillan, 1959). The critique of C. B. Martin is developed more fully in his *Religious Belief* (Ithaca, N.Y.: Cornell University Press, 1959) and in R. Hepburn, *Christianity and Paradox* (C. A. Watts, 1958). Other important recent treatments include W. P. Alston's "Ineffability" in *Philosophical Review* (1956), R. M. Gale's "Mysticism and Philosophy" in *Journal of Philosophy* (1960) and K. Nielsen's "Christian Positivism and the Appeal to Religious Experience" in *Journal of Religion* (1962).

Prayer is discussed in P. Geach, "Praying for things to Happen" in his *God and the Soul* (London: Routledge & Kegan Paul, 1969) and in D. Z. Phillips, *The Concept of Prayer* (Routledge, 1965) and in the literature cited there.

On the relationship between morality and religion, the reader can consult G. E. M. Anscombe, "Modern Moral Philosophy" in *Philosophy* (1958), K. Nielsen, "On the Independence of Morality from Religion" in *Mind* (1961), P. Brown, "Religious Morality" in *Mind* (1963), and D. Z. Phillips, "Moral and Religious Conception of Duty" in *Mind* (1964).

While much of the discussion of the doctrines of the immortality of the soul and the resurrection of the body are carried on in the context of more general discussions of the mind-body problem, there are some independent